L. C.; Henry J. Thomas.

Countee Cullen   D.H. Lawrence

Charles Dickens   Jonathan Swift   Daniel Defoe

Bernard Shaw   Phillis Wheatley   Stephen Crane

Benjamin Lasseter

Langston   Bret Harte   Henry W. Longfellow

car wilde   Thornton Wilder   Edgar A Poe

Ernest Hemingway   J. Austen

Sinclair Lewis   Herman Melville   R Edu Gonl

Juan Turgeneur   A Bradstreet

S. Eliot   Jack London   Thomas Hardy

MACMILLAN LITERATURE SERIES

SIGNATURE EDITION

DISCOVERING LITERATURE

INTRODUCING LITERATURE

ENJOYING LITERATURE

UNDERSTANDING LITERATURE

APPRECIATING LITERATURE

AMERICAN LITERATURE

ENGLISH LITERATURE
WITH WORLD MASTERPIECES

WORLD LITERATURE

FRONT COVER, detail, and BACK COVER: *The Morning Bell,* 1866,
oil on canvas, Winslow Homer, American (1836–1910).
Yale University Art Gallery. Bequest of Stephen Carlton Clark, B.A. 1903.

GENERAL ADVISERS

READING AND INSTRUCTIONAL METHODS
Jack Cassidy
Professor of Education
Millersville University
Millersville, Pennsylvania

THINKING SKILLS
Eric Cooper
Former Director, Comprehension and Cognition
Project, The College Board
New York, New York

TEACHER'S PROFESSIONAL RESOURCES
Robert DiYanni
Professor of English
Pace University
Pleasantville, New York

SPEAKING AND LISTENING SKILLS
R. Brian Loxley
Communications Consultant
New York, New York

CONSULTANTS

Susan G. Bennett, Humboldt State University, Arcata, California

Jean Canning, English Coordinator K–9, Summit School System, Summit, New Jersey

Pat Endsley, Manager, Curriculum Instructional Services, Berkeley Unified School District, Berkeley, California

Marta McMahon Heise, English Teacher, Churchill Junior High School, East Brunswick, New Jersey

Beverly McColley, English Teacher, Brandon Junior High School, Virginia Beach, Virginia

Jean Morgan, English Teacher, Indian Hill Schools, Cincinnati, Ohio

L. Carol O'Neal, Coordinator of English and Language Arts, Clayton County Public Schools, Jonesboro, Georgia

Judi Purvis, Secondary Language Arts Appraiser, Carrollton–Farmers Branch Independent School District, Texas

Carla Robbins, English Teacher, North Davidson Junior High School, Lexington, North Carolina

Donna Rosenberg, English Teacher, Author, Consultant, Winnetka, Illinois

WRITERS
Instructional Text

Cosmo F. Ferrara, Writer and Consultant, Former Department Chair

Gale Cornelia Flynn, Poet and Writer, Former English Teacher

Richard Foerster, Educational Writer

Meish Goldish, Educational Writer, Former English Teacher

Philip McFarland, English Teacher

Eileen Hillary Oshinsky, Educational Writer

Derrick Tseng, Educational Writer

WRITERS
Thinking Skills Handbook

Beau F. Jones-Davis, North Central Regional Educational Laboratory, Elmhurst, Illinois

Susan Sardy, Yeshiva University, New York, New York

John Sherk, University of Missouri, Kansas City, Missouri

Teacher's Classroom Resources

Stanlee Brimberg, Bank Street School for Children, New York, New York

Ellen Davis, Friendswood Independent School District, Texas

Judith H. McGee, Coordinator of Secondary Education, Athens Independent School District, Texas

David Nicholson, Riverdale Country School, Bronx, New York

The publisher is grateful for assistance and comments from the following people:

Gerald Dwight, Cherry Hill High School West, Cherry Hill, New Jersey

José Flores, Center for Mexican American Studies, University of Texas, Austin

Francisco Jiménez, Santa Clara University, Santa Clara, California

Nancy Murvine, Tatnall Middle School, Wilmington, Delaware

James S. Russell, Aptos, California

MACMILLAN LITERATURE SERIES

INTRODUCING LITERATURE

SIGNATURE EDITION

GLENCOE

Macmillan/McGraw-Hill

New York, New York   Columbus, Ohio   Mission Hills, California   Peoria, Illinois

Send all inquiries to:
Glencoe
15319 Chatsworth Street
P.O. Box 9609
Mission Hills, CA 91346-9609

Pupil's Edition ISBN 0-02-635041-6/7
Teacher's Annotated Edition ISBN 0-02-635042-4/7

3 4 5 6 7 8 9   97 96 95 94

ACKNOWLEDGMENTS

Grateful acknowledgment is given authors, publishers, and agents for permission to reprint the following copyrighted material. Every effort has been made to determine copyright owners. In the case of any omissions, the Publisher will be pleased to make suitable acknowledgments in future editions.

Bill Berger Associates, Inc.
MONA GARDNER: "The Dinner Party." Reprinted by permission of *Bill Berger Associates, Inc.*

Brandt & Brandt Literary Agents, Inc.
JOAN AIKEN: "All You've Ever Wanted" from *Smoke from Cromwell's Time.* Published by Doubleday & Co., Inc. Copyright 1959, 1966, 1969, 1970 by Joan Aiken. Reprinted by permission of Brandt & Brandt Literary Agents, Inc.

Gwendolyn Brooks
GWENDOLYN BROOKS: "Home" from *Blacks.* Copyright 1987.

Christ's College
W. H. D. ROUSE: "The Flood" (retitled "Deucalion") from *Gods, Heroes, and Men of Ancient Greece.* Reprinted by permission of the Master, Fellows and Scholars of Christ's College, Cambridge, England.

Don Congdon Associates, Inc.
RUSSELL BAKER: Excerpts from *Growing Up.* Copyright © 1982 by Russell Baker.
RAY BRADBURY: "The Sound of Summer Running" from *Dandelion Wine.* Copyright © 1956 by Ray Bradbury.
JACK FINNEY: "The Third Level." Copyright © 1950 by Crowell-Collier, renewed 1977 by Jack Finney.
The preceding selections were reprinted by permission of Don Congdon Associates, Inc.

Harold Courlander
HAROLD COURLANDER: "The Fire on the Mountain" from *The Fire on the Mountain.* Copyright © 1950 by Holt, Rinehart and Winston. Reprinted by permission of Harold Courlander.

Devin-Adair Publishers
MICHAEL MCLAVERTY: "The Wild Duck's Nest" from *The Game Cock and Other Stories.* Reprinted by permission of Devin-Adair Publishers, Old Greenwich, CT.

Doubleday & Company, Inc.
ISAAC ASIMOV: "The Fun They Had" from *Earth Is Room Enough.* Copyright © 1957 by Isaac Asimov.
BASHŌ: "Bamboo Grove" from *An Introduction to Haiku* translated by Harold Henderson, Copyright © 1958 by Harold G. Henderson.

Copyrights and Acknowledgments continue on pages 622–624, which represent a continuation of the copyright page.

A LETTER TO THE STUDENT

You are about to begin reading a new collection of stories, poems, plays, and other works of literature. This kind of collection is called an *anthology*— a word you ought to get to know. When the ancient Greeks invented the word, it meant "a gathering of flowers," a bouquet or a garland. Now we apply the word to literature instead of flowers, but it still keeps its most important meaning: It is a gathering together of objects that can give us a great deal of enjoyment.

As you read this anthology, you will notice that the stories, poems, and plays become more interesting the more you think about them. In fact, one of your main goals as you read this book is to learn to *think about literature*. Of course you have done a great deal of this kind of thinking already. For instance, every time you read a story and you think, "This character is like me," you are using the thinking skill called *comparing*. Now you will be thinking about literature in a more organized way.

Before you begin a selection, this anthology will provide you with a question or a statement to help you set a *purpose* as you read. When you finish each selection, you will see Study Questions that are divided into three parts to help you think about the selection in an organized way: first *recalling* the events of the selection, then *interpreting* the meaning of those events, and then *extending* the meaning of those events into your own experience.

Near the back of this book you will find a special section called "Student's Resources: Lessons in Active Learning." The handbooks that make up this section are practical guides for responding to literature by speaking, thinking, reading and studying, and writing. Each handbook lesson is designed to help you grow as an active, independent reader and thinker, to help you take charge of your own learning.

Reading and thinking go hand in hand. *Introducing Literature* offers you the chance to think clearly about the literature you read. By learning what makes literature work, you will make everything you read—long after you have finished this book—even more enjoyable.

CONTENTS

INTRODUCING LITERATURE

The first unit presents four types of literature.
Each selection in this unit focuses on the general theme "achieving goals."

THE SHORT STORY

POETRY

PREVIEW: Poetry *209*

NONFICTION

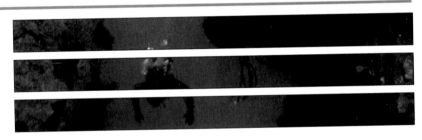

DRAMA

GREEK MYTHS
AND WORLD
FOLK TALES

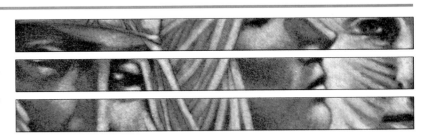

LITERARY FOCUS: **World Folk Tales**   *452*

ACTIVE READING: Myths and Folk Tales   *478*
Distinguishing Fantasy from Reality • Identifying Causes and Effects •
Understanding Character Motivation

LITERARY SKILLS REVIEW: Myths and Folk Tales   *482*

THEMES REVIEW: Myths and Folk Tales   *483*

PREVIEW: The Novel   *485*

LITERARY FOCUS

John Steinbeck .... The Red Pony 487

ACTIVE READING: The Novel   *534*
Preparing for a Test • Paraphrasing Information in a Novel • Making an Outline

LITERARY SKILLS REVIEW: The Novel   *538*

THEMES REVIEW: The Novel   *539*

STUDENT'S RESOURCES

Preview
Introducing
Literature

Have you ever dreamed of living a thousand years in the past? Have you ever wondered what it is like to be a sailor, an astronaut, a detective? Would you like to visit another country or defeat a monster or simply take a long walk through a winter forest? You *can* take part in all these experiences—through the power of literature and your own imagination.

Literature is a kind of entertainment. However, it is also something much more. By reading about the lives and challenges of other people, you may come to understand more about your own life. Literature is like a house with a great number of windows. As you look out through each window, you see a different part of the world. As you learn about the world, you learn about yourself.

People create literature to express their emotions and ideas about life. Since literature comes in several forms, writers must decide *which* form of literature to use. One writer may create a story, while another may compose a poem, a piece of nonfiction, or a drama—all on the same idea. Each literary form offers writers different opportunities to express what they have to say.

This unit introduces four different types of literature, or literary forms: stories, poems, nonfiction, and drama. You will read one example of each form in order to recognize its distinct qualities. You will also compare and contrast the four forms to understand their similarities and differences. In the rest of this book, you will find additional examples of each of these types of literature.

Although a poem differs in appearance from a story and nonfiction differs in appearance from a drama, all four types of literature may still focus on the same idea, or topic. In this unit all the selections concern individuals who have goals they want to achieve. As you read, think about how each character strives to reach a goal, to succeed, to make a dream come true.

Born in India, British writer Rudyard Kipling (1865–1936) became world famous for his action-packed novels, short stories, and poems. In 1907 Kipling was awarded the Nobel Prize for Literature, one of the highest honors a writer can receive. One of his best-known works is *The Jungle Book,* a collection of short stories including "Rikki-tikki-tavi." This adventure is based on the author's childhood memories of India.

■ How does Kipling make you care about the characters?

Rudyard Kipling

Rikki-tikki-tavi

This is the story of the great war that Rikki-tikki-tavi fought single-handed, through the bathrooms of the big bungalow in Segowlee cantonment.[1] Darzee, the tailorbird, helped him, and Chuchundra,[2] the muskrat, who never comes out into the middle of the floor, but always creeps round by the wall, gave him advice; but Rikki-tikki did the real fighting.

He was a mongoose, rather like a little cat in his fur and his tail, but quite like a weasel in his head and his habits. His eyes and the end of his restless nose were pink; he could scratch himself anywhere he pleased, with any leg, front or back, that he chose to use; he could fluff up his tail till it looked like a bottle brush, and his war cry, as he scuttled through the long grass, was *"Rikk-tikk-tikki-tikki-tchk!"*

One day, a high summer flood washed him out of the burrow where he lived with his father and mother, and carried him, kicking and clucking, down a roadside ditch. He found a little wisp of grass floating there, and clung to it till he lost his senses. When he revived, he was lying in the hot sun on the middle of a garden path, very draggled indeed, and a small boy was saying: "Here's a dead mongoose. Let's have a funeral."

"No," said his mother; "let's take him in and dry him. Perhaps he isn't really dead."

They took him into the house, and a big man picked him up between his finger and thumb and said he was not dead but half choked; so they wrapped him in cotton wool and warmed him, and he opened his eyes and sneezed.

"Now," said the big man (he was an Englishman who had just moved into the bungalow), "don't frighten him, and we'll see what he'll do."

---

1. **Segowlee** [sē gou′lē] **cantonment:** British military post in Segowlee, India.
2. **Chuchundra** [chōō chun′drə]

It is the hardest thing in the world to frighten a mongoose, because he is eaten up from nose to tail with curiosity. The motto of all the mongoose family is "Run and find out"; and Rikki-tikki was a true mongoose. He looked at the cotton wool, decided that it was not good to eat, ran all round the table, sat up and put his fur in order, scratched himself, and jumped on the small boy's shoulder.

"Don't be frightened, Teddy," said his father. "That's his way of making friends."

"Ouch! He's tickling under my chin," said Teddy.

Rikki-tikki looked down between the boy's collar and neck, snuffed at his ear, and climbed down to the floor, where he sat rubbing his nose.

"Good gracious," said Teddy's mother, "and that's a wild creature! I suppose he's so tame because we've been kind to him."

"All mongooses are like that," said her husband. "If Teddy doesn't pick him up by the tail, or try to put him in a cage, he'll run in and out of the house all day long. Let's give him something to eat."

They gave him a little piece of raw meat. Rikki-tikki liked it immensely, and when it was finished he went out into the veranda and sat in the sunshine and fluffed up his fur to make it dry to the roots. Then he felt better.

"There are more things to find out about in this house," he said to himself, "than all my family could find out in all their lives. I shall certainly stay and find out."

He spent all that day roaming over the house. He nearly drowned himself in the bathtubs, put his nose into the ink on a writing table, and burned it on the end of the big man's cigar, for he climbed up in the big man's lap to see how writing was done. At nightfall he ran into Teddy's nursery to watch how kerosene lamps were lighted, and when Teddy went to bed Rikki-tikki climbed up too;

but he was a restless companion, because he had to get up and attend to every noise all through the night and find out what made it. Teddy's mother and father came in, the last thing, to look at their boy, and Rikki-tikki was awake on the pillow. "I don't like that," said Teddy's mother; "he may bite the child."

"He'll do no such thing," said the father. "Teddy's safer with that little beast than if he had a bloodhound to watch him. If a snake came into the nursery now—"

But Teddy's mother wouldn't think of anything so awful.

Early in the morning Rikki-tikki came to early breakfast in the veranda, riding on Teddy's shoulder, and they gave him banana and some boiled egg; and he sat on all their laps one after the other, because every well-brought-up mongoose always hopes to be a house mongoose someday and have rooms to run about in, and Rikki-tikki's mother (she used to live in the general's house at Segowlee) had carefully told Rikki what to do if ever he came across Englishmen.

Then Rikki-tikki went out into the garden to see what was to be seen. It was a large garden, only half cultivated, with bushes as big as summer houses of roses, lime and orange trees, clumps of bamboos, and thickets of high grass. Rikki-tikki licked his lips. "This is a splendid hunting ground," he said, and his tail grew bottle-brushy at the thought of it, and he scuttled up and down the garden, snuffling here and there till he heard very sorrowful voices in a thornbush.

It was Darzee, the tailorbird, and his wife. They had made a beautiful nest by pulling two big leaves together and stitching them up the edges with fibers, and had filled the hollow with cotton and downy fluff. The nest swayed to and fro, as they sat on the brim and cried.

"What is the matter?" asked Rikki-tikki.

"We are very miserable," said Darzee. "One

of our babies fell out of the nest yesterday, and Nag[3] ate him."

"H'm!" said Rikki-tikki; "that is very sad—but I am a stranger here. Who is Nag?"

Darzee and his wife only cowered down in the nest without answering, for from the thick grass at the foot of the bush came a low hiss—a horrid cold sound that made Rikki-tikki jump back two clear feet. Then inch by inch out of the grass rose up the head and spread hood of Nag, the big black cobra, and he was five feet long from tongue to tail. When he had lifted one third of himself clear of the ground, he stayed balancing to and fro exactly as a dandelion tuft balances in the wind, and he looked at Rikki-tikki with the wicked snake's eyes that never change their expression, whatever the snake may be thinking of.

"Who is Nag?" he said. "*I* am Nag. The great god Brahm[4] put his mark upon all our

---

3. **Nag** [näg]
4. **Brahm** [bräm]: the chief spirit and creator of the universe in the Hindu religion.

people when the first cobra spread his hood to keep the sun off Brahm as he slept. Look, and be afraid!"

He spread out his hood more than ever, and Rikki-tikki saw the spectacle mark on the back of it that looks exactly like the eye part of a hook-and-eye fastening. He was afraid for the minute; but it is impossible for a mongoose to stay frightened for any length of time, and though Rikki-tikki had never met a live cobra before, his mother had fed him on dead ones, and he knew that all a grown mongoose's business in life was to fight and eat snakes. Nag knew that too, and at the bottom of his cold heart he was afraid.

"Well," said Rikki-tikki, and his tail began to fluff up again, "marks or no marks, do you think it is right for you to eat fledglings out of a nest?"

Nag was thinking to himself, and watching the least little movement in the grass behind Rikki-tikki. He knew that mongooses in the garden meant death sooner or later for him and his family, but he wanted to get Rikki-tikki off his guard. So he dropped his head a little and put it on one side.

"Let us talk," he said. "You eat eggs. Why should not I eat birds?"

"Behind you! Look behind you!" sang Darzee.

Rikki-tikki knew better than to waste time in staring. He jumped up in the air as high as he could go, and just under him whizzed by the head of Nagaina,[5] Nag's wicked wife. She had crept up behind him as he was talking, to make an end of him; and he heard her savage hiss as the stroke missed. He came down almost across her back, and if he had been an old mongoose, he would have known that then was the time to break her back with one bite; but he was afraid of the terrible lash-

---

5. **Nagaina** [nə gī′nə]

ing return stroke of the cobra. He bit, indeed, but did not bite long enough, and he jumped clear of the whisking tail, leaving Nagaina torn and angry.

"Wicked, wicked Darzee!" said Nag, lashing up as high as he could reach toward the nest in the thornbush; but Darzee had built it out of the reach of snakes, and it only swayed to and fro.

Rikki-tikki felt his eyes growing red and hot (when a mongoose's eyes grow red, he is angry), and he sat back on his tail and hind legs like a little kangaroo, and looked all around him, and chattered with rage. But Nag and Nagaina had disappeared into the grass. When a snake misses its stroke, it never says anything or gives any sign of what it means to do next. Rikki-tikki did not care to follow them, for he did not feel sure that he could manage two snakes at once. So he trotted off to the gravel path near the house, and sat down to think. It was a serious matter for him.

If you read the old books of natural history, you will find they say that when the mongoose fights the snake and happens to get bitten, he runs off and eats some herb that cures him. That is not true. The victory is only a matter of quickness of eye and quickness of foot—snake's blow against mongoose's jump—and as no eye can follow the motion of a snake's head when it strikes, that makes things much more wonderful than any magic herb. Rikki-tikki knew he was a young mongoose, and it made him all the more pleased to think that he had managed to escape a blow from behind. It gave him confidence in himself, and when Teddy came running down the path, Rikki-tikki was ready to be petted.

But just as Teddy was stooping, something flinched a little in the dust, and a tiny voice said: "Be careful. I am death!" It was Karait, the dusty brown snakeling that lies for choice on the dusty earth; and his bite is as dangerous as the cobra's. But he is so small that nobody thinks of him, and so he does the more harm to people.

Rikki-tikki's eyes grew red again, and he danced up to Karait with the peculiar rocking, swaying motion that he had inherited from his family. It looks very funny, but it is so perfectly balanced a gait that you can fly off from it at any angle you please; and in dealing with snakes this is an advantage. If Rikki-tikki had only known, he was doing a much more dangerous thing than fighting Nag, for Karait is so small, and can turn so quickly, that unless Rikki bit him close to the back of the head, he would get the return stroke in his eye or lip. But Rikki did not know: his eyes were all red, and he rocked back and forth, looking for a good place to hold. Karait struck out. Rikki jumped sideways and tried to run in, but the wicked little dusty gray head lashed within a fraction of his shoulder, and he had to jump over the body, and the head followed his heels close.

Teddy shouted to the house: "Oh, look here! Our mongoose is killing a snake"; and Rikki-tikki heard a scream from Teddy's mother. His father ran out with a stick, but by the time he came up, Karait had lunged out once too far, and Rikki-tikki had sprung, jumped on the snake's back, dropped his head far between his forelegs, bitten as high up the back as he could get hold, and rolled away. That bite paralyzed Karait, and Rikki-tikki was just going to eat him up from the tail, after the custom of his family at dinner, when he remembered that a full meal makes a slow mongoose, and if he wanted all his strength and quickness ready, he must keep himself thin.

He went away for a dust bath under the castor-oil bushes, while Teddy's father beat the dead Karait. "What is the use of that?"

thought Rikki-tikki. "I have settled it all"; and then Teddy's mother picked him up from the dust and hugged him, crying that he had saved Teddy from death, and Teddy's father said that he was a providence, and Teddy looked on with big scared eyes. Rikki-tikki was rather amused at all the fuss, which, of course, he did not understand. Teddy's mother might just as well have petted Teddy for playing in the dust. Rikki was thoroughly enjoying himself.

That night, at dinner, walking to and fro among the wineglasses on the table, he could have stuffed himself three times over with nice things; but he remembered Nag and Nagaina, and though it was very pleasant to be patted and petted by Teddy's mother, and to sit on Teddy's shoulder, his eyes would get red from time to time, and he would go off into his long war cry of *"Rikk-tikk-tikki-tikki-tchk!"*

Teddy carried him off to bed and insisted on Rikki-tikki sleeping under his chin. Rikki-tikki was too well bred to bite or scratch, but as soon as Teddy was asleep he went off for his nightly walk round the house, and in the dark he ran up against Chuchundra, the muskrat, creeping round by the wall. Chuchundra is a brokenhearted little beast. He whimpers and cheeps all the night, trying to make up his mind to run into the middle of the room, but he never gets there.

"Don't kill me," said Chuchundra, almost weeping. "Rikki-tikki, don't kill me."

"Do you think a snake-killer kills muskrats?" said Rikki-tikki scornfully.

"Those who kill snakes get killed by snakes," said Chuchundra, more sorrowfully than ever. "And how am I to be sure that Nag won't mistake me for you some dark night?"

"There's not the least danger," said Rikki-tikki; "but Nag is in the garden, and I know you don't go there."

"My cousin Chua, the rat, told me—" said Chuchundra, and then he stopped.

"Told you what?"

"H'sh! Nag is everywhere, Rikki-tikki. You should have talked to Chua in the garden."

"I didn't—so you must tell me. Quick, Chuchundra, or I'll bite you!"

Chuchundra sat down and cried till the tears rolled off his whiskers. "I am a very poor man," he sobbed. "I never had spirit enough to run out into the middle of the room. H'sh! I mustn't tell you anything. Can't you *hear*, Rikki-tikki?"

Rikki-tikki listened. The house was as still as still, but he thought he could just catch the faintest *scratch-scratch* in the world—a noise as faint as that of a wasp walking on a windowpane—the dry scratch of a snake's scales on brickwork.

"That's Nag or Nagaina," he said to himself; "and he is crawling into the bathroom sluice.[6] You're right, Chuchundra; I should have talked to Chua."

He stole off to Teddy's bathroom, but there was nothing there, and then to Teddy's mother's bathroom. At the bottom of the smooth plaster wall there was a brick pulled out to make a sluice for the bath water, and as Rikki-tikki stole in by the masonry curb where the bath is put, he heard Nag and Nagaina whispering together outside in the moonlight.

"When the house is emptied of people," said Nagaina to her husband, "*he* will have to go away, and then the garden will be our own again. Go in quietly, and remember that the big man who killed Karait is the first one to bite. Then come out and tell me, and we will hunt for Rikki-tikki together."

"But are you sure that there is anything to be gained by killing the people?" said Nag.

"Everything. When there were no people in the bungalow, did we have any mongoose in the garden? So long as the bungalow is empty, we are king and queen of the garden; and remember that as soon as our eggs in the melon bed hatch (as they may tomorrow), our children will need room and quiet."

"I had not thought of that," said Nag. "I will go, but there is no need that we should hunt for Rikki-tikki afterward. I will kill the big man and his wife, and the child if I can, and come away quietly. Then the bungalow will be empty, and Rikki-tikki will go."

Rikki-tikki tingled all over with rage and hatred at this, and then Nag's head came through the sluice, and his five feet of cold body followed it. Angry as he was, Rikki-tikki was very frightened as he saw the size of the big cobra. Nag coiled himself up, raised his head, and looked into the bathroom in the dark, and Rikki could see his eyes glitter.

"Now, if I kill him there, Nagaina will know; and if I fight him on the open floor, the odds are in his favor. What am I to do?" said Rikki-tikki-tavi.

Nag waved to and fro, and then Rikki-tikki heard him drinking from the biggest water jar that was used to fill the bath. "That is good," said the snake. "Now, when Karait was killed, the big man had a stick. He may have that stick still, but when he comes in to bathe in the morning he will not have a stick. I shall wait here till he comes. Nagaina—do you hear me? I shall wait here in the cool till daytime."

There was no answer from outside, so Rikki-tikki knew Nagaina had gone away. Nag coiled himself down, coil by coil, round the bulge at the bottom of the water jar, and Rikki-tikki stayed still as death. After an hour he began to move, muscle by muscle, toward the jar. Nag was asleep, and Rikki-tikki looked at his big back, wondering which would be the best place for a good hold. "If I don't break his back at the first jump," said Rikki, "he

---

6. **sluice** [slo͞os]: passageway for draining water.

can still fight; and if he fights—O Rikki!" He looked at the thickness of the neck below the hood, but that was too much for him; and a bite near the tail would only make Nag savage.

"It must be the head," he said at last; "the head above the hood; and when I am once there, I must not let go."

Then he jumped. The head was lying a little clear of the water jar, under the curve of it; and, as his teeth met, Rikki braced his back against the bulge of the red earthenware to hold down the head. This gave him just one second's purchase,[7] and he made the most of it. Then he was battered to and fro as a rat is shaken by a dog—to and fro on the floor, up and down, and round in great circles; but his eyes were red, and he held on as the body cartwhipped over the floor, upsetting the tin dipper and the soap dish and the fleshbrush, and banged against the tin side of the bath. As he held, he closed his jaws tighter and tighter, for he made sure[8] he would be banged to death, and, for the honor of his family, he preferred to be found with his teeth locked. He was dizzy, aching, and felt shaken to pieces when something went off like a thunderclap just behind him; a hot wind knocked him senseless, and red fire singed his fur. The big man had been wakened by the noise, and

---

7. **purchase:** here, advantage.

---

8. **made sure:** here, thought.

had fired both barrels of a shotgun into Nag just behind the hood.

Rikki-tikki held on with his eyes shut, for now he was quite sure he was dead; but the head did not move, and the big man picked him up and said: "It's the mongoose again, Alice; the little chap has saved *our* lives now." Then Teddy's mother came in with a very white face, and saw what was left of Nag, and Rikki-tikki dragged himself to Teddy's bedroom and spent half the rest of the night shaking himself tenderly to find out whether he really was broken into forty pieces, as he fancied.

When morning came he was very stiff, but well pleased with his doings. "Now I have Nagaina to settle with, and she will be worse than five Nags, and there's no knowing when the eggs she spoke of will hatch. Goodness! I must go and see Darzee," he said.

Without waiting for breakfast, Rikki-tikki ran to the thornbush where Darzee was singing a song of triumph at the top of his voice. The news of Nag's death was all over the garden, for the sweeper had thrown the body on the rubbish heap.

"Oh, you stupid tuft of feathers!" said Rikki-tikki angrily. "Is this the time to sing?"

"Nag is dead—is dead—is dead!" sang Darzee. "The valiant Rikki-tikki caught him by the head and held fast. The big man brought the bang-stick, and Nag fell in two pieces! He will never eat my babies again."

"All that's true enough; but where's Nagaina?" said Rikki-tikki, looking carefully round him.

"Nagaina came to the bathroom sluice and called for Nag," Darzee went on; "and Nag came out on the end of a stick—the sweeper picked him up on the end of a stick and threw him upon the rubbish heap. Let us sing about the great, the red-eyed Rikki-tikki!" And Darzee filled his throat and sang.

"If I could get up to your nest, I'd roll all your babies out!" said Rikki-tikki. "You don't know when to do the right thing at the right time. You're safe enough in your nest there, but it's war for me down here. Stop singing a minute, Darzee."

"For the great, the beautiful Rikki-tikki's sake I will stop," said Darzee. "What is it, O Killer of the terrible Nag?"

"Where is Nagaina, for the third time?"

"On the rubbish heap by the stables, mourning for Nag. Great is Rikki-tikki with the white teeth."

"Bother[9] my white teeth! Have you ever heard where she keeps her eggs?"

"In the melon bed, on the end nearest the wall, where the sun strikes nearly all day. She hid them there weeks ago."

"And you never thought it worthwhile to tell me? The end nearest the wall, you said?"

"Rikki-tikki. you are not going to eat her eggs?"

"Not eat exactly; no. Darzee, if you have a grain of sense you will fly off to the stables and pretend that your wing is broken, and let Nagaina chase you away to this bush! I must get to the melon bed, and if I went there now she'd see me."

Darzee was a featherbrained little fellow who could never hold more than one idea at a time in his head; and just because he knew that Nagaina's children were born in eggs like his own, he didn't think at first that it was fair to kill them. But his wife was a sensible bird, and she knew that cobras' eggs meant young cobras later on; so she flew off from the nest, and left Darzee to keep the babies warm, and continue his song about the death of Nag. Darzee was very like a man in some ways.

She fluttered in front of Nagaina by the rubbish heap and cried out, "Oh, my wing is

_____

9. **Bother:** here, never mind.

broken! The boy in the house threw a stone at me and broke it." Then she fluttered more desperately than ever.

Nagaina lifted up her head and hissed, "You warned Rikki-tikki when I would have killed him. Indeed and truly, you've chosen a bad place to be lame in." And she moved toward Darzee's wife, slipping along over the dust.

"The boy broke it with a stone!" shrieked Darzee's wife.

"Well! It may be some consolation to you when you're dead to know that I shall settle accounts with the boy. My husband lies on the rubbish heap this morning, but before night the boy in the house will lie very still. What is the use of running away? I am sure to catch you. Little fool, look at me!"

Darzee's wife knew better than to do *that*, for a bird who looks at a snake's eyes gets so frightened that she cannot move. Darzee's wife fluttered on, piping sorrowfully, and never leaving the ground, and Nagaina quickened her pace.

Rikki-tikki heard them going up the path from the stables, and he raced for the end of the melon patch near the wall. There, in the warm litter about the melons, very cunningly hidden, he found twenty-five eggs, about the size of a bantam's eggs,[10] but with whitish skin instead of shell.

"I was not a day too soon," he said; for he could see the baby cobras curled up inside the skin, and he knew that the minute they were hatched they could each kill a man or a mongoose. He bit off the tops of the eggs as fast as he could, taking care to crush the young cobras, and turned over the litter from time to time to see whether he had missed any. At last there were only three eggs left, and Rikki-

tikki began to chuckle to himself, when he heard Darzee's wife screaming:

"Rikki-tikki, I led Nagaina toward the house, and she has gone into the veranda, and—oh, come quickly—she means killing!"

Rikki-tikki smashed two eggs, and tumbled backward down the melon bed with the third egg in his mouth, and scuttled to the veranda as hard as he could put foot to the ground. Teddy and his mother and father were there at early breakfast; but Rikki-tikki saw that they were not eating anything. They sat stone-still, and their faces were white. Nagaina was coiled up on the matting by Teddy's chair, within easy striking distance of Teddy's bare leg, and she was swaying to and fro singing a song of triumph.

"Son of the big man that killed Nag," she hissed, "stay still. I am not ready yet. Wait a little. Keep very still, all you three. If you move I strike, and if you do not move I strike. Oh, foolish people, who killed my Nag!"

Teddy's eyes were fixed on his father, and all his father could do was to whisper, "Sit still, Teddy. You mustn't move. Teddy, keep still."

10. **bantam's eggs:** tiny eggs of the bantam, a small fowl.

Then Rikki-tikki came up and cried: "Turn round, Nagaina; turn and fight!"

"All in good time," said she, without moving her eyes. "I will settle my account with *you* presently. Look at your friends, Rikki-tikki. They are still and white; they are afraid. They dare not move, and if you come a step nearer I strike."

"Look at your eggs," said Rikki-tikki, "in the melon bed near the wall. Go and look, Nagaina."

The big snake turned half round and saw the egg on the veranda. "Ah-h! Give it to me," she said.

Rikki-tikki put his paws one on each side of the egg, and his eyes were blood-red. "What price for a snake's egg? For a young cobra? For a young king cobra? For the last—the very last of the brood? The ants are eating all the others down by the melon bed."

Nagaina spun clear round, forgetting everything for the sake of the one egg; and Rikki-tikki saw Teddy's father shoot out a big hand, catch Teddy by the shoulder, and drag him across the little table with the teacups, safe and out of reach of Nagaina.

"Tricked! Tricked! Tricked! *Rikk-tck-tck!*" chuckled Rikki-tikki. "The boy is safe, and it was I—I—I that caught Nag by the hood last night in the bathroom." Then he began to jump up and down, all four feet together, his head close to the floor. "He threw me to and fro, but he could not shake me off. He was dead before the big man blew him in two. I did it. *Rikki-tikki-tck-tck!* Come then, Nagaina. Come and fight with me. You shall not be a widow long."

Nagaina saw that she had lost her chance of killing Teddy, and the egg lay between Rikki-tikki's paws. "Give me the egg, Rikki-tikki. Give me the last of my eggs, and I will go away and never come back," she said, lowering her hood.

"Yes, you will go away, and you will never come back; for you will go to the rubbish heap with Nag. Fight, widow! The big man has gone for his gun! Fight!"

Rikki-tikki was bounding all round Nagaina, keeping just out of reach of her stroke, his little eyes like hot coals. Nagaina gathered herself together and flung out at him. Rikki-tikki jumped up and backward. Again and

again and again she struck, and each time her head came with a whack on the matting of the veranda, and she gathered herself together like a watchspring. Then Rikki-tikki danced in a circle to get behind her, and Nagaina spun round to keep her head to his head, so that the rustle of her tail on the matting sounded like dry leaves blown along by the wind.

He had forgotten the egg. It still lay on the veranda, and Nagaina came nearer and nearer to it, till at last, while Rikki-tikki was drawing breath, she caught it in her mouth, turned to the veranda steps, and flew like an arrow down the path, with Rikki-tikki behind her. When the cobra runs for her life, she goes like a whiplash flicked across a horse's neck.

Rikki-tikki knew that he must catch her, or all the trouble would begin again. She headed straight for the long grass by the thornbush, and as he was running Rikki-tikki heard Darzee singing his foolish little song of triumph. But Darzee's wife was wiser. She flew off her nest as Nagaina came along, and flapped her wings about Nagaina's head. If Darzee had helped they might have turned her; but Nagaina only lowered her hood and went on. Still, the instant's delay brought Rikki-tikki up to her, and as she plunged into the rathole where she and Nag used to live, his little white teeth were clenched on her tail, and he went down with her—and very few mongooses, however wise and old they may be, care to follow a cobra into its hole. It was dark in the hole; and Rikki-tikki never knew when it might open out and give Nagaina room to turn and strike at him. He held on savagely and struck out his feet to act as brakes on the dark slope of the hot, moist earth.

Then the grass by the mouth of the hole stopped waving, and Darzee said: "It is all over with Rikki-tikki! We must sing his death song. Valiant Rikki-tikki is dead. For Nagaina will surely kill him underground."

So he sang a very mournful song that he made up all on the spur of the minute, and just as he got to the most touching part the grass quivered again, and Rikki-tikki, covered with dirt, dragged himself out of the hole leg by leg, licking his whiskers. Darzee stopped with a little shout. Rikki-tikki shook some of the dust out of his fur and sneezed. "It is all over," he said. "The widow will never come out again." And the red ants that live between the grass stems heard him, and began to troop down one after another to see if he had spoken the truth.

Rikki-tikki curled himself up in the grass and slept where he was—slept and slept till it was late in the afternoon, for he had done a hard day's work.

"Now," he said, when he awoke, "I will go back to the house. Tell the coppersmith, Darzee, and he will tell the garden that Nagaina is dead."

The coppersmith is a bird who makes a noise exactly like the beating of a little hammer on a copper pot; and the reason he is always making it is because he is the town crier to every Indian garden, and tells all the news to everybody who cares to listen. As Rikki-tikki went up the path, he heard his "attention" notes like a tiny dinner gong; and then the steady *"Ding-dong-tock! Nag is dead—dong! Nagaina is dead! Ding-dong-tock!"* That set all the birds in the garden singing, and the frogs croaking, for Nag and Nagaina used to eat frogs as well as little birds.

When Rikki got to the house, Teddy and Teddy's mother (she still looked very white, for she had been fainting) and Teddy's father came out and almost cried over him; and that night he ate all that was given him till he could eat no more, and went to bed on Teddy's shoulder, where Teddy's mother saw him when she came to look late at night.

"He saved our lives and Teddy's life," she said to her husband. "Just think, he saved all our lives!"

Rikki-tikki woke up with a jump, for all mongooses are light sleepers.

"Oh, it's you," said he. "What are you bothering for? All the cobras are dead; and if they weren't, I'm here."

Rikki-tikki had a right to be proud of himself; but he did not grow too proud, and he kept that garden as a mongoose should keep it, with tooth and jump and spring and bite, till never a cobra dared show its head inside the walls.

STUDY QUESTIONS

Recalling

1. In whose house does Rikki find himself? How does he get there?
2. Why didn't Rikki break Nagaina's back when he first had the opportunity?
3. Why did the cobras feel it was necessary to kill the people in the house?
4. How was Nag finally killed? What ultimately happened to Nagaina?

Interpreting

5. Which characters in the story would you describe as good and which as evil? Why?
6. Why didn't the other animals come to Rikki's rescue in Nagaina's rat hole? Was Rikki foolish or wise for following Nagaina there? Explain.
7. What lessons about survival did Rikki learn?

Extending

8. Imagine Rikki had been killed by Nagaina at the end of the story. How would this turn of events have affected your feelings about the story?

READING AND LITERARY FOCUS

The Short Story

A **short story** is a fictional account of events written in prose paragraphs. Generally each event leads to the next. In the beginning of a story, one or more characters may face a problem that gets more complicated as the story progresses. The problem is settled in some way by the end of the story. A story may have a happy ending, a sad ending, or an ending that offers a mixture of human emotions.

Think about a story you may have read or heard—The Wizard of Oz, for example. In that story a girl named Dorothy runs from home to protect her dog. This problem gets more complicated when a cyclone blows Dorothy to a strange land. The difficulty ends when Dorothy awakes at home to discover she has only suffered a bad dream.

The events in a story usually occur in a specific time and place. The time and place may change as the story continues. For example, The Wizard of Oz begins on a farm in Kansas. The action eventually moves to the land of Oz and then back to Kansas. The story seems to take place over several days, but in the end we realize that it actually takes place during the course of a dream.

Authors often wish to express their personal ideas about life, and so they create stories to help illustrate those ideas. The author of The Wizard of Oz wanted to express the idea that living in a strange environment can help people better appreciate the joy and security of their own surroundings. As Dorothy puts it at the end of the story, "There's no place like home."

You will find more stories beginning on page 53.

Thinking About the Short Story

1. Who are the main characters in "Rikki-tikki-tavi"?
2. What problems do the characters in "Rikki-tikki-tavi" face? How are the problems settled by the end of the story?

VOCABULARY

Synonyms

A **synonym** is a word that has the same or nearly the same meaning as another word. *Begin* and *start* are synonyms. The italicized words below are from "Rikki-tikki-tavi." Choose the word that is nearest the meaning of each *italicized* word, *as the word is used in the story.* Write the number of each item and the letter of your choice on a separate sheet.

1. a *valiant* hero
   (a) war
   (b) famous
   (c) brave
   (d) large
2. *cowered* behind a chair
   (a) bent
   (b) afraid
   (c) sat
   (d) stood
3. remarked *scornfully*
   (a) loudly
   (b) quietly
   (c) cleverly
   (d) hatefully
4. slow *gait*
   (a) fence
   (b) speed
   (c) walk
   (d) horse
5. sneaked *cunningly*
   (a) awkwardly
   (b) slyly
   (c) quickly
   (d) slowly

COMPOSITION

Answering an Essay Question

■ Although Rikki is a mongoose and Teddy is a person, both face the problem of survival. Write an essay that answers the following question: How is the problem Rikki faces similar to or different from the problem Teddy faces? First make a general statement. Then identify the specific dangers that threaten Rikki. Next identify the dangers that threaten Teddy. Finally, explain how these problems are similar or different. *For help with this assignment, see Lesson 1 in the Writing About Literature Handbook at the back of this book.*

Writing a Story

■ Write your own story about an animal. Think of a problem that the animal faces, and decide how the problem will be solved. Make sure each event in the story leads logically to the next event. Describe your characters and setting clearly. *For help with this assignment, see Lesson 4 in the Writing About Literature Handbook at the back of this book.*

CHALLENGE

Class Play

■ Work together with several classmates to perform part or all of "Rikki-tikki-tavi" as a play. Write speeches for the characters. Also provide directions that tell the performers how to say their lines and how to move.

British poet John Masefield (1878–1967), orphaned as a child, went to sea at age fourteen. When he returned to England five years later, he took a job on a newspaper and decided to become a writer. By 1930 he had become very popular and was named Poet Laureate of England, the country's official poet. Masefield's exciting experiences at sea inspired many of his best poems, including "Roadways."

■ Identify the vivid details that show how well Masefield knew the "salt green tossing sea."

John Masefield

Roadways

One road leads to London,
    One road runs to Wales,[1]
My road leads me seawards
    To the white dipping sails.

One road leads to the river,
    As it goes singing slow;
My road leads to shipping
    Where the bronzed sailors go.

Leads me, lures me, calls me
    To salt green tossing sea;
A road without earth's road-dust
    Is the right road for me.

A wet road heaving, shining
    And wild with seagull's cries,
A mad salt sea-wind blowing
    The salt spray in my eyes.

My road calls me, lures me
    West, east, south, and north;
Most roads lead men homewards,
    My road leads me forth.

---

1. **Wales:** a division of the United Kingdom.

STUDY QUESTIONS

Recalling

1. In lines 3 and 7 where does the poet say his road leads?
2. According to lines 9 and 17, what does the poet's road do to him?
3. In stanza 4 what specific details of the sea does the poet mention?
4. According to lines 19–20, how is the poet's road different from the roads most people take?

Interpreting

5. What do you think the poet means by "a road without earth's road-dust"?
6. Would the poet rather be at home or at sea? How do you know?
7. The "roads" in this poem might mean more than just roads. What larger thing could they represent?

Extending

8. Why do you think the sea has a strong attraction for some people?

READING AND LITERARY FOCUS

Poetry

Poetry is imaginative writing in which language, images, sound, and rhythm combine to create a special emotional effect. The poet carefully chooses words that create vivid pictures and stir particular feelings in the reader. In "Roadways," for example, the phrase "salt green tossing sea" creates a detailed, imaginative picture and stirs particular feelings as we imagine it.

The speaker of a poem is, simply, the person or thing that "speaks" or "tells" the poem. Often the speaker is the poet, but sometimes the poet creates a different speaker, such as another person, an animal, or an object. The speaker of "Roadways" is the poet, Masefield.

The poet usually arranges lines in units called stanzas. The lines often have a regular rhythm, or beat. Masefield's poem, for example, has a regular rhythm that imitates the back-and-forth movement of the waves, as seen in the following lines:

> One road leads to London,
> One road runs to Wales,
> My road leads me seawards
> To the white dipping sails.

Many poems also contain rhyme. For example, in the first stanza of Masefield's poem, the words *Wales* in line 2 and *sails* in line 4 rhyme.

Just like authors of stories, authors of poems write to express their ideas and visions about life in general. Some poets tell stories in poems to illustrate their ideas. Other poets express their thoughts and emotions more directly. For example, in "Roadways" the poet makes his love of the sea quite clear through his colorful descriptions and straightforward expression of emotion.

You will find more poems beginning on page 209.

Thinking About Poetry

1. How many stanzas does "Roadways" have? How many lines are in each stanza?
2. Which lines in each stanza rhyme?
3. Based on the details in the poem, what picture of the sea do you form in your mind? Which words and phrases help you most to form that picture?

VOCABULARY

Analogies

Analogies are comparisons that are stated as double relationships—for example, *A* is to *B* as *C* is to *D*. On tests analogies are written as two pairs of words—A : B :: C : D. You may be given the first pair and asked to find or complete a second pair that has the same kind of relationship. For example, in the analogy FLOWER : CARNATION :: TREE : ELM, the first word in each pair names a general category, and the second word names a specific member of that category.

Analogies can state the following kinds of relationships, among others:

synonyms (SMART : INTELLIGENT)
opposites (GOOD : BAD)
cause and effect (NOISE : HEADACHE)
different grammatical forms of the same word
(TRANSPORTING : TRANSPORTATION)

The following numbered items are analogies that need to be completed. The third word in each item comes from "Roadways." Decide how the first two words in each item are related. Then from the four choices that follow each numbered item, choose the word that best completes the second pair. Write the number of each item and the letter of your choice on a separate sheet.

1. SKYWARDS : ASTRONAUT :: SEAWARDS :
   (a) rocket   (c) ship
   (b) sailor   (d) water

2. ATTEMPTS : TRIES :: LURES :
   (a) denies   (c) attracts
   (b) succeeds   (d) tackles

3. SOAKED : RAIN :: BRONZED
   (a) sun   (c) yellow
   (b) dry   (d) wind

4. RAISING : UP :: DIPPING :
   (a) lifting   (c) sails
   (b) side   (d) down

5. AWAY : LEAVE :: HOMEWARDS :
   (a) travel   (c) return
   (b) house   (d) going

COMPARING THEMES

1. Rikki-tikki-tavi and the speaker in "Roadways" each have goals to achieve. Whose goals would you call career goals and whose survival goals?
2. How do the goals of Rikki and the speaker both require bravery?

Anne Morrow Lindbergh (born 1906) has written many books and articles about her adventures. In the early days of airplanes, she often made long and dangerous flights with her husband, Charles Lindbergh, the pilot who in 1927 made the first solo flight across the Atlantic Ocean. "Morning—'The Bird Perched for Flight' " is from *Earth Shine*, Anne Morrow Lindbergh's book about space exploration. The selection describes the takeoff of *Apollo 8*, a lunar rocket launched on December 21, 1968, from Cape Canaveral, Florida.

▨ As you read, locate details that lend a sense of tension and great importance to this brief event.

Anne Morrow Lindbergh

Morning—"The Bird Perched for Flight"

We wake to the alarm at four-thirty and leave our motel at five-fifteen. The three astronauts must be already climbing into their seats at the top of their "thirty-six-story" rocket, poised for flight. The pilgrimage of sightseers has started to the Cape.[1] Already the buses have left and lines of cars are on the roads. It is dark, a little chilly, with a sky full of stars. As we approach the Cape we see again the rocket and its launching tower from far off over the lagoon. It is still illumined with searchlights, but last night's vision has vanished. It is no longer tender or biological but simply a machine, the newest and most perfected creation of a scientific age—hard, weighty metal.

We watch the launching with some of the astronauts and their families, from a site near the Vehicle Assembly Building. Our cars are parked on a slight rise of ground. People get out, walk about restlessly, set up cameras and adjust their binoculars. The launch pad is about three miles away, near the beach. We look across Florida marsh grass and palmet-

---

1. **the Cape:** Cape Kennedy (now called Cape Canaveral), a peninsula on the east central coast of Florida; the launch site of many American space shots.

tos. A cabbage palm stands up black against a shadowy sky, just left of the rocket and its launching tower. As dawn flushes the horizon, an egret[2] rises and lazily glides across the flats between us and the pad. It is a still morning. Ducks call from nearby inlets. Vapor trails of a high-flying plane turn pink in an almost cloudless sky. Stars pale in the blue.

With the morning light, Apollo 8 and its launching tower become clearer, harder, and more defined. One can see the details of installation. The dark sections on the smooth sides of the rocket, marking its stages, cut up the single fluid line. Vapor steams furiously off its side. No longer stark and simple, this morning the rocket is complicated, mechanical, earth-bound. Too weighty for flight, one feels.

People stop talking, stand in front of their cars, and raise binoculars to their eyes. We peer nervously at the launch site and then at our wrist watches. Radio voices blare unnaturally loud from car windows. "Now only thirty minutes to launch time . . . fifteen minutes . . . six minutes . . . thirty seconds to go . . . twenty . . . T minus fifteen . . . fourteen . . . thirteen . . . twelve . . . eleven . . . ten . . . nine. . . . Ignition!"

A jet of steam shoots from the pad below the rocket. "Ahhhh!" The crowd gasps, almost in unison. Now great flames spurt, leap, belch out across the horizon. Clouds of smoke billow up on either side of the rocket, completely hiding its base. From the midst of this holocaust,[3] the rocket begins to rise—slowly, as in a dream, so slowly it seems to hang suspended on the cloud of fire and smoke. It's impossible—it can't rise. Yes, it rises, but heavily, as if the giant weight is pulled by an invisible hand out of the atmosphere, like the lead on a plumb line[4] from the depths of the sea. Slowly it rises and—because of our distance—silently, as in a dream.

Suddenly the noise breaks, jumps across our three separating miles—a shattering roar of explosions, a trip hammer over one's head, under one's feet, through one's body. The earth shakes; cars rattle; vibrations beat in the chest. A roll of thunder, prolonged, prolonged, prolonged.

I drop the binoculars and put my hands to my ears, holding my head to keep it steady. My throat tightens—am I going to cry?—my eyes are fixed on the rocket, mesmerized[5] by its slow ascent.

The foreground is now full of birds; a great flock of ducks, herons, small birds, rise pell-mell from the marshes at the noise. Fluttering in alarm and confusion, they scatter in all directions as if it were the end of the world. In the seconds I take to look at them, the rocket has left the tower.

It is up and away, a comet boring through the sky, no longer the vulnerable untried child, no longer the earth-bound machine, or the weight at the end of a line, but sheer terrifying force, blasting upward on its own titanic[6] power.

It has gone miles into the sky. It is blurred by a cloud. No, it has made its own cloud—a huge vapor trail, which hides it. Out of the cloud something falls, cartwheeling down, smoking. "The first-stage cutoff,"[7] someone says. Where is the rocket itself?

There, above the cloud now, reappears the

---

2. **egret** [ē′grit]: type of white-plumed heron, or wading bird with long legs and a long neck; it is most commonly found in the southern United States.
3. **holocaust** [hol′ə kôst′]: thorough destruction by fire.

---

4. **lead . . . line:** A plumb line is used to determine the depth of water or the straightness of a wall. A lead weight hangs at the end of the line to keep it vertical.
5. **mesmerized** [mez′mə rīzd′]: hypnotized.
6. **titanic** [tī tan′ik]: huge and powerful like the Titans, a race of giants in Greek mythology.
7. **"The . . . cutoff":** The spaceship is propelled by several rockets that are fired in stages. The first-stage rocket is cut off a few minutes after the launch and falls back to earth.

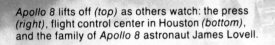

Apollo 8 lifts off *(top)* as others watch: the press *(right)*, flight control center in Houston *(bottom)*, and the family of *Apollo 8* astronaut James Lovell.

rocket, only a very bright star, diminishing every second. Soon out of sight, off to lunar space.

One looks earthward again. It is curiously still and empty. A cloud of brown smoke hangs motionless on the horizon. Its long shadow reaches us across the grass. The launch pad is empty. The abandoned launching tower is being sprayed with jets of water to cool it down. It steams in the bright morning air. Still dazed, people stumble into cars and start the slow, jammed trek back to town. The monotone of radio voices continues. One clings to this last thread of contact with something incredibly beautiful that has vanished.

"Where are they—where are they now?" In eleven minutes we get word. They are in earth orbit. They "look good" in the laconic[8] space talk that comes down from over a hundred miles above earth. And one realizes again that it is the men above all that matter, the individuals who man the machine, give it heart, sight, speech, intelligence, and direction; and the men on earth who are backing them up, monitoring their every move, even to their heartbeats. This is not sheer power, it is power under control of man.

We drive slowly back to town. Above us the white vapor trail of the rocket is being scattered by wind into feathery shapes of heron's wings—the only mark in the sky of the morning's launching.

_____

8. **laconic** [lə kon′ik]: using few words.

STUDY QUESTIONS

Recalling

1. At what time of day is the rocket launched?
2. List several details that describe the way the spectators prepare for the launch.
3. According to the narrator, how does the way _Apollo 8_ looks in the morning differ from the way it looked the night before?
4. What details of the actual blastoff does the narrator give?

Interpreting

5. What is the mood of the crowd before the launch? In what way, if any, does the mood change after the rocket is in orbit?
6. The narrator describes the entire event in the present tense instead of in the past tense. What kind of effect does the use of the present tense create in the selection?
7. What does the narrator mean by saying that the launch "is not sheer power, it is power under control of man"?

Extending

8. The spectators make a great effort to be present at an event lasting only a few minutes. Why do you think they desire so much to be at this event?

READING AND LITERARY FOCUS

Nonfiction

Nonfiction is factual prose writing. It deals with real experiences. While a story or poem may tell of imaginary events, nonfiction focuses on actual events. "Rikki-tikki-tavi," for example, is a fictional story about a mongoose. An encyclopedia article about mongooses is an example of nonfiction.

Nonfiction can be divided into two main categories: (1) essays and (2) biographies and autobiographies. An **essay** is an article expressing the writer's observations or opinions on one particular subject. Essays have been written on every imaginable subject—for example, on politics, science, sports, and entertainment.

A **biography** is the story of someone's life written by another person. Many biographies are about famous people (such as Abraham Lincoln) and are by famous authors (such as the poet Carl Sandburg). An **autobiography** is the story of a person's life written by that person. Eleanor Roosevelt wrote an autobiography describing her experiences as first lady.

Like authors of stories and poems, writers of nonfiction want to express their ideas about life. They may state their ideas directly or suggest ideas through the details they provide. For example, a writer of a factual essay may express directly the benefits of physical exercise. Another author may write a biography of a famous athlete. In so doing the author may suggest—without directly stating—that exercise is helpful for everyone. This suggestion could be made by showing how helpful exercise was in the athlete's life.

You will find more nonfiction selections beginning on page 289.

Thinking About Nonfiction

1. Would you classify "Morning—'The Bird Perched for Flight' " as an essay, a biography, or an autobiography? Give reasons for your choice.
2. What personal ideas about space exploration does Lindbergh communicate through her description of the *Apollo 8* takeoff?

VOCABULARY

Context Clues

Sometimes you can figure out a word's meaning by its **context,** or the words and sentences that surround it. Look carefully at the following sentences from Lindbergh's "Morning—'The Bird Perched for Flight.' "

The pilgrimage of sightseers has started to the Cape. Already the buses have left and lines of cars are on the roads.

Suppose you did not know the meaning of *pilgrimage.* The writer says that sightseers are traveling in buses and cars to the Cape. From this clue you may conclude that a *pilgrimage* is a trip or journey.

The following passages come from the selection. Choose the best meaning for each italicized word by studying its *context.* That is, examine the ideas found in the sentence in which the word appears or in surrounding sentences. Write the number of each item and the letter of your choice on a separate sheet.

1. It is still *illumined* with searchlights, but last night's vision has vanished.
   (a) heated   (c) lighted
   (b) started   (d) faded

2. No longer *stark* and simple, this morning the rocket is complicated, mechanical, earth-bound.
   (a) long   (c) solid
   (b) new   (d) plain

3. The launch pad is empty. The *abandoned* launching tower is being sprayed with jets of water to cool it down.
   (a) deserted   (c) safe
   (b) crowded   (d) cold

4. There, above the cloud now, reappears the rocket, only a very bright star, *diminishing* every second. Soon out of sight, off to lunar space.
   (a) growing   (c) falling
   (b) lessening   (d) freezing

5. Clouds of smoke *billow* up on either side of the rocket, completely hiding its base.
   (a) stand   (c) walk
   (b) rise   (d) warm

COMPARING THEMES

■ The spectators' concerns about *Apollo 8* reflect, in a larger sense, the goals of an entire nation. Compare these national goals to the personal goals sought by Rikki-tikki-tavi and by the speaker in "Roadways." In what ways are they similar and in what ways different?

Sir Arthur Conan Doyle (1859–1930), a Scottish physician, became so successful at creating mystery stories that he finally gave up his medical practice to devote all his time to writing. Many people consider his fictional character Sherlock Holmes to be the world's greatest detective. In fact, Conan Doyle once wrote a story in which Sherlock Holmes died; his devoted readers insisted he bring Holmes back to life.

■ As you read, try to find the clues Holmes will use to help him solve his baffling mystery.

A Dramatization by Michael and Mollie Hardwick
Based on the Story by Sir Arthur Conan Doyle

The Speckled Band

CHARACTERS

SHERLOCK HOLMES: great English detective

DR. WATSON: a physician and Holmes's friend

HELEN STONER: distressed young woman

DR. GRIMESBY ROYLOTT: Helen's stepfather; a physician from an upper-class but poor family

MRS. HUDSON: Holmes's housekeeper; middle-aged

Scene: The action takes place in and around London, England. The time is the 1890s.

Scene 1.

SHERLOCK HOLMES's *parlor. Early morning.*

[*A coffeepot stands on a small table.* HOLMES, *warming his back at the fire, is talking with* MRS. HUDSON, *who stands in the parlor doorway.*]

HOLMES. All right, Mrs. Hudson. I'll see the lady at once.

MRS. HUDSON. Very good, Mr. Holmes.

[*She turns to exit and collides with* WATSON, *who is bustling in.*]

WATSON. Oops!

MRS. HUDSON. I beg your pardon, sir.

WATSON. My fault entirely, Mrs. Hudson.

[MRS. HUDSON *exits, closing the door.* WATSON, *rubbing his hands briskly together, crosses to the coffee things and pours himself a cup.*]

Morning, Holmes!

HOLMES. Good morning, my dear Watson! You're just in time.

WATSON. Eh? What for?

HOLMES. We have a client.

WATSON. What—already!

HOLMES. It seems that a young lady has arrived in a considerable state of excitement.

WATSON. Aha!

HOLMES. Now, when young ladies wander about the metropolis[1] at this hour of the morning I presume they have something very pressing to communicate. Should it prove so, I'm sure you would wish to follow the case from the outset?

WATSON. My dear fellow, I wouldn't miss it for anything! Young lady, d'ye say?

HOLMES. Watson!

[*A knock at the parlor door.* MRS. HUDSON *enters.*]

MRS. HUDSON. Miss Helen Stoner, sir.

[*She steps aside to admit* HELEN, *then goes out, closing the door.* HOLMES *advances with hand outstretched, as* WATSON *hastily lays aside his coffee cup with interest.*]

HOLMES. Good morning, madam. My name is Sherlock Holmes.

HELEN. [*Her voice betrays tension.*] Good morning, Mr. Holmes.

HOLMES. And this is my intimate friend and colleague, Dr. Watson.

WATSON. How d'ye do, ma'am?

HELEN. How do you do, Doctor?

WATSON. You're cold, ma'am! Let me pour you a cup of coffee.

[*He starts off towards the coffee, but* HELEN *checks him.*]

HELEN. No coffee, thank you. It's not . . . the cold.

WATSON. But you're shivering!

HELEN. From fear, Dr. Watson. From terror!

[HOLMES *moves to her and steers her to a fireside chair. He takes the one opposite her,* WATSON *assuming his position at* HOLMES*'s elbow.*]

HOLMES. Don't be afraid, Miss Stoner. We shall soon set matters right.

HELEN. If only you can!

HOLMES. You have come in by train this morning, I see.

HELEN. [*Surprised.*] How do you know that?

HOLMES. [*Pointing.*] There is the second half of a return ticket tucked into your left glove.

HELEN. Oh!

HOLMES. I see you also had a good ride in a dogcart,[2] along heavy roads, on your way to the station.

HELEN. Yes! But I don't see how you can possibly . . .

HOLMES. [*Interrupting her.*] There is no mystery, my dear madam. The left arm of your jacket is spattered with mud in no less than seven places. The marks are perfectly fresh. Only a dogcart throws up mud in that way.

HELEN. [*Urgently.*] Mr. Holmes, I have no one to turn to! No one!

---

1. **metropolis** [mi trop′ə lis]: large city; in this case, London.

2. **dogcart:** small open carriage.

HOLMES. Calm yourself, dear lady.

HELEN. [*Sobbing.*] I can stand this strain no longer! [HELEN *dabs at her eyes.*]

HOLMES. Tell me what I can do for you.

HELEN. [*Recovering.*] Forgive me, Mr. Holmes. If . . . if you can throw a little light through the darkness which seems to surround me . . .

HOLMES. Let us hope so.

HELEN. I . . . I must tell you that I can't pay for your services at present. But in a month or two I shall be married and have control of my own income.

WATSON. [*A little disappointed.*] Er, congratulations!

HOLMES. My profession is its own reward. Now kindly let us hear everything that may help us to form an opinion.

HELEN. Very well. [*She settles back, a little more relaxed.*] My mother was the young widow of Major General Stoner.

WATSON. Bengal Artillery?[3]

HELEN. Yes.

WATSON. [*Impressed.*] By Jove!

[*He catches a meaningful glance from* HOLMES.]

Sorry, Holmes! Pray go on, ma'am.

HELEN. When my twin sister, Julia, and I were two my mother remarried to Dr. Grimesby Roylott,[4] of Stoke Moran, on the western border of Surrey.[5] About eight years ago my mother was killed in a railway accident at Crewe.[6]

[WATSON *makes a sympathetic sound.*]

HOLMES. Leaving you and your sister in the care of your stepfather.

HELEN. Exactly, Mr. Holmes. My mother had a great deal of money. She bequeathed it all to Dr. Roylott, with a provision that a certain annual sum should be allowed to my sister and me in the event of our marriage.

HOLMES. I understand. If I'm not mistaken, the Roylott family is one of the oldest Saxon[7] families in England.

HELEN. And at one time amongst the richest, too. But the fortune was wasted in the last century by four successive heirs. The last

---

3. **Bengal Artillery:** branch of the British Army located in northeast India, which was a British colony at the time.
4. **Grimesby Roylott** [grĭmz′bē roi′lĭt]
5. **Surrey:** county in southwestern England.

6. **Crewe** [krōō]: city that is the site of a great railroad junction, about 150 miles northwest of London.
7. **Saxon:** The Saxons were a German tribe that conquered Britain during the fifth and sixth centuries. Dr. Roylott's family is therefore one of the oldest in Britain.

squire[8] dragged out his existence as an aristocratic pauper,[9] and all my stepfather inherited was a few acres of land and a 200-year-old house.

HOLMES. When was this?

HELEN. Oh, a good many years before he married my mother. He saw that he must adapt himself to conditions, so he took a medical degree. He went out to Calcutta[10] and established a large practice. Unfortunately . . . [*She hesitates.*]

HOLMES. Yes?

HELEN. He . . . in a fit of anger, he beat his butler to death.

WATSON. Good heavens!

HELEN. He escaped a capital sentence,[11] but spent several years in prison.

HOLMES. And it was after his release that he married your mother?

HELEN. That is so. We all came back to England together, and my stepfather tried to establish a new practice here. But then . . . my mother was killed, and he took Julia and me to live with him in the ancestral home at Stoke Moran. It . . . it was about this time that a terrible change came over him.

HOLMES. A change? Of what kind?

HELEN. There was a series of disgraceful quarrels and brawls with anyone giving him the least offense. Two of them ended in the police court. My stepfather is a man of immense strength and absolutely uncontrollable anger.

Only last week he threw the local blacksmith over a parapet[12] into a stream.

[WATSON *whistles.*]

WATSON. [*Apologetically.*] Er, I beg your pardon!

HELEN. He's become the terror of the village, until his only friends are the wandering gypsies. He gives them leave to camp on what remains of the estate. Oh, and he has his animals.

WATSON. He's farming now?

HELEN. Nothing like that, I'm afraid, Doctor. He has a passion for Indian animals. At this moment he has a cheetah and a baboon[13] wandering quite freely in the grounds.

WATSON. Jove!

HOLMES. But your story is incomplete, Miss Stoner.

HELEN. I'm sorry. I was just going to add that, with this state of affairs, no servant would stay in the house, and so my poor sister and I had all the housework to do. You can imagine we had little pleasure in our lives.

[HOLMES *nods sympathetically.*]

Poor Julia's hair had already begun to turn white at the time of her death.

[HOLMES *leans forward interestedly.*]

HOLMES. Your sister is dead, then?

HELEN. She died just two years ago. She was thirty. It . . . it was just a fortnight[14] before she should have been married.

---

8. **squire:** owner of a large amount of rural property.
9. **artistocratic** [ə ris′tə krat′ik] **pauper:** *Aristocratic* refers to the upper classes. A *pauper* is a poor person.
10. **Calcutta:** large city in northeastern India.
11. **capital sentence:** death penalty.

12. **parapet** [par′ə pit′]: low wall.
13. **cheetah . . . baboon:** A cheetah is a large, spotted cat, a member of the leopard family. A baboon is a large and fierce type of monkey.
14. **fortnight:** fourteen nights, or two weeks.

HOLMES. [*Halting her with a gesture.*] Miss Stoner—pray be precise about the details from this point.

HELEN. That will be easy. Every event of that dreadful time is seared into my memory.

HOLMES. Quite so.

HELEN. As I told you, the manor house is very old. Only one wing is now inhabited. The bedrooms are on the ground floor, all in a row, opening out into the same corridor. The first is Dr. Roylott's, the second was my sister's, the third mine. Do I make myself plain?

HOLMES. Perfectly. Watson?

WATSON. Three bedrooms in a row—your stepfather's, your late sister's, and then your own. Yes, I've got it.

HELEN. The windows of all three rooms open on to the lawn. Well, on that fatal night . . .

HOLMES. [*Interrupting her.*] One moment, Miss Stoner. You are about to tell us of your sister's death?

HELEN. Why, yes!

HOLMES. I see. And we understand, do we not, that some time before this event occurred, your sister had announced her intention of marrying?

HELEN. That's correct. Only a short while before, actually. She'd met her fiancé during a visit to our aunt's house at Harrow.[15] He was a major of Marines, on half-pay.[16]

HOLMES. Did your stepfather oppose the match?

---

15. **Harrow:** section of London.
16. **half-pay:** reduced wages received by a military officer who is not in actual service.

HELEN. No.

HOLMES. Then pray continue.

HELEN. On the night in question, Julia and I were sitting in her room, talking about her wedding arrangements. Dr. Roylott was in his room next door. We could smell his cigar. Well, I rose to leave my sister at eleven o'clock, but she stopped me at the door and asked something rather strange.

WATSON. What was that?

HELEN. Whether I had ever heard anyone whistle in the dead of the night.

WATSON. Whistle?

HELEN. I told her I hadn't. Then she said that on the past three nights she had been woken by a long, low whistle. She couldn't tell where it came from, and we put it down to the gypsies in the plantation nearby. Then I went off to my room, and I locked my door and went to bed.

HOLMES. You locked your door?

HELEN. I heard her key turn, too, as usual. With a cheetah and a baboon at large we had no feeling of security if our doors weren't locked.

HOLMES. I understand.

HELEN. I couldn't sleep that night. It was very wild outside, with the wind howling and the rain beating and splashing. Suddenly, amidst all the noise, I heard my sister scream. I turned my key and rushed into the corridor. Just as I did so, I seemed to hear a low whistle. I was in time to see my sister's door swing slowly open. I was rooted to the spot. I didn't know what I expected to see come out. Then, by the light of the corridor lamp, I saw my sister emerge. She was swaying . . . her face was blanched[17] with terror . . . her hands seemed to be groping for help . . . Oh!

[HELEN *buries her face in her hands.* HOLMES *and* WATSON *exchange mystified glances.*]

HOLMES. Take your time, ma'am.

HELEN. [*Recovering with a determined effort.*] I must tell you it all. I . . . ran to my sister. I threw my arms round her. But at that moment her knees seemed to give way and she fell to the ground. She . . . she writhed,[18] as though in terrible pain. I thought she hadn't recognized me, but as I bent over her she suddenly shrieked out . . . "Helen! It was a band! The speckled band!"

HOLMES. "The speckled band?" Those were her exact words?

HELEN. I shall never forget them. It was the last time I heard her voice. As my stepfather came out of his room, pulling on his dressing gown,[19] she died in my arms. [*Faintly.*] Such was the dreadful end of my beloved sister.

HOLMES. This whistle you say you heard—can you be sure?

HELEN. I have asked myself that sometimes.

WATSON. The wind and rain, Holmes. The old house creaking.

HELEN. I still think it was a whistle. That was what I swore to the Coroner.[20]

HOLMES. Was your sister dressed?

HELEN. No, she was in her nightdress. We

found a spent match in one of her hands, and a matchbox in the other.

HOLMES. Showing that she had struck a light and looked around when she was alarmed. That is important.

WATSON. What conclusion did the Coroner come to, Miss Stoner?

HELEN. He was unable to find any satisfactory cause of death. Her door had been locked on the inside. Her window was shut and locked. She must have been quite alone when whatever it was happened to her.

WATSON. Were there any marks of violence on her?

HELEN. None at all.

WATSON. What about poison?

HELEN. The doctors could find no traces.

HOLMES. Miss Stoner . . .

---

17. **blanched:** very pale.
18. **writhed** [rīthd]: twisted and turned.
19. **dressing gown:** bathrobe or lounging robe.
20. **Coroner:** official responsible for determining the cause of any suspicious or violent death.

HELEN. Yes, Mr. Holmes?

HOLMES. What do *you* think this unfortunate lady died of?

HELEN. I believe she died of fear, Mr. Holmes. Of pure terror.

HOLMES. And what do you imagine frightened her?

HELEN. [*Shaking her head slowly.*] I don't know.

WATSON. [*Inspired.*] Holmes—that reference to a "speckled band." Well, couldn't that be to do with the gypsies who were near? A *band* of gypsies . . . or . . . or even those spotted hand-kerchief things they wear on their heads. Speckled bands?

HOLMES. An interesting idea, Watson. These are very deep waters. Miss Stoner, please bring your narrative up to date now.

HELEN. Very well. All that was two years ago, as I told you. Since then, my life has been lonelier and unhappier than ever. However, a dear friend whom I've known for years has asked me to marry him. We . . . we're to be married in a few weeks' time.

HOLMES. What is your stepfather's view of that?

HELEN. He's offered no opposition whatever. But a strange thing has happened . . . suffi-cient to terrify me.

HOLMES. Please go on.

HELEN. Two days ago some building repairs were ordered and my bedroom wall is affected. I have had to move into the room my sister occupied at the time of her death.

WATSON. Next to your stepfather's.

HELEN. Yes. I'm . . . I'm sleeping in the very bed poor Julia slept in. You can imagine my

terror last night, then, when I heard that same low whistling sound.

WATSON. Great heavens!

HELEN. I sprang up and lit the lamp. But there was nothing to be seen in the room. I was too shaken to go to bed again. I got dressed, and as soon as it was daylight I slipped down to the Crown Inn and got a dogcart to drive me to the station at Leatherhead. My object was to see you, Mr. Holmes, and to ask your ad-vice.

HOLMES. You were wise to do so, Miss Stoner. But have you told me everything?

HELEN. Yes, I have.

HOLMES. I fancy you have not!

HELEN. Mr. Holmes!

[HOLMES *leans forward and turns back the fringe of dress at one of her wrists.*]

HOLMES. If you will permit me? Thank you. You see, Watson?

[WATSON *peers.*]

WATSON. Those are bruises from four fingers and a thumb!

HOLMES. Precisely. You have been cruelly used, madam.

[*He withdraws his hand.*]

HELEN. [*Flustered.*] He . . . he is a hard man. But he *is* my stepfather. He . . . doesn't know his own strength. That is all.

HOLMES. If you insist. Miss Stoner, there are a thousand details that I should like to know before we decide on a course of action. If we were to come to Stoke Moran today . . .

HELEN. Today!

HOLMES. Believe me, there isn't a moment to lose. If we came, would it be possible for us to see over these rooms without your stepfather's knowledge?

[HELEN *gets to her feet.*]

HELEN. He spoke of coming to town today on some important business. He will probably be away from home all day.

HOLMES. [*Getting up.*] Excellent! Will your servants be discreet?

HELEN. We only have a housekeeper. She's old and foolish. I could easily get her out of the way.

HOLMES. Then we shall come—that is, if you're not averse to the trip, Watson?

WATSON. By no means.

HELEN. I should like to do one or two things, now that I'm in town. I shall be back by the twelve o'clock train, and be at Stoke Moran in time to meet you.

HOLMES. Capital!

[*He guides her towards the door.*]

You're *sure* you won't stay for some breakfast?

HELEN. [*Hesitates.*] Well . . .

[HOLMES *whips open the door and bows.*]

HOLMES. Then you may expect to see us early this afternoon. Good day, Miss Stoner.

HELEN. Good day, gentlemen.

[*She exits.*]

WATSON. Good day.

[HOLMES *closes the door.*]

Holmes! You invite her to breakfast, then almost push her out!

HOLMES. [*Seriously.*] We have some business of our own to attend to before we go down there. What do you think of it all, Watson?

WATSON. [*Troubled.*] Dark and sinister—that's what I think of it, Holmes.

HOLMES. Dark enough and sinister enough.

WATSON. But, Holmes—if she's correct in saying the door and window of her sister's room were locked, then the girl must have been absolutely alone when she met her death.

HOLMES. Death in a sealed room, in fact?

WATSON. Natural causes. No other explanation. [*Scratching his head.*] But then, what about that whistling in the night—and that speckled band business?

HOLMES. I was hoping *you* were going to provide me with those answers, my dear Watson.

WATSON. Well, you'll have to hope again!

HOLMES. [*Mock dismay.*] Dear me!

WATSON. Have you any ideas?

HOLMES. We have whistles at night, a band of gypsies . . .

WATSON. Yes.

HOLMES. . . . a doctor who has a financial interest in preventing his stepdaughter's marriage.

WATSON. Ah, yes!

HOLMES. And we have a dying reference to a speckled band. Now, if we combine all these elements, I think there is good ground to believe that the mystery may be cleared up.

WATSON. Well, then—the gypsies: what did they do?

HOLMES. I can't imagine.

WATSON. Neither can I!

HOLMES. It's precisely for that reason that we're going to Stoke Moran today.

[*A disturbance outside the parlor door, caused by* MRS. HUDSON *approaching, protesting vigorously, and* ROYLOTT *insisting on being allowed to pass.*]

I want to see just how much can be explained . . . What in the name of . . .?

[*The parlor door is flung open, revealing* ROYLOTT *in a challenging attitude.*]

ROYLOTT. Which of you two is Holmes?

MRS. HUDSON. [*At his elbow.*] I tried to prevent this gentleman, sir. He would insist.

HOLMES. [*Calmly.*] That's all right, Mrs. Hudson. Kindly close the door as you go.

MRS. HUDSON. Yes, sir.

[MRS. HUDSON *goes, closing the door.* ROYLOTT *advances belligerently upon* HOLMES.]

ROYLOTT. You're Holmes, then?

HOLMES. That is my name, sir. But you have the advantage of me.

ROYLOTT. I am Dr. Grimesby Roylott, of Stoke Moran.

HOLMES. Indeed, Doctor! Pray take a seat. This is your professional colleague, Dr. Watson.

[ROYLOTT *ignores both the seat and* WATSON.]

ROYLOTT. I'll do nothing of the kind! My step-daughter has been here. I know she has! What has she been saying to you?

HOLMES. It *is* a little cold for the time of the year.

ROYLOTT. *What has she been saying?*

HOLMES. But I've heard that the crocuses[21] promise well.

ROYLOTT. [*Infuriated.*] You think you can put

me off, do you? But I know you, you scoundrel! You're Holmes, the meddler!

[HOLMES *chuckles.*]

Holmes, the busybody!

[HOLMES *chuckles louder.*]

Holmes, the Scotland Yard Jack-in-Office![22]

[HOLMES *laughs out loud.*]

HOLMES. Your conversation is most entertaining, Dr. Roylott. When you go out, do close the door, please. [*Clasping his shoulders as though cold.*] There's a decided draft.

[ROYLOTT, *beside himself with fury, waves his fists in the air.* WATSON *quietly picks up a bottle, ready to wade in.* HOLMES *stands quite still and allows the tempest to rage.*]

ROYLOTT. I will go when I've had my say. [*Shaking his fist under* HOLMES's *nose.*] Don't you dare meddle with my affairs! I know the girl has been here. I warn you, Holmes, I'm a dangerous man to fall foul of!

[*He looks towards the fireplace, then strides over and picks up the poker.*[23]]

See here!

[WATSON *raises his bottle in readiness, but* ROYLOTT *grasps the poker in both hands and begins to bend it.*]

I'll show you . . . how I could bend you . . . for two pins!

[*With a grunt he gets the poker almost to a right angle before relaxing the pressure. He holds the bent poker aloft for* HOLMES *and* WATSON *to see.*]

See!

---

21. **crocuses** [krō′kəs əz]: flowers that appear in early spring.

22. **Scotland . . . Office:** Scotland Yard is the headquarters of the London police force. *Jack-in-office* is a term for an arrogant minor official.
23. **poker:** iron bar used for stirring a fire.

[ROYLOTT *hurls the poker into the fireplace with a clatter.*]

That's what I could do to you.

[*He turns and strides to the door.*]

See that you keep yourself out of my grip!

[ROYLOTT *jerks open the door and exits, slamming it behind him.* WATSON *puts down his bottle and joins* HOLMES. *They laugh heartily.*]

WATSON. I *say*, Holmes!

HOLMES. He seems a very amiable fellow!

[HOLMES *saunters to the fireplace and picks up the poker to examine it.*]

If he'd stayed a moment I might have shown him something.

[HOLMES *suddenly takes a two-handed grip on the poker and, with a single jerk, bends it straight again.* WATSON *applauds.*]

WATSON. Bravo, Holmes!

[HOLMES *puts the poker back with the other fire irons.*]

"Scotland Yard Jack-in-Office," eh?

HOLMES. The insolence! Confusing *me* with the official police force!

WATSON. I hope he won't make that dear little lady suffer.

HOLMES. He's shown us that this is too serious a matter for any dawdling. Don't you see, Watson? His stepdaughters only come into their inheritance if they marry. One was about to do so, and died mysteriously two weeks beforehand. Now the other intends marriage, and the old, mysterious signs return.

WATSON. Serious business, all right.

HOLMES. I'll ring for our breakfast. . . .

[HOLMES *rings the bell. Curtain.*]

Scene 2.

A country railway station. That afternoon.

[HELEN *enters as men and women—obviously passengers off a train—hurry away from left to exit right.* HELEN *peers past them and raises her hand to attract the attention of* HOLMES *and* WATSON, *as they enter.* HOLMES *wears his ulster and deerstalker,*[24] WATSON *his usual city clothes.*]

HELEN. Mr. Holmes, Dr. Watson! I've been waiting so eagerly for your train.

[*They shake hands.*]

WATSON. We meet again, Miss Stoner.

HOLMES. Is everything well with you, madam?

HELEN. It's all turned out splendidly. Dr. Roylott is away in town, as I expected. It's unlikely he'll be back before evening.

HOLMES. Oh, we had the pleasure of making the Doctor's acquaintance ourselves.

HELEN. Where?

[*She peers past them fearfully.*]

In the train?

WATSON. He came to our rooms. Threw his weight about a bit, too. Trying to warn us off.

HELEN. He . . . he followed me there?

HOLMES. So it appears.

HELEN. What will he say when he returns?

HOLMES. He had better be on his guard. He may find there is someone more cunning than himself on *his* track.

HELEN. Then . . . Mr. Holmes, you really believe my stepfather has something to do with this mystery?

HOLMES. Judge for yourself, Miss Stoner. I found time before we left London to slip down to Doctors' Commons[25] and examine your late mother's will. The total income left by her to your stepfather amounted to eleven hundred pounds[26] a year, all derived from farm properties. But agricultural prices have fallen heavily since her death. The income has dwindled, I should say, to not much over seven hundred and fifty pounds.

HELEN. But what has this to do with anything?

HOLMES. Your mother stipulated that each daughter could claim an income of two hundred and fifty pounds a year in case of marriage. So, if both of you had married, your stepfather would have been left with what he might consider a pittance.[27]

HELEN. [*Slowly.*] I see! Then . . . then even *one* marriage would reduce his income by about a third!

HOLMES. Exactly. My morning's work has proved that your stepfather has the strongest motives for standing in the way of your marriage. Your sister's marriage was prevented by some mysterious means, resulting in her death. And now . . . [*He breaks off.*] Now, we must make the best use of our time. If you will kindly take us at once to the house?

HELEN. Of course. Please come this way, gentlemen.

[*She leads them off to exit right.*]

---

24. **ulster and deerstalker:** An ulster is a very long, heavy overcoat, with a belt and attached cape. A deerstalker is a hunter's cap with visors in front and back. Both items have become associated with the character of Sherlock Holmes.

25. **Doctors' Commons:** offices in London for Doctors of Civil Law.
26. **pounds:** The pound is the basic unit of British currency. In the 1890s it was worth about five dollars.
27. **pittance** [pit′əns]: small amount.

Scene 3.

The bedroom wing at Stoke Moran. Shortly afterward.

[*We see the interiors of two adjoining bedrooms. In that to the audience's left hand, the bed is away from the dividing wall. A small safe stands in the corner, and there is a saucer on top of the safe. A wooden chair has its back to the back wall, in which a window is optional. A leather thong, or dogwhip,*[28] *with its thin end knotted into a small loop, lies on the chair. An unlighted oil lamp stands on a bedside table. High up in the*

dividing wall is a ventilator. In the right-hand room, the bed—a metal, hospital type—stands against the dividing wall, with its foot to the audience. Dangling over it, attached to a point immediately above the ventilator in the dividing wall, is a bell rope.[29] *A small table stands beside the bed, and there is a small chair nearby. There is a window in the back wall, capable of opening and shutting.*

HOLMES, WATSON, *and* HELEN, *attired as in*

---

28. **dogwhip:** leash.

---

29. **bell rope:** rope attached to a wire that leads to a bell in the servants' quarters. When the rope is pulled, the bell rings to summon a servant.

the previous scene, stand in the right-hand room, HOLMES *and* WATSON *looking about them.*]

HOLMES. And this room, in which you are now sleeping, was formerly your late sister's?

HELEN. Yes. This . . . is where she met her death.

HOLMES. [*Pointing to the dividing wall.*] Dr. Roylott's room is next door in that direction?

HELEN. Yes. [*Pointing the other way.*] My own room . . . my usual room, is that way.

HOLMES. I think you said you are sleeping here while alterations are going on?

HELEN. Well . . . I've looked into my room once or twice. No work seems to be in progress. No workmen have been here.

WATSON. Sounds like an excuse to get you to move into here.

HELEN. I had wondered . . .

HOLMES. Then let us examine this room. Now, as both you and your sister locked your doors at night, you were quite unapproachable from the corridor.

[HOLMES *points towards the audience.*]

HELEN. Absolutely.

HOLMES. And the window was locked when your sister met her death?

[WATSON *goes to the window, handles the catch and tests it.*]

HELEN. Yes.

WATSON. Perfectly firm. Couldn't budge that from outside.

HOLMES. Then, what else have we?

[*He spots the bell rope.*]

Bless my soul! A bell rope!

HELEN. Yes. It rings in the housekeeper's room.

WATSON. Looks quite new. Didn't know they still made 'em.

HELEN. Oh, that one was only put in a couple of years ago.

HOLMES. Your sister asked for it, I suppose?

HELEN. No. I never heard of her using it. We always got what we needed for ourselves.

HOLMES. Indeed! Care to give it a tug, Watson?

WATSON. Certainly!

[*He goes to do so, then checks.*[30]]

What about the housekeeper? She'll hear it.

HELEN. It's all right. She's in the wash house[31] for the afternoon.

WATSON. Righto!

[*He tugs at the rope, but there is no give in it, and no ring is heard. He tries again, with no result.*]

That's funny!

[*He tugs once more.*]

Doesn't seem to work. No give in it at all.

HOLMES. Let me see.

[*He tugs the rope, then looks up to the top of it.*]

There's a simple explanation. This bell rope is a dummy.

HELEN. A dummy? You mean, it won't ring?

HOLMES. It isn't even attached to a bell wire.

---

30. **checks:** stops.
31. **wash house:** small building separate from the main house and serving as the household's laundry.

WATSON. Strange, Holmes!

HOLMES. And interesting. Look—you can see it's fastened to a hook, just above the little opening of the ventilator.

HELEN. I never noticed that before. How very absurd!

HOLMES. There are one or two seemingly absurd points about this room. Have you noticed, for instance, that the ventilator appears to connect with the adjoining room?

HELEN. I . . . Yes, I suppose it does!

WATSON. Take a fool of a builder to ventilate one room from another, wouldn't it? Could just as easily have put it in the outside wall.

HELEN. [*Nervously.*] The . . . the ventilator was a recent addition, too.

HOLMES. Done about the same time as the bell rope, I fancy.

HELEN. Why, yes! There were several little changes about that time.

HOLMES. They seem to have been of a most interesting character. A dummy bell rope and a ventilator that doesn't ventilate! Ah, well! With your permission, Miss Stoner, we shall now carry our researches into Dr. Roylott's own room.

HELEN. [*Apprehensively.*] Ce . . . certainly, Mr. Holmes.

[HELEN *leads the way "out of room" by approaching the audience and miming*[32] *the opening of the door, which* WATSON, *bringing up the rear, "closes" after he has passed through.* HELEN *goes through the motions of opening* ROYLOTT's *door to the next room, and they all go in,* WATSON *"clos-*

---

32. **miming:** gesturing without words or solid objects. The "door" must remain imaginary because a real door would block the audience's view of the action.

ing the door" behind them. HOLMES *glances round.*]

HOLMES. Hm! Sparsely furnished, I see.

HELEN. It is, rather.

HOLMES. And a safe!

[*He goes to stand in front of the safe.*]

What's in it?

HELEN. My stepfather's business papers.

HOLMES. You've seen inside it, then?

HELEN. Only once, some years ago. It was full of papers then.

HOLMES. There isn't a cat in it, for example?

WATSON. *Cat* in a *safe,* Holmes?

[HOLMES *picks up the saucer and shows it to them.*]

HOLMES. Look at this. What's a saucer of milk doing here?

HELEN. I can't think. We don't keep a cat. But there's the cheetah—and the baboon.

HOLMES. Well, a cheetah is just a big cat, I suppose—and yet I dare say a saucer of milk would hardly satisfy its needs!

[HOLMES *replaces the saucer and looks at the chair. He picks up the leather thong.*]

Hello! Here *is* something interesting!

WATSON. Looks like a dog leash! That milk's for a dog, then.

HELEN. But we haven't a dog!

[HOLMES *catches up the looped end of the thong with his free hand and examines it closely,* WATSON *peering at it also.*]

HOLMES. Tied to make a loop at the end. What do you make of that, Watson?

WATSON. Dashed if I know! Certainly wouldn't get a dog's neck through that. What d'you think, Holmes?

HOLMES. I think that it's a wicked world—and that when a clever man turns his brains to crime, it's wickedest of all. Now, I must just examine this chair.

[HOLMES *takes a magnifying glass from his pocket and peers through it at the seat of the chair.* WATSON *and* HELEN *exchange baffled glances.* HOLMES *straightens up and puts his glass away.*]

Yes—that point's quite settled, then.

WATSON. Eh?

HOLMES. [*Seriously.*] Miss Stoner . . .

HELEN. Yes, Mr. Holmes?

HOLMES. It is essential that you should follow my advice in every single respect. Your life may depend on it.

HELEN. My . . . my life! I . . . I'm in your hands.

HOLMES. In the first place, my friend and I must spend the night in your room.

HELEN. [*Horrified.*] Mr. Holmes!

HOLMES. Please allow me to explain. I believe the village inn is straight over there?

[*He points towards the window.*]

HELEN. Yes—The Crown.

HOLMES. Your window should be visible from it, I think. Now, when your stepfather comes back, you must confine yourself to this room with a headache. Don't let him near you. You understand?

HELEN. Yes.

HOLMES. When you pretend to retire for the night, unfasten your window and shine a light from it as a signal to us. You must then withdraw quietly from the room and go and spend the night in the room you used to occupy. Could you manage to do that?

HELEN. Yes, easily. But what will you do?

HOLMES. We shall come over from the inn and spend the night in the room next to this. We shall investigate the cause of this whistling noise that has disturbed you.

HELEN. I see. Mr. . . . Mr. Holmes—I believe you have already made up your mind.

HOLMES. Perhaps I have.

HELEN. Then, for pity's sake, tell me what caused my sister's death!

HOLMES. I should prefer to have clearer proof before I speak. And now, Miss Stoner, we must leave you.

HELEN. [*Moving to the "door."*] Very well.

[HELEN *"opens the door" and they follow her out,* WATSON *"closing" it.*]

HOLMES. Miss Stoner—perhaps Dr. Watson and I should wait in your room for a moment, while you make sure the coast is clear for us to leave. If Dr. Roylott returned unexpectedly and found us, our journey would have been in vain.

HELEN. Please go in, then. I won't be a moment.

[*She exits quickly, right.* HOLMES *and* WATSON *reenter the right-hand room,* WATSON *"closing the door."*]

WATSON. Well, Holmes?

HOLMES. You know, Watson, I really have some scruples about bringing you back here tonight. There's a distinct element of danger.

WATSON. Can I be of assistance?

HOLMES. Your presence might be invaluable.

WATSON. Then I shall certainly come!

[HOLMES *claps him on the shoulder.*]

HOLMES. It's very kind of you.

WATSON. Holmes—you speak of danger. You've evidently seen more here than I have.

HOLMES. I imagine you've seen as much as I. But I fancy I've deduced a little more.

WATSON. [*Glancing round.*] I don't see anything remarkable—except that bell rope.

HOLMES. You can see the ventilator, too.

WATSON. Yes—but, hang it, I don't think it's all *that* unusual to have a ventilator between two rooms!

HOLMES. Before we even came to Stoke Moran I knew we should find a ventilator.

WATSON. You did!

HOLMES. You remember in her statement she said that when she and her sister were talking in this room they could smell Roylott's cigar next door?

WATSON. I remember.

HOLMES. The windows and doors were presumably closed—so I deduced a ventilator.

WATSON. Hah! Pretty obvious, I suppose.

HOLMES. [*Sarcastically.*] Oh, yes!

WATSON. [*Gazing at the ventilator.*] But what harm can there be in that?

HOLMES. At least there's a curious coincidence of dates. A ventilator is made, a bell rope is hung, and a lady who sleeps in this room dies. By the way, did you notice anything peculiar about the bed?

WATSON. The bed?

[*He bends down to peer at the bed, and prods it tentatively.*]

Can't see anything wrong with it.

HOLMES. It's clamped to the floor.

WATSON. What!

[*He examines the feet, then straightens up.*]

Jove!

HOLMES. The bed can't be moved. It must always be in the same relative position to the ventilator and the bell rope.

[WATSON's *eyes travel from one thing to the other.*]

WATSON. Holmes! Now I'm beginning to see!

HOLMES. Capital, my dear Watson!

WATSON. We . . . we're only just in time!

HOLMES. When a doctor does go wrong, Watson, he is the first of criminals. He has nerve and he has knowledge. Palmer and Pritchard were among the heads of their profession. This man strikes even deeper. But I think we shall be able to strike deeper still.

[HELEN *enters right.*]

We shall have horrors enough before the night is over. So let's go and have a quiet pipe and turn our minds for a few hours to something more cheerful.

[HELEN *enters the room.*]

HELEN. All clear, Mr. Holmes. You know the way to go.

HOLMES. Then good-bye, Miss Stoner—and be brave. If you do as I have told you, we shall soon drive away these dangers that threaten you.

[WATSON *nods to* HELEN. HOLMES *and* WATSON *leave the room and exit right, leaving her gazing hopefully after them. Blackout.*]

Scene 4.

The same place. That night.

[The setting as before, only now the stage remains in darkness. All is still. After a few moments the glimmer of a bull's-eye lamp[33] can be seen approaching from outside the window of the right-hand room. The window is opened and WATSON, *holding the lamp, climbs stealthily through, followed by* HOLMES, *who carries his walking cane.* WATSON *closes the window. The stage lighting must now simulate[34] the moderate illumination from their lamp—just sufficient to enable the details of the room and the action to be seen. The left-hand room is dark.]*

WATSON. So far, so good!

HOLMES. [*In a lowered voice.*] Keep your voice down, Watson. Just make sure she's locked the door securely.

---

33. **bull's-eye lamp:** lantern with outward-curving glass.
34. **simulate** [sim′yə lāt′]: create the appearance of.

*[*WATSON *goes through the motions of trying the door and turning a key.*]*

WATSON. She's left the key on the inside for us. I've locked it now.

HOLMES. Wise woman! Now, he's still in the parlor. I glimpsed him as we crossed the lawn. When he comes, he must believe Miss Stoner is in here, asleep.

WATSON. Hadn't we better sit in the dark?

HOLMES. I think not. It will be all right, so long as he can catch no glimmer through the ventilator.

*[*WATSON *places their lamp carefully on the bedside table. The bed and the bell rope above it must be clearly seen, but the ventilator must remain in shadow.* HOLMES *draws out the small chair and places it facing the bed and the bell rope.]*

Watson, I will sit on the bed, and you in the chair.

[WATSON *looks at the bed, and then, ruefully,*[35] *at the hard chair.*]

WATSON. Oh, all right!

[*He sits on the chair.* HOLMES *sits near the foot of the bed.*]

HOLMES. Don't go to sleep.

WATSON. Fat chance of that!

HOLMES. Your life may depend on it. Have your pistol ready, in case we should need it.

WATSON. Right.

[*He draws his revolver and holds it on his knees.* HOLMES *keeps his cane in his hands. A smell of cigar smoke becomes apparent.*]

HOLMES. Now, is everything understood?

WATSON. So far. I only wish you'd tell me . . .

[*He breaks off and sniffs.*]

HOLMES. [*Lowering his voice further.*] What is it?

[WATSON *sniffs again.*]

WATSON. [*Low.*] A cigar! He's in there!

HOLMES. He'd enter silently and without a light, not to wake up Miss Stoner. Now, Watson, listen—and watch!

[*They sit absolutely still and silent, their eyes towards the ventilator. After a few movements a snakelike hissing is heard from that direction. A snake begins to make its way down the bell rope and stops halfway. There is a low whistle from the next room.* HOLMES *leaps up and lashes at the snake with his cane.* WATSON *jumps up, the snake slithers quickly up the bell rope and out of sight.*]

---

35. **ruefully:** regretfully.

HOLMES. [*Shouting.*] You saw it, Watson? You saw it?

WATSON. I . . . I think I . . .

[HOLMES *seizes the lamp and shines it at the ventilator, but the snake has disappeared.* ROYLOTT, *in the next room, screams.*]

HOLMES. Quickly, Watson! Roylott's room!

[ROYLOTT *continues to scream. They rush to their door,* HOLMES *carrying the lamp.* WATSON *"unlocks the door" and they run to the left-hand room and run in. The stage lighting, simulating their lamp, reveals* ROYLOTT, *slumped silently on his chair with the snake coiled round his head and the leather thong dangling limply from his hand. The safe door is ajar.*]

WATSON. Holmes! Round his head! A snake!

HOLMES. The band—the speckled band!

[HOLMES *crosses carefully to* ROYLOTT.]

It's a swamp adder—the deadliest snake in India! He's dead already.

[WATSON *approaches cautiously, his revolver at the ready.*]

WATSON. Great heavens!

HOLMES. Violence does, in truth, recoil upon the violent. The schemer falls into the pit which he digs for another.

WATSON. Never mind that, Holmes! Shall I shoot it?

HOLMES. No.

[*He hands the lamp to* WATSON, *then moves carefully to* ROYLOTT *and takes the thong from his hand.*]

This noose in the dog leash will do it. It's obviously intended for this.

[HOLMES *carefully dangles the noose on to the snake, as though capturing it, then, with a swift movement, gathers the reptile up in his hands, holding it firmly by neck and tail.*]

HOLMES. Quickly, Watson! The safe!

[WATSON *hurriedly obeys, opening the safe door wide.* HOLMES *pops the snake inside and slams the door. They stand silently for a moment.*]

WATSON. Whew!

[HOLMES *draws out a handkerchief and mops his brow. Then, taking out a box of matches, he goes to the table lamp and lights it. As the stage lights come up gradually to illuminate the whole room,* WATSON *blows their own lamp out and sets it down.*]

HOLMES. You may put your trusty friend away, Watson. He won't be needed now.

[WATSON *pats his revolver with a grin and returns it to his pocket.* HOLMES *subsides on to the bed.* WATSON *goes to* ROYLOTT *and examines him briefly.*]

WATSON. He's dead, all right. But, Holmes—what made you suspect you'd find a snake?

HOLMES. When I examined Miss Stoner's room, it became clear to me that whatever danger threatened could not come either from the window or the door. The discovery that the bell rope leading from near the ventilator was a dummy, and that her bed was clamped to the floor, instantly made me suspicious that the rope was there as a bridge.

WATSON. I thought as much!

HOLMES. The idea of a snake occurred to me at once. When I coupled it with the knowledge that Dr. Roylott was a fancier of creatures from India, I felt sure I was on the right track.

WATSON. I see!

HOLMES. The idea of using a form of poison which couldn't possibly be discovered by any chemical test was just what would occur to a clever and ruthless man with Eastern experience. It would be a sharp-eyed coroner who could distinguish two little dark punctures in the victim's skin.

WATSON. That's quite so. Miss Stoner didn't mention any such thing being found on her sister. But, then, what about the whistle? I heard it plainly.

HOLMES. So did I. You see, he would put the snake through the ventilator with the certainty that it would crawl down the rope and land on the bed. But he couldn't be sure that it would bite the occupant of the bed. She might escape every night for a week before she fell a victim. Therefore, he had to be able to recall the snake before the morning.

WATSON. By *whistling* to it?

HOLMES. The equivalent of the snake charmer's flute.[36] He probably trained it by means of that saucer of milk.[37]

WATSON. Remarkable!

HOLMES. I had come to these conclusions before I even entered this room for the first time. You remember I examined the seat of that chair through my lens?

WATSON. Yes. What was that for?

HOLMES. Simply to confirm to myself that he had been in the habit of standing on it in order to reach the ventilator. When I saw the safe, the saucer of milk, and this loop of whip-

---

36. **snake charmer's flute:** A snake charmer is an entertainer who seems to hypnotize a snake by playing a flute or similar instrument.
37. **milk:** Many types of snakes are fond of milk.

cord, any doubts I might still have had were dispelled.

WATSON. [*Slowly.*] Holmes . . .

HOLMES. Yes, my dear Watson?

WATSON. I'm rather glad I didn't know any of this before we settled down in that room next door. When I think of that creature, sliding down the bell rope towards us . . . !

HOLMES. Well, at least *I* sat on the bed and gave you the chair.

WATSON. So you did! And *you* knew what to expect!

HOLMES. As soon as I heard the creature hiss I knew for certain what we were up against. I don't mind admitting I was glad to use my stick on it.

WATSON. Did you *hope* to drive it back into here?

HOLMES. No, I wouldn't say that. Some of my blows got home and must have roused its snakish temper. It fled through the ventilator and fastened on the first person it saw.

[HOLMES *gets to his feet and stands before* ROYLOTT, *looking down at him.*]

We must inform the country police of what has happened. No doubt I'm indirectly responsible for Dr. Grimesby Roylott's death—but I can't say it's likely to weigh very heavily upon my conscience.

[*Curtain, as they stand contemplating the dead man.*]

STUDY QUESTIONS

Recalling

1. How does Holmes know that Helen has traveled to his office by train? What else is Holmes able to conclude simply by observing Helen's appearance?
2. What does Watson guess that the "speckled band" may be?
3. Briefly describe Roylott's behavior in Holmes's office.
4. According to Holmes, what four elements should be combined to clear up the mystery?
5. What does the "speckled band" actually turn out to be? List five facts that caused Holmes to suspect its true identity.

Interpreting

6. What do we learn of Roylott's personality from his behavior in Holmes's office?

7. What evidence in the play indicates Holmes's keen skill as a detective?
8. Besides his skill as a detective, name two other aspects of Holmes's personality that we learn from the drama. Give examples to support each aspect.
9. In what way does the play emphasize the idea of good triumphing over evil?

Extending

10. Imagine you were watching a performance of *The Speckled Band.* What parts would you probably find most exciting? What elements make these parts so suspenseful?

READING AND LITERARY FOCUS

Drama

A **drama** is a play or story that is meant to be performed before an audience. A drama always includes two important elements. One element is the dialogue, or lines that the characters speak. The other element is the stage directions, or instructions that tell actors how to say their lines and how to move on stage.

Read the following excerpt from *The Speckled Band:*

HOLMES. [*In a lowered voice.*] Keep your voice down, Watson. Just make sure she's locked the door securely.

[*Watson goes through the motions of trying the door and turning a key.*]

The stage directions appear in brackets. The first direction tells an actor how to speak. The second direction tells an actor how to move. The dialogue, spoken by Holmes, begins, "Keep your voice down. . . ."

A drama is usually divided into acts or scenes. A new act or scene usually begins whenever the time or setting of the action changes.

Authors of plays, or playwrights, write to express their personal views about life. The behavior and experiences of characters on stage reflect the playwright's vision of life in general. For example, a play about a greedy person who ends up friendless may illustrate the playwright's belief that greed is an undesirable trait.

You will find more drama selections beginning on page 341.

Thinking About Drama

1. Find three examples of stage directions that tell actors how to move as they perform *The Speckled Band.* Find three more directions telling actors how to speak.
2. What are the time and location of each scene in *The Speckled Band*? How much time passes in the entire drama?
3. Based on the play's events, what do you feel were the playwright's feelings about people who disobey the law?

COMPOSITION

Writing a Drama Review

■ Write a drama review of *The Speckled Band.* Begin by giving general information about the drama and its author. Then describe the setting of the play. Next describe the main characters, and summarize the plot. End your review by stating your opinion of the drama, backed by details from the play. *For help with this assignment, see Lesson 9 in the Writing About Literature Handbook at the back of this book.*

Writing a Scene

■ Imagine that Holmes and Watson had entered Roylott's room before the snake killed him. Write a dramatic scene that reveals what might have happened then. Make sure the characters, setting, and plot remain believable. Also make sure the problem is settled somehow by the end of the scene. *For help with this assignment, see Lesson 10 in the Writing About Literature Handbook at the back of this book.*

CHALLENGE

Puzzles

■ Write your favorite puzzle or riddle on a piece of paper. Have your teacher collect all the puzzles and read each one aloud. See how many of your classmates' puzzles and riddles you can solve.

COMPARING THEMES

1. Considering that Helen's life is in danger, how are her goals similar to those of Rikki-tikki-tavi?
2. How do Sherlock Holmes and the speaker in "Roadways" both pursue career goals?
3. How are the goals of individuals in the drama different from the national goals in "Morning— 'The Bird Perched for Flight' "?

Active Reading

Introducing Literature

Recognizing Differences and Similarities

This unit contains four forms, or types, of literature—a story, a poem, a piece of nonfiction, and a drama. One difference among the four is that they take different shapes on the page. For example, in "Rikki-tikki-tavi" and in "Morning—'The Bird Perched for Flight,'" the sentences occur in paragraphs. In "Roadways" the lines group into stanzas. *The Speckled Band* presents a combination of dialogue and stage directions. Furthermore, you read the four types of literature differently because you are told that the story, poem, and drama are fiction and that the remaining selection is nonfiction.

In spite of these differences, however, all four selections have some common points. For example, all four selections tell about individuals in a particular time and place, or *setting.* In the story and nonfiction selections you rely on prose descriptions to learn about the setting. In the drama you find the setting established in stage directions. The setting in the poem becomes clear through the images, or pictures, that the poet's carefully chosen words suggest to you. Likewise, all four selections describe events and have people or other characters in them.

Differences and similarities also occur in the ways you learn about the personal ideas of the authors. In two of the selections in this unit you can discover the author's personal beliefs rather easily. That is, Masefield and Lindbergh state their ideas directly in the poem and in the essay. On the other hand, as you read Kipling's story and the play based on Conan Doyle's work, you must "read between the lines" and figure out just what the author is trying to say. Even though two authors are direct and two are indirect in this unit, all four share a common concern. They are all interested in showing how individuals reach goals.

Activity 1   Look back at the four selections in this unit to complete each of the following items.

1. Find a description of setting in each of the four selections. Also tell where each description appears: in a paragraph, in a stanza, or in stage directions.
2. For two of the selections, find a place that describes the feelings of a character.

3. For the selections by Masefield and Lindbergh, find a statement that expresses a personal belief of the author's.
4. Only one of the four selections relates events that could only be fictional. Identify the selection, and tell why you know it is fictional.

Understanding Purpose and Audience

Every day you read different types of writing. In the morning you may read a humorous short story in your literature book. That afternoon you may study an encyclopedia article about prehistoric animals. At night you may browse through advertisements in the newspaper. Each type of writing is different because the authors wrote each one with a special purpose and audience in mind.

The *purpose* is the reason an author writes something. No doubt the author of a humorous story wants to *entertain* readers. On the other hand, the purpose of an encyclopedia article is usually to *inform* readers about that subject. Different still, the purpose of an advertisement is to *persuade* readers to purchase merchandise. As a responsible reader, you must ask yourself each time you read, "What is the author's purpose in writing this?" If the purpose is to entertain, question whether the author succeeds in doing so and why. If the purpose is to inform, think about what you are learning from the material. Finally, if the author wants to persuade you, carefully analyze each argument, and question whether or not you agree with it. Keeping all these points in mind will help you receive the most benefit from your reading.

Authors are also concerned with their readers, or *audience.* Before writing, authors must know who will read their work. The answer helps them decide on a style, or how they will word their ideas. For example, authors of stories for young children are not likely to use difficult vocabulary or lengthy sentences. By contrast, people who write essays for medical journals may assume their audience consists of professionals who are already familiar with any technical language they may use. To help you evaluate your reading, you should always keep in mind the audience for whom the writing was intended. If you fail to understand an article, ask yourself if the work was possibly intended for an audience different from yourself. Furthermore, if you wish to recommend reading to a friend, decide first if your friend will be a suitable audience for that selection. Consider whether the material may be too easy or difficult or if the topic will be of interest.

Activity 2 Identify the purpose of each type of writing below as either *to entertain, to inform,* or *to persuade.*

1. a dictionary
2. a joke book
3. a political speech
4. a news bulletin

Activity 3 Identify a likely audience for each type of writing below.

1. a friendly letter
2. a school composition
3. a business letter
4. a "Letter to the Editor"

Adjusting Rate of Reading

People do not always walk at the same speed. They may walk slowly if they want to appreciate the details of a street scene, or they may walk quickly if they are late for an appointment. In other words, their *purpose* may determine their pace. Sometimes the speed at which people walk depends on the *situation.* They may have to walk more slowly when they are downtown during a rush hour than when downtown on a deserted weekend.

Similarly, the rate at which you read changes. It varies according to your *purpose* and the *situation.* Consider the following descriptions of when reading rates may change.

First, let's consider *why* you are reading. Suppose you are an actor learning a part in *The Speckled Band.* You will read more slowly than your normal rate because your purpose is to memorize the lines. You will also read the lines over and over again. If you are reading a book purely for entertainment, you may move at a quick pace to find out how it ends—or slowly in order to savor the language.

Second, let's look at *what* you are reading. A short poem can be so packed with meaning and wonders of language that it may take you longer to read its fourteen lines than it will take you to read a fourteen-page story. Of course, not all poems require very slow reading and not all stories are easygoing. You can breeze through some poems and may have to proceed very slowly through some stories.

Activity 4 For each situation below, identify whether your reading rate would be *slow, medium,* or *fast,* and tell why.

1. You read an easy novel for your own enjoyment.
2. You read a textbook chapter to prepare a science experiment.
3. You read a newspaper review of a movie you want to see.

4. You read a biography to do a book report for class.
5. You read a poem aloud to a child while babysitting.
6. You read the directions for playing a new game you bought.

Skimming and Scanning

To complete the selections in this unit, you probably read at your normal rate. At times, however, you may want to do a much more rapid kind of reading, called skimming. When you *skim*, you quickly look over a selection—or even an entire book—in order to get a general impression of it. At the library you may skim a book to decide whether to use it for a report. While doing homework, you may first skim the contents of a chapter that you will read more carefully later. Even when just relaxing with a magazine or newspaper, you may skim the headlines of articles to decide which to read in more detail.

You can skim an entire book just by glancing at its title, the table of contents, and perhaps the index. This glance tells you generally what kind of material the book contains. To skim a particular chapter or selection, look first at its main title and any subtitles that appear within it. Also notice any words in italicized or bold print, and glance quickly at pictures and captions. This "sneak preview" will give you a rough idea of the contents.

Another type of rapid reading is scanning. When you *scan*, you look over a page for one specific piece of information. You may be searching for a particular word, phrase, sentence, fact, or figure. Suppose, for example, you cannot remember the name of the boy in "Rikki-tikki-tavi." You will run your eye across each page of the story until it falls on the name Teddy. Scanning, as you can tell, is an even faster type of reading than skimming.

Activity 5 Answer each item below by scanning or skimming for the necessary information.

1. What kind of writing is *not* included in this book: Greek myths, Scandinavian myths, folk tales?
2. Scan the Table of Contents to discover the title of a selection in the book that is written by O. Henry.
3. Based on its title and pictures, what do you think the selection by Jerry Izenberg (page 296) is about?
4. Scan the Table of Contents to identify the author of the poem "Smells."
5. What is Sherlock Holmes's opening line in *The Speckled Band*?

Literary Skills Review

Introducing Literature

Guide for Reading Literature

Use this guide to help you understand and appreciate the characteristics of the four types of literature presented so far in this book—stories, poems, nonfiction, and drama. The other units of the book will deal with each type in more detail and will also present three other types of literature—myths, folk tales, and the novel.

The Short Story

1. Who are the **characters**? What **problems** do they face?
2. What **events** take place to make the characters' problems more complicated? What happens at the end of the story?
3. **When and where** does the story take place?
4. What **idea about life** does the story express?

Poetry

1. What **vivid pictures** does the poem present?
2. Does the poem have a regular **rhythm**? Which lines **rhyme**?
3. Which groups of lines in the poem form separate **stanzas**?
4. What **idea about life** does the poem express?

Nonfiction

1. What is the subject of the **essay**? What main **fact** or **detail** does the essay include?
2. Who is the subject of the **biography** or **autobiography**? What main **event** in the person's life is mentioned?
3. What **idea about life** does the writer express?

Drama

1. Who are the characters who speak the **dialogue**?
2. **When and where** does the play take place? What additional information do the **stage directions** provide?
3. What major **event** takes place in each act and scene of the play?
4. What **idea about life** does the play express?

Themes Review

Introducing Literature

Throughout the long history of literature, writers have drawn upon certain general themes time after time. For example, many poems, stories, plays, and other literary works concern people who strive to achieve goals. However, each writer who writes about the general theme "goals" says something very specific about it.

When we read two works dealing with the same general theme, we should notice that each writer presents a specific view of that theme. For example, both "Rikki-tikki-tavi" (page 2) and "The Speckled Band" (page 23) deal with the general theme "goals." "Rikki-tikki-tavi" expresses the following specific theme: "People can face any danger when their goal is protecting those whom they love." *The Speckled Band* expresses a different specific theme: "Intelligence and careful observation can enable someone to achieve the goal of solving a mystery." A general theme can be a word or phrase, such as "goals." A specific theme can be stated as a complete sentence.

1. Both Masefield's "Roadways" and Lindbergh's "Morning—'The Bird Perched for Flight' " deal with the general theme "goals." What specific theme related to goals does each work express?

2. What do two of the following selections say about the qualities needed to achieve a goal?
   "Rikki-tikki-tavi"   "Morning—'The Bird Perched for
   "Roadways"   Flight' "

3. What do two of the following selections say about why we strive to achieve goals?
   "Rikki-tikki-tavi"   "Morning—'The Bird Perched for
   "Roadways"   Flight' "
                          The Speckled Band

Preview
The Short Story

A **short story** is a brief work of prose fiction. Most stories are short enough to be read in one sitting. In that brief time stories can amaze us. They can transport us to thrilling adventures. They can show us truths about human nature. They can create fantastic make-believe worlds. In fact, a short story can pack great understanding and entertainment into only a few pages.

Every story has several important elements, including plot, character, setting, and theme. These are the events, people, places, and ideas that make a short story a complete world. Each element plays an important role in the story. In most good stories these elements work together. In fact, we sometimes cannot talk about one element without also mentioning the others. This combination of elements forms a story's total effect, or overall impact on the reader.

The stories on the following pages are divided into five groups. Each of the first four groups represents one of the elements: plot, character, setting, and theme. A final group shows how the elements combine to form a story's total effect. Knowing the four elements is an important step to understanding the short story. In turn, this understanding adds to our reading pleasure.

PLOT

Arthur C. Clarke (born 1917) is an award-winning writer of science fiction. Clarke was born in England, and he studied physics and mathematics at King's College in London. The film *2001: A Space Odyssey* was based on Clarke's short story "The Sentinel." Clarke uses his knowledge of astronomy and space travel in many of his science-fiction stories. "Feathered Friend," a story about workers in outer space, takes place in the future.

■ What actual practice of the past turns out to be the basis for this story?

Arthur C. Clarke

Feathered Friend

To the best of my knowledge, there's never been a regulation that forbids one to keep pets in a space station. No one ever thought it was necessary—and even had such a rule existed, I am quite certain that Sven Olsen would have ignored it.

With a name like that, you will picture Sven at once as a six-foot-six Nordic[1] giant, built like a bull and with a voice to match. Had this been so, his chances of getting a job in space would have been very slim; actually he was a wiry little fellow, like most of the early spacers, and managed to qualify easily for the 150-pound bonus that kept so many of us on a reducing diet.

Sven was one of our best construction men, and excelled at the tricky and specialized work of collecting assorted girders[2] as they floated around in free fall, making them do

the slow-motion, three-dimensional ballet that would get them into their right positions, and fusing the pieces together when they were precisely dovetailed[3] into the intended pattern. I never tired of watching him and his gang as the station grew under their hands like a giant jigsaw puzzle; it was a skilled and difficult job, for a space suit is not the most convenient of garbs in which to work. However, Sven's team had one great advantage over the construction gangs you see putting up skyscrapers down on Earth. They could step back and admire their handiwork without being abruptly parted from it by gravity. . . .

Don't ask me why Sven wanted a pet, or why he chose the one he did. I'm not a psychologist, but I must admit that his selection was very sensible. Claribel weighed practically nothing, her food requirements were

---

1. **Nordic:** northern European, Scandinavian.
2. **girders** [gur'dərz]: large steel beams.

3. **precisely** [pri sīs'lē] **dovetailed** [duv'tāld']: exactly fit.

infinitesimal[4]—and she was not worried, as most animals would have been, by the absence of gravity.

I first became aware that Claribel was aboard when I was sitting in the little cubbyhole laughingly called my office, checking through my lists of technical stores to decide what items we'd be running out of next. When I heard the musical whistle beside my ear, I assumed that it had come over the station intercom, and waited for an announcement to follow. It didn't; instead, there was a long and involved pattern of melody that made me look up with such a start that I forgot all about the angle beam just behind my head. When

the stars had ceased to explode before my eyes, I had my first view of Claribel.

She was a small yellow canary, hanging in the air as motionless as a hummingbird—and with much less effort, for her wings were quietly folded along her sides. We stared at each other for a minute; then, before I had quite recovered my wits, she did a curious kind of backward loop I'm sure no earthbound canary had ever managed, and departed with a few leisurely flicks. It was quite obvious that she'd already learned how to operate in the absence of gravity, and did not believe in doing unnecessary work.

Sven didn't confess to her ownership for several days, and by that time it no longer mattered, because Claribel was a general pet.

---

4. **infinitesimal** [in'fi nə tes'ə məl]: almost nothing.

He had smuggled her up on the last ferry from Earth, when he came back from leave—partly, he claimed, out of sheer scientific curiosity. He wanted to see just how a bird would operate when it had no weight but could still use its wings.

Claribel thrived and grew fat. On the whole, we had little trouble concealing our unauthorized guest when VIPs[5] from Earth came visiting. A space station has more hiding places than you can count; the only problem was that Claribel got rather noisy when she was upset, and we sometimes had to think fast to explain the curious peeps and whistles that came from ventilating shafts and storage bulkheads.[6] There were a couple of narrow escapes—but then who would dream of looking for a canary in a space station?

We were now on twelve-hour watches, which was not as bad as it sounds, since you need little sleep in space. Though of course there is no "day" and "night" when you are floating in permanent sunlight, it was still convenient to stick to the terms. Certainly when I woke up that "morning" it felt like 6:00 A.M. on Earth. I had a nagging headache, and vague memories of fitful, disturbed dreams. It took me ages to undo my bunk straps, and I was still only half awake when I joined the remainder of the duty crew in the mess.[7] Breakfast was unusually quiet, and there was one seat vacant.

"Where's Sven?" I asked, not very much caring.

"He's looking for Claribel," someone answered. "Says he can't find her anywhere. She usually wakes him up."

Before I could retort[8] that she usually woke me up, too, Sven came in through the doorway, and we could see at once that something was wrong. He slowly opened his hand, and there lay a tiny bundle of yellow feathers, with two clenched claws sticking pathetically up into the air.

"What happened?" we asked, all equally distressed.

"I don't know," said Sven mournfully. "I just found her like this."

"Let's have a look at her," said Jock Duncan, our cook-doctor-dietitian. We all waited in hushed silence while he held Claribel against his ear in an attempt to detect any heartbeat.

Presently he shook his head. "I can't hear anything, but that doesn't prove she's dead. I've never listened to a canary's heart," he added rather apologetically.

"Give her a shot of oxygen," suggested somebody, pointing to the green-banded emergency cylinder in its recess beside the door. Everyone agreed that this was an excellent idea, and Claribel was tucked snugly into a face mask that was large enough to serve as a complete oxygen tent for her.

To our delighted surprise, she revived at once. Beaming broadly, Sven removed the mask, and she hopped onto his finger. She gave her series of "Come to the cookhouse, boys" trills—then promptly keeled over again.

"I don't get it," lamented Sven. "What's wrong with her? She's never done this before."

For the last few minutes, something had been tugging at my memory. My mind seemed to be very sluggish that morning, as if I was still unable to cast off the burden of sleep. I felt that I could do with some of that oxygen—but before I could reach the mask, understanding exploded in my brain. I whirled on the duty engineer and said urgently:

"Jim! There's something wrong with the air! That's why Claribel's passed out. I've just

5. **VIPs:** very important persons.
6. **bulkheads:** compartments.
7. **mess:** place where a group of people have meals together.
8. **retort** [ri tôrt']: reply.

remembered that miners used to carry canaries down to warn them of gas."[9]

"Nonsense!" said Jim. "The alarms would have gone off. We've got duplicate circuits, operating independently."

"Er—the second alarm circuit isn't connected up yet," his assistant reminded him. That shook Jim; he left without a word, while we stood arguing and passing the oxygen bottle around like a pipe of peace.

He came back ten minutes later with a sheepish expression. It was one of those accidents that couldn't possibly happen; we'd had one of our rare eclipses by Earth's shadow[10] that night; part of the air purifier had frozen up, and the single alarm in the circuit had failed to go off. Half a million dollars' worth of chemical and electronic engineering had let us down completely. Without Claribel, we should soon have been slightly dead.

So now, if you visit any space station, don't be surprised if you hear an inexplicable snatch of bird song. There's no need to be alarmed: on the contrary, in fact. It will mean that you're being doubly safeguarded, at practically no extra expense.

---

9. **miners . . . gas:** Coal miners brought canaries into the mines to warn them of dangerous coal gas. The birds were affected by the gas before humans were.

---

10. **eclipses . . . shadow:** The shadow of the earth blocked the station off from the sun.

STUDY QUESTIONS

Recalling

1. Who is Claribel? How does she come to be in the space station?
2. Tell what happens when Claribel visits the storyteller's cubbyhole.
3. Describe Claribel's condition when Sven brings her to breakfast one morning.
4. As he watches Claribel, what does the storyteller suddenly realize about the station? What leads him to this conclusion?
5. In the next-to-last paragraph what does the storyteller say about the station's expensive equipment? What does he say would have happened without Claribel?

Interpreting

6. Name two ways in which Claribel proves to be a friend to the workers in the station.
7. What does this story suggest about the drawbacks in depending completely on technology?

Extending

8. Experts now say that keeping a pet can often be beneficial to one's health. Why might having a pet be good for someone?

READING AND LITERARY FOCUS

Plot and Suspense

From beginning to end, the events of a story are related to one another. They form a sequence, or pattern, in which each event leads logically to the next. This sequence of events is called the story's **plot.** When we read a story, we become very involved in its plot. We want to know what will happen next and how the story will end. This interest in the outcome of a story is called **suspense.**

Suspense builds as the events of the plot unfold. For example, *The Speckled Band* (page 23) builds suspense from beginning to end. At the beginning of the play, we want to know what caused Julia Stoner's death. As we learn more about her family, we become curious about her stepfather, the strange Dr. Grimesby Roylott. Finally, we are caught up in Sherlock Holmes's attempt to unravel the mystery and learn just what the mysterious speckled band is.

Thinking About Plot and Suspense

1. List in order the six or seven major events in the plot of "Feathered Friend." Begin with the visit of Claribel to the storyteller's cubbyhole.
2. Explain how the following sentence adds to the story's suspense: "Sven came in through the doorway, and we could see at once that something was wrong."

VOCABULARY

Synonyms

A **synonym** is a word that has the same or nearly the same meaning as another word. For example, *speak* and *talk* are synonyms. The italicized words in the following numbered items come from "Feathered Friend." Choose the word that is nearest the meaning of each italicized word, *as the word is used in the selection.* Write the number of each item and the letter of your choice on a separate sheet.

1. *regulation* forbidding pets
   (a) invitation   (c) crime
   (b) rule   (d) disapprove
2. *infinitesimal* portion of vegetables
   (a) tiny   (c) graceful
   (b) expand   (d) terrifying
3. *thrived* in that climate
   (a) sang   (c) studied
   (b) froze   (d) flourished
4. *fitful,* disturbed dreams
   (a) healthy   (c) restless
   (b) hopeful   (d) calm

5. could not *detect* a pulse
   (a) have   (c) found
   (b) find   (d) inspector

COMPOSITION

Answering an Essay Question

■ Do the events of "Feathered Friend" seem believable to you, or do they seem farfetched? Write a brief essay explaining your opinion. Begin by rephrasing the question as the first sentence of your answer. Then back up your opinion with at least two examples of events from the story. *For help with this assignment, see Lesson 1 in the Writing About Literature Handbook at the back of this book.*

Writing a Report

■ Imagine that you work in the space station described in the story and that your duties include writing reports to Earth. Write an official report about the emergency in which the station's air-purifying system failed. Begin by describing what happened to the system as a result of the eclipse. Then explain Claribel's role in saving everyone's life. End with a recommendation about the use of canaries in space stations.

CHALLENGE

Research and Oral Report

■ Find out more about the use of canaries to test the air in mines. Begin by looking in the encyclopedia under the entries "Mining" and "Canary." At the library look in the card catalogue under these headings and others (such as "Miners, Occupational Safety of"). Take notes on your readings, and present your findings in an oral report to the class.

Shirley Jackson (1918–1965) is known both for her tales of horror and for her humorous portraits of her family. She was born in California, but she spent most of her adult life in Vermont with her husband and four children. Jackson used her hectic household as the basis for several books, such as *Life Among the Savages* and *Raising Demons.* "The Sneaker Crisis" relates a zany family emergency.

■ How believable do you find Jackson's portrayal of family life in this story?

Shirley Jackson

The Sneaker Crisis

Day after day I went around the house picking things up. I picked up books and shoes and toys and socks and shirts and gloves and boots and hats and handkerchiefs and puzzle pieces and pennies and pencils and stuffed rabbits and bones the dogs had left under the living-room chairs. I also picked up tin soldiers and plastic cars and baseball gloves and sweaters and children's pocketbooks with nickels inside and little pieces of lint off the floor.

Every time I picked up something I put it down again somewhere else where it belonged better than it did in the place I found it. Nine times out of ten, I did not notice what I was picking up or where I put it until sometime later when someone in the family needed it. Then, when Sally said where were her crayons I could answer at once: kitchen windowsill, left. If Barry wanted his cowboy hat I could reply: playroom, far end of bookcase. If Jannie wanted her arithmetic homework, I could tell her it was under the ashtray on the dining-room buffet.

I could locate the little nut that came off Laurie's bike wheel, and the directions for winding the living-room clock. I could find the recipe for the turkey cutlets Sally admired and the top to my husband's fountain pen. I could even find, ordinarily, the little plastic strips which went inside the collar of his nylon shirt.

If I could not respond at once, identifying object and location in unhesitating answer to the question, the article was very apt to remain permanently lost. Like Jannie's pink Easter-egg hat, which disappeared—let me see—it was the day Laurie got into the fight with the Haynes boys, and the porch rocker got broken—make it the end of October.

We had many small places in our big house where an Easter-egg hat could get itself hopelessly hidden, so when Jannie asked one night at dinner, the end of October, "Who took my Easter-egg hat?" and I found myself without an immediate answer, it was clear that the hat had taken itself off, and although we searched half-heartedly, Jannie had to wear a scarf around her head until the weather got cold enough to wear her long-tailed knitted cap.

Laurie's sneaker was of considerably more moment, since, of course, he could not play basketball with a scarf tied around his left foot. He came to the top of the back stairs of a Saturday morning and inquired gently who had stolen his sneaker.

I opened my mouth to answer, found my mind blank, and closed my mouth again. Laurie came halfway down the stairs and bawled, "Moooooom, where'd my *sneaker* get to?" and I still could not answer. "I neeeeeed my *sneaker*," Laurie howled. "I got to play baaaaaaasketball."

He crashed down the stairs and into the study, where I sat reading the morning paper and drinking a cup of coffee. "I got to play basketball. I can't play on the basketball court without sneakers. So I need—"

"Have you looked? In your room? Under your bed?"

"Yeah, sure." He thought. "It's not there, though."

"Outdoors?"

"Now what would my sneaker be doing outdoors, I ask you? You think I get dressed and undressed on the lawn?"

"Well," I said helplessly, "you had it last Saturday."

"I *know* I had it last Saturday."

"Wait." I went and stood at the foot of the back stairs and called, "Jannie?"

There was a pause. Then Jannie said, sniffling, "Yes?"

"Good heavens," I said, "are you reading *Little Women*[1] again?"

Jannie sniffled. "Just the part where Beth dies."

"Look," I said, "the sun is shining, the sky is blue and—"

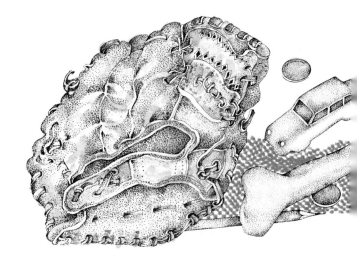

"You seen my sneaker?" Laurie yelled from in back of me.

"No."

"You *sure*?"

Jannie came to the top of the stairs, wiping her eyes. "Hey," she said, "maybe some girl took it. For a keepsake."

"Wha?" said Laurie incredulously. "Took my *sneaker*?"

"Like Mr. Brooke did Meg's glove, in *Little Women*, because he was in love with her and they got married."

"*Wha?*" For a minute Laurie stared at her. Then he turned deliberately and went back to the study. "My sister," he announced formally to his father, "has snapped her twigs."

"That so?" said his father.

"Well, he did," Jannie insisted, coming down the stairs. "He took it and hid it and when Jo found out she—"

"Sally, Barry," I was calling from the back door. "Has either of you seen Laurie's sneaker?"

Sally and Barry were dancing on the lawn. When I called, they circled toward the house, going "cheep-cheep."

"We're little birds," Sally explained, coming closer. "Cheep-cheep."

---

1. ***Little Women:*** novel by Louisa May Alcott (1832–1888) about four girls—Meg, Jo, Beth, and Amy—growing up in Massachusetts.

"Have you seen Laurie's sneaker?"

"Cheep-cheep."

"Well?"

Barry thought. "I have unseen it," he remarked. "I did unsee Laurie's sneaker a day and a day and a day and a day and *many* mornings ago."

"Splendid," I said. "Sally?"

"No. But don't worry. I shall get it back for dear Laurie, dear Mommy."

"If you mean magic, you better not let your father hear you, young lady. No," I said to Laurie, "they haven't."

"But I will find it, Laurie dear, never fear, Laurie dear, I will your sneaker find for you."

"Yeah. So what'm I gonna do?" he asked me. "Play basketball in my socks or something?"

"Are you *sure* you looked under your bed?"

He looked at me in the manner his favorite television detective reserves for ladies who double-talk the cops. "Yeah," he said. "Yeah, lady. I'm sure."

"Daddy won't notice," Sally said to Barry. "All this will take is just a little bit of golden magic and Daddy will never notice and there will be dear Laurie's sneaker."

"Can I do magic, too?"

"You can be my dear helper. You can carry the shovel."

I went into the study and sat down, and Laurie followed.

"And he kept it for weeks and weeks next to his heart," Jannie was explaining to her father, "and she was looking for it just like Laurie, but Mr. Brooke had it all the time."

"How about that little dark-haired girl?" my husband asked Laurie. "The one who keeps calling you so much?"

"Nah," Laurie said. "She's tipped, anyhow. Besides, how could she get my sneaker?" He slapped his forehead. "A veritable[2] madhouse," he said. "Lose a sneaker and they start criticizing your friends and trying to make out she stole it. Bah."

He flung himself violently into a chair and threw his arms dramatically into the air and let them fall resignedly.[3] "Never *find* anything around here," he explained. "Nothing's ever where you *put* it. If *she*—"

"If by *she* you mean *me*—" I began ominously.[4]

---

2. **veritable** [ver′i tə bəl]: actual, real.

3. **resignedly** [ri zī′nid lē]: in a defeated way.

4. **ominously** [om′ə nəs lē]: in a threatening way.

"Always coming and picking things up and putting them away where a person can't find them. Always—"

"If you'd put things away neatly when you take them off instead of just throwing everything under your bed—" I stopped to think. "Have you looked under your bed?"

Laurie threw his arms wide. "Why was I ever born?"

Jannie nodded. "In *Beverly Lee, Girl Detective*," she said, "when the secret plans for the old armory get lost, Beverly Lee and her girlfriend Piggy, *they* look for clues."

"A broken shoelace?" my husband suggested.

"When did you see them last?" I asked reasonably. "Seems to me if you could remember when you had them last—"

"Yeah. Well," Laurie said, scowling, "I *know* I had them last Saturday. But then I took them off and I remember they were on my bookcase because I had to remember to make that map for geography and that was for Wednesday when we had gym—say!" He opened his eyes wide. "Gym. I wore them Wednesday to school for gym. So I had them on Wednesday."

"And Wednesday," I put in, "was the day you were so late getting home from school. And you never got your chores done, and I kept dinner till six-thirty."

"That girl called, too," my husband put in.

"And I must of had my sneakers on all that time, because I never had time because *she* made me do my chores and then I had to rush through dinner because—because—"

"You were going to the dance," Jannie said, triumphant. "You got all dressed up, so *naturally* you put on shoes."

"Hey!" Laurie gestured wildly. "I got dressed—"

"You took a shower," I said. "I remember because—"

He shuddered. "I took a shower because

she wouldn't let me have my good blue pants from the cleaners *unless* I took a shower."

"No gentleman escorts a lady to a public function unless he has bathed and dressed himself in completely clean clothes," my husband said.

"So I undressed in the bathroom because I always do, and then when I went out I had this towel around me and I was carrying my clothes and the sneaker and I—"

"I saw it," I said suddenly. "I did see it after all. I came upstairs to get two aspirin after you had finally gone to the dance, and I remember the way the bathroom looked—floor sopping and dirty towels all over and the soap and—"

"The sneaker," Laurie said impatiently. "Keep on the subject. The sneaker, the sneaker."

I meditated. "It was lying just inside the door, and one wet towel was half on top of it. And I . . . and I . . ." I thought. "What *did* I do?"

"Think, think, think." Laurie stood over me flapping his hands.

"Look," I said. "I go around this house and I go around this house and I *go* around this house and I pick up shoes and socks and shirts and hats and gloves and handkerchiefs and books and toys and I always put them

down again, some place where they belong. Now when I went upstairs and saw that mess of a bathroom I had to clean up, I would have taken the soap and put it in the soap dish. And I would have taken the bath mat and put it over the edge of the tub. And I would have taken the towels—"

"And put them in the hamper," Laurie said impatiently. "We know."

"You do? Because I have often wondered what happens all the times I say to you to put the towels—"

"Yeah, so next time I'll remember sure. What about the sneaker."

"Anyway they were wet so I couldn't put them in the hamper. I would have hung them over the shower rail to dry so *then* I could put them in the hamper. And then I would have picked up the sneaker—"

"Laurie's sneaker is weaker and creaker and cleaker and breaker and fleaker and greaker. . . ." Sally wound through the study, eyes shut, chanting. Barry came behind her, doing an odd little two-step. Sally had a pail of sand and a shovel and she was making scattering motions.

"Now *wait* a minute here," my husband began.

"It's all right," Sally said, opening one eye. "I'm just pretending. This is only sand."

"We're just untending," Barry explained reassuringly. "Bleaker and sneaker and weaker and deaker."

They filed out. My husband studied the floor morosely.

"That certainly looked like magic to *me*," he said, "and I don't *like* it. Going to have footwear popping up all over, right through the floor, probably wreck the foundations."

"Reconstruct the scene of the crime," Jannie said suddenly. "Because Beverly Lee, Girl Detective, and her girlfriend Piggy, that's what *they* did—in *The Mystery of the Broken Candle*, when they had to find the missing

will. They reconstructed the scene of the crime. They got everybody there and put everything the way it was—"

"Say!" Laurie looked at her admiringly. "You're charged, girl. Come on," he said, making for the stairs, and stopped to look compellingly at me. "Come *on*," he said.

"And creaker and beaker and leaker and veaker."

"Gangway, birdbait," Laurie said. He stopped to pat his younger sister on the head. "You keep sprinkling that there magic, Perfessor. Size six-and-a-half, white."

"Kindly do not poke the Sally," said Sally, drawing away stiffly.

"Unpoke, unpoke," Barry said.

"Come on," Laurie said to me. He called ahead to Jannie, "You get the towels wet and throw them on the floor. I'll get the other sneaker and when she comes we'll have it all ready."

"You might as well take two more aspirin," my husband said.

Wearily, I headed up the stairs, sand grinding underfoot. The bathroom is at the head of the stairs, and by the time I was near the top I could see that everything was prepared. Rigorously,[5] I put my mind back three days.

It is eight-thirty in the evening, I told myself. I am coming upstairs to get myself two aspirin. Laurie has just gone to the dance; I have just told him good-bye, get home early, behave yourself, be careful, do you have a clean handkerchief? Jannie is reading. Sally and Barry are asleep. It is eight-thirty Wednesday evening. I am coming to get two aspirin.

I came to the top of the stairs, and sighed. The bathroom floor was sopping; the bath mat was soaked and crumpled; wet towels lay on the floor. In the corner, half under a wet towel, was one white sneaker. I asked myself through my teeth how old people had to get

---

5. **Rigorously** [rig′ər əs lē]: in an exact, precise way.

before they learned to pick up after themselves and after all our efforts to raise our children in a decent and clean house here they still behaved like pigs and the sooner Laurie grew up and got married and had a wife to pick up after him the better off I would be and maybe I would just take his allowance and hire a full-time nursemaid for him.

I picked up the bath mat and hung it over the edge of the tub. I put the soap in the soap dish and hung the towels over the shower rail. I picked up the sneaker and went to the other side of the hall to the linen closet to get clean towels and a dry bath mat, and Laurie and Jannie burst out of the guest room shouting, "You see? You see?"

Jannie said excitedly, "Just like Beverly Lee and it turned out it *was* the caretaker all the time."

"Look, look," Laurie said, pointing. I had the door of the linen closet open, and I reached up onto the towel shelf and took down Jannie's Easter-egg hat.

"What?" I said, surprised.

"That's my hat," Jannie said.

"Why would I want to put your hat in the linen closet?" I demanded.

"Don't be silly."

"My nice, pink Easter-egg hat," Jannie said, pleased.

"Craazy," Laurie remarked. "Opens the closet and there's the hat. Craazy." He pushed past me and began to paw through the towels.

"Ridiculous," I said. "I *never* put hats in linen closets. Linen closets are where I keep towels and sheets and extra blankets, not hats."

"Not sneakers, either." Laurie stood back and dusted his hands.

"You pick up every one of those towels," I said, annoyed. "And then you and your sister can get right in there and clean up that bathroom. And the next time I find that pink hat lying around I am going to burn it. And you

can tell Beverly Lee, Girl Detective—"

"Any luck?" my husband called from the foot of the stairs.

"Certainly not." I started down. "Of all the idiotic notions and now its too late in the year *any*way for a hat like that."

"Sneaker, sneaker, sneaker!" It was Sally and Barry, in glory. Laurie raced past me down the stairs. "Got it? Sal," he yelled, "you *got* it?"

Proudly, the little procession wound around to the front hall. Sally was still scattering sand, but Barry was bearing the sneaker on high. "Gee," Laurie said. "Hey, kids, thanks. Where was it?"

"Under your bed," Sally said. "We did a lot of"—she glanced at her father—"blagic," she said. "And then we went up and looked. Very good, Barry."

"Very good, Sally," Barry said.

"Gosh." Laurie was pleased. He turned and gave me an affectionate pat on the head. "Boy," he said, "are *you* ever a tippy old lady." Then, in a burst of gratitude, he added, "I'm going to go down right now on my bike and get you kids each a popsicle."

"Well, me, too, I should *think*," Jannie said indignantly. "After all, it was me thought of reconstructing the crime, and in *Elsie Dinsmore*[6] when Elsie—"

"What is this crime talk?" I said. "Anyone would think that instead of spending all my time picking up and putting away—"

"The sneaker," Laurie said to me, gesturing. "The other sneaker. I got to get down and get those popsicles, so let's have it."

"What?" I said.

"The sneaker, dear. The one you just had upstairs, for heaven's sake."

Uncomfortably, I looked down at my empty hands. "Now let's see," I said. "I had it just a minute ago. . . ."

---

6. *Elsie Dinsmore:* series of novels by Martha F. Finley.

STUDY QUESTIONS

Recalling

1. What important object has Laurie lost?
2. Name two suggestions that Jannie makes.
3. Explain the series of events that lead the mother to look in the linen closet. What does she find there?
4. Who finds the missing item, and where? What new problem arises at the end of the story?

Interpreting

5. Briefly describe each member of the family.
6. Point out one incident in the story that is funny because it is unexpected.
7. What overall picture of the family does this story create? Give three examples.

Extending

8. How might the behavior of people involved in a *real* crisis be different from that of the family during the sneaker crisis?

READING AND LITERARY FOCUS

Climax and Resolution

As we read a story, we become more and more interested in the events of the plot. We want to know how the problems in the story will be solved and how the story will end. Our rising interest in a story's plot follows the pattern in this diagram:

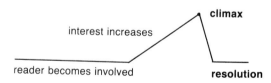

The plot builds to a **climax,** the point of our highest interest and greatest emotional involvement in the story. After the climax we know how the story's problems will be solved. The plot continues to a **resolution,** the story's final outcome.

In the plot of "Feathered Friend" (page 54), the climax occurs when the storyteller realizes that

something is wrong with the air and sends Jim to check the purifier. After this point we understand why Claribel has been losing consciousness and why all the workers are sleepy. In the resolution we learn that the purifier failed because of an eclipse and that Claribel saved everyone's life.

Thinking About Climax and Resolution

1. What is the climax of "The Sneaker Crisis"?
2. What is the story's resolution?

VOCABULARY

Sentence Completions

Each of the following sentences contains a blank with four possible words for completing the sentence. The words are from "The Sneaker Crisis." Choose the word that best completes each sentence. Write the number of each sentence and the letter of your choice on a separate sheet.

1. Gail wore her grandmother's locket as a ___.
   (a) shoelace   (c) keepsake
   (b) handkerchief (d) procession
2. We dressed ___ for the ball.
   (a) permanently   (c) violently
   (b) incredulously (d) formally
3. I exercise ___ to keep in shape.
   (a) morosely   (c) admiringly
   (b) rigorously   (d) indignantly
4. The detective is ___ the crime.
   (a) reconstructing (c) sopping
   (b) reassuring   (d) unhesitating
5. "What time is it?" he politely ___.
   (a) bawled   (c) commanded
   (b) sneered   (d) inquired

CHALLENGE

Staging a Scene

■ Work with other students, and stage one section of "The Sneaker Crisis" as a skit. Decide which family member you will be and how you will speak and behave.

Joan Aiken (born 1924) began writing when she was five years old and always planned to be a writer. Her plans are understandable, since she is the daughter of the American poet Conrad Aiken and the sister of two other writers. She has written several novels, as well as stories and plays for young people.

◼ What aspects of the following story do you think would especially appeal to young readers? What elements in the story might appeal to readers of all ages?

Joan Aiken

All You've Ever Wanted

Matilda, you will agree, was a most unfortunate child. Not only had she three names each worse than the others—Matilda, Eliza, and Agatha—but her father and mother died shortly after she was born, and she was brought up exclusively by her six aunts. These were all energetic women, and so on Monday Matilda was taught algebra and arithmetic by her Aunt Aggie, on Tuesday biology by her Aunt Beattie, on Wednesday classics by her Aunt Cissie, on Thursday dancing and deportment by her Aunt Dorrie, on Friday essentials by her Aunt Effie, and on Saturday French by her Aunt Florrie. Friday was the most alarming day, as Matilda never knew beforehand what Aunt Effie would decide on as the day's essentials—sometimes it was cooking, or revolver practice, or washing, or boilermaking ("For you never know what a girl may need nowadays," as Aunt Effie rightly observed).

So that by Sunday, Matilda was often worn out, and thanked her stars that her seventh aunt, Gertie, had left for foreign parts many years before, and never threatened to come back and teach her geology or grammar on the only day when she was able to do as she liked.

However, poor Matilda was not entirely free from her Aunt Gertie, for on her seventh birthday, and each one after it, she received a little poem wishing her well, written on pink paper, decorated with silver flowers, and signed "Gertrude Isabel Jones, to her niece, with much affection." And the terrible disadvantage of the poems, pretty though they were, was that the wishes in them invariably came true. For instance, the one on her eighth birthday read:

Now you're eight Matilda dear
May shining gifts your place adorn
And each day through the coming year
Awake you with a rosy morn.

The shining gifts were all very well—they consisted of a torch,[1] a luminous watch, pins,

---

1. **torch:** flashlight.

needles, a steel soapbox, and a useful little silver brooch which said "Matilda" in case she ever forgot her name—but the rosy morns were a great mistake. As you know, a red sky in the morning is the shepherd's warning, and the fatal results of Aunt Gertie's well-meaning verse were that it rained every day for the entire year.

Another one read:

Each morning make another friend
Who'll be with you till light doth end.
Cheery and frolicsome and gay,
To pass the sunny hours away.

For the rest of her life Matilda was overwhelmed by the number of friends she made in the course of that year—three hundred and sixty-five of them. Every morning she found another of them, anxious to cheer her and frolic with her, and the aunts complained that her lessons were being constantly interrupted. The worst of it was that she did not really like all the friends—some of them were so *very* cheery and frolicsome, and insisted on pillow fights when she had a toothache, or sometimes twenty-one of them would get together and make her play hockey, which she hated. She was not even consoled by the fact that all her hours were sunny, because she was so busy in passing them away that she had no time to enjoy them.

Long miles and weary though you stray
Your friends are never far away,
And every day though you may roam,
Yet night will find you back at home

was another inconvenient wish. Matilda found herself forced to go for long, tiresome walks in all weathers, and it was no comfort to know that her friends were never far away, for although they often passed her on bicycles or in cars, they never gave her lifts.

However, as she grew older, the poems became less troublesome, and she began to enjoy bluebirds twittering in the garden, and endless vases of roses on her windowsill. Nobody knew where Aunt Gertie lived, and she never put in an address with her birthday greetings. It was therefore impossible to write and thank her for her varied good wishes, or hint that they might have been more carefully worded. But Matilda looked forward to meeting her one day, and thought that she must be a most interesting person.

"You never knew what Gertrude would be up to next," said Aunt Cissie. "She was a thoughtless girl, and got into endless scrapes, but I will say for her, she was very good-hearted."

When Matilda was nineteen she took a job in the Ministry of Alarm and Despondency, a very cheerful place where, instead of typewriter ribbon, they used red tape, and there was a large laundry basket near the main entrance labeled The Usual Channels, where all the letters were put which people did not want to answer themselves. Once every three months the letters were re-sorted and dealt out afresh to different people.

Matilda got on very well here and was perfectly happy. She went to see her six aunts on Sundays, and had almost forgotten the seventh by the time that her twentieth birthday had arrived. Her aunt, however, had not forgotten her.

On the morning of her birthday Matilda woke very late, and had to rush off to work, cramming her letters unopened into her pocket, to be read later on in the morning. She had no time to read them until ten minutes to eleven, but that, she told herself, was as it should be, since, as she had been born at eleven in the morning, her birthday did not really begin till then.

Most of the letters were from her three hundred and sixty-five friends, but the usual pink and silver envelope was there, and she opened it with the usual feeling of slight uncertainty.

> May all your leisure hours be blest
> Your work prove full of interest,
> Your life hold many happy hours
> And all your way be strewn with flowers,

said the pink and silver slip in her fingers. "From your affectionate Aunt Gertrude."

Matilda was still pondering this when a gong sounded in the passage outside. This was the signal for everyone to leave their work and dash down the passage to a trolley[2] which sold them buns and coffee. Matilda left her letters and dashed with the rest. Sipping her coffee and gossiping with her friends, she had forgotten the poem, when the voice of the Minister of Alarm and Despondency himself came down the corridor.

"What is all this? What does this mean?" he was saying.

The group around the trolley turned to see what he was talking about. And then Matilda flushed scarlet and spilled some of her coffee on the floor. For all along the respectable brown carpeting of the passage were growing flowers in the most riotous profusion[3]—daisies, campanulas, crocuses, mimosas, foxgloves, tulips, and lotuses. In some places the passage looked more like a jungle than anything else. Out of this jungle the little red-faced figure of the Minister fought its way.

"Who did it?" he said. But nobody answered.

---

2. **trolley:** cart.

3. **profusion** [prə fū′zhən]: great amount.

Matilda went quietly away from the chattering group and pushed through the vegetation to her room, leaving a trail of buttercups and rhododendrons across the floor to her desk.

"I can't keep this quiet," she thought desperately. And she was quite right. Mr. Willoughby, who presided over the General Gloom Division, noticed almost immediately that when his secretary came into his room, there was something unusual about her.

"Miss Jones," he said, "I don't like to be personal, but have you noticed that wherever you go, you leave a trail of mixed flowers?"

Poor Matilda burst into tears.

"I know, I don't know *what* I shall do about it," she sobbed.

Mr. Willoughby was not used to secretaries who burst into tears, let alone ones who left lobelias, primroses, and the rarer forms of cactus behind them when they entered the room.

"It's very pretty," he said, "but not very practical. Already it's almost impossible to get along the passage, and I shudder to think what this room will be like when these have grown a bit higher. I really don't think you can go on with it, Miss Jones."

"You don't think I do it on purpose, do you?" said Matilda, sniffing into her handkerchief. "I can't stop it. They just keep on coming."

"In that case, I am afraid," replied Mr. Willoughby, "that you will not be able to keep on coming. We really cannot have the Ministry overgrown in this way. I shall be very sorry to lose you, Miss Jones. You have been most efficient. What caused this unfortunate disability, may I ask?"

"It's a kind of spell," Matilda said, shaking the damp out of her handkerchief onto a fine polyanthus.

"But my dear girl," Mr. Willoughby exclaimed testily, "you have a National Magic

Insurance card, haven't you? Good heavens—why don't you go to the Public Magician?"

"I never thought of that," she confessed. "I'll go at lunchtime."

Fortunately for Matilda the Public Magician's office lay just across the square from where she worked, so that she did not cause too much disturbance, though the Borough Council could never account for the rare and exotic flowers which suddenly sprang up in the middle of their dusty lawns.

The Public Magician received her briskly, examined her with an occultiscope, and asked her to state particulars of her trouble.

"It's a spell," said Matilda, looking down at a pink Christmas rose growing unseasonably beside her chair.

"In that case we can soon help you. Fill in that form, *if* you please." He pushed a printed slip at her across the table.

It said: "To be filled in by persons suffering from spells, incantations, philters, evil eye, etc."

Matilda filled in name and address of patient, nature of spell, and date, but when she came to name and address of person by whom spell was cast, she paused.

"I don't know her address," she said.

"Then I'm afraid you'll have to find it. Can't do anything without an address," the Public Magician replied.

Matilda went out into the street very disheartened. The Public Magician would do nothing better than advise her to put an advertisement into the *Times* and the *International Sorcerers' Bulletin,* which she accordingly did:

AUNT GERTRUDE please communicate. Matilda much distressed by last poem.

While she was in the post office sending off her advertisements (and causing a good deal of confusion by the number of forget-me-nots she left about), she wrote and posted[4] her resignation to Mr. Willoughby, and then went sadly to the nearest underground[5] station.

"Ain'tcher left something behind?" a man said to her at the top of the escalator. She looked back at the trail of daffodils across the station entrance and hurried anxiously down the stairs. As she ran around a corner at the bottom, angry shouts told her that blooming lilies had interfered with the works and the escalator had stopped.

She tried to hide in the gloom at the far end of the platform, but a furious station official found her.

"Wotcher mean by it?" he said, shaking her elbow. "It'll take three days to put the station right, and look at my platform!"

The stone slabs were split and pushed aside by vast peonies, which kept growing, and threatened to block the line.

"It isn't my fault—really it isn't," poor Matilda stammered.

"The company can sue you for this, you know," he began, when a train came in. Pushing past him, she squeezed into the nearest door.

She began to thank her stars for the escape, but it was too soon. A powerful and penetrating smell of onions rose around her feet where the white flowers of wild garlic had sprung.

When Aunt Gertie finally read the advertisement in a ten-months-old copy of the *International Sorcerers' Bulletin,* she packed her luggage and took the next airplane back to England. For she was still just as Aunt Cissie had described her—thoughtless, but very good-hearted.

"Where is the poor child?" she asked Aunt Aggie.

"I should say she was poor," her sister re-

---

4. **posted:** mailed.
5. **underground:** subway train.

plied tartly. "It's a pity you didn't come home before, instead of making her life a misery for twelve years. You'll find her out in the summerhouse."[6]

Matilda had been living out there ever since she left the Ministry of Alarm and Despondency, because her aunts kindly but firmly, and quite reasonably, said that they could not have the house filled with vegetation.

She had an ax, with which she cut down the worst growths every evening, and for the rest of the time she kept as still as she could, and earned some money by doing odd jobs of typing and sewing.

"My poor dear child," Aunt Gertie said breathlessly, "I had no idea that my little verses would have this sort of effect. Whatever shall we do?"

"Please do something," Matilda implored her, sniffing. This time it was not tears, but a cold she had caught from living in perpetual drafts.

"My dear, there isn't anything I can do. It's bound to last till the end of the year—that sort of spell is completely unalterable."

"Well, at least can you stop sending me the verses?" asked Matilda. "I don't want to sound ungrateful."

"Even that I can't do," her aunt said gloomily. "It's a banker's order at the Magician's Bank. One a year from seven to twenty-one. Oh dear, and I thought it would be such *fun* for you. At least you only have one more, though."

"Yes, but heaven knows what that'll be." Matilda sneezed despondently and put another sheet of paper into her typewriter. There seemed to be nothing to do but wait. However, they did decide that it might be a good thing to go and see the Public Magician on the morning of Matilda's twenty-first birthday.

Aunt Gertie paid the taxi driver and tipped him heavily not to grumble about the mass of delphiniums sprouting out of the mat of his cab.

"Good heavens, if it isn't Gertrude Jones!" the Public Magician exclaimed. "Haven't seen you since we were at college together. How are you? Same old irresponsible Gertie? Remember that hospital you endowed with endless beds and the trouble it caused? And the row[7] with the cigarette manufacturers over the extra million boxes of cigarettes for the soldiers?"

When the situation was explained to him he laughed heartily.

"Just like you, Gertie. Well-meaning isn't the word."

At eleven promptly, Matilda opened her pink envelope.

> Matilda, now you're twenty-one,
> May you have every sort of fun;
> May you have all you've ever wanted,
> And every future wish be granted.

"Every future wish be granted—then I wish Aunt Gertie would lose her power of wishing," cried Matilda; and immediately Aunt Gertie did.

But as Aunt Gertie with her usual thoughtlessness had said, "May you have all you've *ever wanted.*" Matilda had quite a lot of rather inconvenient things to dispose of, including a lion cub and a baby hippopotamus.

---

6. **summerhouse:** small garden building without walls.

7. **row** [rou]: argument.

STUDY QUESTIONS

Recalling

1. What happens to the birthday wishes that Matilda receives each year from her Aunt Gertie? How does Matilda come to feel about these wishes as she grows older?
2. Explain why Matilda loses her job.
3. Why does Matilda need to contact Gertie? How does she do so?
4. What does Gertie tell her about the wishes?
5. What problem does Gertie's final wish solve? How, specifically, is the problem solved?
6. What new problem does the final wish create for Matilda?

Interpreting

7. Does this story take place in the real world? How can you tell?
8. Explain how Gertie's birthday wishes show that she is both "thoughtless" and "good-hearted."
9. What point does the story make about wishes in general? About how wishes change over time?

Extending

10. Assume that you could have "all you've ever wanted." Do you think your wishes might be different now from what they would be when you are twenty-one? Why or why not?

READING AND LITERARY FOCUS

Chronology; Cause and Effect

The events in a story's plot should take place in a logical order. That is, the reader should be able to see how each event leads to the next one. Most stories follow **chronological order,** the time order in which events naturally happen. For example, a person wakes up *before* getting out of bed and eats breakfast *after* getting up.

Events are also related by **cause and effect,** which means that each event causes others to happen. For example, a man wakes up at 6:00 A.M. *because* he has set his alarm for that time. As a *result* of waking so early, he falls asleep on the bus and misses his stop. When we read a story, we should always be able to understand how events are related to each other and why they occur.

Thinking About Chronology; Cause and Effect

1. List in chronological order six main events in "All You've Ever Wanted."
2. What causes Matilda to make the wish that she does at the end of the story? What is the effect, or result, of this wish?

COMPOSITION

Writing About Plot

■ Write an essay about the plot of "All You've Ever Wanted." First pick the four or five most important events in the plot, and explain how these events are related to each other. Then tell which event is the climax of the story, and explain why this event is the peak of reader interest. End by identifying the resolution and explaining how it is the logical outcome of the climax.

Writing a Story

■ Invent another birthday wish (besides those mentioned in the story) sent by Aunt Gertrude to Mathilda. Write a short story about what happens to Mathilda as a result of that wish. Make sure that the events of your story are related to one another in a logical way. Also, be sure to describe your characters and the setting clearly. *For help with this assignment, see Lesson 4 in the Writing About Literature Handbook at the back of this book.*

Paul Annixter (born 1894) is the pen name of Howard Sturtzel. He was born in Minneapolis, Minnesota, and has been writing since the age of nineteen. Annixter is best known for his stories about nature and animal life. "Last Cover" tells the story of a fox.

▪ What more important story does the story tell about the relationships between two brothers and between a father and son?

Paul Annixter

Last Cover

I'm not sure I can tell you what you want to know about my brother; but everything about the pet fox is important, so I'll tell all that from the beginning.

It goes back to a winter afternoon after I'd hunted the woods all day for a sign of our lost pet. I remember the way my mother looked up as I came into the kitchen. Without my speaking, she knew what had happened. For six hours I had walked, reading signs, looking for a delicate print in the damp soil or even a hair that might have told of a red fox passing that way—but I had found nothing.

"Did you go up in the foothills?" Mom asked.

I nodded. My face was stiff from held-back tears. My brother, Colin, who was going on twelve, got it all from one look at me and went into a heartbroken, almost silent, crying.

Three weeks before, Bandit, the pet fox Colin and I had raised from a tiny kit, had disappeared, and not even a rumor had been heard of him since.

"He'd have had to go off soon anyway," Mom comforted. "A big, lolloping fellow like him, he's got to live his life same as us. But he may come back. That fox set a lot of store by you boys in spite of his wild ways."

"He set a lot of store by our food, anyway," Father said. He sat in a chair by the kitchen window mending a piece of harness. "We'll be seeing a lot more of that fellow, never fear. That fox learned to pine for table scraps and young chickens. He was getting to be an egg thief, too, and he's not likely to forget that."

"That was only pranking when he was little," Colin said desperately.

From the first, the tame fox had made tension in the family. It was Father who said we'd better name him Bandit, after he'd made away with his first young chicken.

"Maybe you know," Father said shortly. "But when an animal turns to egg sucking he's usually incurable. He'd better not come pranking around my chicken run again."

It was late February, and I remember the bleak, dead cold that had set in, cold that was a rare thing for our Carolina hills. Flocks of sparrows and snowbirds had appeared to peck hungrily at all that the pigs and chickens didn't eat.

"This one's a killer," Father would say of a morning, looking out at the whitened barn roof. "This one will make the shoats[1] squeal."

A fire snapped all day in our cookstove and another in the stone fireplace in the living room, but still the farmhouse was never warm. The leafless woods were bleak and empty, and I spoke of that to Father when I came back from my search.

"It's always a sad time in the woods when the seven sleepers are under cover," he said.

"What sleepers are they?" I asked. Father was full of woods lore.

"Why, all the animals that have got sense enough to hole up and stay hid in weather like this. Let's see, how was it the old rhyme named them?

> Surly bear and sooty bat,
> Brown chuck and masked coon,
> Chippy-munk and sly skunk,
> And all the mouses
> 'Cept in men's houses.

"And man would have joined them and made it eight, Granther Yeary always said, if he'd had a little more sense."

"I was wondering if the red fox mightn't make it eight," Mom said.

Father shook his head. "Late winter's a high time for foxes. Time when they're out deviling, not sleeping."

My chest felt hollow. I wanted to cry like Colin over our lost fox, but at fourteen a boy doesn't cry. Colin had squatted down on the floor and got out his small hammer and nails to start another new frame for a new picture. Maybe then he'd make a drawing for the frame and be able to forget his misery. It had been

that way with him since he was five.

I thought of the new dress Mom had brought home a few days before in a heavy cardboard box. That box cover would be fine for Colin to draw on. I spoke of it, and Mom's glance thanked me as she went to get it. She and I worried a lot about Colin. He was small for his age, delicate and blond, his hair much lighter and softer than mine, his eyes deep and wide and blue. He was often sick, and I knew the fear Mom had that he might be predestined.[2] I'm just ordinary, like Father. I'm the sort of stuff that can take it—tough and strong—but Colin was always sort of special.

Mom lighted the lamp. Colin began cutting his white cardboard carefully, fitting it into his frame. Father's sharp glance turned on him now and again.

"There goes the boy making another frame before there's a picture for it," he said. "It's too much like cutting out a man's suit for a fellow that's, say, twelve years old. Who knows whether he'll grow into it?"

Mom was into him then, quick. "Not a single frame of Colin's has ever gone to waste. The boy has real talent, Sumter, and it's time you realized it."

"Of course he has," Father said. "All kids have 'em. But they get over 'em."

"It isn't the pox[3] we're talking of," Mom sniffed.

"In a way it is. Ever since you started talking up Colin's art, I've had an invalid for help around the place."

Father wasn't as hard as he made out, I knew, but he had to hold a balance against all Mom's frothing.[4] For him the thing was the land and all that pertained to it. I was following in Father's footsteps, true to form, but Colin threatened to break the family tradition

---

1. **shoats:** young hogs.

2. **predestined** [prē des'tind]: decided before; here, doomed to die young.
3. **the pox:** chicken pox.
4. **frothing:** here, enthusiasm.

with his leaning toward art, with Mom "aiding and abetting him," as Father liked to put it. For the past two years she had had dreams of my brother becoming a real artist and going away to the city to study.

It wasn't that Father had no understanding of such things. I could remember, through the years, Colin lying on his stomach in the front room making pencil sketches, and how a good drawing would catch Father's eyes halfway across the room, and how he would sometimes gather up two or three of them to study, frowning and muttering, one hand in his beard, while a great pride rose in Colin, and in me too. Most of Colin's drawings were of the woods and wild things, and there Father was a master critic. He made out to scorn what seemed to him a passive "white-livered"[5] interpretation of nature through brush and pencil instead of rod and rifle.

At supper that night Colin could scarcely eat. Ever since he'd been able to walk, my brother had had a growing love of wild things, but Bandit had been like his very own, a gift of the woods. One afternoon a year and a half before, Father and Laban Small had been running a vixen through the hills with their dogs. With the last of her strength the she-fox had made for her den, not far from our house. The dogs had overtaken her and killed her just before she reached it. When Father and Laban came up, they'd found Colin crouched nearby holding her cub in his arms.

Father had been for killing the cub, which was still too young to shift for itself, but Colin's grief had brought Mom into it. We'd taken the young fox into the kitchen, all of us, except Father, gone a bit silly over the little thing. Colin had held it in his arms and fed it warm milk from a spoon.

"Watch out with all your soft ways," Father had warned, standing in the doorway. "You'll

---

5. **white-livered:** sickly, timid.

make too much of him. Remember, you can't make a dog out of a fox. Half of that little critter has to love, but the other half is a wild hunter. You boys will mean a whole lot to him while he's a kit, but there'll come a day when you won't mean a thing to him and he'll leave you shorn."

For two weeks after that Colin had nursed the cub, weaning it from milk to bits of meat. For a year they were always together. The cub grew fast. It was soon following Colin and me about the barnyard. It turned out to be a patch fox, with a saddle of darker fur across its shoulders.

I haven't the words to tell you what the fox meant to us. It was far more wonderful owning him than owning any dog. There was something rare and secret like the spirit of the woods about him, and back of his calm, straw-gold eyes was the sense of a brain the equal to a man's. The fox became Colin's whole life.

Each day, going and coming from school, Colin and I took long side trips through the woods, looking for Bandit. Wild things' memories were short, we knew; we'd have to find him soon or the old bond would be broken.

Ever since I was ten I'd been allowed to hunt with Father, so I was good at reading signs. But, in a way, Colin knew more about the woods and wild things than Father or me. What came to me from long observation, Colin seemed to know by instinct.

It was Colin who felt out, like an Indian, the stretch of woods where Bandit had his den, who found the first slim, small fox-print in the damp earth. And then, on an afternoon in March, we saw him. I remember the day well, the racing clouds, the wind rattling the tops of the pine trees and swaying the Spanish moss. Bandit had just come out of a clump of laurel; in the maze of leaves behind him we caught a glimpse of a slim red vixen, so we knew he had found a mate. She melted from sight like a shadow, but Bandit turned to watch us, his mouth open, his tongue lolling as he smiled his old foxy smile. On his thin chops, I saw a telltale chicken feather.

Colin moved silently forward, his movements so quiet and casual he seemed to be standing still. He called Bandit's name, and the fox held his ground, drawn to us with all his senses. For a few moments he let Colin actually put an arm about him. It was then I knew that he loved us still, for all of Father's warnings. He really loved us back, with a fierce, secret love no tame thing ever gave. But the urge of his life just then was toward his new mate. Suddenly, he whirled about and disappeared in the laurels.

Colin looked at me with glowing eyes. "We haven't really lost him, Stan. When he gets through with his spring sparking[6] he may come back. But we've got to show ourselves to him a lot, so he won't forget."

"It's a go," I said.

"Promise not to say a word to Father," Colin said, and I agreed. For I knew by the chicken feather that Bandit had been up to no good.

A week later the woods were budding and the thickets[7] were rustling with all manner of wild things scurrying on the love scent. Colin managed to get a glimpse of Bandit every few days. He couldn't get close though, for the spring running was a lot more important to a fox than any human beings were.

Every now and then Colin got out his framed box cover and looked at it, but he never drew anything on it; he never even picked up his pencil. I remember wondering if what Father had said about framing a picture before you had one had spoiled something for him.

_____
6. **sparking:** courting.
7. **thickets:** thick growths of bushes.

I was helping Father with the planting now, but Colin managed to be in the woods every day. By degrees he learned Bandit's range, where he drank and rested and where he was likely to be according to the time of day. One day he told me how he had petted Bandit again, and how they had walked together a long way in the woods. All this time we had kept his secret from Father.

As summer came on, Bandit began to live up to the prediction Father had made. Accustomed to human beings he moved without fear about the scattered farms of the region, raiding barns and hen runs that other foxes wouldn't have dared go near. And he taught his wild mate to do the same. Almost every night they got into some poultry house, and by late June Bandit was not only killing chickens and ducks but feeding on eggs and young chicks whenever he got the chance.

Stories of his doings came to us from many sources, for he was still easily recognized by the dark patch on his shoulders. Many a farmer took a shot at him as he fled and some of them set out on his trail with dogs, but they always returned home without even sighting him. Bandit was familiar with all the dogs in the region, and he knew a hundred tricks to confound them. He got a reputation that year beyond that of any fox our hills had known. His confidence grew, and he gave up wild hunting altogether and lived entirely off the poultry farmers. By late September the hill farmers banded together to hunt him down.

It was Father who brought home that news one night. All time-honored rules of the fox chase were to be broken in this hunt; if the dogs couldn't bring Bandit down, he was to be shot on sight. I was stricken and furious. I remember the misery of Colin's face in the lamplight. Father, who took pride in all the ritual of the hunt, had refused to be a party to such an affair, though in justice he could

do nothing but sanction[8] any sort of hunt, for Bandit, as old Sam Wetherwax put it, had been "purely getting in the Lord's hair."

The hunt began next morning, and it was the biggest turnout our hills had known. There were at least twenty mounted men in the party and as many dogs. Father and I were working in the lower field as they passed along the river road. Most of the hunters carried rifles, and they looked ugly.

---

8. **sanction:** approve of.

Twice during the morning I went up to the house to find Colin, but he was nowhere around. As we worked, Father and I could follow the progress of the hunt by the distant hound music on the breeze. We could tell just where the hunters first caught sight of the fox and where Bandit was leading the dogs during the first hour. We knew as well as if we'd seen it how Bandit roused another fox along Turkey Branch and forced it to run for him, and how the dogs swept after it for twenty minutes before they sensed their mistake.

Noon came, and Colin had not come in to eat. After dinner Father didn't go back to the field. He moped about, listening to the hound talk. He didn't like what was on any more than I did, and now and again I caught his smile of satisfaction when we heard the broken, angry notes of the hunting horn, telling that the dogs had lost the trail or had run another fox.

I was restless, and I went up into the hills in midafternoon. I ranged the woods for miles, thinking all the time of Colin. Time lost all meaning for me, and the short day was nearing an end, when I heard the horn talking again, telling that the fox had put over another trick. All day he had deviled the dogs and mocked the hunters. This new trick and the coming night would work to save him. I was wildly glad, as I moved down toward Turkey Branch and stood listening for a time by the deep, shaded pool where for years we boys had gone swimming, sailed boats, and dreamed summer dreams.

Suddenly, out of the corner of my eye, I saw the sharp ears and thin, pointed mask of a fox—in the water almost beneath me. It was Bandit, craftily submerged there, all but his head, resting in the cool water of the pool and the shadow of the two big beeches that spread above it. He must have run forty miles or more since morning. And he must have hidden in this place before. His knowing, crafty mask blended perfectly with the shadows and a mass of drift and branches that had collected by the bank of the pool. He was so still that a pair of thrushes flew up from the spot as I came up, not knowing he was there.

Bandit's bright, harried eyes were looking right at me. But I did not look at him direct. Some woods instinct, swifter than thought, kept me from it. So he and I met as in another world, indirectly, with feeling but without sign or greeting.

Suddenly I saw that Colin was standing almost beside me. Silently as a water snake, he had come out of the bushes and stood there. Our eyes met, and a quick and secret smile passed between us. It was a rare moment in which I really "met" my brother, when something of his essence flowed into me and I knew all of him. I've never lost it since.

My eyes still turned from the fox, my heart pounding. I moved quietly away, and Colin moved with me. We whistled softly as we went, pretending to busy ourselves along the bank of the stream. There was magic in it, as if by will we wove a web of protection about the fox, a ring-pass-not that none might penetrate. It was so, too, we felt, in the brain of Bandit, and that doubled the charm. To us he was still our little pet that we had carried about in our arms on countless summer afternoons.

Two hundred yards upstream, we stopped beside slim, fresh tracks in the mud where Bandit had entered the branch. The tracks angled upstream. But in the water the wily creature had turned down.

We climbed the far bank to wait, and Colin told me how Bandit's secret had been his secret ever since an afternoon three months before, when he'd watched the fox swim downstream to hide in the deep pool. Today he'd waited on the bank, feeling that Bandit, hard pressed by the dogs, might again seek the pool for sanctuary.

We looked back once as we turned homeward. He still had not moved. We didn't know until later that he was killed that same night by a chance hunter, as he crept out from his hiding place.

That evening Colin worked a long time on his framed box cover that had lain about the house untouched all summer. He kept at it all the next day too. I had never seen him work so hard. I seemed to sense in the air the feeling he was putting into it, how he was *believ-*

ing his picture into being. It was evening before he finished it. Without a word he handed it to Father. Mom and I went and looked over his shoulder.

It was a delicate and intricate pencil drawing of the deep branch pool, and there was Bandit's head and watching, fear-filled eyes hiding there amid the leaves and shadows, woven craftily into the maze of twigs and branches, as if by nature's art itself. Hardly a fox there at all, but the place where he was— or should have been. I recognized it instantly, but Mom gave a sort of incredulous sniff.

"I'll declare," she said. "It's mazy[9] as a puzzle. It just looks like a lot of sticks and leaves to me."

---

9. **mazy** [māz′ē]: like a maze; confusing.

Long minutes of study passed before Father's eye picked out the picture's secret, as few men's could have done. I laid that to Father's being a born hunter. That was a picture that might have been done especially for him. In fact, I guess it was.

Finally he turned to Colin with his deep, slow smile. "So that's how Bandit fooled them all," he said. He sat holding the picture with a sort of tenderness for a long time, while we glowed in the warmth of the shared secret. That was Colin's moment. Colin's art stopped being a pox[10] to Father right there. And later, when the time came for Colin to go to art school, it was Father who was his solid backer.

---

10. **pox:** annoyance.

STUDY QUESTIONS

Recalling

1. What kind of special talent does Colin have? Explain what Father "made out to scorn" when he looks at Colin's work early in the story.
2. Tell how Bandit became the family pet. What warning did Father give about Bandit?
3. In what sense does Colin know "more about the woods and wild things" than his brother and father? According to Stan, how did Colin find Bandit after the fox ran away?
4. How does Bandit at first outwit the fox hunt? What finally happens to him?
5. What does Colin finally do with the box cover? According to the last paragraph, how does Father treat Colin's talent after he sees the box cover?

Interpreting

6. How are Colin and his father different?

7. Why do you think Father changes his mind about Colin's work?
8. Use examples from the story to show how Bandit at first causes tensions in the family but finally brings the family together.

Extending

9. Why might it be difficult to choose an occupation different from that of most of the people we know?

READING AND LITERARY FOCUS

External Conflict

Most plots present a conflict of some kind. A **conflict** is a struggle between two opposing forces. The details of the conflict grab our interest as we begin to read a story. At the story's climax we see how the conflict will be solved. The resolution reveals the conflict's final outcome.

An **external conflict** occurs when a character

struggles against an outside force. For example, Rikki-tikki-tavi's battle with the snakes (page 2) and Matilda's attempt to undo her aunt's magic (page 66) are both external conflicts. There are several specific kinds of external conflict. One kind is a person's struggle against nature, as in the case of a family escaping from a flood. Another kind is a conflict between two people, as in an argument or a contest. Still another kind occurs when a person struggles against society, as when a citizen tries to change a law.

Thinking About External Conflict

■ Identify two external conflicts in "Last Cover," and tell how each is resolved.

VOCABULARY

Using the Dictionary

A **dictionary** is a book that lists words in alphabetical order and also presents meanings and other information about those words. See the following sample entry for the word *instinct*:

> **in·stinct** (in'stingkt) *n.* **1.** unlearned, inborn disposition, common to all members of a species, to behave in a fixed way when moved by a particular set of stimuli. **2.** natural aptitude or tendency; talent. [Latin *īnstinctus* impulse, from *īnstinctus,* past participle of *īnstinguere* to impel.]
>
> —*Macmillan Dictionary*

Each word listed is called an **entry word.** Entry words are divided into syllables by dots or spaces. For example, the entry here shows that *instinct* has two syllables. The dictionary shows us where to divide the word when we write it on two lines.

The **pronunciation** is the way a word is spoken. The dictionary gives a word's pronunciation in parentheses after the entry word. The letters used in the pronunciation are called a **phonetic alphabet.** The dictionary's **pronunciation key** explains the sounds of these letters.

A word's **part of speech** tells how it is used in a sentence. The abbreviation for a word's part of speech is usually given after the pronunciation. For example, the word *instinct* is a noun and is marked *n.* Some words can be used as different parts of speech. For example, *cover* can be used as either a noun or a verb.

The **definition,** or meaning, of a word usually follows the part of speech. Many words have more than one definition. These different definitions are numbered, and the most common meaning is usually listed first.

Most dictionaries also give the word's **etymology,** or origin and history. The etymology usually is shown in brackets either before or after the definition. For example, the word *instinct* comes from a Latin word, *īnstinctus,* which means "impulse." This word in turn was based on the Latin verb *īnstinguere,* meaning "to impel."

To help us find a word, each dictionary page has two guide words at the top. These **guide words** are the first and last entry words on the page. All the other entry words fall alphabetically between the two guide words.

The italicized words in the following questions are from "Last Cover." Use a dictionary to answer the questions.

1. What is the first meaning of *harness* as a noun?
2. What pronunciation is given for *surly*?
3. Where would you divide *hollow* if you could not fit it on one line?
4. What is the origin of the word *invalid*?
5. What does the word *pertained* mean, and what is its origin?

Sherwood Anderson (1876–1941) grew up in a poor family that lived in small towns in Ohio. He eventually settled in Chicago, where he was encouraged to write by poets Vachel Lindsay and Carl Sandburg. He used his boyhood experiences as the basis of his most famous book, *Winesburg, Ohio*, published in 1919. Like the stories in that book, "Stolen Day" gives a special twist to the details of ordinary, everyday life.

■ Do you think the boy in this story is typical of other people his age?

Sherwood Anderson

Stolen Day

It must be that all children are actors. The whole thing started with a boy on our street named Walter, who had inflammatory rheumatism.[1] That's what they called it. He didn't have to go to school.

Still, he could walk about. He could go fishing in the creek or the waterworks pond. There was a place up at the pond where in the spring the water came tumbling over the dam and formed a deep pool. It was a good place. Sometimes you could get some big ones there.

I went down that way on my way to school one spring morning. It was out of my way but I wanted to see if Walter was there.

He was, inflammatory rheumatism and all. There he was, sitting with a fish pole in his hand. He had been able to walk down there all right.

It was then that my own legs began to hurt. My back too. I went on to school but, at the recess time, I began to cry. I did it when the teacher, Sarah Suggett, had come out into the schoolhouse yard.

She came right over to me.

"I ache all over," I said. I did, too.

I kept on crying and it worked all right.

"You'd better go on home," she said.

So I went. I limped painfully away. I kept on limping until I got out of the schoolhouse street.

Then I felt better. I still had inflammatory rheumatism pretty bad but I could get along better.

I must have done some thinking on the way home.

"I'd better not say I have inflammatory rheumatism," I decided. "Maybe if you've got that, you swell up."

I thought I'd better go around to where Walter was and ask him about that, so I did—but he wasn't there.

"They must not be biting today," I thought.

I had a feeling that, if I said I had inflammatory rheumatism, Mother or my brothers

---

1. **inflammatory** [in flam′ə tôr′ē] **rheumatism** [rōō′mə tiz′əm]: disease characterized by painful swelling and stiffness in the joints.

and my sister Stella might laugh. They did laugh at me pretty often, and I didn't like it at all.

"Just the same," I said to myself, "I have got it." I began to hurt and ache again.

I went home and sat on the front steps of our house. I sat there a long time. There wasn't anyone at home but Mother and the two little ones. Ray would have been four or five then and Earl might have been three.

It was Earl who saw me there. I had got tired of sitting and was lying on the porch. Earl was always a quiet, solemn little fellow.

He must have said something to Mother, for presently she came.

"What's the matter with you? Why aren't you in school?" she asked.

I came pretty near telling her right out that I had inflammatory rheumatism, but I thought I'd better not. Mother and Father had been speaking of Walter's case at the table just the day before. "It affects the heart," Father had said. That frightened me when I thought of it. "I might die," I thought. "I might just suddenly die right here; my heart might stop beating."

On the day before, I had been running a race with my brother Irve. We were up at the fairgrounds after school, and there was a half-mile track.

"I'll bet you can't run a half mile," he said. "I bet you I could beat you running clear around the track."

And so we did it and I beat him, but afterward my heart did seem to beat pretty hard. I remembered that, lying there on the porch. "It's a wonder, with my inflammatory rheumatism and all, I didn't just drop down dead," I thought. The thought frightened me a lot. I ached worse than ever.

"I ache, Ma," I said. "I just ache."

She made me go in the house and upstairs and get into bed.

It wasn't so good. It was spring. I was up there for perhaps an hour, maybe two, and then I felt better.

I got up and went downstairs. "I feel better, Ma," I said.

Mother said she was glad. She was pretty busy that day and hadn't paid much attention to me. She had made me get into bed upstairs and then hadn't even come up to see how I was.

I didn't think much of that when I was up there; but when I got downstairs where she was, and when, after I had said I felt better and she only said she was glad and went right on with her work, I began to ache again.

I thought, "I'll bet I die of it. I bet I do."

I went out to the front porch and sat down. I was pretty sore at Mother.

"If she really knew the truth, that I have inflammatory rheumatism and I may just drop down dead any time, I'll bet she wouldn't care about that either," I thought.

I was getting more and more angry the more thinking I did.

"I know what I'm going to do," I thought; "I'm going to go fishing."

I thought that, feeling the way I did, I might be sitting on the high bank just above the deep pool where the water went over the dam, and suddenly my heart would stop beating.

And then, of course, I'd pitch forward, over the bank into the pool; and, if I wasn't dead when I hit the water, I'd drown sure.

They would all come home to supper and they'd miss me.

"But where is he?"

Then Mother would remember that I'd come home from school aching.

She'd go upstairs, and I wouldn't be there. One day during the year before, there was a child got drowned in a spring. It was one of the Wyatt children.

Right down at the end of the street there was a spring under a birch tree, and there had been a barrel sunk in the ground.

Everyone had always been saying the spring ought to be kept covered, but it wasn't.

So the Wyatt child went down there, played around alone, and fell in and got drowned.

Mother was the one who had found the drowned child. She had gone to get a pail of water, and there the child was, drowned and dead.

This had been in the evening when we were all at home, and Mother had come running up the street with the dead, dripping child in her arms. She was making for the Wyatt house as hard as she could run, and she was pale.

She had a terrible look on her face, I remembered then.

"So," I thought, "they'll miss me, and there'll be a search made. Very likely there'll be someone who has seen me sitting by the pond fishing, and there'll be a big alarm and all the town will turn out and they'll drag the pond."

I was having a grand time, having died.

Maybe, after they found me and had got me out of the deep pool, Mother would grab me up in her arms and run home with me as she had run with the Wyatt child.

I got up from the porch and went around the house. I got my fishing pole and lit out for the pool below the dam. Mother was busy—she always was—and didn't see me go. When I got there, I thought I'd better not sit too near the edge of the high bank.

By this time I didn't ache hardly at all, but I thought,

"With inflammatory rheumatism you can't tell," I thought.

"It probably comes and goes," I thought.

"Walter has it and he goes fishing," I thought.

I had got my line into the pool and suddenly I got a bite. It was a regular whopper; I knew that. I'd never had a bite like that.

I knew what it was. It was one of Mr. Fenn's big carp.

Mr. Fenn was a man who had a big pond

of his own. He sold ice in the summer, and the pond was to make the ice. He had bought some big carp and put them into his pond; and then, earlier in the spring when there was a freshet,[2] his dam had gone out.

So the carp had got into our creek, and one or two big ones had been caught—but none of them by a boy like me.

The carp was pulling and I was pulling and I was afraid he'd break my line, so I just tumbled down the high bank, holding onto the line and got right into the pool. We had it out, there in the pool. We struggled. We wrestled. Then I got a hand under his gills and got him out.

He was a big one all right. He was nearly half as big as I was myself. I had him on the bank and I kept one hand under his gills and I ran.

I never ran so hard in my life. He was slippery, and now and then he wriggled out of my arms; once I stumbled and fell on him, but I got him home.

---

2. **freshet:** sudden overflowing of a stream because of heavy rain or melting snow.

So there it was. I was a big hero that day. Mother got a washtub and filled it with water. She put the fish in it, and all the neighbors came to look. I got into dry clothes and went down to supper—and then I made a break that spoiled my day.

There we were, all of us, at the table, and suddenly Father asked what had been the matter with me at school. He had met the teacher, Sarah Suggett, on the street, and she told him how I had become ill.

"What was the matter with you?" Father asked; and before I thought what I was saying, I let it out.

"I had the inflammatory rheumatism," I said—and a shout went up. It made me sick to hear them, the way they all laughed.

It brought back all the aching again, and like a fool I began to cry.

"Well, I *have* got it—I *have*," I cried, and I got up from the table and ran upstairs.

I stayed there until Mother came up. I knew it would be a long time before I heard the last of the inflammatory rheumatism. I was sick all night, but the aching I now had wasn't in my legs or in my back.

STUDY QUESTIONS

Recalling

1. Why does Walter not go to school? What is he able to do anyway?
2. What illness does the boy telling the story decide that he has? Why does he not tell his family about it?
3. When the boy comes home from school, what does his mother tell him to do? How does he spend his day?
4. At dinner what does he tell his father was the matter, and how do the others react?
5. In the final sentence what does the boy say about the "aching" he now has?

Interpreting

6. After seeing Walter at the pool, why might the boy decide that he himself is ill?
7. How does the boy's family seem to treat him? What might their treatment have to do with his decision that he is ill?

8. What do you think the story's last sentence means? What lesson do you think the boy has learned?

Extending

9. What advice would you give the storyteller if you were his friend?

READING AND LITERARY FOCUS

Internal Conflict

Most stories involve a **conflict,** or struggle between opposing forces. Conflicts may be either external or internal. An **internal conflict** is a struggle that takes place within a person's mind. For example, in "Last Cover" Father experiences an internal conflict during the hunt for Bandit. He believes that the farmers have the right to hunt Bandit because the fox is a menace to their chickens. Yet Father also disapproves of the way the hunters have abandoned the usual rules of hunting. He is therefore glad whenever Bandit manages to lead the farmers astray.

Thinking About Internal Conflict

What internal conflict takes place within the boy in "Stolen Day"? Tell how that conflict is resolved.

Flashback

Most stories are written in chronological order, or the time order in which events naturally occur. Sometimes authors interrupt that order to show us an event that happened in the past. A **flashback** is a scene that breaks the normal time order of a plot to show a past event. Very often a flashback gives important background information. For example, in "Last Cover" the narrative begins just after Bandit runs away, but the time sequence is interrupted for a flashback telling how Bandit came to be a family pet.

Thinking About Flashback

Relate one flashback in "Stolen Day." What information does it add to the story?

COMPOSITION

Writing About Plot

Write an essay about the plot of "Stolen Day." Begin by identifying the most important conflict in the story. Explain what causes this conflict, and tell what problems make it difficult for the boy in the story to resolve his conflict. End by telling the final outcome of the story's conflict. *For help with this assignment, see Lesson 2 in the Writing About Literature Handbook at the back of this book.*

Writing a Nonfiction Narrative

Write a true narrative about an experience in which you discovered something about yourself. Begin by explaining when the experience occurred and what the circumstances of your life were at the time. Then describe the experience itself. End by explaining what you learned as a result of the experience. *For help with this assignment, see Lesson 8 in the Writing About Literature Handbook at the back of this book.*

CHALLENGE

Literary Criticism

Literary critic Alfred Kazin says of Sherwood Anderson:

> His great subject always was personal freedom, the yearning for freedom, the delight in freedom.

In what sense do the boy's actions in "Stolen Day" come from a "yearning for freedom"? What does his freedom cost him?

Fred Gipson (1908–1973) was a noted writer of westerns and other stories about the great American outdoors. He was born in Mason, Texas, and lived on a farm there for most of his life. Gipson's best-known work is *Old Yeller*, a novel that takes place in rural Texas. The novel is about a big homely yellow—or "yeller"—dog that makes his home with a farm family.

■ In the following selection from his novel, how does Old Yeller help the family with whom he lives?

Fred Gipson

Old Yeller and the Bear

from **Old Yeller**

That little Arliss! From the time he'd grown up big enough to get out of the cabin, he'd made a practice of trying to catch and keep every living thing that ran, flew, jumped, or crawled.

Every night before Mama let him go to bed, she'd make Arliss empty his pockets of whatever he'd captured during the day. Generally, it would be a tangled-up mess of grasshoppers and worms and praying bugs and little rusty tree lizards. One time he brought in a horned toad that got so mad he swelled out round and flat as a Mexican *tortilla*[1] and bled at the eyes. Sometimes it was stuff like a young bird that had fallen out of its nest before it could fly, or a green-speckled spring frog, or a striped water snake. And once he turned out of his pocket a wadded-up baby copperhead that nearly threw Mama into spasms. We

never did figure out why the snake hadn't bitten him, but Mama took no more chances on snakes. She switched Arliss hard for catching that snake.

Then, after the yeller dog came, Little Arliss started catching even bigger game. Like cottontail rabbits and chaparral birds[2] and a baby possum that sulled[3] and lay like dead for the first several hours until he finally decided that Arliss wasn't going to hurt him.

Of course, it was Old Yeller that was doing the catching. He'd run the game down and turn it over to Little Arliss. Then Little Arliss could come in and tell Mama a big fib about how he caught it himself.

I watched them one day when they caught a blue catfish out of Birdsong Creek. The fish had fed out into water so shallow that his top fin was sticking out. About the time I saw it,

---

1. **tortilla** [tôr tē′yə]: round, flat cake made from corn meal.

2. **chaparral** [shap′ə ral′] **birds:** long-tailed desert birds.
3. **sulled:** sulked.

Old Yeller and Little Arliss did, too. They made a run at it. The fish went scooting away toward deeper water, only Yeller was too fast for him. He pounced on the fish and shut his big mouth down over it and went romping to the bank, where he dropped it down on the grass and let it flop. And here came Little Arliss to fall on it like I guess he'd been doing everything else. The minute he got his hands on it, the fish finned him and he went to crying.

But he wouldn't turn the fish loose. He just grabbed it up and went running and squawling toward the house, where he gave the fish to Mama. His hands were all bloody by then, where the fish had finned him. They swelled up and got mighty sore; not even a mesquite[4] thorn hurts as bad as a sharp fish fin when it's run deep into your hand.

But as soon as Mama had wrapped his hands in a poultice[5] of mashed-up prickly-pear root to draw out the poison, Little Arliss forgot all about his hurt. And that night when we ate the fish for supper, he told the biggest windy I ever heard about how he'd dived 'way down into a deep hole under the rocks and dragged that fish out and nearly got drowned before he could swim to the bank with it.

But when I tried to tell Mama what really happened, she wouldn't let me. "Now, this is Arliss' story," she said. "You let him tell it the way he wants to."

I told Mama then, I said: "Mama, that old yeller dog is going to make the biggest liar in Texas out of Little Arliss."

But Mama just laughed at me, like she always laughed at Little Arliss' big windies after she'd gotten off where he couldn't hear her. She said for me to let Little Arliss alone. She said that if he ever told a bigger whopper than the ones I used to tell, she had yet to hear it.

Well, I hushed then. If Mama wanted Little Arliss to grow up to be the biggest liar in Texas, I guessed it wasn't any of my business.

All of which, I figure, is what led up to Little Arliss' catching the bear. I think Mama had let him tell so many big yarns about his catching live game that he'd begun to believe them himself.

When it happened, I was down the creek a ways, splitting rails to fix up the yard fence where the bulls had torn it down. I'd been down there since dinner, working in a stand of tall slim post oaks. I'd chop down a tree, trim off the branches as far up as I wanted, then cut away the rest of the top. After that I'd start splitting the log.

I'd split the log by driving steel wedges into the wood. I'd start at the big end and hammer in a wedge with the back side of my ax. This would start a little split running lengthways of the log. Then I'd take a second wedge and drive it into this split. This would split the log further along and, at the same time, loosen the first wedge. I'd then knock the first wedge loose and move it up in front of the second one.

Driving one wedge ahead of the other like that, I could finally split a log in two halves. Then I'd go to work on the halves, splitting them apart. That way, from each log, I'd come out with four rails.

Swinging that chopping ax was sure hard work. The sweat poured off me. My back muscles ached. The ax got so heavy I could hardly swing it. My breath got harder and harder to breathe.

An hour before sundown, I was worn down to a nub. It seemed like I couldn't hit another lick. Papa could have lasted till past sundown, but I didn't see how I could. I shouldered my ax and started toward the cabin, trying to think up some excuse to tell Mama to keep her from knowing I was played clear out.

That's when I heard Little Arliss scream.

---

4. **mesquite** [mes kēt′]: small thorny tree that grows in desert regions.
5. **poultice** [pōl′tis]: hot, moist mixture applied to an inflamed part of the body as a type of medication.

Well, Little Arliss was a screamer by nature. He'd scream when he was happy and scream when he was mad, and a lot of times he'd scream just to hear himself make a noise. Generally, we paid no more mind to his screaming than we did to the gobble of a wild turkey.

But this time was different. The second I heard his screaming, I felt my heart flop clear over. This time I knew Little Arliss was in real trouble.

I tore out up the trail leading toward the cabin. A minute before, I'd been so tired out with my rail splitting that I couldn't have struck a trot. But now I raced through the tall trees in that creek bottom, covering ground like a scared wolf.

Little Arliss' second scream, when it came, was louder and shriller and more frantic-sounding than the first. Mixed with it was a whimpering crying sound that I knew didn't come from him. It was a sound I'd heard before and seemed like I ought to know what it was, but right then I couldn't place it.

Then, from way off to one side came a sound that I would have recognized anywhere. It was the coughing roar of a charging bear. I'd just heard it once in my life. That was the time Mama had shot and wounded a hog-killing bear, and Papa had had to finish it off with a knife to keep it from getting her.

My heart went to pushing up into my throat, nearly choking off my wind. I strained for every lick of speed I could get out of my running legs. I didn't know what sort of fix Little Arliss had got himself into, but I knew that it had to do with a mad bear, which was enough.

The way the late sun slanted through the trees had the trail all cross-banded with streaks of bright light and dark shade. I ran through these bright and dark patches so fast that the changing light nearly blinded me. Then, suddenly, I raced out into the open

where I could see ahead. And what I saw sent a chill clear through to the marrow of my bones. There was Little Arliss, down in that spring hole again. He was lying half in and half out of the water, holding onto the hind leg of a little black bear cub no bigger than a small coon. The bear cub was out on the bank, whimpering and crying and clawing the rocks with all three of his other feet, trying to pull away. But Little Arliss was holding on for all he was worth, scared now and screaming his head off—too scared to let go.

How the bear cub ever came to prowl close enough for Little Arliss to grab him, I don't know. And why he didn't turn on him and

ning down the slant toward the spring, screaming at Arliss, telling him to turn the bear cub loose. But Little Arliss wouldn't do it. All he'd do was hang onto that hind leg and let out one shrill shriek after another as fast as he could suck in a breath.

Now the she-bear was charging across the shallows in the creek. She was knocking sheets of water high in the bright sun, charging with her fur up and her long teeth bared, filling the canyon with that awful coughing roar. And no matter how fast Mama ran or how fast I ran, the she-bear was going to get there first!

I think I nearly went blind then, picturing what was going to happen to Little Arliss. I know that I opened my mouth to scream and not any sound came out.

Then, just as the bear went lunging up the creek bank toward Little Arliss and her cub, a flash of yellow came streaking out of the brush.

It was that big yeller dog. He was roaring like a mad bull. He wasn't one third as big and heavy as the she-bear, but when he piled into her from one side, he rolled her clear off her feet. They went down in a wild, roaring tangle of twisting bodies and scrambling feet and slashing fangs.

As I raced past them, I saw the bear lunge up to stand on her hind feet like a man while she clawed at the body of the yeller dog hanging to her throat. I didn't wait to see more. Without ever checking my stride, I ran in and jerked Little Arliss loose from the cub. I grabbed him by the wrist and yanked him up out of that water and slung him toward Mama like he was a half-empty sack of corn. I screamed at Mama. "Grab him, Mama! Grab him and run!" Then I swung my chopping ax high and wheeled, aiming to cave in the she-bear's head with the first lick.

But I never did strike. I didn't need to. Old Yeller hadn't let the bear get close enough. He

bite loose, I couldn't figure out, either. Unless he was like Little Arliss, too scared to think.

But all of that didn't matter now. What mattered was the bear cub's mama. She'd heard the cries of her baby and was coming to save him. She was coming so fast that she had the brush popping and breaking as she crashed through and over it. I could see her black heavy figure piling off down the slant on the far side of Birdsong Creek. She was roaring mad and ready to kill.

And worst of all, I could see that I'd never get there in time!

Mama couldn't either. She'd heard Arliss, too, and here she came from the cabin, run-

couldn't handle her; she was too big and strong for that. She'd stand there on her hind feet, hunched over, and take a roaring swing at him with one of those big front claws. She'd slap him head over heels. She'd knock him so far that it didn't look like he could possibly get back there before she charged again, but he always did. He'd hit the ground rolling, yelling his head off with the pain of the blow, but somehow he'd always roll to his feet; and here he'd come again, ready to tie into her for another round.

I stood there with my ax raised, watching them for a long moment. Then, from up toward the house, I heard Mama calling: "Come away from there, Travis. Hurry, Son! Run!"

That spooked me. Up till then, I'd been ready to tie into that bear myself. Now, suddenly, I was scared out of my wits again. I ran toward the cabin.

But like it was, Old Yeller nearly beat me there. I didn't see it, of course, but Mama said that the minute Old Yeller saw we were all in the clear and out of danger, he threw the fight to that she-bear and lit out for the house. The bear chased him for a little piece, but at the rate Old Yeller was leaving her behind, Mama said it looked like the bear was backing up.

But if the big yeller dog was scared or hurt in any way when he came dashing into the house, he didn't show it. He sure didn't show it like we all did. Little Arliss had hushed his screaming, but he was trembling all over and clinging to Mama like he'd never let her go. And Mama was sitting in the middle of the floor, holding him up close and crying like she'd never stop. And me, I was close to crying, myself.

Old Yeller, though, all he did was come bounding in to jump on us and lick us in the face and bark so loud that there, inside the cabin, the noise nearly made us deaf.

The way he acted, you might have thought that bear fight hadn't been anything more than a rowdy romp that we'd all taken part in for the fun of it.

Till Little Arliss got us mixed up in that bear fight, I guess I'd been looking on him about like most boys look on their little brothers. I liked him, all right, but I didn't have a lot of use for him. What with his always playing in our drinking water and getting in the way of my chopping ax and howling his head off and chunking me with rocks when he got mad, it didn't seem to me like he was hardly worth the bother of putting up with.

But that day when I saw him in the spring, so helpless against the angry she-bear, I learned different. I knew then that I loved him as much as I did Mama and Papa, maybe in some ways even a little bit more.

So it was only natural for me to come to love the dog that saved him.

After that, I couldn't do enough for Old Yeller. What if he was a big, ugly, meat-stealing rascal? What if he did fall over and yell bloody murder every time I looked crossways at him? What if he had run off when he ought to have helped with the fighting bulls? None of that made a lick of difference now. He'd pitched in and saved Little Arliss when I couldn't possibly have done it, and that was enough for me.

I petted him and made over him till he was wiggling all over to show how happy he was. I felt mean about how I'd treated him and did everything I could to let him know. I searched his feet and pulled out a long mesquite thorn that had become embedded between his toes. I held him down and had Mama hand me a stick with a coal of fire on it so I could burn off three big bloated ticks that I found inside one of his ears. I washed him with lye soap and water, then rubbed salty bacon grease into his hair all over to rout the fleas. And that night after dark, when he sneaked into bed with me and Little Arliss, I let him sleep there and never said a word about it to Mama.

STUDY QUESTIONS

Recalling

1. How does Arliss actually catch the blue catfish? What story does Arliss tell about his catch?
2. Why does the she-bear come after Arliss?
3. Describe the fight between Old Yeller and the she-bear. When does Old Yeller finally run from the bear?
4. What does Travis realize about his feelings for his brother? In what way do Travis' feelings toward Old Yeller change?

Interpreting

5. Identify two virtues that Old Yeller shows.
6. How old would you say Travis is? Which of his actions seem to be those of a grown man? Which seem to be those of a boy?

Extending

7. Why might a narrow escape from tragedy bring the members of a family closer together?

READING AND LITERARY FOCUS

Episode from a Novel

"Old Yeller and the Bear" is an **excerpt,** or passage, from the novel *Old Yeller.* A **novel** is a long work of narrative fiction. In general, an excerpt from a longer work can begin and end at any point within that work. The excerpt from *Old Yeller* might more specifically be considered an episode. An **episode** is a self-contained incident within a novel. It has a clear beginning and ending. It is like a short story within the longer narrative of the novel.

Each episode adds new situations and sometimes new conflicts to the novel's plot. These episodes also help to develop the characters and themes presented in the novel. For example, the novel *Old Yeller* includes several episodes in which Old Yeller helps the members of the family with whom he lives. The dog thus becomes more ad-mirable and heroic as the novel goes on. Episodes like "Old Yeller and the Bear" are enjoyable to read for themselves alone. In addition, they can give us the flavor of the novel as a whole.

Thinking About an Episode from a Novel

■ On the basis of this episode, make up two questions about which you would like to learn more in the rest of *Old Yeller.*

Foreshadowing and Predicting Outcomes

Writers often use clues known as **foreshadowing** to prepare readers for future developments in a story or novel. For example, in "Last Cover" we see that Colin is very close to the fox, Bandit. Therefore, we are prepared for his discovery of Bandit's hiding place. Because foreshadowing makes us look ahead to what is coming, it helps us to predict the outcome of the narrative.

Thinking About Foreshadowing

1. In "Old Yeller and the Bear" find one clue that foreshadows Old Yeller's rescue of Little Arliss.
2. In the novel *Old Yeller* Old Yeller dies as the result of his attempt to protect the family from a wolf. Tell how "Old Yeller and the Bear" foreshadows this outcome.

COMPARING STORIES

1. "Feathered Friend," "The Sneaker Crisis," "All You've Ever Wanted," and "Old Yeller and the Bear" all involve a crisis of some kind. Choose two or more of these stories, and show how the crisis in each story is different. In what way are the differences in the crises typical of the overall differences in the stories?
2. In "Last Cover," "Stolen Day," and "Old Yeller and the Bear" family relationships are an important part of the plot. Compare the way relationships between parents and children are portrayed in two or more of these stories.

CHARACTER

Count Leo Tolstoy (1828–1910) is one of Russia's greatest writers and one of the world's greatest novelists. In 1854 he fought in the Crimean War, a war between Russia and Great Britain, France, and Turkey. After Tolstoy retired from the army, he returned to his estate to farm the land. There he opened a school for the children of the poor.

■ Consider the values that are important to the king and to the judge in the following story.

Leo Tolstoy

A Just Judge

An Algerian[1] king named Bauakas wanted to find out whether or not it was true, as he had been told, that in one of his cities there lived a just judge who could instantly discern the truth, and from whom no rogue was ever able to conceal himself. Bauakas exchanged clothes with a merchant and went on horseback to the city where the judge lived.

At the entrance to the city a cripple approached the king and begged alms[2] of him. Bauakas gave him money and was about to continue on his way, but the cripple clung to his clothing.

"What do you wish?" asked the king. "Haven't I given you money?"

"You gave me alms," said the cripple, "now grant me one favor. Let me ride with you as far as the city square, otherwise the horses and camels may trample me."

Bauakas sat the cripple behind him on the horse and took him as far as the city square. There he halted his horse, but the cripple refused to dismount.

"We have arrived at the square, why don't you get off?" asked Bauakas.

"Why should I?" the beggar replied. "This horse belongs to me. If you are unwilling to return it, we shall have to go to court."

Hearing their quarrel, people gathered around them shouting:

"Go to the judge! He will decide between you!"

Bauakas and the cripple went to the judge. There were others in court, and the judge called upon each one in turn. Before he came to Bauakas and the cripple he heard a scholar and a peasant. They had come to court over a woman: the peasant said she was his wife, and the scholar said she was his. The judge heard them both, remained silent for a moment, and then said:

"Leave the woman here with me, and come back tomorrow."

When they had gone, a butcher and an oil

---

1. **Algerian** [al jēr′ē ən]: from Algeria, a country in northern Africa.
2. **alms:** money or gifts for the poor.

merchant came before the judge. The butcher was covered with blood, and the oil merchant with oil. In his hand the butcher held some money, and the oil merchant held onto the butcher's hand.

"I was buying oil from this man," the butcher said, "and when I took out my purse to pay him, he seized me by the hand and tried to take all my money away from me. That is why we have come to you—I holding onto my purse, and he holding onto my hand. But the money is mine, and he is a thief."

Then the oil merchant spoke. "That is not true," he said. "The butcher came to me to buy oil, and after I had poured him a full jug, he asked me to change a gold piece for him. When I took out my money and placed it upon a bench, he seized it and tried to run off. I caught him by the hand, as you see, and brought him here to you."

The judge remained silent for a moment, then said: "Leave the money here with me, and come back tomorrow."

When his turn came, Bauakas told what had happened. The judge listened to him, and then asked the beggar to speak.

"All that he said is untrue," said the beggar. "He was sitting on the ground, and as I rode through the city he asked me to let him ride with me. I sat him behind me on my horse and took him where he wanted to go. But when we got there he refused to get off and said that the horse was his, which is not true."

The judge thought for a moment, then said, "Leave the horse here with me, and come back tomorrow."

The following day many people gathered in court to hear the judge's decisions.

First came the scholar and the peasant.

"Take your wife," the judge said to the scholar, "and the peasant shall be given fifty strokes of the lash."

The scholar took his wife, and the peasant was given his punishment.

Then the judge called the butcher.

"The money is yours," he said to him. And

pointing to the oil merchant he said: "Give him fifty strokes of the lash."

He next called Bauakas and the cripple.

"Would you be able to recognize your horse among twenty others?" he asked Bauakas.

"I would," he replied.

"And you?" he asked the cripple.

"I would," said the cripple.

"Come with me," the judge said to Bauakas.

They went to the stable. Bauakas instantly pointed out his horse among the twenty others. Then the judge called the cripple to the stable and told him to point out the horse. The cripple recognized the horse and pointed to it. The judge then returned to his seat.

"Take the horse, it is yours," he said to Bauakas. "Give the beggar fifty strokes of the lash."

When the judge left the court and went home, Bauakas followed him.

"What do you want?" asked the judge. "Are you not satisfied with my decision?"

"I am satisfied," said Bauakas. "But I should like to learn how you knew that the woman was the wife of the scholar, that the money belonged to the butcher, and that the horse was mine and not the beggar's."

"This is how I knew about the woman: in the morning I sent for her and said: 'Please fill my inkwell.' She took the inkwell, washed it quickly and deftly, and filled it with ink; therefore it was work she was accustomed to. If she had been the wife of the peasant she would not have known how to do it. This showed me that the scholar was telling the truth.

"And this is how I knew about the money: I put it into a cup full of water, and in the morning I looked to see if any oil had risen to the surface. If the money had belonged to the oil merchant it would have been soiled by his oily hands. There was no oil on the water; therefore, the butcher was telling the truth.

"It was more difficult to find out about the horse. The cripple recognized it among twenty others, even as you did. However, I did not take you both to the stable to see which of you knew the horse, but to see which of you the horse knew. When you approached it, it turned its head and stretched its neck toward you; but when the cripple touched it, it laid back its ears and lifted one hoof. Therefore I knew that you were the horse's real master."

Then Bauakas said to the judge: "I am not a merchant, but King Bauakas. I came here in order to see if what is said of you is true. I see now that you are a wise judge. Ask whatever you wish of me, and you shall have it as a reward."

"I need no reward," replied the judge. "I am content that my king has praised me."

STUDY QUESTIONS

Recalling

1. As the story opens, what does King Bauakas wish to find out? What disguise does he use?
2. Summarize the way in which the beggar takes advantage of the disguised king.
3. How does the judge figure out the truth in the dispute between Bauakas and the beggar? In how many other cases that day does the judge figure out the truth?
4. After Bauakas reveals that he is the king, what does he offer the judge? What does the judge reply?

5. What does the king admire in the judge?
6. What does your answer to question 5 reveal about the kind of ruler the king is?
7. Were you surprised that the judge refused the king's reward? Why or why not?

Extending

8. What are some of the ways in which truth is determined in courts today?

READING AND LITERARY FOCUS

Character

A **character** is a person or animal in a story. Each character has certain qualities, or **character traits,** that we discover as we read the story. For example, in "The Sneaker Crisis" (page 59) we learn that Laurie is sloppy, unimaginative, and somewhat spoiled and that his sister Jannie is sloppy, romantic, and fond of reading.

Some characters stay the same throughout a story. Other characters change as they respond to the story's events or to the influence of other characters. For example, in "Last Cover" (page 73) the mother does not change. The father, on the other hand, does change. He grows more understanding of Colin's painting.

Thinking About Character

1. Describe three qualities, or character traits, of the king and the judge in "A Just Judge."
2. Does either character change in the course of the story?

VOCABULARY

Context Clues

Sometimes you can figure out the meaning of an unfamiliar word by examining its **context,** or the words and sentences that surround it. Consider the context of the italicized word in this passage from "A Just Judge":

When I took out my purse to pay him, he *seized* me by my hand and tried to take all my money away.

Seized may be unfamiliar, but the phrase "by my hand" and the attempt to take the money away are context clues to the meaning of *seized.* Judging from its context, *seized* must mean "grabbed."

Each of the following passages from "A Just Judge" has an italicized word, which may be unfamiliar. Choose the *best* meaning for the italicized word by studying the context, or surrounding words and sentences. Write the number of each passage and the letter of your choice on a separate sheet.

1. . . . In one of his cities there lived a just judge who could instantly *discern* the truth, and from whom no rogue was ever able to conceal himself.
   (a) recognize   (c) frown
   (b) conceal   (d) ignore
2. At the entrance to the city a cripple approached the king and begged *alms* of him. Bauakas gave him money. . . .
   (a) directions   (c) political pamphlets
   (b) pardon   (d) money for the poor
3. Bauakas sat the cripple behind him on the horse and took him as far as the city square. There he halted his horse, but the cripple refused to *dismount.*
   (a) climb up   (c) answer
   (b) get off   (d) dismay
4. "Take the horse, it is yours," [the judge] said to Bauakas. "Give the beggar fifty strokes of the *lash.*"
   (a) noose   (c) golf club
   (b) clock   (d) whip
5. She took the inkwell, washed it quickly and *deftly,* and filled it with ink; therefore it was work she was accustomed to.
   (a) skillfully   (c) slowly
   (b) awkwardly   (d) angrily

Paul Darcy Boles (1916–1984) lived in Atlanta, Georgia. He won many awards for his novels and short stories. "Lucas and Jake" appears in his short story collection *I Thought You Were a Unicorn*. It tells the story of an elderly zoo keeper and a lion at the zoo.

■ As you read the story, consider what the zoo keeper and the lion might have in common.

Paul Darcy Boles

Lucas and Jake

It was the time when he could relax a little, letting go in all the clean sun that showered down on this part of the zoo.

So Lucas, who would be sixty-five next Tuesday, July sixteenth, was sitting on a box beside Jake's cage down on one of the side paths where not many sightseers came. He was eating a winesap apple, a fine specimen of its kind. He took distinct pleasure in biting into it with teeth that were largely his own.

All morning he'd been thinking back to when he'd been a boy and, on a day like this, would have been footloose and free as a big bird. He'd always liked zoo work, even if it didn't give you much status with friends and fellow men. Yet a man needed somebody to look up to him. An admirer, maybe a relative. Lucas didn't have one ring-tailed relative, admiring or not, on earth.

He finished his apple, flipped its core into a trash can and leaned back, hugging his knees and cutting[1] an eye at Jake.

Jake lay quiet, cinnamon-colored body shadowed, just a few flecks of sunlight picking out bits of his mane, one splash of light in his left eye. The eye, large and golden, resembled some strange pirate coin. Jake possessed awful[2] patience. He could watch an inconsequential[3] bug on the cage floor hours on end, not even his tail twitching, its very tuft[4] motionless.

Lucas sat up as two boys came around the lilac bush and moved toward Jake's cage. And Lucas's mustache bristled a bit. His eyes got the stern cool look of a TV Westerner's—a town marshal, summing up transients.[5]

The older boy, about twelve, padded along on sneakers soundless as a brace[6] of leopards. The younger, eight or nine, with a thatch of sheep-doggish hair, was fiddling with a Yo-Yo.

_____

1. **cutting:** moving suddenly.

_____

2. **awful:** amazing.
3. **inconsequential** [in kon′sə kwen′chəl]: unimportant.
4. **tuft:** here, the clump of fur at the end of a lion's tail.
5. **transients** [tran′shəntz]: here, strangers.
6. **brace:** pair.

It reeled out smartly enough, but when he tried to flip it back it nearly banged his nose.

Both stopped at the cage and looked in at Jake. Lucas waited for their first smidge of smart talk. But the bigger boy's voice sounded thoughtful, not smart talking at all. "Wonder how come they keep him here, Paddy? Not back with all the others?"

The smaller boy shrugged. He went on making his Yo-Yo climb up and roll down. "Maybe he *likes* it here."

That was as good an answer as Lucas had ever heard from a layman who couldn't know anything solid about lions. Most people thought they were lion experts.

The bigger boy's eyes widened toward Lucas. "Sir, how come he's here? Not messing around with the other lions up at the moat?"

Paddy let his Yo-Yo spin to a stop. He wanted to know too.

Lucas cleared his throat. But before he could say word one, information fountained out of the taller boy: "My name's Ridefield Tarrant. This is Patrick McGoll. Call him Paddy, sir. We came out on the bus. We each had two bits for Saturday. I didn't like the baboons, they make me nervous barking. But I sure like the lions and the tigers. Especially lions." He drew fresh breath. "We could have gone seen *Dancers in the Dark Night of Time*, adults only, we know how to sneak in. But it felt like a better day for animals."

When he was sure Ridefield had finished, Lucas nodded. "You can't miss, with animals." He waited; the word coast still seemed clear. "You asked about this lion. His name's Jake. They keep Jake all by himself for"—Jake coughed—"for certain secret reasons."

Ridefield's face lighted all over. He owned very black hair and eyes like a bold Indian's. He was polite, but in a flash Lucas could tell nobody was ever going to break his inquiring spirit. The knowledge made Lucas happy

about something in the universe no man ever really had a name for: glory, ecstasy; he wouldn't know.

With a glance at his own bronzed knuckles, hard as oak roots soaking up sunlight, Lucas nodded again. "Going to tell you boys the secret. Because you look like you want to know. Listen real close."

Ridefield Tarrant was leaning toward Lucas like an arrow set on the bowstring, and the mouth of Paddy McGoll had come a trifle open like that of a young bird expecting food.

Lucas narrowed his eyes. "Ever hear of a Cape lion?"

Their heads shook.

"Well"—Lucas shook his head—"only the kings of the whole lion breed. That's all they are, gents. Never in your life see a Cape lion doing push-ups on a barrel in a circus. No, sir! Wouldn't catch him dead in such a place." Almost casually, Lucas added, "Jake's a Cape lion."

"Yike," murmured Ridefield.

Lucas folded his arms. "Yep. Took from his mother when he was a young brave. Fought all the way. Killed . . . more'n you could count. Notice the bars of this here now cage." He pointed. "Put Jake in a cage with *lighter* bars, why, he'd be right out among you with a baseball bat. Put him up at the moat with the rest, he'd eat 'em like cornflakes. Cornflakes." Lucas touched his mustache reflectively. "He's my sole and particular charge. Jake's my special talent."

At this moment Jake twitched his left ear to discourage a bluebottle fly. Paddy McGoll stiffened like a little post with hair all over the top of it. Ridges and valleys leaped into the leather of Lucas's forehead. They vanished into the tufts of white hair which made him resemble a tough Santa Claus. "Now, I hope I did right to tell you, gents. Most people, you tell 'em about Jake, they'd write to editors

Lucas snorted. "Birds. They're all right, but a lion like Jake—now, he teaches you something. Well, c'mon."

The three started off. Lucas noted that Ridefield and Paddy were walking backward, taking one last look.

And it was just then that Paddy did the foolish thing. It happened because his Yo-Yo finger was too small for the string's loop. Suddenly, there went the whole Yo-Yo, string and all, sailing between the cage bars and coming to rest with a clack eight inches in front of Jake's nose.

"*Yike,*" breathed Ridefield.

Lucas could feel all the radiance of the day pour itself into his veins as though he himself were about twelve again, or even nine, tough as nails, but desperately searching for a key to the whole world and all the whirling planets. Low-voiced, he said, "Don't move an inch."

Ridefield's nostrils were white. Paddy stood as if whacked to the spot with spikes. Lucas walked back to Jake's cage.

He could hear the soda water fizz of Jake's breath through great nostrils. The gold coins of the eyes—sometimes pale green, at other times so full of sun they, too, were like suns—were tightly covered. Jake's chin lay on the backs of his paws.

Lucas put his right arm between the bars. The arm moved very slowly. Then his fingers were touching the Yo-Yo, his arm actually brushing Jake's whiskers. Lucas drew his arm out, stepped back to the boys, said, "Here y'ar," and put the Yo-Yo in Paddy's fingers.

Ridefield tried to speak, and couldn't. He stuck his right hand up to Lucas, and Lucas shook it. Then Paddy, dropping the Yo-Yo into a pocket, stuck his hand out, and he and Lucas shook. Then Ridefield and Paddy moved off. It was as if they held something so

about him, stir up trouble. I'd hate for the zoo to have to shoot him."

Ridefield said, "I won't say a thing! Neither will Paddy."

Paddy nodded. "I don't write so good, anyhow. In penmanship I use my fingers instead of my wrists. I wouldn't *tell* anybody."

"Good." Lucas stood. He felt his joints creak, but the looseness of the sun was warming him too. "Well, I got to be going. I won't be far off—but I hate to leave you here alone with him—"

Ridefield spoke rather swiftly. "We'll be going, we haven't seen the birds yet."

tremendous they might burst. Strength and wonder and greatness, all understood, all there . . .

They were out of sight around the lilac bush before Lucas smiled. It was the smile of a man who'd earned something: more than status. And after a moment Lucas strolled back to Jake's cage. He thrust his arm in, took hold of the mane, which felt like rope fibers, and gave it a minor tug.

All at once Jake came awake, the eyes staring at Lucas with green-gold enigmatic[7] quiet. Jake was no Cape lion. But he might have been. *All* animals of this kind were brave and glorious. If they got old and preferred to sleep,

if they couldn't really be terrible any longer, or even roar much, that was their business. In some definite way Lucas felt he'd done something for Jake today; for the whole kingdom of lions.

He couldn't have put a finger on it. He tousled the dark mane, felt of the veinous surface behind the left ear—soft as a velvet mouse—and drew his arm back out of the cage. He turned away; there was plenty to do, and he didn't want to get chewed out for not doing it. He walked off.

Behind him, alone again to sleep out his years quietly, Jake kept his eyes open for a few more seconds. Then the eyelids trembled. The eyes shut. The body lay unmoving, powerful, in the huge green afternoon.

---

7. **enigmatic** [en′ig mat′ik]: mysterious.

STUDY QUESTIONS

Recalling

1. How old is Lucas? Does he have any relatives?
2. According to the third paragraph, what does Lucas feel a man needs?
3. What "secret" does Lucas tell the two boys to explain why Jake is alone in a cage? What does Lucas say is his own "special talent"?
4. What happens to Paddy's Yo-Yo?
5. What sort of smile does Lucas smile when the boys are out of sight?
6. What do we learn about Jake in the third paragraph from the end?

Interpreting

7. How does Lucas feel about Jake? Why do you think he feels that way?
8. What do you think Lucas gains as a result of the incident with the two boys?

Extending

9. Describe your own experiences at a zoo where wild animals are kept in captivity.

READING AND LITERARY FOCUS

Making Inferences from Details of Character

Details bring a story to life by telling us important information about characters. To understand a character completely, pay attention to details and make inferences from them. An **inference** is a conclusion that we arrive at by analyzing the information that we have.

Details about a character's actions, appearance, and conversation help us to decide what the character is like. For example, in "Lucas and Jake" we know that Lucas is nearly sixty-five and takes pleasure in still having teeth that are largely his own. From these details we can infer that Lucas is concerned but not upset about getting old.

Thinking About Making Inferences

■ What inference can we make about Lucas' concern for Jake from the details about his bristling mustache, his stern cool look, and his expectation of "smart talk" when the two boys approach the cage?

CHALLENGE

Research and Oral Report

■ Use the library to locate information about the natural habitat of lions. Find out how lions live and whether or not they often threaten human beings. Also find out if there is such a thing as a Cape lion. You may wish to read *Born Free* by Joy Adamson for some of your information. Present your findings in an oral report to the class.

Betty Smith (1904–1972) grew up in the Williamsburg section of Brooklyn, New York. Her family was very poor, and Smith was able to attend school only until the eighth grade. Late in life she returned to school and became interested in drama and writing. Her most famous book is *A Tree Grows in Brooklyn*, a novel based on her own childhood. The following selection is an excerpt from the novel.

■ What do Francie and Neeley try to win?

Betty Smith

Christmas in Brooklyn

from **A Tree Grows in Brooklyn**

Christmas was a charmed time in Brooklyn. It was in the air long before it came. The first hint of it was Mr. Morton going around the schools teaching Christmas carols, but the first sure sign was the store windows.

—You have to be a child to know how wonderful is a store window filled with dolls and sleds and other toys. And this wonder came free to Francie. It was nearly as good as actually having the toys to be permitted to look at them through the glass window.

Oh, what a thrill there was for Francie when she turned a street corner and saw another store all fixed up for Christmas! Ah, the clean, shining window with cotton batting sprinkled with stardust for a carpet. There were flaxen-haired dolls, and others, which Francie liked better, who had hair the color of good coffee with lots of cream in it. Their faces were perfectly tinted, and they wore clothes the like of which Francie had never seen on earth. The dolls stood upright in flimsy cardboard boxes. They stood with the help of a bit of tape passed around the neck and ankles and through holes at the back of the box. Oh, the deep-blue eyes framed by thick lashes that stared straight into a little girl's heart, and the perfect miniature hands extended, appealingly asking, "Please, won't *you* be my mama?" And Francie had never had a doll except a two-inch one that cost a nickel.

And the sleds! (Or, as the Williamsburg[1] children called them, the sleighs.) There was a child's dream of heaven come true! A new sled with a flower someone had dreamed up painted on it—a deep-blue flower with bright-green leaves—the ebony-black painted runners, the smooth steering bar made of hardwood and gleaming varnish over all! And the names painted on them! *Rosebud! Magnolia! Snow King! The Flyer!* Thought Francie, "If I could only have one of those, I'd never ask God for another thing."

There were roller skates made of shining

---

1. **Williamsburg:** area in Brooklyn.

nickel with straps of good brown leather and silvered, nervous wheels, tensed for rolling, needing but a breath to start them turning as they lay crossed one over the other, sprinkled with mica[2] snow on a bed of cloudlike cotton.

There were other marvelous things. Francie couldn't take them all in. Her head spun, she was dizzy with the impact of all the seeing and all the making up of stories about the toys in the shopwindows.

The spruce trees began coming into the neighborhood the week before Christmas. Their branches were corded to hold back the glory of their spreading and probably to make shipping easier. Vendors rented space on the curb before a store and stretched a rope from pole to pole and leaned the trees against it. All day they walked up and down this one-sided avenue of aromatic leaning trees, blowing on stiff ungloved fingers and looking with bleak hope at those people who paused. A few ordered a tree set aside for the day; others stopped to price, inspect, and conjecture.[3] But most came to touch the boughs and surreptitiously[4] pinch a fingerful of spruce needles together to release the fragrance. And the air was cold and still and full of the pine smell and the smell of tangerines, which appeared in the stores only at Christmastime, and the mean street was truly wonderful for a little while.

There was a cruel custom in the neighborhood. It was about the trees still unsold when midnight of Christmas Eve approached. There was a saying that if you waited until then, you wouldn't have to buy a tree, that "they'd chuck 'em at you." This was literally true.

At midnight the kids gathered where there were unsold trees. The man threw each tree in turn, starting with the biggest. Kids volunteered to stand up against the throwing. If a boy didn't fall down under the impact, the tree was his. If he fell, he forfeited his chance of winning a tree. Only the toughest boys and some of the young men elected to be hit by the big trees. The others waited shrewdly until a tree came up that they could stand against. The littlest kids waited for the tiny, foot-high trees and shrieked in delight when they won one.

On the Christmas Eve when Francie was ten and Neeley nine, Mama consented to let them go down and have their first try for a tree. Francie had picked out her tree earlier in the day. She had stood near it all afternoon and evening, praying that no one would buy it. To her joy, it was still there at midnight. It was the biggest tree in the neighborhood, and its price was so high that no one could afford to buy it. It was ten feet high. Its branches were bound with new white rope, and it came to a sure pure point at the top.

The man took this tree out first. Before Francie could speak up, a neighborhood bully, a boy of eighteen known as Punky Perkins, stepped forward and ordered the man to chuck the tree at him. The man hated the way Punky was so confident. He looked around and asked, "Anybody else want to take a chance on it?"

Francie stepped forward. "Me, mister."

A spurt of derisive laughter came from the tree man. The kids snickered. A few adults who had gathered to watch the fun, guffawed.

"Aw, g'wan. You're too little," the tree man objected.

"Me and my brother. We're not too little together."

She pulled Neeley forward. The man looked at them—a thin girl of ten with starveling hollows in her cheeks but with the chin still

2. **mica** [mī'kə]: here, artificial.
3. **conjecture** [kən jek'chər]: form opinions.
4. **surreptitiously** [sur'əp tish'əs lē]: secretly.

baby-round. He looked at the little boy with his fair hair and round blue eyes—Neeley Nolan, all innocence and trust.

"Two ain't fair," yelped Punky.

"Shut your trap," advised the man, who held all power in that hour. "These here kids is got nerve. Stand back, the rest of youse. These kids is goin' to have a show at this tree."

The others made a wavering line. Francie and Neeley stood at one end of it and the big man with the big tree at the other. It was a human funnel with Francie and her brother making the small end of it. The man flexed his great arms to throw the great tree. He noticed how tiny the children looked at the end of the short lane. For the split part of a moment, the tree man went through a kind of Gethsemane.[5]

"Oh," his soul agonized, "why don't I just give them the tree, say Merry Christmas and let 'em go? What's the tree to me? I can't sell it this year, and it won't keep till next year."

The kids watched him solemnly as he stood there in his moment of thought. "But then," he rationalized,[6] "if I did that, all the others would expect to get 'em handed to 'em. And next year nobody at all would buy a tree off me. They'd all wait to get 'em handed to 'em on a silver plate. I ain't a big enough man to give this tree away for nothin'. No, I ain't big enough. I ain't big enough to do a thing like that. I gotta think of myself and my own kids."

He finally came to his conclusion. "Them two kids is gotta live in this world. They *got* to get used to it. They got to learn to give and to take punishment. And it ain't give but *take, take, take* all the time in this world." As

he threw the tree with all his strength, his heart wailed out, "It's a rotten world!"

Francie saw the tree leave his hands. There was a split bit of being when time and space had no meaning. The whole world stood still as something dark and monstrous came through the air. The tree came toward her blotting out all memory of her ever having lived. There was nothing, nothing but pungent[7] darkness and something that grew and grew as it rushed at her. She staggered as the tree hit them. Neeley went to his knees, but she pulled him up fiercely before he could go down. There was a mighty swishing sound as the tree settled. Everything was dark, green, and prickly. Then she felt a sharp pain at the side of her head where the trunk of the tree had hit her. She felt Neeley trembling.

When some of the older boys pulled the tree

---

5. **Gethsemane** [geth sem′ə nē]: here, suffering and doubt. (In the Bible Gethsemane was the place where Jesus suffered and was betrayed and arrested.)
6. **rationalized** [rash′ən əl īzd′]: made explanations or excuses for his actions.

7. **pungent** [pun′jənt]: sharp-smelling.

away, they found Francie and her brother standing upright, hand in hand. Blood was coming from scratches on Neeley's face. He looked more like a baby than ever with his bewildered blue eyes and the fairness of his skin made more noticeable because of the clear red blood. But they were smiling. Had they not won the biggest tree in the neighborhood! Some boys hollered "Hooray!" A few adults clapped. The tree man eulogized[8] them by screaming, "And now get out of here with your tree. . . ."

It wasn't easy dragging that tree home. They had to pull it inch by inch. They were handicapped by a boy who ran alongside yelping, "Free ride! All aboard!" who'd jump on and make them drag him along. But he got sick of the game eventually and went away.

In a way, it was good that it took them so long to get the tree home. It made their triumph more drawn out. Francie glowed when she heard a lady say, "I never saw such a big tree!" A man called after them, "You kids musta robbed a bank to buy such a big tree." The cop on the corner stopped them, examined the tree, and solemnly offered to buy it for ten cents, fifteen cents if they'd deliver it to his home.

Francie nearly burst with pride, although she knew he was joking. She said she wouldn't sell it for a dollar even. He shook his head and said she was foolish not to grab the offer. He went up to a quarter, but Francie kept smiling and shaking her head no.

It was like acting in a Christmas play where the setting was a street corner and the time, a frosty Christmas Eve, and the characters, a kind cop, her brother, and herself. Francie knew all the dialogue. The cop gave his lines right and Francie picked up her cues

happily and the stage directions were the smiles between the spoken lines.

They had to call up Papa to help them get the tree up the narrow stairs. Papa came running down.

Papa's amazement at the size of the tree was flattering. He pretended to believe that it wasn't theirs. Francie had a lot of fun convincing him, although she knew all the while that the whole thing was make-believe. Papa pulled in front and Francie and Neeley pushed in back, and they began forcing the big tree up the three narrow flights of stairs. Papa was so excited that he started singing, not caring that it was rather late at night. He sang "Holy Night." The narrow walls took up his clear sweet voice, held it for a breath, and gave it back with doubled sweetness. Doors creaked open and families gathered on the landings, pleased and amazed at the something unexpected being added to that moment of their lives. . . .

They set the tree up in the front room after spreading a sheet to protect the carpet of pink roses from falling pine needles. The tree stood in a big tin bucket with broken bricks to hold it upright.

When the rope was cut away, the branches spread out to fill the whole room. They draped over the piano, and it was so crowded that some of the chairs stood among the branches. There was no money to buy tree decorations or lights. But the great tree standing there was enough. The room was cold. It was a poor year, that one, too poor for them to buy the extra coal for the front-room stove. The room smelled cold and clean and aromatic. Every day, during the week the tree stood there, Francie put on her sweater and cap and went in and sat under the tree. She sat there and enjoyed the smell and the dark greenness of it.

---

8. **eulogized** [ū′lə jīzd′]: praised.

STUDY QUESTIONS

Recalling

1. What is the neighborhood custom involving Christmas trees on Christmas Eve? Who usually volunteers to try for the big trees?
2. What happens to Francie and Neeley when the tree vendor throws the tree at them? What does Francie feel as they drag the tree home?
3. According to the last paragraph, what is there no money to buy? What does Francie do every day of Christmas week?

Interpreting

4. Based on the details given in the story about the Christmas tree "chucking," what character traits would you say Francie displays?
5. What details make the last paragraph surprising and touching?

READING AND LITERARY FOCUS

Character Motivation

Motivation is a feeling or goal that causes a character to behave in a certain way. We must try to understand a character's motives, or reasons for behavior, if we want to know why the character does something. In "Lucas and Jake" (page 96), for example, we know that Lucas pretends Jake is a ferocious Cape lion. We understand that Lucas presents Jake this way because he is near retirement and wants to earn respect both for his job and for the lion he has tended for so many years. We know that Lucas is not telling the truth. However, because we know his motives, we find him a true-to-life character for whom we can feel sympathy and understanding.

Thinking About Character Motivation

1. What motivates Francie to try for the big tree?
2. What are the tree vendor's motives for throwing the large tree at Francie and Neeley even though he realizes it is a cruel thing to do?

VOCABULARY

Suffixes

A **suffix** is a word part added to the end of a word. Adding a suffix can change the meaning of a word. Suffixes are listed in most dictionaries.

You can often figure out the meaning of a word by examining its suffix. In the word *greenness,* for example, the suffix -*ness* means "the quality, state, or condition of being." Therefore, *greenness* means "the quality, state, or condition of being green." Here are some common suffixes:

Suffix	Meaning
-able	able to or capable of being
-er, -or	one who or that which
-ful	full of
-ic	like or pertaining to
-like	resembling or like

The following words are from "Christmas in Brooklyn." Copy each word, underline the suffix, and explain the meaning of the word.

1. wonderful
2. vendor
3. cloudlike
4. aromatic
5. noticeable

COMPOSITION

Writing About Character

■ Write a paragraph describing two of Francie's character traits. First tell what traits you are describing. Then explain which details in the story helped you to choose these traits to describe Francie's character. The details may be about Francie's actions, appearance, or conversation.

Writing a Diary Entry

■ Pretend that you are Neeley. Write the diary entry that he might have written about the large Christmas tree. Try to capture reactions that Neeley would be likely to have.

Isaac Asimov (1920–1992) was one of America's busiest writers. In addition to science-fiction works such as *I, Robot* and *Foundation Trilogy*, he wrote many nonfiction works about science. Asimov studied to be a scientist, and his science fiction is based on facts. In "The Fun They Had" he considered some of the ways that computers may be used by schoolchildren of the future.

■ Can you find any similarities between the school of the future and school as you know it today?

Isaac Asimov

The Fun They Had

Margie even wrote about it that night in her diary. On the page headed May 17, 2157, she wrote, "Today Tommy found a real book!"

It was a very old book. Margie's grandfather once said that when he was a little boy, *his* grandfather told him that there was a time when all stories were printed on paper.

They turned the pages, which were yellow and crinkly; and it was awfully funny to read words that stood still instead of moving the way they were supposed to—on a screen, you know. And then, when they turned back to the page before, it had the same words on it that it had had when they read it the first time.

"Gee," said Tommy, "what a waste. When you're through with the book, you just throw it away, I guess. Our television screen must have had a million books on it, and it's good for plenty more. I wouldn't throw *it* away."

"Same with mine," said Margie. She was eleven and hadn't seen as many telebooks as Tommy had. He was thirteen.

She said, "Where did you find it?"

"In my house." He pointed without looking, because he was busy reading. "In the attic."

"What's it about?"

"School."

Margie was scornful. "School? What's there to write about school? I hate school."

Margie always hated school, but now she hated it more than ever. The mechanical teacher had been giving her test after test in geography, and she had been doing worse and worse until her mother had shaken her head sorrowfully and sent for the County Inspector.

He was a round little man with a red face and a whole box of tools with dials and wires. He smiled at Margie and gave her an apple, then took the teacher apart. Margie had hoped he wouldn't know how to put it together again, but he knew how all right; and, after an hour or so, there it was again, large and black and ugly, with a big screen on which all the lessons were shown and the questions were asked. That wasn't so bad. The part Margie hated most was the slot where she had to put homework and test papers. She always had to write them out in a punch code they made her learn when she was six years old, and the mechanical teacher calculated the mark in no time.

The Inspector had smiled after he was finished and patted Margie's head. He said to her mother, "It's not the little girl's fault, Mrs. Jones. I think the geography sector was geared a little too quick. Those things happen sometimes. I've slowed it up to an average ten-year level. Actually, the overall pattern of her progress is quite satisfactory." And he patted Margie's head again.

Margie was disappointed. She had been hoping they would take the teacher away altogether. They had once taken Tommy's teacher away for nearly a month because the history sector had blanked out completely.

So she said to Tommy, "Why would anyone write about school?"

Tommy looked at her with very superior eyes. "Because it's not our kind of school, stupid. This is the old kind of school that they had hundreds and hundreds of years ago." He added loftily, pronouncing the word carefully, "*Centuries* ago."

Margie was hurt. "Well, I don't know what kind of school they had all that time ago." She read the book over his shoulder for a while, then said, "Anyway, they had a teacher."

"Sure they had a teacher, but it wasn't a *regular* teacher. It was a man."

"A man? How could a man be a teacher?"

"Well, he just told the boys and girls things and gave them homework and asked them questions."

"A man isn't smart enough."

"Sure he is. My father knows as much as my teacher."

"He can't. A man can't know as much as a teacher."

"He knows almost as much, I betcha."

Margie wasn't prepared to dispute that. She said, "I wouldn't want a strange man in my house to teach me."

Tommy screamed with laughter. "You

don't know much, Margie. The teachers didn't live in the house. They had a special building, and all the kids went there."

"And all the kids learned the same things?"

"Sure, if they were the same age."

"But my mother says a teacher has to be adjusted to fit the mind of each boy and girl it teaches, and that each kid has to be taught differently."

"Just the same, they didn't do it that way then. If you don't like it, you don't have to read the book."

"I didn't say I didn't like it," Margie said quickly. She wanted to read about those funny schools.

They weren't even half-finished when Margie's mother called, "Margie! School!"

Margie looked up. "Not yet, Mamma."

"Now!" said Mrs. Jones. "And it's probably time for Tommy, too."

Margie said to Tommy, "Can I read the book some more with you after school?"

"Maybe," he said nonchalantly. He walked away whistling, the dusty old book tucked beneath his arm.

Margie went into the schoolroom. It was right next to her bedroom, and the mechanical teacher was on and waiting for her. It was always on at the same time every day except Saturday and Sunday, because her mother said little girls learned better if they learned at regular hours.

The screen was lit up, and it said, "Today's arithmetic lesson is on the addition of proper fractions. Please insert yesterday's homework in the proper slot."

Margie did so with a sigh. She was thinking about the old schools they had when her grandfather's grandfather was a little boy. All the kids from the whole neighborhood came, laughing and shouting in the schoolyard, sitting together in the schoolroom, going home together at the end of the day. They learned the same things, so they could help one another on the homework and talk about it.

And the teachers were people. . . .

The mechanical teacher was flashing on the screen, "When we add the fractions ½ and ¼—"

Margie was thinking about how the kids must have loved it in the old days. She was thinking about the fun they had.

When we add the fractions:

$$\frac{1}{2} \text{ and } \frac{1}{4}$$

STUDY QUESTIONS

Recalling

1. In what year does the story take place, according to the first paragraph? What does Margie report in her diary for May 17?
2. Describe the books that Margie and Tommy use in their schoolwork.
3. What are their teachers like? Where do these teachers "live" and work?
4. What is the old book about? What does Margie conclude about kids "in the old days," according to the last paragraph?

Interpreting

5. When Margie thinks about school "in the old days," what kind of school do we realize she means?
6. Identify two specific ways in which school "in the old days" is different from school as Margie knows it. What does Margie seem to dislike about her form of education?
7. What does this story suggest computers can never replace?

Extending

8. Do you think we can use computers in education but avoid problems like Margie's?

READING AND LITERARY FOCUS

Characterization

Characterization refers both to the personality of a character and to the method by which an author reveals that personality. An author may directly state opinions about a character's personality. For example, in "Christmas in Brooklyn"

(page 101) Smith states that Punky is a bully.

More often an author reveals a character's personality indirectly just by presenting us with the character's own words and actions. We can then form our own opinions about the character. In "Christmas in Brooklyn" the author lets Francie talk for herself: When the tree vendor says she is too small to catch the big tree she says, "Me and my brother. We're not too little together." We then conclude that Francie is a determined character. The author also shows us Francie in action. When she and Neeley caught the tree, "she staggered as the tree hit them. Neeley went to his knees, but she pulled him up fiercely before he could go down." We form the opinion that Francie is brave.

In addition, an author can reveal a character's personality by telling us what others say about the character. For example, the words of the neighbors show how impressed they are with Francie's achievement: Francie "heard a lady say, 'I never saw such a big tree!' A man called after them, 'You kids musta robbed a bank to buy such a big tree.' "

Thinking About Characterization

1. Find two opinions that the author states directly about Margie in "The Fun They Had."
2. Find something Margie says and something she does. What do you learn about her from each?

CHALLENGE

Research and Oral Report

■ Try to find a book that is at least fifty years old. Does the book seem old-fashioned and out of date? Why? Do you have any of the feelings that Margie had for Tommy's old book? Share your discoveries with the class.

Leslie Marmon Silko (born 1948) grew up on the Laguna Pueblo in New Mexico. She has written novels, poetry, and short stories exploring her Pueblo Indian heritage. One important part of that heritage is a strong attachment to nature.

■ See how nature and its creatures affect the characters in the following story.

Leslie Silko

Uncle Tony's Goat

We had a hard time finding the right kind of string to use. We knew we needed gut to string our bows the way the men did, but we were little kids and we didn't know how to get any. So Kenny went to his house and brought back a ball of white cotton string that his mother used to string red chili with. It was thick and soft and it didn't make very good bowstring. As soon as we got the bows made we sat down again on the sand bank above the stream and started skinning willow twigs for arrows. It was past noon, and the tall willows behind us made cool shade. There were lots of little minnows that day, flashing in the shallow water, swimming back and forth wildly like they weren't sure if they really wanted to go up or down the stream; it was a day for minnows that we were always hoping for—we could have filled our rusty coffee cans and old pickle jars full. But this was the first time for making bows and arrows, and the minnows weren't much different from the sand or the rocks now. The secret is the arrows. The ones we made were crooked, and when we shot them they didn't go straight—

they flew around in arcs and curves; so we crawled through the leaves and branches, deep into the willow groves, looking for the best, the straightest willow branches. But even after we skinned the sticky wet bark from them and whittled the knobs off, they still weren't straight. Finally we went ahead and made notches at the end of each arrow to hook in the bowstring, and we started practicing, thinking maybe we could learn to shoot the crooked arrows straight.

We left the river each of us with a handful of damp, yellow arrows and our fresh-skinned willow bows. We walked slowly and shot arrows at bushes, big rocks, and the juniper tree that grows by Pino's sheep pen. They were working better just like we had figured; they still didn't fly straight, but now we could compensate for that by the way we aimed them. We were going up to the church to shoot at the cats old Sister Julian kept outside the cloister.[1] We didn't want to hurt anything, just to have new kinds of things to shoot at.

---

1. **cloister:** convent, a building where nuns live.

But before we got to the church we went past the grassy hill where my uncle Tony's goats were grazing. A few of them were lying down chewing their cud peacefully, and they didn't seem to notice us. The billy goat was lying down, but he was watching us closely like he already knew about little kids. His yellow goat eyes didn't blink, and he stared with a wide, hostile look. The grazing goats made good deer for our bows. We shot all our arrows at the nanny goats and their kids; they skipped away from the careening[2] arrows and never lost the rhythm of their greedy chewing as they continued to nibble the weeds and grass on the hillside. The billy goat was lying there watching us and taking us into his memory. As we ran down the road toward the church and Sister Julian's cats, I looked back, and my uncle Tony's billy goat was still watching me.

My uncle and my father were sitting on the bench outside the house when we walked by. It was September now, and the farming was almost over, except for bringing home the melons and a few pumpkins. They were mending ropes and bridles and feeling the afternoon sun. We held our bows and arrows out in front of us so they could see them. My father smiled and kept braiding the strips of leather in his hand, but my uncle Tony put down the bridle and pieces of scrap leather he was working on and looked at each of us kids slowly. He was old, getting some white hair—he was my mother's oldest brother, the one that scolded us when we told lies or broke things.

"You'd better not be shooting at things," he said, "only at rocks or trees. Something will get hurt. Maybe even one of you."

We all nodded in agreement and tried to hold the bows and arrows less conspicuously down at our sides; when he turned back to his work we hurried away before he took the bows away from us like he did the time we made the slingshot. He caught us shooting rocks at an old wrecked car; its windows were all busted out anyway, but he took the slingshot away. I always wondered what he did with it and with the knives we made ourselves out of tin cans. When I was much older I asked my mother, "What did he ever do with those knives and slingshots he took away from us?" She was kneading bread on the kitchen table at the time and was probably busy thinking about the fire in the oven outside. "I don't know," she said; "you ought to ask him yourself." But I never did. I thought about it lots of times, but I never did. It would have been like getting caught all over again.

The goats were valuable. We got milk and meat from them. My uncle was careful to see that all the goats were treated properly; the worst scolding my older sister ever got was when my mother caught her and some of her friends chasing the newborn kids. My mother kept saying over and over again, "It's a good thing I saw you; what if your uncle had seen you?" and even though we kids were very young then, we understood very well what she meant.

The billy goat never forgot the bows and arrows, even after the bows had cracked and split and the crooked, whittled arrows were all lost. This goat was big and black and important to my uncle Tony because he'd paid a lot to get him and because he wasn't an ordinary goat. Uncle Tony had bought him from a white man, and then he'd hauled him in the back of the pickup all the way from Quemado.[3] And my uncle was the only person who could touch this goat. If a stranger or one of us kids got too near him, the mane on the billy goat's neck would stand on end and the

---

2. **careening** [kə rēn′ing]: swaying without control.

3. **Quemado** [kā mä′dō]: town in western New Mexico.

goat would rear up on his hind legs and dance forward trying to reach the person with his long, spiral horns. This billy goat smelled bad, and none of us cared if we couldn't pet him. But my uncle took good care of this goat. The goat would let Uncle Tony brush him with the horse brush and scratch him around the base of his horns. Uncle Tony talked to the billy goat—in the morning when he unpenned the goats and in the evening when he gave them their hay and closed the gate for the night. I never paid too much attention to what he said to the billy goat; usually it was something like "Get up, big goat! You've slept long enough," or "Move over, big goat, and let the others have something to eat."

We all had chores to do around home. My sister helped out around the house mostly,

and I was supposed to carry water from the hydrant and bring in kindling. I helped my father look after the horses and pigs, and Uncle Tony milked the goats and fed them. One morning near the end of September I was out feeding the pigs their table scraps and pig mash; I'd given the pigs their food, and I was watching them squeal and snap at each other as they crowded into the feed trough. Behind me I could hear the milk squirting into the eight-pound lard pail that Uncle Tony used for milking.

When he finished milking he noticed me standing there; he motioned toward the goats still inside the pen. "Run the rest of them out," he said as he untied the two milk goats and carried the milk to the house.

I was seven years old, and I understood

that everyone, including my uncle, expected me to handle more chores; so I hurried over to the goat pen and swung the tall wire gate open. The does[4] and kids came prancing out. They trotted daintily past the pigpen and scattered out, intent on finding leaves and grass to eat. It wasn't until then I noticed that the billy goat hadn't come out of the little wooden shed inside the goat pen. I stood outside the pen and tried to look inside the wooden shelter, but it was still early and the morning sun left the inside of the shelter in deep shadow. I stood there for a while, hoping that he would come out by himself, but I realized that he'd recognized me and that he wouldn't come out. I understood right away what was happening and my fear of him was in my bowels and down my neck; I was shaking.

Finally my uncle came out of the house; it was time for breakfast. "What's wrong?" he called out from the door.

"The billy goat won't come out," I yelled back, hoping he would look disgusted and come do it himself.

"Get in there and get him out," he said as he went back into the house.

I looked around quickly for a stick or broom handle, or even a big rock, but I couldn't find anything. I walked into the pen slowly, concentrating on the darkness beyond the shed door; I circled to the back of the shed and kicked at the boards, hoping to make the billy goat run out. I put my eye up to a crack between the boards, and I could see he was standing up now and that his yellow eyes were on mine.

My mother was yelling at me to hurry up, and Uncle Tony was watching. I stepped around into the low doorway, and the goat charged toward me, feet first. I had dirt in my mouth and up my nose and there was blood

___
4. **does** [dōz]: adult female goats.

running past my eye; my head ached. Uncle Tony carried me to the house; his face was stiff with anger, and I remembered what he'd always told us about animals; they won't bother you unless you bother them first. I didn't start to cry until my mother hugged me close and wiped my face with a damp wash rag. It was only a little cut above my eyebrow, and she sent me to school anyway with a Band-Aid on my forehead.

Uncle Tony locked the billy goat in the pen. He didn't say what he was going to do with the goat, but when he left with my father to haul firewood, he made sure the gate to the pen was wired tightly shut. He looked at the goat quietly and with sadness; he said something to the goat, but the yellow eyes stared past him.

"What's he going to do with the goat?" I asked my mother before I went to catch the school bus.

"He ought to get rid of it," she said. "We can't have that goat knocking people down for no good reason."

I didn't feel good at school. The teacher sent me to the nurse's office and the nurse made me lie down. Whenever I closed my eyes I could see the goat and my uncle, and I felt a stiffness in my throat and chest. I got off the school bus slowly, so the other kids would go ahead without me. I walked slowly and wished I could be away from home for a while. I could go over to Grandma's house, but she would ask me if my mother knew where I was and I would have to say no, and she would make me go home first to ask. So I walked very slowly, because I didn't want to see the black goat's hide hanging over the corral fence.

When I got to the house I didn't see a goat hide or the goat, but Uncle Tony was on his horse and my mother was standing beside the horse holding a canteen and a flour sack bundle tied with brown string. I was frightened at what this meant. My uncle looked down at me from the saddle.

"The goat ran away," he said. "Jumped out of the pen somehow. I saw him just as he went over the hill beyond the river. He stopped at the top of the hill and he looked back this way."

Uncle Tony nodded at my mother and me and then he left; we watched his old roan[5] splash across the stream and labor up the steep path beyond the river. Then they were over the top of the hill and gone.

Uncle Tony was gone for three days. He came home early on the morning of the fourth day, before we had eaten breakfast or fed the animals. He was glad to be home, he said, because he was getting too old for such long rides. He called me over and looked closely at the cut above my eye. It had scabbed over good, and I wasn't wearing a Band-Aid any more; he examined it very carefully before he let me go. He stirred some sugar into his coffee.

"That goat," he said. "I followed him for three days. He was headed south, going straight to Quemado. I never could catch up to him." My uncle shook his head. "The first time I saw him he was already in the piñon[6] forest, halfway into the mountains already. I could see him most of the time, off in the distance a mile or two. He would stop sometimes and look back." Uncle Tony paused and drank some more coffee. "I stopped at night. I had to. He stopped too, and in the morning we would start out again. The trail just gets higher and steeper. Yesterday morning there was frost on top of the blanket when I woke up and we were in the big pines and red oak leaves. I couldn't see him any more because the forest is too thick. So I turned around." Tony finished the cup of coffee. "He's probably in Quemado by now."

I looked at him again, standing there by the door, ready to go milk the nanny goats.

"There wasn't ever a goat like that one," he said, "but if that's the way he's going to act, O.K. then. That goat got mad too easy anyway."

He smiled at me and his voice was strong and happy when he said this.

---

5. **roan** [rōn]: reddish-brown horse.

6. **piñon** [pin′yən]: pine tree.

STUDY QUESTIONS

Recalling

1. What do Kenny and the narrator, or storyteller, do when they encounter the goats on the hill?
2. According to the storyteller, what does the billy goat do when the children shoot arrows at the nanny goats and their kids?
3. Summarize what happens when the storyteller attempts to run the goats from the pen.
4. According to the storyteller's mother, why must Uncle Tony get rid of the billy goat?

5. What is the narrator afraid he will see when he returns from school? Why doesn't he see it?

Interpreting

6. Why do you think the billy goat acts as he does when the storyteller attempts to run the goats from the pen? Does Uncle Tony understand why the billy goat acts as he does?
7. Does the goat deserve to be destroyed as Uncle Tony plans? Why or why not?
8. How does the storyteller's attitude toward the goat change in the course of the story?

9. What has the storyteller learned from his experience with Uncle Tony's goat?

READING AND LITERARY FOCUS

First-Person Narrator

The **narrator** of a short story is the person who tells the story. Some stories are told by a **first-person narrator,** who actually takes part in the story and refers to herself or himself as "I." For example, "Uncle Tony's Goat" is told by a child who takes part in the events of the story and describes those events to the reader.

Keep in mind that a first-person narrator is not the author. Leslie Silko, the author of "Uncle Tony's Goat," is a woman. She creates all the characters in the story, including a fictional boy character who is the first-person narrator.

A first-person narrator often makes the story seem more true to life. However, a first-person narrator cannot give a complete view of the story. He or she can only guess the thoughts and feelings of the other characters. The narrator of "Uncle Tony's Goat" can tell you what he is feeling, but he can only guess what Uncle Tony is feeling.

Thinking About First-Person Narrator

1. Find one example in "Uncle Tony's Goat" of the narrator telling you his own thoughts or feelings.
2. Name one other story in this book that has a first-person narrator.

VOCABULARY

Sentence Completions

Each of the following sentences contains a blank with four possible words for completing the sentence. Choose the word that completes each sentence correctly. Write the number of each item and the letter of your choice on a separate sheet.

1. The dance was performed lightly and ___.
   (a) ponderously (c) dismally
   (b) daintily (d) virtually

2. They had to ___ the logs to the mill.
   (a) bombast (c) haul
   (b) lather (d) compensate

3. They climbed up the ___ staircase to the tower.
   (a) spiral (c) level
   (b) hilt (d) preside

4. It was a(n) ___ prize.
   (a) inclement (c) latter
   (b) valuable (d) torrent

5. For some reason the visitor was very ___.
   (a) stark (c) hostile
   (b) dilated (d) embedded

COMPOSITION

Writing a Character Sketch

■ Write a character sketch of the narrator of "Uncle Tony's Goat." First tell who the narrator is and how old he is. Then identify three character traits of the narrator. Give examples of his actions, words, thoughts, and feelings to explain each character trait. *For help with this assignment, see Lesson 3 in the Writing About Literature Handbook at the back of this book.*

Retelling a Story

■ Write "Uncle Tony's Goat" as if the goat were telling the story. Make the goat the first-person narrator, and include the goat's thoughts and feelings instead of those of the boy now telling the story. Be sure to show how the goat feels about the activities of the boys and of Uncle Tony.

CHALLENGE

Narration

■ Choose an incident from today's news. Describe the incident as if you were one of the people who witnessed the news event. Include your opinions as well as a description of what happened.

Jessamyn West (1907–1984) was born in Indiana and moved with her family to a ranch in California when she was six. One of her most famous books, *Cress Delahanty*, is a collection of stories about a young girl. Many of the stories are based on experiences West had when she was growing up. Cress Delahanty, like Jessamyn West, is the daughter of a California rancher.

■ As you read the story, look for details that tell what kind of person Cress is.

Jessamyn West

Thirteen

It was a hot August morning, Saturday, six-thirty o'clock, and Mr. and Mrs. Delahanty still lingered at the breakfast table. Six-thirty is midmorning for a rancher in summer; but Mrs. Delahanty hadn't finished talking about the hat.

"It's perfectly clear why she wants it," she said.

It wasn't perfectly clear to Mr. Delahanty. Besides, he thought it would be interesting to know what one woman thinks of another's reasons for buying a hat, even though the second is only thirteen and her daughter.

"Why?" he asked.

"Edwin," said Mrs. Delahanty.

Mr. Delahanty put down his coffee which was too hot, anyway, for a hot morning.

"Edwin!" he exclaimed.

"Oh yes," Mrs. Delahanty assured him.

Mr. Delahanty decided to drink his coffee. After drinking, he asked, "How does the hat figure in it?"

"I think Cress thinks this hat would make Edwin see her in a new light. Frail and feminine."

"Better let her have it, hadn't you?" asked Mr. Delahanty. "Not that I like the idea of encouraging Edwin in any way."

"This hat," Mrs. Delahanty said, "wouldn't encourage anyone. This hat . . . Oh, Cress," she cried, "don't slip around that way. You gave me a start. What are you doing up this hour of the day anyway?"

During summer vacation Cress, unless she had projects of her own afoot, had to be routed from bed.

"I couldn't sleep," she said. She could tell from their faces that they had been talking about her. "And I wanted to ask Father something before he went out to work." She sat down at the table and turned toward her father as if they were two together, though seated unfortunately at a table with a stranger. "Can I call the store and tell them that if they'll hold the hat, you'll come in and look at it with me when we go to town tonight?"

"I've looked at it, Cress," said her mother.

"Mother," said Cress very sweetly, "I was speaking to Father. May I?"

"You don't have to ask permission of me, Cress, to speak to your father."

"Thank you, Mother," said Cress. "May I, Father?"

"Well," said Mr. Delahanty, "I don't suppose there'd be any harm in taking a look. Would there, Gertrude? Though you mustn't count on me for any expert advice about a hat, Cress."

Cress leaned toward her father. "Daddy," she said—she hadn't called her father Daddy for years but somehow the word seemed right and natural to her this morning—"Daddy, if you thought a hat was beautiful and becoming, I'd know it was beautiful and becoming. Or if you thought it was ugly and unsuitable, I'd know it was ugly and unsuitable. Do you know what, Daddy," Cress said and leaned toward her father, admiring the philosophic lines which ran, not from his nose to his mouth and which she thought made people look sour, but from his cheek bone to his jaw bone. "Do you know what?"

"No, Cress," said Mr. Delahanty, "I don't. But I'm waiting to be told."

"I think you probably have instinctive taste."

Mrs. Delahanty laughed, quite loud and long for so early in the morning.

Cress looked at her mother with a mingling of shock and disapproval on her face.

"Were you laughing at me or Daddy, Mother?" she asked politely.

"The two of you," said Mrs. Delahanty. "You and your daddy. Your daddy, Cress, can't tell a bonnet from a bushel basket. Not if the basket has a flower on it, anyway."

"Well, Gertrude," said Mr. Delahanty, "I may not be an expert on hats. I grant you that. But I think I know a pretty hat when I see one."

"That's why I want you to see this hat, Daddy," cried Cress. "It's so downright beautiful."

"That hat, Cress," said her mother, "is the most unsuitable object for a girl of thirteen years to put on her head I ever laid my eyes on."

"Just what do you mean by unsuitable, Gertrude?" asked Mr. Delahanty.

"I mean that hat was never intended for a thirteen-year-old girl. It's for an older— woman," concluded Mrs. Delahanty, wasting irony.

Mr. Delahanty poured himself a glass of milk. "You mean it ties under the chin?" he asked. "Or has . . ." he took a drink of milk, visibly running out of what suggested to him the hat of an older woman.

"Or has a black veil?" Cress helped him.

"No," said Mrs. Delahanty, "it hasn't got a black veil and it doesn't tie under the chin. But every single other thing on this earth that hat has got."

"Now, Gertrude," said Mr. Delahanty, "maybe you'd just better tell me what this hat is really like."

Mrs. Delahanty had a musing look in her eyes. "John, do you remember the chamber of commerce[1] dinner last fall? In Santa Ana?"[2]

"I remember we were there."

"Do you remember the table decorations?"

"No," said Mr. Delahanty, "I can't say I remember the table decorations."

"Well, it's a pity you can't, because then you would know what this hat looks like."

Cress did not like the way her mother had of being funny about serious matters. It was objectionable in anyone, in any mature person that is, and particularly so in a mother. When I have a child, Cress thought, I'll be serious and understanding the rest of my days.

---

1. **chamber of commerce:** organization that promotes business in a community.
2. **Santa Ana:** city in southern California.

"The table decorations," said Mrs. Delahanty reminiscently, "were horns of plenty, made out of straw mats. And out of them came spilling every fruit, grain, and flower ever grown in Orange County. Cress's hat would look right at home on that table."

"Oh Mother!" cried Cress.

"Except," said Mrs. Delahanty, "that those horns of plenty were of natural-colored straw, while this hat . . ." she paused, searching the room for some object with which to compare it, "while this hat," she concluded, "is an indescribable color."

"Oh Mother," cried Cress again. "It isn't. It's flamingo red."

"I've always considered red a nice warm color," said Mr. Delahanty.

"This is the warmest red, if it *is* red," agreed Mrs. Delahanty, "you ever laid eyes on. And its size!" Once again Mrs. Delahanty's eyes searched the kitchen without finding a comparable object. "It's just unbelievable," she said, shaking her head.

"Which all adds up to saying, I gather," said Mr. Delahanty, "that this hat Cress wants is large and flowered. Is that right, Cress? Is that the way it strikes you?"

The way the hat struck Cress was so overwhelming that she felt she might search the whole world over and still not find any word, any comparison which would explain it or the way she felt about it. The hat was summertime. It was deep and broad like summer. It caused soft scallops of shadow, like summer shadows under the densest trees, to fall across her face. It was like a poem; it was as much, "The rose is in full bloom, the riches of Flora[3] are lavishly strown," as though Keats[4] when he wrote had been thinking of it. The person wearing it would be languorous,[5] gentle, and delicate. Looking at herself in the store mirror with that hat on, she had heard herself saying to Edwin, "If you'll be kind enough to give me your arm I think I'd like to stroll a little before the dew comes out." And she had seen how she would look, saying that, glancing appealingly upward at Edwin from under the brim of the shadow-casting, summery, flower-laden hat.

"Well, Cress?" asked her father.

"Oh, yes!" said Cress. "That's how it strikes me. May I call the store and say you'll come in tonight to look at it?"

"There's no rush, is there?" asked Mr. Delahanty. "Could look Monday as well as tonight, couldn't we?"

"The rush," said Cress, "is because I want it to wear to the beach tomorrow. That is, if you approve of it, Daddy."

"What's the idea, Cress?" asked her father. "A hat to the beach? You usually put on your bathing cap before we leave the house."

"Tomorrow," said Cress, "I'm not going to go thrashing about in the water. I'm going to walk about and observe."

"You're not going to be able to observe much, Cress," said her mother, "with that hat hanging down over your eyes."

Cress ignored this. "Father, may or may not I call the S.Q.R.? You don't have to promise to buy it or like it. Only to look at it."

"I guess looking never did any harm," said Mr. Delahanty.

"Now you've gone and done it," said Mrs. Delahanty, when Cress had gone.

"Done what?" asked Mr. Delahanty, innocently.

"Promised her that monstrosity. And all in the world she wants it for is to parade around Balboa in it tomorrow hoping Edwin will catch sight of her."

---

3. **Flora:** Roman goddess of flowers.
4. **Keats:** John Keats (1795–1821), English poet.

5. **languorous** [lang′gər əs]: in a tender, soft mood.

"Is Edwin at Balboa?"

"His family is. And as far as I know they haven't abandoned him."

"I didn't promise to buy the hat," protested Mr. Delahanty. "All I said I'd do was look at it."

Wearing the hat, Cress felt just as she had known she would: gentle and fragile and drooping. Beautiful, too. Running, with it on, would be utterly out of the question. Even sitting with it on had its difficulties, for the hat with its burden of fruits and flowers had to be balanced just so.

"Father," she called from the back seat, "will you please roll up your window? It's blowing my hat."

"Cress," said Mr. Delahanty, "it's at least ninety in here now and I'm not going to roll this window up another inch. We're barely getting enough fresh air to keep us alive as it is."

"It's blowing the flowers off my hat," cried Cress.

"A few will never be missed," said Mr. Delahanty.

Mrs. Delahanty leaned across her husband and rolled up his window.

"How I could signal, if the need suddenly arose, I don't know," Mr. Delahanty told her, "apart from the fact that I'm suffocating right now."

"Nonsense," said Mrs. Delahanty. "Besides we'll be there in a few minutes."

"Steer for me for a minute, will you, Gertrude?" asked Mr. Delahanty. "I want to get out of this coat before I have a heat stroke."

How ridiculous! Cress felt just right. Warm, summery warm, of course, but though the car windows were tightly closed she could feel the freshness of the sea breeze which was bending the brown grass by the roadside, shaking the palm fronds, ruffling the white leghorns'[6] tails up over their backs like untidy skirts. She could smell the strange salt freshness of the sea, the far, non-land scent of its never-quiet water; and suddenly, in a little gap between two brown hills, she saw the sea itself, blue in the hot air, rippling and glinting

---

6. **leghorns:** small chickens.

under the sun like the scales of big silver-blue fish. Cress sighed so deeply with pleasure that her hat rocked unsteadily and she righted it, holding it for a minute with both hands at just the angle which she hoped it would have when Edwin saw her.

Because Edwin would see her, of course. It was impossible to believe that she, having become the owner of the most beautiful hat, should be in the same town with Edwin, without his seeing it and her.

After her father parked the car, he got out his own and her mother's bathing suits; then the two of them stood for a time looking at her.

"Well, times change," said Mr. Delahanty. "Times change. I never thought I'd live to see the day, Cress, when you'd elect to tramp up and down the boardwalk on a hot day instead of going swimming with us."

"I'm going to walk and observe," said Cress holding onto her hat which was hard to control in the stiff sea breeze which was blowing. "I'm getting a little old for just sporting around in the water."

"Observe," said Mr. Delahanty, seriously regarding her. "I can only hope, Cress, the shoe won't be too decidedly on the other foot."

"Now, John," said Mrs. Delahanty, and though she wasn't ordinarily a mother much given to kissing, she managed to get sufficiently under the brim of Cress's hat to give her a loving kiss.

"You're all right, Crescent," she said. "That hat's a little unusual, but I don't know that I'd want a daughter of mine trigged out like everyone else. Have a good time. And I hope you see Edwin."

"Oh Mother," said Cress earnestly, for the knowledge of her mother's understanding was as comforting to her as confession after sin.

"Run on now," said Mrs. Delahanty.

"We'll meet you at Tiny's at four," said her father, "and have some ice cream before we go home."

At first, Cress was so certain of seeing Edwin that she walked along the boardwalk, really observing and truly, except for the difficulties she had keeping her hat righted, enjoying the sights and smells of the town and the sea. Now and then in front of a plate glass window which served her as mirror she stopped to admire her hat, to get it on straight again and to poke up the stray hairs which kept dangling down from her not very solid kid-curler curls. Her mother had tried to persuade her not to wear a middy and skirt, saying they didn't go well with her hat. She was glad she hadn't listened to her. A middy was a nautical costume, and what, unless you actually went to sea, was more nautical than the shore? And her hat was the heart of summer, and where was the heart of summer to be found if not in August at the beach? No, looking at herself in the plate glass windows she passed, she was very content with what she saw: under the large hat her neck looked slender and reedlike, a blossom's stem; her eyes were shadowed, her entire aspect gentle, and even, she thought, mysterious. She was glad she had worn her high-heeled patent leather pumps, too. They made her teeter a little, but a swaying gait, she thought, suited the day, the hat, and her own personality; besides denying in the sharpest way possible the tomboy she was afraid Edwin thought her, and who would, no doubt, have worn sneakers.

What with observing, keeping her hat on straight, and practicing on occasional strangers the look of melting surprise with which she planned to greet Edwin, the first hour went by quickly. After the quietness of the ranch, where a whole day often passed with no other sounds than her own and her father's and mother's voices, and where the chief diversions, perhaps, were those of digging up a trap-door spider, or freeing a butcher-bird's victim, the sights and sounds of a beach town on a Sunday afternoon were almost too exciting to be borne.

First, there was the strange light touch of the penetrating wind off the sea on her warm inland body. Then there was the constant, half-heard beat of the surf, hissing as it ran smoothly up the sand, thundering as it crashed against the rocks of the breakwater.[7] There were all the smells of salt and seaweed, of fish and water and wind. There were all the human smells too of the hundreds of people who filled the boardwalk: ladies in print dresses smelling like passing gardens; swimmers with their scents of sun-tan oils and skin lotions; there were the smells of the eating places: of mustard and onions, of hamburgers frying; and the sudden sharp smell of stacks of dill pickles, as brisk in the nose as a sudden unintended inhalation of sea water. There was the smell of frying fish from the many fish grottos. And outside these places, in the middle of the boardwalk like miniature, land-locked seas, the glass tanks, where passers-by might admire the grace and color of their dinners before eating them. It was hard to say who did the most looking; fish outward from these sidewalk aquariums, at the strange pale gill-less pedestrians, or pedestrians inward at the finny swimmers.

Cress liked them both. Solemn fish and passers-by, some also solemn, with problems sun and water had not made them forget. For the first hour this was enough for Cress: being a part of this abundance and knowing that at any minute she would see Edwin. For in a town of one street how could she miss him?

Then suddenly the first hour was gone by;

it was past three and already the wind seemed a little sharper, the sun less bright, the boardwalk less crowded. More of her hair had come uncurled; her hat took more righting to keep it straight; her neck ached from holding her head high enough to see out from under the hat's brim; occasional stabs of pain shot up the calves of legs unaccustomed to the pull of high heels. A thought, with the swiftness of a stone dropping through water, settled in her mind: he isn't coming. It was a possibility she had not even thought about before. She had thought he would *have* to come. The hat was *for* him. The day was *for* him. How could she possibly, without seeing him, meet her father and mother, say yes, say no, eat ice cream, get in the car, go home, take off her hat, go to bed, sleep?

It was fifteen after three. At first she had been willing that Edwin see her first. Now, she searched every figure, every slight, short man or boy's figure, for as great a distance as she could make them out, saying, "Be Edwin." So strongly did she will it that she thought she might, by determination alone, transform a stranger into Edwin.

It was three-thirty. It was fifteen of four. Her hat was on one side, her mouth weary from practicing her smile on strangers, the pleat out of her freshly starched skirt, her feet mere stumps of pain. Still, she would not give up. "Edwin, appear, Edwin appear," she willed.

Edwin did appear, crossing the street a block away, small and neat and thin in white duck[8] pants and a white shirt. He crossed and turned toward Cress, walking steadily toward her. In two minutes or three he would see her, and see the hat and notice her new gentleness. All tiredness and pain left Cress. She could very easily have flown, or played a piece

---

7. **breakwater:** wall that protects an area from waves.

8. **duck:** made of light cotton fabric.

she had never seen before on the piano, or kissed a mad dog and not been bitten. She had just time to arrange herself, resettle her hat, give her now completely uncurled hair a quick comb upward. To do this she took her hat off, stood on tiptoe, and with fingers which trembled with excitement managed to get it up onto the top of one of the rectangular glass aquariums which by chance stood conveniently before her in the middle of the sidewalk.

Before she, herself, understood what had happened someone was jovially yelling, "Hey, sis, bread crumbs is what you feed them," and there was her hat, slowly, gracefully settling among the startled fish of the aquarium.

The man who had yelled was a short fat man, wearing pants, but no shirt or under-

shirt. He had sand in the hair on his chest; like dandruff, Cress thought wildly, unable for shame to raise her eyes to his face. "What's the idea, sis?" he asked.

Forcing her eyes away from the sandy dandruff, Cress saw that her hat, still gradually, gracefully floundering, was bleeding flamingo red into the aquarium, so that the amazed fish now swam in sunset waters.

"I thought it had a top," she whispered to no one in particular.

"The hat, sis?" asked the shirtless man.

"The glass place for the fish," Cress whispered. "I thought it had a top."

"It didn't, sis."

"I was resting my hat on it," Cress whispered, "while I fixed my hair."

"You was resting your hat on air, sis."

It was a field day for fish and humans. It was a great occasion for fish, who had had nothing more exciting to look forward to than death in the frying pan: a big blunt-nosed fish swam at the hat as if to ram it; smaller fish circled it curiously; nervous fish parted the darkening waters in a fishy frenzy. It was a glorious moment for humans, too, a sight they had never expected to see. Someone, a worthy man dedicated to service, brought out the fish grotto proprietor. He came in his white apron and tall chef's hat, brandishing a long-handled ladle and happy at first to see his fish arousing so much interest. He shouldered his way through the crowd, his blood-shot eyes bright with pleasure, until he caught sight of vermilion[9] waters, frantic fish, and the heart of summer, still partially afloat among them. He had had a long hard day frying fish. This was the last straw, fish dying without frying.

"In God's name," he cried, sadly, "who is murdering my fish?"

Cress was too frightened to reply.

"She is," said the fat man, pointing. "Sis, here, done it."

"What does she mean?" the fish grotto proprietor cried. Cress opened her mouth, but not a sound came out. She was as speechless as the fish.

"Sis here was resting her hat on the top of the aquarium," explained the fat man.

"There ain't no top," said the fish grotto owner. "Is she blind?"

"More or less, I reckon," said the fat man. "You kind of blind, sis?" he asked kindly.

Cress was able only to moan a little. With a long shudder, like a capsized ship coming to rest, her hat settled to the bottom of the aquarium. It lay there at a crazy angle, one side held up by a small castle with which the

"It dropped," said Cress. "It fell right out of my hands."

"Gravity, sis," said the fat man. "It was gravity."

"Will it make the fish sick?" asked Cress.

"Make 'em die, sis, in my opinion."

"What'll I do?" asked Cress.

"Watch 'em die," said the fat man comfortably. "That big one's a goner already."

Cress wanted to die herself. She willed it very hard, but she couldn't. She couldn't even faint, though she held her breath and willed her heart to stop beating. But a sort of numbness did come over her, making all the voices blurred and indistinct, making all the people, and there were dozens, hundreds it seemed to Cress, now pressed about the aquarium, distant and hazy.

---

9. **vermilion** [vər mil′yən]: bright red.

fish grotto proprietor had attempted to give his aquarium a romantic, gothic[10] air. Out of a castle window one frightened fish eye peered, trying to penetrate the murky waters, make out if this was the end of the world for fish. It looked to be. Flowers and fruits were now adding their colors to that of the flamingo red straw. Streaks of purple from pansies and violets, puffs of sulphurous[11] yellow from the daisies, veins of green from stems and flowers richly marbled the general red of the water. And the hat, in form as well as color, was suffering a sea change. It was softening up, flattening out. Each minute it looked less and less like a hat.

Cress finally found her voice. "Save my hat," she whispered.

"It's too late," the fish grotto proprietor said, "to speak of saving anything. Hat or fishes. They are all goners. Let 'em die together."

"Die?" asked Cress.

"Poisoned," said the fish proprietor, pointing to his frantic fish, the vari-colored water. "What've you got agin fish, kid?"

"I like fish," Cress whispered.

"She likes fish," said the fat man. "Hate to consider what she might do if she didn't." Those who had gathered about the aquarium laughed. Somewhere among them must be Edwin, Cress thought: seeing her, seeing her face trembling with the effort not to cry, seeing her beautiful hat, its colors fading out amongst an aquarium full of fish. The laughter was not malicious; it was lazy Sunday afternoon laughter; lazy Sunday afternoon laughers, watching, as if at play, to see what the fish proprietor would do, if he were villain or hero, straight man or clown. But it might as well have been malicious; it shamed Cress to the bone.

"Poisoned," declared the fish proprietor again, gloomily, "deliberately poisoned."

"I think you're mistaken about their being poisoned."

It was impossible, Cress thought, that anyone should be defending her: let alone Edwin—Edwin, who was always a victim himself.

"I think that color is probaby from pure vegetable dyes," said Edwin. Edwin's face was as white as his shirt and Cress could see that his upper lip trembled. But he was defending her, defying the fish grotto proprietor, not ashamed to be on the side of a person who had been publicly laughed at.

"It might even be good for the fish," suggested Edwin, "that pure vegetable dye."

"Good for them!" cried the fish proprietor. "Them fish have been scared to death at the very least, poison or no poison. Hats descending on them! I wouldn't feed them fish to a cat now. Their nervous systems have been shook up. You related to this girl?"

"No," said Edwin.

"Well, someone," said the fish proprietor, coming to the crux of the matter, "has got to pay for my ruined fish."

"That'll be me, I reckon," said Mr. Delahanty who, without enthusiasm, was pushing his way through the crowd. He took the ladle from the fish owner's hand, and being a tall man was able, by stretching a little, to fetch up the hat, heavy and dripping from the bottom of the aquarium. He held the hat toward Cress, who without a word took it. Then Mr. Delahanty handed the ladle back to its owner.

"I'll pay ten dollars," he said.

"Twenty-five," said the fish grotto proprietor. "Not a cent less. Those were fancy fish and not to be picked up every day in the week."

"Eleven," said Mr. Delahanty.

"I was fond of those fish," said their owner. "They were pets, so to speak."

"Eleven fifty," said Mr. Delahanty.

---

10. **gothic:** mysterious.
11. **sulphurous** [sul′fər əs]: like the chemical sulphur.

"It was cruelty to animals putting that hat in with them. I could turn you in to the S.P.C.A."[12]

"Twelve," said Mr. Delahanty.

They settled for fifteen, Mr. Delahanty getting the fish.

Cress, the hat, and the fish, in an oversized kettle loaned by the fish man, occupied the back of the car on the trip home. It was a slow trip because speed tended to slosh the water in the kettle, together with a fish or two, out on the floor. It was a silent trip because Cress was thinking, and because up in the front seat, while Mr. and Mrs. Delahanty had plenty to say, they didn't want to be overheard by Cress.

They were nearly home before Mrs. Delahanty said, very low, "What a terrible thing to happen! It might mark her emotionally for life."

Mr. Delahanty agreed. "It wouldn't have been so bad though if that Edwin hadn't had to turn up in time to see it all."

"I know. She wanted to be such a lady—for him. That hat . . . and the curls . . . and then the hat in with the fish, the curls gone, and all those people laughing. I'm a grown person, John, but I just don't think I could live down such a thing."

Mrs. Delahanty looked quickly around.

"Cress," she cried, "what have you got that hat on your head for?"

"It'll shrink if I don't," said Cress very calmly.

"Well, let it. Let it shrink. And you've got all those colors dribbling down your face and neck."

"I'm trying to keep them mopped up," said Cress, mopping some more.

"Throw that hat away," ordered Mrs. Delahanty. "Toss it out the window, Cress. You don't ever have to wear it again. We'll get you a new one."

"Oh no," cried Cress, "I love it. I'm going to keep it all my life."

"Keep it all your life?" Mrs. Delahanty asked, feeling rather dazed. "Cress, that hat didn't look too good in the first place. I can't begin to tell you what it looks like now. Throw it away!"

"No," said Cress stubbornly. "I want to keep it to remember today by."

"Remember today," repeated Mrs. Delahanty, who was beginning to feel increasingly that she and her daughter were not speaking of the same day at all. "Why in the world do you want to remember today?"

"Because of the brave way Edwin defended me," said Cress.

"Oh," said Mrs. Delahanty faintly.

"He was really wonderful, Mother. He defied that man."

"I'm afraid we missed that, Cress."

"And I was stricken, Mother, really stricken. It was the first time Edwin ever saw me stricken. He didn't even know I could be. He's always been the stricken one so far. The most I'd dared hope for was to be gentle. Then," said Cress with great satisfaction, "stricken."

There was complete silence in the car for some time. "Don't you think I was, Mother?" Cress asked anxiously.

"Yes," said Mrs. Delahanty with conviction, "I think that's about the word for it."

"And whenever I wear this hat, he'll remember."

Mrs. Delahanty took her husband's handkerchief from his pocket and handed it back to her daughter. "Tuck this around your neck, Cress. It'll keep those colors from staining your middy."

With one hand Cress tucked the handkerchief about her neck, with the other she kept her hat in place.

---

12. **S.P.C.A.:** Society for Prevention of Cruelty to Animals.

STUDY QUESTIONS

Recalling

1. Describe the hat that Cress wants. Why?
2. What does Cress's father agree to do in the opening scene of the story? What does he actually do when he and Cress go to town?
3. Summarize Cress's plans for her day at the beach. What happens to spoil her plans?
4. What does the fish proprietor insist Cress has done? What does Edwin say? What does Mr. Delahanty give the proprietor?
5. According to the final paragraphs, why is Cress pleased? Why will she keep the hat?

Interpreting

6. Does Cress get along well with her parents? Describe three instances that reveal the Delahantys' feelings for their daughter.
7. Do you think Cress is really the "gentle" and "stricken" person she wants Edwin to think she is? Why or why not?
8. Is Cress a humorous character? Might some of her words, thoughts, and actions be considered funny? Explain.

READING AND LITERARY FOCUS

Third-Person Narrator

A story with a **third-person narrator** is told by the author. The author acts as a narrator who stands outside the story and refers to all the characters as "he" or "she." Unlike a first-person narrator (see page 115), a third-person narrator can give a full view of the story. The third-person narrator can tell us what every character is thinking and can show us events that happen to many different characters. For example, in "Thirteen" the narrator tells what Mr. Delahanty thinks as he and Mrs. Delahanty discuss the hat that their daughter, Cress, wants: "He thought it would be interesting to know what one woman thinks of another's reasons for buying a hat." Later the narrator tells what

Cress is thinking while she is hoping Edwin will appear: "A thought . . . settled in her mind: he isn't coming."

Thinking About Third-Person Narrator

■ Find two other examples of Cress's thoughts and feelings revealed by the narrator.

COMPOSITION

Writing About Plot

■ Write a paragraph about the plot of "Thirteen." What is the conflict? Whom is the conflict between? What problems make it difficult for Cress to resolve the conflict? How does the story conclude? *For help with this assignment, see Lesson 2 in the Writing About Literature Handbook at the back of this book.*

Writing a Scene

■ Write a short scene in which Cress and Edwin discuss the events at the end of "Thirteen." The scene should take place a week later at the beach. Decide whether or not Cress is wearing her hat. Try to capture the way Cress and Edwin behave in "Thirteen." *For help with this assignment, see Lesson 10 in the Writing About Literature Handbook at the back of this book.*

COMPARING STORIES

1. Compare the characterization in "A Just Judge" (page 92) with the characterization in any other story on pages 96–126. In which story do the characters seem more realistic and why?
2. Choose one character from two or more of the following stories: "Lucas and Jake," "Christmas in Brooklyn," "The Fun They Had," "Uncle Tony's Goat," and "Thirteen." Which character seems to learn the most about himself or herself in the course of the story? Do any of the characters remain the same? Give examples.

SETTING

Mari Sandoz (1901–1966) grew up outside Ellsworth, Nebraska, near what is now called the Sandoz Bridge. Her father struggled hard to make a living as a frontier farmer. In addition to writing, Sandoz taught school and worked as a proofreader for newspapers in Lincoln, Nebraska. She was interested in Nebraskan history, and many of her stories use details from frontier life.

■ As you read "The Birdman," pay special attention to the place in which the story unfolds.

Mari Sandoz

The Birdman

Long before the sun struck the face of Lookout Mountain, curls of smoke rose from the earth houses at its feet. Women hurried to the springs for water. Boys ran through the village. Dogs barked. The men brought out the weapons and gear of the hunt for admiration and repair. Today would begin the preparations for the ceremonial that would bring the buffalo from the land of the warm wind.

It was time. The long snows of winter had eaten deep into the caches[1] of dried meat and corn and pumpkin rings. But soon there would be new meat for the pots and the drying racks, new robes and skins for sewing with the bone awls[2] and needles of the women. And with these things would come great glory for the buffalo hunters.

Seeing this, young Birdman drew his robe around him and stalked out of the village, carrying neither bow nor arrow—only his flintheaded spear which everyone derided as much too heavy and much too strong for birds and rabbits.

Climbing the steep slope out of Reams Creek to the high plain spreading away southwestward, he circled back to where it broke in the high limestone-capped bluff[3] called Lookout Mountain. There he squatted in his robe and scowled down upon the gray earth homes of his people, scattered in little groups far up and down the benches[4] of the creek valley.

Below him the women moved about their labors. Several were working with bone diggers and willow baskets and the warming clay pits, for there was pottery to make, and the winter-bared patches of willow thatching[5] on

---

1. **caches** [kash′əz]: stores; supplies.
2. **awls** [ôlz]: pointed tools used to make small holes in leather.

3. **bluff:** high, steep cliff.
4. **benches:** strips of elevated, flat land.
5. **thatching:** roof covering made from woven leaves.

the house roofs must be covered before the late spring rains came. At the creek an old woman tied a long string of buffalo bladders to a stake to soak, complainingly, Birdman knew, and with no faith that there would soon be fresh ones for the molding of the pottery.

About the earth houses the men were preparing for the buffalo ceremonial and the coming of the herds from the south, the older with pipe and story and the sacred things for tomorrow's rites, the younger with mighty testing of bow and arrow and great plans for the surround. Others sharpened the knives and spears that might, with one blow under the shoulder, bring the buffalo to his knees.

But the testing of buffalo bows and the sharpening of spearheads was not for him on the top of Lookout Mountain. He was a birdman and sat long hours in the chill waters with an eye-holed pumpkin over his head. When the ducks came he moved slowly, very slowly, as though drifting in the evening winds, until he was among the gossiping birds. Then he pulled them under by the feet, each so swiftly that there was no time for outcry, their mates noticing only to watch this curious diving until Birdman had all his two hands could hold. And twice a year came the flying wedges of geese out of the evening horizon. Once he caught two white-throated geese at one time.

But Birdman was not so named for these things alone. Upon a far bluff was an old pit, and when the hunting eagle soared the sky like a flake of soot from burning cornstalks, the hunter threw the drifted sand from the pit with the shoulder blade of a buffalo and repaired the light covering of willows.[6] When it was old to the eye he caught a young ante-lope or a rabbit, and with its side opened red, tied it firmly to a center pole. Then he waited in the pit and when the circling eagle dropped like a stone upon his prey, Birdman reached up from below and swiftly clutched the powerful legs. He must get them both, and in one hand, to leave the other free for defense against the sharp tearing beak, the threshing wings.

In the first fierce rush of his anger, the eagle would beat down the light network of willow and strike again and again upon Birdman's unprotected head and shoulders, his sharp beak cutting and tearing the flesh, while the wings were as war clubs. But never once did the bird hunter release his hold and at last his thumb always closed on the sinewed, pulsing throat.

Sometimes it was hours before he could rise and bear his kill to the village, the wings spread longer than any man and the torn flesh of the hunter speaking of a battle that would bear recounting for many a moon.

He knew that it was no small thing to be called Birdman, but it was not enough. He would be a buffalo hunter also and as he looked down upon the earth houses of his people on the second bench above the river, Birdman was angry. Even now the house builders were perhaps seeking him to help place the center posts about the fire pit in a new house or to mold the clay about the firehole in the roof. Or perhaps his aunt wanted him to help plant the pumpkin in the creek bends where the sod would yield to the shovel of bone from buffalo killed by those who were now sharpening their spears for the hunt.

As the sun climbed in the sky, a drowsiness settled over the gray earth houses above the tree-tufted creek. They were greening fast today, and on the horizon shimmered a pale heat dance. No wind stirred the spare sand grass upon the slope. Two grouse flew across

---

6. **hunter . . . willows:** The Birdman hollows out the pit and covers it with twigs and leaves. Then he hides inside to set a trap for the eagle.

the valley, cackling low, uneasily. Birdman marked their flight, but not as carefully as was his habit. The sun was as the ash fire in winter, soothing. Gradually he was drowsy too and slept for a long time.

He awoke to hunger and to a breathless stillness and a green-gray sky. Below him the women were flying to finish their work, to gather in the soaking bladders, the garments and the robes spread to air. Over them the clouds darkened and began to roll and tumble like the floodwaters of the creek rolled when they rose over the cornfields or perhaps even the lower houses, crumbling their earth shells.

Birdman watched the valley below darken into an unnatural opaqueness.[7] The air sang with a high, thin sound that grew into a roar. A dust cloud swept out of the horizon toward Lookout Mountain. Then the wind struck, from every side at one time. The grass ran like milling[8] buffalo. Trees leaned, turned half around, and went down like sticks.

Hard on the wind came sheets of rain and earth-shaking thunder. Birdman dropped over the limestone cap of the mountain, squeezed himself under an overhanging cliff, and pulled his robe about him. Let the storm howl like the wolves in midwinter, the thunder fall like great boulders from high places!

A long time afterward the silence came back. Birdman stretched his cramped knees and looked out from his robe. Reams Creek was a swirling, gray river, scattering mud,

7. **opaqueness** [ō pāk′nes]: darkness, dullness.

8. **milling:** moving around aimlessly.

branches, even whole trees over the lower cornfields. The new yellow clay was washed as paint over the ground. The trees tucked in the draws[9] were broken; many that stood alone bared their uprooted feet to the air.

The creek lapped sullenly at the houses along the lower bench. The women ran for the higher ground with their bundles, shooing their children before them, while the men threw up earth embankments.[10] Birdman saw that he must return to the village. As he wrapped his robe about him he heard a faint roar as of far but mighty thunder—a low, steady thunder that shook the earth. He looked around. Across the horizon lay a dark line. At first he could not believe it. But even as he watched, it grew—the buffalo were coming, stampeded by the storm.

One moment he hesitated before giving the customary signal. Then, without warning his village, he grasped his spear and clinging to his flying robe, he ran over the plain toward the herd, leaping gullies and washouts[11] like an antelope. As the dark mass neared he saw that it was breaking. Little herds, unpressed from behind, were gradually swinging to the sides.

One of these dark fingers pointed along the breaks of Reams Creek. Birdman, recalling the many accounts of the great hunters of his people, thought swiftly. To the left was the broad plain down which the larger herd was sweeping. Coming straight toward him were about a hundred of the muddy animals, heads down, running blindly, certain death to everything in their path. For one instant he was only a birdman and, wishing to rid himself of spear and robe, wanted to run as the antelope and the coyote ran, with no pretense of courage. But instead he threw himself into a washout to wait, the earth trembling under his body. Even now he wondered if he should not signal to the village for those who make the surrounds, those who do it well and bring meat to the drying racks. But already it was too late. Besides, his anger with himself stiffened his determination. As the dark herd was upon him he rose and with a loud cry he waved the dark robe before him.

For a second the leaders hesitated. Then the thrust of those behind drove them on. Birdman leaped sideways, flung his robe into the mud-caked faces, and with a mighty thrust buried his spear under the shoulder of the nearest. Inexpertly he overbalanced and went down but the herd, already swerved, swept past him toward the bluff. At the brink the leaders could not stop and those behind followed.

Birdman found himself unhurt. As he looked down upon the muddy, bleeding side of the dead buffalo, his spear deep, an exultation[12] rose in him and he threw back his head and began to run. At the edge of the bluff overlooking Reams Creek he stopped and looked down. Below was a writhing mass of buffalo; some, less crippled, were dragging their heavy bodies onward.

And already up the benchland from the village came the first of the runners with their spears. Birdman stood straight and tall against the sky and signaled to his people. Here were robes enough to keep the women tanning for a long moon, fresh bladders about which to mold their pottery. Here was much meat for the pots and the drying racks and tongue and hump enough to feast all the people—to whom he would be Birdman no longer.

---

9. **draws:** grooves worn into the ground by running water.
10. **embankments:** barriers that hold back water.
11. **washouts:** holes made in the earth by water.

---

12. **exultation** [eg′zul tā′shən]: joy.

STUDY QUESTIONS

Recalling

1. What ceremonies are about to begin as the story opens?
2. What has Birdman hunted in the past? Describe his methods of hunting.
3. What does Birdman want to become?
4. What does Birdman do to fulfill his ambition? Explain how he provides his people with many robes and enough meat for a feast.

Interpreting

5. What qualities make Birdman a good hunter? Give examples from the story.
6. Why do you think being called Birdman is not enough for him?
7. What is the climax of the story? What conflicting emotions does Birdman feel at this point?
8. What change do you notice in Birdman by the end of the story?

Extending

9. Do you think it is better to have ambition than to be satisfied with your present state? Explain.

READING AND LITERARY FOCUS

Setting and Atmosphere

The **setting** is the time and place in which a story occurs. The setting includes the historical period, geographic area, landscape, season, weather, and culture in which the action takes place. We can picture the setting from the **descriptive details** given in the story. For example, in "Last Cover" (page 73) the narrator includes descriptive details about his home that tell us that the story takes place in the South ("our Carolina hills") on a farm near the woods.

A vivid description of a story's setting can cre-ate an **atmosphere,** or mood, that runs through the story. For example, in "The Birdman" the narrator's descriptions of the sky and land just before the storm create an atmosphere of expectancy. We sense that something important is about to happen. The description of the setting thus adds to the story's suspense as Birdman waits for his prey.

Thinking About Setting and Atmosphere

1. Describe the setting of "The Birdman." In what region do you think the story is set?
2. Does "The Birdman" take place in the modern world? How do you know?
3. Reread the first paragraph of the story. What atmosphere is created by that paragraph? What details help create this atmosphere?

COMPOSITION

Writing About Setting

■ Write a composition explaining how descriptive details make the setting of "The Birdman" come alive for the reader. Begin with a statement giving your general impression of the setting. Then choose several details, and explain how each adds to your picture of the setting. Look for details that appeal to different senses—for example, to the senses of sight, sound, and smell.

Writing a Poem

■ Write a poem about Birdman's activities in this story. For example, you might write a poem about his skill as a hunter of birds or his courage in hunting the buffalo. You may find some ideas for your poem in "A Song of Greatness" (page 215), which is a traditional poem of the Chippewa people. *For general help with writing poetry, see Lesson 6 in the Writing About Literature Handbook at the back of this book.*

© 1982 Jill Krementz

Isaac Bashevis Singer (1904–1991) grew up in Poland and came to the United States in 1935. Singer wrote in Yiddish, a language related to German and spoken by eastern European Jews. He often translated his own stories into English. In 1978 Singer received the Nobel Prize for Literature. Many of Singer's stories are based on Jewish folklore.

■ As you read "The Snow in Chelm" —a seemingly simple tale of a foolish village—look for insights about people in general.

Isaac B. Singer

The Snow in Chelm[1]

Chelm was a village of fools, fools young and old. One night someone spied the moon reflected in a barrel of water. The people of Chelm imagined it had fallen in. They sealed the barrel so that the moon would not escape. When the barrel was opened in the morning and the moon wasn't there, the villagers decided it had been stolen. They sent for the police, and when the thief couldn't be found, the fools of Chelm cried and moaned.

Of all the fools of Chelm, the most famous were its seven Elders.[2] Because they were the village's oldest and greatest fools, they ruled in Chelm. They had white beards and high foreheads from too much thinking.

Once, on a Hanukkah[3] night, the snow fell all evening. It covered all of Chelm like a silver tablecloth. The moon shone; the stars twinkled; the snow shimmered like pearls and diamonds.

That evening the seven Elders were sitting and pondering, wrinkling their foreheads. The village was in need of money, and they did not know where to get it. Suddenly the oldest of them all, Gronam[4] the Great Fool, exclaimed, "The snow is silver!"

"I see pearls in the snow!" another shouted.

"And I see diamonds!" a third called out.

It became clear to the Elders of Chelm that a treasure had fallen from the sky.

But soon they began to worry. The people of Chelm liked to go walking, and they would most certainly trample the treasure. What was to be done? Silly Tudras[5] had an idea.

---

1. **Chelm** [ᴋʜelm]
2. **Elders:** older, influential members of a community.
3. **Hanukkah** [hä′nə kə]: joyous, winter Jewish holiday that lasts for eight days.

4. **Gronam** [grō′näm]
5. **Tudras** [too′dräs]

Peasant Life, Marc Chagall, 1925.

"Let's send a messenger to knock on all the windows and let the people know that they must remain in their houses until all the silver, all the pearls, and all the diamonds are safely gathered up."

For a while the Elders were satisfied. They rubbed their hands in approval of the clever idea. But then Dopey Lekisch[6] called out in consternation, "The messenger himself will trample the treasure."

The Elders realized that Lekisch was right, and again they wrinkled their high foreheads in an effort to solve the problem.

"I've got it!" exclaimed Shmerel[7] the Ox.

"Tell us, tell us," pleaded the Elders.

"The messenger must not go on foot. He must be carried on a table so that his feet will not tread on the precious snow."

Everybody was delighted with Shmerel the Ox's solution; and the Elders, clapping their hands, admired their own wisdom.

The Elders immediately sent to the kitchen for Gimpel[8] the errand boy and stood him on a table. Now who was going to carry the table? It was lucky that in the kitchen there were Treitle[9] the cook, Berel[10] the potato peeler, Yukel[11] the salad mixer, and Yontel,[12] who was in charge of the community goat. All four were ordered to lift up the table on which Gimpel stood. Each one took hold of a leg. On top stood Gimpel, grasping a wooden hammer with which to tap on the villagers' windows. Off they went.

At each window Gimpel knocked with the hammer and called out, "No one leaves the house tonight. A treasure has fallen from the sky, and it is forbidden to step on it."

The people of Chelm obeyed the Elders and remained in their houses all night. Meanwhile the Elders themselves sat up trying to figure out how to make the best use of the treasure once it had been gathered up.

Silly Tudras proposed that they sell it and buy a goose which lays golden eggs. Thus the community would be provided with a steady income.

Dopey Lekisch had another idea. Why not buy eyeglasses that make things look bigger for all the inhabitants of Chelm? Then the houses, the streets, the stores would all look bigger, and of course if Chelm *looked* bigger, then it *would be* bigger. It would no longer be a village, but a big city.

There were other, equally clever ideas. But while the Elders were weighing their various plans, morning came and the sun rose. They looked out of the window, and, alas, they saw the snow had been trampled. The heavy boots of the table carriers had destroyed the treasure.

The Elders of Chelm clutched at their white beards and admitted to one another that they had made a mistake. Perhaps, they reasoned, four others should have carried the four men who had carried the table that held Gimpel the errand boy?

After long deliberations the Elders decided that if next Hanukkah a treasure would again fall down from the sky, that is exactly what they would do.

Although the villagers remained without a treasure, they were full of hope for the next year and praised their Elders, who they knew could always be counted on to find a way, no matter how difficult the problem.

---

6. **Lekisch** [leʹkēsh]
7. **Shmerel** [shmerʹəl]
8. **Gimpel** [gimʹpəl]
9. **Treitle** [trāʹtəl]
10. **Berel** [berʹəl]
11. **Yukel** [ūʹkəl]
12. **Yontel** [yònʹtəl]

STUDY QUESTIONS

Recalling

1. What does the story's first sentence tell us about Chelm?
2. Of what is the town in need? What do the Elders see in the snow?
3. What two problems does the snow present, and what do the Elders do to solve each problem?
4. What do the Elders discover the next morning? What do they decide to do next Hanukkah?

Interpreting

5. Explain in your own words how the Elders show that they are the most famous fools in Chelm.
6. What link can you see between what the village needs and what the Elders see in the snow?
7. Do you think the story could take place in another setting? Explain.

Extending

8. What does the story suggest about how people sometimes behave when they see the chance of wealth?

VOCABULARY

Antonyms

Antonyms are words that have opposite or nearly opposite meanings. *Sleep* and *wake* are antonyms. The capitalized words in the following numbered items are from "The Snow in Chelm." Choose the word that is most nearly opposite the meaning of each capitalized word, *as it is used in the selection*. Write the number of each item and the letter of your choice on a separate sheet.

1. SHIMMERED: (a) shone (b) shook (c) darkened (d) glimmered
2. PONDERED: (a) ignored (b) considered (c) weighed (d) thought over
3. WRINKLING: (a) smoothing (b) furrowing (c) creasing (d) blinking
4. TRAMPLE: (a) crush (b) walk on (c) step around (d) smash
5. CONSTERNATION: (a) concern (b) confidence (c) fear (d) friendship

COMPOSITION

Answering an Essay Question

■ Why is the setting of "The Snow in Chelm," which is a town inhabited entirely by fools, important to what happens in the story? Write an essay answering this question. Begin with a sentence that restates the question. Then briefly summarize the action of the story. Finally, explain how the story's action suits the setting. Use examples from the story to support your statements. *For help with this assignment, see Lesson 1 in the Writing About Literature Handbook at the back of this book.*

Writing a Sequel

■ Write another incident about the town of Chelm. You might, for example, relate what happens on the following Hanukkah when the Elders carry out the plan described in the story. Try to imitate the story's silliness.

CHALLENGE

Literary Criticism

■ The American novelist Bernard Malamud once said that Isaac Bashevis Singer's stories "uniquely combine elements of fantasy, comedy, love." What elements of fantasy and of comedy do you find in "The Snow in Chelm"? Is love—or at least affection—also an element in this story? Explain. Give examples from the story to support your answers.

William Saroyan (1908–1981) published his first stories when he was still a teen-ager. His well-known works include *My Name Is Aram, The Human Comedy,* and *The Time of Your Life.* Saroyan wrote often of his Armenian American heritage and of his boyhood in Fresno, California. In the following story he tells about a beautiful bird and a man who appreciates the bird's beauty.

■ What makes the man's love of the bird's beauty especially touching?

William Saroyan

The Hummingbird That Lived Through Winter

There was a hummingbird once which in the wintertime did not leave our neighborhood in Fresno, California.

I'll tell you about it.

Across the street lived old Dikran, who was almost blind. He was past eighty and his wife was only a few years younger. They had a little house that was as neat inside as it was ordinary outside—except for old Dikran's garden, which was the best thing of its kind in the world. Plants, bushes, trees—all strong, in sweet black moist earth whose guardian was old Dikran. All things from the sky loved this spot in our poor neighborhood, and old Dikran loved *them.*

One freezing Sunday, in the dead of winter, as I came home from Sunday School I saw old Dikran standing in the middle of the street trying to distinguish what was in his hand. Instead of going into our house to the fire, as I had wanted to do, I stood on the steps of the front porch and watched the old man. He would turn around and look upward at his

trees and then back to the palm of his hand. He stood in the street at least two minutes and then at last he came to me. He held his hand out, and in Armenian he said, "What is this in my hand?"

I looked.

"It is a hummingbird," I said half in English and half in Armenian. Hummingbird I said in English because I didn't know its name in Armenian.

"What is that?" old Dikran asked.

"The little bird," I said. "You know. The one that comes in the summer and stands in the air and then shoots away. The one with the wings that beat so fast you can't see them. It's in your hand. It's dying."

"Come with me," the old man said. "I can't see, and the wife's at church. I can feel its heart beating. Is it in a bad way? Look again, once."

I looked again. It was a sad thing to behold. This wonderful little creature of summertime in the big rough hand of the old peasant. Here it was in the cold of winter, absolutely helpless and pathetic, not suspended in a shaft of summer light, not the most alive thing in the world, but the most helpless and heartbreaking.

"It's dying," I said.

The old man lifted his hand to his mouth and blew warm breath on the little thing in his hand which he could not even see. "Stay now," he said in Armenian. "It is not long till summer. Stay, swift and lovely."

We went into the kitchen of his little house, and while he blew warm breath on the bird he told me what to do.

"Put a tablespoon of honey over the gas fire and pour it into my hand, but be sure it is not too hot."

This was done.

After a moment the hummingbird began to show signs of fresh life. The warmth of the room, the vapor of the warm honey—and, well, the will and love of the old man. Soon the old man could feel the change in his hand, and after a moment or two the hummingbird began to take little dabs of the honey.

"It will live," the old man announced. "Stay and watch."

The transformation was incredible. The old man kept his hand generously open, and I expected the helpless bird to shoot upward out of his hand, suspend itself in space, and scare the life out of me—which is exactly what happened. The new life of the little bird was magnificent. It spun about in the little kitchen, going to the window, coming back to the heat, suspending, circling as if it were summertime and it had never felt better in its whole life.

The old man sat on the plain chair, blind but attentive. He listened carefully and tried to see, but of course he couldn't. He kept asking about the bird, how it seemed to be, whether it showed signs of weakening again, what its spirit was, and whether or not it appeared to be restless; and I kept describing the bird to him.

When the bird was restless and wanted to go, the old man said, "Open the window and let it go."

"Will it live?" I asked.

"It is alive now and wants to go," he said. "Open the window."

I opened the window, the hummingbird stirred about here and there, feeling the cold from the outside, suspended itself in the area of the open window, stirring this way and that, and then it was gone.

"Close the window," the old man said.

We talked a minute or two and then I went home.

The old man claimed the hummingbird lived through that winter, but I never knew for sure. I saw hummingbirds again when summer came, but I couldn't tell one from the other.

One day in the summer I asked the old man.

"Did it live?"

"The little bird?" he said.

"Yes," I said. "That we gave the honey to. You remember. The little bird that was dying in the winter. Did it live?"

"Look about you," the old man said. "Do you see the bird?"

"I see humming*birds*," I said.

"Each of them is our bird," the old man said. "Each of them, each of them," he said swiftly and gently.

STUDY QUESTIONS

Recalling

1. Why can't Dikran identify the bird in his hand?
2. In what condition is the bird at the beginning of the story?
3. What do Dikran and the narrator do to help the bird? What do they finally do with the bird?
4. What does Dikran say the next summer when the narrator asks if the bird lived?

Interpreting

5. What qualities does Dikran display in this story?
6. What does Dikran's last remark mean? What message about nature might it suggest?

Extending

7. Name some things that most people can do to protect natural creatures.

READING AND LITERARY FOCUS

Making Inferences from Details of Setting

Even when a story includes only a few details, we can picture the setting by making inferences from these details. An **inference** is a conclusion that we draw from the information we have. For example, we may hear about a restaurant in which all of the tables are empty at dinner time. We may also hear that the paint on the walls is peeling and that the windows are dusty. From these details we can infer that the restaurant is not doing well.

Thinking About Making Inferences

■ Study the details that describe Dikran's house, garden, and kitchen. What inferences about Dikran's home can you make from these details?

VOCABULARY

Using a Glossary

A **glossary** is an alphabetical list of words usually found at the end of a textbook. Like a dictionary, a glossary gives the **definitions,** or meanings, of the words. Many glossaries also give **pronunciations** of words, explaining how the word is spoken. The letters used in the pronunciation are called a **phonetic alphabet.** Many glossaries have **pronunciation keys** to explain the sounds of these letters. Glossaries often also give the parts of speech of words. The **part of speech** tells how a word is used in a sentence. The abbreviation for a word's part of speech is often given after the pronunciation.

Unlike a dictionary, a glossary includes only certain words that are found within the textbook. For example, the glossary in a book about chemistry lists words that refer to the study of chemistry. The Glossary at the back of this book lists words from the selections. Many words have more than one meaning. However, the words in the Glossary for this book are defined as they are used in the selections.

Use the Glossary at the back of this book to answer the numbered questions about the italicized words from "The Hummingbird That Lived Through Winter."

1. What part of speech is *distinguish*?
2. What is the meaning of *suspended*?
3. Is the *a* in *vapor* to be pronounced like the *a* in *at* or like the *a* in *ape*?
4. On what syllable does the main stress of *transformation* fall?
5. What is the meaning of *pathetic*?

Walter Braden ("Jack") Finney (born 1911) is a noted writer of suspense stories and science fiction. One of his novels was the basis of the classic science-fiction movie *The Invasion of the Body Snatchers.* Finney's recent works include *Forgotten News,* a nonfiction collection, and *Time and Again,* a novel about time travel. Time travel also plays an important role in this story.

■ What does the story make you think about the past? What does it suggest about the present?

Jack Finney

The Third Level

The presidents of the New York Central and the New York, New Haven and Hartford railroads[1] will swear on a stack of timetables that there are only two. But I say there are three, because I've *been* on the third level at Grand Central Station.[2] Yes, I've taken the obvious step: I talked to a psychiatrist friend of mine, among others. I told him about the third level at Grand Central Station, and he said it was a waking-dream wish fulfillment.[3] He said I was unhappy. That made my wife kind of mad, but he explained that he meant the modern world is full of insecurity, fear, war, worry and all the rest of it, and that I just want to escape. Well, who doesn't? Everybody I know wants to escape, but they don't wander down into any third level at Grand Central Station.

But that's the reason, he said, and my friends all agreed. Everything points to it, they claimed. My stamp collecting, for example; that's a "temporary refuge from reality." Well, maybe, but my grandfather didn't need any refuge from reality; things were pretty nice and peaceful in his day, from all I hear, and he started my collection. It's a nice collection, too, blocks of four of practically every U.S. issue, first-day covers, and so on. President Roosevelt[4] collected stamps, too, you know.

Anyway, here's what happened at Grand Central. One night last summer I worked late at the office. I was in a hurry to get uptown to my apartment so I decided to take the subway from Grand Central because it's faster than the bus.

Now, I don't know why this should have happened to me. I'm just an ordinary guy named Charley, thirty-one years old, and I was wearing a tan gabardine[5] suit and a straw hat

---

1. **New York Central . . . railroads:** railroads that connected New York City with upstate New York and Connecticut. New Haven and Hartford are cities in Connecticut.
2. **Grand Central Station:** large, busy railroad station in New York City.
3. **waking-dream wish fulfillment:** daydream or fantasy in which an unconscious wish seems to come true.

4. **President Roosevelt:** U.S. President (1933–1945).
5. **gabardine** [gab′ər dēn′]: strong fabric used in suits.

with a fancy band; I passed a dozen men who looked just like me. And I wasn't trying to escape from anything; I just wanted to get home to Louisa, my wife.

I turned into Grand Central from Vanderbilt Avenue, and went down the steps to the first level, where you take trains like the Twentieth Century.[6] Then I walked down another flight to the second level, where the suburban trains leave from, ducked into an arched doorway heading for the subway—and got lost. That's easy to do. I've been in and out of Grand Central hundreds of times, but I'm always bumping into new doorways and stairs and corridors. Once I got into a tunnel about a mile long and came out in the lobby of the Roosevelt Hotel. Another time I came up in an office building on Forty-sixth Street, three blocks away.

Sometimes I think Grand Central is growing like a tree, pushing out new corridors and staircases like roots. There's probably a long tunnel that nobody knows about feeling its way under the city right now, on its way to Times Square, and maybe another to Central Park. And maybe—because for so many people through the years Grand Central *has* been an exit, a way of escape—maybe that's how the tunnel I got into . . . But I never told my psychiatrist friend about that idea.

The corridor I was in began angling left and slanting downward and I thought that was wrong, but I kept on walking. All I could hear was the empty sound of my own footsteps and I didn't pass a soul. Then I heard that sort of hollow roar ahead that means open space and people talking. The tunnel turned sharp left; I went down a short flight of stairs and came out on the third level at Grand Central Station. For just a moment I thought I was back on the second level, but I saw the room was smaller, there were fewer ticket windows and train gates, and the information booth in the center was wood and old-looking. And the man in the booth wore a green eyeshade and long black sleeve protectors. The lights were dim and sort of flickering. Then I saw why; they were open-flame gaslights.

There were brass spittoons on the floor, and across the station a glint of light caught my eye; a man was pulling a gold watch from his vest pocket. He snapped open the cover, glanced at his watch and frowned. He wore a derby hat, a black four-button suit with tiny lapels, and he had a big, black, handlebar mustache. Then I looked around and saw that everyone in the station was dressed like eighteen-ninety-something; I never saw so many beards, sideburns and fancy mustaches in my life. A woman walked in through the train gate; she wore a dress with leg-of-mutton sleeves and skirts to the top of her high-buttoned shoes. Back of her, out on the tracks, I caught a glimpse of a locomotive, a very small Currier & Ives[7] locomotive with a funnel-shaped stack. And then I knew.

To make sure, I walked over to a newsboy and glanced at the stack of papers at his feet. It was *The World*; and *The World* hasn't been published for years. The lead story said something about President Cleveland.[8] I've found that front page since, in the Public Library files, and it was printed June 11, 1894.

I turned toward the ticket windows knowing that here—on the third level at Grand Central—I could buy tickets that would take Louisa and me anywhere in the United States

---

6. **the Twentieth Century:** train that connected New York City and Chicago.

7. **Currier & Ives:** printing firm in the 1800s that published pictures of American people and events.
8. **President Cleveland:** Grover Cleveland (1837–1908), twenty-second and twenty-fourth president of the United States (1885–1889, 1893–1897).

we wanted to go. In the year 1894. And I wanted two tickets to Galesburg,[9] Illinois.

Have you ever been there? It's a wonderful town still, with big old frame houses, huge lawns, and tremendous trees whose branches meet overhead and roof the streets. And in 1894, summer evenings were twice as long, and people sat out on their lawns, the men smoking cigars and talking quietly, the women waving palm-leaf fans, with the fireflies all around, in a peaceful world. To be

back there with the First World War still twenty years off, and World War II over forty years in the future . . . I wanted two tickets for that.

The clerk figured the fare—he glanced at my fancy hatband, but he figured the fare—and I had enough for two coach tickets, one way. But when I counted out the money and looked up, the clerk was staring at me. He nodded at the bills. "That ain't money, mister," he said, "and if you're trying to skin[10]

---

9. **Galesburg:** small city in western Illinois.

10. **skin:** cheat.

me, you won't get very far," and he glanced at the cash drawer beside him. Of course the money was old-style bills, half again as big as the money we use nowadays, and different-looking. I turned away and got out fast. There's nothing nice about jail, even in 1894.

And that was that. I left the same way I came, I suppose. Next day, during lunch hour, I drew three hundred dollars out of the bank, nearly all we had, and bought old-style currency (that *really* worried my psychiatrist friend). You can buy old money at almost any coin dealer's, but you have to pay a premium. My three hundred dollars bought less than two hundred in old-style bills, but I didn't care; eggs were thirteen cents a dozen in 1894.

But I've never again found the corridor that leads to the third level at Grand Central Station, although I've tried often enough.

Louisa was pretty worried when I told her all this, and didn't want me to look for the third level any more, and after a while I stopped; I went back to my stamps. But now we're *both* looking, every weekend, because now we have proof that the third level is still there. My friend Sam Weiner disappeared! Nobody knew where, but I sort of suspected because Sam's a city boy, and I used to tell him about Galesburg—I went to school there—and he always said he liked the sound of the place. And that's where he is, all right. In 1894.

Because one night, fussing with my stamp collection, I found—Well, do you know what a first-day cover is? When a new stamp is issued, stamp collectors buy some and use them to mail envelopes to themselves on the very first day of sale; and the postmark proves the date. The envelope is called a first-day cover. They're never opened; you just put blank paper in the envelope.

That night, among my oldest first-day covers, I found one that shouldn't have been there. But there it was. It was there because someone had mailed it to my grandfather at his home in Galesburg; that's what the address on the envelope said. And it had been there since July 18, 1894—the postmark showed that—yet I didn't remember it at all. The stamp was a six-cent, dull brown, with a picture of President Garfield.[11] Naturally, when the envelope came to Granddad in the mail, it went right into his collection and stayed there—till I took it out and opened it.

The paper inside wasn't blank. It read:

> *941 Willard Street*
> *Galesburg, Illinois*
> *July 18, 1894*

Charley:

I got to wishing that you were right. Then I got to believing you were right. And, Charley, it's true; I found the third level! I've been here two weeks, and right now, down the street at the Dalys', someone is playing a piano, and they're all out on the front porch singing "Seeing Nelly Home." And I'm invited over for lemonade. Come on back, Charley and Louisa. Keep looking till you find the third level! It's worth it, believe me!

The note is signed *Sam*.

At the stamp and coin store I go to, I found out that Sam bought eight hundred dollars' worth of old-style currency. That ought to set him up in a nice little hay, feed and grain business; he always said that's what he really wished he could do, and he certainly can't go back to his old business. Not in Galesburg, Illinois, in 1894. His old business? Why, Sam was my psychiatrist.

---

11. **President Garfield:** James A. Garfield (1831–1881), twentieth president of the United States (1881).

Recalling

1. How does Charley get to the "third level" at the beginning of the story?
2. Describe the place and people that Charley sees when he finds the third level.
3. When Charley is at the ticket window on the third level, to what place and time does he want to go?
4. What proof convinces Charley's wife that the third level really exists?
5. In his letter what does Sam tell Charley and his wife to do? Why?

Interpreting

6. Use two examples to explain how Charley concludes that he has left the present when he wanders into the third level.
7. Why does Charley want to go back in time?

Extending

8. If you could travel to another time—past or future—where would you go?

READING AND LITERARY FOCUS

Comparison/Contrast

A **comparison** points out the similarities between two or more items. A **contrast** points out the differences. In a story a writer may help us to see one place more clearly by comparing it with another place. For example, in "Feathered Friend" (page 54), Arthur C. Clarke helps us see the space station more vividly by comparing construction work in space with construction work on Earth's skyscrapers.

An author often uses contrasts to make a point or express an opinion. For example, if a story is set during the Great Depression of the 1930s, the author might contrast details of Depression life with details of life today in order to show us that life was harder during the Depression.

Thinking About Comparison/Contrast

■ What basic contrast does "The Third Level" make between the present as Charley knows it and the past? What opinion is Charley expressing through this contrast?

CHALLENGE

Debate

■ With another student taking the other side, debate the question of whether life in nineteenth-century America would be preferable to life in the present day. Prepare for the debate by researching facts that support your opinion. You might also think about answering arguments that your opponent is likely to raise.

COMPARING STORIES

1. Compare and contrast the settings of at least two of the following stories: "The Birdman," "The Snow in Chelm," and "The Third Level." First comment on how the characters in each story seem to feel about the place in which they live. Then tell which characters seem better able to deal with their settings by the end of the story.
2. In which of the following three stories is the weather most important: "The Birdman," "The Snow in Chelm," or "The Hummingbird That Lived Through Winter"? How is the weather important in the other stories?

THEME

Ivan Turgenev [toor gā'nyəf] (1818–1883) was one of Russia's first writers to win international fame. Although he came from a wealthy family, he was dedicated to helping the poor. As a writer he is especially noted for his sensitive descriptions of the lives of poor farmers. "The Sparrow" describes a hunter's encounter with a simple event of nature.

◾ What does the hunter learn from his experience?

Ivan Turgenev

The Sparrow

I was returning from a day's hunting and was walking toward the house along an alley[1] in my garden. My dog was running ahead of me.

Suddenly she slowed her pace and began to advance stealthily, as though she had caught scent of game.

I looked down the path and saw a young sparrow with a streak of yellow near its beak and a bit of puff on its head. It had fallen out of the nest. (A strong wind was swaying the birch trees.) The tiny bird sat there trying helplessly to use its barely grown wings.

My dog was stealing[2] up to the infant sparrow when, abruptly, an old black-chested bird fell like a stone right in front of the dog's face, and with all its feathers standing on end, misshapen, uttering a desperate and pitiful chirp, it hopped once and then again in the direction of the dog's open jaw.

The bird had thrown itself in front of the dog to shield its young one, but its own small body was trembling with terror, its little voice was frenzied and hoarse, and it was numb with fright—it was sacrificing itself!

What a huge monster the dog must have seemed to the mother sparrow! Nevertheless, it could not bear to stay on its high, safe perch in the tree. A force stronger than its will to remain alive made it hurl itself to the rescue.

My Treasure, the dog, stopped still and then backed up. Evidently she, too, recognized that force. . . .

I hastened to call off the puzzled dog and went on my way, awed.[3]

Yes, do not laugh. I was awed by that small, heroic bird—by its impulse of love.

Love, I felt more than ever, is stronger than death and the fear of death. Only through love is life sustained and nourished.[4]

---

1. **alley:** here, a walk bordered by trees or shrubs in a garden.
2. **stealing:** moving in a secret, sly way.

3. **awed:** moved by deep feelings of respect and wonder.
4. **sustained** [sə stānd'] **and nourished** [nur'ishd]: here, supported and made worthwhile.

STUDY QUESTIONS

Recalling

1. What do the man and his dog encounter as they return from a day's hunting?
2. What falls "like a stone right in front of the dog's face"? According to the fifth paragraph, what does the man realize the mother is doing?
3. How does the dog react to the mother?
4. What two emotions does the sparrow experience, according to the man?
5. What conclusion does the man reach in the final paragraph?

Interpreting

6. What is it about the incident that "awes" the man?

Extending

7. Retell an experience of an animal's being protective.

READING AND LITERARY FOCUS

Stated Theme

An author usually writes a story in order to communicate a general message about life. The message may state a moral truth or it may be a general observation about nature, society, or human behavior. This message is the **theme,** or main idea, of the story. Some stories have a **stated theme,** a theme the author announces directly. Such a theme is often stated in a sentence near the end of a story. It may be expressed by one of the characters or by the author. A story with a stated theme usually has details that support the theme.

The moral lesson at the end of a **fable**—a very brief story told to teach the lesson—can sometimes be a good example of stated theme. Aesop's fable about the tortoise and the hare tells of a race between these two animals. The hare easily takes the lead and confidently stops for a nap by the roadside. The tortoise plods on, passes the sleeping hare, and crosses the finish line first. The fable ends with the statement "Slow and steady wins the race."

Thinking About Stated Theme

■ What is the theme of "The Sparrow"? Is it a stated theme? Why or why not?

COMPOSITION

Writing About Theme

■ Write a paragraph in which you show that the events of "The Sparrow" support the theme. First state the theme of the story. Then describe the events of the story. Finally, tell why you think they lead the man to his general conclusion about love.

Writing a Fable

■ A fable is a short tale that presents a lesson in story form. This lesson is called a **moral.** Choose a famous moral as your theme. Then write a brief story in which a character learns from experience that the moral is true. Finally, use the moral as the last sentence of your story. You may want to use one of the following morals as the stated theme of your story:

a. Haste makes waste.
b. Too many cooks spoil the broth.
c. The grass is always greener on the other side of the fence.

Mark Twain (1835–1910) is the pen name of Samuel Clemens, one of America's greatest authors. Twain grew up in Hannibal, Missouri, a town on the Mississippi River. In 1864 Twain headed west to Nevada to look for gold, but then he began a writing career. Many of his most famous works are based on his boyhood experiences on the Mississippi River. "The Glorious Whitewasher" is from *The Adventures of Tom Sawyer.*

■ What does Tom learn about human nature as he paints a fence?

Mark Twain

The Glorious Whitewasher

from **The Adventures of Tom Sawyer**

Saturday morning was come, and all the summer world was bright and fresh, and brimming with life. There was a song in every heart; and if the heart was young the music issued at the lips. There was cheer in every face and a spring in every step. The locust trees were in bloom and the fragrance of the blossoms filled the air. Cardiff Hill, beyond the village and above it, was green with vegetation; and it lay just far enough away to seem a Delectable Land, dreamy, reposeful, and inviting.

Tom appeared on the sidewalk with a bucket of whitewash and a long-handled brush. He surveyed[1] the fence, and all gladness left him and a deep melancholy settled down upon his spirit. Thirty yards of board fence nine feet high. Life to him seemed hollow, and existence but a burden. Sighing, he dipped his brush and passed it along the topmost plank; repeated the operation; did it again; compared the insignificant whitewashed streak with the far-reaching continent of unwhitewashed fence, and sat down on a tree-box discouraged. . . .

He began to think of the fun he had planned for this day, and his sorrows multiplied. Soon the free boys would come tripping along on all sorts of delicious expeditions, and they would make a world of fun of him for having to work—the very thought of it burnt him like fire. He got out his worldly wealth and examined it—bits of toys, marbles, and trash; enough to buy an exchange of *work*, maybe, but not half enough to buy so much as half an hour of pure freedom. So he returned his straitened means[2] to his pocket and gave up the idea of trying to buy the boys.

1. **surveyed** [sər vād']: examined.

2. **straitened means:** limited possessions.

At this dark and hopeless moment an inspiration burst upon him! Nothing less than a great, magnificent inspiration.

He took up his brush and went tranquilly to work. Ben Rogers hove in sight[3] presently—the very boy, of all boys, whose ridicule he had been dreading. Ben's gait was the hop-skip-and-jump—proof enough that his heart was light and his anticipations high. He was eating an apple, and giving a long, melodious whoop, at intervals, followed by a deep-toned ding-dong-dong, ding-dong-dong, for he was personating a steamboat. As he drew near, he slackened speed, took the middle of the street, leaned far over to starboard[4] and rounded to[5] ponderously and with laborious pomp and circumstance[6]—for he was personating the *Big Missouri*, and considered himself to be drawing nine feet of water. He was boat and captain and engine bells combined, so he had to imagine himself standing on his own hurricane deck giving the orders and executing them:

"Stop her sir! Ting-a-ling-ling!" The headway[7] ran almost out and he drew up slowly toward the sidewalk.

"Ship up to back! Ting-a-ling-ling!" His arms straightened and stiffened down his sides.

"Set her back on the stabboard! Ting-a-ling-ling! Chow! Ch-chow-wow! Chow!" His right hand, meantime, describing stately circles—for it was representing a forty-foot wheel.[8]

"Let her go back on the labboard![9] Ting-a-ling-ling! Chow-ch-chow-chow!" The left hand began to describe circles. . . .

Tom went on whitewashing—paid no attention to the steamboat. Ben stared a moment and then said:

"Hi-*yi! You're* up a stump, ain't you!"

No answer. Tom surveyed his last touch with the eye of an artist, then he gave his brush another gentle sweep and surveyed the result, as before. Ben ranged up alongside of him. Tom's mouth watered for the apple, but he stuck to his work. Ben said:

"Hello, old chap, you got to work, hey?"

Tom wheeled suddenly and said:

"Why, it's you, Ben! I warn't noticing."

"*Say—I*'m going in a-swimming, *I* am. Don't you wish you could? But of course you'd druther *work*—wouldn't you? Course you would!"

Tom contemplated the boy a bit, and said:

"What do you call work?"

"Why, ain't *that* work?"

Tom resumed his whitewashing, and answered carelessly:

"Well, maybe it is, and maybe it ain't. All I know is, it suits Tom Sawyer."

"Oh come now, you don't mean to let on that you *like* it?"

The brush continued to move.

"Like it? Well, I don't see why I oughtn't to like it. Does a boy get a chance to whitewash a fence every day?"

That put the thing in a new light. Ben stopped nibbling his apple. Tom swept his brush daintily back and forth—stepped back to note the effect—added a touch here and there—criticized the effect again—Ben watching every move and getting more and more interested, more and more absorbed. Presently he said:

---

3. **hove in sight:** came into view.
4. **starboard:** right side of a boat facing forward; here, meaning "to the right."
5. **rounded to:** turned to face into the wind.
6. **pomp and circumstance:** showy display and formality.
7. **headway:** forward motion.
8. **forty-foot wheel:** Mississippi River steamboats are usually propelled by large paddle wheels at their sides or backs.

---

9. **labboard:** larboard, the left side of a boat.

"Say, Tom, let *me* whitewash a little."

Tom considered, was about to consent; but he altered his mind:

"No—no—I reckon it wouldn't hardly do, Ben. You see, Aunt Polly's awful particular about this fence—right here on the street, you know—but if it was the back fence I wouldn't mind and *she* wouldn't. Yes, she's awful particular about this fence; it's got to be done very careful; I reckon there ain't one boy in a thousand, maybe two thousand, that can do it the way it's got to be done."

"No—is that so? Oh come, now—lemme just try. Only just a little—I'd let *you*, if you was me, Tom."

"Ben, I'd like to, honest Injun; but Aunt

sweated in the sun, the retired artist sat on a barrel in the shade close by, dangled his legs, munched his apple, and planned the slaughter of more innocents. There was no lack of material; boys happened along every little while; they came to jeer, but remained to whitewash. By the time Ben was fagged out, Tom had traded the next chance to Billy Fisher for a kite, in good repair; and when *he* played out, Johnny Miller bought in for a dead rat and a string to swing it with—and so on, and so on, hour after hour. And when the middle of the afternoon came, from being a poor poverty-stricken boy in the morning, Tom was literally rolling in wealth. He had besides the things before mentioned, twelve marbles, part of a jew's-harp, a piece of blue bottle glass to look through, a spool cannon, a key that wouldn't unlock anything, a fragment of chalk, a glass stopper of a decanter,[11] a tin soldier, a couple of tadpoles, six firecrackers, a kitten with only one eye, a brass doorknob, a dog collar—but no dog—the handle of a knife, four pieces of orange peel, and a dilapidated old window sash.

He had had a nice, good, idle time all the while—plenty of company—and the fence had three coats of whitewash on it! If he hadn't run out of whitewash, he would have bankrupted every boy in the village.

Tom said to himself that it was not such a hollow world, after all. He had discovered a great law of human action, without knowing it—namely, that in order to make a man or a boy covet a thing, it is only necessary to make the thing difficult to attain. If he had been a great and wise philosopher, like the writer of this book, he would now have comprehended that Work consists of whatever a body is *obliged* to do and that Play consists of whatever a body is not obliged to do. . . .

Polly—well, Jim wanted to do it, but she wouldn't let him; Sid wanted to do it, and she wouldn't let Sid. Now don't you see how I'm fixed? If you was to tackle this fence and anything was to happen to it—"

"Oh, shucks, I'll be just as careful. Now lemme try. Say—I'll give you the core of my apple."

"Well, here—No, Ben, now don't. I'm afeared—"

"I'll give you *all* of it!"

Tom gave up the brush with reluctance in his face, but alacrity[10] in his heart. And while the late steamer *Big Missouri* worked and

---

10. **alacrity** [ə lak′rə tē]: eagerness.

11. **decanter:** decorative glass bottle.

STUDY QUESTIONS

Recalling

1. What chore must Tom do as the story opens? What does Tom say when Ben asks if Tom likes the chore?
2. What does Ben give Tom for a chance to help?
3. What happens to the other boys who come to jeer? Name at least three things that Tom has earned since the beginning of the story.
4. According to the final paragraph, what "great law of human action" has Tom learned?

Interpreting

5. Explain in your own words the strategy Tom uses to get the other boys to help him.
6. What character traits does Tom display?
7. State the theme of this selection.

Extending

8. Have you ever enjoyed doing a chore that you thought would be unpleasant or boring? Why?

VOCABULARY

Antonyms

Antonyms are words that have opposite or nearly opposite meanings. For example, *old* and *new* are antonyms. The words in capitals are from "The Glorious Whitewasher." Choose the word that is *most nearly the opposite* of each word in capitals, *as the word is used in the story*. Write the number of each item and the letter of your choice on a separate sheet.

1. INSIGNIFICANT: (a) busy (b) important (c) small (d) absorbent
2. RIDICULE: (a) laughter (b) tardiness (c) praise (d) inhibition
3. TRANQUILLY: (a) easily (b) happily (c) gracefully (d) loudly
4. RELUCTANCE: (a) eagerness (b) hesitation (c) reliance (d) specialty
5. COVET: (a) hide (b) dislike (c) regret (d) direct

COMPOSITION

Writing an Opinion

■ Write a paragraph in which you give your opinion of the theme of "The Glorious Whitewasher." First state the theme of the story. Then tell whether you agree or disagree with Twain's generalization about human nature. Give specific reasons for your opinion.

Writing a Dialogue

■ Imagine that it is the day after "The Glorious Whitewasher" takes place. Tom has more whitewash and sees you walking down the street. It is hot, and you are going swimming. Write the dialogue that you both have as you meet and discuss painting the fence. Is Tom able to convince you to paint it? If so, what item do you give him in return for such an opportunity? If not, how are you able to resist Tom's arguments?

CHALLENGE

Picture Research

■ Look in the library for pictures of steamboats that traveled up and down the Mississippi River during the nineteenth century. Look under *steamboat* in the encyclopedia and under Currier and Ives in the card catalogue. Currier and Ives were nineteenth-century printers who were famous for their colorful prints of steamboats.

From 1938 to 1942, Ray Bradbury (born 1920) earned his living by selling newspapers on a Los Angeles street corner. Soon afterward he sold his first story. Now he is one of America's most highly respected writers of science fiction. "The Sound of Summer Running" is not science fiction, but it does include flights of fancy.

■ Look for the magical things that happen when the boy's imagination moves into high gear.

Ray Bradbury

The Sound of Summer Running

Late that night, going home from the show with his mother and father and his brother Tom, Douglas saw the tennis shoes in the bright store window. He glanced quickly away, but his ankles were seized, his feet suspended, then rushed. The earth spun; the shop awnings slammed their canvas wings overhead with the thrust of his body running. His mother and father and brother walked quietly on both sides of him. Douglas walked backward, watching the tennis shoes in the midnight window left behind.

"It was a nice movie," said Mother.

Douglas murmured, "It was. . . ."

It was June and long past time for buying the special shoes that were quiet as a summer rain falling on the walks. June and the earth full of raw power and everything everywhere in motion. The grass was still pouring in from the country, surrounding the sidewalks, stranding the houses. Any moment the town would capsize, go down and leave not a stir in the clover and weeds. And here Douglas stood, trapped on the dead cement and the red-brick streets, hardly able to move.

"Dad!" He blurted it out. "Back there in that window, those Cream-Sponge Para Lite-foot Shoes . . ."

His father didn't even turn. "Suppose you tell me why you need a new pair of sneakers. Can you do that?"

"Well . . ."

It was because they felt the way it feels every summer when you take off your shoes for the first time and run in the grass. They felt like it feels sticking your feet out of the hot covers in wintertime to let the cold wind from the open window blow on them suddenly and you let them stay out a long time until you pull them back in under the covers again to feel them, like packed snow. The tennis shoes felt like it always feels the first time every year wading in the slow waters of the creek and seeing your feet below, half an inch further downstream, with refraction,[1] than the real part of you above water.

"Dad," said Douglas, "it's hard to explain."

Somehow the people who made tennis shoes knew what boys needed and wanted. They put marshmallows and coiled springs in the soles and they wove the rest out of grasses bleached and fired in the wilderness. Somewhere deep in the soft loam of the shoes the thin hard sinews of the buck deer were hidden. The people that made the shoes must have watched a lot of winds blow the trees and a lot of rivers going down to the lakes. Whatever it was, it was in the shoes, and it was summer.

Douglas tried to get all this in words.

"Yes," said Father, "but what's wrong with last year's sneakers? Why can't you dig *them* out of the closet?"

Well, he felt sorry for boys who lived in California where they wore tennis shoes all year and never knew what it was to get winter off your feet, peel off the iron leather shoes all full of snow and rain and run barefoot for a day and then lace on the first new tennis shoes of the season, which was better than barefoot. The magic was always in the new pair of shoes. The magic might die by the first of September, but now in late June there was still plenty of magic, and shoes like these could jump you over trees and rivers and houses. And if you wanted, they could jump you over fences and sidewalks and dogs.

"Don't you see?" said Douglas. "I just *can't* use last year's pair."

For last year's pair were dead inside. They had been fine when he started them out, last year. But by the end of summer, every year, you always found out, you always knew, you couldn't really jump over rivers and trees and houses in them, and they were dead. But this was a new year, and he felt that this time, with this new pair of shoes, he could do anything, anything at all.

They walked up on the steps to their house. "Save your money," said Dad. "In five or six weeks—"

"Summer'll be over!"

Lights out, with Tom asleep, Douglas lay watching his feet, far away down there at the end of the bed in the moonlight, free of the heavy iron shoes, the big chunks of winter fallen away from them.

"Reasons. I've got to think of reasons for the shoes."

Well, as anyone knew, the hills around town were wild with friends putting cows to riot, playing barometer to the atmospheric changes, taking sun, peeling like calendars each day to take more sun. To catch those friends, you must run much faster than foxes or squirrels. As for the town, it steamed with enemies grown irritable with heat, so remembering every winter argument and insult. *Find friends, ditch enemies!* That was the Cream-Sponge Para Litefoot motto. *Does the world run too fast? Want to be alert, stay alert? Litefoot, then! Litefoot!*

He held his coin bank up and heard the faint small tinkling, the airy weight of money there.

Whatever you want, he thought, you got to make your own way. During the night now, let's find that path through the forest. . . .

Downtown, the store lights went out, one by one. A wind blew in the window. It was like a river going downstream and his feet wanting to go with it.

In his dreams he heard a rabbit running running running in the deep warm grass.

Old Mr. Sanderson moved through his

---

1. **refraction** [ri frak'shən]: bending of a ray of light as it enters water. Refraction causes items that stand in water to seem bent.

shoe store as the proprietor of a pet shop must move through his shop where are kenneled animals from everywhere in the world, touching each one briefly along the way. Mr. Sanderson brushed his hands over the shoes in the window, and some of them were like cats to him and some were like dogs; he touched each pair with concern, adjusting laces, fixing tongues. Then he stood in the exact center of the carpet and looked around, nodding.

There was a sound of growing thunder.

One moment, the door to Sanderson's Shoe Emporium[2] was empty. The next, Douglas Spaulding stood clumsily there, staring down at his leather shoes as if these heavy things could not be pulled up out of the cement. The thunder had stopped when his shoes stopped. Now, with painful slowness, daring to look only at the money in his cupped hand, Douglas moved out of the bright sunlight of Saturday noon. He made careful stacks of nickels, dimes, and quarters on the counter, like someone playing chess and worried if the next move carried him out into sun or deep into shadow.

"Don't say a word!" said Mr. Sanderson.

Douglas froze.

"First, I know just what you want to buy," said Mr. Sanderson. "Second, I see you every afternoon at my window; you think I don't see? You're wrong. Third, to give it its full name, you want the Royal Crown Cream-Sponge Para Litefoot Tennis Shoes: 'LIKE MENTHOL ON YOUR FEET!' Fourth, you want credit."

"No!" cried Douglas, breathing hard, as if he'd run all night in his dreams. "I got something better than credit to offer!" he gasped. "Before I tell, Mr. Sanderson, you got to do me one small favor. Can you remember when was the last time you yourself wore a pair of Litefoot sneakers, sir?"

2. **Emporium** [em pôr′ē əm]: store.

Mr. Sanderson's face darkened. "Oh, ten, twenty, say, thirty years ago. Why . . .?"

"Mr. Sanderson, don't you think you owe it to your customers, sir, to at least try the tennis shoes you sell, for just one minute, so you know how they feel? People forget if they don't keep testing things. Candy-store man samples his own stuff, I should think. So . . ."

"You may have noticed," said the old man, "I'm wearing shoes."

"But not sneakers, sir! How you going to sell sneakers unless you can rave about them and how you going to rave about them unless you know them?"

Mr. Sanderson backed off a little distance from the boy's fever, one hand to his chin. "Well . . ."

"Mr. Sanderson," said Douglas, "you sell me something and I'll sell you something just as valuable."

"Is it absolutely necessary to the sale that I put on a pair of the sneakers, boy?" said the old man.

"I sure wish you could, sir!"

The old man sighed. A minute later, seated panting quietly, he laced the tennis shoes to his long narrow feet. They looked detached and alien down there next to the dark cuffs of his business suit. Mr. Sanderson stood up.

"How do they *feel?*" asked the boy.

"How do they feel, he asks; they feel fine." He started to sit down.

"Please!" Douglas held out his hand. "Mr. Sanderson, now could you kind of rock back and forth a little, sponge around, bounce kind of, while I tell you the rest? It's this: I give you my money, you give me the shoes, I owe you a dollar. But, Mr. Sanderson, *but*—soon as I get those shoes on, you know what *happens?*"

"What?"

"Bang! I deliver your packages, pick up packages, bring you coffee, burn your trash, run to the post office, telegraph office, library!

You'll see twelve of me in and out, in and out, every minute. Feel those shoes, Mr. Sanderson, *feel* how fast they'd take me? All those springs inside? Feel all the running inside? Feel how they kind of grab hold and can't let you alone and don't like you just *standing* there? Feel how quick I'd be doing the things you'd rather not bother with? You stay in the nice cool store while I'm jumping all around town! But it's not me really, it's the shoes. They're going like mad down alleys, cutting corners, and back! There they go!"

Mr. Sanderson stood amazed with the rush of words. When the words got going the flow carried him; he began to sink deep in the shoes, to flex his toes, limber his arches, test his ankles. He rocked softly, secretly, back and forth in a small breeze from the open door. The tennis shoes silently hushed themselves deep in the carpet, sank as in a jungle grass, in loam and resilient clay. He gave one solemn bounce of his heels in the yeasty dough, in the yielding and welcoming earth. Emotions hurried over his face as if many colored lights had been switched on and off. His mouth hung slightly open. Slowly he gentled and rocked himself to a halt, and the boy's voice faded and they stood there looking at each other in a tremendous and natural silence.

A few people drifted by on the sidewalk outside, in the hot sun.

Still the man and boy stood there, the boy glowing, the man with revelation in his face.

"Boy," said the old man at last, "in five years, how would you like a job selling shoes in this emporium?"

"Gosh, thanks, Mr. Sanderson, but I don't know what I'm going to be yet."

"Anything you want to be, son," said the old man, "you'll be. No one will ever stop you."

The old man walked lightly across the store to the wall of ten thousand boxes, came back with some shoes for the boy, and wrote up a list on some paper while the boy was lacing the shoes on his feet and then standing there, waiting.

The old man held out his list. "A dozen things you got to do for me this afternoon. Finish them, we're even Stephen, and you're fired."

"Thanks, Mr. Sanderson!" Douglas bounded away.

"Stop!" cried the old man.

Douglas pulled up and turned.

Mr. Sanderson leaned forward. "How do they *feel*?"

The boy looked down at his feet deep in the rivers, in the fields of wheat, in the wind that already was rushing him out of town. He looked up at the old man, his eyes burning, his mouth moving, but no sound came out.

"Antelopes?" said the old man, looking from the boy's face to his shoes. "Gazelles?"

The boy thought about it, hesitated, and nodded a quick nod. Almost immediately he vanished. He just spun about with a whisper and went off. The door stood empty. The sound of the tennis shoes faded in the jungle heat.

Mr. Sanderson stood in the sun-blazed door, listening. From a long time ago, when he dreamed as a boy, he remembered the sound. Beautiful creatures leaping under the sky, gone through brush, under trees, away, and only the soft echo their running left behind.

"Antelopes," said Mr. Sanderson. "Gazelles."

He bent to pick up the boy's abandoned winter shoes, heavy with forgotten rains and long-melted snows. Moving out of the blazing sun, walking softly, lightly, slowly, he headed back toward civilization. . . .

STUDY QUESTIONS

Recalling

1. What time of year is it when the story begins?
2. Why can't Douglas use last year's sneakers?
3. Give two reasons Douglas thinks of for buying new sneakers.
4. What bargain does Douglas strike with Mr. Sanderson?

Interpreting

5. Find Douglas' examples of the way a new pair of sneakers feels. What do the examples have in common?
6. Why does Douglas ask Mr. Sanderson to put on the sneakers?
7. Why do you think Mr. Sanderson accepts Douglas' deal?
8. Do you agree with Mr. Sanderson that Douglas can be anyone he wants to be? Explain with examples from the story.

Extending

9. What special meanings does summer have for you?

READING AND LITERARY FOCUS

Implied Theme

The **theme** is the main idea of a story. Usually this idea is a general statement about life. An **implied theme** is not stated directly. It is gradually revealed to readers by the other elements of the story. We can discover a story's theme by remembering the following points:

- A character may learn a lesson about life from the events of the story.
- A character's personality traits may tell us the author's ideas about people in general.
- Details of setting may tell us the author's idea of the world in general.

- The title may suggest the author's opinion of what happens in the story.

For example, a character in a story is in trouble. He turns to his best friend for help, but his friend cannot help him. Instead, someone he hardly knows comes to his rescue. The implied theme of this story might be that "true friends are those who help in times of need." You should be able to state the theme of a story in one sentence.

Thinking About Implied Theme

■ State the theme of "The Sound of Summer Running" in a sentence. What aspects of character, setting, or title led you to this theme?

COMPOSITION

Writing a Character Sketch

■ Write a character sketch of Douglas in which you discuss his outstanding traits. Examine Douglas' actions, thoughts, words, and feelings in order to determine those traits. *For help with this assignment, see Lesson 3 in the Writing About Literature Handbook at the back of this book.*

Writing a Vivid Description

■ Douglas thinks of vivid experiences that convey the feeling he gets when wearing new sneakers. What experiences might Douglas think of to describe the feelings that accompany the items listed below? Choose one item from the list, and describe the feelings Douglas might have about it. Use vivid language in your description.

a. Seeing an "A" on his big report
b. Having a pebble in his shoe
c. Standing before the class to give a speech
d. Wearing formal clothes
e. Drinking hot chocolate after being in the cold

Mona Gardner (1900–1981) was born in Seattle, Washington. She lived in Hong Kong, South Africa, and California, among other places, and she also traveled widely. Many of her novels and stories are set in Asia. "The Dinner Party," her best-known short story, takes place in India earlier this century, when India was still a colony ruled by Great Britain.

■ As you read the story, look for its theme.

Mona Gardner

The Dinner Party

The country is India. A colonial official and his wife are giving a large dinner party. They are seated with their guests—army officers and government attachés[1] and their wives, and a visiting American naturalist—in their spacious dining room, which has a bare marble floor, open rafters,[2] and wide glass doors opening onto a veranda.

A spirited discussion springs up between a young girl who insists that women have outgrown the jumping-on-a-chair-at-the-sight-of-a-mouse era and a colonel who says that they haven't.

"A woman's unfailing reaction in any crisis," the colonel says, "is to scream. And while a man may feel like it, he has that ounce more of nerve control than a woman has. And that last ounce is what counts."

The American does not join in the argument but watches the other guests. As he looks, he sees a strange expression come over the face of the hostess. She is staring straight ahead, her muscles contracting slightly. With a slight gesture she summons the servant standing behind her chair and whispers to him. The servant's eyes widen, and he quickly leaves the room.

Of the guests, none except the American notices this or sees the servant place a bowl of milk on the veranda just outside the open doors.

The American comes to with a start. In India, milk in a bowl means only one thing—bait for a snake. He realizes there must be a cobra in the room. He looks up at the rafters—the likeliest place—but they are bare. Three corners of the room are empty, and in the fourth the servants are waiting to serve the next course. There is only one place left—under the table.

His first impulse is to jump back and warn the others, but he knows the commotion would frighten the cobra into striking. He speaks quickly, the tone of his voice so arresting that it sobers everyone.

"I want to know just what control everyone

---

1. **attachés** [at′ə shäz′]: persons with special duties on the staff of an ambassador or minister to another country.
2. **rafters:** ceiling beams.

at this table has. I will count three hundred—that's five minutes—and not one of you is to move a muscle. Those who move will forfeit fifty rupees.[3] Ready!"

The twenty people sit like stone images while he counts. He is saying " . . . two hundred and eighty . . . " when, out of the corner of his eye, he sees the cobra emerge and make for the bowl of milk. Screams ring out as he jumps to slam the veranda doors safely shut.

"You were right, Colonel!" the host exclaims. "A man has just shown us an example of perfect control."

"Just a minute," the American says, turning to his hostess. "Mrs. Wynnes,[4] how did you know that cobra was in the room?"

A faint smile lights up the woman's face as she replies: "Because it was crawling across my foot."

---

3. **rupees** [rōo′pēz]: Indian coins. One rupee was worth about ten cents at the time of the story.

4. **Wynnes** [win′əs]

STUDY QUESTIONS

Recalling

1. On what topic do the colonel and the young girl disagree?
2. What does the American notice?
3. What does the American realize the bowl of milk means?
4. Summarize what the American says to make sure that everyone remains perfectly still.
5. After the American slams the veranda doors shut, what does the host say to the colonel? What does the hostess reveal?

Interpreting

6. In what way does the story's end relate to the discussion between the girl and the colonel?
7. What qualities or virtues do both the American and the hostess display?
8. What is the implied theme of this story?

VOCABULARY

Synonyms

A **synonym** is a word that has the same or nearly the same meaning as another word. *Fast* and *quick* are synonyms. The following phrases are from "The Dinner Party." In each phrase one word is in italics. Choose the word that is *nearest the meaning* of each italicized word, *as the word is used in the story*. Write the number of each item and the letter of your choice on a separate sheet.

1. glass doors opening onto a *veranda*
   (a) porch
   (b) attic
   (c) garage
   (d) chimney

2. a *spirited* discussion
   (a) breathless
   (b) ghostly
   (c) jointed
   (d) lively

3. muscles *contracting* slightly
   (a) expanding
   (b) tightening
   (c) building
   (d) pact

4. *summons* the servant
   (a) tickets
   (b) assists
   (c) insults
   (d) calls

5. looks up at the *rafters*
   (a) clouds
   (b) ferries
   (c) beams
   (d) chandelier

CHALLENGE

Oral Research Report

■ Do library research on cobras. How large are they? In what countries are they found? Do they have any unusual habits? Do they have a natural enemy? Share your findings with the class.

Gwendolyn Brooks (born 1917) is best known as a poet. She won the Pulitzer Prize for poetry in 1949 and succeeded Carl Sandburg as poet laureate (official poet) of Illinois. She grew up in Illinois and sets many of her poems and stories there. *Annie Allen*, her Pulitzer Prize–winning poetry collection, is about a black girl growing up in Chicago. The following story is from *Maud Martha*, which explores the same topic in prose.

■ What problem do Maud Martha and her family face in "Home"?

Gwendolyn Brooks

Home

What had been wanted was this always, this always to last, the talking softly on this porch, with the snake plant in the jardiniere[1] in the southwest corner, and the obstinate slip from Aunt Eppie's magnificent Michigan fern at the left side of the friendly door. Mama, Maud Martha, and Helen rocked slowly in their rocking chairs, and looked at the late afternoon light on the lawn and at the emphatic iron of the fence and at the poplar tree. These things might soon be theirs no longer. Those shafts and pools of light, the tree, the graceful iron, might soon be viewed possessively by different eyes.

Papa was to have gone that noon, during his lunch hour, to the office of the Home Owners' Loan. If he had not succeeded in getting another extension, they would be leaving this house in which they had lived for more than fourteen years. There was little hope. The Home Owners' Loan was hard. They sat, making their plans.

"We'll be moving into a nice flat[2] somewhere," said Mama. "Somewhere on South Park, or Michigan, or in Washington Park Court." Those flats, as the girls and Mama knew well, were burdens on wages twice the size of Papa's. This was not mentioned now.

"They're much prettier than this old house," said Helen. "I have friends I'd just as soon not bring here. And I have other friends that wouldn't come down this far for anything, unless they were in a taxi."

Yesterday, Maud Martha would have attacked her. Tomorrow she might. Today she said nothing. She merely gazed at a little hopping robin in the tree, her tree, and tried to keep the fronts of her eyes dry.

"Well, I do know," said Mama, turning her hands over and over, "that I've been getting tireder and tireder of doing that firing.[3] From October to April, there's firing to be done."

"But lately we've been helping, Harry and

---

1. **jardiniere** [järd'ən ēr']: decorative pot for plants.

2. **flat:** apartment.
3. **firing:** starting and tending a wood or coal fire.

I," said Maud Martha. "And sometimes in March and April and in October, and even in November, we could build a little fire in the fireplace. Sometimes the weather was just right for that."

She knew, from the way they looked at her, that this had been a mistake. They did not want to cry.

But she felt that the little line of white, sometimes ridged with smoked purple, and all that cream-shot saffron[4] would never drift across any western sky except that in back of this house. The rain would drum with as sweet a dullness nowhere but here. The birds on South Park were mechanical birds, no better than the poor caught canaries in those "rich" women's sun parlors.

"It's just going to kill Papa!" burst out Maud Martha. "He loves this house! He *lives* for this house!"

"He lives for us," said Helen. "It's us he loves. He wouldn't want the house, except for us."

"And he'll have us," added Mama, "wherever."

"You know," Helen sighed, "if you want to know the truth, this is a relief. If this hadn't come up, we would have gone on, just dragged on, hanging out here forever."

"It might," allowed Mama, "be an act of God. God may just have reached down and picked up the reins."

"Yes," Maud Martha cracked in, "that's what you always say—that God knows best."

Her mother looked at her quickly, decided the statement was not suspect, looked away.

Helen saw Papa coming. "There's Papa," said Helen.

They could not tell a thing from the way Papa was walking. It was that same dear little staccato walk,[5] one shoulder down, then the other, then repeat, and repeat. They watched his progress. He passed the Kennedys', he passed the vacant lot, he passed Mrs. Blakemore's. They wanted to hurl themselves over the fence, into the street, and shake the truth out of his collar. He opened his gate—the gate—and still his stride and face told them nothing.

"Hello," he said.

Mama got up and followed him through the front door. The girls knew better than to go in too.

Presently Mama's head emerged. Her eyes were lamps turned on.

"It's all right," she exclaimed. "He got it. It's all over. Everything is all right."

The door slammed shut. Mama's footsteps hurried away.

"I think," said Helen, rocking rapidly, "I think I'll give a party. I haven't given a party since I was eleven. I'd like some of my friends to just casually see that we're homeowners."

---

4. **saffron** [saf′rən]: orange-yellow color.

5. **staccato** [stə kä′tō] **walk:** a way of walking marked by short, quick, sharp steps.

Recalling

1. What problem does the family face as the story opens? For how long have they lived in their house?
2. What does Helen say about the flats into which the family may have to move?
3. For what does Papa live, according to Maud Martha? What does Helen say to that?
4. What news does Papa bring home?
5. According to the last paragraph, why does Helen want to throw a party?

Interpreting

6. How does the family feel about their house?
7. Why do you think Mama and Helen speak hopefully about moving at the beginning of the story?
8. Although the house is important to the family, what is even more important? Based on your answer, what is the implied theme of the story?

Extending

9. What are some of the things that make a home important to the people who live in it?

READING AND LITERARY FOCUS

Dialogue

Dialogue is conversation between characters. Dialogue presents the exact words of the characters. In short stories these words are put in quotation marks. When a new speech begins, the story gets a new paragraph. Dialogue often includes a tag line such as "he said" or "she asked" to identify the person who is speaking. However, as a dialogue progresses, these tag lines may be dropped. For example:

"Now you've gone and done it," said Mrs. Delahanty, when Cress had gone.

"Done what?" asked Mr. Delahanty, innocently.

"Promised her that monstrosity. And all in the world she wants it for is to parade around Balboa in it tomorrow hoping Edwin will catch sight of her."

We receive information from dialogue. From what characters say we learn about their thoughts and feelings. We also learn what they think about other characters. From dialogue we can make inferences about the characters' personalities and the theme of the story.

Thinking About Dialogue

1. From the dialogue in "Home," what do we learn about the character of the father?
2. Which lines of dialogue point to the theme of the story?

VOCABULARY

Sentence Completions

Each of the following sentences contains a blank with four possible words for completing the sentence. The words are from "Home." Choose the word that best completes each sentence, using the word *as it is used in the selection*. Write the number of each item and the letter of your choice on a separate sheet.

1. The ___ mule refused to budge.
   - (a) lively
   - (b) willing
   - (c) obstinate
   - (d) reserved
2. He responded with a very ___ "No."
   - (a) detailed
   - (b) emphatic
   - (c) brandishing
   - (d) observant
3. They guarded the treasure ___.
   - (a) possessively
   - (b) abruptly
   - (c) carelessly
   - (d) respectively
4. Randy asked the teacher for an ___ on his paper.
   - (a) annulment
   - (b) application
   - (c) easement
   - (d) extension
5. They decided that watering the neighbor's plants would not be a ___.
   - (a) keepsake
   - (b) dedication
   - (c) burden
   - (d) loan

Jesse Stuart (1907–1984) sometimes scrawled poems on empty potato sacks at the farm where he grew up. He went to a one-room schoolhouse but could not attend school regularly because of his farm chores. After graduation he taught school for a time. His poetry and stories deal mostly with the Kentucky hill people whom he knew all his life. The following story is about two farm families clearing their land.

■ What other kind of "clearing" occurs in the story?

Jesse Stuart

The Clearing

Finn and I were pruning the plum trees around our garden when a rock came cracking among the branches of the tree I was pruning.

"Where did that come from?" I asked Finn, who was on the ground below piling the branches.

"I don't know," he said.

Then we heard the Hinton boys laughing on the other side of the valley. I went back to pruning. In less than a minute, a rock hit the limb above my head, and another rock hit at Finn's feet. Then I came down from the tree. Finn and I started throwing rocks. In a few minutes, rocks were falling like hailstones around them and around us. The land was rocky on both sides of the valley, and there were plenty of rocks to throw.

One of their rocks hit Finn on the foot, and one of our rocks hit the largest Hinton boy's head.

"Think of it," Finn said. "We fight before we know each other's names! What will it be as time goes on?"

We fought all afternoon with rocks. At sunset the Hinton boys took off up the path and over the hill. We went home. When Pa asked why we hadn't finished pruning the trees, we told him.

"I told you," he said to Mom. "You'll see whether we can live apart!"

"Wait until we get to know each other," Mom said.

"But how are we ever going to know people like them?" Pa asked.

"Oh, something will happen," she replied calmly. "You'll see."

The next day, Mort Hinton was with his boys. They climbed higher on the hill, cutting the briers and brush and tree branches and stacking them neatly into piles. Finn and I pruned our trees.

"I'll say one thing for the Hintons," Mom said. "They're good workers."

"When they don't throw rocks," Finn said.

On the fourth day, my guinea hens[1] flew across the valley where the Hintons were clearing land.

"Get these hens back on your side of the valley," Mort Hinton yelled. "Get 'em back where they belong."

I didn't want to put my hens in the hen house. But I had to. I knew Mort Hinton would kill them. I wanted to tell him that they would help his land. They'd get rid of insects that might destroy his crop. But I was afraid to tell him anything.

A week had passed before my guinea hens got out and flew across the valley.

"If you don't keep your hens on your side of the valley," Mort Hinton hollered to me, "I'll wring their necks."

That night I put my guinea hens in again. I fixed the hen house so they couldn't get out and roam the hills as they had always done. While Finn, Pa, and I cleared land on one side of the valley, the Hintons cleared on the other side.

Though we'd never been close enough to the Hintons to talk with them, and we didn't want to get that close, we found ourselves trying to do more work than the four of them. Each day, that early March, rain or sunshine, four Hintons worked on their side of the valley, and Pa, Finn, and I worked on our side. One day a Hinton boy hollered at us, "You can't clear as much land as we can."

"Don't answer him," Pa said.

When April came and the Hintons had finished clearing the hill and had burned the brush, Mort Hinton brought a skinny mule hitched to a plow and started plowing the new ground. He plowed slowly the first day. The second day my hens got out again and flew across the valley to the plowed ground. Mort Hinton caught two of them. The others flew back home when he tried to catch them. Then he yelled across to where we were plowing our new ground and told us what he had done.

"Your hens were on his land," Mom said. "He told you to keep them off his land."

Mort Hinton plowed his new ground by working from daylight until dusk, while the boys carried armloads of roots from the field and stacked them in great heaps. By the first of May, they had made this ground soil like a garden. Then came a rainy season in early May, and they carried baskets of tobacco plants and set them in the newly plowed rows.

"They're workers, all right," Pa said.

On a dark night about a week later, I watched a moving light from my upstairs window. It came from the direction of the Hintons', over the hill and down into the valley below our house. In a few minutes, I heard footsteps on the porch. Then there was a loud knock on our door. I heard Pa get out of bed and open the door.

"I'm Mort Hinton," a voice said. "My wife sent for your wife."

I heard Mom getting out of bed.

"I'll be ready in a minute," she called out.

Neither Pa nor Mort said another word.

"I'll be back when everything is all right," Mom said as she hurried off.

I watched the lantern fade from sight as Mort Hinton and Mom went down the path into the deep valley below the house. In two minutes or more, it flashed into sight again when they reached Hinton's tobacco field. The light moved swiftly up and over the hill.

The next morning, Pa cooked breakfast for us. He muttered about the Hintons as he stood near the hot stove frying eggs.

"They are friendly enough when they need something over there," Pa said.

---

1. **guinea** [gin′ē] **hens:** fowl with featherless heads, round bodies, and speckled feathers.

We were ready to sit down to breakfast when Mom came home.

"Dollie Hinton's got a healthy girl baby," were Mom's first words as she sat down for a cup of coffee.

"What did they name the baby?" Glenna asked.

"They've not named her yet," Mom said. "I think they plan to call her Ethel. They're tickled to death. Three boys and now a girl!"

"What kind of people are they, anyway?" Pa asked.

"Like other people," Mom said. "They don't have much furniture in their house. They're working hard to pay for their farm."

"Will they be any better neighbors?" Pa asked.

"I think so," Mom said. "That hill over there is not a fence between us any longer."

"There's more than a hill between us," I said. "What about my hens Mort Hinton caught? Did he say anything about 'em last night?"

"And what about the Hinton boy that hit me on the foot with a rock?" Finn said. "I'd like to meet up with him sometime."

By the time we had finished our breakfast, Mort Hinton was plowing the young tobacco. His three sons were hoeing the tender plants with long-handled hoes.

"You'd think Mr. Hinton would be sleepy," Mom said. "He didn't go to bed last night. And the boys slept on the hay in the barn loft."

Pa, Finn, and I didn't have too much sympathy for the Hintons. Through the dining-room window, we could look across the valley and watch Mort keep the plow moving steadily. We watched his boys dig with their hoes, never looking up from the ground.

"This will be a dry, sunny day," Pa said. "We'll burn the brush piles on the rest of our clearing."

We gathered our pitchforks, hoes, and rakes and went to the hill where we had cleared ground all spring. There were hundreds of brush piles on our twenty acres of cleared ground. The wind was still. The sun had dried the dew from the leaves that carpeted the ground between the brush piles.

"It's the right time to burn," Pa said. "I can't feel any wind. The brush has aged in these piles until it is as dry as powder."

Pa struck a match to the brush pile at the bottom of the clearing. The fire started with little leaps over the leaf-carpeted ground. Finn, Pa, and I set fire to the bottom of the clearing until we had a continuous line of fire going up the slope. Then a wind sprang up from nowhere. And when flames leaped from brush pile to brush pile, Pa looked at me.

"This is out of control," Pa said. "Grab a hoe and start raking a ring."

"I'm afraid we can't stop it," Finn said. "We'll have to work fast to save the orchards."

"Run to the house and get Sal and Glenna," Pa yelled.

"Look, Pa," Finn said, pointing down the hill.

Mort Hinton was in front. He was running up the hill. His three sons were running behind him, each with a hoe across his shoulder.

"It's out of control," Pa shouted to Mort before he reached us.

"We've come to help," Mort said.

"Can we keep it from the orchards?" Pa asked.

"Let's run to the top of the hill and fire against it," Mort said. "I've burnt hundreds of acres of clearings on hillsides, and I always fire the top first and let it burn down! I fire the bottom last. Maybe we'll not be too late to save the orchards!"

Mort ran up the hill and we followed. Finn and I didn't speak to his boys, and they didn't speak to us. But when we started raking a ring side by side, we started talking to the Hintons. We forgot about the rock fight. Now wasn't the time to remember it, when flames down under the hill were shooting twenty to thirty feet high. In no time, we raked the ring across the top of the clearing. And the fire Mort Hinton set along the ring burned fiercely

down the hill and made the ring wider and wider. Only once did fire blow across the ring, and Pa stopped it then.

As soon as we had this spot under control, we raked a ring down the west side near the peach orchard. Mort set a line of fire along this ring and let it burn toward the middle of the clearing. Then we raked a ring on the east side and fired against the fire that was approaching our plum trees and our house. Soon the leaping flames met in the clearing. We had the fire under control. Our clearing was burned clean as a whistle.

"How much do I owe you?" Pa asked Mort Hinton.

"You don't owe me anything," Mort said. "We're just paying you back for the help your wife gave us."

"Then let's go to the house for dinner," Pa said.

"Some other time," Mort said. "We must go home and see about Dollie and the baby."

As we went down the hill, Finn and I talked with the Hinton boys about fishing and wild-bee trees, while Pa and Mort laughed and talked about weather and crops.

STUDY QUESTIONS

Recalling

1. What happens the first time Finn and the narrator encounter the Hinton boys?
2. What is the one good thing Mom says about the Hintons near the beginning of the story?
3. What does Mort Hinton threaten to do if guinea hens come onto his land?
4. What favor does Mort Hinton come to ask one night? What do he and his sons do to repay the favor?
5. At the end of the story, what do Finn and the narrator do as they go down the hill?

Interpreting

6. What change occurs in the way the two families behave toward each other? What do the boys realize about one another at the end of the story?
7. Is the theme of this story stated or implied? What is the theme?

Extending

8. Why is it good to be on friendly terms with neighbors? What are some of the ways to help neighbors?

READING AND LITERARY FOCUS

Title

The **title**, or name, of a short story usually refers to an important plot event, to a character, or to the setting of the story. For example, the title "The Hummingbird That Lived Through Winter" reveals an important plot event—the hummingbird lived through the winter. The title "The Just Judge" draws attention to an important character. The title "The Snow in Chelm" tells where the story is set and at what time of year it takes place.

Sometimes a title can also be a clue to the story's theme, or main idea. For example, the title "The Sound of Summer Running" hints at the idea that summer is a time for activity. When we read the story, we see that indeed the story focuses on a young man's excitement about summertime activities. We should try to recognize the insight the title gives into the meaning of a story.

Thinking About Title

1. To what major plot event does the title of "The Clearing" refer?
2. What else does *clearing* mean? How does this second meaning direct attention to the theme of the story?

COMPOSITION

Writing About Plot

■ Write a paragraph about the plot of "The Clearing." First explain what the conflict is. Then tell between whom the conflict exists. Explain the problems that make it difficult for the characters to resolve the conflict. Finally, tell how the story ends. *For help with this assignment, see Lesson 2 in the Writing About Literature Handbook at the back of this book.*

Writing Story Titles

■ Give new titles to two of the short stories in this section on theme, pages 144–167. Each of your titles should relate to the story's plot, characters, or setting. Your titles should also point to the story's theme. Try to create one title that has a double meaning, as does the title "The Clearing." In a paragraph tell why you have chosen these new titles.

COMPARING STORIES

1. Compare at least two of the following characters. Who acts more bravely? Explain.

   a. the mother sparrow in "The Sparrow"
   b. the hostess in "The Dinner Party"
   c. the narrator's mother in "The Clearing"

2. Compare two or more of the following stories: "The Glorious Whitewasher," "The Sound of Summer Running," and "Home." In which story is devotion to a cause strongest?

THE TOTAL EFFECT

When we read a good story, we are caught up in the world that it creates. We want to find out what will happen in the plot. We begin to think of the characters as people whom we know. We step into the **setting,** or time and place in which the story occurs. We try to understand the **theme**—what the author may be saying to us about life in general.

The more we enter into a story, the more we enjoy it. We can enter into a story more fully if we become aware of each element in it. If we are active, alert readers, we will notice each twist in the plot. We will pick up more information about the characters, setting, and theme. We will also see how these elements all work together to create a **total effect,** the story's overall impact.

Different people will notice different things in any story. However, an active reader will always think about the individual elements and their total effect. The following points can remind you of how each element adds to a story's total effect:

Reminders for Active Reading of Short Stories

1. The **title** can help you to understand the story's theme.
2. The **plot** revolves around a conflict. Suspense builds until the climax. The resolution is the final outcome.
3. Personalities of **characters** are revealed by what they do or say, by what others say about them, and by what the author says about them.
4. **Setting** is the time and place of a story. Setting can also create atmosphere, or mood.
5. The **theme,** or main idea, of a story can be stated directly, or it can be implied by the other elements.

Model for Active Reading

On the following pages you will see how an alert reader used these reminders while reading "A Secret for Two." Notes in the margin represent comments and questions that the reader formed while becoming involved in the story. Each note gives a page reference for further information about the item in question. Read the selection first for your own enjoyment. Then read it again with the notes, and try to answer the questions in the notes. Later you can use the process followed in this model as you read any short story.

Quentin James Reynolds (1902–1965) grew up in Brooklyn, New York. He studied law and then went into journalism. During World War II Reynolds became famous as a war correspondent, covering the battle fronts in North Africa and Europe. Reynolds was also a sportswriter and an author of short stories. "A Secret for Two" is one of his best-known works.

How does he surprise us in this story?

Quentin Reynolds

A Secret for Two

Montreal[1] is a very large city, but, like all large cities, it has some very small streets. Streets, for instance, like Prince Edward Street, which is only four blocks long, ending in a cul-de-sac.[2] No one knew Prince Edward Street as well as did Pierre Dupin,[3] for Pierre had delivered milk to the families on the street for thirty years now.

During the past fifteen years the horse which drew the milk wagon used by Pierre was a large white horse named Joseph. In Montreal, especially in that part of Montreal which is very French, the animals, like children, are often given the names of saints. When the big white horse first came to the Provincale[4] Milk Company, he didn't have a name. They told Pierre that he could use the white horse henceforth. Pierre stroked the softness of the horse's neck; he stroked the sheen of its splendid belly, and he looked into the eyes of the horse.

The **setting** (p. 131) is the time and place in which a story occurs. What is the setting of this story?

The **narrator** (p. 115 and p. 126) is the person who tells a story. Is this story told by a first-person narrator or a third-person narrator?

---

1. **Montreal** [mon′trē ôl′]: large city in the province of Quebec in southeastern Canada. French and English are the official languages, but French is widely spoken.
2. **cul-de-sac** [kul′də sak′]: street that is closed at one end; dead end.
3. **Pierre Dupin** [pē är′ dü pan′]
4. **Provincale** [prō van säl′]

"That is a kind horse, a gentle and a faithful horse," Pierre said, "and I can see a beautiful spirit shining out of the eyes of the horse. I will name him after good St. Joseph, who was also kind and gentle and faithful and a beautiful spirit."

Within a year Joseph knew the milk route as well as Pierre. Pierre used to boast that he didn't need reins—he never touched them. Each morning Pierre arrived at the stables of the Provincale Milk Company at five o'clock. The wagon would be loaded and Joseph hitched to it. Pierre would call *"Bon jour, vieille ami,"*[5] as he climbed into his seat and Joseph would turn his head and the other drivers would smile and say that the horse would smile at Pierre. Then Jacques,[6] the foreman, would say, "All right, Pierre, go on," and Pierre would call softly to Joseph, *"Avance, mon ami,"*[7] and this splendid combination would stalk proudly down the street.

The wagon, without any direction from Pierre, would roll three blocks down St. Catherine Street, then turn right two blocks along Roslyn Avenue; then left, for that was Prince Edward Street. The horse would stop at the first house, allow Pierre perhaps thirty seconds to get down from his seat and put a bottle of milk at the front door and would then go on, skipping two houses and stopping at the third. So down the length of the street. Then Joseph, still without any direction from Pierre, would turn around and come back along the other side. Yes, Joseph was a smart horse.

Pierre would boast at the stable of Joseph's skill. "I never touch the reins. He knows just where to stop. Why, a blind man could handle my route with Joseph pulling the wagon."

So it went on for years—always the same. Pierre and Joseph both grew old together, but gradually, not suddenly. Pierre's huge walrus mustache was pure white now and Joseph didn't lift his knees so high or raise his head quite as much. Jacques, the foreman of the stables, never noticed that they were both getting old until Pierre appeared one day carrying a heavy walking stick.

"Hey, Pierre," Jacques laughed. "Maybe you got the gout,[8] hey?"

"Mais oui,"[9] Jacques," Pierre said uncertainly. "One grows old. One's legs get tired."

---

5. *Bon jour, vieille ami* [bôn zhoor′ vē ā′ äm ē′]: French for "hello, old friend."
6. *Jacques* [zhäk]
7. *Avance, mon ami* [ä väns′ môn äm ē′]: French for "forward, my friend."
8. **gout** [gout]: disease that causes swelling of the joints.
9. *Mais oui* [mä wē′]: French for "but yes."

Characterization (p. 109) is the method by which an author reveals a character's personality. What do we learn about Joseph from Pierre's statements here? What trait of Joseph's does the narrator *directly state* in paragraph 5?

Details lead us to **make inferences** (p. 100), or draw conclusions about a story. What can you infer about Pierre's feelings for his job and Joseph from these details?

The **conflict** (p. 79 and p. 85) is the problem around which the story revolves. What is the conflict in this story?

"You should teach the horse to carry the milk to the front door for you," Jacques told him. "He does everything else."

He knew every one of the forty families he served on Prince Edward Street. The cooks knew that Pierre could neither read nor write, so instead of following the usual custom of leaving a note in an empty bottle if an additional quart of milk was needed they would sing out when they heard the rumble of his wagon wheels over the cobbled street, "Bring an extra quart this morning, Pierre."

Pierre had a remarkable memory. When he arrived at the stable he'd always remember to tell Jacques, "The Paquins[10] took an extra quart this morning; the Lemoines[11] bought a pint of cream."

Jacques would note these things in a little book he always carried. Most of the drivers had to make out the weekly bills and collect the money, but Jacques, liking Pierre, had always excused him from this task. All Pierre had to do was to arrive at five in the morning, walk to his wagon, which was always in the same spot at the curb, and deliver his milk. He returned some two hours later, got stiffly from his seat, called a cheery *"Au 'voir"*[12] to Jacques and then limped slowly down the street.

One morning the president of the Provincale Milk Company came to inspect the early morning deliveries. Jacques pointed Pierre out to him and said, "Watch how he talks to that horse. See how the horse listens and how he turns his head toward Pierre? See the look in that horse's eyes? You know, I think those two share a secret. I have often noticed it. It is as though they both sometimes chuckle at us as they go off on their route. Pierre is a good man, Monsieur[13] President, but he gets old. Would it be too bold for me to suggest that he be retired and be given perhaps a small pension?" he added anxiously.

"But of course," the president laughed. "I know his record. He has been on this route now for thirty years and never once has there been a complaint. Tell him it is time he rested. His salary will go on just the same."

But Pierre refused to retire. He was panic-stricken at the thought of not driving Joseph every day. "We are two old men," he said to Jacques. "Let us wear out together. When Joseph is ready to retire—then I, too, will quit."

> **Dialogue** (p. 161) is conversation between characters. What reference to the title occurs in Jacques's dialogue with the company president?

> **Motivation** (p. 105) is the reason that a character acts in a certain way. Why does Pierre refuse to retire?

---

10. **Paquins** [pä kan′]
11. **Lemoines** [lə mwan′]
12. *Au 'voir* [ō vwär′]: au revoir, French for "good-bye."
13. **Monsieur** [mə syœ′]: French for "mister."

Jacques, who was a kind man, understood. There was something about Pierre and Joseph which made a man smile tenderly. It was as though each drew some hidden strength from the other. When Pierre was sitting in his seat, and when Joseph was hitched to the wagon, neither seemed old. But when they finished their work, then Pierre would limp down the street slowly, seeming very old indeed, and the horse's head would drop and he would walk very wearily to his stall.

Then one morning Jacques had dreadful news for Pierre when he arrived. It was a cold morning and still pitch-dark. The air was like iced wine that morning and the snow which had fallen during the night glistened like a million diamonds piled together.

Jacques said, "Pierre, your horse, Joseph, did not wake this morning. He was very old, Pierre, he was twenty-five, and that is like seventy-five for a man."

"Yes," Pierre said, slowly. "Yes, I am seventy-five. And I cannot see Joseph again."

"Of course you can," Jacques soothed. "He is over in his stall, looking very peaceful. Go over and see him."

Pierre took one step forward then turned. "No . . . no . . . you don't understand, Jacques."

Jacques clapped him on the shoulder. "We'll find another horse just as good as Joseph. Why, in a month you'll teach him to know your route as well as Joseph did. We'll . . ."

The look in Pierre's eyes stopped him. For years Pierre had worn a heavy cap, the peak of which came low over his eyes, keeping the bitter morning wind out of them. Now Jacques looked into Pierre's eyes and he saw something which startled him. He saw a dead, lifeless look in them. The eyes were mirroring the grief that was in Pierre's heart and his soul. It was as though his heart and soul had died.

"Take today off, Pierre," Jacques said, but already Pierre was hobbling off down the street, and had one been near one would have seen tears streaming down his cheeks and have heard half-smothered sobs. Pierre walked to the corner and stepped into the street. There was a warning yell from the driver of a huge truck that was coming fast and there was a scream of brakes, but Pierre apparently heard neither.

Five minutes later an ambulance driver said, "He's dead. Was killed instantly."

Jacques and several of the milk-wagon drivers had arrived and they looked down at the still figure.

"I couldn't help it," the driver of the truck protested, "he

Atmosphere (p. 131), or mood, is created by details of setting. What atmosphere is created in this paragraph? How does this paragraph fore-shadow (p. 91), or hint at, the news Jacques tells Pierre in the next paragraph?

The plot moves toward a cli-max (p. 65), the point of our highest interest. Afterward the plot continues to a resolution, the story's final outcome. What are the climax and reso-lution that follow in this story?

walked right into my truck. He never saw it, I guess. Why, he walked into it as though he was blind."

The ambulance doctor bent down. "Blind? Of course the man was blind. See those cataracts?[14] This man has been blind for five years." He turned to Jacques, "You say he worked for you? Didn't you know he was blind?"

"No . . . no . . ." Jacques said, softly. "None of us knew. Only one knew—a friend of his named Joseph. . . . It was a secret, I think, just between those two."

The **title** (p. 166) of a story can be a clue to the story's **theme** (p. 145 and p. 156), the idea about life that the story communicates. What does the title of this story mean? What is the story's theme?

---

14. **cataracts** [kat′ə rakts′]: lenses of the eyes that have become cloudy.

STUDY QUESTIONS

Recalling

1. What is Pierre's job? Who is Joseph, and how does he get his name?
2. In the sixth paragraph what boast does Pierre make about Joseph?
3. What does the company president offer Pierre? What is Pierre's answer?
4. What eventually happens to Joseph? What then happens to Pierre?
5. What does the ambulance doctor reveal about Pierre?

Interpreting

6. In your own words tell what sort of relationship Pierre and Joseph share.
7. Why do you think Pierre keeps his problem a secret? What does this behavior suggest about him?
8. Point out two places where foreshadowing prepares us for the story's surprise ending.
9. What does the story say about friendship?

COMPOSITION

Writing a Character Sketch

■ Write a character sketch of Pierre in "A Secret for Two." First briefly identify Pierre, explaining who he is, how old he is, what he does for a living, and so on. Then discuss what you consider to be Pierre's outstanding traits as a character. For each trait give one or two examples of Pierre's behavior in "A Secret for Two." *For help with this assignment, see Lesson 3 in the Writing About Literature Handbook at the back of this book.*

Writing a Story

■ Write a story that has a surprise ending. Be sure that your story's sequence of events is logical. Describe your characters and setting clearly. You may want to give your reader a hint or two to foreshadow the ending. *For help with this assignment, see Lesson 4 in the Writing About Literature Handbook at the back of this book.*

O. Henry (1862–1910), whose real name was William Sydney Porter, is one of America's most colorful writers. He grew up in Greensboro, North Carolina. He then moved to Texas, writing for a Houston newspaper and working in an Austin bank. He also spent time in New Orleans and Honduras before finally settling in New York City. He completed twelve volumes of short stories. Many of them are famous for surprise endings.

■ Which characters are surprised by the events of "After Twenty Years"?

O. Henry

After Twenty Years

The policeman on the beat moved up the avenue impressively. The impressiveness was habitual and not for show, for spectators were few. The time was barely ten o'clock at night, but chilly gusts of wind with a taste of rain in them had well nigh[1] depeopled the streets.

Trying doors as he went, twirling his club with many intricate and artful movements, turning now and then to cast his watchful eye down the pacific thoroughfare,[2] the officer, with his stalwart[3] form and slight swagger,[4] made a fine picture of a guardian of the peace. The vicinity was one that kept early hours. Now and then you might see the lights of a cigar store or of an all-night lunch counter; but the majority of the doors belonged to business places that had long since been closed.

When about midway of a certain block, the policeman suddenly slowed his walk. In the doorway of a darkened hardware store a man leaned, with an unlighted cigar in his mouth. As the policeman walked up to him, the man spoke up quickly.

"It's all right, officer," he said, reassuringly. "I'm just waiting for a friend. It's an appointment made twenty years ago. Sounds a little funny to you, doesn't it? Well, I'll explain if you'd like to make certain it's all straight. About that long ago there used to be a restaurant where this store stands—'Big Joe' Brady's restaurant."

"Until five years ago," said the policeman. "It was torn down then."

The man in the doorway struck a match and lit his cigar. The light showed a pale, square-jawed face with keen eyes, and a little white scar near his right eyebrow. His scarfpin was a large diamond, oddly set.

"Twenty years ago tonight," said the man, "I dined here at 'Big Joe' Brady's with Jimmy Wells, my best chum, and the finest chap in the world. He and I were raised here in New York, just like two brothers, together. I was eighteen and Jimmy was twenty. The next

---
1. **well nigh** [nī]: almost.
2. **pacific thoroughfare:** quiet street.
3. **stalwart** [stôl'wərt]: strong, brave.
4. **swagger:** bold walk.

morning I was to start for the West to make my fortune. You couldn't have dragged Jimmy out of New York, he thought it was the only place on earth. Well, we agreed that night that we would meet here again exactly twenty years from that date and time, no matter what our conditions might be or from what distance we might have to come. We figured that in twenty years each of us ought to have our destiny worked out and our fortunes made, whatever they were going to be."

"It sounds pretty interesting," said the policeman. "Rather a long time between meets, though, it seems to me. Haven't you heard from your friend since you left?"

"Well, yes, for a time we corresponded," said the other. "But after a year or two we lost track of each other. You see, the West is a pretty big proposition, and I kept hustling around over it pretty lively. But I know Jimmy will meet me here if he's still alive, for he always was the truest, staunchest[5] old chap in the world. He'll never forget. I came a thousand miles to stand in this door tonight, and it's worth it if my old partner turns up."

The waiting man pulled out a handsome watch, the lids of it set with small diamonds.

"Three minutes to ten," he announced. "It was exactly ten o'clock when we parted here at the restaurant door."

"Did pretty well out West, didn't you?" asked the policeman.

"You bet! I hope Jimmy has done half as well. He was a kind of plodder, though, good fellow as he was. I've had to compete with some of the sharpest wits going to get my pile. A man gets in a groove in New York. It takes the West to put a razor-edge on him."

The policeman twirled his club and took a step or two.

"I'll be on my way. Hope your friend comes

___

5. **staunchest** [stônch′ist]: most dependable.

around all right. Going to call time on him sharp?"

"I should say not!" said the other. "I'll give him half an hour at least. If Jimmy is alive on earth he'll be here by that time. So long, Officer."

"Good-night, sir," said the policeman, passing on along his beat, trying doors as he went.

There was now a fine, cold drizzle falling, and the wind had risen from its uncertain puffs into a steady blow. The few foot passengers astir in that quarter hurried dismally and silently along with coat collars turned high and pocketed hands. And in the door of the hardware store the man who had come a thousand miles to fill an appointment, uncertain almost to absurdity, with the friend of his youth, smoked his cigar and waited.

About twenty minutes he waited, and then a tall man in a long overcoat, with collar turned up to his ears, hurried across from the opposite side of the street. He went directly to the waiting man.

"Is that you, Bob?" he asked doubtfully.

"Is that you, Jimmy Wells?" cried the man in the door.

"Bless my heart!" exclaimed the new arrival, grasping both the other's hands with his own. "It's Bob, sure as fate. I was certain I'd find you here if you were still in existence. Well, well, well!—twenty years is a long time. The old restaurant's gone, Bob; I wish it had lasted, so we could have had another dinner there. How has the West treated you, old man?"

"Bully; it has given me everything I asked it for. You've changed lots, Jimmy. I never thought you were so tall by two or three inches."

"Oh, I grew a bit after I was twenty."

"Doing well in New York, Jimmy?"

"Moderately. I have a position in one of the city's departments. Come on, Bob; we'll go around to a place I know of, and have a good long talk about old times."

The two men started up the street, arm in arm. The man from the West, his egotism enlarged by success, was beginning to outline the history of his career. The other, submerged in his overcoat, listened with interest.

At the corner stood a drugstore, brilliant with electric lights. When they came into this glare each of them turned simultaneously to gaze upon the other's face.

The man from the West stopped suddenly and released his arm.

"You're not Jimmy Wells," he snapped. "Twenty years is a long time, but not long enough to change a man's nose from a Roman to a pug."

"It sometimes changes a good man into a bad one," said the tall man. "You've been under arrest for ten minutes, 'Silky' Bob. Chicago thinks you may have dropped over our way and wires us she wants to have a chat with you. Going quietly, are you? That's sensible. Now, before we go to the station here's a note I was asked to hand to you. You may read it here at the window. It's from Patrolman Wells."

The man from the West unfolded the little piece of paper handed him. His hand was steady when he began to read, but it trembled a little by the time he had finished. The note was rather short.

Bob:
  I was at the appointed place on time. When you struck the match to light your cigar I saw it was the face of the man wanted in Chicago. Somehow I couldn't do it myself, so I went around and got a plainclothesman to do the job.

Jimmy

STUDY QUESTIONS

Recalling

1. For whom is the man from the West waiting? What promise did he make twenty years ago?
2. What does the Westerner tell the policeman on the beat about Jimmy's character?
3. According to the Westerner, what happens to someone in New York? In contrast, what does the West do to a person?
4. After the policeman on the beat leaves, who approaches the Westerner? Tell what happens after the two men see each other's faces.
5. What does Jimmy reveal in his note?

Interpreting

6. What sort of person is "Silky" Bob? Give examples of his appearance and behavior.
7. What sort of person do you think Jimmy Wells is? Describe his internal conflict.
8. In what way has Jimmy been less successful than his friend? In what way has he been more successful?
9. What do you think this story is saying about success? What might it be saying about people's expectations of the future?

READING AND LITERARY FOCUS

The Total Effect: Irony

In the works you have read so far, you have studied the most important elements of short stories: plot, character, setting, and theme. Keep in mind that these elements are all part of a unified story. They work together to create a **total effect**—the story's overall impact on the reader.

The total effect of one story can differ dramatically from the total effect of another story. For example, the total effect of one story—such as "Home" (page 159)—may be its true-to-life quality. The total effect of another story—such as "The Sneaker Crisis" (page 59)—may be its ability to make us laugh.

In some stories the total effect is one of irony. A story is **ironic** when it focuses on the difference between the way things seem to be and the way they actually are. For example, the total effect in "A Secret for Two" (page 169) is one of touching irony. Pierre seems to be a proud milkman; at the story's end we learn that he is blind and relies completely on his horse. Pierre and Joseph seem to be good partners. At the end of the story, we learn that their relationship goes much deeper and is actually a matter of life and death. The plot, characters, setting, and theme of the story all contribute to the total effect of irony.

Thinking About the Total Effect

1. **Plot:** As "After Twenty Years" opens, what does "Silky" Bob expect to happen? What unexpected event happens to him at the story's end?
2. **Character:** What do we think about the policeman on the beat and about Bob at the beginning of the story? What surprising facts do we learn about each at the story's end?
3. **Setting:** How does the darkness of the street help Jimmy to keep his identity secret?
4. **Theme:** What idea does the story communicate about life and the way people can change?
5. **Total Effect:** Based on your answers to the preceding questions, describe the story's total effect, or overall impact, on you.

CHALLENGE

Literary Criticism

■ Critic Martin Seymour-Smith describes the basic pattern in an O. Henry story:

> a beginning calculated to arouse curiosity and provoke a guess; a demonstration that this . . . guess is wrong; a surprise ending with the famous ingenious "twist."

Does "After Twenty Years" follow this pattern? Explain with examples from the story.

In World War II Roald Dahl (1916–1990) served as a fighter pilot in Britain's Royal Air Force. His first collection of stories dealt with his wartime experiences. He wrote many more short stories, a number of which are full of suspense. He was also the author of *Charlie and the Chocolate Factory,* an award-winning book for children. "The Wish" is a story about a dangerous journey.

■ In what sense is the journey in "The Wish" unusual? What actually creates the dangers in the story?

Roald Dahl

The Wish

Under the palm of one hand the child became aware of the scab of an old cut on his kneecap. He bent forward to examine it closely. A scab was always a fascinating thing; it presented a special challenge he was never able to resist.

Yes, he thought, I will pick it off, even if it isn't ready, even if the middle of it sticks, even if it hurts like anything.

With a fingernail he began to explore cautiously around the edges of the scab. He got the nail underneath, and when he raised it, but ever so slightly, it suddenly came off, the whole hard brown scab came off beautifully, leaving an interesting little circle of smooth red skin.

Nice. Very nice indeed. He rubbed the circle and it didn't hurt. He picked up the scab, put it on his thigh, and flipped it with a finger so that it flew away and landed on the edge of the carpet, the enormous red and black and yellow carpet that stretched the whole length of the hall from the stairs on which he sat to the front door in the distance. A tremendous carpet. Bigger than the tennis lawn. Much

bigger than that. He regarded it gravely, settling his eyes upon it with mild pleasure. He had never really noticed it before, but now, all of a sudden, the colors seemed to brighten mysteriously and spring out at him in a most dazzling way.

You see, he told himself, I know how it is. The red parts of the carpet are red-hot lumps of coal. What I must do is this: I must walk all the way along it to the front door without touching them. If I touch the red I will be burnt. As a matter of fact, I will be burnt up completely. And the black parts of the carpet . . . yes, the black parts are snakes, poisonous snakes, adders mostly, and cobras, thick like tree trunks round the middle, and if I touch one of *them,* I'll be bitten and I'll die before tea time. And if I get across safely, without being burnt and without being bitten, I will be given a puppy for my birthday tomorrow.

He got to his feet and climbed higher up the stairs to obtain a better view of this vast tapestry of color and death. Was it possible? Was there enough yellow? Yellow was the only color he was allowed to walk on. Could it be

He came slowly down the stairs and advanced to the edge of the carpet. He extended one small sandaled foot and placed it cautiously upon a patch of yellow. Then he brought the other foot up, and there was just enough room for him to stand with the two feet together. There! He had started! His bright oval face was curiously intent,[1] a shade whiter perhaps than before, and he was holding his arms out sideways to assist his balance. He took another step, lifting his foot high over a patch of black, aiming carefully with his toe for a narrow channel of yellow on the other side. When he had completed the second step he paused to rest, standing very stiff and still. The narrow channel of yellow ran forward unbroken for at least five yards and he advanced gingerly along it, bit by bit, as though walking a tightrope. Where it finally curled off sideways, he had to take another long stride, this time over a vicious looking mixture of black and red. Halfway across he began to wobble. He waved his arms around wildly, windmill fashion, to keep his balance, and he got across safely and rested again on the other side. He was quite breathless now, and so tense he stood high on his toes all the time, arms out sideways, fists clenched. He was on a big safe island of yellow. There was

done? This was not a journey to be undertaken lightly; the risks were too great for that. The child's face—a fringe of white-gold hair, two large blue eyes, a small pointed chin— peered down anxiously over the banisters. The yellow was a bit thin in places and there were one or two widish gaps, but it did seem to go all the way along to the other end. For someone who had only yesterday triumphantly traveled the whole length of the brick path from the stables to the summerhouse without touching the cracks, this carpet thing should not be too difficult. Except for the snakes. The mere thought of snakes sent a fine electricity of fear running like pins down the backs of his legs and under the soles of his feet.

---

1. **intent:** firmly fixed; determined.

lots of room on it—he couldn't possibly fall off—and he stood there resting, hesitating, waiting, wishing he could stay forever on this big safe yellow island. But the fear of not getting the puppy compelled him to go on.

Step by step, he edged further ahead, and between each one he paused to decide exactly where next he should put his foot. Once, he had a choice of ways, either to left or right, and he chose the left because although it seemed the more difficult, there was not so much black in that direction. The black was what made him nervous. He glanced quickly over his shoulder to see how far he had come. Nearly halfway. There could be no turning back now. He was in the middle and he couldn't turn back and he couldn't jump off sideways either because it was too far, and when he looked at all the red and all the black that lay ahead of him, he felt that old sudden sickening surge of panic in his chest—like last Easter time, that afternoon when he got lost all alone in the darkest part of Piper's Wood.

He took another step, placing his foot carefully upon the only little piece of yellow within reach, and this time the point of the foot came within a centimeter[2] of some black. It wasn't touching the black, he could see it wasn't touching, he could see the small line of yellow separating the toe of his sandal from the black; but the snake stirred as though sensing the nearness, and raised its head and gazed at the foot with bright beady eyes, watching to see if it was going to touch.

"I'm not touching you! You mustn't bite me! You know I'm not touching you!"

Another snake slid up noiselessly beside the first, raised its head, two heads now, two pairs of eyes staring at the foot, gazing at a little naked place just below the sandal strap where the skin showed through. The child went high up on his toes and stayed there, frozen stiff with terror. It was minutes before he dared to move again.

The next step would have to be a really long one. There was this deep curling river of black that ran clear across the width of the carpet, and he was forced by his position to cross it at its widest part. He thought first of trying to jump it, but decided he couldn't be sure of landing accurately on the narrow band of yellow on the other side. He took a deep breath, lifted one foot, and inch by inch he pushed it out in front of him, far far out, then down and down until at last the tip of his sandal was across and resting safely on the edge of the yellow. He leaned forward, transferring his weight to this front foot. Then he tried to bring the back foot up as well. He strained and pulled and jerked his body, but the legs were too wide apart and he couldn't make it. He tried to get back again. He couldn't do that either. He was doing the splits and he was properly stuck. He glanced down and saw this deep curling river of black underneath him. Parts of it were stirring now, and uncoiling and sliding and beginning to shine with a dreadful oily glister.[3] He wobbled, waved his arms frantically to keep his balance, but that seemed to make it worse. He was starting to go over. He was going over to the right, quite slowly he was going over, then faster and faster, and at the last moment, instinctively he put out a hand to break the fall and the next thing he saw was this bare hand of his going right into the middle of a great glistening mass of black and he gave one piercing cry of terror as it touched.

Outside in the sunshine, far away behind the house, the mother was looking for her son.

---

2. **centimeter:** about two-fifths of an inch.

3. **glister:** shine.

STUDY QUESTIONS

Recalling

1. Explain what the boy imagines the red and black parts of the carpet to be.
2. What does the boy think he must do to cross the carpet safely? What does he believe he will be given if he succeeds?
3. Does the boy succeed in crossing? Explain.

Interpreting

4. How old do you think the boy in the story is? Why do you think so?
5. What else can you infer, or figure out, about the boy? For example, does he seem to have friends? Why might he want a puppy?
6. Where do the danger and excitement of the plot actually take place?
7. What is the effect of the very last sentence?
8. What idea about the imagination does the story communicate?

Extending

9. Why might children be more likely than adults to be carried away by their imagination?

VOCABULARY

Analogies

Analogies are comparisons that are stated as double relationships: for example, *A* is to *B* as *C* is to *D*. On tests analogies are written as two pairs of words, *A* : *B* :: *C* : *D*. You may be given the first pair and asked to find or complete a second pair that has the same kind of relationship. For example, in the analogy WARM : HOT :: LOUD : DEAFENING, the words in each pair are different degrees of the same quality.

Analogies can state many different kinds of relationships. Here are some examples:

- synonyms (FALL : AUTUMN)
- opposites (UP : DOWN)
- cause and effect (NIGHTMARE : FRIGHT)

The following numbered items are analogies that need to be completed. The third word in each item comes from "The Wish." Decide how the first two words in each item are related. Then from the four choices that follow each item, choose the word that best completes the second pair.

1. DRESS : SEW :: TAPESTRY :
   (a) paint   (c) hang
   (b) clean   (d) weave

2. EXPAND : GROW :: WOBBLE :
   (a) fix   (c) fall
   (b) shake   (d) unsafe

3. MESSY : NEAT :: CLENCHED :
   (a) fist   (c) tight
   (b) relaxed   (d) squeezed

4. FREEZING : COLD :: DAZZLING :
   (a) bright   (c) dark
   (b) sun   (d) warm

5. SOARING : EAGLE :: UNCOILING :
   (a) straight   (c) spring
   (b) winding   (d) rattlesnake

COMPOSITION

Writing About Setting

■ Contrast the actual setting of "The Wish" with the setting that the boy imagines. Begin by explaining briefly where the boy is and where he imagines himself to be. Then choose two or three details from the actual setting, and explain what each becomes in the boy's imagination. End by saying which setting seems more "real" to you by the end of the story. Why?

Writing an Imaginative Description

■ Write an imaginative description of something that is actually quite ordinary, as Roald Dahl does in "The Wish." For example, you might write about wallpaper, a school bulletin board, or the pattern on someone's clothing. Your composition could begin: "Sometimes the wallpaper in my room makes me think of. . . ."

Michael McLaverty (born 1904) comes from Belfast, Northern Ireland. He originally planned to become a scientist, studying experimental physics in college. In 1938 he published his first novel. He considers his best work to be *Lost Fields*, which concerns a grandmother who lives in the city but longs for the country life she once knew.

■ What signs can you find in "The Wild Duck's Nest" of McLaverty's love of nature? What signs can you find of the scientist's attention to detail?

Michael McLaverty

The Wild Duck's Nest

The sun was setting, spilling gold light on the low western hills of Rathlin Island.[1] A small boy walked jauntily[2] along a hoof-printed path that wriggled between the folds of these hills and opened out into a craterlike valley on the clifftop. Presently he stopped as if remembering something, then suddenly he left the path, and began running up one of the hills. When he reached the top he was out of breath and stood watching streaks of light radiating from golden-edged clouds, the scene reminding him of a picture he had seen of the Transfiguration.[3] A short distance below him was the cow standing at the edge of a reedy lake. Colm[4] ran down to meet her waving his stick in the air, and the wind rumbling in his ears made him give an exultant[5] whoop which splashed upon the hills in a shower of echoed sound. A flock of gulls lying on the short grass near the lake rose up languidly,[6] drifting like blown snowflakes over the rim of the cliff.

The lake faced west and was fed by a stream, the drainings of the semicircling hills. One side was open to the winds from the sea and in winter a little outlet trickled over the cliffs making a black vein in their gray sides. The boy lifted stones and began throwing them into the lake, weaving web after web on its calm surface. Then he skimmed the water with flat stones, some of them jumping the surface and coming to rest on the other side. He was delighted with himself and after listening to his echoing shouts of delight he ran to fetch his cow. Gently he tapped her on the side and reluctantly she went towards the brown-mudded path that led out of the valley. The boy was about to throw a final stone into the lake when a bird flew low over his head, its neck astrain, and its orange-colored legs clear in the soft light. It was a wild duck. It circled the lake twice, thrice, coming lower each time and then with a nervous flapping of wings it skidded along the

---

1. **Rathlin Island:** small island off the coast of Northern Ireland.
2. **jauntily:** in a carefree way.
3. **Transfiguration:** New Testament event in which Christ's appearance is miraculously changed.
4. **Colm** [kol′um]
5. **exultant** [ig zult′ənt]: joyful.

6. **languidly** [lang′gwid lē]: without energy.

of sedge[8] and separated from the bank by a narrow channel of water. The water wasn't too deep—he could wade across with care.

Rolling up his short trousers he began to wade, his arms outstretched, and his legs brown and stunted in the mountain water. As he drew near the islet, his feet sank in the cold mud and bubbles winked up at him. He went more carefully and nervously. Then one trouser leg fell and dipped into the water; the boy dropped his hands to roll it up, he un-balanced, made a splashing sound, and the bird arose with a squawk and whirred away over the cliffs. For a moment the boy stood frightened. Then he clambered onto the wet-soaked sod of land, which was spattered with sea gulls' feathers and bits of wind-blown rushes.

Into each hummock[9] he looked, pulling back the long grass. At last he came on the nest, facing seawards. Two flat rocks dimpled the face of the water and between them was a neck of land matted with coarse grass containing the nest. It was untidily built of dried rushes, straw and feathers, and in it lay one solitary egg. Colm was delighted. He looked around and saw no one. The nest was his. He lifted the egg, smooth and green as the sky, with a faint tinge of yellow like the reflected light from a buttercup; and then he felt he had done wrong. He put it back. He knew he shouldn't have touched it and he wondered would the bird forsake the nest. A vague sadness stole over him and he felt in his heart he had sinned. Carefully smoothing out his footprints he hurriedly left the islet and ran after his cow. The sun had now set and the cold shiver of evening enveloped him, chilling his body and saddening his mind.

In the morning he was up and away to

surface, its legs breaking the water into a series of silvery arcs. Its wings closed, it lit silently, gave a slight shiver, and began pecking indifferently at the water.

Colm with dilated eyes eagerly watched it making for the farther end of the lake. It meandered between tall bulrushes,[7] its body black and solid as stone against the graying water. Then as if it had sunk it was gone. The boy ran stealthily along the bank looking away from the lake, pretending indifference. When he came opposite to where he had last seen the bird he stopped and peered through the sighing reeds whose shadows streaked the water in a maze of black strokes. In front of him was a soddy islet guarded by the spears

---

7. **bulrushes:** tall grass that grows in shallow water.

8. **sedge:** grassy marsh plant.
9. **hummock:** low mound of earth.

school. He took the grass rut that edged the road, for it was softer on the bare feet. His house was the last on the western headland and after a mile or so he was joined by Paddy McFall; both boys dressed in similar hand-knitted blue jerseys and gray trousers carried homemade schoolbags. Colm was full of the nest and as soon as he joined his companion he said eagerly: "Paddy, I've a nest—a wild duck's with one egg."

"And how do you know it's a wild duck's?" asked Paddy, slightly jealous.

"Sure I saw her with my own two eyes, her brown speckled back with a crow's patch on it, and her yellow legs—"

"Where is it?" interrupted Paddy in a challenging tone.

"I'm not going to tell you, for you'd rob it!"

"Aach! I suppose it's a tame duck's you have or maybe an old gull's."

Colm put out his tongue at him. "A lot you know!" he said; "for a gull's egg has spots and this one is greenish-white, for I had it in my hand."

And then the words he didn't want to hear rushed from Paddy in a mocking chant. "You had it in your hand! . . . She'll forsake it! She'll forsake it! She'll forsake it!" he said, skipping along the road before him.

Colm felt as if he would choke or cry with vexation.[10]

His mind told him that Paddy was right, but somehow he couldn't give in to it and he replied: "She'll not forsake it! She'll not! I know she'll not!"

But in school his faith wavered. Through the windows he could see moving sheets of rain—rain that dribbled down the panes filling his mind with thoughts of the lake creased and chilled by wind; the nest sodden and black with wetness; and the egg cold as a cave stone. He shivered from the thoughts and fidgeted with the inkwell cover, sliding it backwards and forwards mechanically. The mischievous look had gone from his eyes and the school day dragged on interminably. But at last they were out in the rain, Colm rushing home as fast as he could.

He was no time at all at his dinner of potatoes and salted fish until he was out in the valley now smoky with drifts of slanting rain. Opposite the islet he entered the water. The wind was blowing into his face, rustling noisily the rushes heavy with the dust of rain. A moss cheeper,[11] swaying on a reed like a mouse, filled the air with light cries of loneliness.

The boy reached the islet, his heart thumping with excitement, wondering did the bird forsake. He went slowly, quietly, onto the strip of land that led to the nest. He rose on his toes, looking over the ledge to see if he could see her. And then every muscle tautened. She was on, her shoulders hunched up, and her bill lying on her breast as if she were asleep. Colm's heart hammered wildly in his ears. She hadn't forsaken. He was about to turn stealthily away. Something happened. The bird moved, her neck straightened, twitching nervously from side to side. The boy's head swam with lightness. He stood transfixed.[12] The wild duck with a panicky flapping, rose heavily, and flew off towards the sea. . . . A guilty silence enveloped the boy. . . . He turned to go away, hesitated, and glanced back at the bare nest; it'd be no harm to have a look. Timidly he approached it, standing straight, and gazing over the edge. There in the nest lay two eggs. He drew in his breath with delight, splashed quickly from the island, and ran off whistling in the rain.

---

10. **vexation:** anger.

11. **moss cheeper:** small songbird.
12. **transfixed:** motionless with amazement.

STUDY QUESTIONS

Recalling

1. Explain where and how Colm finds the nest.
2. What does Colm see in the nest, and what does he do? What does he immediately wonder?
3. Repeat Paddy's "mocking chant" when Colm tells him about the nest. What does Colm say?
4. What does Colm see when he returns to the nest?

Interpreting

5. Why is Colm delighted when he looks into the nest on his return? What does he know then?
6. What do Colm's actions and thoughts show about his feelings toward nature?
7. What does the story tell us about how we should treat nature?

Extending

8. Why might someone be especially thrilled by being accepted by a wild creature?

READING AND LITERARY FOCUS

The Total Effect

The various elements in a story—plot, character, setting, and theme—all work together to create the story's **total effect,** its overall impact on the reader. No one element is isolated from the rest. As we see in "The Wild Duck's Nest," for instance, a character's feelings can influence the events of the plot; these feelings can themselves be affected by the setting.

Thinking About the Total Effect

1. **Plot and Character:** Which events in the plot are the result of Colm's decisions? Choose one of his actions, and explain what motivates it.
2. **Setting and Plot:** Find an example in which the setting influences the story's events.
3. **Setting and Character:** Describe the atmosphere of the story. In what way might the story's atmosphere influence Colm's state of mind?
4. **Theme:** What would you say is the theme of the story? How do the plot, Colm's character, and the setting help you understand this theme?
5. **Total Effect:** What would you say is the total effect of "The Wild Duck's Nest"?

VOCABULARY

Sentence Completions

Each of the following sentences contains a blank with four possible words for completing the sentence. The words all come from "The Wild Duck's Nest." Choose the word that best completes each sentence. Write the number of each sentence and the letter of your choice on a separate sheet.

1. Light was ___ from the clouds.
   (a) radiating   (c) speckled
   (b) wading   (d) sodden
2. The sleepy man rose ___ from his chair.
   (a) jauntily   (c) stealthily
   (b) languidly   (d) interminably
3. I built a hut on the small ___ in the river.
   (a) maze   (c) sedge
   (b) islet   (d) vexation
4. After the storm a(n) ___ leaf was left on the tree.
   (a) exultant   (c) dilated
   (b) thrice   (d) solitary
5. We worried that the cat would ___ her kittens.
   (a) meander   (c) transfix
   (b) forsake   (d) hesitate

Washington Irving (1783–1859) was the first American writer to win international fame. His *Sketch Book* (1819), a collection of stories greatly admired throughout Europe, included Irving's two most famous tales, "Rip Van Winkle" and "The Legend of Sleepy Hollow." Both of these stories take place in the Hudson River valley of New York State. "Rip Van Winkle" is based on an old German legend, yet it is considered an American classic.

■ What does it say about early America and the changes that the Revolution brought?

Washington Irving

Rip Van Winkle (slightly abridged)

Whoever has made a voyage up the Hudson[1] must remember the Catskill Mountains.[2] They are a branch of the great Appalachian family,[3] and are seen away to the west of the river, swelling up to a noble height, and lording it over the surrounding country. Every change of season, every change of weather, indeed, every hour of the day, produces some change in the magical hues and shapes of these mountains, and they are regarded by all the good wives, far and near, as perfect barometers. When the weather is fair and settled, they are clothed in blue and purple, and print their bold outlines on the clear evening sky; but, sometimes, when the rest of the landscape is cloudless, they will gather a hood of gray vapors about their summits, which,

in the last rays of the setting sun, will glow and light up like a crown of glory.

At the foot of these fairy mountains, the voyager may have seen the light smoke curling up from a village, whose shingle roofs gleam among the trees, just where the blue tints of the upland melt away into the fresh green of the nearer landscape. It is a little village, of great antiquity, having been founded by some of the Dutch colonists, in the early times of the province. There were some of the houses of the original settlers standing within a few years,[4] built of small yellow bricks brought from Holland, having latticed windows and gable fronts, surmounted with weathercocks.

In that same village, and in one of these very houses, which was sadly timeworn and weather-beaten, there lived many years since, while the country was yet a province of Great Britain, a simple, good-natured fellow, of the

---

1. **Hudson:** Hudson River in eastern New York State.
2. **Catskill Mountains:** mountain range in southeastern New York State.
3. **Appalachian** [ap'ə lăch'ən] **family:** mountain chain that extends from southeastern Canada to northern Alabama and includes the Catskills.

4. **within a few years:** until a few years ago, about 1820.

name of Rip Van Winkle. He was a descendant of the Van Winkles who figured so gallantly in the chivalrous days of Peter Stuyvesant.[5] He inherited, however, but little of the martial character of his ancestors. I have observed that he was a simple, good-natured man; he was, moreover, a kind neighbor, and an obedient, henpecked husband. Indeed, to the latter circumstance might be owing that meekness of spirit which gained him such universal popularity; for those men are most apt to be conciliating[6] abroad who are under the discipline of shrews at home. Their tempers, doubtless, are rendered pliant in the fiery furnace of domestic trouble, which is worth all the sermons in the world for teaching the virtues of patience and long-suffering. A quarrelsome wife may, therefore, in some respects, be considered a tolerable blessing; and if so, Rip Van Winkle was thrice blessed.

Certain it is, that he was a great favorite among all the good wives of the village, who took his part in all family squabbles, and never failed, whenever they talked those matters over in their evening gossipings, to lay all the blame on Dame Van Winkle. The children of the village, too, would shout with joy whenever he approached. He assisted at their sports, made their playthings, taught them to fly kites and shoot marbles, and told them long stories of ghosts, witches, and Indians. Whenever he went dodging about the village, he was surrounded by a troop of them, hanging on his coat skirts, clambering on his back, and playing a thousand tricks on him with impunity;[7] and not a dog would bark at him throughout the neighborhood.

The great error in Rip's character was an insuperable dislike of all kinds of profitable labor. It could not be from the want of perseverance; for he would sit on a wet rock, with a rod as long and heavy as a Tartar's lance,[8] and fish all day without a murmur, even though he should not be encouraged by a single nibble. He would carry a fowling piece[9] on his shoulder for hours together, trudging through woods and swamps, and up hill and down dale, to shoot a few squirrels or wild pigeons. He would never refuse to assist a neighbor even in the roughest toil, and was a foremost man at all country frolics for husking Indian corn, or building stone fences. The women of the village, too, used to employ him to run their errands, and to do such little odd jobs as their less obliging husbands would not do for them. In a word, Rip was ready to attend to anybody's business but his own; but as to doing family duty, and keeping his farm in order, he found it impossible.

In fact, he declared it was of no use to work on his farm; it was the most pestilent[10] little piece of ground in the whole country; everything about it went wrong, and would go wrong, in spite of him. His fences were continually falling to pieces; his cow would either go astray or get among the cabbages; weeds were sure to grow quicker in his fields than anywhere else; the rain always made a point of setting in just as he had some outdoor work to do; so that his estate had dwindled away under his management, acre by acre, until there was little more left than a mere patch of Indian corn and potatoes, and was the worst-conditioned farm in the neighborhood.

His children, too, were as ragged and wild

---

5. **Peter Stuyvesant** [stī′və sənt]: (1592–1672), last governor of the Dutch colony of New Netherland. The colony was taken by the British in 1664 and renamed New York.
6. **conciliating** [kən sil′ē āt′ing]: friendly, good-natured.
7. **with impunity** [im pū′nə tē]: without fear of punishment.

8. **Tartar's** [tar′tərz] **lance:** long spear of a Mongolian tribesman.
9. **fowling piece:** light gun used for shooting wild birds.
10. **pestilent** [pes′tə lənt]: troublesome.

as if they belonged to nobody. His son Rip promised to inherit the habits, with the old clothes, of his father. He was generally seen trooping like a colt at his mother's heels, equipped in a pair of his father's castoff galligaskins,[11] which he had to hold up with one hand, as a fine lady does her train in bad weather.

Rip Van Winkle, however, was one of those happy mortals, of foolish, well-oiled dispositions, who take the world easy, eat white bread or brown, whichever can be got with least thought or trouble, and would rather starve on a penny than work for a pound.[12] If left to himself, he would have whistled life away in perfect contentment, but his wife kept continually dinning in his ears about his idleness, his carelessness, and the ruin he was bringing on his family. Morning, noon, and night, her tongue was incessantly going, and everything he said or did was sure to produce a torrent of household eloquence. Rip had but one way of replying to all lectures of the kind, and that, by frequent use, had grown into a habit. He shrugged his shoulders, shook his head, cast up his eyes, but said nothing. This, however, always provoked a fresh volley from his wife; so that he would take to the outside of the house—the only side which, in truth, belongs to a henpecked husband.

Rip's sole domestic adherent[13] was his dog Wolf, who was as much henpecked as his master; for Dame Van Winkle regarded them as companions in idleness, and even looked upon Wolf with an evil eye, as the cause of his master's going so often astray. True it is, in

---

11. **galligaskins** [gal'ə gas'kinz]: loose knee-length trousers.
12. **pound:** basic unit of British currency, which was used in the colonies.

13. **adherent:** supporter.

all points of spirit befitting an honorable dog, he was as courageous an animal as ever scoured the woods—but what courage can withstand the terrors of a woman's tongue? The moment Wolf entered the house his crest fell, his tail drooped to the ground, or curled between his legs, he sneaked about with a gallows air, casting many a sidelong glance at Dame Van Winkle, and at the least flourish of a broomstick or ladle, he would fly to the door, yelping.

Times grew worse and worse with Rip Van Winkle as years of matrimony rolled on; a tart temper never mellows with age, and a sharp tongue is the only edged tool that grows keener with constant use. For a long while he used to console himself, when driven from home, by frequenting a kind of perpetual club of the sages, philosophers, and other idle personages of the village, which held its sessions on a bench before a small inn, designated by a portrait of His Majesty George the Third.[14] Here they used to sit in the shade through a long, lazy summer's day, talking listlessly over village gossip, or telling endless sleepy stories about nothing. But it would have been worth any statesman's money to have heard the profound discussions that sometimes took place, when by chance an old newspaper fell into their hands from some passing traveler. How solemnly they would listen to the contents, as drawled out by Derrick Van Bummel, the schoolmaster, a dapper, learned little man, who was not to be daunted by the most gigantic word in the dictionary; and how sagely they would deliberate upon public events some months after they had taken place.

The opinions of this club were completely controlled by Nicholas Vedder, a patriarch[15] of the village, and landlord of the inn, at the door of which he took his seat from morning till night, just moving sufficiently to avoid the sun and keep in the shade of a large tree; so that the neighbors could tell the hour by his movements as accurately as by a sundial. It is true he was rarely heard to speak, but smoked his pipe incessantly. His adherents, however, perfectly understood him, and knew how to gather his opinions. When anything that was read or related displeased him, he was observed to smoke his pipe vehemently, and to send forth short, frequent, and angry puffs; but when pleased, he would inhale the smoke slowly and tranquilly, and emit it in light and placid clouds; and sometimes, taking the pipe from his mouth, and letting the fragrant vapor curl about his nose, would gravely nod his head in token of perfect approbation.

From even this stronghold the unlucky Rip was at length routed by his wife, who would suddenly break in upon the tranquillity of the assemblage and call the members all to naught; nor was that august[16] personage, Nicholas Vedder himself, sacred from the daring tongue of this terrible shrew, who charged him outright with encouraging her husband in habits of idleness.

Poor Rip was at last reduced almost to despair; and his only alternative, to escape from the labor of the farm and clamor of his wife, was to take gun in hand and stroll away into the woods. Here he would sometimes seat himself at the foot of a tree, and share the contents of his wallet[17] with Wolf, with whom he sympathized as a fellow sufferer in persecution. "Poor Wolf," he would say, "thy mis-

---

14. **His Majesty George the Third:** (1738–1820) King of England and, until the American Revolution in 1776, ruler of the American colonies.

15. **patriarch** [pā′trē ärk]: old man who is honored and respected.
16. **august:** dignified; worthy of respect.
17. **wallet:** here, bag for carrying supplies.

tress leads thee a dog's life of it; but never mind, my lad, whilst I live thou shalt never want a friend to stand by thee!" Wolf would wag his tail, look wistfully in his master's face, and if dogs can feel pity, I believe he returned the sentiment with all his heart.

In a long ramble of the kind on a fine autumnal day, Rip had unconsciously scrambled to one of the highest parts of the Catskill Mountains. He was after his favorite sport of squirrel shooting, and the still solitudes[18] had echoed and reechoed with the reports of his gun. Panting and fatigued, he threw himself, late in the afternoon, on a green knoll, covered with mountain herbage, that crowned the brow of a precipice. From an opening between the trees he could overlook all the lower country for many a mile of rich woodland. He saw at a distance the lordly Hudson, far, far below him, moving on its silent but majestic course, with the reflection of a purple cloud, or the sail of a lagging bark,[19] here and there sleeping on its glassy bosom, and at last losing itself in the blue highlands.

On the other side he looked down into a deep mountain glen, wild, lonely, and shagged, the bottom filled with fragments from the overhanging cliffs, and scarcely lighted by the reflected rays of the setting sun. For some time Rip lay musing on this scene. Evening was gradually advancing. The mountains began to throw their long blue shadows over the valleys. He saw that it would be dark before he could reach the village, and he heaved a heavy sigh when he thought of encountering the terrors of Dame Van Winkle.

As he was about to descend, he heard a voice from the distance, hallooing, "Rip Van Winkle! Rip Van Winkle!" He looked round, but could see nothing but a crow winging its solitary flight across the mountain. He thought his fancy[20] must have deceived him, and turned again to descend, when he heard the same cry ring through the still evening air: "Rip Van Winkle! Rip Van Winkle!" At the same time Wolf bristled up his back, and giving a low growl, skulked to his master's side, looking fearfully down into the glen. Rip now felt a vague apprehension stealing over him; he looked anxiously in the same direction, and perceived a strange figure slowly toiling up the rocks, and bending under the weight of something he carried on his back. He was surprised to see any human being in this lonely and unfrequented place, but supposing it to be someone of the neighborhood in need of his assistance, he hastened down to yield it.

On nearer approach he was still more surprised at the singularity of the stranger's appearance. He was a short, square-built old fellow, with thick, bushy hair and a grizzled beard. His dress was of the antique Dutch fashion—a cloth jerkin[21] strapped round the waist—several pairs of breeches, the outer one of ample volume, decorated with rows of buttons down the sides, and bunches at the knees. He bore on his shoulder a stout keg that seemed full of liquor, and made signs for Rip to approach and assist him with the load. Though rather shy and distrustful of this new acquaintance, Rip complied with his usual readiness; and mutually relieving one another, they clambered up a narrow gully, apparently the dry bed of a mountain torrent. As they ascended, Rip every now and then heard long rolling peals, like distant thunder, that seemed to issue out of a deep ravine, or

---

18. **still solitudes** [sol′ə tōōdz′]: quiet, lonely places.
19. **bark:** small boat.

20. **fancy:** imagination.
21. **jerkin:** short, fitted jacket, often made of leather.

rather cleft, between lofty rocks, toward which their rugged path conducted. He paused for an instant, but supposing it to be the muttering of one of those transient thundershowers which often take place in mountain heights, he proceeded. Passing through the ravine, they came to a hollow, like a small amphitheater,[22] surrounded by perpendicular precipices, over the brinks of which trees shot their branches, so that you only caught glimpses of the azure sky and the bright evening cloud. During the whole time Rip and his companion had labored on in silence; for though Rip marveled greatly what could be the object of carrying a keg of liquor up this wild mountain, yet there was something strange and incomprehensible about the unknown, that inspired awe and checked familiarity.

On entering the amphitheater, new objects of wonder presented themselves. On a level spot in the center was a company of odd-looking personages playing at ninepins. They were dressed in a quaint, outlandish fashion; some wore short doublets,[23] others jerkins, with long knives in their belts, and most of them had enormous breeches, of style similar to that of the guide's. Their visages,[24] too, were peculiar. One had a large beard, broad face, and small piggish eyes. The face of another seemed to consist entirely of nose, and was surmounted by a white sugar-loaf hat,[25] set off with a litle red cock's tail. They all had beards, of various shapes and colors. There was one who seemed to be the commander. He was a stout old gentleman, with a weather-beaten countenance; he wore a laced doublet, broad belt and hanger,[26] high-crowned hat

and feather, red stockings, and high-heeled shoes, with roses in them. The whole group reminded Rip of the figures in an old Flemish[27] painting, in the parlor of the village parson, which had been brought over from Holland at the time of the settlement.

What seemed particularly odd to Rip was that, though these folks were evidently amusing themselves, yet they maintained the gravest faces, the most mysterious silence, and were the most melancholy party of pleasure he had ever witnessed. Nothing interrupted the stillness of the scene but the noise of the balls, which, whenever they were rolled, echoed along the mountains like rumbling peals of thunder.

As Rip and his companion approached them, they suddenly stopped their play, and stared at him with such fixed, statuelike gaze, and such strange, lackluster countenances, that his heart turned within him, and his knees smote together. His companion now emptied the contents of the keg into large flagons,[28] and made signs to him to wait upon the company. He obeyed with fear and trembling; they quaffed[29] the liquor in profound silence, and then returned to their game.

By degrees Rip's awe and apprehension subsided. He even ventured, when no eye was fixed upon him, to taste the beverage, which he found had much of the flavor of excellent Holland gin. He was naturally a thirsty soul, and was soon tempted to repeat the draft.[30] One taste provoked another; and he repeated his visits to the flagon so often that at length his senses were overpowered, his eyes swam in his head, his head gradually declined, and he fell into a deep sleep.

---

22. **amphitheater** [am'fə thē'ə tər]: round open stadium surrounded by tiers of seats.
23. **doublets** [dub'lits]: tight waist-length jackets.
24. **visages** [viz'ij əz]: faces.
25. **sugar-loaf hat:** tall, cone-shaped hat.
26. **hanger:** short sword.

27. **Flemish:** of Flanders, an area of western Europe, now part of France, Belgium, and the Netherlands.
28. **flagons** [flag'ənz]: large containers for liquids, with handles and spouts.
29. **quaffed** [kwafd]: drank.
30. **draft:** here, drink.

On waking, he found himself on the green knoll whence he had first seen the old man of the glen. He rubbed his eyes—it was a bright sunny morning. The birds were hopping and twittering among the bushes, and the eagle was wheeling aloft, and breasting the pure mountain breeze. "Surely," thought Rip, "I have not slept here all night." He recalled the occurrences before he fell asleep. The strange man with a keg of liquor—the mountain ravine—the wild retreat among the rocks—the woebegone party at ninepins—the flagon—"Oh! that flagon! that wicked flagon!" thought Rip—"what excuse shall I make to Dame Van Winkle?"

He looked round for his gun, but in place of the clean, well-oiled fowling piece, he found an old firelock lying by him, the barrel incrusted with rust, the lock falling off, and the stock worm-eaten. He now suspected that the grave roisters[31] of the mountain had put a trick upon him, and, having dosed him with liquor, had robbed him of his gun. Wolf, too, had disappeared, but he might have strayed away after a squirrel or partridge. He whistled after him and shouted his name, but all in vain; the echoes repeated his whistle and shout, but no dog was to be seen.

He determined to revisit the scene of the last evening's gambol,[32] and if he met with any of the party, to demand his dog and gun. As he rose to walk, he found himself stiff in the joints. "These mountain beds do not agree with me," thought Rip, "and if this frolic should lay me up with a fit of the rheumatism, I shall have a blessed time with Dame Van Winkle." With some difficulty he got down into the glen. He found the gully up which he and his companion had ascended the preceding evening; but to his astonishment a mountain stream was now foaming down it, leaping from rock to rock, and filling the glen with babbling murmurs. He, however, made shift to scramble up its sides, working his toilsome way through thickets of birch, sassafras, and witch hazel, and sometimes tripped up or entangled by the wild grapevines that twisted their coils or tendrils from tree to tree, and spread a kind of network in his path.

At length he reached to where the ravine had opened through the cliffs to the amphitheater; but no traces of such opening remained. The rocks presented a high wall over which the torrent came tumbling in a sheet of feathery foam, and fell into a broad, deep basin, black from the shadows of the surrounding forest. Here, then, poor Rip was brought to a stand. He again called and whistled after his dog; he was only answered by the cawing of a flock of idle crows, who seemed to look down and scoff at the poor man's perplexities.[33] What was to be done? The morning was passing away, and Rip felt famished for want of his breakfast. He grieved to give up his dog and gun; he dreaded to meet his wife; but it would not do to starve among the mountains. He shook his head, shouldered the rusty firelock, and, with a heart full of trouble and anxiety, turned his steps homeward.

As he approached the village, he met a number of people, but none whom he knew, which somewhat surprised him, for he had thought himself acquainted with everyone in the country round. Their dress, too, was of a different fashion from that to which he was accustomed. They all stared at him with equal marks of surprise, and whenever they cast their eyes upon him, invariably stroked their chins. The recurrence of this gesture induced Rip to do the same, when, to his astonish-

---

31. **roisters:** roisterers; noisy merrymakers.
32. **gambol:** fun; play.

33. **perplexities** [pər plek′sə tēz]: confusions.

ment, he found his beard had grown a foot long!

He had now entered the outskirts of the village. A troop of strange children ran at his heels, hooting after him, and pointing at his gray beard. The dogs, too, not one of which he recognized for an old acquaintance, barked at him as he passed. The very village was altered; it was larger and more populous. There were rows of houses which he had never seen before, and those which had been his familiar haunts had disappeared. Strange names were over the doors—strange faces at the windows—everything was strange. His mind now misgave him; he began to doubt whether both he and the world around him were not bewitched. Surely this was his native village, which he had left but the day before. There stood the Catskill Mountains—there ran the silver Hudson at a distance—there was every hill and dale precisely as it had always been—Rip was sorely perplexed. "That flagon last night," thought he, "has addled[34] my poor head sadly."

It was with some difficulty that he found the way to his own house, which he approached with silent awe, expecting every moment to hear the shrill voice of Dame Van Winkle. He found the house gone to decay—the roof fallen in, the windows shattered, and the doors off the hinges. A half-starved dog that looked like Wolf was skulking about it. Rip called him by name, but the cur snarled, showed his teeth, and passed on. This was an unkind cut indeed. "My very dog," sighed poor Rip, "has forgotten me!"

He entered the house, which, to tell the truth, Dame Van Winkle had always kept in neat order. It was empty, forlorn, and apparently abandoned. This desolateness overcame all his fears—he called loudly for his wife and children—the lonely chambers rang for a moment with his voice, and then all again was silence.

He now hurried forth, and hastened to his old resort, the village inn—but it too was gone. A large, rickety wooden building stood in its place, with great gaping windows, some of them broken and mended with old hats and petticoats, and over the door was painted, "The Union Hotel, by Jonathan Doolittle." Instead of the great tree that used to shelter the quiet little Dutch inn of yore, there now was reared a tall naked pole, with something on the top that looked like a red nightcap,[35] and from it was fluttering a flag, on which was a singular assemblage of stars and stripes—all this was strange and incomprehensible. He recognized on the sign, however, the ruby face of King George, under which he had smoked so many a peaceful pipe; but even this was singularly changed. The red coat was changed for one of blue and buff, a sword was held in the hand instead of a scepter, the head was decorated with a cocked hat,[36] and underneath was painted in large characters, GENERAL WASHINGTON.

There was, as usual, a crowd of folk about the door, but none that Rip recollected. The very character of the people seemed changed. There was a busy, bustling tone about it, instead of the accustomed tranquillity. He looked in vain for the sage Nicholas Vedder, with his broad face, double chin, and fair long pipe, uttering clouds of tobacco smoke instead of idle speeches; or Van Bummel, the schoolmaster, doling forth the contents of an ancient newspaper. In place of these, a lean, bilious-looking[37] fellow, with his pockets full of handbills, was talking vehemently about

---

34. **addled:** confused.

35. **red nightcap:** refers to a liberty cap, a red cloth cap that was a symbol of freedom.
36. **cocked hat:** three-cornered hat.
37. **bilious** [bil'yəs]-**looking:** appearing bad-tempered.

rights of citizens—elections—members of Congress—liberty—Bunker's Hill—heroes of seventy-six—and other words, which were a perfect Babylonish jargon[38] to the bewildered Van Winkle.

The appearance of Rip, with his long, grizzled beard, his rusty fowling piece, his uncouth dress, and an army of women and children at his heels, soon attracted the attention of the tavern politicians. They crowded round him, eyeing him from head to foot with great curiosity. The orator bustled up to him, and drawing him partly aside, inquired "on which side he voted?" Rip stared in vacant stupidity. Another short but busy little fellow pulled him by the arm, and, rising on tiptoe, inquired in his ear, "whether he was Federal or Democrat?"[39] Rip was equally at a loss to comprehend the question, when a knowing, self-important old gentleman, in a sharp cocked hat, made his way through the crowd, putting them to the right and left with his elbows as he passed, and planting himself before Van Winkle, with one arm akimbo,[40] the other resting on his cane, his keen eyes and sharp hat penetrating, as it were, into his very soul, demanded in an austere tone, "what brought him to the election with a gun on his shoulder, and a mob at his heels; and whether he meant to breed a riot in the village?"

"Alas! gentlemen," cried Rip, somewhat dismayed, "I am a poor quiet man, a native of the place, and a loyal subject of the King, God bless him!"

Here a general shout burst from the bystanders—"A Tory![41] a Tory! a spy! a refugee! hustle him! away with him!" It was with great difficulty that the self-important man in the cocked hat restored order; and demanded again of the unknown culprit, what he came there for, and whom he was seeking. The poor man humbly assured him that he meant no harm, but merely came there in search of some of his neighbors, who used to keep about the tavern.

"Well—who are they?—name them."

Rip bethought himself a moment, and inquired, "Where's Nicholas Vedder?"

There was a silence for a little while, when an old man replied, in a thin, piping voice, "Nicholas Vedder! why, he is dead and gone these eighteen years! There was a wooden tombstone in the churchyard that used to tell all about him, but that's rotten and gone too."

"Where's Brom Dutcher?"

"Oh, he went off to the army in the beginning of the war; some say he was killed at the storming of Stony Point[42]—others say he was drowned in a squall at the foot of Anthony's Nose.[43] I don't know—he never came back again."

"Where's Van Bummel, the schoolmaster?"

"He went off to the wars too, was a great militia general, and is now in Congress."

Rip's heart died away at hearing of these sad changes in his home and friends, and finding himself thus alone in the world. Every answer puzzled him, too, by treating of such enormous lapses of time, and of matters which he could not understand: war—Congress—Stony Point; he had no courage to ask after any more friends, but cried out in despair, "Does nobody here know Rip Van Winkle?"

---

38. **Babylonish jargon:** language that cannot be understood. In the Old Testament of the Bible, the people of Babylon tried to build a tower to heaven. God stopped the project by causing all the people to speak different languages.

39. **Federal or Democrat:** member of the Federalist Party or the Democrat-Republican Party, the two political parties in the early years of the United States.

40. **akimbo:** holding the hand on the hip with the elbow out.

41. **Tory:** American who sided with the British during the American Revolution.

42. **Stony Point:** village on the Hudson River.

43. **Anthony's Nose:** mountain on the Hudson River.

"Oh, Rip Van Winkle!" exclaimed two or three; "oh, to be sure! that's Rip Van Winkle yonder, leaning against the tree."

Rip looked, and beheld a precise copy of himself, as he went up the mountain; apparently as lazy, and certainly as ragged. The poor fellow was now completely bewildered. He doubted his own identity, and whether he was himself or another man. In the midst of his bewilderment, the man in the cocked hat demanded who he was, and what was his name.

"God knows," exclaimed he, at his wit's end; "I'm not myself—I'm somebody else—that's me yonder—no—that's somebody else got into my shoes—I was myself last night, but I fell asleep on the mountain, and they've changed my gun, and everything's changed, and I'm changed, and I can't tell what's my name, or who I am!"

The bystanders began now to look at each other, nod, wink significantly, and tap their fingers against their foreheads. There was a whisper, also, about securing the gun, and keeping the old fellow from doing mischief, at the very suggestion of which the self-important man in the cocked hat retired quickly. At this critical moment a fresh, comely[44] woman pressed through the throng to get a peep at the gray-bearded man. She had a chubby child in her arms, which, frightened at his looks, began to cry. "Hush, Rip," cried she, "hush, you little fool; the old man won't hurt you." The name of the child, the air of the mother, the tone of her voice, all awakened a train of recollections in his mind. "What is your name, my good woman?" asked he.

"Judith Gardenier."

"And your father's name?"

"Ah, poor man, Rip Van Winkle was his name, but it's twenty years since he went away from home with his gun, and never has

been heard of since—his dog came home without him; but whether he shot himself, or was carried away by the Indians, nobody can tell. I was then but a little girl."

Rip had but one question more to ask; but he put it with a faltering voice: "Where's your mother?"

"Oh, she too had died but a short time since; she broke a blood vessel in a fit of passion at a New England peddler."

There was a drop of comfort, at least, in this intelligence.[45] The honest man could contain himself no longer. He caught his daughter and her child in his arms. "I am your father!" cried he—"Young Rip Van Winkle once—old Rip Van Winkle now!—Does nobody know poor Rip Van Winkle?"

All stood amazed, until an old woman, tottering out from among the crowd, put her hand to her brow, and peering under it in his face for a moment, exclaimed, "Sure enough! it is Rip Van Winkle—it is himself! Welcome home again, old neighbor. Why, where have you been these twenty long years?"

Rip's story was soon told, for the whole twenty years had been to him as but one night. The neighbors stared when they heard it; some were seen to wink at each other, and put their tongues in their cheeks; and the self-important man in the cocked hat, who, when the alarm was over, had returned to the field, screwed down the corners of his mouth, and shook his head—upon which there was a general shaking of the head throughout the assemblage.

It was determined, however, to take the opinion of old Peter Vanderdonk, who was seen slowly advancing up the road. He was a descendant of the historian of that name, who wrote one of the earliest accounts of the province. Peter was the most ancient inhabitant

---

44. **comely** [kum'lē]: beautiful.

45. **intelligence:** here, news.

of the village, and well versed in all the wonderful events and traditions of the neighborhood. He recollected Rip at once, and corroborated his story in the most satisfactory manner. He assured the company that it was a fact, handed down from his ancestor the historian, that the Catskill Mountains had always been haunted by strange beings. That it was affirmed that the great Henry Hudson, the first discoverer of the river and country, kept a kind of vigil there every twenty years, with his crew of the *Half-Moon*; being permitted in this way to revisit the scenes of his enterprise and keep a guardian eye upon the river and the great city called by his name. That his father had once seen them in their old Dutch dresses playing at ninepins in a hollow of the mountain; and that he himself had heard, one summer afternoon, the sound of their balls, like distant peals of thunder.

To make a long story short, the company broke up, and returned to the more important concerns of the election. Rip's daughter took him home to live with her; she had a snug, well-furnished house, and a stout, cheery farmer for a husband, whom Rip recollected for one of the urchins that used to climb upon his back. As to Rip's son and heir, who was the ditto of himself, seen leaning against the tree, he was employed to work on the farm; but showed an hereditary disposition to attend to anything else but his business.

Rip now resumed his old walks and habits; he soon found many of his former cronies, though all rather the worse for the wear and tear of time; and preferred making friends among the rising generation, with whom he soon grew into great favor.

Having nothing to do at home, and being arrived at that happy age when a man can be idle with impunity, he took his place once more on the bench at the inn door, and was reverenced as one of the patriarchs of the village, and a chronicle of the old times "before the war." It was some time before he could get into the regular track of gossip, or could be made to comprehend the strange events that had taken place during his sleep. How that there had been a Revolutionary War—that the country had thrown off the yoke of old England—and that, instead of being a subject of His Majesty George the Third, he was now a free citizen of the United States. Rip, in fact, was no politician; the changes of states and empires made but little impression on him; but there was one species of despotism under which he had long groaned, and that was—petticoat government. Happily that was at an end; he had got his neck out of the yoke of matrimony, and could go in and out whenever he pleased, without dreading the tyranny of Dame Van Winkle. Whenever her name was mentioned, however, he shook his head, shrugged his shoulders, and cast up his eyes; which might pass either for an expression of resignation to his fate, or joy at his deliverance.

He used to tell his story to every stranger that arrived at Mr. Doolittle's hotel. He was observed, at first, to vary on some points every time he told it, which was, doubtless, owing to his having so recently awaked. It at last settled down precisely to the tale I have related, and not a man, woman, or child in the neighborhood but knew it by heart. Some always pretended to doubt the reality of it, and insisted that Rip had been out of his head, and that this was one point on which he always remained flighty. The old Dutch inhabitants, however, almost universally gave it full credit. Even to this day they never hear a thunderstorm of a summer afternoon about the Catskills but they say Henry Hudson and his crew are at their game of ninepins; and it is a common wish of all henpecked husbands in the neighborhood, when life hangs heavy on their hands, that they might have a quieting draft out of Rip Van Winkle's flagon.

STUDY QUESTIONS

Recalling

1. What does the narrator say is the "great error" in Rip's character? What is the chief flaw of Rip's wife?

2. Briefly describe the strangers Rip meets in the mountains. What does drinking their beverage cause Rip to do?

3. When Rip returns to the town, what changes does he see in the area around the inn? Mention one other change that Rip notices.

4. What does Peter Vanderdonk tell Rip and the villagers about the men in the mountains?

5. Describe Rip's life after his return to the town. Summarize the historical events that occurred during his absence.

Interpreting

6. What sort of person is Rip Van Winkle? What conflict exists between Rip and his wife?

7. In what ways is Rip's life better after his sleep?

8. What similarity can you see between Rip's loss of his wife and the historical events that occurred in America while he was asleep?

Extending

9. If you were to sleep through the next twenty years, what sort of world do you think you would wake up to find?

READING AND LITERARY FOCUS

Stereotypes

A **stereotype** is a kind of character who has only a few personality traits and is more a category than a real, individualized person. For example, the strong, silent cowboy is a stereotype. We see the same stereotypes appearing in many different pieces of literature. For instance, the innocent heroine and the wicked villain are both stereotypes that often appear in literature.

Stereotyped characters do not usually change in a work. They are also not fully believable because their virtues or flaws are exaggerated. Stereotypes appear in many fairy tales, folk tales, legends, and other literature that is meant to teach a lesson.

Thinking About Stereotypes

■ Prove that Rip Van Winkle and his wife are stereotypes. Why might the use of stereotypes be appropriate in "Rip Van Winkle"?

The Total Effect

Plot, character, setting, and theme all contribute to a story's **total effect**—its overall impact on the reader. Each story produces its own special impact because of its combination of unique ingredients. For example, "The Wish" (page 179) combines an everyday setting (a hallway) with a very young and very imaginative boy. The result is an unusual, exciting journey that takes place entirely in the boy's mind. The story's total effect is amusing and suspenseful at the same time because we enter into the boy's imaginary adventure.

Thinking About the Total Effect

1. **Plot:** Explain how the total effect of "Rip Van Winkle" would have been different if Rip had simply lost his memory instead of sleeping for twenty years. Would you have liked the story more or less?

2. **Character:** How do the cartoonlike characters add to the total effect of the story?

3. **Setting:** Point out three details that help you see the historical period in which "Rip Van Winkle" is set. What does the long-ago setting add to the story's total effect?

4. **Theme:** What idea about change and the passage of time is suggested by "Rip Van Winkle"? What does this idea add to the story's total effect?

5. **Total Effect:** "Rip Van Winkle" combines its own special ingredients—a fanciful plot based on an old legend; simple, comic characters; and

an early American setting. Did you find the total effect of this story amusing, realistic, dreamlike, suspenseful, moving, or some combination of these or of other qualities?

VOCABULARY

Context Clues

Sometimes you can figure out the meaning of an unfamiliar word by examining its **context,** or the words and sentences that surround it. Consider the context of the word *visages* in this passage from "Rip Van Winkle":

Their visages, too, were peculiar. One had a large beard, broad face, and small piggish eyes. The face of another seemed to consist entirely of nose.

The passage goes on to give examples of peculiar faces. Therefore, we know that *visage* must mean "face."

The passages in the following numbered items come from "Rip Van Winkle." From the four choices that follow each item, select the best meaning for the italicized word in each passage. Write the number of each item and the letter of your choice on a separate sheet.

1. . . . and sometimes, taking the pipe from his mouth, and letting the fragrant vapor curl about his nose, [he] would gravely nod his head in token of perfect *approbation.*
   - (a) approval
   - (b) disapproval
   - (c) anger
   - (d) confusion

2. Morning, noon, and night, her tongue was *incessantly* going. . . .
   - (a) continuously
   - (b) intelligently
   - (c) pleasantly
   - (d) widely

3. Panting and fatigued, he threw himself, late in the afternoon, on a green knoll, covered with mountain herbage, that crowned the brow of the *precipice.*
   - (a) waterfall
   - (b) forehead
   - (c) rainfall
   - (d) steep slope

4. He . . . made signs for Rip to approach and assist him with the load. . . . Rip *complied* with his usual readiness; and mutually relieving one another, they clambered up a narrow gully. . . .
   - (a) refused
   - (b) agreed
   - (c) fainted
   - (d) ran away

5. He entered the house, which . . . Dame Van Winkle had always kept in neat order. It was empty, forlorn, and apparently abandoned. This *desolateness* overcame all his fears. . . .
   - (a) beauty
   - (b) richness
   - (c) coziness
   - (d) vacancy

COMPARING STORIES

1. Both "A Secret for Two" and "After Twenty Years" are stories that revolve around surprises. Which story had a more surprising end for you? Explain.

2. Compare and contrast the ideas about friendship presented in "A Secret for Two" and "After Twenty Years."

3. "The Wish" and "Rip Van Winkle" both present special kinds of journeys. On what kind of journey does the main character go in each story? What happens to the main character in each story?

4. Compare the boy in "The Wish" with Colm in "The Wild Duck's Nest." What similarities can you see in their responses to their surroundings? In what ways are they different?

Active Reading

The Short Story

Interpreting Details in Stories

Reading literature is an experience that involves your imagination. By paying close attention to the details in a story, you can imagine the total picture that an author has in mind. You are able to picture every shape and color of the setting. The details help you visualize everything about characters, including their dress, facial expressions, voice, and body movements. Through detail, each action becomes a lifelike moment filled with sound and motion. As a good reader, you should always try to see and hear literature with your imagination.

Read the following passage from "Old Yeller and the Bear." Try to picture and listen to the scene as you read.

> Now the she-bear was charging across the shallows in the creek. She was knocking sheets of water high in the bright sun, charging with her fur up and her long teeth bared, filling the canyon with that awful coughing roar. And no matter how fast Mama ran or how fast I ran, the she-bear was going to get there first!

Activity 1 Study the following two pictures. Then answer each of the numbered items.

1. Which picture more accurately portrays the bear's body movement and facial expression? Why?
2. Which picture more accurately depicts the creek? Why?
3. Which picture has a more appropriate shade of light? Why?
4. Which picture has a more appropriate background? Why?
5. Identify two sounds you can hear in the passage.

Making Inferences About Stories

Details are stated directly in a story. Look for the details that are stated directly in the following sentence from "Old Yeller and the Bear":

> Then, just as the bear went lunging up the creek bank toward Little Arliss and her cub, a flash of yellow came streaking out of the brush.

The sentence contains several clearly stated details. For example, the passage tells you that a bear was moving toward Arliss and the cub. It also tells you that a flash of yellow came from the brush.

Sometimes in a story, however, you come to understand more about characters, events, or actions than what is stated directly. You draw conclusions, or make inferences, about the characters, events, or actions.

An *inference* is a conclusion that is based on details that are stated. For example, after reading the sentence from "Old Yeller and the Bear," you may have asked yourself, "What was the flash of yellow?" The details do not tell. The flash of yellow could be anything—from a bolt of lightning to a flying banana peel. You must ask yourself what would be a *reasonable* inference to make from the details. You know that Old Yeller often hunted with Arliss. You also know that the dog was yellow. Therefore, a reasonable inference to make is that the "flash of yellow" was Old Yeller.

Making inferences as you read is a valuable skill. It helps you to feel a part of the story and to stay involved in the action. If you make inferences, you will want to keep reading to discover if your conclusions are correct. Usually, you will learn later in the story if your inferences were on the mark. Regarding the "flash of yellow," the very next sentence of the story says that "it was that big yeller dog." Even if the rest of the story does not directly confirm your inferences, you can still consider them reasonable if you base them on details that are stated directly in passages appearing in the story.

Activity 2 Read the following passage. Then make inferences to complete each numbered sentence with the correct answer. Be prepared to tell what details helped you make each inference.

As I raced past them, I saw the bear lunge up to stand on her hind feet like a man while she clawed at the body of the yeller dog hanging to her throat. I didn't wait to see more. Without ever checking my stride, I ran in and jerked Little Arliss loose from the cub. I grabbed him by the wrist and yanked him up out of that water and slung him toward Mama like he was a half-empty sack of corn. I screamed at Mama. "Grab him, Mama! Grab him and run!" Then I swung my chopping ax high and wheeled, aiming to cave in the she-bear's head with the first lick.

1. You may assume from the details that Old Yeller was ___.
   a. bigger than the bear   c. faster than the bear
   b. smaller than the bear   d. slower than the bear

2. The speaker "didn't wait to see more" because ___.
   a. he had no time to waste   c. his vision became blurry
   b. fighting upset him   d. he wanted to run away

3. The speaker swung his ax intending to ___.
   a. wound the bear   c. knock the bear over
   b. knock the bear out   d. kill the bear

4. The speaker probably assumed the bear would ___.
   a. run away   c. attack his family
   b. chase Old Yeller   d. grab her cub

5. From his actions you may assume the speaker's main concern was ___.
   a. his own safety   c. Arliss' safety
   b. the dog's safety   d. his mother's safety

Predicting Outcomes in Stories

As you read stories, you may make many types of inferences. One type involves predicting outcomes. Of course, you are not expected to guess the ending of every story you read. On the contrary, many good stories have endings that are meant to surprise you. However, you may use details to predict the outcomes of individual conversations, actions, or events within that story. In other words, you may be able to figure out what will happen next. As a good reader, you should always try to anticipate future developments, based on everything you have learned about the characters and events so far.

For example, in "Old Yeller and the Bear" Travis, the narrator and Arliss' older brother, describes a moment in which a bear is racing toward her cub and Arliss:

> She was roaring mad and ready to kill. And worst of all, I could see that I'd never get there in time! Mama couldn't either.

From the details in the description, it appears that the bear will attack Arliss before Travis or Mama can rescue him. Later, of course, you learn that Old Yeller suddenly arrives to save Arliss. However, until this moment it seems that the bear will attack. Expecting this outcome adds suspense to the story.

Activity 3 Read each of the following situations and the three outcomes listed afterward. Choose the outcome you feel is most likely to occur, based on details in "Old Yeller and the Bear." Then explain why you chose the outcome you did.

1. Toward the end of the book *Old Yeller*, a mad wolf is about to attack Travis' family. Considering what you already know about the characters and previous events, which of these outcomes do you predict will occur? Defend your answer.
   a. The wolf will attack the family and kill Mama and Arliss.
   b. Old Yeller will see the wolf and run away forever.
   c. Old Yeller will fight the wolf and save the family.
2. Old Yeller gets rabies at the end of the book. If he is allowed to live, he will be a danger to people around him. Based on what you already know about Travis, what action do you think he will take? Defend your answer.
   a. Travis will accept the responsibility of killing Old Yeller.
   b. Travis will allow Old Yeller to live with his family.
   c. Travis will give Old Yeller away to a neighbor.

Literary Skills Review

The Short Story

Guide for Reading the Short Story

As you read short stories, use this guide to understand how an author combines different techniques to create a fictional world.

Plot

1. What type of **conflict** does the main character face?
2. What is the **climax,** the point of our highest interest and involvement?
3. What is the **resolution,** or final outcome?
4. What events of the plot create **suspense**?

Character

1. Who are the important **characters** in the story?
2. What **character traits** do the characters show?
3. What **motivations** do characters have for their actions?
4. What does the author **directly tell** about the characters?
5. What do the characters' **words and actions** reveal about their personalities?
6. Does the author use a character in the story as a **first-person narrator**?
7. Does the author tell the story, acting as a **third-person narrator**?

Setting

1. **When and where** does the story take place?
2. What **details** describe the time and place of the story?
3. What **atmosphere,** or mood, does the setting create?

Theme

1. What is the story's **theme,** or main idea?
2. Is the theme directly **stated,** or is it **implied**?
3. In what sense is the theme a **generalization** of what happens in the story?
4. In what ways does the story's **title** point to its theme?

Themes Review

The Short Story

Authors write in order to communicate their ideas. Certain general themes—for example, "love"—appear in all types of literature because they concern people everywhere.

When we read two works dealing with the same general theme, we can consider each author's specific idea about that theme. The general theme is expressed as a single word or phrase, such as "love," while the specific theme can be stated as a sentence. For example, consider what two stories say about the general theme "love." The specific theme of "All You've Ever Wanted" is "Love can cause problems." The specific theme of "A Secret for Two" is "Love can provide a reason for living."

1. What specific points do "Last Cover" and "Thirteen" make about the general theme "love"?

2. For two of the following stories, explain the specific point that the author makes about the general theme "animals."
   "Feathered Friend"   "Lucas and Jake"
   "Uncle Tony's Goat"   "The Hummingbird . . ."
   "Old Yeller and the Bear" "The Wild Duck's Nest"

3. Explain what specific idea two of the following stories express about the general theme "communities."
   "A Just Judge"   "The Birdman"
   "The Snow in Chelm"   "The Clearing"
   "After Twenty Years" "Rip Van Winkle"

4. Select two of the following stories, and tell what specific view of family life each conveys.
   "All You've Ever Wanted" "The Sneaker Crisis"
   "Stolen Day"   "Christmas in Brooklyn"
   "The Sparrow"   "Home"

5. From the following lists choose one story and one other work. Tell what specific point each work makes about the general theme "challenges and goals."
   Stories: "The Fun They Had"   "The Third Level"
                 "The Wish"   "The Dinner Party"
                 "The Sound of Summer   "The Glorious White-
                   Running"   washer"
   Other: "Roadways"   *The Speckled Band*

Preview
Poetry

Poetry is like a circus. It is full of color, motion, and excitement. It entertains, delights, and inspires its audience. Like a circus, poetry appeals to our senses: A poem can please the eyes, sing to the ears, tickle the taste buds, and create a sense of wonder along the way.

Poetry is different from prose, the kind of writing we read in short stories, novels, and newspapers. Poetry squeezes meaning into a small number of words and lines, while prose is often longer and looser. A line of prose stretches from margin to margin across a page. A line of poetry, however, ends in a specific place because the poet wants to make a special effect. Prose is often written in paragraphs, but poetry is often written in groups of lines called **stanzas.** The language of prose re-creates the words and rhythms of everyday speech. The language of the poet is the language of suggestion, exaggeration, and comparison. It inspires the reader to look at the world in fresh, new ways. Some writers use poetry instead of prose when they want to express personal feelings in a brief, rhythmic, colorful way. Other writers use poetry when they want to tell stories in a compact, musical fashion that cannot be created in a short story, novel, or play.

In the pages ahead we will look at the basic elements of poetry: sound, language, form, and meaning. We will also look at many different kinds of poetry, from the traditional to the experimental. Finally, we will see how the elements of poetry work together to draw a unique and personal reaction from the reader.

THE SOUND OF POETRY

As with the circus tent, where the sound of the clapping crowd first pulls you inside, it is sound that first draws you into a poem. Because words have sound, they can be combined to make patterns of sound. By choosing and combining sounds in a special way, a poet can make sounds as loud and dramatic as a lion's roar or as hushed as a crowd during a high-wire act. The sound of poetry is not just decoration. It is an important part of the overall meaning and total effect of the poem. Read the following poems aloud, and listen carefully to the many different sounds they make.

Woody Guthrie (1912–1967) was a folk singer and songwriter. He roamed all over America working at odd jobs. While he traveled, he wrote and sang songs about the people he met and the land he saw.

As you read the words for "This Land Is Your Land," remember the music that Guthrie wrote to go with them.

The Chippewa are American Indians who, in their early days, hunted, fished, and gathered wild plants in their homeland around the Great Lakes and throughout the Great Plains. "A Song of Greatness" is a traditional Chippewa song that has been handed down from generation to generation for hundreds of years.

As you read "A Song," think of why it has been handed down for so many years.

Like Woody Guthrie, Carl Sandburg (1878–1967) traveled throughout our country getting to know the people, their stories, and their customs. Sometimes called our national poet, he captured the struggles and hopes of the American people and their land.

■ As you read "Buffalo Dusk," think about why Sandburg sets the poem at dusk, the beginning of darkness.

Born in Pennsylvania in 1901, Robert Francis has written poetry, essays, and fiction and has lectured throughout the United States.

■ As you read "Seagulls," notice how Francis' use of repetition adds to the poem's music and balance.

Theodore Roethke [ret′kē] (1908–1963) spent much time during his early years in his family's huge greenhouse, or indoor garden. His experiences there probably developed his sensitivity to the details of nature. "The Sloth" is about a strange South American animal known for its slow movement, its hooklike claws, and its ability to hang and walk upside down. The word *slothful*, which means "lazy," comes from the sloth's name and habits.

■ What is slothful about the creature in Roethke's poem?

Louise Bogan (1897–1970) was a person who preferred privacy and wanted to remain anonymous, or unacknowledged. Nonetheless, she became a well-known poet, critic, and lecturer. Bogan won many prizes for her poems, which were praised for their simple traditional form and for their compact use of language.

■ Read "Train Tune" aloud. In what way does it remind you of the sound of a train?

Edgar Allan Poe (1809–1849) is well known as the father of the horror tale and the detective story. He is equally famous for his highly musical poetry. As an adult Poe led an unhappy and lonely life. He was often ill, he was very poor, and his wife, Virginia, died while she was still in her twenties. "Annabel Lee," thought to be about his beloved dead wife, illustrates the haunting melody often found in Poe's poems.

■ What strong emotions flow on this melody?

Eleanor Farjeon (1881–1965) was an English author who wrote music, poems, plays, novels, nursery rhymes, and games. Her poems are often playful and full of humor.

■ Notice how her use of sound adds to the overall effect of "Cat!"

Woody Guthrie

This Land Is Your Land

Refrain
This land is your land, this land is my land
From California to the New York island;
From the redwood forest to the Gulf Stream waters;[1]
This land was made for you and me.

5 As I was walking that ribbon of highway,
I saw above me that endless skyway.
I saw below me that golden valley,
This land was made for you and me.

I've roamed and rambled and I followed my footsteps
10 To the sparkling sands of her diamond deserts,
And all around me a voice was sounding,
"This land was made for you and me."

When the sun comes shining and I was strolling
And the wheatfields waving and the dust clouds rolling,
15 As the fog was lifting a voice was chanting,
"This land was made for you and me."

———————
1. **From the redwood . . . waters:** from the giant evergreen trees on the West Coast to the warm ocean currents along the East Coast.

STUDY QUESTIONS

Recalling

1. To whom does the singer say the land belongs? What borders of the United States does the singer mention in lines 2 and 3 of the song?
2. List at least four of the features of the land that are described in lines 6, 7, 10, 14, and 15. What are some of the adjectives that Guthrie uses?
3. Which words in particular describe how the singer gets from place to place?

Interpreting

4. How does the singer feel about our country? What words and details in the song convey the singer's feelings to you?
5. In lines 11 and 15 the singer refers to a voice. Whose voice might it be? Why?

Extending

6. How does "This Land Is Your Land" make you feel about the United States? Why?

READING AND LITERARY FOCUS

The Music of Poetry

Poems and songs are close cousins. Long ago poems were not just recited; they were often sung. The poet's song was accompanied by a harplike instrument, and meaning and music were closely combined. Though poets no longer play music with their poems, the songlike qualities of poetry remain. For example, like some songs, some poems have a **refrain,** a line or group of lines repeated at regular intervals. The first four lines of "This Land Is Your Land" are a refrain.

Though a poem provides no tune to whistle or hum, the words a poet uses in a poem create definite patterns of sound. The poet may repeat syllables, consonants, vowels, words, word groups, or even entire lines. A poet relies on the patterns of sound to stress a poem's meaning. For example, in "This Land Is Your Land" the words *from* and *to* are repeated in lines 2 and 3. Repetition of these words helps to emphasize the idea of the land's size.

Thinking About the Music of Poetry

■ Find one or two other lines in "This Land Is Your Land" that contain a pattern of sound. Does this pattern stress the song's meaning?

CHALLENGE

Song Verse

■ Write an extra verse (a four-line section) for "This Land Is Your Land." The verse should include details about your own town. You might begin as follows:

This town is your town, this town is my town . . .

A Song of Greatness

When I hear the old men
Telling of heroes,
Telling of great deeds
Of ancient days—
5 When I hear that telling,
Then I think within me
I, too, am one of these.

When I hear the people
Praising great ones,
10 Then I know that I too—
Shall be esteemed;
I, too, when my time comes
Shall do mightily.

STUDY QUESTIONS

Recalling

1. What do the old men tell of the ancient days? What does the singer (the "I" in the song) think of when he hears them?
2. Whom do the people praise? What two things does the singer know when he hears the people?

Interpreting

3. How old is the singer? Which lines of the song helped you find your answer?
4. How does the singer feel about himself and his people? Explain your answer.

Extending

5. Do you think that any popular songs of today will be handed down from generation to generation? If so, which songs would they be, and what messages would they give to future generations?

READING AND LITERARY FOCUS

The Beginning of Poetry

Poems did not begin on paper. They began as songs, and long before they were written down, these songs were passed on by word of mouth. At one time a member of the tribe was the keeper of the people's history. How was the tribal poet able to remember the details of hundreds of years of past events without writing anything down?

The tribal poet used certain memory tricks to help remember long songs or poems. Often the poet repeated certain lines more than once, sometimes varying a word or part of a word. The poet also made sure that each line had a certain number of syllables or a certain number of rhythmic beats. In "A Song of Greatness" each line has either four, five, or six syllables. Lines 1, 5, and 8 all begin with the words "When I hear." These memory tricks helped many poems survive until they could be written down so that we can enjoy and appreciate them today.

Thinking About the Beginning of Poetry

■ If you were a tribal poet, what specific memory tricks would help you remember this poem?

COMPOSITION

Writing About a Title

■ Explain how the title "A Song of Greatness" captures the experience described in the poem. First tell what experience the speaker is describing in the poem, and explain what it means to him. Then explain how the title is appropriate to that experience.

Writing a Description

■ Imagine that you are the speaker of "A Song of Greatness." Your time has come, and you have done "mightily." For example, you may have won some kind of competition. In a short paragraph identify your accomplishment, and describe what you have done and how you feel about your achievement. Finally, describe the way your "ancestors" might feel about what you have done.

Carl Sandburg

Buffalo Dusk

The buffaloes are gone.
And those who saw the buffaloes are gone.
Those who saw the buffaloes by thousands and how they pawed
   the prairie sod into dust with their hoofs, their great heads
   down pawing on in a great pageant of dusk,
Those who saw the buffaloes are gone.
5 And the buffaloes are gone.

STUDY QUESTIONS

Recalling

1. Where are the buffaloes and those who saw them?
2. What did the buffaloes once do with their hoofs and their heads?
3. How many buffaloes does Sandburg suggest once roamed the prairie? Explain your answer.

Interpreting

4. Does the word *dusk* have any relation to the buffaloes' fate? Use examples from the poem to explain your answer.
5. Why do you think Sandburg called this poem "Buffalo Dusk"?

Extending

6. What does this poem tell you about the nation's past? Does it present a lesson for its future?

READING AND LITERARY FOCUS

Repetition

Ever since the earliest days, poets have used repetition to create special effects in their poetry. **Repetition** is the repeated use of sounds, words, phrases, or lines. Repetition increases the importance of the items that are repeated. It also helps tie the work together into a unified whole. In "This Land Is Your Land," for example, each verse ends with the line, "This land was made for you and me." This repetition ties together the idea that the land, with all its vastness and variety, belongs to everyone. In addition, repetition creates the reassuring sense that we are returning to something familiar.

Thinking About Repetition

■ What words and lines are repeated in "Buffalo Dusk"? What does this repetition add to the emotional force of the poem?

COMPOSITION

Writing About Words in a Poem

■ In a paragraph show how Sandburg suggests the power of the buffaloes in his poem "Buffalo Dusk." First identify the words Sandburg uses to refer directly to the buffaloes' strength. Then identify the words that suggest their strength indirectly.

Writing a Poem with Repetition

■ Write a five-line poem in which you describe the loss of something you have valued. Imitating Sandburg's poem, construct your first sentence to fit the following formula: "The ____ are [or is] gone." In the next three lines write descriptions of some of the specific activities or qualities of the lost object that you especially miss. Then, as Sandburg does, repeat your first line as the last line of your poem.

CHALLENGE

Research and Oral Report

■ After doing research in the library, present an oral report on the fate of the American buffalo. You may want to answer the following questions in your report: How close to extinction, or total disappearance, did the buffalo come? What factors contributed to their great decrease in number? What efforts have been made to save them? How many buffaloes are in the United States today?

Robert Francis

Seagulls

Between the under and the upper blue
All day the seagulls climb and swerve and soar,
Arc[1] intersecting arc, curve over curve.

And you may watch them weaving a long time
5   And never see their pattern twice the same
And never see their pattern once imperfect.

Take any moment they are in the air—
If you could change them, if you had the power
How would you place them other than they are?

10 What we have labored all our lives to have
And failed, these birds effortlessly achieve:
Freedom that flows in form and still is free.

_____

1. **Arc:** curved line.

STUDY QUESTIONS

Recalling

1. According to line 3, how do the seagulls fly?
2. What might you never see the same or imperfect?
3. What question is asked in the poem?
4. What do the birds effortlessly achieve, according to the last line?

Interpreting

5. How does the poem's speaker feel about the seagulls and their flight? Explain your answer.
6. Who is Francis referring to with the word _we?_ What have the birds achieved that we have not?
7. What comment about nature do you think Francis is making in "Seagulls"?

READING AND LITERARY FOCUS

Alliteration

A special sound effect of poetry, **alliteration** is the repetition of consonant sounds, most often at the beginnings of words. The following line from Francis' "Seagulls" is an example of alliteration:

All day the <u>s</u>eagulls climb and <u>s</u>werve and <u>s</u>oar . . .

Alliteration adds to the musical quality of a poem by creating echoes among the sounds.

Thinking About Alliteration

■ Find two other examples of alliteration in "Seagulls," and tell how they support the overall meaning of the poem.

Theodore Roethke

The Sloth

In moving-slow he has no peer.
You ask him something in his ear;
He thinks about it for a Year;

And then, before he says a Word
5 There, upside down (unlike a bird)
He will assume that you have heard—

A most EX-as-per-at-ing Lug.[1]
But should you call his manner Smug,
He'll sigh and give his branch a Hug;

10 Then off again to Sleep he goes,
Still swaying gently by his Toes,
And you just know he knows he knows.

---

1. **Lug:** lazy person.

STUDY QUESTIONS

Recalling

1. In what area does the sloth have no "peer," or equal? What does he do if you ask him something?
2. What about the sloth is "unlike a bird," according to line 5? What does he assume you have done?
3. What will the sloth do if you say he is smug?

Interpreting

4. Why do you think the poet divided the word *exasperating* in line 7 into syllables? Why might he have capitalized the first two letters of that word?
5. In the last line of the poem, what do you think the sloth "knows he knows"?

READING AND LITERARY FOCUS

Rhyme

Rhyme is a characteristic of poetry, but it is not a requirement. All poems do not rhyme. **Rhyme** is the repetition of the same or similar sounds in words that appear near each other in a poem. Most rhymes are **end rhymes**—that is, they come at the ends of lines of poetry. The following lines from "The Sloth" exemplify end rhyme:

> Then off again to Sleep he *goes*,
> Still swaying gently by his *Toes*,
> And you just know he knows he *knows*.

The words *goes, toes,* and *knows* are considered **perfect rhymes** because after their first consonant sounds their remaining sounds are alike. Notice that to rhyme, words do not have to be spelled alike. *Knows* and *toes* are perfect rhymes because they sound alike even though they are spelled differently. However, while *nose* and *lose* may look similar, they do not rhyme.

Thinking About Rhyme

1. How many different end rhymes can you find in "The Sloth"? Which lines in each of the stanzas rhyme?
2. Find two examples in "The Sloth" of rhymes with endings that are not spelled alike.

VOCABULARY

Synonyms

A **synonym** is a word that has the same or nearly the same meaning as another word. For example, the words *huge* and *large* are synonyms.

The italicized words below are from Roethke's "Sloth." Choose the word that is *nearest* the meaning of the italicized word *as it is used in the poem.* Write the number of each item and the letter of your choice on a separate piece of paper.

1. I *assume* that
   (a) confess
   (b) succeed
   (c) confusing
   (d) suppose
2. an *exasperating* day
   (a) delightful
   (b) afraid
   (c) breathing
   (d) annoying
3. a *smug* fellow
   (a) tired
   (b) rude
   (c) self-satisfied
   (d) slowly
4. the *swaying* trees
   (a) bouncing
   (b) swinging
   (c) heavy
   (d) slippery

Louise Bogan

Train Tune

Back through clouds
Back through clearing
Back through distance
Back through silence

5 Back through groves
Back through garlands
Back by rivers
Back below mountains

Back through lightning
10 Back through cities
Back through stars
Back through hours

Back through plains
Back through flowers
15 Back through birds
Back through rain

Back through smoke
Back through noon
Back along love
20 Back through midnight

Detail, *Rain, Steam, Speed,* J. M. W. Turner (1775–1851).

STUDY QUESTIONS

Recalling

1. List two places that the train goes back through. Then list two words that refer to time and two words that refer to nature.

2. Where in the poem does Bogan refer to an emotion? Is this the only emotion she mentions?

Interpreting

3. Describe the repetition in "Train Tune." In what lines does the repetition change? Why might Bogan have made these lines different?

4. In what ways is this poem a tune? If this poem were untitled, would it still make sense?

Extending

5. Is this a simple or a complex poem?

Edgar Allan Poe

Annabel Lee

It was many and many a year ago,
  In a kingdom by the sea,
That a maiden there lived whom you may know
  By the name of Annabel Lee;
5 And this maiden she lived with no other thought
    Than to love and be loved by me.

I was a child and *she* was a child,
  In this kingdom by the sea,
But we loved with a love that was more than love—
10   I and my Annabel Lee—
With a love that the wingèd seraphs[1] of Heaven
  Coveted[2] her and me.

And this was the reason that, long ago,
  In this kingdom by the sea,
15 A wind blew out of a cloud, chilling
    My beautiful Annabel Lee;
So that her highborn kinsmen[3] came
  And bore her away from me,
To shut her up in a sepulcher[4]
20   In this kingdom by the sea.

The angels, not half so happy in Heaven,
  Went envying her and me:
Yes!—that was the reason (as all men know,
  In this kingdom by the sea)
25 That the wind came out of the cloud by night,
  Chilling and killing my Annabel Lee.

But our love it was stronger by far than the love
  Of those who were older than we—
  Of many far wiser than we—

---

1. **seraphs** [ser'əfs]: angels.
2. **Coveted:** envied.
3. **kinsmen:** male relatives.
4. **sepulcher** [sep'əl kər]: tomb.

The Girl I Left Behind Me, Eastman Johnson (1824–1906).

30 And neither the angels in Heaven above,
      Nor the demons down under the sea,
    Can ever dissever[5] my soul from the soul
      Of the beautiful Annabel Lee:

    For the moon never beams, without bringing me dreams
35   Of the beautiful Annabel Lee;
    And the stars never rise, but I feel the bright eyes
      Of the beautiful Annabel Lee:
    And so, all the nighttide,[6] I lie down by the side
    Of my darling—my darling—my life and my bride,
40   In the sepulcher there by the sea—
      In her tomb by the sounding sea.

---

5. **dissever** [di sev′ər]: separate.
6. **nighttide:** nighttime.

STUDY QUESTIONS

Recalling

1. According to lines 1–4, when and where did the events of the poem take place? Who lived there?
2. In lines 5–7 what was Annabel Lee's only thought? How old were Annabel Lee and the speaker (the "I" in the poem) at the time?
3. In lines 11–26 why did a wind blow "out of a cloud"? What did it do to Annabel Lee? Where did her "highborn kinsmen" take her?
4. In lines 27–29 how does the speaker describe the love he and Annabel Lee had for each other? In lines 38–41 what does the speaker say he does "all the nighttide"?

Interpreting

5. Using your own words, in three or four sentences summarize the story of this poem.
6. Describe the speaker's love for Annabel Lee, based on what he tells about it in the poem.
7. Give three examples of Poe's use of rhyme and repetition. How do these add to the poem's eerie mood?

Extending

8. Do you agree or disagree with the expression "It is better to have loved and lost than never to have loved at all"? How do you think the speaker of "Annabel Lee" would feel about this expression?

READING AND LITERARY FOCUS

Rhythm

Like a song, a poem has rhythm. The word *rhythm* comes from the Greek word for "flow" and refers to any repeated pattern. In poetry **rhythm** is the pattern of beats made by stressed and unstressed syllables in the lines of a poem. The rhythm in "Annabel Lee" usually repeats in sets of three syllables. Two unstressed syllables (marked ˘) are followed by one stressed syllable (marked ′). Every line has at least one set of two syllables:

    And this maiden she lived with no other thought

    Than to love and be loved by me.

Sometimes a line of poetry has sets of only two syllables, the first unstressed and the second

Annabel Lee 225

stressed. For example, these lines from the American poet John Greenleaf Whittier have sets of unstressed and stressed syllables:

The sún thăt brief Dĕcémbĕr dáy

Rŏse chéerlĕss ŏver hílls ŏf gráy.

Sometimes in a set of two syllables, the first syllable is stressed, and the second is unstressed:

Báck thrŏugh líghtnĭng

Báck thrŏugh cítiĕs

The matching of rhythm with meaning is important in a poem. For instance, a lively, excited rhythm would match a poem about a baseball game.

In reading a poem we need to pay attention to the pattern of beats. However, we should not stress the beats too much, or the poem will become sing-song. Instead, we need to pay attention to the words and their meaning. We need also to vary the flow of the rhythm by pausing now and then for emphasis, or emotional effect. Pauses are an important part of a poem's rhythm. Just as the rhythm of a dribbled basketball is created by the bounce-silence-bounce-silence pattern, the rhythm of a poem is emphasized by pauses. In poems pauses can be created by punctuation, rhyme, line breaks (where a line ends), and stanza breaks (where a group of lines ends).

Thinking About Rhythm

1. Read "Train Tune" aloud, and note the syllables in each line. Is the pattern of stressed and unstressed syllables always the same? Does the rhythm seem to match the poem?
2. Copy the first six lines of "Annabel Lee" on a separate sheet, and mark the stressed and unstressed syllables. Do the stresses follow a pattern, or are they irregular?

COMPOSITION

Writing About Pauses

■ In poems pauses can be created by punctuation, rhyme, line breaks (where a line ends), and stanza breaks (where a group of lines ends). In a paragraph identify two kinds of pauses used in "Annabel Lee." Describe each kind of pause, and give an example of each. Then explain what kind of special effect each gives to the poem.

Writing a Poem with Rhythm

■ Write an unrhymed poem of five or more lines. Begin each line with the phrase "I like . . ." In your poem use a pattern of stressed and unstressed syllables that is similar to the one in "Train Tune" (page 222). For example, the poem below is about one particular thing (summer), and the first four lines identify things that the poet likes about summer.

I like hotdogs
I like pickles
I like beaches
I like sunshine
I like summer

CHALLENGE

Group Story

■ Create an oral mystery story with your class. Each person should add one sentence to the mystery at each turn. Continue until the mystery is solved. You might want to begin your mystery with the following sentence:

At midnight one rainy night Willy and his sister Nettie were awakened by a crash in the dining room.

Cat and Yellow Butterfly, Chinese hanging scroll, Hsü Pei-hung (1895–1953).

Eleanor Farjeon

Cat!

> *Cat!*
> Scat!
> After her, after her,
> Sleeky flatterer,
> 5 Spitfire[1] chatterer,
> Scatter her, scatter her
>   Off her mat!
>   *Wuff!*
>   *Wuff!*
> 10   Treat her rough!
> Git her, git her,
> Whiskery spitter!
> Catch her, catch her,
> Green-eyed scratcher!
> 15   Slathery
>   Slithery
>   Hisser,
>   Don't miss her!
> Run till you're dithery,[2]
> 20   Hithery
>   Thithery[3]
>   *Pftts! pftts!*
>   How she spits!
>   *Spitch! Spatch!*
> 25   Can't she scratch!
> Scritching the bark
> Of the sycamore tree,
> She's reached her ark
> And's hissing at me
> 30   *Pftts! pftts!*
>   *Wuff! wuff!*
>   Scat,
>   Cat!
>   That's
> 35   *That!*

---

1. **Spitfire:** quick-tempered.
2. **dithery:** nervous and confused; in a dither.
3. **Hithery / Thithery:** mixed up from running hither and thither, this way and that way.

Cat! 227

STUDY QUESTIONS

Recalling

1. Where is the cat at the beginning of the poem? Where is she at the end of the poem?
2. List at least two actions that the cat takes.

Interpreting

3. Which lines tell who is chasing the cat?
4. Who is telling what is happening in the poem? What does the cat do to her pursuer?
5. List two examples each of repetition, rhyme, and alliteration. What do these sound effects add to "Cat!"?

READING AND LITERARY FOCUS

Onomatopoeia

Onomatopoeia [on′ə mat′ə pē′ə] is the use of a word or phrase that actually imitates or suggests the sound of what it describes. For example, the word *hiss* sounds exactly like what it means—"the sound of an angry cat." Other words with sounds that suggest their meaning are *whinny, cluck, sizzle,* and *buzz.* Onomatopoeia is a sound effect that both reinforces the meaning of a poem and adds to its musical quality.

Thinking About Onomatopoeia

■ Find three examples of onomatopoeia in "Cat!" What do these words add to the meaning or the mood of the poem?

CHALLENGE

Illustration

■ Draw a comic strip of the action between the two animals in "Cat!" In cartoon balloons include the sounds they make in the poem.

COMPARING POEMS

■ Compare the use of sound in two or more of the poems in this section: "This Land Is Your Land," "A Song of Greatness," "Buffalo Dusk," "Seagulls," "The Sloth," "Train Tune," "Annabel Lee," and "Cat!" For example, you might want to compare the use of repetition in "This Land Is Your Land," "A Song of Greatness," and "Buffalo Dusk." You might compare the use of alliteration in "Seagulls" and "Annabel Lee." You might also compare the use of rhyme in "The Sloth" and "Annabel Lee" and the use of rhythm in "Train Tune" and "Cat!" How important is the sound of each poem to its meaning?

THE LANGUAGE OF POETRY

A poem catches your attention by spotlighting colors, tastes, smells, textures, and movements. To make a poem seem more real the poet chooses language that appeals to your senses. To portray a scene or idea a poet uses **figurative language**—words that make unusual comparisons or create unexpected effects. In doing so the poet arranges words to create memorable impressions. As you read the poems ahead, think about the ways each poet uses language to make sharp and vivid pictures.

Rachel Field (1894–1942) was born in New York and raised in New England. She wrote poetry, plays, and novels but is best remembered for her children's books. She was the first woman to win the Newbery Medal, an award given each year to a deserving work of literature for young people.

■ As you read "Something Told the Wild Geese," try to picture in your mind the scene Field describes.

Christopher Morley (1890–1957) was a poet, editor, and novelist who wrote more than fifty books in his lifetime. This poem is his tribute to one of the five senses that he feels has been neglected.

■ What tells you right away what sense it is?

John Ciardi (1916–1986) was a poet, editor, translator, and professor. Ciardi's poems are playful but simple and have often been praised for their gracefulness.

■ What comparison does Ciardi make in "The River Is a Piece of Sky"?

James Whitcomb Riley (1849–1916) was born in Indiana, which is sometimes called the Hoosier State. Riley wrote poems depicting his happy childhood and the people and scenery of his home. "When the Frost Is on the Punkin" is written in **dialect,** a form of speech spoken by the people of a particular region.

■ As you read this poem by "the Hoosier poet," try to picture the scene of old-fashioned country life he describes.

The Dinka are an African tribe that live to the west of the White Nile River in the southern Sudan. They are a nomadic people, which means that they move from place to place, usually with the change of seasons. The Dinka are especially known for their cattle herds.

■ As you read this tribal poem, notice how the images convey the poet's feelings about the bull.

Carl Sandburg (1878–1967) once defined poetry as "a yellow-silk handkerchief knotted with riddles, sealed in a balloon tied to the tail of a kite flying in a white wind against a blue sky in spring." From this definition you can see how important imagery and concrete language were to Sandburg.

■ As you read his delicate poem "Fog," keep in mind how Sandburg uses concrete language to create his imagery.

Born in Springfield, Illinois, Vachel Lindsay (1879–1931) wanted to bring poetry to the American people. He spent much of his life traveling and reciting his popular poems. He often performed his poems in return for food and lodging. Lindsay's poems are known for their rhythmic, musical qualities and for their vivid images.

■ How many images can you find in "To a Golden-Haired Girl in a Louisiana Town"?

Rachel Field

Something Told the Wild Geese

Something told the wild geese
    It was time to go.
Though the fields lay golden
    Something whispered,—"Snow."
5 Leaves were green and stirring,
    Berries, luster-glossed,
But beneath warm feathers
    Something cautioned,—"Frost."
All the sagging orchards
10   Steamed with amber[1] spice,
But each wild breast stiffened
    At remembered ice.
Something told the wild geese
    It was time to fly,—
15 Summer sun was on their wings,
    Winter in their cry.

---

1. **amber:** golden.

STUDY QUESTIONS

Recalling

1. What did "something" tell the wild geese?
2. What did "something" whisper to them? What did it caution?
3. What was on the geese's wings? What was in their cry?

Interpreting

4. To what does "something" refer?
5. In what season is this poem set? Which details tell you so?

Extending

6. What sounds, tastes, and smells do you associate with each of the seasons?

Christopher Morley

Smells

Why is it that the poets tell
So little of the sense of smell?
These are the odors I love well:

The smell of coffee freshly ground;
5   Or rich plum pudding, holly-crowned;
Or onions fried and deeply browned.

The fragrance of a fumy[1] pipe;
The smell of apples, newly ripe;
And printer's ink on leaden type.

10   Woods by moonlight in September
Breathe most sweet; and I remember
Many a smoky campfire ember.

Camphor,[2] turpentine,[3] and tea,
The balsam[4] of a Christmas tree,
15   These are whiffs of gramarye[5] . . .
A ship smells best of all to me!

---

1. **fumy** [fūm′ē]: smoky.
2. **Camphor** [kam′fer]: strong-smelling substance that comes from the wood of the camphor tree, used to protect clothes from moths.
3. **turpentine:** liquid that comes from substances secreted by pine trees, used as paint thinner.
4. **balsam** [bôl′səm]: pleasant-smelling gummy oil that comes from certain evergreen trees.
5. **gramarye** [gram′ər ē]: enchantment or magic.

STUDY QUESTIONS

Recalling

1. What is the subject of Morley's poem? When do you first know that?
2. List at least five types of smell presented in this poem.
3. What smells best of all to Morley?

Interpreting

4. In general, how does Morley feel about the things he is describing? Use examples from the poem to explain your answer.
5. Why might Morley consider the sensations he describes to be "gramarye," or magic?

Extending

6. Are there any smells that you would classify as "gramarye"? If so, what would they be?

READING AND LITERARY FOCUS

Imagery

An **image** is a picture, or likeness, that a poet creates with words. Poetic images are most often visual, or related to sight. These images help us picture in our minds what a poem is describing. However, not all images are visual. They may appeal to any of our five senses. Images may help us to imagine the way something may look, feel, taste, sound, or smell. For example, in describing an apple you may mention the snap of its stem when you pick it (sound), the shiny red color of its smooth skin (sight and touch), and the crisp sweetness when you bite into it (taste and smell).

The combination of images in a poem is called imagery. **Imagery** is the language that appeals to the senses. By reminding us of our own experiences, images are a key to the poet's message.

Thinking About Imagery

1. Find five images in "Something Told the Wild Geese." To which of the five senses do they appeal?
2. Do all of the images in "Smells" refer to the sense of smell? Find at least two or three images that appeal to one or more of the other four senses.

COMPOSITION

Writing About Images

■ Sometimes a poet may create an image with one word, but sometimes it takes several words to create a single image. In a paragraph first identify the one-word images in "Smells." Then identify the images that require several words. Finally, tell why these images bring out the meaning of the poem.

Writing an Adjective Poem

■ Write a poem of at least three lines in which you celebrate one of the five senses. In your title state what that sense is, as Morley does. Then, using only adjectives (words that modify, or describe, a noun or a pronoun), bring the sense to life. For example, the following poem is about sound:

Sound
Roaring, crashing,
Screeching, squealing,
Soft, soft,
Echoing,
Still.

For general help with writing poetry, see Lesson 6 in the Writing About Literature Handbook at the back of this book.

John Ciardi

The River Is a Piece of Sky

From the top of a bridge
The river below
Is a piece of sky—

      —Until you throw
5   —A penny in
      —Or a cockleshell[1]
      —Or a pebble or two
      —Or a bicycle bell
      —Or a cobblestone
10   —Or a fat man's cane—

And then you can see
It's a river again.

The difference you'll see
When you drop your penny:
15 The river has splashes,
The sky hasn't any.

---

1. **cockleshell:** heartshaped, two-part shell
of various shellfish called cockles.

STUDY QUESTIONS

Recalling

1. Where is the speaker of the poem standing? What does the river look like to him?
2. List three or four objects that you might throw in the river.
3. When do you see the difference between the sky and a river? According to lines 15 and 16, how are the river and the sky different?

Interpreting

4. Why do you think a river is like a piece of sky when you look at it "from the top of a bridge"? What are some ways that a river and the sky are alike?
5. How many rhyming words are in the poem? What are they?

Extending

6. Why do you think people are fascinated by reflections?

READING AND LITERARY FOCUS

Concrete Language

Since poems are short a poet needs to create images quickly and clearly. A poet usually chooses **concrete,** or specific, words instead of **abstract,** or general, words to describe images. For example, in "Something Told the Wild Geese," Field's concrete description ". . . the sagging orchards/ Steamed with amber spice" is much more specific than the general description "fields of trees." The picture that we have in our minds of Field's orchard is much richer and more detailed than the image we could possibly have of just "fields of trees." Field uses concrete language—or words that appeal to our senses of sight, hearing, taste, smell, and touch—to help us envision the picture she wants us to see.

Thinking About Concrete Language

■ Make a list of the images Ciardi uses in "The River Is a Piece of Sky." Put a *C* next to all the concrete images and a *G* next to the general images.

VOCABULARY

Modifiers

Modifiers are words or groups of words that describe or limit other words. They often help to make the meaning of the main words vivid and exact. Modifiers make images easier to picture by adding number, color, or other information about the senses. Look carefully at the following phrases:

thirty green, slimy snakes
big black bat

Think about the relationship of the modifiers, which are italicized, to the words they modify. Also think about what these modifiers add to the meaning of the main word.

On a separate sheet write at least one modifier that could fill each of the following blanks. Then tell to which of the five senses each of your modifiers appeals.

1. the _____ tea
2. ten _____ spiders
3. a _____ jacket
4. the _____ leaves
5. a _____ student

James Whitcomb Riley

When the Frost
Is on the Punkin

When the frost is on the punkin and the fodder's in the shock,[1]
And you hear the kyouck and gobble of the struttin' turkey cock,
And the clackin' of the guineys,[2] and the cluckin' of the hens,
And the rooster's hallylooyer as he tiptoes on the fence;
5 O, it's then's the time a feller is a-feelin' at his best,
With the risin' sun to greet him from a night of peaceful rest,
As he leaves the house, bareheaded, and goes out to feed the stock,[3]
When the frost is on the punkin and the fodder's in the shock.

---

1. **fodder's . . . shock:** Animal feed, such as cornstalks and alfalfa, tied upright in a bundle (shock).
2. **guineys** [gin'ēz]: guinea fowl, bird related to the pheasant.
3. **stock:** farm animals.

They's something kindo' harty-like about the atmusfere
10 When the heat of summer's over and the coolin' fall is here—
Of course we miss the flowers, and the blossums on the trees,
And the mumble of the hummin'birds and buzzin' of the bees;
But the air's so appetizin'; and the landscape through the haze
Of a crisp and sunny morning of the airly autumn days
15 Is a pictur' that no painter has the colorin' to mock[4]—
When the frost is on the punkin and the fodder's in the shock.

The husky, rusty russel of the tossels[5] of the corn,
And the raspin' of the tangled leaves, as golden as the morn;
The stubble in the furries[6]—kindo' lonesome-like, but still
20 A-preachin' sermuns to us of the barns they growed to fill;
The strawstack in the medder,[7] and the reaper in the shed;
The hosses in theyr stalls below—the clover overhead!—
O, it sets my hart a-clickin' like the tickin' of a clock,
When the frost is on the punkin and the fodder's in the shock!

25 Then your apples all is gethered, and the ones a feller keeps
Is poured around the celler floor in red and yeller heaps;
And your cider makin's over, and your wimmern[8] folks is through
With theyr mince[9] and apple butter, and theyr souse[10] and sausage, too!
I don't know how to tell it—but ef sich a thing could be
30 As the Angels wantin' boardin', and they'd call around on *me*—
I'd want to 'commodate[11] 'em—all the whole indurin' flock—
When the frost is on the punkin and the fodder's in the shock!

---

4. **mock:** imitate.
5. **tossels:** tassels; the flowers at the top of corn stalks.
6. **furries:** furrows; grooves made in the ground by a plow.
7. **medder:** meadow.
8. **wimmern:** women.
9. **mince:** mixture of chopped apples, raisins, spices, and sometimes meat, used as pie filling.
10. **souse:** pickled foods.
11. **'commodate:** accommodate; provide food and lodging.

Recalling

1. What is on the "punkin" when a "feller" feels his best? Where is the fodder?
2. What about summer does the poet miss? List four things that the poet likes about autumn.
3. What "russel" and "raspin'" does the poet hear in lines 17–19? What does "the stubble in the furries" preach about?
4. If they were to come to his farm at this time, to whom would the poet offer food and lodging, according to the last stanza?

Interpreting

5. What does the old-fashioned dialect add to the poem? In what way would the poem seem different without the dialect?
6. What might the poet mean in lines 13–15?
7. How do you think Riley feels about autumn? Support your opinion with examples.

READING AND LITERARY FOCUS

The Precise Word

Poets must be especially careful about using exactly the right word because poetry tries to say a great deal in just a few words. A poet may choose a particular word for a variety of reasons. For instance, the word may rhyme with another word, or its sound may echo its sense. It may add a double meaning or a tricky twist to the poem. It may also create a vivid picture or highlight a certain emotion.

Thinking About the Precise Word

1. Look at the word *hallylooer* in line 4 of "When the Frost Is on the Punkin." What effect is created by substituting the word *crowing* in its place?
2. Substitute other, more familiar words for Riley's regional ones. How is the poem changed? Which version do you prefer and why?

VOCABULARY

Dialect

The most used and recognized form of speech in the United States is standard American English. A variation of a language is called dialect. **Dialect** is the special form of speech that belongs to a particular group or region. A dialect uses some vocabulary that differs from that of standard English. For example, a large sandwich made on a long tube roll may be called a submarine, a zeppelin, a grinder, or a hoagie, depending on the part of the country in which you live. A dialect may also play with the spellings of standard English as well as with their sounds, forms, and meanings.

Here is a list of words from "When the Frost Is on the Punkin." All of these words are examples of Hoosier, or Indiana, dialect. List these words on a separate sheet, and beside them give the standard English form of each.

1. punkin
2. kyouck
3. guineys
4. hallylooer
5. kindo'
6. harty-like
7. atmusfere
8. yeller

COMPOSITION

Writing About Onomatopoeia

■ In a paragraph describe Riley's use of onomatopoeia in "When the Frost Is on the Punkin." Pay particular attention to words that imitate the sounds of farm animals. Give examples of onomatopoeia from the poem, and explain what they add to the poem's overall effect.

Writing an Advertisement

■ Imagine that you are a real-estate agent trying to sell the farm that Riley describes in his poem. In a paragraph write down what you would want possible buyers to know about the farm. Emphasize those features that you think would make it most attractive to buyers.

Dinka Traditional

The Magnificent Bull

My bull is white like the silver fish in the river
white like the shimmering crane bird on the river bank
white like fresh milk!
His roar is like the thunder to the Turkish cannon[1] on the steep shore.
5 My bull is dark like the raincloud in the storm.
He is like summer and winter.
Half of him is dark like the storm cloud,
half of him is light like sunshine.
His back shines like the morning star.
10 His brow is red like the beak of the Hornbill.[2]
His forehead is like a flag, calling the people from a distance,
He resembles the rainbow.

I will water him at the river,
With my spear I shall drive my enemies.
15 Let them water their herds at the well;
the river belongs to me and my bull.
Drink, my bull, from the river; I am here
to guard you with my spear.

---

1. **Turkish cannon:** During the 1800s much of the Sudan was occupied by Turkish and Egyptian forces.
2. **Hornbill:** bird of Africa and Asia known for its brightly colored bill.

STUDY QUESTIONS

Recalling

1. In lines 1–3 to what three things does the poet compare his bull? What color are these things?
2. According to lines 5–8, in what ways is the bull dark, and in what ways is he light? What seasons does he resemble?
3. Describe the bull's back, brow, and forehead. In line 12 what does the poet say the bull resembles?
4. Where will the poet water his bull? What will he do to his enemies? Where will they water their bulls?

Interpreting

5. How does the poet feel about his bull? Use the poem to support your answer.
6. List four or five examples of concrete images in this poem. What do they contribute to the overall effect of the poem?

Extending

7. The word *magnificent* comes from the Latin *magnus,* meaning "great." Think of some examples of other stories or poems you have read in which the animal was considered great. What qualities did the animal have?

READING AND LITERARY FOCUS

Simile

A **simile** is a direct comparison of two seemingly unlike things using a comparing word such as *like* or *as*. For example, the following are similes from "When the Frost Is on the Punkin": "the tangled leaves, *as* golden *as* the morn" and "it sets my hart a-clickin' *like* the tickin' of a clock."

The things that are being compared in a simile are basically not alike, but they do share some characteristics. For instance, think about the examples of similes just given. In the fall leaves turn a golden color that is like the morning sun, and a

heart and a clock both beat. Be careful not to confuse other statements using the words *like* or *as* with similes. For example, although "the rooster's hallylooyer as he tiptoes on the fence" uses the word *as,* it is not a comparison and therefore not a simile.

Thinking About Simile

1. List five similes from "The Magnificent Bull."
2. Reread the poem leaving out all the similes. Is the new poem as easy to visualize?

COMPOSITION

Writing About Color Imagery

■ In a paragraph write about the use of color imagery in "The Magnificent Bull." Be certain to mention all the color references and to point out how you think these color images bring the bull to life for the reader.

Writing a Poem with Similes

■ Write a nonrhyming poem in which each line begins with one of the colors of the rainbow (violet, indigo, blue, green, yellow, orange, and red) followed by the words "is like ____." Fill in the blank with a concrete example of something that is that color. Try to think of unusual examples. For example, instead of saying, "Red is like the color of a rose," you might say, "Red is like the color of a tired student's eyes." Put your colors in the order in which they appear in a rainbow. *For general help with writing poetry, see Lesson 6 in the Writing About Literature Handbook at the back of this book.*

CHALLENGE

Illustration

■ Draw or paint a picture of the bull described in "The Magnificent Bull." Be faithful to the details in the poem, particularly to the colors described.

Carl Sandburg

Fog

The fog comes
on little cat feet.

It sits looking
over harbor and city
5 on silent haunches
and then moves on.

STUDY QUESTIONS

Recalling
1. How does the fog arrive? What does it look at?
2. On what does the fog sit? What does the fog finally do?

Interpreting
3. Explain how Sandburg creates a feeling of motion in "Fog." Indicate words or phrases that show the stages of the fog's movement.
4. What qualities of fog does Sandburg suggest without directly mentioning them? Name the specific words in the poem that suggest these qualities.

Extending
5. What is meant by saying that a person is "in a fog"? What similarities does this type of fog have with actual fog?

CHALLENGE

Pantomime
■ Pantomime, or act without words, the actions described in "Fog."

Vachel Lindsay

To a Golden-Haired Girl in a Louisiana Town

You are a sunrise,
If a star should rise instead of the sun.
You are a moonrise,
If a star should come, in the place of the moon.
5 You are the Spring,
If a face should bloom,
Instead of an apple-bough.
You are my love
If your heart is as kind
10 As your young eyes now.

STUDY QUESTIONS

Recalling

1. To whom is the poem addressed? How do you know this?
2. In lines 1, 3, 5, and 8 what four things does the poet say the girl is to him?
3. What conditions, or "if" clauses, does the speaker add immediately after lines 1, 3, 5, and 8?

Interpreting

4. How does the speaker feel about the person he describes? Use examples from the poem to support your answer.
5. What do the conditions, or "if" clauses, add to the poem? Which condition seems to be most important to the speaker? Why do you think so?
6. Why do you think nature images are so often used in love poems?

READING AND LITERARY FOCUS

Metaphor

Like a simile, a **metaphor** is a comparison of two basically different things. In a metaphor, however, the comparison is not stated directly, and the words *like* or *as* do not appear. For example, Ciardi's title "The River Is a Piece of Sky" is a metaphor, while "the river is *like* a piece of sky" is a simile. Examples of metaphors by other poets include "hope is a tattered flag" (Sandburg) and "the sun is a huntress young" (Lindsay). Like similes, metaphors create images. They can bring a poem to life in colorful, unexpected ways.

Similes and metaphors always compare ideas from two different categories. You cannot, for example, create a simile or a metaphor by comparing one person with another. Instead, you must compare the person with something that is not a human being, such as an animal:

That quarterback is a gazelle.

Thinking About Metaphor

1. Identify the metaphor in "Fog." Do you like the metaphor? Why or why not?
2. Find three metaphors in "To a Golden-Haired Girl in a Louisiana Town."

VOCABULARY

Compound Words

A **compound word** is a combination of two or more words that acts as a single word. Some compound words are actually written as one word. For example, the words *door* and *knob* are joined into the single word *doorknob*. Sometimes, however, the compound word is joined with one or several hyphens, as in *sister-in-law*. Other two-word phrases like *high school* and *post office* are not actually joined into single words, but they do combine to form a single meaning.

1. Reread Lindsay's poem "To a Golden-Haired Girl in a Louisiana Town," and locate all of the compound words in the poem.
2. List some compound words that you know.
3. On a separate sheet make three columns labeled "Closed Words," "Hyphenated Words," and "Open Compounds." List each word from questions 1 and 2 in the correct column.

COMPARING POEMS

■ Compare the imagery of the poems in one of the following groups:

"Something Told the Wild Geese" and "Smells"

"The Magnificent Bull" and "When the Frost Is on the Punkin"

"The River Is a Piece of Sky," "Fog," and "To a Golden-Haired Girl in a Louisiana Town"

To which of the senses do the images in each of the poems appeal? Which poem could most easily be turned into a painting? Why?

THE FORM OF POETRY

The form of a poem is its overall pattern. You can get a sense of form simply by looking at a poem on the page. The poem may be broken into even parts, like bread cut into slices, or it may be presented uninterrupted, as a whole, uncut loaf. The lines of the poem may be similar in length or quite different, creating a visual pattern on the paper. Words may even be arranged to form a picture. A poet can construct a poem by using a known pattern or by making one up. In either case the finished creation will have shape and form. The following poems are good examples of the many shapes poetry can take.

Robert Frost (1874–1963) received a gold medal from Congress in honor of his poetry. Frost grew up in New England and spent much of his adult life struggling to make a living from farming and part-time teaching. Frost's poetry describes country life, depicting common experiences in uncommon ways. His poems are known for plain language and natural rhythms.

■ What country chores does Frost describe in "The Pasture"?

In addition to writing poetry, William Carlos Williams (1883–1963) practiced medicine for nearly forty years in his home town in New Jersey. Williams' poems are concerned with the details of daily life, which he portrays with clear, precise images. His great gift is his ability to make poetry from the most ordinary objects and experiences.

■ How many ordinary things are mentioned in Williams' poem?

Bashō (1644–1694), one of Japan's most famous poets, was born into the samurai, or feudal-warrior, class. During his lifetime he served in the court of a noble, entered a monastery, taught poetry, and wrote many popular poems. Just before Bashō died he called his students and friends to his bedside and recited for them his final poem.

■ Most of Bashō's poems, including "Bamboo Grove," follow a special form, called haiku [hī′kōō].

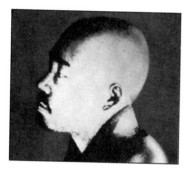

Like Bashō, Shiki (1867–1902) is famous for writing haiku. Shiki lived during a time when western ideas were being introduced in Japan. He was worried that the new ideas might take over completely, and he worked to preserve the best of his nation's culture. Many of Shiki's finest poems are about the history and traditions of Japan.

■ What does Shiki compare in his haiku reprinted here?

Richard Wright (1908–1960) was born in Mississippi. He moved to New York City in 1937, and his famous first novel, *Native Son*, was published several years later. In "A Balmy Spring Wind" Wright uses the traditional form of Japanese haiku.

■ Can you distinguish Wright's haiku from the earlier ones by Bashō and Shiki?

Carmen Tafolla was born in San Antonio, Texas, in 1951. She won first prize in the 1987 National Chicano Literature Competition sponsored by the University of California. Her publications include the poetry collections *Get Your Tortillas Together* and *Curandera*, in which the poem "Voyage" appears.

■ What is the price a person must sometimes pay for being an individual and taking a different road, as the speaker does in "Voyage"?

An anonymous poem is written by an author whose name is not known. Often anonymous poems were passed on orally from generation to generation before they were written down. It is impossible to trace their authors. "There Was an Old Man of Peru" and "A Mouse in Her Room," which are called limericks, are anonymous. In fact, many limericks are anonymous.

■ What strange situations do these limericks describe?

Born in New York in 1897, David McCord grew up in Oregon. He is a well-known poet and watercolor artist. "Write a Limerick Now" urges you to make up your own limerick.

Born in 1932, John Updike is known mainly as a novelist and short story writer although he has written several books of poetry. Like William Carlos Williams, Updike writes about the ordinary things of everyday life. The poem on page 255 is about such an ordinary object—a pendulum, which is a device that hangs from a fixed point and swings to-and-fro.

■ Who is the subject of Updike's poem?

Mary Ellen Solt was born in Iowa in 1920. Her poetry has been praised for its unique playfulness. She stresses the visual qualities of poems—the way they look on the page. In "Forsythia" the series of dots and dashes between the letters are not mere decoration. They are the Morse code symbols for each of the letters that spell out *forsythia*, a bush that blooms with bright yellow flowers at the beginning of spring.

■ What does Solt's poem look like?

Robert Frost

The Pasture

I'm going out to clean the pasture spring;
I'll only stop to rake the leaves away
(And wait to watch the water clear, I may):
I sha'n't be gone long.—You come too.

5   I'm going out to fetch the little calf
That's standing by the mother. It's so young
It totters when she licks it with her tongue.
I sha'n't be gone long.—You come too.

STUDY QUESTIONS

Recalling

1. What is the speaker going out to clean? What will he stop to do? Will he wait for anything?
2. Will he be gone long? Does he ask anyone to go with him?
3. What will the speaker fetch? What does the calf do when its mother licks it?
4. What line does the poet repeat?

Interpreting

5. Imagine and describe the speaker of "The Pasture."
6. Who might be the person who is invited to "come too"? Could it be the reader?
7. What is the effect of the period followed by the dash in lines 4 and 8? How would the poem change without this punctuation?
8. How does Frost make a common country chore special? Use examples from the poem to explain your answer.

Extending

9. What chores can you think of that might make a person feel good?

READING AND LITERARY FOCUS

End-Stopped Lines

In a poem an **end-stopped line** is one in which a pause occurs naturally at the end of a line. An end-stopped line that ends with a colon, period, question mark, or exclamation point requires the reader to stop completely before going on to the next line. An end-stopped line that ends with a comma, semicolon, or dash directs the reader to pause for a brief time before continuing. The following lines from "The Magnificent Bull" show several kinds of end-stopped lines:

> I will water him at the river,
> With my spear I shall drive my enemies.
> Let them water their herds at the well;
> the river belongs to me and my bull.

Thinking About End-Stopped Lines

1. Which lines in "The Pasture" are end-stopped? What punctuation marks does Frost use to indicate pauses at the ends of lines?
2. Read "The Pasture" out loud twice. First stop at the end of each line. Then pause only when the punctuation directs you to do so. Which reading makes the poem easier to understand?

William Carlos Williams

Poem

As the cat
climbed over
the top of

the jamcloset
5   first the right
forefoot

carefully
then the hind
stepped down

10   into the pit of
the empty
flowerpot.

Recalling

1. Over what did the cat climb? With which two feet did it step?
2. Into what did the cat step?

Interpreting

3. Which word in the poem seems to characterize the cat's movement best?
4. Is Williams' language concrete, abstract, or a combination of the two? How complete an image do you get from this poem? Explain your answer with examples from the poem.

Extending

5. Why does a cat make a good subject for a poem? What other animals might be interesting to write about? List three or four animals.

READING AND LITERARY FOCUS

Run-On Lines

As you have learned, when a line of poetry has an end stop, you should pause. However, when a line does not have an end stop, you should go on reading until you come to a mark of punctuation or some other break. A line without an end stop is called a **run-on line,** because its meaning is contained in more than a one-line unit. In a run-on line the meaning is carried over from one line to the next. Sometimes it takes several run-on lines to complete a thought. For example, Sandburg's "Fog," a six-line poem, can be read as two sentences. The slashes show where Sandburg broke the lines of the poem.

The fog comes / on little cat feet. / It sits looking / over harbor and city / on silent haunches / and then moves on.

Thinking About Run-On Lines

■ How many sentences are there in "Poem"? What punctuation does Williams use?

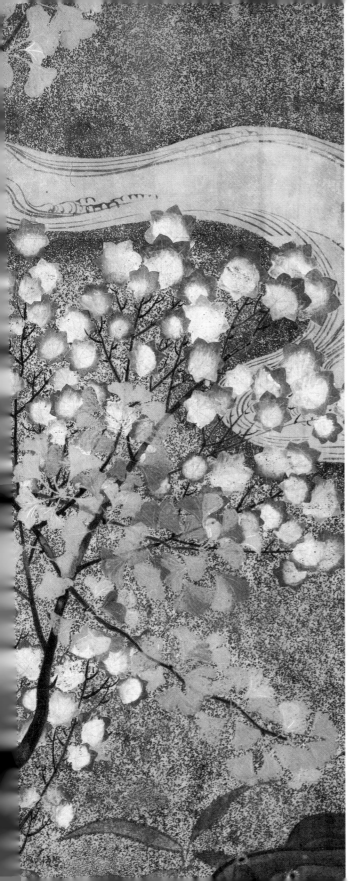

Bashō

Bamboo Grove

Song of the cuckoo:
   in the grove of great bamboos,
     moonlight seeping through.

Shiki

The New and the Old

Railroad tracks; a flight
   of wild geese close above them
     in the moonlit night.

Richard Wright

A Balmy Spring Wind

A balmy spring wind
Reminding me of something
I cannot recall

Detail from Japanese painting. Sotatsu–Korin School,
seventeenth–eighteenth century.

STUDY QUESTIONS

Recalling

1. Where does Bashō's poem take place? What can be heard there? What "seeps" through the grove?
2. About what two things does Shiki write? At what time of day does his poem take place?
3. What is the subject of Wright's poem? What does it remind him of?

Interpreting

4. Explain the importance of the colon in "Bamboo Grove." What effect does it have on the two parts of the poem?
5. Compare the two subjects of Shiki's poem. How are they different, and how are they similar?
6. What contradictions does Wright present? Could what he describes actually occur? Explain your answer.

READING AND LITERARY FOCUS

Haiku

A **haiku** is a three-line poem, usually about nature. The entire poem contains just seventeen syllables, five in the first line and the third line, seven in the second line. The form was developed in Japan in the seventeenth century. A haiku usually presents one or two vivid images without direct comment but often with a suggestion of a deeper meaning. For example, the haiku "Bamboo Grove" presents the image of a thick grove of tall bamboos dimly illuminated by moonlight. A cuckoo sings. The haiku suggests a fleeting, delicate moment in nature.

Thinking About Haiku

1. Explain why the poem by Shiki is an example of haiku.
2. Is Wright's poem different from the Japanese haiku? Why or why not?

COMPOSITION

Writing About Haiku

■ In a paragraph show how each of the preceding poems appeals to the senses. For each haiku tell which sense is most important. Give an example from each haiku to prove your point.

Writing Haiku

■ Write a haiku that expresses an idea or describes a brief moment that you remember. It may be about a person, a place, an object, an animal, or an event. Remember that a haiku is written in three lines. The pattern of syllables is five-seven-five, and there is usually no rhyme. You may want to follow Richard Wright's haiku:

1. In the first line use five syllables to state your subject.
2. In the second line use seven syllables to describe your subject.
3. In the third line use five syllables to define a word in the second line.

Here is an example:

A hammering noise
Interrupting my reading
About silent swans

For general help with writing poetry, see Lesson 6 in the Writing About Literature Handbook at the back of this book.

CHALLENGE

Collage

■ A **collage** is a picture made from assembling scraps of materials (bits of string, rubber bands, magazine pictures, paint, glitter, cloth, and so on). Paste your materials on a flat surface to make a collage that illustrates the scene described in "Bamboo Grove."

Carmen Tafolla

Voyage

I was the fourth ship
    Behind Niña, Pinta, and Santa María,[1]
    Lost at sea while watching a seagull,
    Following the wind and sunset skies,
5   While the others set their charts.

I was the fourth ship.
    Breathing in salt and flying with clouds,
    Sailing moonbreezes and starvision nights,
    Rolling into the wave and savoring its lull,
10   While the others pointed their prows.

I was the fourth ship.
    Playfully in love with the sea,
    Eternally entwined with the sky,
    Forever vowed to my voyage,
15   While the others shouted "Land."

---

1. **Niña, Pinta, Santa María:** ships commanded by Christopher Columbus on his first voyage to the New World.

STUDY QUESTIONS

Recalling

1. Who is the speaker of the poem?
2. According to line 3, what happened to the fourth ship? What was it doing when this occurred?
3. Name three specific actions taken by the Niña, the Pinta, and the Santa María.

Interpreting

4. How does the fourth ship feel about nature? Support your answer with specific examples.
5. For what reason do you think the poet leaves the fourth ship unnamed?
6. How does the fourth ship's purpose differ from that of the other three? Which of the ships seem more interested in the voyage? The destination?

READING AND LITERARY FOCUS

The Stanza

Sometimes the shape of a poem is determined by groupings of lines and the spaces between them. Poetry is often arranged in these groups of lines, which are called **stanzas.**

A stanza forms a visual unit on the page. It is divided from the rest of the poem by a space above and below it. Generally—but not always—each stanza in a poem contains the same number of lines. These equal divisions give a poem a sense of order and balance. Sometimes a stanza is also used as a division of thought, functioning as the paragraph does in prose. For example, in Robert Frost's "Pasture" (page 247) the speaker tells of cleaning the pasture spring in the first stanza. In the second stanza he speaks of another chore—fetching the little calf. Each stanza has four lines.

Thinking About the Stanza

1. How many stanzas does "Voyage" have? How many lines are in each?
2. In what ways is the organization of each of these stanzas alike?

VOCABULARY

The Thesaurus

A **synonym** is a word that has the same or nearly the same meaning as another word. The words *joy* and *happiness* are synonyms.

A **thesaurus** is a book that contains synonyms. Some thesauruses list key words in alphabetical order like dictionaries. Each key word is followed by its synonyms. Another type of thesaurus, *Roget's Thesaurus,* organizes words into groups that are listed by number. Guide numbers rather than guide words help you to find entries. An index of words in alphabetical order is located at the back of the book.

Suppose that you want to find a synonym for the word *screen.* First find *screen* in the index of *Roget's Thesaurus.* Then look at the group of words listed after *screen.* Notice that a number follows each word. If you want to use *screen* in the sense of "shade," for example, you will look up number 424.

Sample from Index
  screen, sieve 260
  shade 424
  hider 530
  defense 717

In the body of the book under number 424, you will find many words from which to choose the exact word that you need.

Sample Thesaurus Entry
  424. SHADE.—awning, screen, curtain; shutter, blind.

The following list of words is from "Voyage." Copy the words onto a separate sheet, and beside each word place a synonym that has the same meaning as the word has in the poem. Use your library's thesaurus to do this exercise.

1. savoring (verb)
2. lull (noun)
3. prows (noun)
4. eternally (adverb)
5. entwined (adjective)

Anonymous

There Was an Old Man of Peru

There was an old man of Peru
Who dreamed he was eating a shoe.
    He awoke in the night
    With a terrible fright
5 And found it was perfectly true!

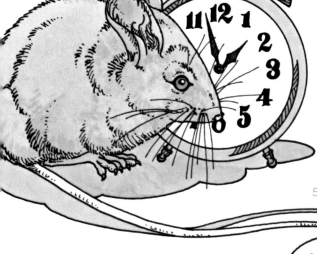

Anonymous

A Mouse in Her Room

A mouse in her room woke Miss Dowd;
She was frightened and screamed very loud,
    Then a happy thought hit her—
    To scare off the critter,
5 She sat up in bed and meowed.

David McCord

Write a Limerick Now

Write a limerick now. Say there was
An old man of some place, what he does,
    Or perhaps what he doesn't.
    Or isn't or wasn't.
5 Want help with it? Give me a buzz.

STUDY QUESTIONS

Recalling

1. In "There Was an Old Man of Peru" where did the old man live? What did he dream? What did he learn when he "awoke in the night"?
2. In "A Mouse in Her Room" what woke Miss Dowd? What did she do at first? How did she scare the "critter"?
3. What does McCord say to write? What does he tell you to say?
4. What question does McCord ask in line 5? What answer does he give?

Interpreting

5. Do you think "There Was an Old Man of Peru" and "A Mouse in Her Room" are humorous? Why or why not?
6. Compare McCord's advice on writing a limerick with the limericks you have read. Are the limericks in keeping with McCord's suggestions? Why or why not?

READING AND LITERARY FOCUS

Limericks

A **limerick** is a humorous five-line poem that follows a specific form. It has three long lines and two short lines. The long lines (lines 1, 2, and 5) rhyme, and the short lines (lines 3 and 4) rhyme. There is a strict pattern of beats, or accented syllables, in these lines. The three long lines usually each have three strong beats, and the two short lines each have two strong beats. Limericks can be foolish as well as funny, and they often end with

an unexpected twist. For instance, "There Was an Old Man of Peru" contains the surprise that the man had actually eaten his shoe. "A Mouse in Her Room" has a woman imitating a cat as its twist.

Thinking About Limericks

1. Tell how the two anonymous limericks presented here follow the form of the limerick.
2. Is McCord's poem a true limerick in terms of form and subject matter? Give specific reasons in your answer.

COMPOSITION

Writing About Limericks

■ In a paragraph state your opinion of limericks, and then support your opinion with evidence. Regardless of whether you have a favorable or unfavorable opinion of limericks, you should mention their form and their humor in your response.

Writing Limericks

■ A good way to begin writing limericks is to think about your name. You can begin as follows:

> There once was a boy [or girl or teenager or student, etc.] named ＿＿

Lines 2 and 5, which will be the same length as line 1, will have to end with words that rhyme with your name. Lines 3 and 4, which will be shorter, should end in a different rhyme. *For general help with writing poetry, see Lesson 6 in the Writing About Literature Handbook at the back of this book.*

John Updike

Pendulum

This lean commuter busies

Himself with being steady;

No matter where he is, he's

Been often there already.

STUDY QUESTIONS

Recalling

1. What adjective is used to describe the commuter? With what does he busy himself?
2. How many times has he been where he is?

Interpreting

3. Why do you think the commuter "busies himself with being steady"? Where might this poem take place?
4. Describe Updike's use of rhyme. Why is the rhyme not as obvious as in other poems?
5. Reread the poem, paying close attention to the movement of your eyes as you read. What kind of motion do they make in order to follow the poem? How does this movement relate to the subject matter and the title of the poem?

Mary Ellen Solt

Forsythia

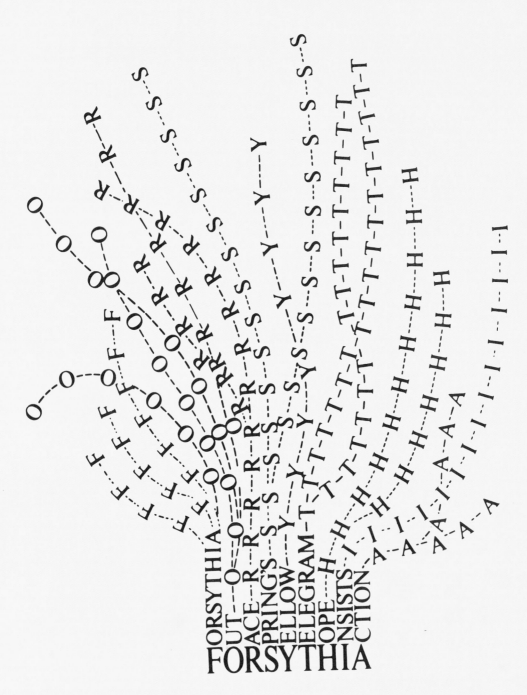

Recalling

1. What word is spelled at the bottom of the poem in large letters?
2. Write the nine words that grow out of the word at the bottom of the poem.

Interpreting

3. Read the "branch words" out loud as a poem. Do they make a sentence? What images do they present? What else do they add to the poem?
4. If you had never seen forsythia, could you tell just by looking at Solt's poem what the bush might look like? Describe it from what you see in the poem.

Extending

5. Think of some creative ways that "Forsythia" could be read in class.

READING AND LITERARY FOCUS

Concrete Poetry

A **concrete** poem is shaped to look like its subject. In concrete poems the placement of letters, words, lines, spaces, and punctuation creates a strong visual effect. To emphasize a poem's visual importance, the author of a concrete poem may even take the poem off the paper and outdoors into the parks, building giant letters of steel, wood, or concrete.

Thinking About Concrete Poetry

■ Are the poems by Updike and Solt concrete? What characteristics make them so?

COMPOSITION

Writing an Opinion

■ In a paragraph express your opinion of concrete poetry. Do you like it? Why or why not? Do you think it makes reading poetry more fun, more difficult, or both? Why? Support your opinions with examples from concrete poems.

Writing a Concrete Poem

■ Write a poem in which the shape of your words on the page suggests the poem's subject matter. If you wish, you may choose to write about one of the following: a rocking horse, a Ping-Pong game, rain, a doughnut, a snake, or a weeping willow.

COMPARING POEMS

1. Compare the forms of the poems in one of the following groups:

   "The Pasture," "Poem," and "Voyage"

   "There Was an Old Man of Peru," "A Mouse in Her Room," and "Write a Limerick Now"

   "Bamboo Grove," "The New and the Old," and "A Balmy Spring Wind"

   "Pendulum" and "Forsythia"

   Tell whether or not each poem's form is based on syllables, stanzas, rhyme, shape, or some combination of these elements.

2. In which of the poems that you have read in this section does form best seem to suit meaning? Explain your answer fully.

THE MEANING OF POETRY

Looking for the meaning of a poem can sometimes be like looking for buried treasure. Sounds, images, and form are a map to guide you on the right course. In some poems meaning is not hidden at all. The poet may state the **theme,** or main idea, of a poem directly in a single line or sentence or even in the poem's title. In other poems—such as a **narrative poem,** which tells a story—the main idea unfolds as the story is told. Sometimes, however, the treasured message of a poem is not so obvious. For example, a **lyric poem,** which expresses a personal vision or an emotion, does not have a story line.

Whether or not the message is on the surface or buried, you should think about the sounds, the images, and the form of the poem first. Then you will be able to discover the meaning. The following poems illustrate both the direct and the indirect ways in which poets convey the meaning of their works.

Alfred Noyes (1880–1958) became a successful poet while still in his twenties. The idea for "The Highwayman" came to Noyes one stormy night as he was standing in a lonely spot about thirty miles from London. It was the very spot where a famous highwayman, or outlaw, had waited to ambush stagecoaches and rob travelers almost two hundred years earlier.

■ Notice how the exciting story of the highwayman unfolds throughout the poem.

Gwendolyn Brooks was born in Kansas in 1917 but grew up in Chicago, where she still lives. She began writing at the age of seven, and her first poem was published when she was thirteen. She won the Pulitzer Prize for *Annie Allen,* a volume of poems about a black girl's growing up. Many of Brooks's poems concentrate on specific places and people.

■ What does the title of the poem on page 266 reveal about the poem?

Marge Piercy was born in Detroit, Michigan, in 1936. She has written poetry, plays, and novels and contributes essays, short stories, and reviews to magazines. Her work often deals with issues about women.

■ As you read "Simple Song," notice how each stanza develops a different thought.

Emily Dickinson (1830–1886) spent most of her life in the town of Amherst, Massachusetts. She had few friends and rarely left her father's house. Only seven of her poems were published during her lifetime. After her death her sister found over 1,700 poems hidden in Dickinson's room, along with instructions to burn them—instructions that her sister did not follow.

■ What unusual comparison does Dickinson make in the poem on page 270?

Alfred Noyes

The Highwayman

Part 1

The wind was a torrent of darkness among the gusty trees,
The moon was a ghostly galleon[1] tossed upon cloudy seas,
The road was a ribbon of moonlight over the purple moor,[2]
And the highwayman came riding—
5   Riding—riding—
The highwayman came riding, up to the old inn door.

He'd a French cocked hat[3] on his forehead, a bunch of lace at his chin,
A coat of the claret[4] velvet, and breeches[5] of brown doeskin;
They fitted with never a wrinkle: his boots were up to the thigh!
10 And he rode with a jeweled twinkle,
    His pistol butts a-twinkle,
His rapier hilt[6] a-twinkle, under the jeweled sky.

Over the cobbles he clattered and clashed in the dark innyard
And he tapped with his whip on the shutters, but all was locked and barred;
15 He whistled a tune to the window, and who should be waiting there
But the landlord's black-eyed daughter,
    Bess, the landlord's daughter,
Plaiting[7] a dark red love knot into her long black hair.

And dark in the dark old innyard a stable wicket[8] creaked
20 Where Tim the ostler[9] listened; his face was white and peaked;
His eyes were hollows of madness, his hair like moldy hay,
But he loved the landlord's daughter,
    The landlord's red-lipped daughter,
Dumb as a dog he listened, and he heard the robber say—

---

1. **galleon** [gal'yən]: large sailing ship.
2. **moor:** wild, marshy land, often covered with purplish-pink flowers called heather.
3. **cocked hat:** hat with turned-up brim forming two or more points.
4. **claret** [klar'it]: deep, purplish-red color.
5. **breeches** [brich'iz]: trousers reaching to the knees.
6. **rapier** [rā'pē ər] **hilt:** sword handle.
7. **Plaiting:** braiding.
8. **wicket:** small door set in a larger door.
9. **ostler** [os'lər]: hostler [hos'lər], person who takes care of horses in a stable.

25 "One kiss, my bonny sweetheart, I'm after a prize tonight,
   But I shall be back with the yellow gold before the morning light;
   Yet, if they press me sharply, and harry[10] me through the day,
   Then look for me by moonlight,
      Watch for me by moonlight,
30 I'll come to thee by moonlight, though hell should bar the way."

   He rose upright in the stirrups; he scarce could reach her hand,
   But she loosened her hair i' the casement![11] His face burned like a brand
   As the black cascade of perfume came tumbling over his breast;
   And he kissed its waves in the moonlight,
35   (Oh, sweet black waves in the moonlight!)
   Then he tugged at his rein in the moonlight, and galloped away to the west.

———————
10. **harry:** attack.
11. **casement:** window that opens outward on hinges along the sides.

Part 2

He did not come in the dawning; he did not come at noon;
And out o' the tawny sunset, before the rise o' the moon,
When the road was a gypsy's ribbon, looping the purple moor,
40 A redcoat troop came marching—
    Marching—marching—
King George's men[12] came marching, up to the old inn door.

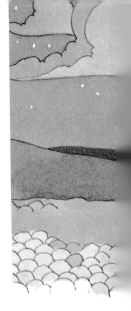

They said no word to the landlord, they drank his ale instead,
But they gagged his daughter and bound her to the foot of her narrow bed;
45 Two of them knelt at her casement, with muskets at their side!
There was death at every window;
    And hell at one dark window;
For Bess could see, through her casement, the road that *he* would ride.

They had tied her up to attention, with many a sniggering jest;
50 They had bound a musket beside her, with the barrel beneath her breast!
"Now keep good watch!" and they kissed her. She heard the dead man say—
Look for me by moonlight;
    Watch for me by moonlight;
I'll come to thee by moonlight, though hell should bar the way!

55 She twisted her hands behind her; but all the knots held good!
She writhed her hands till her fingers were wet with sweat or blood!
They stretched and strained in the darkness, and the hours crawled by like years,
Till, now, on the stroke of midnight,
    Cold, on the stroke of midnight,
60 The tip of one finger touched it! The trigger at least was hers!

The tip of one finger touched it; she strove no more for the rest!
Up, she stood to attention, with the barrel beneath her breast,
She would not risk their hearing: she would not strive again;
For the road lay bare in the moonlight;
65   Blank and bare in the moonlight;
And the blood in her veins in the moonlight throbbed to her love's refrain.

Tlot-tlot; tlot-tlot! Had they heard it? The horse hoofs ringing clear;
Tlot-tlot, tlot-tlot, in the distance? Were they deaf that they did not hear?
Down the ribbon of moonlight, over the brow of the hill,

---

12. **King George's men:** soldiers of George III (1738–1820), king of Great
Britain during the American Revolution.

70 The highwayman came riding,
     Riding, riding!
The redcoats looked to their priming![13] She stood up, straight and still!

Tlot-tlot, in the frosty silence! *Tlot-tlot*, in the echoing night!
Nearer he came and nearer! Her face was like a light!
75 Her eyes grew wide for a moment; she drew one last deep breath,
Then her finger moved in the moonlight,
     Her musket shattered the moonlight,
Shattered her breast in the moonlight and warned him—with her death.

He turned; he spurred to the westward; he did not know who stood
80 Bowed, with her head o'er the musket, drenched with her own red blood!
Not till the dawn he heard it, his face grew gray to hear
How Bess, the landlord's daughter,
     The landlord's black-eyed daughter,
Had watched for her love in the moonlight, and died in the darkness there.

85 Back, he spurred like a madman, shrieking a curse to the sky,
With the white road smoking behind him, and his rapier brandished high!
Blood-red were his spurs i' the golden noon; wine-red his velvet coat,
When they shot him down on the highway,
     Down like a dog on the highway,
90 And he lay in his blood on the highway, with a bunch of lace at his throat.

---

13. **priming:** gunpowder.

And still of a winter's night, they say, when the wind is in the trees,
When the moon is a ghostly galleon tossed upon cloudy seas,
When the road is a ribbon of moonlight over the purple moor,
A highwayman comes riding—
95 *Riding—riding—*
A highwayman comes riding, up to the old inn door.

Over the cobbles he clatters and clangs in the dark innyard;
And he taps with his whip on the shutters, but all is locked and barred;
He whistles a tune to the window, and who should be waiting there
100 *But the landlord's black-eyed daughter,*
Bess, the landlord's daughter,
Plaiting a dark red love knot into her long black hair.

STUDY QUESTIONS

Recalling

1. Using lines 1–6, describe the night on which the poem takes place, and identify the highwayman's destination.
2. Describe the person (lines 20–24) who overhears the highwayman's conversation with Bess.
3. What does the highwayman say in lines 25–30? What does he do in lines 31–36?
4. What do King George's men do to the landlord's daughter in lines 44–50? For whom are they waiting?
5. According to lines 76–78, how does Bess warn the returning highwayman? What happens to the highwayman in lines 85–90?
6. According to lines 91–102, what legend about the highwayman and Bess still lives?

Interpreting

7. Who might have warned the redcoats that the highwayman would return to the inn? Why do you think that the person warned them?

8. What sacrifice does Bess make? For what reason do you think she makes it? Do you think her act is heroic or foolish? Is the highwayman also heroic? Explain your answer.
9. What different actions take place in the moonlight? What role, or function, does moonlight play in the poem?
10. How would the poem be different if it ended at line 90?

READING AND LITERARY FOCUS

Narrative Poetry

A **narrative poem** tells a story in verse. Like a short story, a narrative poem has plot, characters, and setting. Often the events of a narrative poem unfold in a **chronological sequence,** or in the order in which they happen in time. "The Highwayman" is told in chronological order. It begins with the highwayman's arrival at the inn yard. The middle of the poem describes his brief visit, his plan to return, and the waiting troops. The poem ends with the highwayman's death.

Not all narrative poems have a beginning, middle, and end. Some focus only on one part of a story, highlighting only a few main events. The poet who tells this kind of story usually creates a vivid and intense emotional effect within the compact form of a poem. In "Annabel Lee" (page 223), for example, Poe focuses only on the death of Annabel Lee. As a result, he heightens the sense of personal loss felt by the narrator.

Thinking About Narrative Poetry

1. Who are the characters in "The Highwayman"? What is the setting?
2. List the complete sequence of events as they are told in "The Highwayman."

VOCABULARY

Sentence Completions

Each of the following sentences contains a blank with four possible words for completing the sentence. Choose the word that completes each sentence correctly and that uses the word *as the word is used in the selection.*

1. The rain fell in a ____.
   (a) torrent   (c) plaiting
   (b) claret   (d) casement

2. As he walked on the ____ in the moonlight, his feet got soggy.
   (a) hilt   (c) ostler
   (b) moor   (d) tawny

3. The milk poured down her chin in a ____.
   (a) landlord   (c) musket
   (b) brand   (d) cascade

4. The ____ look on the woman's face made him uncomfortable.
   (a) sniggering   (c) brandished
   (b) priming   (d) writhed

COMPOSITION

Comparing Poetry and Prose

■ The story line of "The Highwayman" could be told quite simply and briefly in prose. In one paragraph explain why you think the poetic version of the story has remained popular for many years. You might mention and give examples of the poem's rhythm, images, and figurative language. Conclude by stating what you think the story would lose or gain if it were written in prose.

Writing a Description

■ Reread the second stanza of Noyes's poem. Notice how he uses vivid images to describe the highwayman's clothing. In a short paragraph describe in detail a particular person's clothing. Begin with a general statement about that person's wardrobe, and then give examples. Try to choose details that will also show something about the character's personality.

Gwendolyn Brooks

Life for My Child Is Simple, and Is Good

Life for my child is simple, and is good.
He knows his wish. Yes, but that is not all,
Because I know mine too.
And we both want joy of undeep and unabiding things,
5 Like kicking over a chair or throwing blocks out of a window
Or tipping over an icebox pan
Or snatching down curtains or fingering an electric outlet
Or a journey or a friend or an illegal kiss.
No. There is more to it than that.
10 It is that he has never been afraid.
Rather, he reaches out and lo the chair falls with a beautiful crash,
And the blocks fall, down on the people's heads,
And the water comes slooshing sloppily out across the floor.
And so forth.
15 Not that success, for him, is sure, infallible.[1]
But never has he been afraid to reach.
His lesions[2] are legion.[3]
But reaching is his rule.

---

1. **infallible:** incapable of error or failure.
2. **lesions** [lē′zhənz]: injuries.
3. **legion:** great in number.

STUDY QUESTIONS

Recalling

1. What do the child and the speaker (the "I" in the poem) both know, according to lines 2–3?
2. List the eight activities from which the child and the speaker wish to derive joy (lines 5–8).
3. Give the three examples from lines 11–13 of the child's successes.
4. What has the child never been afraid to do? What is his "rule"?

Interpreting

5. What is the relationship between speaker and child? How do you know?
6. What literal, or exact, meaning does Brooks give the word *reaching*? What larger meaning does she imply?
7. What, according to this poem, is more important than just having a wish to do something?

Extending

8. Is it important to "reach" out? Why or why not?

READING AND LITERARY FOCUS

Stated Theme

The **theme,** or main idea, of a piece of literature is usually a statement that expresses the author's attitude about life. Certain themes have appeared again and again in literature—themes about love, nature, heroism, time. In poetry these abstract concepts are made concrete by the examples the poet uses to illustrate them. Some poems have a **stated theme,** a theme that the author expresses directly. A poem with a stated theme often has many examples that support the theme. The theme is usually expressed in a sentence.

In order to find the theme of a poem, first ask yourself why the author wrote the poem. Then try to state the poem's central thought, or theme, in a single sentence. Finally, make sure the examples or supporting details are consistent with the theme you have chosen. For example, Sandburg probably wrote "Buffalo Dusk" to call attention to the disappearance of thousands of buffaloes. The theme of the poem, stated in a sentence, is "It is sad that the buffaloes have disappeared." Examples from the poem include a description of thousands of buffaloes pawing the prairie and the statement "The buffaloes are gone."

It is easy to confuse theme and topic. The **topic** is the broad subject an author writes about in a piece of literature. The topic is usually stated in a word or phrase. For example, buffaloes are the topic of Sandburg's poem "Buffalo Dusk."

Thinking About Stated Theme

1. What is the theme of Brooks's poem? Is it stated directly? Do examples support the theme?
2. What is the topic of Brooks's poem?

VOCABULARY

Word Origins

The origin of a word refers to its history, or heritage—where it came from, what it originally meant, and how its meaning and form have changed over the years. The origin of a word is called its **etymology,** and you can find the etymology for a particular word by looking up the word in a dictionary. You will usually find that word's etymology in parentheses or brackets just after the pronunciation or at the end of the definitions. This information will tell you from which language or languages the word comes, its original meaning, and forms that the word took in its development.

The information given about a word's etymology varies from dictionary to dictionary. For instance, in the following sample entries the *Scribner Dictionary* tells you that the word *journey* comes from the Old French word *journee* and goes back to the Latin word *diurnus*. *Webster's New World Dictionary* says that *journey* comes from the Middle English word *journee* and traces the word's development back to the Latin word *dies*. The dictionary that you use may present different information. Before you learn about a word's etymology, be sure to consult your dictionary's key to abbreviations and symbols.

> **jour·ney** (jur′nē) *pl.,* **-neys.** *n.* **1.** trip, esp. one over a considerable distance or taking considerable time: *a journey across the United States.* **2.** distance traveled, or that can be traveled, in a specified time: *a four days' journey from here.* —*v.i.,* **-neyed, -ney·ing,** to make a trip; travel. —*v.t.* to travel over or through. [Old French *journee* day, a day's travel, a day's work, going back to Latin *diurnus* daily, from *diēs* day.]
>
> —*Macmillan Dictionary*

Using a good dictionary, copy down the etymologies for each of the words listed below, all of which come from Brooks's poem "Life for My Child Is Simple, and Is Good."

1. afraid
2. beautiful
3. infallible
4. lesion
5. legion

Marge Piercy

Simple Song

When we are going toward someone we say
You are just like me
your thoughts are my brothers
word matches word
5 how easy to be together.

When we are leaving someone we say
how strange you are
we cannot communicate
we can never agree
10 how hard, hard and weary to be together.

We are not different nor alike
but each strange in his leather body
sealed in skin and reaching out clumsy hands
and loving is an act
15 that cannot outlive
the open hand
the open eye
the door in the chest standing open.

268

STUDY QUESTIONS

Recalling

1. According to the speaker, what four things do we say when we are "going toward someone"?
2. What four things do we say when we are leaving someone?
3. What are three things that loving cannot outlive?

Interpreting

4. What do you think Piercy means by "going toward someone"? By "leaving someone"? Do you agree with what Piercy says about going toward and away from someone? Why or why not?
5. Do you agree with what Piercy says about love? Do you think this poem is basically positive or negative? Use examples from the poem to support your answer.

Extending

6. Why do you think people sometimes have difficulty communicating? List three or four reasons.

READING AND LITERARY FOCUS

Implied Theme

Some poems have a **stated theme,** or one that the poet expresses directly. Often, however, a poet will prefer to imply a theme indirectly rather than state it outright. An **implied theme** is one that gradually becomes clear as the poem unfolds. You can figure out an implied theme by paying attention to the title, examples, or supporting details and by thinking about the poet's purpose in writing.

For example, in "Something Told the Wild Geese" you can guess that the poem will be about the "something" referred to in the title. As the poem unfolds, supporting details tell you that "something" whispered "snow" and "frost." Other details tell you that the season is changing from summer to fall and that the geese are responding to the changes in weather. The poet's purpose seems to be to write about nature and its creatures. Therefore, the implied theme might be stated as "Nature communicates with its creatures in subtle and mysterious ways."

Thinking About Implied Theme

■ What is the theme of "Simple Song"? Is it stated directly, or is it implied? Explain your answer by examining the title, the supporting details, and the author's purpose in writing.

COMPOSITION

Writing About a Poem

■ Examine the use of lines in either Brooks's or Piercy's poem. Write about the poet's use of lines, answering the following questions: (1) Are the lines in the poem alike or different in length? (2) How do the line lengths emphasize certain points? (3) Are the lines end-stopped (page 247), run-on (page 248), or both?

Writing a Description

■ In a paragraph describe a person who does not want to communicate with anyone. Imagine that you are in the same room with this person. Describe the person's movements and clothing. For example, perhaps the person's collar is turned up so that others cannot see his or her face. Describe at least four things that make the person unfriendly.

Emily Dickinson

I'm Nobody!
Who Are You?

I'm nobody! Who are you?
   Are you nobody, too?
Then there's a pair of us—don't tell!
   They'd banish[1] us, you know.

5 How dreary to be somebody!
   How public like a frog
To tell your name the livelong day
   To an admiring bog![2]

---

1. **banish:** send away; force to leave.
2. **bog:** swamp.

STUDY QUESTIONS

Recalling

1. What word does the speaker use to describe herself in line 1? What two questions does she ask of the reader in lines 1–2?
2. What does she advise the reader not to tell? What would happen if the reader did tell?
3. According to line 5, what would the speaker find "dreary"? What animal does the speaker mention in lines 6–8? What does that animal do?

Interpreting

4. Whom do you think the speaker is referring to with the word *they* in line 4?
5. What simile does the poet use in the second stanza? What two things are being compared?
6. What do you think the word *bog* suggests about people who want to be "somebodies"?

Extending

7. List at least three advantages and three disadvantages of being in the public eye.

READING AND LITERARY FOCUS

Lyric Poetry

A **lyric poem** is a brief, often musical expression of the poet's thoughts and feelings. It may follow a variety of forms, but its main purpose is to communicate the emotions of the poet. Most lyric poems use vivid images and imaginative similes and metaphors. Lyric poems are usually about a particular thing—a moment, a feeling, a memory—that stirs the poet's imagination. "This Land Is Your Land" (page 213) is a lyric poem filled with vivid and varied images of the United States. Likewise, "When the Frost Is on the Punkin" (page 236) is a lyric poem that offers in rich detail the poet's vision of an autumn morning.

The word *lyric* comes from *lyre,* the guitarlike instrument that poets played when they sang their poems many centuries ago. Poets no longer sing their own poems, but we still use the word *lyric* to refer to the words of songs and to the kind of poetry that is brief, musical, and emotional.

Thinking About Lyric Poetry

■ What makes "I'm Nobody! Who Are You?" a lyric poem? Point to at least two specific examples from the poem in your answer.

COMPARING POEMS

■ Compare at least two of the following poems:

"Life for My Child Is Simple, and Is Good," "Simple Song," and "I'm Nobody! Who Are You?"

State the theme of each poem you are comparing. What do the themes have in common? In what way are they different? Which theme is most meaningful to you? Why?

THE TOTAL EFFECT

The **total effect** of a poem is its overall impact. All the poetic elements—sound, language, form, and meaning—come together.

Vachel Lindsay (1879–1931) earned the nickname Vagabond Poet because as a young man he walked from Illinois to New Mexico, reciting his poems along the way.

■ Notice how Lindsay contrasts the old with the new in the poem on page 274.

Walt Whitman (1819–1892) was born and raised on Long Island, New York, where he worked at everything from carpentry to teaching. He loved variety not only in jobs but also in the people and places of America. *Leaves of Grass,* his famous collection of poetry, celebrates the variety and vastness of this country. Breaking with traditional forms, rhythms, and subjects, Whitman wrote in his poems about both the ugly and the beautiful.

■ What two questions does he ask in "Miracles"?

Walter de la Mare (1873–1956) spent most of his life near London, England. He wrote poems that have been described as mysterious and dreamlike. His poems often leap beyond the real world into fantasy.

■ As you read "The Listeners," think about the relationship between the real and the imaginary.

E. E. Cummings (1894–1962) is considered one of the most inventive poets of this century. His full name was Edward Estlin Cummings. He often experimented with punctuation, spelling, word order, and form. In the poem presented here you will notice sentences that do not have all the standard capital letters and periods (see, for example, the sentences in lines 4 and 5).

■ What is the subject of his dramatic poem, "All in Green Went My Love Riding"?

The Total Effect

Like a spectator watching the many acts of a circus all at once, the reader of a poem does not separate the elements of a poem one from the other but instead takes them in all at the same time. Each of the following poems creates a strong and moving total effect.

When you come across a poem, you should read it twice, first aloud and then silently. Listen to the sounds, and let the images form pictures in your mind. Then examine the details and techniques, and decide on the theme, or main idea. When you understand the poem's individual parts you should read it once more to experience it as a whole and to recognize its total effect.

Getting the most out of a poem is easier when you know what to look for. Of course, each person will react to a poem differently. An active reader, however, will always consider the following points when reading a poem.

Reminders for Active Reading of Poetry

1. The **title** mirrors the poet's main idea or concern.
2. The **sound** of the poem—its use of rhyme, rhythm, onomatopoeia, repetition, and alliteration—matches the poem's subject and mood.
3. **Imagery** and **figures of speech,** such as simile and metaphor, engage your senses.
4. A **narrative poem** tells a story; a **lyric poem** expresses emotions.

Model for Active Reading

With the following poem, "Flower-Fed Buffaloes" by Vachel Lindsay, you can see how an alert reader approaches poetry. First read the poem aloud, and then read it silently. Then consider the notes to the right of it as an aid in understanding the poem. Finally, read the poem again to appreciate its total effect.

Vachel Lindsay

Flower-Fed Buffaloes

The flower-fed buffaloes of the spring
In the days of long ago,
Ranged where the locomotives sing
And the prairie flowers lie low—
5 The tossing, blooming, perfumed grass
Is swept away by wheat,
Wheels and wheels and wheels spin by
In the spring that still is sweet,
But the flower-fed buffaloes of the spring
10 Left us long ago.
They gore[1] no more, they bellow no more,
They trundle[2] around the hills no more—
With the Blackfeet, lying low,
With the Pawnees,[3] lying low.
15 Lying low.

---

1. **gore:** pierce with their horns.
2. **trundle:** move as if on wheels.
3. **Blackfeet, Pawnees:** referring to the Blackfoot and Pawnee tribes, Plains Indians of the Midwest who once hunted buffalo.

Alliteration (p. 219) is the repetition of consonant sounds at the beginnings of words. What sound is repeated in the title?

An **image** (p. 233) helps a reader to make a mental picture. What image is found in line 5? To which senses does the image appeal?

Rhythm (p. 225) is the pattern of beats made by stressed and unstressed syllables. Do lines 8–11 have a regular or irregular pattern of beats?

The **repetition** (p. 218) of words helps give poetry its meaning. Which words are repeated in the last three lines?

STUDY QUESTIONS

Recalling

1. Where did the buffaloes "range" in the "days of long ago"? What has the wheat swept away?
2. What "spin by" now? What is still sweet?
3. When did the buffaloes leave? Who left with them? Where are they now?

Interpreting

4. What effect does the phrase "flower-fed" have in your picture of the buffaloes? What effect does it have on the overall mood of the poem?
5. What comparisons between the past and present does Lindsay make?
6. What meanings do you think Lindsay intended for the phrase "lying low"? Apply this phrase to the prairie flowers, buffaloes, and Indians.

Extending

7. Do you agree or disagree with the following statement: "Progress always has its price." How does this statement apply to "Flower-Fed Buffaloes"?

CHALLENGE

Research and Oral Report

■ Choose one of the poets you have studied, and learn about his or her life, work, and appearance. To do your research you may check a general encyclopedia or a biographical reference work such as the *Dictionary of American Biography, Webster's Biographical Dictionary,* or *Current Biography.* You can find these reference works in most libraries. Present your findings in a brief oral report to the class.

Walt Whitman

Miracles

Why, who makes much of a miracle?
As to me I know of nothing else but miracles,
Whether I walk the streets of Manhattan,
Or dart my sight over the roofs of houses toward the sky,
5 Or wade with naked feet along the beach just in the edge of the water,
Or stand under trees in the woods,
Or talk by day with any one I love . . .
Or sit at table at dinner with the rest,
Or look at strangers opposite me riding in the car.
10 Or watch honey-bees busy around the hive of a summer forenoon,
Or animals feeding in the fields,
Or birds, or the wonderfulness of the sundown, or of stars
      shining so quiet and bright,
Or the exquisite delicate thin curve of the new moon in spring;
These with the rest, one and all, are to me miracles,
15 The whole referring, yet each distinct and in its place.

To me every hour of the light and dark is a miracle,
Every cubic inch of space is a miracle,
Every square yard of the surface of the earth is spread with the same,
Every foot of the interior swarms with the same.

20 To me the sea is a continual miracle,
The fishes that swim—the rocks—the motion of the waves—the
      ships with men in them,
What stranger miracles are there?

STUDY QUESTIONS

Recalling

1. What question does the speaker ask in line 1? What answer does he give in line 2?
2. In what kinds of locations does the speaker experience miracles?
3. List four events that the speaker identifies as miracles relating to human beings and five relating to nature.

Interpreting

4. Does Whitman include all five senses in his list of miracles? Give examples from the poem.
5. What is the theme of "Miracles"? Is it stated or implied?
6. Is "Miracles" a lyric poem? Support your answer with specific reasons.

Extending

7. What else might Whitman include in a list of miracles? Think of four or five possibilities.

READING AND LITERARY FOCUS

The Total Effect

To appreciate the total effect of a poem, read it once to take it in as a whole. Then read it a second time to examine each of the devices or techniques—sound, language, imagery, form, and meaning—that make up the poem. Finally, read the poem once more, this time bringing to it your own experiences and imagination. The result will be the total effect, a personal response unlike that of anyone else.

Thinking About the Total Effect

■ What specific techniques of sound and imagery help to create the total effect that "Miracles" has on you?

COMPOSITION

Writing About Poetry

■ In a paragraph or two write about the total effect of "Miracles." First describe the poem's overall impact on you. Then give examples of the sounds, imagery, and figurative language that help to create that effect. *For help with this assignment, see Lesson 5 in the Writing About Literature Handbook at the back of this book.*

Writing a Noun Poem

■ Whitman uses many nouns in his poem. Try writing a poem that is made exclusively of nouns. Here are two examples:

Beaches	Chores
Woods	Friends
Strangers	Films
Ships	Weekends
Miracles	

Notice how the nouns in the first lines can be said to "add up" to the noun in the final line. Your poem should be four or five lines long. It may rhyme but does not have to.

Walter de la Mare

The Listeners

"Is there anybody there?" said the Traveler,
    Knocking on the moonlit door;
And his horse in the silence champed the grasses
    Of the forest's ferny floor:
5 And a bird flew up out of the turret,
    Above the Traveler's head:
And he smote[1] upon the door again a second time;
    "Is there anybody there?" he said.
But no one descended to the Traveler;
10   No head from the leaf-fringed sill
Leaned over and looked into his gray eyes,
    Where he stood perplexed and still.
But only a host of phantom[2] listeners
    That dwelt in the lone house then
15 Stood listening in the quiet of the moonlight
    To that voice from the world of men:
Stood thronging the faint moonbeams on the dark stair
    That goes down to the empty hall,
Hearkening[3] in an air stirred and shaken
20   By the lonely Traveler's call.
And he felt in his heart their strangeness,
    Their stillness answering his cry,
While his horse moved, cropping the dark turf,[4]
    'Neath the starred and leafy sky;
25 For he suddenly smote on the door, even
    Louder, and lifted his head—
"Tell them I came, and no one answered,
    That I kept my word," he said.
Never the least stir made the listeners,
30   Though every word he spake[5]
Fell echoing through the shadowiness of the still house
    From the one man left awake:
Aye, they heard his foot upon the stirrup,
    And the sound of iron on stone,
35 And how the silence surged softly backward,
    When the plunging hoofs were gone.

---

1. **smote:** hit hard.
2. **phantom:** ghostly.
3. **Hearkening:** listening.
4. **cropping . . . turf:** nibbling the grass.
5. **spake:** spoke.

STUDY QUESTIONS

Recalling

1. What question does the Traveler ask twice? Who listened as he called?
2. What was "stirred and shaken" by his call? According to lines 21–22, what did the Traveler feel in his heart?
3. What does the Traveler tell the listeners in lines 27–28? What do the listeners do?
4. According to lines 33–36, what do the listeners hear?

Interpreting

5. Describe the setting of the poem. Describe the mood, or the atmosphere, of the poem. In what ways does the setting enhance the mood of the story?
6. How much does the poem actually tell you about the Traveler's mission? What effect does leaving out details have on the poem?
7. Identify the techniques of sound, language, imagery, and form that contribute to the total effect of this poem.

Extending

8. Why do you think it is important to "keep your word"?

VOCABULARY

Sentence Completions

Each of the following sentences contains a blank with four possible words for completing the sentence. The words are from "The Listeners." Choose the word that completes the sentence correctly and that uses the word as it is used in the selection. Write the number of each item and the letter of your choice on a separate sheet.

1. The elevator ____ to the first floor.
   (a) succeeded   (c) descended
   (b) blamed   (d) except
2. He was ____ by the test.
   (a) maybe   (c) possibly
   (b) perplexed   (d) erased
3. The ____ was bright.
   (a) moonlight   (c) cavity
   (b) thunder   (d) glee
4. The horse nibbled the ____.
   (a) sprint   (c) turf
   (b) cane   (d) tardy

COMPOSITION

Writing About Plot

■ Analyze the plot of "The Listeners" by discussing its major parts. For example: What is the conflict? Whom is the conflict between? What problems make it difficult for the main character to resolve the conflict? How does the story conclude? *For help with this assignment, see Lesson 2 in the Writing About Literature Handbook at the back of this book.*

Writing a Story

■ Change de la Mare's poem into a story. Add details of plot and character, and give the story a clear sense of beginning, middle, and end. Include dialogue and detailed descriptions of setting. *For help with this assignment, see Lesson 4 in the Writing About Literature Handbook at the back of this book.*

E. E. Cummings

All in Green Went My Love Riding

All in green went my love riding
on a great horse of gold
into the silver dawn.

four lean hounds crouched low and smiling
5 the merry deer ran before.

Fleeter be they than dappled[1] dreams
the swift sweet deer
the red rare deer.

Four red roebuck[2] at a white water
10 the cruel bugle sang before.

Horn at hip went my love riding
riding the echo down
into the silver dawn.

four lean hounds crouched low and smiling
15 the level meadows ran before.

Softer be they than slippered sleep
the lean lithe deer
the fleet flown deer.

Four fleet does[3] at a gold valley
20 the famished arrow sang before.

Bow at belt went my love riding
riding the mountain down
into the silver dawn.

four lean hounds crouched low and smiling
25 the sheer peaks ran before.

Paler be they than daunting[4] death
the sleek slim deer
the tall tense deer.

Four tall stags[5] at a green mountain
30 the lucky hunter sang before.

All in green went my love riding
on a great horse of gold
into the silver dawn.

four lean hounds crouched low and smiling
35 my heart fell dead before.

1. **dappled:** spotted.
2. **roebuck:** male of the roe, a variety of small deer.

3. **does:** adult female deer.
4. **daunting** [dônt'ing]: frightening.
5. **stags:** adult male deer.

STUDY QUESTIONS

Recalling

1. Tell what is happening in lines 1–5. Mention the adjectives used in those lines.
2. Describe the deer as pictured in lines 6–8, and tell what enter the picture in line 9 and then in line 19.
3. Identify the hunter's weapons, which are referred to in lines 20 and 21.
4. What adjective does the speaker use to describe the hunter in line 30? What prey finally falls to the hunter in line 35?

Interpreting

5. What feelings does the speaker have for the hunter, or rider, through line 30?
6. Assuming that the speaker does not actually die at the end of the poem, what might she mean by "my heart fell dead"?
7. Which lines have strong alliteration (see page 219)? State your reaction to those lines.
8. What generalization might you make about the color adjectives in this poem? What do they do to the picture you form of the events in this poem?

Extending

9. The title is the first line of the poem. What alternative title might you create for this poem? Be prepared to defend your choice.

COMPOSITION

Writing About Poetry

▣ In a paragraph or two write about the total effect of "All in Green Went My Love Riding." First describe the poem's overall impact on you. Then give examples of the sounds, imagery, and figurative language that help to create that effect. *For help with this assignment, see Lesson 5 in the Writing About Literature Handbook at the back of this book.*

Writing a Poem with Metaphors

▣ In Cummings' poem love is compared to a hunt. Write a three-line poem in which each line is a metaphor. All three lines should relate to one another. Here is an example; each line is about a display of human affection:

> Laughter is electricity.
> Smiles are crescent moons.
> Hugs are campfires glowing in the dark.

Remember that a metaphor always compares ideas from two different categories. For example, you do not have a metaphor when you compare one person with another person, but you do have a metaphor when you compare a person to an animal or an object. *For general help with writing poetry, see Lesson 6 in the Writing About Literature Handbook at the back of this book.*

CHALLENGE

Collage

▣ A **collage** is a picture made from assembling scraps of materials—string, magazine pictures, paint, glitter, cloth. Make a collage that captures a scene from "All in Green Went My Love Riding." Pay special attention to the colors, shapes, and textures described in the poem.

COMPARING POEMS

▣ Compare the poems in one of the following groups:

"Flower-Fed Buffaloes" and "All in Green Went My Love Riding"

"Miracles" and "The Listeners"

Which poem moves you the most? Why? In your opinion which of the poems best uses the following elements—sound, imagery, form, and theme—in creating a powerful total effect? Give specific reasons and examples in your answer.

Active Reading

Poetry

Interpreting Details in Poetry

Poems, like stories, are made up of details. Only by paying careful attention to the details in a poem can you *sense* each image, whether it appeals to sight, sound, taste, touch, or smell. Furthermore, you need the details in order to experience the emotions of poetry, which range from exhilaration to regret, from calm to confusion.

Activity 1   Consider the following excerpt from the poem "All in Green Went My Love Riding." Then, based on the details in the poem, answer the questions.

> All in green went my love riding
> on a great horse of gold
> into the silver dawn.
>
> four lean hounds crouched low and smiling
> the merry deer ran before.
>
> Fleeter be they than dappled dreams
> the swift sweet deer
> the red rare deer.
>
> Four red roebuck at a white water
> the cruel bugle sang before.

1. Which color is *not* mentioned in the passage?
   a. white   c. blue
   b. red   d. green
2. In a painting depicting the scene, what is the least number of animals you would see?
   a. one   c. eight
   b. four   d. nine
3. What is the time of day in the poem?
   a. early morning   c. late afternoon
   b. around noon   d. near midnight
4. What sound is mentioned in the poem?
   a. a horse neighing   c. hounds barking
   b. a bugle blowing   d. water rushing
5. What feeling does the speaker have for the animals?
   a. coldness   c. admiration
   b. envy   d. embarrassment

Making Inferences in Poetry

Using details within a poem, you can form pictures, or images. Read the following stanza from "Seagulls," looking for its many details.

> Between the under and the upper blue
> All day the seagulls climb and swerve and soar,
> Arc intersecting arc, curve over curve.

Among the details in these lines is the mention of three actions by the seagulls—climbing, swerving, and soaring. The poem also mentions the time of the action—all day. These details help you picture the scene.

Details in a poem can also help you make inferences, which will help you picture the scene in the poem more clearly. An *inference* is a conclusion that is based on the details that are stated. For example, the previous stanza talks about "the under and the upper blue." To what do these expressions refer? You have to make a reasonable guess, or inference, from the details. First of all, the poem is talking about seagulls, which, as their name implies, are generally found near the sea. Second, details tell us that the seagulls are climbing and soaring, which means they are most likely outdoors. Therefore, a reasonable inference to make from the details is that "the under and the upper blue" refers to the sea and the sky, respectively.

Now try using the details in the poem to decide which of the following three pictures best represents the movement of the seagulls.

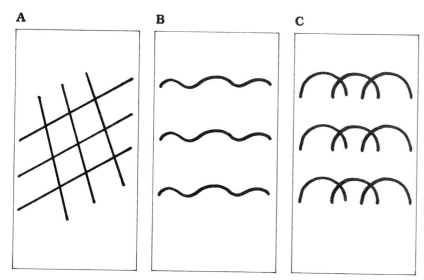

A   B   C

The poem describes the movement of the seagulls as "arc intersecting arc, curve over curve." Picture A shows no curves, only straight lines. Picture B has curves, but they do not intersect. Only Picture C shows intersecting curves and arcs. Therefore, based on details in the poem, you may infer that Picture C best represents the seagulls' movement.

Activity 2 Read the following poem. Then complete each numbered sentence with the best answer. Be prepared to tell what details helped you make each inference.

> Something told the wild geese
>   It was time to go.
> Though the fields lay golden
>   Something whispered,—"Snow."
> Leaves were green and stirring,
>   Berries, luster-glossed,
> But beneath warm feathers
>   Something cautioned,—"Frost."
> All the sagging orchards
>   Steamed with amber spice,
> But each wild breast stiffened
>   At remembered ice.
> Something told the wild geese
>   It was time to fly,—
> Summer sun was on their wings,
>   Winter in their cry.

1. The month in which the scene occurs is most likely ____.
   a. June
   b. September
   c. December
   d. April
2. The "something" that told the geese to go is probably ____.
   a. duck hunters
   b. other birds
   c. the coming of winter
   d. the hot sun
3. The wild geese will probably ____.
   a. build larger nests
   b. get rid of their food
   c. hide from each other
   d. fly away soon
4. The orchards are probably sagging because of ____.
   a. ripe fruit
   b. heavy snow
   c. geese on the branches
   d. clinging icicles
5. In a painting depicting the poem, the color that would least likely appear is ____.
   a. green
   b. gold
   c. brown
   d. pink

Activity 3 Read the following excerpt from a poem. Then complete each numbered sentence with the best answer. Be prepared to tell what details helped you make each inference.

> And he felt in his heart their strangeness,
>   Their stillness answering his cry,
> While his horse moved, cropping the dark turf,
>   'Neath the starred and leafy sky;
> For he suddenly smote on the door, even
>   Louder, and lifted his head—
> "Tell them I came, and no one answered,
>   That I kept my word," he said.
> Never the least stir made the listeners,
>   Though every word he spake
> Fell echoing through the shadowiness of the still house
>   From the one man left awake:
> Aye, they heard his foot upon the stirrup,
>   And the sound of iron on stone,
> And how the silence surged softly backward,
>   When the plunging hoofs were gone.

1. A sound you probably would *not* hear in the poem is ____.
   a. knocking on a door
   b. the pounding of a heart
   c. the chewing of a horse
   d. the echoes of a voice
2. The "sound of iron on stone" probably refers to ____.
   a. a door knocker against a door
   b. horseshoes on the ground
   c. boots on a street
   d. windows banging shut
3. The time of the poem seems to be ____.
   a. dawn
   b. dusk
   c. night
   d. afternoon
4. The speaker's actions suggest that he may feel ____.
   a. annoyed
   b. exhausted
   c. relieved
   d. embarrassed
5. The "listeners" in the poem are ____.
   a. ghosts in the house
   b. never clearly identified
   c. relatives of the speaker
   d. horses near the house

Literary Skills Review

Poetry

Guide for Reading Poetry

As you read poems, use this guide to help you notice and appreciate the techniques that appeal to our senses and our emotions.

Sound

1. What examples can you find of **repetition, alliteration, onomatopoeia,** and **rhyme**? What effect does each create?
2. What is the poem's **rhythm**? Is the rhythm appropriate to the subject matter of the poem?

Language

1. What **images** does the poem contain? To what senses do the images appeal?
2. What vivid **word choices** does the poet make?
3. What **similes** and **metaphors** does the poem contain?

Form

1. Is the poem divided into **stanzas**?
2. In a **concrete poem** what unusual shape does the poem have?

Meaning

1. What events in the poem form a **narrative**?
2. What thoughts and feelings does the poet share in a **lyric**?
3. What is the **theme** of the poem? Is it directly or indirectly stated?

Themes Review

Poetry

Since literature began, writers have written about certain general themes. For example, a general theme such as "communities" appears in poems, stories, plays, and other types of literature. However, each writer who uses this general theme says something very specific about it. For example, "A Song of Greatness" conveys the following specific theme: "A great community inspires individuals to become great." "Voyage" offers another specific view of "communities": "An individual may depart from his community." A general theme can be a word, while a specific theme can be stated as a sentence.

1. What specific point about the general theme "communities" does Emily Dickinson express in "I'm Nobody! Who Are You?"

2. Choose two of the following poems, and tell what specific theme each expresses about the general theme "animals."
   "The Sloth"   "The Magnificent Bull"   "Buffalo Dusk"
   "Cat!"   "Flower-Fed Buffaloes"   "Poem"
   "Seagulls"   "Something Told the Wild   "A Mouse in Her
                    Geese"   Room"

3. Choose two of the following poems, and tell what specific theme each expresses about the general theme "the land."
   "Fog"   "This Land Is Your Land"   "A Balmy Spring
   "Forsythia"   "The New and the Old"   Wind"
   "Miracles"   "When the Frost Is on the   "Bamboo Grove"
   "The Pasture"   Punkin"   "The River . . ."

4. From the following lists choose one poem and one story. What specific view does each express about "love"?
   Poems: "Life for My Child . . ."   "Simple Song"
                  "To a Golden-Haired . . ."   "All in Green
                  "Annabel Lee"   Went . . ."
   Stories: "A Secret for Two"   "Thirteen"

5. From the following lists choose one poem and one story. What specific view does each express about "imagination"?
   Poems: "Train Tune"   "Pendulum"
                  "There Was an Old Man"   "Smells"
                  "Write a Limerick Now"   "The Listeners"
   Stories: "Last Cover"   "Stolen Day"

Preview
Nonfiction

Nonfiction is factual prose writing. Unlike fiction and poetry, nonfiction always tells us about incidents that really happened and people who really lived. However, writers of nonfiction give us more than the facts about their subjects. They choose, arrange, and interpret these facts in a certain way and thus reveal their own opinions about their subjects. Sometimes they also reveal their own personalities and ways of looking at the world.

Nonfiction includes a wide variety of writing. It can range, for example, from a play-by-play account of a football game, to the diary of a ten-year-old girl, to a scientific book on the brain, to a humorous magazine article about life without television. However, all writers of nonfiction are guided by three things as they write: their subject, their purpose, and their audience. The **subject** is the specific topic about which the author is writing. An author's **purpose** might be, for example, to entertain, inform, persuade, or present an idea to the reader. The **audience** is the type of reader for whom the work is intended. Many nonfiction works are written for experts, while others are meant for casual readers. Authors select information and write in a way that will suit their subjects, achieve their purposes, and be understood by their audiences.

The following nonfiction selections include autobiography, biography, and essays. An **autobiography** is the story of a person's life written by that person. A **biography** is the story of a person's life written by someone else. An **essay** is a short nonfiction work that can deal with any subject. Essays may be narrative, descriptive, expository, or persuasive. Narrative essays tell true stories, while descriptive essays create pictures of their subjects. Expository essays present facts or explain ideas, and persuasive essays try to convince readers to accept an opinion or take action.

AUTOBIOGRAPHY AND BIOGRAPHY

Russell Baker was born in 1925 in Virginia and grew up in New Jersey and Maryland. He has been a writer for the *New York Times* since 1962 and has commented about our society with humor and intelligence. His widely read newspaper column won the Pulitzer Prize for Distinguished Commentary in 1979.

Baker won a second Pulitzer Prize in 1983 for his autobiography, *Growing Up.* Baker grew up in the 1930s during the time of America's worst economic distress—the Great Depression. His family was poor but determined to make a better life. His autobiography paints memorable portraits of himself as a boy and as a young man. It also tells about his younger sister, Doris, and their strong and loving mother.

■ Why does Baker show us these particular incidents from his boyhood?

Russell Baker

from **Growing Up**

The paper route earned me three dollars a week, sometimes four, and my mother, in addition to her commissions on magazine sales, also had her monthly check coming from Uncle Willie, but we'd been in Baltimore a year before I knew how desperate things were for her. One Saturday morning she told me she'd need Doris and me to go with her to pick up some food. I had a small wagon she'd bought me to make it easier to move the Sunday papers, and she said I'd better bring it along. The three of us set off eastward, passing the grocery stores we usually shopped at, and kept walking until we came to Fremont Avenue, a grim street of dilapidation[1] and poverty.

"This is where we go," she said when we reached the corner of Fremont and Fayette Street. It looked like a grocery, with big plate-glass windows and people lugging out cardboard cartons and bulging bags, but it wasn't. I knew very well what it was.

"Are we going on relief?" I asked her.

"Don't ask questions about things you don't know anything about," she said. "Bring that wagon inside." . . .

From then on I assumed we were paupers.[2] For this reason I was often astonished when my mother did me some deed of generosity, as when she bought me my first Sunday suit with long pants. The changeover from

1. **dilapidation** [di lap'ə dā'shən]: ruin.

2. **paupers:** very poor people.

knickers[3] to long pants was the ritual recognition that a boy had reached adolescence, or "the awkward age," as everybody called it. The "teenager," like the atomic bomb, was still uninvented, and there were few concessions to adolescence, but the change to long pants was a ritual of recognition. There was no ceremony about it. You were taken downtown one day and your escort—my mother in my case—casually said to the suit salesman, "Let's see what you've got in long pants."

For me the ritual was performed in the glossy, mirrored splendor of Bond's clothing store on Liberty Street. She had taken me for a Sunday suit and, having decided I looked too gawky in knickers, said, "Let's see what you've got in long pants." My physique at this time was described by relatives and friends with such irritating words as "beanpole," "skinny," and "all bones." My mother, seeing me through eyes that loved, chose to call me "a tall man."

The suit salesman displayed a dazzling assortment of garments. Suit designers made no concessions to youth; suits for boys were just like suits for men, only smaller. My mother expressed a preference for something with the double-breasted[4] cut. "A tall man looks good in a double-breasted suit," she said.

The salesman agreed. Gary Cooper,[5] he said, looked especially good in double-breasted suits. He produced one. I tried it on. It was a hard fabric, built to endure. The color was green, not the green of new grass in spring, but the green of copper patina[6] on old statues. The green was relieved by thin, light gray stripes, as though the designer had started to create cloth for a bunco artist,[7] then changed his mind and decided to appeal to bankers.

"Well, I just don't know," my mother said.

Her taste in clothes was sound rather than flamboyant, but I considered the suit smashing, and would have nothing else. The price was $20, which was expensive even though it came with two pairs of pants, and upon hearing it I said, "We can't afford it."

"That's what you think, mister," she said to me. "It's worth a little money to have the man of the house look like a gentleman."

In conference with the salesman, it was agreed that she would pay three dollars down and three dollars a month until the cost was amortized.[8] On my attenuated[9] physique, this magnificent, striped, green, double-breasted suit hung like window drapes on a scarecrow. My mother could imagine Gary Cooper's shoulders gradually filling out the jacket, but she insisted that Bond's do something about the voluminous excesses of the pants, which in the seat area could have accommodated both me and a watermelon. The salesman assured her that Bond's famous tailors would adjust the trousers without difficulty. They did so. When finally I had the suit home and put it on for its first trip to church, so much fabric had been removed from the seat that the two hip pockets were located with seams kissing right over my spine.

My mother was dazzled. With visions of a budding Gary Cooper under her wing, she said, "Now you look like somebody I can be proud of," and off to church we went.

---

3. **knickers** [nik'ərz]: knee-length trousers.
4. **double-breasted:** with two rows of buttons.
5. **Gary Cooper** (1901–1961): American actor famous for his height and good looks.
6. **patina** [pat'ən ə]: any finish that results from age; in this case the green film that is produced when copper or bronze reacts to the oxygen in the air.

7. **bunco artist:** dishonest person; cheater.
8. **amortized** [am'ər tīzd']: paid off through a series of smaller payments.
9. **attenuated** [ə ten'ū āt'əd]: extremely thin.

She was a magician at stretching a dollar. That December, with Christmas approaching, she was out at work and Doris was in the kitchen when I barged into her bedroom one afternoon in search of a safety pin. Since her bedroom opened onto a community hallway, she kept the door locked, but needing the pin, I took the key from its hiding place, unlocked the door, and stepped in. Standing against the wall was a big, black bicycle with balloon tires. I recognized it instantly. It was the same secondhand bike I'd been admiring in a Baltimore Street shop window. I'd even asked about the price. It was horrendous. Something like $15. Somehow my mother had scraped together enough for a down payment and meant to surprise me with the bicycle on Christmas morning.

Russell Baker and his sister, Doris, as children.

I was overwhelmed by the discovery that she had squandered such money on me and sickened by the knowledge that, bursting into her room like this, I had robbed her of the pleasure of seeing me astonished and delighted on Christmas day. I hadn't wanted to know her lovely secret; still, stumbling upon it like this made me feel as though I'd struck a blow against her happiness. I backed out, put the key back in its hiding place, and brooded privately.

I resolved that between now and Christmas I must do nothing, absolutely nothing, to reveal the slightest hint of my terrible knowledge. I must avoid the least word, the faintest intonation, the weakest gesture that might reveal my possession of her secret. Nothing must deny her the happiness of seeing me stunned with amazement on Christmas day.

In the privacy of my bedroom I began composing and testing exclamations of delight: "Wow!" "A bike with balloon tires! I don't believe it!" "I'm the luckiest boy alive!" And so on. They all owed a lot to movies in which boys like Mickey Rooney[10] had seen their wildest dreams come true, and I realized that, with my lack of acting talent, all of them were going to sound false at the critical moment when I wanted to cry out my love spontaneously from the heart. Maybe it would be better to say nothing but appear to be shocked into such deep pleasure that speech had escaped me. I wasn't sure, though. I'd seen speechless gratitude in the movies too, and it never really worked until the actors managed to cry a few quiet tears. I doubted I could cry on cue, so I began thinking about other expressions of speechless amazement. In front of a hand-held mirror in my bedroom I tried the whole range of expressions: mouth agape

10. **Mickey Rooney** (born 1920): American actor known for his portrayals of all-American boys.

and eyes wide; hands slapped firmly against both cheeks to keep the jaw from falling off; ear-to-ear grin with all teeth fully exposed while hugging the torso with both arms. These and more I practiced for several days without acquiring confidence in any of them. I decided to wait until Christmas morning and see if anything came naturally.

Christmas was the one occasion on which my mother surrendered to unabashed sentimentality. A week beforehand she always concocted homemade root beer, sealed it in canning jars, and stored it in the bathroom for the yeast to ferment. Now and then, sitting in the adjoining kitchen, we heard a loud thump from the bathroom and knew one of the jars had exploded, but she always made enough to allow for breakage. She took girlish delight in keeping her brightly wrapped gifts hidden in closets. Christmas Eve she spent in frenzies of baking—cakes, pies, gingerbread cookies cut and decorated to look like miniature brown pine trees and Santa Clauses. In the afternoon she took Doris and me to the street corner where trees were piled high and searched through them until she found one that satisfied our taste for fullness and symmetry. It was my job and Doris's to set the tree up in the parlor and weigh it with ornaments, lights, and silver icicles, while she prepared Christmas Eve dinner. This was a ritual meal at which the centerpiece was always oysters. She disliked oysters but always ate them on Christmas Eve. Oysters were the centerpiece of the traditional Christmas Eve supper she remembered from her girlhood in Virginia. By serving them she perpetuated the customs of Papa's household.[11]

She did not place her gifts under the tree that night until Doris and I had gone to bed.

We were far beyond believing in Santa Claus, but she insisted on preserving the forms of the childhood myth that these were presents from some divine philanthropist. She planned all year for this annual orgy of spending and girded for it by putting small deposits month after month into her Christmas Club account at the bank.

That Christmas morning she roused us early, "to see what Santa Claus brought," she said with just the right tone of irony to indicate we were all old enough to know who Santa Claus was. I came out of my bedroom with my presents for her and Doris, and Doris came with hers. My mother's had been placed under the tree during the night. There were a few small glittering packages, a big doll for

Russell Baker's mother.

---

11. **Papa's household:** Baker refers to the household of his mother's father.

Doris, but no bicycle. I must have looked disappointed.

"It looks like Santa Claus didn't do too well by you this year, Buddy," she said, as I opened packages. A shirt. A necktie. I said something halfhearted like, "It's the thought that counts," but what I felt was bitter disappointment. I supposed she'd found the bike intolerably expensive and sent it back.

"Wait a minute!" she cried, snapping her fingers. "There's something in my bedroom I forgot all about."

She beckoned to Doris, the two of them went out, and a moment later came back wheeling between them the big black two-wheeler with balloon tires. I didn't have to fake my delight, after all. The three of us—Doris, my mother, and I—were people bred to repress the emotional expressions of love, but I did something that startled both my mother and me. I threw my arms around her spontaneously and kissed her.

"All right now, don't carry on about it. It's only a bicycle," she said.

Still, I knew that she was as happy as I was to see her so happy.

STUDY QUESTIONS

Recalling

1. Why do Russell, Doris, and their mother take the wagon to Fremont Avenue?
2. What does Russell assume about his family after the incident with the wagon? What "often astonished" him about his mother?
3. What does Russell say when he learns the price of the green suit? What is his mother's answer?
4. Why does Russell practice being surprised before Christmas?
5. Tell what happens on Christmas morning.

Interpreting

6. What are Mrs. Baker's main qualities as her son presents her? Give examples of actions that show these qualities.
7. Toward whom or what does Baker show humor in his account of his childhood? Toward whom or what does he show tenderness?
8. What do you think Baker wants us to understand about his family?

Extending

9. Why might people take special joy in surprising those they love?

READING AND LITERARY FOCUS

Autobiography

An **autobiography** is the story of a person's life written by that person. In writing an autobiography an author tells the most meaningful events in his or her life and passes along the insights gained with the passage of time.

In *Growing Up* Russell Baker relates the events of his childhood through the eyes of the boy who experienced them. He also shares with us the observations of the adult who has come to understand those events. We see, for example, the twelve-year-old Russell staring at a hand-held mirror, seriously practicing expressions of surprise. At the same time we see what Baker as an adult has come to realize: how funny—and how touching—these actions must have been.

Thinking About Autobiography

1. How do you think the boy Russell felt about his family and their circumstances, according to this selection? Give examples.
2. Find one comment by Baker that shows an adult's understanding rather than a boy's viewpoint. Suggest one or two ways in which the adult and the boy are different.

Purpose in Nonfiction

We enjoy any work more when we remember that the writer had a particular **purpose** for writing it. An author writes a work of nonfiction in order to *do* something. For example, an author may write in order to make us laugh, explain something, praise or blame someone, share a realization with us, or persuade us to change our minds about an issue. An author may even combine several of these goals or have another purpose altogether.

Authors writing about similar subjects will create very different works if they write for different purposes. For example, one author may write about an incident from the past chiefly to inform us about the way people lived sixty years ago. Another may focus on the funny aspects of a past incident in order to amuse us. Another may want to justify his or her past behavior. Still another may tell us about the past in order to express the idea that the most important things remain the same, no matter how times change. The writer chooses information and writes in a style that will accomplish the purpose that he or she has in mind.

Thinking About Purpose

◼ For what purpose do you think Russell Baker wrote this chapter from *Growing Up*? Choose one incident or statement from the selection, and show how it helps accomplish this purpose.

VOCABULARY

Synonyms

A **synonym** is a word that has the same or nearly the same meaning as another word. For example, *shout* and *yell* are synonyms. The italicized words in the following numbered items are from *Growing Up*. From the four choices that follow each numbered item, choose the word that is nearest the meaning of the italicized word *as it is used in the selection.* Write the number of each item and the letter of your choice on a separate sheet.

1. *flamboyant* costume
   - (a) colorful
   - (b) burning
   - (c) heavy
   - (d) quiet
2. *brooded* quietly for hours
   - (a) slept
   - (b) talked
   - (c) ate
   - (d) thought deeply
3. had *squandered* such money on me
   - (a) saved
   - (b) found
   - (c) wasted
   - (d) hidden
4. answered *spontaneously*
   - (a) much later
   - (b) naturally
   - (c) strangely
   - (d) humorously
5. *concocted* a feast
   - (a) found
   - (b) ate
   - (c) threw away
   - (d) put together

COMPOSITION

Writing About Autobiography

◼ Any work of nonfiction has a central idea. This idea may be a particular point about the subject or an insight about life in general. To convey this idea, the author may use various techniques such as relating facts, providing details, and giving examples. Write about Baker's central idea in this selection from *Growing Up.* Cite and give examples of the specific techniques that he uses to communicate this idea. *For help with this assignment, see Lesson 7 in the Writing About Literature Handbook at the back of this book.*

Writing a Nonfiction Narrative

◼ Write a narrative telling of an experience in which you learned something about yourself or about another person. Begin by briefly stating what the experience was and what you learned. Then relate the facts and details of the experience, and end by telling why you learned what you learned. *For help with this assignment, see Lesson 8 in the Writing About Literature Handbook at the back of this book.*

Jerry Izenberg (born 1930) has been a sportswriter since the 1950s. His column appears daily in over forty newspapers, and he is also the author of six books. In recent years he has been a television and radio commentator.

"Roberto Clemente: A Bittersweet Memoir" is a short biographical piece about Roberto Clemente, who played with the Pittsburgh Pirates for eighteen years and was elected to baseball's Hall of Fame in 1973. In 1972 he was killed in a plane crash while on his way to help victims of an earthquake in Central America.

■ Clemente was only thirty-eight when he died; had he "lived a full life"?

Jerry Izenberg

Roberto Clemente: A Bittersweet Memoir

The record book will tell you that Roberto Clemente collected 3,000 hits during his major-league career. It will say that he came to bat 9,454 times, that he drove in 1,305 runs, and played 2,433 games over an eighteen-year span.

But it won't tell you about Carolina,[1] Puerto Rico, and the old square, and the narrow, twisting streets, and the roots that produced him. It won't tell you about the Julio Coronado[2] School and a remarkable woman named María Isabella Casares,[3] whom he called "Teacher" until the day he died and who helped to shape his life in times of despair and depression. It won't tell you about a man

named Pedro Zarrilla,[4] who found him on a country softball team and put him in the uniform of the Santurce[5] club and who nursed him from a promising young athlete to a major-league superstar.

And most of all, those cold numbers won't begin to delineate[6] the man Roberto Clemente was. To even begin to understand what this magnificent athlete was all about, you have to work backward. The search begins at the site of its ending.

The car moves easily through the predawn streets of San Juan. It turns down a bumpy secondary road and moves past small shanty-towns. Then there is another turn, onto hard-

---

1. **Carolina** [kä rō lē′nə]
2. **Julio Coronado** [hōō′lē ō kō rō nä′<u>th</u>ō]
3. **María Isabella Casares** [mä rē′ə ēs ä bä′lä kä sä′räs]

4. **Pedro Zarrilla** [pād′rō sä rē′yä]
5. **Santurce** [sän tōōr′sä]
6. **delineate** [di lin′ē āt′]: describe.

packed dirt and sand, and although the light has not yet quite begun to break, you can sense the nearness of the ocean. You can hear its waves, pounding harshly against the jagged rocks. You can smell its saltiness. The car noses to a stop, and the driver says, "From here you must walk." The place is called Punta Maldonado.[7]

"This is the nearest place," the driver tells me. "This is where they came by the thousands on that New Year's eve and New Year's day. Out there," he says, gesturing with his right hand, "out there, perhaps a mile and a half from where we stand. That's where we think the plane went down."

The final hours of Roberto Clemente were like this. Just a month or so before, he had agreed to take a junior-league baseball team to Nicaragua and manage it in an all-star game in Managua.[8] He had met people and made friends there. He was not a man who made friends casually. He had always said -that the people you wanted to give your friendship to were the people to whom you had to be willing to give something—no matter what the price.

Just two weeks after he returned from that trip, Managua, Nicaragua, exploded into flames. The earth trembled, and people died. It was the worst earthquake anywhere in the hemisphere in a long time.

Back in Puerto Rico, a television personality named Luis Vigereaux[9] heard the news and was moved to try to help the victims. He needed someone to whom the people would listen, someone who could say what had to be said and get the work done that had to be done and help the people who had to be helped.

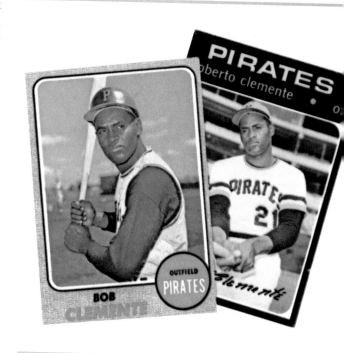

OUTFIELD PIRATES

BOB CLEMENTE

"I knew," Luis Vigereaux said, "that Roberto was such a person, perhaps the only such person who would be willing to help."

And so the mercy project, which would eventually claim Roberto's life, began. He appeared on television. But he needed a staging area. The city agreed to give him Sixto Escobar[10] Stadium.

"Bring what you can," he told the people. "Bring medicine . . . bring clothes . . . bring food . . . bring shoes . . . bring yourself to help us load. We need so much. Whatever you bring, we will use."

And the people of San Juan came. They walked through the heat, and they drove old cars and battered little trucks, and the mound of supplies grew and grew. Within two days, the first mercy planes left for Nicaragua.

Meanwhile, a ship had been chartered and

_____

7. **Punta Maldonado** [poon'tä mäl dō nä'thō]
8. **Managua** [mä nä'gwä]: capital city of Nicaragua.
9. **Luis Vigereaux** [loo ēs' vē gär ō']

10. **Sixto Escobar** [sēs'tō es cō bär']

Roberto Clemente: A Bittersweet Memoir 297

loaded. And as it prepared to steam away, unhappy stories began to drift back from Nicaragua. Not all the supplies that had been flown in, it was rumored, were getting through. Puerto Ricans, who had flown the planes, had no passports, and Nicaragua was in a state of panic.

"We have people there who must be protected. Black-market types[11] must not be allowed to get their hands on these supplies," Clemente told Luis Vigereaux. "Someone must make sure—particularly before the ship gets there. I'm going on the next plane."

The plane they had rented was an old DC-7. It was scheduled to take off at 4 P.M. on December 31, 1972. Long before takeoff time, it was apparent that the plane needed more work. It had even taxied onto the runway and then turned back. The trouble, a mechanic who was at the airstrip that day conjectured, "had to do with both port engines.[12] We worked on them most of the afternoon."

The departure time was delayed an hour, and then two, and then three. At 9 P.M., even as the first stirrings of the annual New Year's eve celebration were beginning in downtown San Juan, the DC-7 taxied onto the runway, received clearance, rumbled down the narrow concrete strip, and pulled away from the earth. It headed out over the Atlantic and banked toward Nicaragua, and its tiny lights disappeared on the horizon.

Just ninety seconds later, the tower at San Juan International Airport received this message from the DC-7 pilot, "We are coming back around."

Just that.

Nothing more.

And then there was a great silence.

"It was almost midnight," recalls Rudy Hernández,[13] a former teammate of Roberto's. "We were having this party in my restaurant. Somebody turned on the radio, and the announcer was saying that Roberto's plane was feared missing. And then, because my place is on the beach, we saw these giant floodlights crisscrossing the waves, and we heard the sound of the helicopters and the little search planes."

Drawn by a common sadness, the people of San Juan began to make their way toward the beach, toward Punta Maldonado. A cold rain had begun to fall. It washed their faces and blended with the tears.

They came by the thousands, and they watched for three days. Towering waves boiled up and made the search virtually impossible. The U.S. Navy sent a team of expert divers into the area, but the battering of the waves defeated them too. Midway through the week, the pilot's body was found in the swift-moving currents to the north. On Saturday, bits of the cockpit were sighted.

And then—nothing else.

Rudy Hernández said, "I have never seen a time or a sadness like that. The streets were empty, the radios silent, except for the constant bulletins about Roberto. Traffic? Forget it. All of us cried. All of us who knew him, and even those who didn't, wept that week. There will never be another like Roberto."

Who was he . . . I mean really?

He was born in Carolina, Puerto Rico. Today the town has about 125,000 people, but when Roberto was born there in 1934, it was roughly one-sixth its current size.

María Isabella Casares is a school teacher. She has taught the children of Carolina for thirty years. Most of her teaching has been

---

11. **Black-market types:** people who sell goods illegally, outside official controls.
12. **port engines:** engines on the left side of the airplane.

13. **Hernández** [är nän′des]

done in tenth-grade history classes. Carolina is her home, and its children are her children. And among all of those whom she calls her own (who are all the children she taught), Roberto Clemente was something even more special to her.

"His father was an overseer on a sugar plantation. He did not make much money," she explained in an empty classroom at Julio Coronado School. "But then, there are no rich children here. There never have been. Roberto was typical of them. I had known him when he was a small boy because my father had run a grocery store in Carolina and Roberto's parents used to shop there."

There is this thing that you have to know about María Isabella Casares before we hear more from her. What you have to know is that she is the model of what a teacher should be. Between her and her students even now, as back when Roberto attended her school, there is this common bond of mutual respect. Earlier in the day, I had watched her teach a class in the history of the Abolition Movement[14] in Puerto Rico. I don't speak much Spanish, but even to me it was clear that this is how a class should be, this is the kind of person who should teach, and these are the kinds of students such a teacher will produce.

With this as a background, what she has to say about Roberto Clemente carries much more impact.

"Each year," she said, "I let my students choose the seats they want to sit in. I remember the first time I saw Roberto. He was a very shy boy, and he went straight to the back of the room and chose the very last seat. Most of the time he would sit with his eyes down. He was an average student. But there was some-thing very special about him. We would talk after class for hours. He wanted to be an engineer, you know, and perhaps he could have been. But then he began to play softball, and one day he came to me and said, 'Teacher, I have a problem.'

"He told me that Pedro Zarrilla, who was one of our most prominent baseball people, had seen him play and that Pedro wanted him to sign a professional contract with the Santurce Crabbers. He asked me what he should do.

"I have thought about that conversation many times. I believe Roberto could have been almost anything, but God gave him a gift that few have, and he chose to use that gift. I remember that on that day I told him, 'This is your chance, Roberto. We are poor people in this town. This is your chance to do some-thing. But if in your heart you prefer not to try, then, Roberto, that will be your problem— and your decision.' "

There was and there always remained a closeness between this boy-soon-to-be-a-man and his favorite teacher.

"Once, a few years ago, I was sick with a very bad back. Roberto, not knowing this, had driven over from Río Piedras,[15] where his house was, to see me," Mrs. Casares recalled.

"Where is the teacher?" Roberto asked Mrs. Casares's stepdaughter that afternoon.

"Teacher is sick, Roberto. She is in bed."

"Teacher," Roberto said, pounding on the bedroom door, "get up and put on your clothes. We are going to the doctor whether you want to or not."

"I got dressed," Mrs. Casares told me, "and he picked me up like a baby and carried me in his arms to the car. He came every day for fifteen days, and most days he had to carry

---

14. **Abolition Movement:** movement to outlaw slavery. Slavery in Puerto Rico began with the Spanish settlement in the 1500s and was abolished in 1873.

15. **Río Piedras** [rē′ō pē ä′dräs]: area on the southern edge of San Juan, just west of Carolina.

me. But I went to the doctor, and he treated me. Afterward, I said to the doctor that I wanted to pay the bill.

" 'Mrs. Casares,' he told me, 'please don't start with that Clemente or he will kill me. He has paid all your bills, and don't you dare tell him I have told you.'

"Well, Roberto was like that. We had been

so close. You know, I think I was there the day he met Vera, the girl he later married. She was one of my students too. I was working part-time in the pharmacy, and he was already a baseball player by then, and one day Vera came into the store.

" 'Teacher,' Roberto asked me, 'who is that girl?'

" 'That's one of my students,' I told him. 'Now, don't you dare bother her. Go out and get someone to introduce you. Behave yourself.'

"He was so proper, you know. That's just what he did, and that's how he met her, and they were married here in Carolina in the big church on the square."

On the night Roberto Clemente's plane disappeared, Mrs. Casares was at home, and a delivery boy from the pharmacy stopped by and told her to turn on the radio and sit down. "I think something has happened to someone who is very close to you, Teacher, and I want to be here in case you need help."

María Isabella Casares heard the news. She is a brave woman, and months later, standing in front of the empty crypt in the cemetery at Carolina where Roberto Clemente was to have been buried, she said, "He was like a son to me. This is why I want to tell you about him. This is why you must make people—particularly our people, our Puerto Rican children—understand what he was. He was like my son, and he is all our sons in a way. We must make sure that the children never forget how beautiful a man he was."

The next person to touch Roberto Clemente was Pedro Zarrilla, who owned the Santurce club. He was the man who discovered Clemente on the country softball team, and he was the man who signed him for a four-hundred-dollar bonus.

"He was a skinny kid," Pedro Zarrilla recalls, "but even then he had those large, powerful hands, which we all noticed right away.

He joined us, and he was nervous. But I watched him, and I said to myself, 'This kid can throw, and this kid can run, and this kid can hit. We will be patient with him.' The season had been through several games before I finally sent him in to play."

Luis Olmo remembers that game. Luis Olmo had been a major-league outfielder with the Brooklyn Dodgers. He had been a splendid ballplayer. Today he is in the insurance business in San Juan. He sat in his office and recalled very well that first moment when Roberto Clemente stepped up to bat.

"I was managing the other team. They had a man on base, and this skinny kid comes out. Well, we had never seen him, so we didn't really know how to pitch to him. I decided to throw him a few bad balls and see if he'd bite.

"He hit the first pitch. It was an outside fast ball and he never should have been able to reach it. But he hit it down the line for a double. He was the best bad-ball hitter I have ever seen, and if you ask major-league pitchers who are pitching today, they will tell you the same thing. After a while, it got so that I just told my pitchers to throw the ball down the middle because he was going to hit it no matter where they put it, and at least if he decided not to swing, we'd have a strike on him.

"I played in the big leagues. I know what I am saying. He was the greatest we ever had . . . maybe one of the greatest anyone ever had. Why did he have to die?"

Once Pedro Zarrilla turned him loose, there was no stopping Roberto Clemente. As Clemente's confidence grew, he began to get better and better. He was the one the crowds came to see out at Sixto Escobar Stadium.

"You know, when Clemente was in the line-up," Pedro Zarrilla says, "there was always this undercurrent of excitement in the ball park. You knew that if he was coming to bat, he would do something spectacular. You knew

that if he was on first base, he was going to try to get to second base. You knew that if he was playing right field and there was a man on third base, then that man on third base already knew what a lot of men on third base in the majors were going to find out—you don't try to get home against Roberto Clemente's arm."

Soon the major-league scouts began to make their moves, and in 1955 Roberto Clemente came to the Pittsburgh Pirates. He was the finest prospect the club had had in a long, long time. But the Pirates of those days were spectacular losers, and even Roberto Clemente couldn't turn them around overnight.

"I will never forget how fast he became a superstar in this town," says Bob Friend, who became a great Pirate pitcher. "Later he would have troubles because he was either hurt or thought he was hurt, and some people would say that he was loafing. But I know he gave it his best shot, and he helped make us winners."

The first winning year was 1960, when the Pirates won the pennant and went on to beat

the Yankees in the seventh game of the World Series. Whitey Ford, who pitched against him twice in that Series, recalls that Roberto actually made himself look bad on an outside pitch to encourage Whitey to come back with it. "I did," Ford recalls, "and he unloaded. Another thing I remember is the way he ran out a routine ground ball in the last game, and when we were a little slow covering, he beat it out. It was something most people forget, but it made the Pirates' victory possible."

The season was over. Roberto Clemente had hit safely in every World Series game. He had batted over .300. He had been a superstar. But when they announced the Most Valuable Player Award voting, Roberto had finished a distant third.

"I really don't think he resented the fact that he didn't win it," Bob Friend says. "What hurt—and in this he was right—was how few votes he got. He felt that he simply wasn't being accepted. He brooded about that a lot. I think his attitude became one of 'well, I'm going to show them from now on so that they will never forget.'

"And you know, he sure did."

Roberto Clemente went home and married Vera. He felt less alone. Now he could go on and prove what it was he had to prove. And he was determined to prove it.

His moment finally came. It took eleven years for the Pirates to win a World Series berth again, and when they did in 1971, it was Roberto Clemente who led the way. I will never forget him as he was during that 1971 Series with the Orioles, a Series that the Pirates figured to lose and in which they, in fact, dropped the first two games down in Baltimore.

When they got back to Pittsburgh for the middle slice of the tournament, Roberto Clemente went to work and led his team. He was a superstar during the five games that fol-

lowed. He was the big man in the Series. He was the MVP.[16] He was everything he had ever dreamed of being on a ball field.

Most important of all, the entire country saw him do it on network television, and never again—even though nobody knew it would end so tragically soon—was anyone ever to doubt his ability.

The following year, Clemente ended the season by collecting his three thousandth hit. Only ten other men had ever done that in the entire history of baseball.

"When I think of Roberto now," says Willie Stargell, his closest friend on the Pirates, "I think of the kind of man he was. There was nothing phony about him. He had his own ideas about how life should be lived, and if you didn't see it that way, then he let you know in so many ways, without words, that it was best you each go your separate ways.

"He was a man who chose his friends carefully. His was a friendship worth having. I didn't think many people took the time and the trouble to try to understand him, and I'll admit it wasn't easy. But he was worth it.

"The way he died, you know, I mean on that plane carrying supplies to Nicaraguans who'd been dying in that earthquake, well, I wasn't surprised he'd go out and do something like that. I wasn't surprised he'd go. I just never thought what happened could happen to him.

"But I know this. He lived a full life. And if he knew at that moment what the Lord had decided, well, I really believe he would have said, 'I'm ready.' "

He was thirty-eight years old when he died. He touched the heart of Puerto Rico in a way that few people ever could. He touched a lot of other hearts too. He touched hearts that beat inside people of all colors of skin.

---

16. **MVP:** abbreviation for "Most Valuable Player."

STUDY QUESTIONS

Recalling

1. According to Izenberg, Roberto Clemente "was not a man who made friends casually." What did Clemente always say we have to be willing to do for the people we choose as our friends?
2. Why did Clemente decide to fly to Nicaragua?
3. How did the people of San Juan react to the news of Clemente's death?
4. Who is María Isabella Casares? What are her reasons for telling Izenberg about Clemente?

Interpreting

5. Show the connection between what Clemente always said we must do for our friends and what he did in the last weeks of his life.
6. Why do you think the people of San Juan responded to Clemente's death as they did?

Extending

7. What qualities do you think make a person a hero? Name one or two heroes of your own.

READING AND LITERARY FOCUS

Biography

A **biography** is the story of a person's life written by someone other than that person. Whether a biography is book-length or only a few pages long, a good biography creates a full, accurate picture of its subject. It also presents the writer's understanding of and opinion about the subject.

Authors of biographies must do **research.** Biographers find information about the lives and times of their subjects in books, newspapers, and letters. In some cases they can **interview** the subject or people who knew the subject personally.

Interviews like those Izenberg used in writing about Roberto Clemente often add depth and color to biographies by providing anecdotes about the subject. An **anecdote** is a brief account of a true event, meant to entertain or inform. Anecdotes usually reveal a person's character by giving examples of his or her behavior. For example, Izenberg reveals Clemente's ideas about friendship when he relates María Casares' anecdote about how Clemente took her to the doctor's office.

Thinking About Biography

1. Pick another anecdote from the selection. What did it tell you about Roberto Clemente?
2. What do you think is Jerry Izenberg's opinion of Roberto Clemente? How can you tell?

VOCABULARY

Using a Pronunciation Key

"Roberto Clemente: A Bittersweet Memoir" contains a number of proper names for which pronunciations are given in the footnotes. The phonetic symbols in these footnotes are explained in the **pronunciation key** in the Glossary at the back of this book.

Using the footnotes and the pronunciation key in the Glossary, answer the following questions.

1. Is the *I* in *Isabella* to be pronounced like the *i* in *ice*, the *e* in *end*, or the *e* in *me*?
2. Is the *J* in *Julio Coronado* to be pronounced like the *j* in *joke*, the *y* in *yes*, or the *h* in *hit*?
3. Is the *eaux* in *Vigereaux* to be pronounced like the *o* in *fork*, the *o* in *old*, or the *o* in *hot*?
4. Is the *e* in *Río Piedras* to be pronounced like the *e* in *me*, the *a* in *ape*, or the *i* in *it*?

CHALLENGE

Further Reading

■ You may enjoy reading other biographies or biographical essays, such as the following:

- *Martin Luther King, Jr.: A Documentary . . . Montgomery to Memphis,* edited by Flipp Schulke.

- *Florence Nightingale* by Elspeth J. Huxley.

ESSAY

James Thurber (1894–1961) is one of America's greatest writers of humor. He was born in Columbus, Ohio, and lost much of his sight as the result of a childhood accident. He became famous for his comic essays, short stories, articles, and cartoons.

Thurber drew on his experiences of childhood and adolescence to write his best-known book, *My Life and Hard Times*, which was published in 1933. The essays and sketches in this collection are based on fact, describing such subjects as the author's unusual relatives and his experiences in college. "The Night the Bed Fell" comes from this book.

▧ Would you like to be a member of the family that Thurber describes in this narrative?

James Thurber

The Night the Bed Fell

I suppose that the high-water mark of my youth in Columbus, Ohio, was the night the bed fell on my father. It makes a better recitation[1] (unless, as some friends of mine have said, one has heard it five or six times) than it does a piece of writing, for it is almost necessary to throw furniture around, shake doors, and bark like a dog, to lend the proper atmosphere and verisimilitude[2] to what is admittedly a somewhat incredible tale. Still, it did take place.

It happened, then, that my father had de-cided to sleep in the attic one night, to be away where he could think. My mother opposed the notion strongly because, she said, the old wooden bed up there was unsafe; it was wobbly, and the heavy headboard would crash down on Father's head in case the bed fell, and kill him. There was no dissuading him, however, and at a quarter past ten he closed the attic door behind him and went up the narrow twisting stairs. We later heard ominous creakings as he crawled into bed. Grandfather, who usually slept in the attic bed when he was with us, had disappeared some days before. (On these occasions he was usually gone six or eight days and returned growling and out of temper, with the news

---

1. **recitation** [res′ə tā′shən]: piece memorized and prepared for public performance.
2. **verisimilitude** [ver′ə si mil′ə tōōd]: appearance of truth.

that the Federal Union[3] was run by a passel of blockheads and that the Army of the Potomac[4] didn't have a chance.)

We had visiting us at this time a nervous first cousin of mine named Briggs Beall, who believed that he was likely to cease breathing when he was asleep. It was his feeling that if he were not awakened every hour during the night, he might die of suffocation. He had been accustomed to setting an alarm clock to ring at intervals until morning, but I persuaded him to abandon this. He slept in my room and I told him that I was such a light sleeper that if anybody quit breathing in the same room with me, I would wake instantly. He tested me the first night—which I had suspected he would—by holding his breath after my regular breathing had convinced him I was asleep. I was not asleep, however, and called to him. This seemed to allay his fears a little, but he took the precaution of putting a glass of spirits of camphor[5] on a little table at the head of his bed. In case I didn't arouse him until he was almost gone, he said, he would sniff the camphor, a powerful reviver.

Briggs was not the only member of his family who had his crotchets.[6] Old Aunt Melissa Beall (who could whistle like a man, with two fingers in her mouth) suffered under the premonition that she was destined to die on South High Street because she had been born on South High Street and married on South High Street. Then there was Aunt Sarah Shoaf, who never went to bed at night without the fear that a burglar was going to get in and blow chloroform[7] under her door through a

tube. To avert this calamity—for she was in greater dread of anesthetics than of losing her household goods—she always piled her money, silverware, and other valuables in a neat stack just outside her bedroom, with a note reading "This is all I have. Please take it and do not use your chloroform, as this is all I have." Aunt Gracie Shoaf also had a burglar phobia,[8] but she met it with more fortitude. She was confident that burglars had been getting into her house every night for forty years. The fact that she never missed anything was to her no proof to the contrary. She always claimed that she scared them off before they could take anything, by throwing shoes down the hallway. When she went to bed, she piled, where she could get at them handily, all the shoes there were about her house. Five minutes after she had turned off the light, she would sit up in bed and say "Hark!" Her husband, who had learned to ignore the whole

3. **Federal Union:** another name for the Union, or Northern, side in the Civil War. Thurber's grandfather believes that the Civil War is still being fought.
4. **Army of the Potomac:** eastern branch of the Union Army in the Civil War.
5. **spirits of camphor:** strong-smelling solution.
6. **crotchets** [kroch′its]: strange or peculiar ideas.
7. **chloroform** [klôr′ə form′]: type of anesthetic, or substance used to cause sleep.

8. **phobia** [fō′bē ə]: unreasonable fear.

situation as long ago as 1903, would either be sound asleep or pretend to be sound asleep. In either case he would not respond to her tugging and pulling, so that presently she would arise, tiptoe to the door, open it slightly, and heave a shoe down the hall in one direction and its mate down the hall in the other direction. Some nights she threw them all, some nights only a couple of pairs.

But I am straying from the remarkable incidents that took place during the night that the bed fell on Father. By midnight we were all in bed. The layout of the rooms and the disposition[9] of their occupants is important to an understanding of what later occurred. In the front room upstairs (just under Father's attic bedroom) were my mother and my brother Herman, who sometimes sang in his sleep, usually "Marching Through Georgia" or "Onward, Christian Soldiers." Briggs Beall and myself were in a room adjoining this one. My brother Roy was in a room across the hall from ours. Our bull terrier, Rex, slept in the hall.

My bed was an army cot, one of those affairs which are made wide enough to sleep on comfortably only by putting up, flat with the middle section, the two sides which ordinarily hang down like the sideboards of a drop-leaf table. When these sides are up, it is perilous to roll too far toward the edge, for then the cot is likely to tip completely over, bringing the whole bed down on top of one, with a tremendous banging crash. This, in fact, is precisely what happened about two o'clock in the morning. (It was my mother who, in recalling the scene later, first referred to it as "the night the bed fell on your father.")

Always a deep sleeper, slow to arouse (I had lied to Briggs), I was at first unconscious of what had happened when the iron cot rolled me onto the floor and toppled over on me. It left me still warmly bundled up and unhurt, for the bed rested above me like a canopy. Hence I did not wake up, only reached the edge of consciousness and went back. The racket, however, instantly awakened my mother, in the next room, who came to the immediate conclusion that her worst dread was realized: the big wooden bed upstairs had fallen on Father. She therefore screamed, "Let's go to your poor father!" It was this shout, rather than the noise of my cot falling, that awakened Herman, in the same room with her. He thought that Mother had become, for no apparent reason, hysterical. "You're all right, Mamma!" he shouted, trying to calm her. They exchanged shout for shout for perhaps ten seconds: "Let's go to your poor father!" and "You're all right!" That woke up Briggs. By this time I was conscious of what was going on, in a vague way, but did not yet realize that I was under my bed instead of on it. Briggs, awakening in the midst of loud shouts of fear and apprehension, came to the

---

9. **disposition** [dis′pə zish′ən]: arrangement; placement or grouping.

quick conclusion that he was suffocating and that we were all trying to "bring him out." With a low moan, he grasped the glass of camphor at the head of his bed and instead of sniffing it poured it over himself. The room reeked of camphor. "Ugf, ahfg," choked Briggs, like a drowning man, for he had almost succeeded in stopping his breath under the deluge of pungent spirits. He leaped out of bed and groped toward the open window, but he came up against one that was closed. With his hand, he beat out the glass, and I could hear it crash and tinkle on the alleyway below. It was at this juncture that I, in trying to get up, had the uncanny sensation of feeling my bed above me! Foggy with sleep, I now suspected, in my turn, that the whole uproar was being made in a frantic endeavor to extricate me from what must be an unheard-of and perilous situation. "Get me out of this!" I bawled. "Get me out!" I think I had the nightmarish belief that I was entombed in a mine. "Gugh," gasped Briggs, floundering in his camphor.

By this time my mother, still shouting, pursued by Herman, still shouting, was trying to open the door to the attic, in order to go up and get my father's body out of the wreckage. The door was stuck, however, and wouldn't yield. Her frantic pulls on it only added to the general banging and confusion. Roy and the dog were now up, the one shouting questions, the other barking.

Father, farthest away and soundest sleeper of all, had by this time been awakened by the battering on the attic door. He decided that the house was on fire. "I'm coming, I'm coming!" he wailed in a slow, sleepy voice—it took him many minutes to regain full consciousness. My mother, still believing he was caught under the bed, detected in his "I'm coming!" the mournful, resigned note of one who is preparing to meet his Maker. "He's dying!" she shouted.

"I'm all right!" Briggs yelled to reassure her. "I'm all right!" He still believed that it was his own closeness to death that was worrying Mother. I found at last the light switch in my room, unlocked the door, and Briggs and I joined the others at the attic door. The dog, who never did like Briggs, jumped for him—assuming that he was the culprit in whatever was going on—and Roy had to throw Rex and hold him. We could hear Father crawling out of bed upstairs. Roy pulled the attic door open with a mighty jerk, and Father came down the stairs, sleepy and irritable but safe and sound. My mother began to weep when she saw him. Rex began to howl. "What in the name of heaven is going on here?" asked Father.

The situation was finally put together like a gigantic jigsaw puzzle. Father caught a cold from prowling around in his bare feet, but there were no other bad results. "I'm glad," said Mother, who always looked on the bright side of things, "that your grandfather wasn't here."

STUDY QUESTIONS

Recalling

1. Why is Mrs. Thurber afraid to let her husband sleep in the attic?
2. Why does Thurber's cousin Briggs keep a glass of camphor by his bed? What promise does Thurber make to him?
3. Name two other members of Thurber's family. What are their "crotchets," or strange ideas?
4. What happens to the author's cot on the famous night? What does Mrs. Thurber think happened?
5. What is Thurber's father actually doing throughout the "emergency"? Where does everyone else in the family end up?

Interpreting

6. What general impression of his family does Thurber create in this account?
7. What side of human nature does Thurber emphasize?

Extending

8. Do you think most people have some sort of "crotchet"? Explain.

READING AND LITERARY FOCUS

Narration

Narration is the type of writing that tells a story. A narrative work can be either fictional or nonfictional, depending on whether the story it tells actually happened. Autobiographies, biographies, narrative essays, short stories, and novels are all forms of narrative writing.

Most narratives are told in **chronological order,** the order in which events naturally occur. Effective narratives usually follow a pattern similar to the plot of a short story. That is, a **conflict,** or problem, of some kind sets in motion a chain of events. These events build to a **climax,** or peak of interest—the point at which we realize how the conflict or problem will be resolved.

Thinking About Narration

■ Tell step by step what happens during the family emergency, beginning with the collapse of the army cot and ending with Mr. Thurber's appearance. What is the narrative's climax?

Humor and Exaggeration

Much of the humor in "The Night the Bed Fell" comes from Thurber's **exaggeration** of his characters and actions. He stretches the truth to make his narrative larger—and funnier—than life normally is. For example, it is normal to be worried about burglars. However, Thurber's Aunt Sarah Shoaf has an exaggerated and much funnier worry. She is so frightened that a burglar will chloroform her that she piles all her valuables outside her door and invites any burglar to take them.

Thinking About Humor and Exaggeration

■ From Thurber's narrative choose one other character or situation that seems exaggerated. What qualities make the person or situation seem larger and funnier than life?

COMPOSITION

Writing About a Narrative Essay

■ Tell what you think was Thurber's purpose in relating what happened on the night the bed fell. For example, do you think he wanted to inform us, to reveal something about his childhood, to entertain us, or to make some point about human nature? Begin by stating what you think is Thurber's purpose. Then use examples from the narrative to support your opinion. End by saying how well you think he succeeded.

Retelling a Narrative

■ Choose one of the characters Thurber describes in "The Night the Bed Fell" (for example, Cousin Briggs or one of Thurber's parents). Write that character's own brief version of what happened on that night.

Marjorie Kinnan Rawlings (1896–1953) was born in Washington, D.C., but spent much of her life on a farm at Cross Creek, Florida. Described by Rawlings as "a bend in a country road," Cross Creek is a wooded, marshy place quite different from the cities in which Rawlings had previously lived. Her experiences in Cross Creek formed the background for her novels and stories, many of which center on children and animals. The most famous of these is *The Yearling*, the novel for which Rawlings won the Pulitzer Prize.

Rawlings wrote of her Florida home in *Cross Creek* (1942), a loosely autobiographical work that formed the basis for the 1983 film *Cross Creek*. The following descriptive essay, which comes from this book, concerns a dog that becomes the author's companion for a time.

■ Do you know why the author treats the dog as she does?

Marjorie Kinnan Rawlings

The Catch-Dog

I was struck, with Harper's bear dogs on the hunt, as with John Clardy's fox hounds, by the sharp line drawn between house dogs and work dogs. Florida hunters believe that any dog allowed the run of the house cannot be made a good sporting or working dog. I cannot agree. I make companions of my pointers and take them with me in my car. It seems to me that my Mad Pat, for instance, hunts with even greater enthusiasm and earnestness than kennel dogs I have known, through his delight in sharing the hunt with me and his desire to please me. Discipline of course must be strict and businesslike and must begin with the puppy. Because of this, I did once a cruel thing to a work dog whose path crossed mine.

The dog and I first met on a warm June evening. I was walking east along the Creek road, a little later than usual. The sun had set. I remember feeling lonely. I was a little uneasy, as well, for the moccasins[1] and ratlers cross the road in the twilight. A ramshackle[2] car came out from the lane that leads to Cow Hammock and turned toward the village. A dog followed it. He ran with the dejection of the forsaken. He was not noticed. A half-mile ahead he stopped disconsolately[3] and began to trot back toward home. I saw that he was of a tawny yellow. He had some-

---

1. **moccasins:** water moccasins, large poisonous snakes found in the southeastern United States.
2. **ramshackle** [ram'shak'əl]: about to fall apart.
3. **disconsolately** [dis kon'sə lit lē]: sorrowfully.

thing of the build of the Belgian police dog. As he came closer, I became aware of his mixed breeding. A black and alien smudge ran down his nose, and his long tail was ignominiously[4] curled, revealing the mongrel. He trotted with a wolflike purpose.

I called to him with some uncertainty as to his nature. The yellow dog stopped. He came to me. I held out my hand and he snuffed it. I touched his rough coat. I pulled one ear. He rubbed his nose briefly against me in a gesture of acceptance. A feeling of friendliness passed over us in the dusk.

I said, "Come, boy," and he turned and walked with me.

It was good, after long months without a dog of my own, to have him beside me. He left me in a few minutes and went ahead, but the link between us was unbroken. Now and then he stopped and looked back, to be sure that I was following. Once he came to me to be touched; to be reassured that we were, truly, together. Studying him, I saw that he was a working dog; the catch-dog, it proved, of my new neighbor in Cow Hammock, who used him to round up his vagrant hogs. The business dog has his own ear marks. He is self-contained. He expects no luxuries of life, no graciousness. He possesses usually a simple integrity. He does his work faithfully and well and takes his pan of cornbread and an occasional bone, not with gratitude, but with the dignity of one who knows he has earned, that day, his keep. His gratitude is reserved for the rare expression of friendliness such as I had given him. That first night he ran well ahead of me and up his home lane, not taking too much for granted the closeness of our relation.

The next day I set out up the road in the late afternoon. I passed the entrance to Cow Hammock.

I called, "Here, boy! Here!"

I expected no response and there was none. I was halfway to Big Hammock when a clicking sound on the gravel road caught my ear. The yellow catch-dog was running to overtake me as though his life depended on it. I waited for him and he bounded about me with the joy of the alien who comes at last to his own. I was as glad as he. We walked that evening in a great content and that time he did not turn up his lane until I passed it with him. After that he waited for me with a faithful regularity. If I went early, I might have to call. Invariably he heard and joined me as soon as he could leave his business. If I went late, he was waiting at the lane. A few strokings of his head and he was satisfied. He went ahead, not far, looking back often over his curled and shameful tail.

Sometimes we romped together. We enjoyed most the game with the bull-bats.[5] We stalked them together. They have a trick of sitting bright-eyed in the road, waiting for the approach. At the last instant they take off, circling to swoop low over their pursuer's head. It is a good game of tag. The yellow dog beat me at it. Often, a bull-bat too sure of himself all but lost his tail feathers. When this happened, the catch-dog raced joyfully around and around, or chased a quite imaginary rabbit.

One evening we loitered, for the approaching night was hot and sultry. As we turned west again, the last red stain of sunset faded from the sky and the road was dark. The catch-dog walked slowly beside me. Suddenly he stiffened. He made a sound, half growl, half moan, deep in his throat. Then he backed against me. I became aware that he was pushing me with his strong hindquarters, moving me away as deliberately as though he pos-

---

4. **ignominiously** [ig′nə min′ē əs lē]: in shame.

5. **bull-bats:** brown, night-flying birds, also known as nighthawks and nightjars.

sessed an arm with which to do so. I backed with him to the far side of the road. On the gray gravel what had been a wide shadow resolved itself into a large rattlesnake that slid now into the grass. The catch-dog and I quivered, for the blood curdles instinctively at such an encounter in the dark. We hurried the rest of the way. Then and afterward we were joined by the closeness of those who, together, have escaped a danger.

One night I heard him being beaten for having gone away when he was wanted. Once he failed me, when an outlaw boar was being cornered. I heard the shrill squealings of the hog and knew that the catch-dog was at his work. He came later to my gate, as though to show me that his failure to join me was not of his intention. He did this sometimes, too, when circumstances kept me from my walking. Otherwise he did not intrude on my life of which, he recognized, he was not a part.

Some weeks after we began our jaunts together I was given the high-bred pointer puppy for which I had been waiting. The puppy was captivating. I devoted myself at once to his care and training. I wanted to raise the handsome young fellow as a companion, so that I was especially anxious to discipline him firmly from the beginning. I ended my evening walks down the highway, going about the grove instead. The puppy was not yet broken to go to heel and I could not risk the distraction of the catch-dog, a rabbit chaser, to disturb his training. Two or three days later the yellow dog came to my gate, wagging his tail. I ignored him and he went away.

A week later I took my young pointer on a leash. We passed the entrance to Cow Hammock. Passing, the catch-dog must have scented us, for some distance on he came after us on the gallop. He was insane with joy. He jumped against me, he went taut proudly, introducing himself to the puppy. He dropped his forelegs to the ground and shook his head,

inviting the new dog to play. The puppy barked shrilly and tugged at the leash. Discipline was hopeless. There was nothing for it but to drive the catch-dog away. I made a menacing gesture. He looked at me unbelieving and did not stir. I picked up a handful of light gravel and threw it in his direction and went on, dragging the puppy behind me. The catch-dog followed. He watched me with bewildered eyes.

I shouted with as much sternness as I could manage to bring from a sick heart, "Get back!" and he stopped and made no further effort to go with us. On the way home, we passed him, lying at the Cow Hammock entrance, his head on his paws. He fluttered his tail a little, as though in hope that I did not, could not, mean my rejection of him. The pointer and I hurried by.

Now we pass as though we were strangers. I am ashamed to face him, having used him in my loneliness, and then betrayed him. He shows no signs of recognition. His tail curves over his back. He trots with a high head, looking straight ahead. He is a work dog, and he must be about his business.

STUDY QUESTIONS

Recalling

1. According to Rawlings, what part does discipline play in raising a dog?
2. When and where does Rawlings meet the catch-dog?
3. How does the dog usually respond when he sees Rawlings?
4. What does Rawlings do when she meets the catch-dog after the pointer puppy comes? How does she feel about her treatment of the dog?

Interpreting

5. Before the puppy comes, what are Rawlings' and the catch-dog's feelings for each other?
6. Do you understand Rawlings' treatment of the catch-dog after the arrival of the puppy? Why or why not?

Extending

7. Why do you think that people and animals become attached to one another?

READING AND LITERARY FOCUS

Description and Details

Description is the type of writing that creates a clear picture of something—a person, animal, object, or place, for example. All works of literature, both fiction and nonfiction, contain description.

Good descriptive writing should create a strong **overall impression** of the subject. This overall impression is made up of many **details:** specific pictures, colors, shapes, sounds, sometimes smells, tastes, textures, and even emotions. For example, Rawlings says of one evening as she walks with the catch-dog:

> One evening we loitered, for the approaching night was hot and sultry. . . . the last red stain of sunset faded from the sky and the road was dark. . . . Suddenly he stiffened. He made a sound, half growl, half moan. . . .

These details call up the senses of feeling (in "hot and sultry"), color ("red stain" and "dark"), movement ("stiffened"), and sound ("half growl, half moan"). They also create the overall impression of a rather ominous scene.

Thinking About Description and Details

1. List the details that Rawlings uses in her first description of the catch-dog.
2. Which details seem to reveal the dog's personality?

COMPOSITION

Writing About Nonfiction

■ Every nonfiction work has a central idea of some kind. What idea about friendship does Marjorie Kinnan Rawlings convey in describing the catch-dog? Cite the specific facts, details, and examples that she uses to convey this idea. *For help with this assignment, see Lesson 7 in the Writing About Literature Handbook at the back of this book.*

Writing a Description

■ In a paragraph write a description of one of the following subjects: (a) a small object, (b) a graceful or clumsy gesture, (c) a musical instrument, or (d) a food you like or dislike very much. Be sure to use details and vivid words.

CHALLENGE

Literary Criticism

■ Toward the end of her book *Cross Creek,* Marjorie Kinnan Rawlings says

> We at the Creek draw our conclusions about the world from our intimate knowledge of one small portion of it.

What conclusions about people and animals might be drawn from Rawlings' account of her relationship with the catch-dog?

© 1982 Jill Krementz

Alice Walker (born 1944) comes from Eatonton, Georgia. She is a teacher and an author. Walker has written a biography of the famous black American writer Langston Hughes. She has also published several collections of stories and poems and three novels. Her novel *The Color Purple* won the American Book Award and the Pulitzer Prize in 1983.

"In Search of Our Mothers' Gardens" pays honor to Walker's mother and thousands of women like her, who kept alive a "creative spark." Walker says of her mother, "Whatever she planted grew as if by magic."

■ What, besides flowers, did Alice Walker's mother plant?

Alice Walker

from **In Search of Our Mothers' Gardens**

In the late 1920s my mother ran away from home to marry my father. By the time she was twenty, she had two children. Five children later, I was born. And this is how I came to know my mother: she seemed a large, soft, loving-eyed woman who was rarely impatient in our home. . . .

She made all the clothes we wore, even my brothers' overalls. She made all the towels and sheets we used. She spent the summers canning vegetables and fruits. She spent the winter evenings making quilts enough to cover all our beds.

During the "working" day, she labored beside—not behind—my father in the fields. Her day began before sunup, and did not end until late at night. There was never a moment for her to sit down, undisturbed, to unravel her own private thoughts; never a time free from interruption—by work or the noisy inquiries of her many children. And yet, it is to my mother—and all our mothers who were not famous—that I went in search of the secret of what has fed that muzzled and often mutilated, but vibrant, creative spirit that the black woman has inherited, and that pops out in wild and unlikely places to this day.

But when, you will ask, did my overworked mother have time to know or care about feeding the creative spirit?

The answer is so simple that many of us have spent years discovering it. We have constantly looked high, when we should have looked high—and low.

Alice Walker at work in her home.

For example: in the Smithsonian Institution[1] in Washington, D.C., there hangs a quilt unlike any other in the world. In fanciful, inspired, and yet simple and identifiable figures, it portrays the story of the Crucifixion.[2] It is considered rare, beyond price. Though it follows no known pattern of quilt-making, and though it is made of bits and pieces of worthless rags, it is obviously the work of a person of powerful imagination and deep spiritual feeling. Below this quilt I saw a note that says it was made by "an anonymous Black woman in Alabama, a hundred years ago."

If we could locate this "anonymous" black woman from Alabama, she would turn out to be one of our grandmothers—an artist who left her mark in the only materials she could afford, and in the only medium her position in society allowed her to use.

And so our mothers and grandmothers have, more often than not anonymously, handed on the creative spark, the seed of the flower they themselves never hoped to see: or like a sealed letter they could not plainly read.

And so it is, certainly, with my own mother. Unlike "Ma" Rainey's[3] songs, which retained their creator's name even while blasting forth from Bessie Smith's[4] mouth, no song or poem will bear my mother's name. Yet so many of the stories that I write, that we all write, are my mother's stories. Only recently did I fully realize this: that through years of listening to my mother's stories of her life, I have absorbed not only the stories themselves, but something of the manner in which she spoke, something of the urgency that involves the knowledge that her stories—like her life—must be recorded. It is probably for this reason that so much of what I have written is about characters whose counterparts in real life are so much older than I am.

But the telling of these stories, which came from my mother's lips as naturally as breathing, was not the only way my mother showed herself as an artist. For stories, too, were subject to being distracted, to dying without conclusion. Dinners must be started, and cotton must be gathered before the big rains. The artist that was and is my mother showed itself to me only after many years. This is what I finally noticed:

Like Mem, a character in *The Third Life of Grange Copeland*,[5] my mother adorned with flowers whatever shabby house we were forced

---

1. **Smithsonian Institution:** group of museums in Washington, D.C., displaying items of historical, scientific, and artistic interest.
2. **Crucifixion:** death of Jesus Christ on the cross.

3. **"Ma" Rainey's:** Gertrude Rainey was an early twentieth-century blues singer and composer of blues songs.
4. **Bessie Smith's:** Bessie Smith (1898?–1937) was a famous American blues singer and a student of "Ma" Rainey's.
5. ***The Third Life of Grange Copeland:*** novel by Alice Walker.

Alice Walker and her daughter, Rebecca.

to live in. And not just your typical straggly country stand of zinnias, either. She planted ambitious gardens—and still does—with over fifty different varieties of plants that bloom profusely from early March until late November. Before she left home for the fields, she watered her flowers, chopped up the grass, and laid out new beds. When she returned from the fields she might divide clumps of bulbs, dig a cold pit,[6] uproot and replant roses, or prune branches from her taller bushes or trees—until night came and it was too dark to see.

Whatever she planted grew as if by magic, and her fame as a grower of flowers spread over three counties. Because of her creativity with her flowers, even my memories of poverty are seen through a screen of blooms—sunflowers, petunias, roses, dahlias, forsythia, spirea, delphiniums, verbena . . . and on and on.

Alice's parents, Minnie Lou and Willie Lee Walker, in the 1930s.

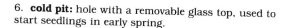
6. **cold pit:** hole with a removable glass top, used to start seedlings in early spring.

And I remember people coming to my mother's yard to be given cuttings from her flowers; I hear again the praise showered on her because whatever rocky soil she landed on, she turned into a garden. A garden so brilliant with colors, so original in its design, so magnificent with life and creativity, that to this day people drive by our house in Georgia—perfect strangers and imperfect strangers—and ask to stand or walk among my mother's art.

I notice that it is only when my mother is working in her flowers that she is radiant, almost to the point of being invisible—except as Creator: hand and eye. She is involved in work her soul must have. Ordering the universe in the image of her personal conception of Beauty.

Her face, as she prepares the Art that is her gift, is a legacy of respect she leaves to me, for all that illuminates and cherishes life. She has handed down respect for the possibilities—and the will to grasp them.

For her, so hindered and intruded upon in so many ways, being an artist has still been a daily part of her life. This ability to hold on, even in very simple ways, is work black women have done for a very long time.

This poem[7] is not enough, but it is something, for the woman who literally covered the holes in our walls with sunflowers:

_____

7. **This poem:** "Women," a poetic tribute by Alice Walker to her mother and women like her.

They were women then
My mama's generation
Husky of voice—Stout of
Step
With fists as well as
Hands
How they battered down
Doors
And ironed
Starched white
Shirts
How they led
Armies
Headragged[8] Generals
Across mined[9]
Fields
Booby-trapped[10]
Kitchens
To discover books
Desks
A place for us
How they knew what we
Must know
Without knowing a page
Of it
Themselves.

Guided by my heritage of a love of beauty and a respect for strength—in search of my mother's garden, I found my own. . . .

_____

8. **Headragged:** with heads covered by kerchiefs.
9. **mined:** containing buried explosives.
10. **Booby-trapped:** containing a dangerous trick disguised to seem harmless.

STUDY QUESTIONS

Recalling
1. What daily tasks occupy Alice Walker's mother?
2. What "secret" does Walker set out to find?
3. Who made the Crucifixion quilt in the museum?
4. In what two ways does Walker's mother show herself as an artist?
5. What legacy has Walker's mother handed down, according to her daughter?

Interpreting

6. What do Walker's mother and the maker of the Crucifixion quilt have in common?
7. In your own words explain what Alice Walker feels she owes her mother and women like her.
8. What do you think Walker means by the final sentence of this essay?

Extending

9. Do you agree that an activity like gardening can be regarded as an art? Why or why not?

READING AND LITERARY FOCUS

Exposition and Thesis Statement

Exposition is the type of writing that presents facts or explains an idea. Sometimes an author directly tells us the central idea of an expository essay in a **thesis statement,** a sentence or two in which the central thought of the work is clearly expressed. The thesis statement of an expository essay often takes the form of a **generalization,** or general statement of some kind. In making a generalization a writer ties together many separate examples.

The thesis statement usually occurs early in the essay. The material that follows the thesis statement supports and develops it with specific facts, incidents, examples, and details. For example, in the selection from *Growing Up,* Russell Baker expresses his central idea in this thesis statement: "For this reason [his family's poverty] I was often astonished when my mother did me some deed of generosity. . . ." The incidents of the suit and the bicycle then support and develop this idea about Baker's mother. Many writers then restate the thesis in new words near the end of the essay.

Thinking About Exposition and Thesis Statement

1. Point out Alice Walker's thesis statement. Find two examples that she uses to back it up.
2. Where does Walker restate her thesis?

VOCABULARY

Analogies

Analogies are comparisons that are stated as double relationships: for example, *A* is to *B* as *C* is to *D.* On tests analogies are written as two pairs of words, *A : B :: C : D.* You may be given the first pair and asked to find or complete a second pair that has the same kind of relationship. For example, in the analogy COLOR : RED :: SHAPE : SQUARE, the first word in each pair names a general category, and the second word names a specific member of that category.

The following numbered items are analogies that need to be completed. The third word in each item comes from "In Search of Our Mothers' Gardens." Decide how the first two words in each item are related. Then from the four choices that follow each numbered item, choose the word that best completes the second pair. Write the number of each item and the letter of your choice.

1. SHARP : BLUNT : : VIBRANT :
   (a) bright   (c) alive
   (b) pointed   (d) dull

2. FAST : SWIFT : : FANCIFUL :
   (a) imaginative   (c) ordinary
   (b) fancy   (d) pleasant

3. APPLES : FRUITS : : DAHLIAS :
   (a) trees   (c) daisies
   (b) flowers   (d) leaves

4. MOIST : MOISTURE : : RADIANT :
   (a) bright   (c) radar
   (b) sun   (d) radiance

CHALLENGE

Outline

■ Outline "In Search of Our Mothers' Gardens." Begin by indicating the central idea of the essay with the Roman numeral *I.* Then list all the supporting ideas with capital letters (*A, B, C,* etc.). Note examples and details with Arabic numerals (*1, 2, 3,* etc.).

James Michener (born 1907) is famous throughout the world as the author of such best-selling novels as *Hawaii* (1960), *Centennial* (1974), and *Space* (1983). Born in New York City, Michener taught social sciences and worked as an editor before entering the Navy during World War II. His wartime experiences in the Solomon Islands of the South Pacific led him to write his first book, *Tales of the South Pacific* (1947), for which he won the Pulitzer Prize. In 1983 Michener was officially named a National Treasure.

▨ Before beginning this essay, write on a slip of paper your *own* answer to Michener's question "When does education stop?" Then decide whether your answer agrees with Michener's.

James Michener

When Does Education Stop?

During the summer vacation a fine-looking young man, who was majoring in literature at a top university, asked for an interview, and before we had talked for five minutes, he launched into his complaint.

"Can you imagine?" he lamented. "During vacation I have to write a three-thousand-word term paper about your books." He felt very sorry for himself.

His whimpering irritated me, and on the spur of the moment I shoved at him a card which had become famous in World War II. It was once used on me. It read:

> Young man, your sad story
> is truly heartbreaking.
> Excuse me while I fetch a
> crying towel.

My complaining visitor reacted as I had done twenty years earlier. He burst into laughter and asked, "Did I sound that bad?"

"Worse!" I snapped. Then I pointed to a novel of mine which he was using as the basis for his term paper. "You're bellyaching about a three-thousand-word paper which at most will occupy you for a month. When I started work on *Hawaii*,[1] I faced the prospect of a three-million-word term paper. And five years of work. Frankly, you sound silly."

This strong language encouraged an excellent discussion of the preparation it takes to write a major novel. Five years of research, months of character development, extensive work on plot and setting, endless speculation

---

1. **Hawaii:** long novel by James Michener, published in 1959.

on psychology and concentrated work on historical backgrounds.

"When I was finally ready to write," I replied under questioning, "I holed up in a bare-wall, no-telephone Waikiki[2] room and stuck at my typewriter every morning for eighteen months. Seven days a week I wrestled with the words that would not come, with ideas that refused to jell. When I broke a tooth, I told the dentist I'd have to see him at night. When DeWitt Wallace, the editor of the *Reader's Digest* and a man to whom I am much indebted, came to Hawaii on vacation, I wanted to hike with him but had to say, 'In the late afternoon. In the morning I work.' "

I explained to my caller that I write all my books slowly, with two fingers on an old typewriter, and the actual task of getting the words on paper is difficult. Nothing I write is good enough to be used in first draft, not even important personal letters, so I am required to rewrite everything at least twice. Important work, like a novel, must be written over and over again, up to six or seven times. For example, *Hawaii* went very slowly and needed constant revision. Since the final version contained about 500,000 words, and since I wrote it all many times, I had to type in my painstaking fashion about 3,000,000 words.

At this news, my visitor whistled and asked, "How many research books did you have to consult?"

"Several thousand. When I started the actual writing, there were about five hundred that I kept in my office."

"How many personal interviews?"

"About two hundred. Each two or three hours long."

"Did you write much that you weren't able to use?"

"I had to throw away about half a million words."

The young scholar looked again at the card and returned it reverently to my desk. "Would you have the energy to undertake such a task again?" he asked.

"I would always like to be engaged in such tasks," I replied, and he turned to other questions.

Young people, especially those in college who should know better, frequently fail to realize that men and women who wish to accomplish anything must apply themselves to tasks of tremendous magnitude. A new vaccine may take years to perfect. A Broadway play is never written, cast and produced in a week. A foreign policy is never evolved in a brief time by diplomats relaxing in Washington, London or Geneva.

The good work of the world is accomplished principally by people who dedicate themselves unstintingly to the big job at hand. Weeks, months, years pass, but the good workman knows that he is gambling on an ultimate achievement which cannot be measured in time spent. Responsible men and women leap to the challenge of jobs that require enormous dedication and years to fulfill, and are happiest when they are so involved.

This means that men and women who hope to make a real contribution to American life must prepare themselves to tackle big jobs, and the interesting fact is that no college or university in the world can give anyone the specific education he will ultimately need. Adults who are unwilling to reeducate themselves periodically are doomed to mediocrity.

I first discovered this fact on Guadalcanal[3]

---

2. **Waikiki** [wī′kē kē′]: famous beach and resort area in Honolulu, Hawaii.

3. **Guadalcanal** [gwäd′əl kə nal′]: one of the Solomon Islands in the southwestern Pacific Ocean; during World War II the site of fighting between American and Japanese forces in 1942–1943.

in 1945, when the war had passed us by and we could see certain victory ahead. Relieved of pressure, our top admirals and generals could have been excused if they loafed, but the ones I knew well in those days took free time and gave themselves orderly courses in new fields. One carrier admiral[4] studied everything he could get on tank warfare. The head of our outfit, William Lowndes Calhoun, spent six hours a day learning French.

I asked him about this. "Admiral, what's this big deal with French?"

"How do I know where I'll be sent when the war's over?" he countered.

But what impressed me most was the next tier of officers, the young Army colonels and the Navy commanders. They divided sharply into two groups: those who spent their spare time learning something and those who didn't. In the years that followed, I noticed in the newspapers that whenever President Truman[5] or President Eisenhower[6] chose men for military positions of great power, they always picked from the officers who had re-educated themselves.

More significant to me personally was my stay with the brilliant doctors of an Army hospital in the jungles of Espiritu Santo.[7] The entire staff of a general hospital in Denver, Colorado, had been picked up and flown out to care for our wounded, and they experienced days of overwork followed by weeks of tedium. In the latter periods the doctors organized voluntary study groups by which to further their professional competence.

By good luck, I was allowed to participate in a group that was analyzing alcoholism, and one night the leader asked me, as we were breaking up, "What are you studying, Michener?" The question stunned me, for I had been studying exactly nothing.

I drove back through the jungle and that very night started working on something that I had been toying with for some months. In a lantern-lit, mosquito-filled tin shack, I started writing *Tales of the South Pacific*.[8]

I have been the typical American in that I have had widely scattered jobs: teacher, businessman, soldier, traveler, writer. And my college education gave me no specific preparation for any of these jobs.

But it gave me something much better. I attended Swarthmore College, outside Philadelphia, and by fantastic luck, I got there just as the college was launching an experiment which was to transform the institution and those of us who participated. At the end of my sophomore year the faculty assembled a group of us and said, "Life does not consist of taking courses in small segments. A productive life consists of finding huge tasks and mastering them with whatever tools of intelligence and energy we have. We are going to turn you loose on some huge tasks. Let's see what you can do with them."

Accordingly, we were excused from all future class attendance and were told, "Pick out three fields that interest you." I chose logic, English history and the novel. The faculty said, "For the next two years go to the library and learn what you can about your fields. At the end of two years we'll bring in some outside experts from Harvard and Yale,[9] whom

---

4. **carrier admiral:** commander of a warship serving as a takeoff and landing area for airplanes.
5. **President Truman:** Harry S. Truman (1884–1972), thirty-third President of the United States (1945–1953).
6. **President Eisenhower:** Dwight D. Eisenhower (1890–1969), thirty-fourth President of the United States (1953–1961).
7. **Espiritu Santo** [e spēˈrē to͞o sänˈtō]: large island in the south Pacific; used as a U.S. air base.

8. ***Tales of the South Pacific:*** Michener's Pulitzer Prize–winning collection of stories about the war in the Pacific; published in 1947.
9. **Harvard and Yale:** two top-ranking American universities.

you've never seen, and they will determine whether or not you have educated yourselves."

What followed was an experience in intellectual grandeur. The Swarthmore professors, realizing that when I was tested they would be tested too, helped me to gain as thorough an education as a young man could absorb. For it was in their interest to see that I understood the fine points of the fields I had chosen.

When the two years ended, the visiting experts arrived and for a week they probed and tested and heckled. At the end of this exciting time one of the examiners told me, "You have the beginning of a real education."

He was right. Nothing that I studied in college has been of use to me in my various jobs. But what I did learn was how to learn, how to organize, how to write term papers. If my education had ended the week I stood before those strange examiners, I would have proved a fairly useless citizen. . . .

While I was reflecting on these matters, my young scholar asked, "If you were a young man today and wanted to be a writer, what kind of education would you seek?"

I replied, "I'd choose some very difficult field and try to master it. I'd seek out professors who really poured it on. Long term papers and many of them, tough laboratory work."

"Why?" he pressed.

"Because we learn only those things at which we have to work very hard. It's ridiculous to give a bright fellow like you a three-thousand-word term paper. It ought to be fifteen thousand words—or thirty. Tackle a real job. Then, when you're through, you're on the way to facing big jobs in adult life." . . .

We parted on that note, but when he had gone, I realized that I had not made my statement nearly strong enough. I should have said, "The world is positively hungry for young men who have dedicated themselves to big jobs. If your present professors aren't training you for such work, quit them and find others who will drive you. If your present college isn't making you work to the limit of your ability, drop out and go to another that will. Because if you don't discipline your brain now, you'll never be prepared for the years when it's a question of work or perish."

Parents or professors who do not encourage their young to tackle big jobs commit a moral crime against those young people. For we know that when the young are properly challenged, they will rise to the occasion and they will prepare themselves for the great work that remains to be done.

STUDY QUESTIONS

Recalling

1. What complaint does the student make to Michener, and what answer does Michener give?
2. How long did Michener work on his novel *Hawaii*? How many research books did he consult?
3. According to Michener, who accomplishes the "good work of the world"?

4. What parting advice does Michener give the student? What does he tell us he "should have said"?

Interpreting

5. What point does Michener make by telling the student about how he wrote *Hawaii*?
6. In general, do you think Michener's experiences add weight to his opinions? Explain why or why not.

7. What answer would Michener give to the question posed in the essay's title?
8. Based on the last two paragraphs, what do you think Michener's purpose may have been in turning his conversation with the student into this article?

Extending
9. Give one example of a situation in which you tackled a difficult job. How did you feel while you were working and after you finished?

READING AND LITERARY FOCUS

Persuasion

Persuasion is the type of writing in which an author attempts to make the reader accept an opinion or take action of some kind. In order to be persuasive, writers need to back up their opinions with **objective evidence** such as facts, incidents, and examples. For example, James Michener backs up his opinions with evidence when he tells us that the officers who received high government appointments were those who re-educated themselves.

Persuasive writers also offer **logical arguments,** or reasons, in support of their opinions. For example, Michener gives a logical argument for the necessity of hard work when he reasons that the discovery of a new vaccine cannot possibly be easy.

Thinking About Persuasion
1. Restate in your own words the opinion that Michener expresses in this essay.
2. Relate one more piece of evidence or logical argument that Michener uses to support his opinion.
3. Does Michener persuade *you*? Why or why not?

Topic Sentence

The **topic sentence** of a paragraph is the sentence that expresses the main idea of the paragraph. Usually the topic sentence appears early in the paragraph, and the remaining sentences support and develop the topic sentence with details. For example, in "When Does Education Stop?" the eighth paragraph begins with the following topic sentence:

> I explained to my caller that I write all my books slowly, with two fingers on an old typewriter, and the actual task of getting the words on paper is difficult.

The sentences that follow add details that show just how slow and difficult the task of writing is for Michener.

Thinking About Topic Sentence
1. What is the topic sentence of the next-to-last paragraph in this essay?
2. From Michener's essay choose any other paragraph that contains more than one sentence, and identify its topic sentence.

COMPOSITION

Writing About a Persuasive Essay
■ Write a brief composition telling how persuasive you found Michener's essay. Begin by stating in your own words the opinion Michener sets forth in his essay. Then tell whether or not he persuaded you to accept this opinion. If he succeeded in persuading you, tell which of his pieces of evidence and arguments you found most convincing and why. If he did not succeed, tell what faults you found in his evidence and arguments.

Writing Persuasion
■ Choose an issue of interest in your school, an issue about which you have a strong opinion. Write an essay expressing your opinion on that issue. Be sure to use facts, incidents, examples, and logical arguments to support your opinion.

THE TOTAL EFFECT

Nonfiction will give you more pleasure when you read it actively and attentively. In particular, you should remember that although a work of nonfiction is factual, it presents one author's version of the truth. When you actively look for clues about the author's intentions, you will be better able to understand and judge what the author is saying about the subject. You will also enjoy nonfiction more if you notice the facts, details, and language that the author uses to create a **total effect**—an overall impact on the reader. The following reminders will help you keep in mind the most important elements of any nonfiction work.

Reminders for Active Reading of Nonfiction

1. The **title** often points to the author's subject, purpose, and audience.
2. The writer of **autobiography** includes both memories and insights about past events.
3. The writer of **biography** presents the facts about an individual's life and opinions about the subject's character.
4. The writer of any form of nonfiction—biography, autobiography, or essays—uses various elements and techniques, including the following:

   - a **thesis statement** or a clearly implied central idea
   - **facts, incidents,** and **examples** supporting this idea
   - **topic sentences** to alert the reader to the main idea in each paragraph
   - **chronological order** or some other clear organization
   - **anecdotes** to reveal character
   - **descriptive details** to create vivid pictures

5. The writer of any piece of nonfiction has a **purpose** in mind. The reader should uncover that purpose.

Model for Active Reading

On the following pages you will see how an alert reader kept in mind these reminders while reading "Beneath the Crags of Malpelo Island." Notes in the margin present the reader's observations about the work. Each notation gives a page reference for further information about the item in question. Read the selection first for your own enjoyment, and then read it along with the notations. Later you can use the process followed in this model as you read any nonfiction work.

Harry Earl Rieseberg (born 1892) studied journalism and business and then entered government service. He eventually worked within the United States Bureau of Navigation. Rieseberg has often appeared on television to speak about underwater exploration, and he has written numerous articles about his own diving experiences. In the following selection Rieseberg tells about a challenge that he found too exciting to turn down.

■ In light of what happens to him, do you think his decision to take on the challenge was wise or foolhardy?

Harry Earl Rieseberg

Beneath the Crags of Malpelo Island[1]

With a smother of foam and bubbles the green water closed over me. When I was not too far down, I signaled the crew above to stop. Since they were new at this business, I wanted to see whether they would answer satisfactorily. When they promptly did so, I adjusted the air pressure in my diving dress and resumed my slow descent.

As I went I thought of the treasure supposedly lying in the wreck below. I thought, too, of the dangers lurking there and of the seven divers who had gone down to the wreck and never returned. Had I known the terror that awaited me, I might have stopped my descent then and there and gone back to the surface and safety.

The whole strange adventure had begun two weeks before in the little seaport town of Buenaventura,[2] Colombia. I had just returned from six months of salvage work[3] on several so-called

Narration (p. 308) tells a story. Where is the author, and what is he doing at the beginning of this true-life story?

The central idea in an essay is often expressed in a **thesis statement** (p. 317). What idea about his experience does Rieseberg express in this paragraph?

---

1. **Malpelo** [mäl pä′lō] **Island:** island in the Pacific Ocean off the western coast of Colombia in South America.
2. **Buenaventura** [bwä′nä vän too′rä]
3. **salvage work:** retrieving sunken cargo.

treasure wrecks in the Gulf[4] waters. I had decided to return to the States for a long-needed rest.

But that was before I met Charlie Boyer in the office of the dock superintendent. Once a diver himself, he was quite interested in my recent experiences. When I mentioned that there were few unrecovered treasure wrecks left on the sea floor along the West Coast, he looked at me sharply and then stared ahead in silence.

I asked him, "What's the strangest thing you've ever heard of in these waters, Boyer?"

For a brief moment he did not reply, then he said, "I think the salvage job off Malpelo Island, to the west of here, is the strangest, Lieutenant. But it's a long, long story."

I settled myself down comfortably to listen.

Many years ago, Boyer said, an unidentified Spanish schooner had hit the rocks off the end of Malpelo Island during a violent storm. The vessel had gone down immediately, with only one man surviving. Rescued from the deserted island, the man revealed that the sunken schooner had carried in its hold a vast sum in gold and silver bars, together with some other valuable cargo. That was all that was ever learned about the ship and its treasure; a few days later the survivor died from exposure.

Seven attempts had been made to recover the mysterious treasure cargo. In each case the diver never came up. All the air and life lines were snapped, and there was no sign of what had caused the series of tragedies.

The story chilled me. But there was a challenge in it.

"Boyer," I said, "if you're willing to take a chance with me on making the eighth attempt, I'll do the diving."

With a broad grin he jumped to his feet. "You mean that, Lieutenant? You aren't superstitious?"

My answer was a flat no.

The next two weeks were busy ones. We secured the best equipment we could in Buenaventura and hired a double crew of husky Colombians. It wasn't long before we were anchored off Malpelo Island and I was going down to the wreck of the ill-fated Spanish schooner.

As I caught the faint outline of the hulk beneath me, I fingered my shark knife nervously. About a hundred feet down, I landed on a rocky ledge that jutted out from the main rock ridge. Among

Anecdotes (p. 303) add background information or colorful details to writing. What information does this anecdote give us?

---

4. **Gulf:** Golfo Tortugas, off the west coast of Colombia.

these sharp crags I had to be mighty careful with my lines. A hard rub on one of their jagged edges might put me in a bad spot. I was glad of one thing: there were no signs whatever of sharks as yet. In fact, not a large fish of any kind appeared among the long streamers of queer stuff that hung in the water around the old hulk.

In a few minutes I had landed on the slime-coated deck of the sunken schooner. The white superstructure[5] shone clean and fresh, as though it had recently been painted. In the faint light that penetrated from above, the wreck looked weird and sinister. It lay there, white and ghostly, with the high black walls of rock around it—much like a gigantic coffin lowered into a watery tomb.

The after-hatch[6] was open, its cover partly off; just forward appeared the companionway.[7] Making certain that neither of my lines was fouled,[8] I loosened my shark knife and strode forward. Climbing down the sand-covered steps to the heavy door of the chamber below, I moved ever more cautiously.

Then I saw it—and stood there, almost paralyzed, for a moment. Beside the half-open door appeared a large round object. *It was a copper diving helmet!*

Quickly I dug it out of the debris and sand. Stooping, I peered closer. In the light of my torch[9] I could see inside that helmet. I gazed down upon a skull—the white jaws wide apart in a set and uncanny grin!

Here was the first of the seven divers who had perished.

As I straightened up, the soft purr of the incoming air stopped abruptly. Then air started to whistle past my ears as it began to leave my suit. I suddenly realized that my air hose was cut. I knew that the great pressure of water at that depth would empty my suit in a few seconds and I should be badly crushed.

Shutting off the intake valve, I felt enough air within my suit to last about five minutes. But for normal decompression[10] I needed more time than that to go up. Now I was in a tough spot. There seemed slight chance for my survival.

Stumbling up the companionway steps, I jerked out my shark

Description is more vivid when it includes specific details (p. 312). What details give us a vivid picture of the ship?

---

5. **superstructure:** part of a ship above the main deck.
6. **after-hatch:** entrance to a ship's lower deck, toward the ship's rear.
7. **companionway:** stairs leading from a ship's deck to the area below.
8. **fouled:** tangled.
9. **torch:** flashlight.
10. **normal decompression:** gradual return to normal atmospheric pressure, which is much less than the pressure in the ocean's depths.

knife. But on the deck nothing was in sight, nothing but those ghostly white planks and sharp black limestone rocks.

Now my suit was deflating fast. I pulled my signal cord quickly, and soon I was being slowly hauled upward. Of course I knew the terrible danger of being hauled up from deep water too fast. Often it causes caisson disease, or the "bends."[11] In fact, it can put a man out for good. At the halfway stage, I signaled for a stop. For a minute or two I hung at that level to lessen the shock.

When, at my signal, the crew started hauling up again, my eyes seemed to be bursting from their sockets. My body felt as if it had been gripped by some giant's hand that was crushing the remaining life from it.

Exposition (p. 317) presents facts or explains ideas. What information or explanation does Rieseberg give here?

---

11. **caisson** [kā′son] . . . **"bends":** chest tightness, joint pains, and violent muscle spasms caused by nitrogen bubbles that form in the body when deep-sea divers return to the surface too quickly.

They pulled me on deck, and the crew boys got my headpiece unscrewed just in time. I lay there helpless, almost unconscious. After undergoing decompression in our makeshift chamber,[12] I rested for two whole days.

On the third day the sea was calm and the day clear. We had rigged up a new air hose; the old one had been cut almost in two. What cut it I didn't know—perhaps some sharp edge on the old hulk or a pointed rock outcrop. Again I climbed over the side of the little salvage craft and sank slowly down past the wall of gloomy rocks.

I circled the entire deck, carefully watching my lines. Everything appeared the same as before—the water seemed as lifeless as ever. I climbed down the companionway toward the chamber below. The grim helmet with its grinning white skull lay where I had left it. This time, without hesitating, I began to dig away the sand that blocked the doorway. Soon I had the opening cleared. I peered in, then cautiously entered.

Inside was a space about fifteen feet wide. It was partly filled with crates and boxes of different sizes. One of the boxes had the top pried off. Excited, I quickly scraped away the thick sand and flashed my torch on the uncovered contents. It revealed several metal bars. Yes, here was the treasure. How much I had no idea, but if it was to be raised, I should have to arrange for steel slings to be dropped down to me. Then, counting the boxes and crates, I prepared to ascend.

Turning to retrace my steps, I noticed that the boxes were piled higher at the opposite end of the chamber, away from the doorway. To the right of these was a huge object heavily wrapped in a large tarpaulin. Striding clumsily across the room, I tore away the length of covering.

There before me was a great bronze statue. It had large eyes, probably made of precious stones. They were of different shades and seemed to be looking at me sorrowfully. At the base of the statue were a number of small bones, whitened and half buried in the sand. Among them two skulls grinned at me eerily. Close by lay a lead-soled boot, with remnants of a diver's suit still clinging to it.

I stood there trembling in the dark, eerie tomb. Then in the light of my torch something snakelike floated into my view. My scalp tightened, and I thought another diver was scheduled to

---

12. **chamber:** area in which the air pressure can be adjusted in order to bring a diver gradually back to normal atmospheric pressure.

"go out." Then, to my relief, I saw that it was only a long piece of rotted tarpaulin. By now my nerves were pretty raw, and I couldn't help thinking of the seven divers who had come down here—to stay.

In the midst of these thoughts I had a weird, uncanny feeling that somebody or something was watching me. So strong was this strange sense of a presence in the lonely, silent tomb that I turned and threw my torchlight about the chamber. It moved over the boxes and crates, played on the wall, and returned finally to the statue. As it shone past the bronze figure, I became faint with terror. For there, from behind the dim outlines of the boxes and crates, a huge shape was rising before my eyes. My heart pounded wildly, for the thing bulked across the doorway—and barring my exit—was a quivering, warty body rocking from side to side. The huge monster was fully fifteen feet across, with a ball of a body at least four to five feet in width. The creature's long, slimy arms, or tentacles, were lined with many great saucer-like cups. And its ghoulish eyes watched my every movement.

Now I knew the fate of the seven lost divers, and I realized that I, too, was trapped in this watery grave. For there was only one way out of the chamber, and that was blocked by the swaying, writhing giant octopus!

Its long tentacles swayed and quivered continuously, almost rhythmically. They caressed the water, wrapping themselves about the crates and boxes. Then the creature crawled slowly along the floor in the sand toward me. I gazed at it in horror and edged backward out of its grasping reach. In spite of its great bulk and spreading arms it moved quickly.

As I watched, I could see the color of the huge, bloated body change from brown to dirty yellow, then to tan, and then to gray and white. And all the while those terrible eyes watched me.

I thought of the statue behind me. As I backed slowly and cautiously toward it, the octopus seemed to realize what my intent was, for it lunged with one of its tentacles directly at me. The powerful arm stirred the sand into a great cloud, the movement was so swift. Then, suddenly, a wild plan occurred to me. It was a slim chance, but a man facing death will clutch at almost any straw.

Backing as far as I could into the corner of the chamber, I drew my shark knife from its sheath and waited. The fourteen-inch blade didn't seem to be an adequate weapon against such a monster, but I was used to the knife. With half a chance, I could let the terrible creature know that he had been in a fight.

Conflict (p. 308) is a struggle between two opposing forces. What conflict does Rieseberg present here?

Now it was enraged, changing from one color to another very quickly, its tentacles reaching always closer. I stood waiting. Desperately, the huge beast sought to clasp its suction-cupped arms about me. Hooking the torch to my belt, I waited just beyond reach. Suddenly an arm shot directly at me.

With a quick side swipe, I sliced through it, almost without knowing that my knife had made contact with flesh. Then another tentacle was severed from the sickening, wart-covered body. As still another arm was thrust at me, I sliced downward at it, lopping it off. Now I saw closely the monster's devilish eyes watching me fixedly with blank, goggling hatred.

A stream of blue-black fluid poured forth from the creature's ink sac,[13] spreading slowly upward and clouding the water all around me. Now I began to wonder whether my plan would succeed. I was desperate, cornered like a rat in a hole.

Another writhing tentacle shot forward. I managed to turn it aside with my knife, but failed to cut it off. But in the next instant, a back-handed blow from the tentacle smashed against my helmet. It hurled me backward against the wooden wall with a force that left me dazed, almost unconscious. Slowly I managed to stagger to my feet. I wasn't a second too soon, for the creature clamped onto my helmet and shook me violently. With a yell that sounded hideous in my own ears, I drove my knife upward at the quivering arm wrapped about my helmet. The blade sliced deep through the boneless arm, its grip relaxing as the sinuous tentacle parted in two.

Now the octopus became wild with rage. Another huge arm groped for me. It flashed out as if to grip my helmet again, but dropped quickly and seized my left leg instead, throwing me off my feet. Again I slashed at it. And, with fiendish cunning, the creature changed its hold to my left arm, pulling me a little nearer to the doorway. I drove my knife upward once more, but luck was against me. The keen blade glanced wildly, and a second later it was wrenched from my hand!

Now I was completely helpless. In desperation I tried to brace myself, but there was nothing to brace against. I could not signal to the salvage ship above for help, because the huge monster's tentacles, those which remained, were staked across my lines. Inch by inch, the huge arm dragged me across the sand-covered floor of that watery tomb. As I came nearer, I could see the terrible

The **topic sentence** (p. 322) states the main point of a paragraph. Show how this paragraph develops the idea stated in the topic sentence.

---

13. **ink sac:** When in danger, an octopus or squid releases an inky fluid to cloud the water and hide itself.

eyes watching me through the clouded water. *The eighth victim that would never return to the surface.*

Suddenly a faint light shone on something that lay on the sand at my feet. *The shark knife!* I saw one last, crazy chance. I must take it or be torn to pieces by the nightmare that clutched me. Quickly I grabbed the steel knife. The tentacle on my left arm tightened, gave a quick jerk. Now I was within arm's reach of the terrible creature's body. I had to act quickly. Again I felt the grip tighten. Swiftly I raised the knife and drove the long blade full into the fearful monster's body at what I was certain was a vital spot. . . .

At the very same moment something tore at my belt, and I felt a savage jerk as a stream of air bubbles shot out from the front of my diving suit. It was punctured.

Then the very air seemed to tear apart. There was a blinding flash and a dull roar as I felt myself being whirled through space. Then came darkness.

The high point of a narrative is its **climax** (p. 308). What happens to Rieseberg at the climax of this narrative?

Later I opened my eyes with a start, a sort of nervous twitch. Surely I must be dreaming, I thought, and closed my eyes for a few seconds. I opened them again and lay blinking, not knowing whether I was in this world or the next. My head cleared gradually and I caught the soft hiss of an air valve and saw that I was in a decompression lock. There were pressure gauges on the wall and a lone figure stood before them, adjusting the valves. Gingerly I rubbed the lump the size of an egg over my right ear and moved in the narrow bunk. The man at the valves turned to look at me. It was Boyer.

He eyed me a moment in silence, then quietly said, "Well, Lieutenant," with a look of concern on his face, "you did come back."

I was stiff and sore and numb—symptoms that tell a diver that he has been under the water too long. But I was fortunate to be alive at all! I wondered how I had managed to get back on the sloop, and Boyer explained:

"When we didn't hear from you for so long, I ordered two of the native divers to go down to see what was the matter. They found you with lines fouled and three tentacles of an octopus about you on the underdeck of the wreck. The creature was dead. They closed the air-pressure valves in your torn suit, cut away the lines and tentacles, and got you clear just in time. The suit was leaking fast, but they were able to get you on board before all the air was gone."

"Thank God, thank God!" I said.

For a moment or two we were silent, thinking of the narrow escape from a terrible death. I stood up, feeling quite groggy, but a lot better than I had expected. On deck I turned to Boyer and remarked, "Boyer, there are two things in this wide world I never want to meet again."

He smiled broadly. "What are they, Lieutenant?" he asked.

"Giant octopi[14] and more octopi!" I answered with a grin.

---

14. **octopi** [äk′tə pī]: plural of *octopus*.

Autobiography (p. 294) is a person's own account of events in his or her life. What have we learned about Rieseberg from reading this autobiographical essay?

STUDY QUESTIONS

Recalling

1. What does Boyer tell Rieseberg about the sunken Spanish ship and the divers who searched for it?
2. Why does Rieseberg cut short his first dive?
3. What besides treasure does Rieseberg find?
4. Describe Rieseberg's struggle in the ship and his rescue.

Interpreting

5. Why do you think Rieseberg decides to look for the sunken treasure?
6. In retelling his experience the author wanted to create a feeling of suspense, or rising interest, in the outcome of a narrative. Do you think he succeeded? At which points was your interest strongest?

Extending

7. What might be the satisfaction in taking on challenging projects?

COMPARING NONFICTION

1. Show how Russell Baker's *Growing Up,* Alice Walker's "In Search of Our Mothers' Gardens," and Jerry Izenberg's "Roberto Clemente: A Bittersweet Memoir" are all tributes. Choose two or more of these selections, and explain to whom each author pays tribute and what each author praises in his or her subject.
2. Russell Baker's *Growing Up,* James Thurber's "The Night the Bed Fell," Marjorie Kinnan Rawlings' "Catch-Dog," and James Michener's "When Does Education Stop?" are all autobiographical in some way. Choose two or more of these selections, and explain what they reveal about their authors' lives.
3. Marjorie Kinnan Rawlings' "Catch-Dog," Alice Walker's "In Search of Our Mothers' Gardens," and Harry Rieseberg's "Beneath the Crags of Malpelo Island" all show human beings interacting with the natural world. Choose two or more of these selections, and explain how their views of this interaction differ.

Active Reading

Nonfiction

Distinguishing Fact from Opinion

Nonfiction is about real people and events. Reading nonfiction means reading factual material. Even so, a nonfiction selection may contain more than facts alone. It may also present the writer's opinions. In order to evaluate fairly the nonfiction you read, you must first be able to distinguish between facts and opinions.

A *fact* is a statement that can be proven true or false. You may prove it by using a reference source or by observing for yourself. An *opinion* is a statement that expresses an individual's personal feelings. Opinions, unlike facts, cannot be proven true or false.

Read the following two sentences from the nonfiction selection "Roberto Clemente: A Bittersweet Memoir."

- The record book will tell you that Roberto Clemente collected 3,000 hits during his major-league career.
- He was the greatest we ever had . . . maybe one of the greatest anyone ever had.

The first sentence states a fact. You can prove it by checking a reference book containing sports statistics. The second sentence offers an opinion. It is a matter of personal belief.

Activity 1   On a separate piece of paper, write whether each of the following sentences states a fact or an opinion. If it states a fact, tell how you can prove the statement.

1. He was born in Carolina, Puerto Rico.
2. Roberto Clemente went home and married Vera.
3. There will never be another like Roberto.
4. In 1955 Roberto Clemente came to the Pittsburgh Pirates.
5. He was the finest prospect the club had had in a long, long time.
6. As Clemente's confidence grew, he began to get better and better.
7. But when they announced the Most Valuable Player Award voting, Roberto had finished a distant third.
8. The following year, Clemente ended the season by collecting his three thousandth hit.
9. He touched the heart of Puerto Rico in a way that few people ever could.

10. He was thirty-eight years old when he died.
11. Just a month or so before, he had agreed to take a junior-league baseball team to Nicaragua and manage it in an all-star game in Managua.
12. He lived a full life.

Evaluating Opinions and Facts

Authors of nonfiction often include their personal opinions in their work. Although these opinions cannot be proven, writers still hope you will agree with their ideas. As a responsible reader, you must first look for facts that support the author's opinions. Then, after carefully considering the facts, you can decide whether you agree or disagree with each opinion. Sometimes you may feel that the facts are not strong enough to support the opinion. Other times you may discover there are actually no facts at all to support the opinion.

Read the following description of Roberto Clemente given by the author:

Roberto Clemente had hit safely in every World Series game. He had batted over .300. He had been a superstar.

The author states his opinion—that Roberto had been a superstar. He offers two facts as supporting evidence. For one thing, Clemente had hit safely in every Series game. For another thing, he had batted over .300. The author uses these facts to support his opinion that Roberto had been a superstar. Now you should consider the facts for yourself. Decide whether or not they are strong enough to make you agree with the author's opinion that Roberto was a superstar.

Activity 2 Identify the facts and opinions that are stated in the following quotations from the selection about Roberto Clemente. Tell whether you think the facts help to support the opinion in each passage. Also identify any passages that contain no facts at all.

1. In 1955 Roberto Clemente came to the Pittsburgh Pirates. He was the finest prospect the club had had in a long, long time.
2. He was a superstar during the five games that followed. He was the big man in the Series. He was the MVP. He was everything he had ever dreamed of being on a ball field.
3. He was a man who chose his friends carefully. His was a friendship worth having.

Activity 3   Read each of the following opinions that you might form after completing the selection about Roberto Clemente. Find the facts in the selection to help support each opinion.

1. Roberto Clemente was very generous.
2. The people of Puerto Rico cared about Roberto Clemente.
3. Pedro Zarrilla was impressed with Roberto Clemente.
4. Roberto was a special person to María Isabella Casares.
5. Baseball players respected Clemente's athletic ability.
6. Roberto Clemente was a brave individual.
7. Roberto did not let depression defeat him.
8. Roberto loved children.
9. Roberto strongly believed in honesty.
10. Roberto was able to do a job well.

Recognizing Persuasive Techniques

In many kinds of nonfiction, the authors want readers to agree with their opinions. In his persuasive essay, for example, James Michener hopes to convince readers that "men and women who wish to accomplish anything must apply themselves to tasks of tremendous magnitude." In her expository essay Alice Walker wishes to convince us that "mothers and grandmothers have, more often than not anonymously, handed on the creative spark, the seed of the flower they themselves never hoped to see. . . ." Regardless of the type of essay—narrative, descriptive, expository, or persuasive—the author tries to persuade us to accept his or her personal belief about the subject matter.

How do writers persuade readers to agree with them? One way, you have learned, is by providing facts to support each opinion. Another way is by using emotion-filled words—words able to create a positive or negative picture for the reader.

For example, in the biographical selection about Roberto Clemente, Jerry Izenberg described the 1955 Pittsburgh Pirates as "spectacular losers." He could have simply called them "a poor team" or "a bad ball club," but he wanted to create a strong, negative picture. Through his choice of language, Izenberg hoped to persuade readers to accept his opinion immediately.

Activity 4   Read each of the following pairs of sentences. One sentence contains a phrase taken from the selection about Roberto Clemente. The other sentence states a similar idea but in a different way. Identify the sentence that creates a more *positive* picture.

1. a. María Isabella Casares helped to shape his life.
   b. María Isabella Casares always told him what to do.
2. a. He was a skinny kid.
   b. He was a slender young man.
3. a. He was an average student.
   b. He wasn't anything special as a student.
4. a. He refused to talk with people as a boy.
   b. He was a very shy boy.
5. a. Some people would say he was reserving his best effort.
   b. Some people would say he was loafing.
6. a. He sulked like a baby about that a lot.
   b. He brooded about that a lot.
7. a. His coach learned to be patient with him.
   b. His coach had to put up with him.
8. a. In the World Series Roberto Clemente led the way.
   b. In the World Series Roberto Clemente hogged the show.
9. a. He was snobbish about which people he would like.
   b. He was a man who chose his friends carefully.
10. a. He had his own ideas about how life should be lived.
    b. No one could tell him anything about how to behave.

Literary Skills Review

Nonfiction

Guide for Reading Nonfiction

As you read nonfiction, use the following guide to help you notice and appreciate the ways that nonfiction writers present their ideas.

Autobiography

1. What seems to be the author's **purpose** in writing this autobiography? That is, does the author want to inform, entertain, or persuade the reader, or does the author want to express an idea about life?
2. About what main **events** and **people** has the author written? What is important about these events and people?
3. What understanding about life or what impression of himself or herself does the author present?

Biography

1. What seems to be the author's **purpose** in writing this biography?
2. About what major **events** of the subject's life has the author written? Why?
3. What opinion of the subject or idea about people in general does the author communicate?
4. What **anecdotes** reveal the subject's human qualities?

Essay

1. What is the **central idea**? That is, what information, idea, or opinion is the author presenting?
2. For what **purpose** and **audience** has the essay been written?
3. If the essay is **narrative,** what major events does it relate? What is the main conflict? What is the outcome?
4. If the essay is **descriptive,** what impression of the subject does it create? What details does it present?
5. If the essay is **expository,** what is the **thesis statement**? How does the rest of the essay support the thesis?
6. If the essay is **persuasive,** what opinion does the author present? What facts, incidents, examples, and reasons back up this opinion?

Themes Review

Nonfiction

Certain universal themes—experiences and concerns common to all people—appear again and again in literature. For example, a general theme such as "challenges" is used in many stories, poems, essays, and plays. However, each writer has something specific and personal to say about challenges. For instance, the specific view of challenges presented in "When Does Education Stop?" (page 318) is "We grow only when we challenge our mental abilities." However, the specific theme of "Beneath the Crags of Malpelo Island" (page 324) is "Accepting a challenge for its own sake can sometimes be riskier than it is worth." Note that the general theme can be a word or phrase, such as "challenges," while the specific theme can be a sentence.

1. What specific point about the general theme "challenges" does Alice Walker make in "In Search of Our Mothers' Gardens"?

2. Choose two of the following selections, and tell what specific point each author makes about the general theme "love and friendship."
   Growing Up   "The Catch-Dog"   "Roberto Clemente"

3. The following selections all deal with the general theme "identity." Choose two of them, and explain what specific point each author makes about identity.
   Growing Up   "In Search of Our   "When Does Education
                  Mothers' Gardens"   Stop?"

4. For one nonfiction selection and one other work, explain the writer's specific view of the general theme "families."
   Nonfiction: *Growing Up*   "The Night the Bed Fell"
   Stories: "Thirteen"   "The Sneaker Crisis"
   Poem: "Life for My
                   Child . . ."

5. Choose from the following titles one nonfiction selection and one poem or story, and explain what specific point each work seems to be making about the general theme "imagination."
   Nonfiction: "In Search of Our   "The Night the Bed Fell"
                   Mothers' Gardens"
   Stories: "The Wish"   "Stolen Day"
   Poems: "The Listeners"   "Write a Limerick Now"

Preview
Drama

Drama is the form of literature that presents stories meant to be performed for an audience. The roots of drama reach far back in human history, to the period of **oral literature,** when stories and songs were spoken rather than written down. Imagine what life was like when few people could read. Occasionally an individual might be gifted with a wonderful memory and ability to tell stories. Whenever such a person would begin to tell a tale, others would gather to be entertained. In time, other persons gifted as mimics might begin to act out parts of the story, presenting lifelike scenes in front of a spellbound audience.

Drama has changed a great deal over time, but it still shows us actions rather than telling us about them as a short story does. Today we can enjoy drama in a number of different ways. We may attend a live production of a play in a theater. We may watch a filmed or taped drama in the movies or on television. We may also read dramatic works—plays, screenplays, and television scripts. Seeing a play or film can be very exciting because of the **staging**—the acting, costumes, sets, lighting, sound effects, and other special effects that bring the work to life. The written script of any dramatic work is made up of **dialogue,** the speeches of the characters; and **stage directions,** the writer's descriptions of settings, characters, and actions. Reading the words of a playwright or screenwriter allows us to stop and take a closer look at the work—a thing we cannot do when we attend a performance.

In the following pages we will take a closer look at two very different dramatic works. *Gregory's Girl* is a screenplay for a 1981 film about the comic adventures of a young man in search of romance. *A Christmas Carol* is a play based on the classic story by the great nineteenth-century English writer Charles Dickens. It shows us a man in search of a new life.

GREGORY'S GIRL

Bill Forsyth

Bill Forsyth, who wrote and directed the film *Gregory's Girl*, grew up in Glasgow, Scotland. He began working in films as a very young man. *Gregory's Girl*—only his second feature film—scored a great success when it was shown in Britain and the United States. Forsyth's script for *Gregory's Girl* won the 1981 Best Screenplay award from the British Academy of Film and Television Arts, an honor similar to the U.S. film industry's Oscars. Forsyth's later films include the highly acclaimed *Local Hero* and *Comfort and Joy.*

Gregory's Girl

In reading the screenplay for *Gregory's Girl*, you need to keep in mind the similarities and differences between films like *Gregory's Girl* and plays like *The Speckled Band*, which appears at the beginning of this book. Because films often use real-life settings, outdoors as well as indoors, they seem more immediately "lifelike" than plays, which take place on a stage in a theater in front of an audience. *Gregory's Girl*, for instance, was filmed in an actual Scottish town and on the grounds of an actual school. Nevertheless, a film like *Gregory's Girl* is as much a work of the imagination as a story or play. That is, it is *fiction* rather than fact; like a story or play, *Gregory's Girl* uses invented situations and characters to present the writer's ideas about life.

■ In what ways are Gregory and the people you meet in the script like people in your own school? What differences do you find?

Key Ideas in *Gregory's Girl*

As you read *Gregory's Girl* think about the following topics. If you keep track of what the screenplay says about each topic, you will begin to understand the most important themes of *Gregory's Girl.*

- The difficulties of growing up
- The need for a sense of humor
- Relationships between young men and young women
- The importance of understanding who you are and what you really need

Susan.   Dorothy.   Gregory.

Adapted from an Original Screenplay by
Bill Forsyth

Gregory's Girl

CHARACTERS

GREGORY: high school soccer player; gangly sixteen-year-old

DOROTHY: high school soccer player; athletic, pretty

STEVE: Gregory's best friend; expert cook

MADELINE: Gregory's younger sister; ten years old

SUSAN: friend of Dorothy; classmate of Gregory

CAROL: friend of Dorothy

MARGO: friend of Dorothy

ANDY: friend and former teammate of Gregory

CHARLIE: friend of Andy

PHIL MENZIES: high school gym teacher and soccer coach

GORDON: ace reporter for the school magazine

ERIC: photographer for the school magazine

RICHARD: friend of Gregory's sister, Madeline; ten years old

A WAITRESS

SOCCER PLAYERS; STUDENTS

Scene: *Scotland. The present day.*

The soccer field of a Scottish high school. The present time.

[*We begin as the* REFEREE *blows his whistle to end the match. Even in the simple business of leaving the field and heading for the dressing room, our team manage to demonstrate some of their ineptness. One boy is reacting in a fit of mild hysterics. He is* GREGORY, *a tall, gangly boy of about sixteen. He is leaving the field in a fit of laughter, shaking his head in disbelief. During the whole scene* PHIL MENZIES, *the young gym teacher and coach, watches sadly from the sidelines. He then walks defeatedly into the dressing room.*]

[*Dressing room. A few minutes have passed, and* GREGORY *is now alone in the dressing room, changing into his school clothes.* PHIL MENZIES *joins him.*]

GREGORY. [*Laughing.*] Terrible game, eh?

MENZIES. [*Grimly.*] Very bad, very very bad.

GREGORY. [*Shaking his head.*] You've got to laugh.

MENZIES. What have you got to laugh about?

[GREGORY *senses a hurt in* MENZIES. *He tries to make amends.*]

GREGORY. Soccer is all about *entertainment.* We give them a good laugh. It's only a game.

MENZIES. It's only *eight* games. Eight games in a row you've lost.

GREGORY. Can't lose them all. [*Consoling* MENZIES.] You push us really hard, no mercy, lots of *discipline,* that's what we need. [*Nods.*] Get tough.

MENZIES. We need *goals,* son; you're not making any goals. That's your job.

GREGORY. [*With a shrug.*] Nobody's perfect. [*Matter-of-fact.*] Its a tricky time for me. I'm doing a lot of growing; it slows you down. Five inches this year. [GREGORY *crouches down so that he's level with* MENZIES, *and their faces are very close together.*] Remember last year I was way down here? [*Smiling at* MENZIES.] Are you growing a mustache?

MENZIES. [*Ignoring this.*] I want to make some changes. I want to try out some other people. Switch the team around. Take some people out. [*A pause.*] I was going to take *you* out.

GREGORY. [*Laughing at the silly idea.*] You don't want to do that.

MENZIES. Yes I do.

GREGORY. [*Still a coaxing smile.*] You don't.

MENZIES. I do.

GREGORY. [*Pauses. Serious.*] You don't.

MENZIES. I might.

GREGORY. What about Andy? He's hardly *started* growing yet. He's going to be *real* trouble.

[MENZIES *is thinking.*]

I'll tell him. . . .

MENZIES. *I'll* tell him. A week's trial as goalie for you. Then I'll decide.

GREGORY. [*New tack.*] Have you got a jersey my size? Andy's a lot smaller.

MENZIES. Don't worry about the jersey. A week as goalie and then I'll *decide.*

GREGORY. [*Resigned.*] You're the boss. Who's getting my position?

MENZIES. I want to try out some new people.

[GREGORY *is dressed now and ready to leave. He makes his way to the door.*]

GREGORY. [*With thumbs up and a winning smile.*] You won't regret this.

Scene 2

Soccer field. Later that day.

[MENZIES *is assembling his hopefuls for the trial session—five* BOYS *in assorted soccer gear.*]

MENZIES. You all know what I'm looking for— a goal scorer—and that means two things: ball control, shooting accuracy and the ability to read the game . . . uh, *three* things.

[*The* BOYS *look on attentively, as if they actually understand him.*]

MENZIES. So this trial will allow me to assess these two—*three* basic aspects of your skills. Right? First, simple ball control. I want you to trot with the ball at your feet, fifty yards and back. Two lines. Go!

[*As the* BOYS *play ineptly,* DOROTHY, *a pretty blonde girl, emerges confidently from the building, dressed in a dark tracksuit.*]

MENZIES. Both sides of the foot! Let me see complete control. . . .

[DOROTHY *approaches the group.* MENZIES *presumes that she is on some errand or other and gives her little attention.*]

MENZIES. I want it faster now—come on! [*A half glance to* DOROTHY.] What d'you want, lass? [*Back to the* BOYS.] Get some pace into it! Anybody can *walk* with a ball! [*To* DORO-THY.] What is it, dear?

DOROTHY. The trial. I'm here for the trial.

MENZIES. This is soccer here, sweetheart. Maybe Miss McAlpine is up to something with the hockey team, I don't know, but this here is soccer, for boys.

DOROTHY. That's right—soccer trials 11 A.M. I saw the notice.

[MENZIES *laughs, trying to stay in control.*]

MENZIES. There's been a slight misunder-standing, dear; it was *boys* I wanted for the trials.

DOROTHY. Didn't say so on the notice—just said "talented players."

[MENZIES *tries getting tougher.*]

MENZIES. That's a shame that you picked it up wrongly, but I'm afraid I can't do anything now.

DOROTHY. You didn't say boys only—you're not allowed to, anyway. I want a trial.

[MENZIES *knows he is losing ground.*]

MENZIES. Not possible, dear, not today. Well, we don't have a spare ball . . . [*Trailing off.*]

[DOROTHY *nods towards an extra ball on the field. She moves for it and with the gentlest of flicks of her foot raises the ball from the ground and seems to float it into her hands.*]

DOROTHY. Here's one.

[DOROTHY *and* MENZIES *face each other. The challenge is open now.* MENZIES *gives in, and hopes he is playing for time. He sets about organizing the boys again. He speaks very quietly now.*]

MENZIES. Two basic skills—control and the other one—trotting with the ball again. Two lines, lots of speed. On you go.

[DOROTHY *joins one of the lines and does her stuff. She moves with the ball as if it were anchored to her feet with elastic. None of the boys can match* DOROTHY's *skill in even this simple exercise. At the gym entrance we see* GREGORY. *His expression reveals definite interest in* DOROTHY. *Back on the soccer field,* MENZIES *is still irritated by* DOROTHY, *but he is also impressed by her. They move on to another exercise.*]

MENZIES. Into two's now, out from the goal. I want to see a shot for the goal. One attack and one defend. Let's see who's first in the net. Go!

[*The six hopefuls line themselves up in three pairs.* DOROTHY *is one of the attacking three. They start off, and the three defenders come out for them.* GREGORY *is now joined by two friends,* ANDY, *whom he replaced as goalkeeper, and* CHARLIE.]

ANDY. What's going on?

GREGORY. She's gorgeous! She's absolutely gorgeous!

ANDY. [*Looks at the players.*] That's Dorothy. . . . She's got funny ears.

[DOROTHY's *ball rips into the net. The* BOYS *are bewildered. They look to* MENZIES *for leadership. He gets tougher.*]

MENZIES. Three shots each at goal now—accuracy. Best of three shots. [*To* DOROTHY.] You first, dear.

[MENZIES *himself defends the goal. The* BOYS *and* DOROTHY *form a line for three shots each at the goal. Three times we see* DOROTHY *hammer the ball past* MENZIES *into the goal tent.*]

GREGORY. [*To himself.*] What a dream . . . what an absolute dream!

MENZIES. [*Giving it up.*] Right, that's it. Just show me some stamina now. Once round the field and back to the dressing rooms. It's only half a mile and should be tackled as a sprint. On your way.

[*The five* BOYS *and* DOROTHY *race off round the field.* MENZIES *turns his back on them and heads for the building. We watch the progress of the race.* DOROTHY *takes the lead immediately and finishes well in front of the rest. She runs up to a halt beside* MENZIES, *and she is hardly out of breath.*]

DOROTHY. Well?

[MENZIES *has no time to be patronizing now.*]

MENZIES. I'll let everyone know in the fullness of time. I'll pass the word on to Miss McAlpine.

DOROTHY. [*Forceful.*] You *know* I was the best!

MENZIES. It's not that simple. It could be out of my hands. We'll have to see. . . .

[MENZIES *moves off for his office.* DOROTHY *follows him.* GREGORY *stands watching nearby.*]

DOROTHY. You've got to put me on the team list. I want to sign something—you've got to let me sign something. . . .

[*The two of them hurry past* GREGORY *and into the building.*]

GREGORY. What a dream. . . .

Scene 3

Cooking class. Later that day.

[*The class is underway, and* GREGORY *comes in late. The pupils work in groups of two to each oven.* GREGORY *arrives at his cooker, where his friend and cooking partner* STEVE *is already working.*]

STEVE. [*A little irritated at* GREGORY's *lateness.*] I've got the biscuit mix started. You get on with the sponge and put the oven on, 450 degrees.

GREGORY. [*Saluting.*] Yes, boss.

[SUSAN, *a petite, very pretty girl with dark hair leaves her own work area and approaches* GREGORY *and* STEVE, *who is the acknowledged expert on cooking.*]

SUSAN. Hey, Steve, can you help me out with this pastry mix thing? [*A glance at* GREGORY.]

STEVE. Pastry? There's more than one kind, you know. Is it rough puff, short crust . . . flaky . . . suet[1]? . . .

SUSAN. Well, Margaret's doing the strudel soup, and I'm doing the pie. It's the eggs for the pastry I'm not sure of. . . .

STEVE. [*Sarcastic.*] Strudel soup, eh? I'd like to try some of that. It's NOODLE soup, and *what* eggs? You don't put eggs in a pastry. It's eight ounces flour, four ounces margarine . . .

GREGORY. [*Helpfully.*] . . . pinch of salt . . .

[SUSAN *takes a long look at* GREGORY; STEVE *ignores him.*]

STEVE. . . . mix it up, into the oven, fifteen minutes, and that's it, OK? No eggs, no strudels, nothing.

SUSAN. Is that all? That's *simple*, really.

[*She wanders off.* STEVE *shakes his head and turns back to* GREGORY's *frantic mixing.*]

STEVE. Take it easy. Take it easy!

GREGORY. Have you ever been in love?

[STEVE *looks uncomfortable, but* GREGORY *goes on blissfully.*]

I'm in love. [*He is absent-mindedly stirring the sponge mix with his finger.*] It's great, I can't eat, when I think about it I feel dizzy, I'm restless—it's wonderful. [*Proudly.*] I bet I don't get any sleep tonight.

---

1. **suet** [soo̅′it]: beef fat.

STEVE. That sounds more like indigestion.

GREGORY. No. I'm serious.

[STEVE *extracts* GREGORY's *finger from the mixing bowl.*]

STEVE. Who is it?

GREGORY. You'll just laugh and tell people.

STEVE. Give us a clue.

GREGORY. [*Reluctantly.*] It's someone on the soccer team.

[STEVE *gives him a look.*]

GREGORY. I mean Dorothy, she came into the team last week. She's in 4A.[2] [*Gesticulating, getting carried away.*] She's a wonderful player, she's a *girl*. She's got long lovely hair, and she smells mmmm, lovely . . . even if you just pass her in the corridor she smells *gorgeous.* . . . She's got teeth, lovely white teeth, white white teeth. . . .

STEVE. Oh, *that* Dorothy, the hair, the teeth, and the smell—*that* Dorothy. And she's on the team?

GREGORY. [*Confidentially.*] Well, I think she's taking my position. She's a really good player. She's some girl.

STEVE. Can she cook? Can she do this?

[STEVE *throws his rolled-out pastry into the air and juggles it with a pizza maker's flourish.*]

GREGORY. [*Very serious.*] Look, Steve, when you're in love, things like that just don't matter.

STEVE. Give me the margarine.

_____
2. **4A:** Like Gregory, Dorothy is a fourth-year student (roughly equivalent to a sophomore or junior in American high schools).

GREGORY. Think she'll love me back?

STEVE. [*Shaking his head.*] No chance. . . . Watch that mix. I told you, nice and slowly— take it easy. . . .

[STEVE *takes* GREGORY's *hands and guides him.*]

GREGORY. What do you mean, "No chance"?

STEVE. [*Takes a look at his gangly, awkward friend.*] No *chance.*

Scene 4

The soccer field. A few days later.

[*In preparation for a practice game,* GREGORY *does his warmup. It consists of a few awkward jumping jacks, a kneebend in which he almost loses his balance, and a lung-clearing cough. Then he runs a bit, stumbling occasionally, with his arms dangling. At the end he collapses gasping on a bench. Meanwhile* DOROTHY *confidently practices with the ball. As the game begins, we see* DOROTHY *at her best, weaving and dancing with the ball.* GREGORY *is defending the goal, but he is most interested in watching* DOROTHY. *He is also talking to his friend* ANDY, *the boy whom he replaced as goalie.* ANDY *hangs around the goal, shaking his head in frustration.*]

ANDY. This is a real farce, a shambles. Nine games lost in a row, and then what do we do? Sack the goalie and put a girl in the forward line. It's a madhouse!

GREGORY. [*His eyes on* DOROTHY.] Watch the game, Andy, watch the game. She's good, she can move!

ANDY. [*Unbelieving.*] It's not right—it's un-natural—it doesn't even *look* nice!

GREGORY. [*Enthusiastically.*] It's *modern*, Andy—it's good! Modern girls, modern boys. . . . It's tremendous! Look—

ANDY. [*Working up a lather.*] Girls weren't *meant* to play soccer; it's too *tough*, too *physical*!

GREGORY. [*Turning his back on the game to chat with* ANDY.] *Tough?* Have you ever watched them play hockey? They're like wild animals. Even at twelve, thirteen—

[*Suddenly the play makes its way towards* GREGORY's *goal.* GREGORY *and* ANDY *both panic.*]

ANDY. [*Hopping about.*] Gregory!!! Watch the ball, go out and meet it, don't wait for it—

GREGORY. [*Running back and forth, trying to follow* ANDY's *advice.*] Watch the ball—meet the ball—

ANDY. [*Frantic.*] Watch the winger[3]—he's coming up fast—wait for the cross[4]. . . !

GREGORY. [*Bobbing like a jack-in-the-box.*] Watch the ball—watch the winger—meet the ball. . . . [*He lunges in the wrong direction, away from the ball, and* DOROTHY *shoots it past him into the unguarded goal.* GREGORY *stares at the ball.*]

DOROTHY. [*Impatient.*] Come on, give me the ball.

[GREGORY *tenderly dusts off the ball and gives it to her. He turns back to* ANDY.]

GREGORY. I took my eye off the ball for a split second. Two microseconds.

---

3. **winger:** soccer team member who plays forward on the right or left side.
4. **cross:** pass from a wing toward center field in a soccer game.

ANDY. [*Impressed by* DOROTHY.] We need more women on this team, more new blood.

GREGORY. [*Proudly.*] Yeah. She's some girl.

Scene 5

The dressing room. A few minutes later.

[GREGORY *is alone now, dressed and drying his hair.* DOROTHY *comes in. She has just come from a shower and has slipped back into her shirt and pants. She is paying a great deal of attention to a small cut on her leg.*]

DOROTHY. Do you have any plaster?[5] There's none in the girls' dressing room.

GREGORY. [*Spluttering and blushing with embarrassment at meeting her here.*] No—maybe—um—I'll get some. What's wrong—does it hurt? Hold on—

DOROTHY. [*Calmly, sitting down, examining her wound.*] Don't panic, it's just a scratch. I only want to save my tights from getting blood on them. That big gorilla on the left wing—I got back at him though. Just before that last corner, I got my boot on his shin and scraped it right down . . . big animal. . . .

[GREGORY'S *face reacts a little delicately to this. He tries to latch onto the mood, however.*]

GREGORY. You'll have a bruise there.

DOROTHY. Not if I let it bleed. That's the idea. I don't bruise easily.

GREGORY. I do. [*Softly.*] I bruise like a peach. [*Hits himself here and there to make a point.*] Boing . . . bruise . . . bop . . . bruise . . . chung . . . bruise.

[DOROTHY *rewards him with a smile. Her attention wanders to a tiny scar on her other knee. She points it out to* GREGORY.]

DOROTHY. See that? I was only three when that happened. On the beach. I was chasing a boy; I wasn't going to hurt him. I fell on a bottle. That'll never go away. Marked for life—I'm imperfect!

[*They laugh.*]

GREGORY. [*Enthusiastically.*] It's nice. I like it.

DOROTHY. Really? [*She smiles.*]

GREGORY. Yes. [*Clowning for her.*] I hurt my arm once, at the joint. Can't get it any higher than this. [*He raises his left arm to head level.*] I used to be able to get it away up here, no bother. [*He raises the same arm.*]

DOROTHY. You just did.

GREGORY. No—it's *this* arm. See? Stuck.

[*He now goes through the same routine with his other arm. They both laugh.* DOROTHY *indicates another scar at the back of her neck, a little bit down her back.*]

DOROTHY. Look at this. That was my big brother. I was only seven—he threw a bike at me. I can only see it in the mirror. It's quite nice, isn't it? . . . Nice shape.

GREGORY. [*Shyly.*] Yeah. [*With more bravado.*] Yeah.

DOROTHY. Renaldo, that was a boy in Italy last summer, he said it was like a new moon. Very romantic—*la luna!* [6]

GREGORY. [*A deep, Italian voice.*] Ah sì, sì, bella! Bella! [7]

---

5. **plaster:** bandage tape.

6. ***la luna*** [lä loo'nä]: Italian for "the moon."
7. ***sì, sì, bella! Bella!*** [sē, sē, bel'ä, bel'ä]: Italian for "yes, yes, beautiful! Beautiful!"

DOROTHY. *Ah, parliamo italiano!* [8]

GREGORY. [*Shrugging apologetically.*] No, not really. Just . . . *bella, bella.*

DOROTHY. Oh, I think it's a wonderful language—so . . . *alive!* I want to live in Italy when I leave school.

GREGORY. [*Awed.*] Oh. . . .

DOROTHY. I can speaka de language. I'm a quarter Italian and a quarter Irish, on my mother's side.

GREGORY. [*Brightening up again.*] Hey, I can speak Irish. . . .

[*They giggle.*]

GREGORY. [*Like an overanimated talk-show host.*] Any major wounds when you were twelve? Fourteen?

[*They both laugh. Just then the door is thrown open, the spell is broken, and in come* GORDON *and* ERIC. GORDON *is the sixteen-year-old ace reporter from the school magazine.* ERIC *is the photographer. They have come to interview* DOROTHY. *They breeze past* GREGORY.]

GORDON. [*Self-assured.*] Dorothy, *there* you are, nice to see you. Good game?

[GREGORY *tries desperately to retrieve their intimacy.*]

GREGORY. Sorry, this is a dressing room; you can't come in here. . . .

[*This gambit*[9] *of* GREGORY's *is completely ignored.*]

GORDON. [*To* DOROTHY.] You know Eric, don't you? I'd like to have a chat with you, for the magazine.

DOROTHY. You want to interview *me?*

GORDON. You bet. We're covering two or three school personalities. You're pretty famous now, you know. [GORDON *is pretty much in command now.*] Eric, pick off a few shots, will you? Get the whole dressing room thing. And some nice big close shots of Dorothy.

[GREGORY *has a last effort. He takes* ERIC *aside.*]

GREGORY. This is no place for a camera, Eric; people take their clothes off in here.

ERIC. [*To* GREGORY, *brushing his appeal aside.*] Could you move over here, please? I want to isolate the lady in the shot. Too many shadows.

[GREGORY, *defeated, sits in his allotted place.*]

GORDON. I like to interview people like this— no preparation, everything nice and natural. Now, tell me, Dorothy, how are the boys taking it, you being on the team now?

[GREGORY *sees another chance.*]

GREGORY. You guys are *so* predictable . . . always trying to make trouble. There are *no* problems at all—we're all very *happy.* Dorothy is a *very good* player. . . .

GORDON. Slow down, Gregory. This is an in-depth interview. Dorothy?

DOROTHY. Things are fine. Some of them thought I wouldn't be heavy enough for a tackle, but I'm quicker than most boys; I can keep out of trouble. I take dancing lessons too, and that helps my balance.

GORDON. [*Nodding wisely.*] You must train a lot, keep in shape. Do you have time for any-

---

8. *parliamo italiano* [pär′lyä′mō ē′tä lyä′nō]: Italian for "we are speaking Italian."
9. **gambit:** move made to gain an advantage.

thing else? What do you do on Saturday nights, for instance?

DOROTHY. Saturday nights are special. I like to do something special.

[GREGORY *has caught* GORDON's *drift and is paying the utmost attention to his technique, because he's appalled by it and also because he wants to know how to do it.*]

GORDON. Hey—how about doing something special *this* Saturday?

GREGORY. [*Fed up.*] Come on! Can't a guy dry his hair in here? This is a dressing room. . . . You go and conduct your business somewhere else.

DOROTHY. [*Getting up.*] I'll go and change too.

GORDON. We'll come with you, Dorothy. You're an interesting girl, you know. I want to find the real Dorothy. OK?

DOROTHY. OK.

GORDON. Cheerio,[10] Gregory.

GREGORY. Arrivederci,[11] Gordon. Hurry back.

[*The three of them leave.* GREGORY *resumes his hair drying, muttering disgustedly.*]

GREGORY. Bella, bella . . . bella Renaldo . . . bella Gordon . . .

Scene 6

The science laboratory. A few days later.

[DOROTHY *is working on an experiment with her friend* SUSAN, *the girl from cooking class.*]

DOROTHY. Pass the sulfuric acid, will you?

SUSAN. What is the pH[12] of that?

DOROTHY. Um . . . [*Checking.*] seven.

SUSAN. [*After a pause, casually.*] How's the soccer going?

DOROTHY. Oh, it's good. [*Looks critically at the specimen* SUSAN *is preparing.*] You need to cut that up a bit. It's too big.

SUSAN. [*Still casually.*] What about the goalie, Gregory? [*Pause.*] What do you make of Gregory?

DOROTHY. [*Considering.*] Well, he's a bit slow, and a bit awkward. [*Nodding.*] Slow and awkward.

SUSAN. [*A little smile.*] He's got a nice laugh.

DOROTHY. [*Back to business.*] Give me the bromide,[13] will you?

Scene 7

Lunchtime in the school cafeteria.

[SUSAN *is sitting alone, reading.* ANDY, *accompanied by his constant companion,* CHARLIE, *attempts to make small talk with her.*]

ANDY. [*Grandly.*] Good afternoon.

[SUSAN *says nothing. A pause.*]

ANDY. [*Another try.*] Do you know, when you sneeze, it comes out your nose at a hundred miles an hour!

[SUSAN *stares at him.*]

ANDY. [*Nodding with enthusiasm.*] It's a well-known fact—*a hundred miles an hour!* [*He

10. **Cheerio:** British expression for "good-bye."
11. *Arrivederci* [ä´rē ve där´chē]: Italian for "good-bye."

12. **pH:** a measure of the degree to which a solution is either acidic or alkaline.
13. **bromide** [brō´mīd]: any chemical compound that includes bromine.

demonstrates.] Ahhh-choooooo!!! Just like that!

[SUSAN *gets up and walks away.* ANDY *looks bewildered.*]

Scene 8

Outside the school. About a week later.

[*We now meet* GREGORY's *little sister,* MADE-
LINE. *She is ten, and she and* GREGORY *are
very close. On her way to meet* GREGORY, *she*

meets her friend RICHARD, *also ten. They are
both amazingly self-possessed.*]

RICHARD. Hello.

MADELINE. Hello.

RICHARD. Carry your bag for you?

MADELINE. I can't see you today. I've got to go
to the big school. Family trouble.

RICHARD. [*Sagely.*] Is it Gregory?

MADELINE. [*Nodding.*] Guess what? He's fallen
in love.

RICHARD. [*Sympathetically.*] That's big trouble. Well, maybe I can see you later on.

MADELINE. Right. Bye.

Scene 9

A shopping mall. A few minutes later.

[*Having met* GREGORY, MADELINE *counsels him as they browse the store windows at the mall.*]

MADELINE. [*Critically.*] You need some new trousers. These baggy ones are awful. I'll talk to Mum about it. Blue ones, Italian. If you're going to start falling in love, you'll have to start taking care of yourself.

GREGORY. Are Italians good dressers?

MADELINE. They have style. And they make nice trousers. . . . I was talking to Steven's sister about Dorothy. She's very attractive. I *knew* you would fall for that type. She wears nice things—she's got style.

GREGORY. [*Agreeing.*] She's one-quarter Italian.

MADELINE. Don't get too serious about her, if you can help it. Have you asked her out yet? [GREGORY *shakes his head.*] I can help you. I can tell you things. You were nice to me when other boys *hated* their sisters.

[*They pause in front of a clothing store.*]

MADELINE. [*Pointing to some sweaters.*] Which color do you like?

GREGORY. If it were brown, it would be OK.

MADELINE. [*Frustrated by his lack of style.*] Brown! You don't think about colors, do you? If you don't take an interest in yourself, how can you expect other people to be interested in you? Talk to Dorothy. Ask her out. She

won't say no, I'll bet you. But don't treat her too special. You're too romantic—it could scare a girl off.

GREGORY. What kind of things should I say?

MADELINE. For heaven's sake, don't plan it, don't think about it. *Do* it!

[*They walk into a café.*]

GREGORY. [*Summing up.*] So, I should think less about love and more about colors.

MADELINE. [*Congratulating him.*] You've got it.

[*A* WAITRESS *comes up for their order.*]

WAITRESS. What would you like?

MADELINE. A ginger beer,[14] with vanilla ice cream and some lime juice, please, and *don't stir it.*

GREGORY. Coffee, please.

WAITRESS. Black or white?[15]

GREGORY. Ummm . . . [*Looks at* MADELINE. *He knows he's going to blow it.*] Brown.

[*A big sigh from* MADELINE, *to tease him.*]

GREGORY. They don't *do* blue coffees here, Madeline. This isn't Italy. No style.

MADELINE. [*More serious.*] Do you dream about her? [GREGORY *nods.*] That means you love her. It's the one you have the dreams about that counts.

GREGORY. [*After a pause.*] What do *you* dream about?

MADELINE. I just dream about ginger beer and ice cream. I'm still a little girl, remember?

---

14. **ginger beer:** soft drink similar to ginger ale but stronger in flavor.
15. **Black or white?:** The waitress is asking whether Gregory wants his coffee without milk or with milk.

STUDY QUESTIONS

Recalling

1. Explain how Dorothy first comes to Gregory's attention. Contrast Dorothy and Gregory as soccer players.
2. In Scene 3 what does Gregory tell Steve about his feelings for Dorothy?
3. What opinions about Gregory do Susan and Dorothy express in Scene 6?
4. What advice does Madeline give her brother as they walk through the mall?

Interpreting

5. What qualities of Gregory's do you find appealing? Think about characters who act as romantic heroes in other films, and point out what qualities Gregory might lack as such a hero.
6. How accurate do you find Susan's and Dorothy's opinions of Gregory?
7. List three or four ways in which Gregory and Dorothy differ as people. Do you think that they will make a good couple? Why or why not?

Extending

8. What advice would *you* give Gregory if you were a friend of his?

READING AND LITERARY FOCUS

Dialogue

Dialogue is the conversation between characters in a literary work. Short stories, novels, and even some poems and nonfiction pieces contain dialogue, but dialogue is absolutely essential in a play or film. Usually the only words spoken in a play or film are the characters' speeches. As audience members we must pay close attention to what these characters say in order to understand what they are like.

At the start of *Gregory's Girl,* we watch a soccer team leaving the field after a game. The first bit of dialogue between Gregory and the coach tells us how the game went. More important, it tells us about Gregory's sense of humor. Rather than moping over the team's defeat, Gregory laughs at himself and his teammates.

Thinking About Dialogue

1. Look again at Scene 5, in which Gregory has his first conversation with Dorothy. What do Dorothy's statements about her "imperfections" show about her? What does Gregory's attempt to speak Italian reveal about him?
2. The stage direction at the beginning of Scene 8 says that Gregory and his sister Madeline are "very close." Find two examples in which their dialogue shows this closeness.

CHALLENGE

Props

▨ Part of the pleasure of reading drama comes from imagining how the scenes would look when performed with costumes, sets, and props (portable articles used by the actors in a scene—for example, the soccer equipment in Scene 2 or the cooking utensils in Scene 3). Choose a scene from *Gregory's Girl* to act out with other students. Bring in appropriate props and items of clothing to make the scene more convincing.

GREGORY's *home, evening. A few days later.*

[STEVE *and* GREGORY *are in the sitting room watching the television. At least* STEVE *is watching it. The program is a cookery demonstration, and* STEVE *reacts to it much as others react to a televised sports match, engrossed and critical.* GREGORY *is uninterested. He would rather be talking about* DOROTHY. *We hear snatches of the sound from the TV. Apart from them the house is empty.*]

GREGORY. Do you know anything about Italians?

STEVE. [*Without taking his eyes from the screen.*] Excellent seafood in the northwest. Some of their regional pasta dishes are good too. Good with salads, very stylish all round. . . . [*To the television.*] Whoa! Whoa! Go easy with the sugar, lady!

GREGORY. [*A frustrated outburst.*] Food! Food! Food! Is that all you think about? [*Turns off the TV.*] You're *unnatural,* pal; you're a freak!

STEVE. [*Responding now.*] You eat it, don't you? I've never seen you turn up your nose at anything I've made. [*As if cut to the quick.*] Hours and hours I've spent making you lovely, lovely things, and all it means to you in the end is *food?*

GREGORY. Look, pal, I don't know whether you've noticed, but I'm going through a *crisis.*

STEVE. Of course I've noticed. What do you want me to do? The whole world's got problems. You're just obsessed by a beautiful, young, *unattainable* girl. So what?

GREGORY. Stop saying things like that—unattainable—obsessed. . . . It's *love.*

STEVE. OK, it's love. Sweep her off her feet,

then. Oh, I forgot, you're the goalkeeper, *she's* the sweeper.

GREGORY. [*Darkly.*] Ha ha.

STEVE. [*Sensibly now.*] Look, one key question: Have you talked to her, asked her for a date? *Anything?*

[GREGORY *shakes his head.*]

STEVE. Well, do it. *Then* complain. [*Turns TV set back on.*]

[GREGORY *thinks for a second or two.*]

GREGORY. If I get a date, can I borrow your white jacket?

STEVE. [*Emphatically.*] No.

[*The doorbell rings. Both of them react to it.*]

STEVE. [*Sarcastically.*] Maybe that's her.

[GREGORY *makes for the door. He looks to the right and left when he opens the door. He's slightly baffled because nobody appears to be there. Then he looks down. He finds* RICHARD, MADELINE'*s friend.*]

RICHARD. I wonder if Maddy is in?

GREGORY. [*Upset at his self-assurance.*] You mean *Madeline.* She's out with her mother.

RICHARD. That's a shame. I thought we could go for a walk. Maybe I could wait. . . .

GREGORY. No. They'll be ages.

RICHARD. Maybe she could phone me later on. She has my number.

GREGORY. Who *are* you anyway? You're talking about my sister, and she doesn't go for walks with *any*body. What's the idea, coming to people's doors, asking for people's sisters. Act your age. See, when *I* was your age—

RICHARD. [*Interrupting.*] You're Gregory, aren't you?

[*He offers* GREGORY *his hand.* GREGORY *gives his without thinking, and his outraged speech trails off.*]

Maddy's told me all about you. How are you feeling? Everything OK?

[GREGORY *gets his outrage underway again.*]

GREGORY. Oho! There's nothing wrong with *me*, son. *You're* the one that should be worried. Dates at your age!

[*He splutters off.* RICHARD *figures he's got a crazy person on his hands.*]

RICHARD. OK, Gregory, fair enough. Richard's the name. Ask Maddy to call me anyway.

[*He beats a rational man's retreat down the path.* GREGORY *feels in command now and shouts after him.*]

GREGORY. The name's *Madeline.* . . .

Scene 11

The school corridor. A few days later.

[*A* GIRL *from the third year catches up with* GREGORY.]

GIRL. Are you Gregory?

[GREGORY *turns around, and puts on an easeful, mature air. Junior girls make him feel comfortable.*]

GREGORY. That's me, sweetheart. Who wants to know?

GIRL. Dorothy wants to see you.

[*This rocks him. The mature act vanishes. He turns to jelly.*]

GREGORY. Dorothy?

GIRL. That's what I said. She'll be in room nine at breaktime, OK?

[*The* GIRL *leaves a stunned* GREGORY. *Then he tears down the corridor, smoothing his hair and straightening his clothes. He finds room nine. After a pause to put on an air of sophistication, he knocks and sticks his head into the room.* DOROTHY *and four* GIRLFRIENDS *are casually draped over chairs and desks.*]

GREGORY. [*A little taken aback.*] Got your message, Dorothy.

DOROTHY. Good. I just wanted to know what you were up to at lunchtime.

GREGORY. [*A new spark of optimism lights up his face.*] Nothing that can't wait a million years.

DOROTHY. Good. Will you help me out with some goal practice?

GREGORY. Yes—sure.

DOROTHY. Good. It'll speed things up. I want to practice goal shots at different angles.

GREGORY. [*Jokingly.*] I'll bring my compass.

[*Just a look from* DOROTHY.]

GREGORY. [*More subdued.*] Good. See you at half-twelve?[16]

DOROTHY. [*Smiling now.*] Fine.

GREGORY. Good. See you.

[GREGORY *tears off down the school corridor, where he eagerly accosts* STEVE.]

GREGORY. [*Breathlessly.*] I'm on the way,

---

16. **half-twelve:** British expression for "eleven-thirty."

Steve. It's off the ground. Romance is in the air. Can I have your white jacket?

STEVE. Hi, pal! No.

GREGORY. I don't want to make a big thing over it, but it's just that the jacket would really help. It would make the—it would put the whole date on a different footing. Just for one night, eh?

STEVE. What are you raving on about?

GREGORY. [*Patiently.*] Me . . . Dorothy . . . *date* . . . it's in the bag! She's *after* me—she wants me to play soccer with her at lunch!

STEVE. Not with my good jacket, you won't.

GREGORY. No—the jacket's for later on, for the *real* date!

[STEVE *shakes his head.*]

GREGORY. Come on, Steve, you gave Pete the jacket last week. Why not me?

STEVE. That's exactly why, Gregory old son. Did you see the state of that coat the day after? Never again.

[*As* GREGORY *begins to protest,* STEVE *sees a way to get off the hook.*]

STEVE. Look, I'll make a deal, old pal . . . you get the date, signed, sealed, delivered . . . and then come and ask for the jacket. . . . Fair?

GREGORY. [*Triumphant.*] It's a deal! Want to throw in your brown shoes as well?

[STEVE *gives him a cutting look.*]

School cafeteria. Lunchtime that day.

[ANDY *and his friend* CHARLIE *have picked up their food.* ANDY *is scanning the dining room,*

looking for a likely couple of girls to sit with. Nudging CHARLIE, *he walks over to* CAROL *and* MARGO.]

ANDY. [*Sociably.*] Good afternoon, ladies. Mind if we join you?

[*The girls give a shrug of acquiescence.* ANDY *gives* CHARLIE *an encouraging look as they sit.*]

ANDY. [*Smiling round the table.*] I'm particularly fond of lamb chops. . . .

[*No great response from the girls so far. They eat on in silence.* ANDY *looks across the table to* CHARLIE, *and makes a kind of "do something, say something" gesture to him. No response from* CHARLIE. ANDY *plows on alone.*]

ANDY. How's your roast beef?

CAROL. [*Dryly.*] It's veal.

ANDY. Oh, *veal!* [*Enthusiastic.*] You know how they make veal? They get the little baby calves and they hang them upside down and they slit their throats and let the blood drip out. It's very interesting, isn't it?

[*The girls put down their forks and leave.*]

The soccer field. The same lunch period.

[*With lunchtime well underway we see* GREGORY *and* DOROTHY *practicing.* GREGORY *is a hopelessly inept goalie. He hops back and forth, clapping his hands together with a great show of energy, shouting encouraging remarks to* DOROTHY, *who again and again kicks the ball past him into the net.*]

GREGORY. This is *great!* I can really use the practice in goal! [*As the ball whizzes past him once more.*] That was a good shot!

[*The ball goes back to* DOROTHY, *who ignores* GREGORY *and gets off another cracking shot.*]

Great shot! You got me that time!

DOROTHY. [*Losing patience.*] Could you stop dancing around so much? It's very distracting.

[*She lines up another shot, and the ball's in the net again.*]

GREGORY. Great! First class! You know, you're some girl. I haven't got *near* the ball yet. . . .

[*Spoken just too soon. The ball is hammered into his stomach. He hits the dirt.*]

DOROTHY. [*Allowing herself a smile.*] Well held. You OK?

GREGORY. [*On his knees, gasping.*] Think I've broke my neckchain.

[GREGORY *fumbles around in the dirt.* DOROTHY *wants to get back to work.*]

DOROTHY. Come on, we've only got another hour. I want to try some shots on the move— come out and tackle me, try and block, then move back and block some more. Use your feet . . . don't grab for the ball.

[*It looks like* GREGORY *is a long way from getting the encouragement to ask Dorothy for that date.*]

GREGORY. [*Gallantly.*] OK! Keep 'em coming, Dorothy!

Scene 14

The cafeteria. The same lunch period.

[ANDY *and* CHARLIE *are very desolate looking. They pick at their food.*]

ANDY. Of course, you know we're in the wrong place.

[*They munch some more.*]

You know where we should be. . . ?

[*Another pause for eating.*]

South America.

[*A glimmer of interest from* CHARLIE.]

There's a town there—do you know the ratio of women to men?

[CHARLIE *looks more interested.*]

Eight to one! Eight South American women per guy! That's the sort of place for us, eh?

[CHARLIE *gives a nod this time.*]

It's called *Caracas.*[17]

[CHARLIE *smiles.*]

Scene 15

Back on the field. The end of the lunch hour.

[*As practice ends,* GREGORY *is panting and sweating. He walks with the stagger of near exhaustion.* DOROTHY *is cool and serene.*]

DOROTHY. Are you happy as a goalie?

GREGORY. [*Heavily breathing.*] S'OK.

DOROTHY. You waste a lot of energy. No control.

GREGORY. [*Bravely.*] I've got tons left! [*Runs in place to demonstrate.*]

DOROTHY. [*Smiling.*] Thanks for the practice.

GREGORY. No sweat, eh? [*He looks down at his own dishevelment.*] Well, *lots* of sweat actually—but no sweat, if you get my meaning.

DOROTHY. Sorry you missed lunch.

GREGORY. Oh, lunch means nothing to me . . . some fresh fruit—

DOROTHY. [*Smiling.*] Double apple pie and custard—

GREGORY. [*Sheepishly.*] That kind of thing.

DOROTHY. I'm off for a shower.

[*With that she moves quickly and beautifully off.* GREGORY *is perplexed and angry with himself for failing to move the relationship forward. Then, with amazing resolve, he sprints after her.*]

GREGORY. [*Breathless but resolute.*] Dorothy! Just wanted to say—any time—for more practice. *Any* time. Just say the word.

DOROTHY. [*Waving good-bye.*] Right. Bye.

GREGORY. [*A big gulp.*] Also . . . would you like to come out with me?

DOROTHY. OK.

---

17. **Caracas** [kə rä′kəs]: capital and largest city of Venezuela, a South American country.

[GREGORY *cannot quite take it in so quickly.*]

GREGORY. I mean on a kind of date. [*Looks around nervously.*]

DOROTHY. I said OK.

[*It is still not making sense to* GREGORY.]

GREGORY. Come on, stop fooling around. I mean a real—

DOROTHY. [*Teasingly exasperated.*] If you're going to argue about it, forget it.

GREGORY. No! No! Fine. [*Thinks.*] When?

DOROTHY. Tonight. Half-past seven, at the clock in the plaza. [*She goes into the building to change.*]

[GREGORY *follows* DOROTHY *into the dressing room, then stands tongue-tied.*]

GREGORY. [*Finally.*] I—uh—just wanted to check—

DOROTHY. Yes?

GREGORY. Tonight.

DOROTHY. Yes, tonight.

GREGORY. Half-past seven.

DOROTHY. Half-past seven.

GREGORY. And you'll be there. [*Pointing to her.*]

DOROTHY. I'll be there.

GREGORY. And *I'll* be there. [*Pointing to himself.*]

DOROTHY. Uh huh.

GREGORY. At the clock.

DOROTHY. At the clock.

[GREGORY *floats out the door and down the corridor, ten feet tall.*]

Scene 16

GREGORY'*s room. That evening.*

[MADELINE *is blow-drying and combing* GREGORY'*s hair at the mirror. She is happy to be fussing over him, and he is wearing the contented, half-drowsy expression of someone being pampered. He is singing to himself.*]

GREGORY. " . . . Heaven, I'm in heaven. . . ."

[*The singing stops.*]

GREGORY. Should I tell her some jokes?

MADELINE. [*Still busy on the hair.*] Maybe.

[*After a pause.*]

GREGORY. Do you know any jokes?

[MADELINE *giggles lightly.* GREGORY *catches her eye in the mirror and starts to giggle.*]

Scene 17

The town plaza. Rendezvous time.

[GREGORY *is waiting in the deserted mall in front of a gigantic clock. He is wearing* STEVE's *white jacket and looks almost stylish, but his tension and anticipation show on his face.*]

GREGORY. [*Practicing different voices.*] Hi there. [*More friendly.*] Hi there! [*With a deep voice and nonchalant swagger.*] Hi, there.

[*He hears the sound of light footsteps before he sees anyone. Alert, he pulls himself to attention. The footsteps get closer and stop beside him. He swings his head round elegantly. He sees* CAROL. *By now his wide nice-guy smile is well underway and it is too late to stop it.*]

CAROL. Hi, Gregory.

GREGORY. [*Starting his wave but losing heart. Still smiling, however.*] Hello, Carol.

CAROL. Waiting for Dorothy?

GREGORY. [*Still with the smile.*] Yes.

CAROL. [*Dealing her blow quickly.*] She's not coming.

GREGORY. [*Nodding.*] Thanks. [*Walks off, trying to whistle nonchalantly. Then comes back.*] Wrong way. [*Starts off the other way.*]

CAROL. Something turned up—to do with her soccer, I think. . . . [CAROL *gives* GREGORY *a long look.*] Is that Steve's jacket?

GREGORY. No. Thanks for the word about Dorothy.

CAROL. S'OK. Couldn't leave you here all night. What will you do now?

[GREGORY *looks at* CAROL. *She's a nice-looking girl with big open eyes.*]

GREGORY. [*Nothing to lose.*] Fancy a walk?

CAROL. Where?

GREGORY. [*Thinks a moment.*] We can go past Capaldi's. I'll buy you some chips.[18]

CAROL. Well, OK. I'm going that way anyway.

[*They walk into the street.* CAROL *suddenly heads for a phone booth.*]

CAROL. Gregory! Hold on a minute!

[*She dodges into the booth. Up until now* CAROL *has been dressed in her conservative school uniform.* GREGORY *is astonished to witness a rapid transformation. She puts on lipstick and eyeliner quickly and expertly and removes her school clothes to reveal a jersey and short skirt underneath. She teases out her hair and changes her shoes for horrific white spike heels.*]

CAROL. [*A sigh of relief.*] I feel like a human being again.

GREGORY. [*A bit frightened by her transformation. He makes a strange little noise and then backs off.*] Uh, look, I've got to go home—I've really enjoyed the walk—

CAROL. *Hold it,* Gregory. I thought we were going for chips!

GREGORY. [*Reluctantly.*] OK, OK. But put your coat on.

CAROL. Oh no! Come on, Gregory, all I'm asking for is a walk up to the chips shop. I've *got* a date—I'm going away. [*Mysteriously.*] I've just got a funny feeling that something *nice* might happen up there . . . so, *come on!* We haven't got all night!

[*And they go.*]

---

18. **chips:** French fried potatoes.

Scene 18

Near the chips shop. A few minutes later.

[GREGORY *and* CAROL *are perched on the back of a concrete bench, nibbling at their chips.*]

CAROL. Do you like Dorothy?

GREGORY. Yes.

CAROL. Can you drive?

GREGORY. Not yet. My father has a car though. Why?

CAROL. Oh nothing, it doesn't matter. . . . It's just that Ricky Swift has a car. He's up at the Physical Ed. College, and his father has a sports shop. Dorothy knows him.

GREGORY. He must be quite old then.

CAROL. Mmmmm. He's nearly nineteen.

GREGORY. Has he got any hair left? [*Retreating into laughter.*] Ricky Swift! Sounds like something out of a comic! Does he fly through the air like Batman? [*In a mock cartoon-type voice.*] Quick, Dorothy, to the Rickmobile!

CAROL. OK, OK. Calm down.

[GREGORY *does calm down. In an instant the hysteria has been washed away, and a sober-faced* GREGORY *gets on with his chips.* CAROL *notices the approach of her friend* MARGO.]

CAROL. Well, I'm off! [*Hailing* MARGO.] Hey, Margo, here's Gregory. Dorothy stood him up, so he's buying everybody chips and telling jokes. [*To* GREGORY.] Have fun, Gregory. You can tell me all about it tomorrow.

[*Then she goes off, leaving* GREGORY *and* MARGO *alone.* MARGO *takes the initiative.*]

MARGO. Well, I'll buy my own chips, but you can keep telling the jokes.

[*As* MARGO *goes into the shop,* GREGORY *spots* ANDY *and* CHARLIE *sitting nearby.*]

GREGORY. [*Confidentially.*] I think Margo's after me.

ANDY. [*Egging him on, eager to see some success in romance somewhere.*] It's a good night for it. Are you taking her to the Country Park?

GREGORY. I don't know. Should I?

ANDY. [*With great confidence.*] Aye, aye!

[GREGORY *sees* MARGO *coming out of the shop and with a hopeful grin waves to* ANDY *and* CHARLIE. *They look at each other, impressed, as* GREGORY *and* MARGO *stroll off.* MARGO *signals* GREGORY *to wait for her while she goes into a phone booth and makes a quick call. We cut to* SUSAN *waiting outside another phone booth and answering a call. After* MARGO *finishes her end of the call, she summons* GREGORY, *who, rather than walking with her, follows warily a few feet behind her. He is not sure what is happening tonight.*]

MARGO. [*Sensing his mood.*] Relax.

GREGORY. Where are we going?

MARGO. Relax. Enjoy it!

GREGORY. [*With a brave smile.*] I am . . . I will. But where are we going? Where are *you* and *I* going? I'm just a bit emotional tonight. OK?

MARGO. That's OK, that's fine. There's nothing wrong with a bit of emotion. [*Impatient.*] Come *on.*

[MARGO *hurries him along, as if they have an appointment somewhere. And very soon they meet* SUSAN, *who has been waiting for them a few blocks away.*]

SUSAN. [*Pleasantly.*] Hello, Gregory. You're all dressed up. Anywhere to go?

[GREGORY *clowns wordlessly for the two*

girls. *Several times he seems about to say something and then thinks better of it. He shrugs, looks at the sky, whistles, and puffs out his cheeks in exaggerated bewilderment. He ends with a sheepish smile.*]

MARGO. Well, *I* have got somewhere to go. See you tomorrow, Susan. [*To* GREGORY.] Bye. [*She leaves.*]

[GREGORY, *left alone with* SUSAN, *laughs at his ridiculous predicament.*]

SUSAN. [*Brightly.*] I believe you're short of a date.

GREGORY. There was a bit of a mix-up earlier on. It's OK.

SUSAN. Would you like to spend some time with me—on a kind of date?

GREGORY. Look, I'm not very sure what's going on. Is this some kind of a joke? All this—with Carol—and Margo—and—[*Looks at her closely.*] It *is* a joke, isn't it?

SUSAN. [*Patiently.*] It's not a joke. It's just the way girls work. They help each other.

GREGORY. Is Dorothy—

SUSAN. [*Gently.*] Dorothy's a good sport. Anyway, how about it, you and me, what do you say? [SUSAN *makes things easier.*] Think about it.

[GREGORY *laughs nervously.*]

Sit down there and think about it.

[GREGORY *sits, giving* SUSAN *a reassuring wave, while* SUSAN *stands nearby whistling.* GREGORY *gets up after a minute or so.*]

GREGORY. OK. A kind of date. Do we start right away?

SUSAN. Yes. We'll go to the Country Park. [*As they walk.*] What we'll do is, we'll just walk and talk. And we don't even need to talk much, either. We'll just see how it goes.

GREGORY. [*Relieved.*] Fine.

SUSAN. I hope you don't think I do this kind of thing all the time.

GREGORY. No. . . . Can we whistle too?

SUSAN. We can whistle too.

Scene 19

The Country Park. A little while later.

[GREGORY *and* SUSAN *continue to walk, whistling.*]

SUSAN. I like your jacket.

GREGORY. I like your skirt.

SUSAN. [*Giggling.*] I like your shirt.

GREGORY. I like your beret.

SUSAN. Thank you.

[*They both laugh and sit down under a tree.*]

GREGORY. [*Relaxed.*] Now this is really good. I'm really enjoying myself.

SUSAN. [*Smiling.*] Good. I'm glad we—bumped into each other. [*She whistles innocently.*]

GREGORY. Do you want to dance? It's really good—you just lie flat down and dance. I'll show you what I mean. I'll start off, and you just join in when you feel confident enough. OK?

[*He lies on his back and begins to wave his arms and wiggle his hands around.* SUSAN *laughs.*]

GREGORY. Just dance.

[SUSAN *reclines beside him, and they con-*

tinue to "dance" in this way as GREGORY *speaks.*]

GREGORY. I'll tell you something, and not a lot of people know this. [*Momentously.*] We are clinging to the surface of this planet while it spins through space at a thousand miles an hour, held only by the mystery force called . . . *gravity!*

SUSAN. [*Amused.*] Wild.

GREGORY. A lot of people panic when you tell them that. They just fall off.

SUSAN. Oh!

GREGORY. But I see you're not falling off. That means you've got the hang of it. That means that you've got—

SUSAN. [*Smiles.*] Natural ability.

GREGORY. Yeah. A thousand miles an hour, eh?

SUSAN. Why are boys obsessed with numbers?

GREGORY. No, we're not.

SUSAN. [*A superior laugh.*] Ah.

GREGORY. Don't stop dancing—you'll fall off.

SUSAN. Listen, I want to tell you something. Do you know when you sneeze, it comes out of your nose at a hundred miles an hour?

GREGORY. Really?

SUSAN. [*Demonstrates with a little sneeze.*] Ah-choo! Just like that.

[GREGORY *and* SUSAN *continue waving their arms around and talking as it grows darker. They gradually move their arms more and more in unison, each following the other's lead in trying out new movements. The whole thing actually begins to look like a kind of dance. Time passes quickly.*]

GREGORY. One more number. . . . Eleven. Home by. I've got to be. . . .

SUSAN. [Getting up.] OK, Mister Spaceman, I'll walk you home.

GREGORY. Really?

SUSAN. Umm hmmm.

GREGORY. I don't want to put you to any trouble.

SUSAN. It's OK.

GREGORY. If you just want to walk to the bridge, that's fine.

SUSAN. All the way home. I don't mind.

GREGORY. OK. I'll do the same for you sometime.

SUSAN. Good!

Scene 20

GREGORY's backdoor. A little while later.

[Moonlight. SUSAN and GREGORY talk softly.]

GREGORY. When can I see you again?

SUSAN. Tomorrow. History. Ten-thirty.

GREGORY. I want a date.

SUSAN. OK, Mister Spaceman. Twelve-thirty in room seventeen. We'll talk about it.

GREGORY. Ten four.[19]

SUSAN. A million and nine. Good night, Mister Spaceman.

[A peck on the cheek, and SUSAN is gone.]

GREGORY. [Watching her.] Three hundred and seventy-five. [Blows a kiss.] Five thousand six hundred and seventy-two. [Blows another kiss.]

---

19. **Ten four:** radio jargon for "message received."

Scene 21

GREGORY's house. A few minutes later.

[MADELINE makes her way quietly to GREGORY's room. It is in darkness as she creeps in and switches on the bed lamp. We find GREGORY not asleep but lying wide awake in bed with his hands folded under his head, smiling.]

MADELINE. How did it go? Are you going to see her again?

GREGORY. Who? Dorothy?

MADELINE. Who else?

GREGORY. [Mysteriously.] Well . . . maybe Susan for instance. . . .

[MADELINE is too eager for news to stand for this coy stuff. She grabs him by the pajama collar and starts banging his head on the pillow.]

MADELINE. Tell me! I'll hurt you. Tell me!!!!!!!

GREGORY. OK, OK! Dorothy didn't show up. But I met Carol and Margo and then Susan. She's lovely. We went to the park. I think she likes me. I'll see her tomorrow.

MADELINE. [With a sympathetic grin.] It's hard work being in love, eh? Especially when you don't know which girl it is?

GREGORY. [Happily.] I'll work on it.

MADELINE. [Sighs and shakes her head in mock bewilderment.] Who's going to be Gregory's girl?

GREGORY. [Laughing.] You are!

[MADELINE pulls the pillow from under his head and shoves it over his face. She jumps off the bed and disappears back to her room. GREGORY lies back, settled for sleep. He stretches over and puts out the light, looking very content.]

The highway. Later that night.

[ANDY *and* CHARLIE *are on the roadside, watching for passing cars.* ANDY *holds a cardboard sign with the word* Caracus *(misspelled) printed on it. Both boys look exhausted.* CHARLIE *is sitting on the curb. He looks at* ANDY *and finally speaks (for the first time in the film).*]

CHARLIE. Come on, Andy. Let's go home.

[ANDY *lets himself be led away by* CHARLIE.]

CHARLIE. That's not the way to spell *Caracas*, anyway.

ANDY. [*Stunned.*] What?! What do you mean?

CHARLIE. [*Patiently.*] *Caracas* is spelled with an *a*. It's *c-a-s*, not *c-u-s*.

ANDY. Well, why didn't you tell me that before?! Could you not have told me that *four hours ago*?! We've been standing here, waiting, for *ages*!

CHARLIE. Well, let's go home. [*Coaxing.*] Come on, we can start again tomorrow. There are some nice girls in the third year. They always go for older guys. There's even some beauties in the second year. . . . [*Reassuring him.*] Andy, I think everything's going to be all right. . . .

STUDY QUESTIONS

Recalling

1. Describe the conditions under which Gregory manages to ask Dorothy for a date.
2. What message does Carol bring Gregory at the mall? Where does she go with him, and whom do they meet?
3. What do Gregory and Susan do and talk about on their "kind of date"?

Interpreting

4. Susan says that girls "help each other." Show how Gregory's evening proves this statement.
5. Contrast Dorothy's treatment of Gregory on the soccer field with Susan's treatment of him during their date. How does he respond to each girl?
6. Prove that Gregory is better matched with Susan than with Dorothy.
7. Who do you think is the *real* "Gregory's girl"? Why?

Extending

8. What do you find in Gregory's world that seems most like your own? What seems different?

READING AND LITERARY FOCUS

Character and Theme

We come to understand **characters** in drama partly by what they say, partly by what they do, and partly by what others say about them or do with them. Of course, some characters are simpler to understand than others. Andy, for instance, remains the same throughout *Gregory's Girl*: wanting to impress girls but never managing to figure out how. Compare the effect he has on Susan in Scene 7, for example, with the effect he has on Carol and her friends in Scene 12. By contrast, Gregory is a more complex character, one who develops in the course of the screenplay.

In fact, Gregory's development helps us understand the theme of the play. The **theme** is the larger, general meaning that grows out of the specific story being told. Although specifically about one Scottish high school student and his friends, *Gregory's Girl* is more generally about young people in most times and places. It portrays that period in our lives when we come to know ourselves better and to understand better what is right for us.

Thinking About Character and Theme

1. How would you describe Gregory's character by the end of the play? How has he changed, and what has happened to make him change?
2. Gregory falls in love with Dorothy, who is very different from him and does not appreciate him. Then he discovers Susan, who likes him and shares his sense of humor. What point might Gregory's situation make about the difference between what we think we want and what we actually need?

Foreshadowing and Predicting Outcomes

Surprises make life and literature more interesting. However, any well-written work contains hints, known as **foreshadowing,** that help us to predict future developments in the plot. For example, Gregory's date turns out to be something quite different from what we and he might have expected. Yet we can see in earlier scenes hints that help us to predict the outcome of his date.

Thinking About Foreshadowing and Predicting Outcomes

1. At what point in the screenplay does Susan first show interest in Gregory?
2. Before Gregory's meeting with Susan, when did you begin to think that his evening might turn out happily?

VOCABULARY

Technical Words

Every occupation or activity develops its own special vocabulary. Carpenters, nurses, sailors, lawyers all use special **technical words** or words that describe their professional activities. Many sports also have their own vocabularies. In the early scenes of *Gregory's Girl,* a number of technical words referring to the game of soccer appear: for example, *goalie, corner, cross,* and *winger.*

To what sports do the following terms apply? Check in a dictionary for definitions of any terms you may not know.

1. field goal
2. dribble
3. touchdown
4. tacking
5. free throw
6. slalom
7. inning
8. deuce
9. spare
10. marathon

COMPOSITION

Comparing Characters

■ Write a three-paragraph composition explaining how Susan and Dorothy differ from each other. Begin by thinking about how each girl treats Gregory. Think also about the effect that each has on him. Then compare the two, pointing out specific ways in which they resemble each other, as well as specific ways in which they differ. End by indicating which girl you like better, and why.

Writing a Scene

■ Consider the brief scenes in which either Andy or Charlie or both appear. Write yet another brief scene presenting the two at school the day after their attempt to hitchhike to Caracas. Set the scene wherever you choose, and show the two boys trying to impress "some nice girls in the third year." Try to capture the way Andy and Charlie speak and behave in *Gregory's Girl.* Be sure to follow the format for writing drama, using dialogue and stage directions. You can use *Gregory's Girl* as a model. *For help with this assignment, see Lesson 10 in the Writing About Literature Handbook at the back of this book.*

A CHRISTMAS CAROL

Charles Dickens

Charles Dickens (1812–1870) was born to a middle-class family living near the seacoast of England. When he was a child, his family moved to nearby London. Dickens became the sole support of his family at the age of twelve, when his parents and younger brothers and sisters entered debtors' prison. Although he eventually achieved great success and prosperity as a writer, Dickens never forgot what it was like to be poor. His works remind us constantly of the need for kindness and generosity in a world in which many people are always hungry.

Perhaps haunted by his childhood experiences of poverty, the adult Dickens lived and worked with a driving energy. He traveled, produced and acted in plays, edited a magazine, had a large family of his own, gave public readings of his works, and, above all, wrote many of the world's greatest stories and novels. His most famous novels include *Oliver Twist*, *The Life and Adventures of Nicholas Nickleby*, *David Copperfield*, *A Tale of Two Cities*, and *Great Expectations*. No other writer could match Dickens' ability to move readers to both laughter and tears. During his lifetime Dickens was more popular in England and America than any other writer who has ever lived. Over a century after his death, his huge popularity survives, as his works continue to reach new admirers with their special combination of humor and heartbreak.

A Christmas Carol

Published in 1843, *A Christmas Carol* is one of Dickens' best loved stories. The play that follows, adapted from that story, begins on Christmas Eve in nineteenth-century London. Dickens' London was a dirty, bustling metropolis that was fast becoming the business capital of the world. It was a place where the extremes of wealth and poverty met daily. Most people had little or no money; a family might have to feed itself on only a few dollars a week. The government did little to help those who could not work, leaving these people to depend on private charity. Throughout his career Dickens fought these conditions, reminding his readers that the most important obligation of human beings is toward one another. Perhaps no work communicates this message more memorably than *A Christmas Carol*.

■ The main character of *A Christmas Carol* is a man named Ebenezer Scrooge. Watch for clues that tell you the kind of person Scrooge is—and how he got that way.

Key Ideas in *A Christmas Carol*

As you read *A Christmas Carol*, think about the following topics. If you keep track of what Dickens says about each topic, you will begin to understand the most important themes of *A Christmas Carol*.

- The emptiness of material goods
- The importance of love and compassion
- The need for social justice
- The possibility for change and personal growth

Scrooge and Bob Cratchit, from a production of *A Christmas Carol* at the Folger Theatre in Washington, D.C.

Bob Cratchit.

Tiny Tim and Scrooge.

A Dramatization by Michael Paller
Based on the Story by Charles Dickens

A Christmas Carol

CHARACTERS

NARRATOR

EBENEZER SCROOGE: bitter old miser

BOB CRATCHIT: Scrooge's penniless clerk

FRED: nephew of Scrooge

JACOB MARLEY (A GHOST): Scrooge's former business partner

The Past

GHOST OF CHRISTMAS PAST

YOUNG EBENEZER: Scrooge as a young boy

FAN: Young Ebenezer's sister

YOUNG SCROOGE: Scrooge as a young man

DICK WILKINS: Young Scrooge's friend

FEZZIWIG: warehouse owner; employer of Young Scrooge

MRS. FEZZIWIG: his wife

LITTLE FEZZIWIGS: their children

BELLE: their eldest daughter; Young Scrooge's fiancée

The Present

GHOST OF CHRISTMAS PRESENT
MRS. CRATCHIT: wife of Bob Cratchit
TINY TIM: the Cratchits' lame son
PETER, BELINDA, MARTHA: the Cratchits' other children
MRS. FRED: Fred's wife
MRS. FRED'S SISTER: her sister
TOPPER: friend of Fred

The Future

GHOST OF CHRISTMAS YET TO COME
FAT MAN, MAN WITH A HANDKERCHIEF, THIN MAN: businessmen
OLD JOE: pawnbroker
MRS. DILBER, CHARWOMAN, UNDERTAKER: clients of Old Joe

Others

TWO PORTLY GENTLEMEN
CHRISTMAS CAROLERS
BOY

Scene: *London, England. The nineteenth century.*

ACT I

[The set has two levels. The first level covers most of the stage; the second level, which is about six inches higher, is much smaller in area than the first.

The play begins in London in the middle of the 1800s. However, it presents a series of events that take place in a number of different locations and at different times. So that the action can flow smoothly from one event to the next, the set should be kept very simple, involving only a few essential pieces of furniture and other items.]

NARRATOR. Once upon a time—of all good days in the year, on Christmas Eve—old Scrooge sat busy in his counting house.[1] It was cold, bleak, biting weather. The city clocks had only just gone three, but it was quite dark already. Oh, but he was a tight-fisted hand at the grindstone,[2] Scrooge!

[The lights come up on SCROOGE's *office. We see* SCROOGE *and his clerk,* BOB CRATCHIT, *who is busily writing at his desk and trying not to notice the cold. A pause.* SCROOGE's *nephew,* FRED, *bursts into the room.]*

FRED. *[Tossing a small gift—a candy cane, or a piece of fruit, perhaps—to* CRATCHIT.] A merry Christmas, uncle! God save you!

SCROOGE. *[Annoyed at the intrusion, he looks up for a moment, but not at* FRED. *Then, back to work.]* Bah. Humbug.

FRED. Christmas a humbug, uncle? You don't mean that, I'm sure.

SCROOGE. I do. "Merry Christmas." What right have you to be merry? What reason have you? You're poor enough.

FRED. Come then, what right have you to be dismal? You're rich enough.

SCROOGE. What's Christmas time to you but a time for paying bills without money? A time for finding yourself a year older but not an hour richer; a time for balancing your books and having every item in 'em presented dead against you. Bah. Humbug!

FRED. Don't be cross, uncle.

SCROOGE. What else can I be when I live in such a world of fools as this? Merry Christmas! Out upon merry Christmas! If I could work my will, every idiot who goes about with "Merry Christmas" on his lips should be boiled with his own pudding, and buried with a stake of holly through his heart. He should!

FRED. Uncle!

SCROOGE. *[Getting up from his desk with a few money bags and crossing to a small safe.]* Nephew! Keep Christmas in your own way, and let me keep it in mine.

FRED. Keep it? But you don't keep it.

SCROOGE. Let me leave it alone, then. Much good may it do you. Much good it has ever done you.

FRED. There are many things from which I have derived good by which I have not profited, I dare say—Christmas among them. It's the only time I know of when men and women open their shut-up hearts and think of less fortunate people as if they really were fellow passengers to the grave, and not another race of creatures. And therefore, uncle, though it

---

1. **counting house:** office used for bookkeeping and other business activities.
2. **grindstone:** literally, a stone used for sharpening knives, scissors, and other utensils. "To keep one's nose to the grindstone" means to work hard.

has never put a scrap of gold or silver in my pocket, I believe that it has done me good, and I say God bless it!

[*He puts a stick of wood on the fire.* CRATCHIT *bursts into applause at the end of the speech.*]

SCROOGE. [*Standing. To* CRATCHIT.] Let me hear another sound from you, and you'll keep your Christmas by losing your situation. [*To* FRED.] You're quite a powerful speaker, sir. I wonder you don't go into Parliament.[3]

FRED. Don't be angry, uncle. Come dine with us tomorrow.

SCROOGE. [*Back at his desk.*] I'll dine with the devil first.

FRED. But why, uncle?

SCROOGE. Why did you get married?

FRED. Because I fell in love.

SCROOGE. [*As if that were the only thing in the world more ridiculous than "Merry Christmas."*] "Because I fell in love." Good afternoon. [*He turns back to his work.*]

FRED. You never came to see me before I married. Why give it as a reason for not coming now?

SCROOGE. Good afternoon.

FRED. I want nothing from you. I ask nothing of you. Why cannot we be friends?

SCROOGE. Good afternoon.

FRED. I am sorry with all my heart to find you so resolute. We have never had any quarrel to which I have been a party. But I have made the visit in homage to Christmas, and I'll keep my Christmas humor to the last. So, a merry

Christmas, uncle! [*From his coat, he pulls a small wrapped package and sets it down on* SCROOGE's *desk. Then, he turns for the door.*]

SCROOGE. Good afternoon!

FRED. [*Turning back.*] And a happy New Year! [*He exits.*]

SCROOGE. Good afternoon! [*Turning on*

---

3. **Parliament** [pär′lə mənt]: legislature in Britain.

CRATCHIT.] And you're another fellow. My clerk, with fifteen shillings[4] a week, a wife and family, talking about a merry Christmas.

[*A knock on the door, and two* PORTLY GENTLEMEN *enter.*]

FIRST PORTLY GENTLEMAN. Scrooge and Marley's, I believe? Have I the pleasure of addressing Mister Scrooge, or Mister Marley?

SCROOGE. Mister Marley has been dead these seven years. He died seven years ago this very night.

SECOND PORTLY GENTLEMAN. [*Handing* SCROOGE *his credentials.*] We have no doubt his liberality is well-represented by his surviving partner. [SCROOGE *examines the credentials and hands them back distastefully.*]

FIRST PORTLY GENTLEMAN. At this festive time of the year, Mister Scrooge, it is more than usually desirable that we should make some slight provision for the poor and destitute, who suffer greatly at the present time. Many thousands are in want of common necessities. Hundreds of thousands are in want of common comforts, sir.

SCROOGE. Are there no prisons?

FIRST PORTLY GENTLEMAN. Plenty of prisons.

SCROOGE. And the workhouses?[5] Are they still in operation?

FIRST PORTLY GENTLEMAN. They are. I wish I could say they were not.

SCROOGE. [*Considering.*] Oh. I was afraid, from what you said at first, that something had occurred to stop them in their useful course. I'm very glad to hear it.

---

4. **shillings:** British coins worth about twenty-five cents in Dickens' time.
5. **workhouses:** institutions that once housed and employed poor people. Dickens' writings eventually helped bring about the end of workhouses.

SECOND PORTLY GENTLEMAN. Under the impression that they scarcely furnish cheer of mind or body, a few of us are endeavoring to raise a fund to buy the poor some meat and drink, and means of warmth. We choose this time because it is a time, of all others, when want is keenly felt, and abundance rejoices. What shall I put you down for? [*He opens a small notebook, prepared to record* SCROOGE's *donation.*]

SCROOGE. Nothing.

SECOND PORTLY GENTLEMAN. You wish to be anonymous?

SCROOGE. I wish to be left alone. Since you ask me what I wish, gentlemen, that is my answer. I don't make myself merry at Christmas, and I can't afford to make idle people merry. I help support the establishments I have mentioned—they cost enough, and those who are badly off must go there.

FIRST PORTLY GENTLEMAN. Many can't go there. And many would rather die.

SCROOGE. If they would rather die, they had better do it, and decrease the surplus population. Besides—I don't know that.

FIRST PORTLY GENTLEMAN. But you might know it.

SCROOGE. It's not my business. It's enough for a man to understand his own business, and not interfere with other people's. Mine occupies me constantly.

SECOND PORTLY GENTLEMAN. But, Mister Scrooge—

SCROOGE. [*Showing them to the door.*] Good afternoon.

SECOND PORTLY GENTLEMAN. I can only say, Mister Scrooge, that I hope you will consider the spirit of the day, and think again. Here is my card.

SCROOGE. [*Taking the card and tearing it slowly.*] Bah. Humbug.

[*The two* PORTLY GENTLEMEN *exit.* SCROOGE *feeds the torn card to the fire.* CHILDREN *singing Christmas carols appear.* SCROOGE *turns and grabs a poker.*[6] *The* CHILDREN, *frightened, stop their singing and run away.* SCROOGE *comes back.*]

SCROOGE. Beggars. Pests.

[*A bell rings. It is five o'clock.* SCROOGE *checks his watch, and* CRATCHIT *bolts from his desk. He approaches* SCROOGE, *who is likewise making ready to leave.*]

SCROOGE. You'll be wanting all day tomorrow, I suppose?

CRATCHIT. If quite convenient, sir.

SCROOGE. [*Taking some coins from a money bag, and paying him.*] It's not convenient, and it's not fair. If I was to stop your wages half-a-crown,[7] you'd think yourself ill-used, I'll be bound. And yet, you don't think me ill-used when I pay a day's wages for no work.

CRATCHIT. It's only once a year, Mister Scrooge.

SCROOGE. A poor excuse for picking a man's pocket every twenty-fifth of December. But I suppose you must have the whole day. Be here all the earlier next morning.

CRATCHIT. Yes, sir. Thank you, Mister Scrooge. [*He moves to exit, then turns back.*] And a merry Christmas, Mister Scrooge. [*He exits.*]

SCROOGE. "A merry Christmas, Mister Scrooge." Bah. Humbug.

---

6. **poker:** iron bar used for stirring a fire.
7. **half-a-crown:** British coin, no longer used, worth about two shillings. Half-a-crown in Dickens' time would be worth several dollars today.

NARRATOR. Scrooge took his melancholy dinner in his usual melancholy tavern; and, having read all the newspapers, and beguiled the rest of the evening with his banker's book, went home to bed.

[SCROOGE *walks up to the front door of his house.*]

NARRATOR. Now, it is a fact that there was nothing at all particular about the knocker on his door, except that it was very large. It is also a fact that Scrooge had seen it, night and morning, during his whole residence in that place; also that Scrooge had as little of what is called fancy about him as any man in the City of London. Let it also be borne in mind that Scrooge had not bestowed one thought on Marley since the last mention of his dead partner that afternoon.

[SCROOGE *moves toward the door, with a candle in his hand.*]

And then, let any man explain, if he can, how it happened that Scrooge, having his key in the lock of the door, saw in the knocker, not a knocker, but—

SCROOGE. —Marley's face!

[*He quickly backs away in shock; the candle goes out. After a pause* SCROOGE *relights the candle and examines the inside of the door—half expecting to be terrified by the sight of* MARLEY'*s head. But there is nothing. He slides two bolts on the door shut.*]

Humbug.

[*Low sound of wind. It quickly fades.*]

Humbug.

[*He sits on a stool by the fire and takes a pan of gruel*[8] *and a spoon from near the*

---

8. **gruel** [grōō′əl]: thin porridge or broth.

fireplace and eats. Suddenly the bells on the wall begin to clang. A loud gong is heard, and the sounds die as quickly as they began.]

Humbug. It's nothing! It's the wind!

[SCROOGE *sits rigidly on his stool. Heavy steps are heard. Chains are being dragged up the stairs.*]

It's humbug still! I won't believe it!

[*A door swings open. There is a crash of thunder, and a bright, eerie light illuminates the doorway.* MARLEY'S GHOST—*in a ragged suit, wrapped in chains—enters.*]

SCROOGE. How now? What do you want with me?

MARLEY. Much.

SCROOGE. Who are you?

MARLEY. Ask me who I was.

SCROOGE. Who *were* you, then?

MARLEY. In life, I was your partner, Jacob Marley.

SCROOGE. Can you sit down?

MARLEY. I can.

SCROOGE. Do it, then.

MARLEY. [*Sits in a chair opposite* SCROOGE.] You don't believe in me.

SCROOGE. I don't.

MARLEY. What evidence would you have of my reality beyond that of your senses?

SCROOGE. I don't know.

MARLEY. Why do you doubt your senses?

SCROOGE. Because a little thing affects them. A slight disorder of the stomach makes them

cheats.[9] You may be an undigested bit of beef, a blot of mustard, a crumb of cheese, a fragment of underdone potato. There's more of gravy than of grave about you, whatever you are. Do you see this toothpick? [*Holding one.*]

MARLEY. I do.

SCROOGE. You are not looking at it.

MARLEY. I see it, notwithstanding.

SCROOGE. I have but to swallow this, and be for the rest of my days persecuted by a legion of goblins, all of my own creation. Humbug, I tell you. Humbug!

[MARLEY *raises a frightful cry—a loud, melancholy wail—which sends* SCROOGE *scurrying behind his stool at the fireplace.*]

SCROOGE. Mercy! Dreadful apparition, why do you trouble me?

MARLEY. Man of worldly mind! Do you believe in me, or not?

SCROOGE. I do, I must. But why do you walk the earth, and why do you come to me?

MARLEY. It is required of every man that the spirit within him should walk abroad among his fellow man, and travel far and wide. If that spirit goes not forth in life, it is condemned to do so after death. It is doomed to wander through the world, and witness what it cannot share but might have shared on earth, and turned to happiness.

SCROOGE. You are wrapped in chains. Tell me why?

MARLEY. I wear the chain I forged in life. I made it, link by link, and yard by yard. I girded it on of my own free will, and of my own free will I wore it. Is its pattern strange to you?

---

9. **cheats:** liars or tricksters.

SCROOGE. It is.

MARLEY. Or would you know the weight and length of the strong coil you bear yourself? It was full as heavy and as long as this, seven Christmas Eves ago. You have labored on it since. It is a ponderous chain!

SCROOGE. Old Jacob Marley, tell me more. Speak comfort to me!

MARLEY. I have none to give. A very little more is all that is permitted me. I cannot rest, I cannot stay, I cannot linger anywhere. My spirit never walked beyond our counting house. In life, my spirit never roved beyond the narrow limits of our money-changing hole. Weary journeys lie before me.

SCROOGE. You must have been very slow about it, Jacob.

MARLEY. Slow?

SCROOGE. Seven years dead, and traveling all the time.

MARLEY. The whole time, on the wings of the wind. No rest, no peace, incessant torture of remorse. [*Again he sends up a wail, and rattles his chains.*]

SCROOGE. But you were always a good man of business, Jacob.

MARLEY. Business! Mankind was my business! The common welfare was my business! Charity, mercy, forbearance were all my business. The dealings of my trade were but a drop in the comprehensive ocean of my business!

SCROOGE. Don't be hard on me, Jacob!

MARLEY. My time is nearly gone. How it is that I appear before you in a shape that you can see, I may not tell. I am here tonight to warn you that you have yet a chance of escaping my fate.

SCROOGE. You were always a good friend to me, Jacob. Thank'ee!

MARLEY. You will be haunted by three Spirits.

SCROOGE. Is that the chance you mentioned, Jacob?

MARLEY. It is.

SCROOGE. I think I'd rather not.

MARLEY. Without their visits, you cannot hope to shun the path I tread. [*He crosses to a window.*] Look you, down upon the people of this planet, your fellow creatures crawling, senses shut, through life. Many of them are known to you. You see them on the streets, in the shops, on the Exchanges.[10] They go about their business, seldom lifting their eyes to the crying children, to the inhuman misery that surrounds them. But what is this misery to what they will know when, gone from this life, they seek to interfere for good in human affairs, and discover that they have lost the power forever? [*Turning to* SCROOGE.] Expect the first Spirit tomorrow, when the bell tolls one.

SCROOGE. Couldn't I take 'em all at once and have it over, Jacob?

MARLEY. Expect the second on the next night at the same hour. The third upon the next night when the last stroke of twelve has ceased to vibrate. Look to see me no more. And, for your own sake, look that you remember what has passed between us!

[*He exits. The door slams shut, and the bolts shoot across. A pause.* SCROOGE *tries the door. It is locked tight. The room is silent.*]

SCROOGE. Bah . . . [*He hasn't the heart to*

---

10. **Exchanges:** places where stocks, bonds, and other securities are bought and sold.

squeeze out a "Humbug." He hurries to bed, hops in, and blows out the light. A peep.] Humbug.

[*The clock chimes one.*]

One! It was past two when I went to bed. An icicle must have gotten into the works.

[*He lights a candle. The room is suddenly lit up, and he sees the* GHOST OF CHRISTMAS PAST.]

SCROOGE. Are you the Spirit, sir, whose coming was foretold me?

CHRISTMAS PAST. [*Gentle, childlike, and somehow far away.*] I am.

SCROOGE. Who and what are you?

CHRISTMAS PAST. I am the Ghost of Christmas Past.

SCROOGE. Long past?

CHRISTMAS PAST. No, your past.

SCROOGE. What business brings you?

CHRISTMAS PAST. Your welfare.

SCROOGE. I'm much obliged, but I can't help thinking that a night of unbroken rest would be more conducive to that end.

CHRISTMAS PAST. Your reclamation,[11] then. Rise, and walk with me.

SCROOGE. [*Getting out of bed, and approaching the* GHOST.] I? But I am mortal, and likely to fall.

CHRISTMAS PAST. Bear but a touch of my hand, and you shall be upheld in more than this!

---

11. **reclamation** [rek′ lə mā′shən]: salvation.

[*He extends his hand, which* SCROOGE *grabs onto, and whisks him up to a different level of the stage.*]

Is this place familiar to you?

[YOUNG EBENEZER *enters with a book in his hand. He takes a stool to the middle of the second level and sits. He opens the book and reads.*]

SCROOGE. Good heavens! I was at school in this place! I was a boy here!

CHRISTMAS PAST. These are but shadows of the things that have been. They have no consciousness of us.

[YOUNG EBENEZER *lifts his eyes from the book and sighs.*]

CHRISTMAS PAST. The school is not quite deserted. A solitary child, neglected by his friends, is left there still.

[YOUNG EBENEZER *begins to hum.*]

SCROOGE. [*Recognizing him and placing a hand on his shoulder.*] Poor boy.

[FAN, YOUNG EBENEZER's *sister, enters. She doesn't see* SCROOGE; *she runs to* YOUNG EBENEZER. *He is ecstatic to see her.*]

FAN. Ebenezer! Dear, dear brother! I have come to take you home!

SCROOGE. Fan!

YOUNG EBENEZER. Home, Fan?

FAN. Yes, home, for good and all. Father is so much kinder than he used to be. He spoke so gently to me one night that I wasn't afraid to ask him once more if you might come home. And he said yes, you should. He sent me in a coach to bring you.

YOUNG EBENEZER. This *is* a merry Christmas, Fan!

FAN. We're to be together all Christmas, and have the merriest time in the world. Let's get your trunk! [*They exit.*]

CHRISTMAS PAST. Always a delicate creature, whom a breath might have withered.

SCROOGE. [*Looking after them.*] But she had a large heart.

CHRISTMAS PAST. So she had. She died a woman, and had, as I think, children.

SCROOGE. One child.

CHRISTMAS PAST. True. Your nephew.

SCROOGE. I wish . . .

CHRISTMAS PAST. What is the matter?

SCROOGE. Nothing, nothing. There were some children singing a Christmas carol at my door last night. I should like to have given them something, that's all. [*The lights go full.*]

CHRISTMAS PAST. Do you know this place?

SCROOGE. [*Something about this place jogs his memory.*] Know it? I was apprenticed[12] here!

[FEZZIWIG, *a warehouse owner to whom* SCROOGE *was apprenticed long ago, bustles in.*]

FEZZIWIG. Yo ho, there! Ebenezer! Dick!

SCROOGE. Why, it's old Fezziwig! Bless his heart, it's Fezziwig, alive again!

[YOUNG SCROOGE *appears, now about twenty-one, as cheerful as old* SCROOGE *is dour. With him is* DICK WILKINS, *also an apprentice, and also about twenty-one.*]

FEZZIWIG. No more work tonight. Christmas Eve, Dick! Christmas, Ebenezer! Let's have

---

12. **was apprenticed:** worked for several years for little or no wages in order to learn a trade.

the place cleared away before a man can say "Jack Robinson!"

[DICK *and* EBENEZER *set to work, clearing away tables and chairs. They clear away a space large enough to permit dancing, singing as they go.*]

SCROOGE. Dick Wilkins, to be sure! Bless me, yes. He was very much attached to me was Dick. Poor Dick. Dear, dear . . .

FEZZIWIG. Hilli-ho! Clear away, my lads, and let's have lots of room here! Hilli-ho, Dick! Ebenezer!

[*As they work, in comes* BELLE FEZZIWIG, SCROOGE'*s fiancée;* MRS. FEZZIWIG; *and the* LITTLE FEZZIWIGS. *There is more singing.*]

FEZZIWIG. [*Quieting the crowd.*] My dears, it's Christmas Eve. A toast to that glorious occasion! May tomorrow, and the whole of the new year find us merry, content, and above all, filled with the happy good will of the season toward all our fellows!

EVERYONE. Bravo! To Christmas!

CHRISTMAS PAST. [*As* GUESTS *gather around a trunk, for the opening of some gifts for the children.*] A small matter, to make these silly folk so full of gratitude.

SCROOGE. Small?

CHRISTMAS PAST. Why, is it not? He has spent but a few pounds of your mortal money—three or four, perhaps. Is that so much that he deserves praise?

SCROOGE. It isn't that at all, Spirit. He had the power to render us happy or unhappy; to make our service light or burdensome. The happiness he gave was quite as great as if it had cost a fortune. . . . [*He is suddenly quiet.*]

CHRISTMAS PAST. What is the matter?

SCROOGE. Nothing particular.

CHRISTMAS PAST. Something, I think.

SCROOGE. No, no. I should like to be able to say a word or two to my clerk just now. That's all.

[*A cheer from the crowd as a toy drum is unwrapped, and a* LITTLE FEZZIWIG *tries it out.*]

FEZZIWIG. My dears, the hour grows late. Before we depart, however, Mrs. Fezziwig and I have an announcement.

SCROOGE. Spirit, show me no more.

FEZZIWIG. As you know, Mrs. Fezziwig and I have labored these many years to rear a very particular child. The fruits of our labor, I am happy to say, are most satisfactory—more than satisfactory. They are summed up in one beautiful word—Belle. [*Applause.*] Now at the very dawn, the very ripeness of her youth and beauty, she has surrendered to the wiles of one of you in this very room. One to whom I've furnished shelter, food, and a warm bed.

DICK WILKINS. A sore back and aching eyes, too!

FEZZIWIG. Yes, I'll not deny he's the hardest-working apprentice ever to balance a book or close an account. Come spring, our lovely Belle shall wed that most industrious of young men, Mister Ebenezer Scrooge! [*Applause.*]

DICK WILKINS. A dance! A dance from the couple!

[*The lights are dimmed, and* YOUNG SCROOGE *and* BELLE *embrace, and dance a slow waltz.*]

SCROOGE. [*Scarcely able to watch.*] Spirit, take me home.

[*As the short dance ends,* YOUNG SCROOGE *and* BELLE *drift apart,* YOUNG SCROOGE *to* SCROOGE's *desk. He sits, and becomes absorbed in his work.* BELLE *approaches him. Some time has passed since the dance.*]

BELLE. It matters little to you; very little. Another idol has displaced me. If it can cheer and comfort you in times to come, as I would have tried to do, I have no just cause to grieve.

YOUNG SCROOGE. [*Annoyed at this distraction.*] What idol has displaced you?

BELLE. A golden one.

YOUNG SCROOGE. This is the even-handed dealing of the world. There is nothing on which it is so hard as poverty; and there is nothing it professes to condemn so severely as the pursuit of wealth.

BELLE. You fear the world too much. All your other hopes have merged into the hope of being beyond the world's reproach. I have seen your nobler aspirations fall off, one by one, until one passion, gain, engrosses you. Have I not?

YOUNG SCROOGE. [*Checking his watch.*] What then? Even if I have grown so much wiser, what then? I am not changed toward you. [*A pause.*] Am I?

BELLE. Our contract is an old one. It was made when we were both poor and content to be so, until in good time we could improve our fortunes. You are changed. When it was made, you were another man.

YOUNG SCROOGE. I was a boy.

BELLE. Your own feeling tells you that you are not what you were. I am. How often I have thought of this does not matter. It is enough that I *have* thought of it, and can release you.

YOUNG SCROOGE. Have I ever sought release?

BELLE. In words, no. Never.

YOUNG SCROOGE. In what, then?

BELLE. In a changed nature, an altered spirit. In everything that made my love of any worth or value in your sight. If we had never had our past, would you seek me out and try to win me now?

YOUNG SCROOGE. You think not.

BELLE. I would think otherwise if I could. But if you were free today, could I believe you would choose a girl with so small a dowry?[13] You, who now weigh everything by gain? Or, if you did choose her, do I not know that your regret would surely follow? I do. And I release you.

13. **dowry:** money or property that a bride brings to her husband.

[*She takes a ring from her finger and presses it into* YOUNG SCROOGE's *hand.*]

With a full heart, for the love of him you once were. May you be happy in the life you have chosen.

[*She exits. A pause.* YOUNG SCROOGE *stands, but does not move.*]

SCROOGE. [*Pleading.*] Go to her, you fool!

[*As* YOUNG SCROOGE *stands there.*]

You fool!

[YOUNG SCROOGE *wraps the ring in a piece of paper and shuts it up in a drawer in the desk.*]

Spirit, show me no more. Why do you delight to torture me?

CHRISTMAS PAST. I told you these were shadows of things that have been. That they are what they are, do not blame me.

SCROOGE. Leave me, take me back! Haunt me no longer!

CHRISTMAS PAST. As you wish.

[*With a wave of his hand, he vanishes, and* SCROOGE *is left alone in the darkness.*]

STUDY QUESTIONS

Recalling

1. In what terms does the Narrator describe Scrooge at the beginning of the play?
2. What is Scrooge's opinion of Christmas? What is Fred's?
3. What is Scrooge's answer to the gentlemen collecting for charity? How does he respond to the carolers?
4. What explanation does Marley's ghost give for his visit to Scrooge? Who else does he say will visit Scrooge?
5. Where does the Ghost of Christmas Past first take Scrooge? Where does he take him next? What does Scrooge see?

6. What reason does Belle give for breaking her engagement to Young Scrooge?

Interpreting

7. Show how Scrooge's treatment of his nephew, Cratchit, the portly gentlemen, and the carolers supports the Narrator's and Marley's statements about him.
8. Explain how old Scrooge is different from his earlier selves, Young Ebenezer and Young Scrooge. How does Young Scrooge himself change?
9. Point to two or three signs of change in old Scrooge by the end of Act I.

READING AND LITERARY FOCUS

Staging

Staging refers to the scenery, lighting, sounds, costumes, and acting that bring a playwright's words to life on stage in front of an audience. When we read a play instead of seeing it in a theater, we enjoy the work more if we try to imagine how the play might come alive through staging.

We can try to envision what staging might add to our enjoyment of *A Christmas Carol*. For example, if we think about how Scrooge's visit to the Fezziwigs' party might be staged, we might imagine a sad old man standing in a cold blue light just to the side of a glowing room, watching his younger self waltz happily with the girl he once loved. Envisioning how this scene might be staged gives us a fuller, more vivid understanding of Scrooge's regret over his wasted life.

Thinking About Staging

■ If you were put in charge of staging the entrance of Marley's ghost, what moment on stage would you want to startle the audience most? What could you do to make that moment even more exciting? For example, what kinds of sound effects would you use? What would Marley's ghost look like?

VOCABULARY

Word Origins

Dickens' *Christmas Carol* created a new noun: A *Scrooge* has come to refer to anyone who is miserly or bad-tempered. Many other words in our language were originally proper names of people—many of them real people (as opposed to fictional characters like Scrooge). Using a dictionary, identify the person to whom the following words originally referred, and explain what each word means now.

1. boycott	6. mackintosh
2. braille	7. sandwich
3. derby	8. shrapnel
4. derrick	9. silhouette
5. guillotine	10. watt

CHALLENGE

Diorama

■ A **diorama** is a three-dimensional scene, either large or small in scale, made out of materials such as wood or cardboard. Make a miniature diorama depicting a scene from Act I of *A Christmas Carol*. Remove the cover from a shoebox, and cut away one of the four sides. Next paint or draw scenery on the remaining three sides and bottom. You may then paste, tape, or staple stand-up characters to the bottom. Decide on the furniture and other elements of the set that you want to portray in your diorama. Think also about how you want your characters to look and what they should wear.

ACT II

[SCROOGE's *bedroom. Immediately afterward.*]

NARRATOR. We left Ebenezer Scrooge in bed, vainly trying to recall and mend his unpleasant past, and wondering what variety of spirits await him in the present and future. Now, being prepared for almost anything, he was by no means prepared for nothing. [*A pause.*] The bell tolled one again. And no shape appeared. Five minutes. [*Pause.*] Ten minutes. [*Pause.*] A quarter of an hour went by. [*Pause.*] Yet nothing came.

[*The light in the fireplace begins to glow brightly. Deep echoing laughter grows louder and louder. When it dies out, a booming voice is heard from behind a quilt.*]

VOICE. Enter, Ebenezer Scrooge! [SCROOGE *gets out of bed, as the quilt drops away, revealing the* GHOST OF CHRISTMAS PRESENT. *His head is crowned by a wreath.*] Come in and know me better, man! [SCROOGE *approaches meekly.*] I am the Ghost of Christmas Present. Look upon me. You have never seen the like of me before!

SCROOGE. Never.

CHRISTMAS PRESENT. You have never walked forth with the younger members of my family, my brothers born in these later years?

SCROOGE. I'm afraid I have not. Have you many brothers, Spirit?

CHRISTMAS PRESENT. More than eighteen hundred.

SCROOGE. A tremendous family to provide for.

CHRISTMAS PRESENT. Nor have I ever seen the likes of *you.* You're so sour, the blood's gone bad in your veins.

SCROOGE. Spirit, conduct me where you will. I went forth last night on compulsion, and I learned a lesson which is working still. Tonight, if you have aught[1] to teach me, let me profit by it.

CHRISTMAS PRESENT. Profit? Touch my robe!

[SCROOGE *does so. Six chimes of a mantle clock.* MRS. CRATCHIT, PETER CRATCHIT, *and* BELINDA CRATCHIT *enter.* MRS. CRATCHIT *covers a table with a tablecloth, and* BELINDA *sets two candlesticks on it.*]

MRS. CRATCHIT. Whatever has gotten your precious father, then? And your brother, Tiny Tim? And Martha wasn't as late last Christmas by half-an-hour. [MARTHA *enters.*]

MARTHA. Here's Martha, mother!

BELINDA. Here's Martha! There's such a goose, Martha!

MRS. CRATCHIT. Why, bless you, my dear, how late you are. They're keeping you longer and longer at the milliner's.[2] [BELINDA *goes to the door to keep watch for* CRATCHIT *and* TINY TIM.]

MARTHA. We had a tremendous deal of work to finish up last night, and had to clear away this morning.

MRS. CRATCHIT. Working on Christmas Eve! Well, never mind so long as you're here. Sit down by the fire, my dear, and have a warm.

BELINDA. Here's father coming! Hide, Martha, hide!

[*Quickly they hide beneath the table.* CRATCHIT *enters, with* TINY TIM *on his shoulder.* TIM *is carrying a crutch.*]

---

1. **aught** [ôt]: anything.
2. **milliner's:** shop where hats are made or sold.

CRATCHIT. Merry Christmas, my dears! [*Putting* TIM *into* PETER's *arms in order that he may take off his coat.*] Merry Christmas, Peter.

PETER. Merry Christmas, father!

CRATCHIT. [*Noticing* MARTHA's *absence.*] Why, where's our Martha?

MRS. CRATCHIT. Not coming.

CRATCHIT. Not coming? Not coming upon Christmas Day?

MRS. CRATCHIT. She had so much work at the milliner's. They sent someone 'round to tell the families that all the girls would be staying.

CRATCHIT. [*Very much let down.*] Oh. Well, if she feels she must stay, we'll abide by her good judgment. But it hardly seems fair . . . to work on Christmas Day.

[*A giggle is heard underneath the table.* CRATCHIT *goes to the table, lifts the tablecloth, and* MARTHA *embraces him.*]

MARTHA. I'm here, father. I can't stand to see you disappointed, even for a joke!

CRATCHIT. Well then, we're all together, after all! Then it *will* be a merry Christmas.

MRS. CRATCHIT. Peter, take Tim off to the wash house. The goose will be ready before we know it.

PETER. [*Who still has* TIM *on his shoulder.*] Right, ma'am. All right, Timothy. This way. [*They exit.*]

MRS. CRATCHIT. And tend to the pudding, Belinda. It mustn't be overdone.

BELINDA. [*Alarmed.*] What if it were? [*She and* MARTHA *exit, determined to save the pudding.*]

MRS. CRATCHIT. [*To* BOB. *They cross to the*

fireplace and sit. MRS. CRATCHIT *takes the bowl of fruit, and peels some apples.*] And how did Tim behave at church?

CRATCHIT. As good as gold—and better. Somehow, he gets thoughtful, sitting by himself so much, and he thinks the strangest things you ever heard. He told me, coming home, that he hoped the people saw him in church, because he was a cripple, and it might be pleasant for them to remember upon Christmas Day who made lame beggars walk and blind men see. [*A pause.*] Then, I trotted us 'round to the shop windows, where he gazed for the longest time at the toys. Sensing his spirits beginning to droop, I galloped straight away to Cornhill Street, where, in honor of its being Christmas, we went down the slide twenty times.

[TINY TIM *enters, followed by* MARTHA.]

TINY TIM. Twenty-five!

CRATCHIT. [*Taking* TIM *on his lap.*] Right you are, Tim. Twenty-five! [*A pause.*] And all along the way, any number of acquaintances stopped us to remark that Tim is looking stronger and heartier every day. . . . [*Another pause.*]

MARTHA. You haven't made the punch yet, father. It can't be Christmas without your special punch.

CRATCHIT. [*Brightening.*] That's a fact. What could I be thinking to forget that? [*Taking a decanter³ from the mantle, he crosses to the table, where* MARTHA *has just placed some mugs and a pitcher.*] Here's Christmas dinner practically on the table, and not a drop of punch in evidence. Easily remedied! [*He adds some of the decanter's contents to the pitcher and stirs.*]

PETER. [*Entering with* BELINDA.] Here we are, perfectly cleaned, and wonderfully starved.

---

3. **decanter:** decorative bottle.

MRS. CRATCHIT. Good. The goose is all but calling to be let out of the oven. Martha, help your father with the punch.

[*She exits.* BELINDA *follows her to the door to stand guard.*]

CRATCHIT. No need, no need. All done, and in a trice.[4]

[MARTHA *helps him distribute mugs around the table.*]

PETER. Remarkable time, father.

CRATCHIT. Let no man say that old Bob Cratchit can't mix his Christmas punch with the swiftest of 'em.

BELINDA. Here's the goose!

[*She exits.* MRS. CRATCHIT *enters proudly bearing the roast goose on its tray.* BELINDA *enters again, carrying the pudding. "Ooh"'s and "ah"'s from the family; universal admiration for both the bird and pudding.*]

PETER. Bravo! A glorious bird! [*They gather around the table.*]

CRATCHIT. Never has there been such a bird! A truly sumptuous-looking fowl, Mrs. Cratchit.

SCROOGE. [*To* CHRISTMAS PRESENT.] So small a goose for so large a family.

CRATCHIT. And a pudding! Have you ever seen such a one? I ask you, Martha.

MARTHA. Never. The girls at the shop would be positively ashamed to display theirs anywhere in the vicinity.

BELINDA. Hear, hear!

TINY TIM. They'd not be seen.

CRATCHIT. And you, Master Peter? Have you

ever set eyes upon the mortal pudding which could equal this wonder?

PETER. In all my years as a Christmas pudding observer, I've never seen a finer.

CRATCHIT. And that's a high compliment indeed. Tell me a higher one, and I'll use it. Mrs. Cratchit, as for myself, I think that it is your greatest success since our marriage.

MRS. CRATCHIT. Well, it's a great weight off my mind. I don't mind confessing I had my doubts about the quantity of flour.

MARTHA. Never fear, mother. It's perfect.

CRATCHIT. [*Tapping his mug with a spoon.*] Now, before plunging into this splendid feast, I'd like to propose a health. [*He raises his mug; the others do the same.*] A merry Christmas to us all, my dears. God bless us.

FAMILY. God bless us!

TINY TIM. God bless us, every one.

SCROOGE. [*With an interest he's never felt before.*] Spirit, tell me if Tiny Tim will live.

CHRISTMAS PRESENT. I see a vacant seat in the poor chimney corner, and a crutch without an owner, carefully preserved. If these shadows remain unaltered by the future, the child will die.

SCROOGE. Kind Spirit, say he will be spared.

CHRISTMAS PRESENT. If these shadows remain unaltered by the future, none other of my race will find him here. [*Turning on* SCROOGE.] What of it? If he be like to die, he had better do it, and decrease the surplus population. [SCROOGE *turns away, stung by his own words.*] Man, if man you be, forbear that wicked cant[5] until you have discovered what the surplus is, and where it is. Will you decide

---

4. **trice:** very short time.

---

5. **cant:** insincere talk.

what men shall live and what men shall die? It might be that, in the sight of Heaven, you are less fit to live than millions like this poor man's child.

SCROOGE. It may be, Spirit. It may be.

CRATCHIT. A toast! A toast, everyone. Mister Scrooge! I give you Mister Scrooge, the founder of the feast.

[*A pall descends upon the proceedings, and the family put their mugs down.*]

MRS. CRATCHIT. The founder of the feast indeed! I wish I had him here. I'd give him a piece of my mind to feast upon, and I hope he'd have good appetite for it.

CRATCHIT. My dear, the children. Christmas Day.

MRS. CRATCHIT. It should be Christmas Day I'm sure, on which we drink the health of such an odious, stingy, hard, unfeeling man as Mister Scrooge. You know he is, Robert. Nobody knows it better than you do.

CRATCHIT. My dear, Christmas Day. [*A pause.*]

MRS. CRATCHIT. I'll drink his health for your sake and the day's. Not for his. A merry Christmas and a happy New Year to him. He'll be very merry and very happy, I have no doubt. [*Raising her mug.*] Mister Scrooge.

FAMILY. [*With no enthusiasm whatsoever.*] Mister Scrooge. [*They drink. A pause.*]

TINY TIM. I wouldn't give tuppence[6] for Mister Scrooge.

BELINDA. Neither would I.

CRATCHIT. Have an open heart, I beg you. It's Christmas, after all. And I think that, in many

---

6. **tuppence** [tup'əns]: two pence, or British pennies.

ways, Mister Scrooge is a great deal less fortunate than we are.

PETER. Impossible.

CRATCHIT. Not at all. Compare our condition with that of Mister Scrooge. He has no family to gather 'round him, no warmth, no cheer. He has none but his own voice to listen to, and none to answer. I believe he is a great deal less fortunate than we.

CHRISTMAS PRESENT. A clerk who makes fifteen shillings a week, and he counts himself more fortunate than you?

CRATCHIT. Remembering those who are less fortunate, let us say grace. [*The family takes hands.*] Kind Father, bless this humble portion. Bless our home, bless our family, bless our happiness. May we share them all with any who should ask, in Your name. Amen.

[*The lights dim and the family vanishes.* SCROOGE *moves toward the family as the lights go out. The* GHOST OF CHRISTMAS PRESENT *stops him.*]

CHRISTMAS PRESENT. You cannot move within that circle.

SCROOGE. Why not, Spirit?

CHRISTMAS PRESENT. Did you not hear the clerk take the measure of his employer? You are drifting alone, outside, and cannot get in. You have no circle.

SCROOGE. There was a time, Spirit, when I had.

CHRISTMAS PRESENT. How many years ago? That kind circle has long since withered, and you have cast it from your heart.

SCROOGE. I deny it, Spirit, I deny it! If any kindness has withered in me, it has done so of its own accord. I had nothing to do with it. If kindness wishes to wither, it withers.

CHRISTMAS PRESENT. Have you not seen, nor heard? You unrepentant little man. You have a long journey to make, and but a short time in which to make it. Let us see another house in this teeming city.

[*With a wave of his hand, the lights come up, and we are in* FRED'*s parlor. Also here are* MRS. FRED, *her* SISTER, *and* TOPPER, *a young friend of theirs.* FRED *has just given them each a long carrot, and they are seated around him, ready for some sort of game.*]

FRED. Everyone have theirs? Good. Now, place it on the end of your nose, like this. [*He places the fat end of the carrot on the tip of his nose. The others do the same.*] Ready? Now repeat after me: [*He assumes a* SCROOGE-*like voice.*] " . . . should be boiled in his own pudding . . ."

THE OTHERS. [*Also intoning as they think* SCROOGE *might.*] " . . . should be boiled in his own pudding . . ."

FRED. " . . . and be buried with a stake of holly through his heart. He should!"

THE OTHERS. " . . . and be buried with a stake of holly through his heart. He should!"

[*They laugh, as* FRED *collects the carrots from them, and places them on the tray next to the punch bowl.*]

FRED. And as I live, he said that Christmas was a humbug! He believed it, too.

MRS. FRED. More shame for him, Fred.

FRED. He's a comical old fellow, that's the truth—though not as pleasant as he might be. However, his offenses carry their own punishment, and I'll have nothing to say against him.

MRS. FRED. I'm sure he's very rich. At least you always tell me so.

FRED. What of that, my dear? His wealth is of no use to him. He doesn't do any good with it. He doesn't make himself comfortable with it. And he hasn't the satisfaction of thinking he is ever going to benefit *us* with it.

[*They laugh at the thought of this unlikely occurrence.*]

MRS. FRED. I have no patience with him.

FRED. Oh, I have. I'm sorry for him. I couldn't be angry with him if I tried. Who suffers by his ill whims? Himself, always. Here he takes it into his head to dislike us and he won't come to dine with us. What's the consequence? [*Tossing it off.*] He doesn't lose much of a dinner.

MRS. FRED. Indeed, I think he loses a very good dinner!

MRS. FRED'S SISTER. He does.

FRED. Well, I'm glad to hear it, because I haven't any faith in these young housekeepers. What do you say, Topper?

TOPPER. [*A young chap who very much has his eye on* MRS. FRED'S SISTER—*and everyone knows it.*] I am a bachelor, and a bachelor is a wretched outcast who has no right to express an opinion on the subject. [*And he promptly squeezes* MRS. FRED'S SISTER, *who responds with a giggle.*]

CHRISTMAS PRESENT. A game is in order, I think.

MRS. FRED'S SISTER. A game! Blindman!

TOPPER. [*Taking it up immediately.*] Blindman's buff![7] An excellent idea!

FRED. I volunteer—

---

7. **blindman's buff:** group game in which a player wearing a blindfold tries to catch and identify another player; also known as *blindman's bluff*.

TOPPER. No, no. Quite all right, Freddy, *I* volunteer. In fact, I insist. [MRS. FRED *nods her head in agreement.*]

FRED. Oh. Your every wish, my dear Topper. [*Searching his pockets.*] Now, where is that blasted handkerchief? Ah, here it is. [*He blindfolds* TOPPER.] Any last requests?

TOPPER. [*Looking in* MRS. FRED'S SISTER's *direction.*] Only one. [*She giggles.*]

FRED. Here we go. One . . . [*He spins* TOPPER *around.*] Two . . . [*Spinning him around again.*] Three . . .

[*Spinning him for a final time, and with a shove, sending him in the direction of* MRS. FRED'S SISTER. FRED, MRS. FRED, *and* TOPPER *try their best to corner* MRS. FRED'S SISTER *for* TOPPER. FRED *fixed the handkerchief so that* TOPPER *can see through it. As for* SCROOGE, *his icy spirit melts bit by bit. He laughs, shouts warnings, and is entirely caught up in the whole thing. The game finally ends with* TOPPER *wrapping his arms around* MRS. FRED'S SISTER.]

TOPPER. Who could this be? [*He removes the handkerchief.*] Well, well, well. I really had no idea. I thought it was dear old Mrs. Fred.

SCROOGE. He knew who it was all along!

FRED. Another game!

MRS. FRED. Another? Let's sit down. [*She does.*]

FRED. A word game, then.

CHRISTMAS PRESENT. My time grows short.

SCROOGE. But there's another game, Spirit. One more game.

CHRISTMAS PRESENT. If you wish. You may not find this one as amusing.

FRED. [*As the others sit around him.*] This

game is called "Yes and No." I think of something, and you have to guess what it is by asking me questions which I can answer either "yes" or "no." [*A pause, as he thinks of a subject.*] All right. I've got it.

TOPPER. What is it? [*They laugh.*]

MRS. FRED. Is it a living thing?

FRED. Yes.

TOPPER. Is it an animal?

FRED. Yes.

MRS. FRED'S SISTER. Is it a tame animal?

FRED. No. It is rather disagreeable.

MRS. FRED. Is it savage, then?

FRED. Yes, fierce.

TOPPER. Does it make a noise?

FRED. Yes.

MRS. FRED'S SISTER. Does it bark?

FRED. In my opinion, no. Though some may differ on that point.

MRS. FRED. Does it meow?

FRED. Definitely not.

SCROOGE. That rules out the cats!

TOPPER. Does it howl?

FRED. No, not its style.

MRS. FRED. Does it growl?

MRS. FRED'S SISTER. Or grunt?

FRED. Yes. I'd say it does both. [*A pause, as they puzzle this out.*]

SCROOGE. He's got 'em stumped! A brilliant boy, Fred!

MRS. FRED. Is it a bear?

FRED. No.

MRS. FRED'S SISTER. Does it live in the jungle?

FRED. No.

TOPPER. Does it live in the zoo?

FRED. No. At least *I* don't think of it as a zoo.

MRS. FRED'S SISTER. [*To* MRS. FRED.] What does that mean? *He* doesn't think of it as a zoo?

TOPPER. [*Catching on.*] It must be a city, then. Does it live in a city?

FRED. Yes.

SCROOGE. Clever boy! But not clever enough for my Fred. That boy's as sharp as a needle!

TOPPER. Is it London?

FRED. Yes.

MRS. FRED. Does it walk the streets?

FRED. Yes.

MRS. FRED'S SISTER. Does anyone lead it?

FRED. Not that I've ever known. Heavens, no.

SCROOGE. Not a dog or a horse, then. Is it a person?

TOPPER. Is it sold in a market?

FRED. No. But it's often found near the Exchange.

MRS. FRED'S SISTER. What sort of animal is found near the Exchange?

MRS. FRED. Is it a sociable creature?

FRED. Most unsociable.

TOPPER. Does it live among others of its kind?

FRED. It positively despises its kind.

MRS. FRED'S SISTER. [*Adding it up.*] It grunts and growls, lives in London, walks the streets

... is disagreeable and unsociable ... [*It suddenly strikes her. Like* FRED, *who can barely suppress it, she bursts into laughter.*]

SCROOGE. I know it! I know it!

MRS. FRED'S SISTER. I've found it out! I know what it is, Fred! I know what it is!

SCROOGE. [*Triumphantly, while* MRS. FRED'S SISTER *is still laughing helplessly.*] It's the tax collector!

MRS. FRED'S SISTER. It's your uncle Scroooooooge!

[SCROOGE *is struck speechless. The others dissolve into laughter and applause.*]

TOPPER. Well, if that's the case, then your reply to the question, "Is it a bear?" ought to have been "yes."

FRED. But he's not a bear.

TOPPER. No, but your negative answer was sufficient to divert our attention from him.

FRED. He's given us plenty of merriment, I'm sure, and it would be ungrateful not to drink his health. I say, "Uncle Scrooge!"

THE OTHERS. Uncle Scrooge! [*They drink.*]

CHRISTMAS PRESENT. [*To* SCROOGE.] You seem to be the source of much merriment.

SCROOGE. Yes, for others. [*Scrutinizing the* GHOST.] Your hair is gray, Spirit. Are spirits' lives so brief?

CHRISTMAS PRESENT. My life upon this globe is very short. It ends tonight.

SCROOGE. Tonight?

CHRISTMAS PRESENT. At midnight. The time grows near.

[*The party disappears, and we hear tolling bells. First, just one, then, two, tolling twelve; wind and thunder crashes.* SCROOGE *and* CHRISTMAS PRESENT *are alone.*]

SCROOGE. What place is this?

CHRISTMAS PRESENT. Children are buried here.

SCROOGE. Children? [*As the bells continue to toll.*]

CHRISTMAS PRESENT. It is the primary requirement for admittance that they be under the age of ten.

SCROOGE. Of what did these children die?

CHRISTMAS PRESENT. Of too cruel a contact with the world. Of cold. Of disease. Of poverty. Of hunger. Of the ruthless neglect of comfortable thousands.

SCROOGE. They are buried so closely. They are almost one on top of the other.

CHRISTMAS PRESENT. A natural occurrence when their numbers are so great, and each child so small.

SCROOGE. But where did all these children come from, that they should end so soon?

CHRISTMAS PRESENT. Are there no prisons? Are there no workhouses? [THE GHOST *begins backing away until he is out of sight.*]

SCROOGE. [*Over loud sounds of wind and chains.*] Spirit! Don't leave me in this place!

[*With a tremendous rolling thunder clap, the window flies open, and there stands* THE GHOST OF CHRISTMAS YET TO COME. *A hood is pulled over his face, and one arm is outstretched accusingly at* SCROOGE. SCROOGE *falls to his knees.*]

SCROOGE. I am in the presence of the Ghost of Christmas Yet to Come?

[*The* GHOST *nods.*]

You are about to show me shadows of the things that have not yet happened, but will happen in the time before us. Is that so, Spirit?

[*Again, just a nod. But* SCROOGE *senses two eyes fixed upon him from deep within the shroud.*]

Ghost of the future, I fear you more than any other specter I have seen. But as I know your purpose is to do me good, and as I hope to live to be another man from what I was, I am prepared to bear you company.

[*A pause, as he waits for some kind of reply.*]

Will you not speak to me?

[*Again, nothing; just the arm, outstretched.*]

Lead on. The night is waning fast, and it is precious time for me, I know. Lead on!

[*A loud thundercrash in the darkness. Lights come up on the London Stock Exchange (although* SCROOGE *does not recognize it yet), and three* BUSINESSMEN, *each with a newspaper, enter. They are the* FAT MAN, *the* MAN WITH THE HANDKERCHIEF, *and the* THIN MAN. *They read their papers as they speak.*]

MAN WITH THE HANDKERCHIEF. Have you heard the news?

FAT MAN. Indeed I have.

THIN MAN. Do you know the details?

FAT MAN. No, I don't know much about it either way. I only know he's dead.

MAN WITH THE HANDKERCHIEF. When did he die?

FAT MAN. Last night, I believe.

THIN MAN. Why, whatever was the matter with him? I thought he'd never die. [*A most significant question.*] What has he done with his money? [*A pause.*]

FAT MAN. I haven't heard. Left it to his company, perhaps. He hasn't left it to me, that's all I know. [*They laugh.*] It's likely to be a very small funeral, for, upon my life, I don't know of anybody going to it. Suppose we make up a party, and volunteer? [*They exchange glances and laugh.*]

MAN WITH THE HANDKERCHIEF. I don't mind going—if a lunch is provided. I'll make the pilgrimage, but I must be fed. [*Another laugh.*]

THIN MAN. Well, I am the most disinterested among you, for I never attend funerals, and I never eat lunch. But I'll offer to go if anybody else will. Come to think of it, I'm not sure I wasn't his most particular friend: we used to stop and speak whenever we met. [*Checking his watch.*] Bye-bye. Don't want to miss the morning's trading. [*He wanders off.*]

FAT MAN. No, no.

[*He and the* MAN WITH THE HANDKERCHIEF *turn aside in private conversation of a business nature, and exit.*]

SCROOGE. [*He speaks to the* GHOST, *but his eyes are scanning the Exchange all the while. Thus, he does not notice that the* GHOST *has momentarily vanished.*] Why, Spirit, this is the Exchange. And these are men of business—very wealthy and very important. They are my very good friends, for I always make a point of standing well in their esteem. [*A pause.*] But if this is the Exchange, and these are my associates, then where am I? I don't seem to be standing in my usual corner. And this is most certainly my time of day. [*Thinking he has found the answer.*] Spirit, I have been revolving in my mind a change of life. Could this be the outcome?

[*We hear thunder, wind, and chains. The lights dim. In the background we see a figure lying on a bed and covered with a sheet. In the foreground we see a pawnshop.*[8] *Enter* MRS. DILBER, *a laundress. She's a withered old woman. She carries* SCROOGE'S *coat, in which are wrapped a pair of boots and a pair of spoons.*

She runs into the CHARWOMAN.[9] *She, too, is an old, ratty grotesque, carrying a bed coverlet, in which is wrapped a white shirt. They stand, frightened, realizing who the other is. Pawning the stolen property of a dead man is against the law.*

Now the UNDERTAKER *enters. In his pockets he carries a quill and an ink pot; in his top hat, a pair of candlesticks. He freezes on seeing the two women. A moment of standoff. Then all three rush in an effort to be first in line at the pawnshop.*]

CHARWOMAN. Let the charwoman alone be first. Let the laundress alone be second, and let the undertaker be third.

[*A pause, as the proposition is thought over. Then, another mad rush to the pawnshop.* OLD JOE, *the proprietor, enters.*]

OLD JOE. You couldn't have met in a better place. We're all suited to our calling. We're well matched.

[*The* CHARWOMAN *opens the coverlet, and lays out her haul for inspection.*]

CHARWOMAN. [*Noticing that the other two are*

---

8. **pawnshop:** establishment where people obtain loans in exchange for articles of personal property.
9. **charwoman:** woman hired to clean homes or offices.

not displaying their take.] Every person has a right to take care of himself. *He* always did.

MRS. DILBER. That's true indeed. No man more so.

CHARWOMAN. Why then, don't stand staring as if you was afraid, woman. Who's the wiser? We're not going to pick holes in each other's coats, I suppose?

MRS. DILBER. No indeed. [*She unrolls the coat on the floor and separates the boots and spoons.*]

UNDERTAKER. I should hope not.

CHARWOMAN. Very well, then, that's enough. Who's the worse for the loss of a few things like these? Not a dead man, I suppose.

MRS. DILBER. Not him.

UNDERTAKER. True enough. If he wanted to dispose of 'em after he was dead, why wasn't he natural in his lifetime? If he had been, he'd have had somebody to look after him when he was struck with death, instead of gasping out his last there, alone.

MRS. DILBER. It's the truest word was ever spoke. It's a judgment on him.

CHARWOMAN. I wish it were a little heavier one. [*To* OLD JOE.] Examine that bundle, Joe, and let me know the value of it.

UNDERTAKER. [*Grabbing her by the hair and forcefully sitting her down.*] No, my dear, you mustn't. [*To* OLD JOE.] Joe, appraise my lot first. [*The* UNDERTAKER *hands him the candlesticks.*]

OLD JOE. [*Examining them critically, holding them up to the light.*] Hmmm . . . umph . . . well, these are originals. Haven't seen their like in at least a half-an-hour. [*He laughs and drops a few coins into the* UNDERTAKER's

hand.] That's to your account, and I wouldn't give another sixpence if I was to be boiled for not doing it.

UNDERTAKER. [*Outraged, he raises his fist.*] Why—

OLD JOE. [*Standing.*] Don't try nothing, old man.

[*Furious, the* UNDERTAKER *exits.*]

OLD JOE. Who's next?

MRS. DILBER. [*Pushing the* CHARWOMAN *aside.*] I'll be next. [*She hands* OLD JOE *the spoons. He looks them over.*] Them's nice items, barely used. Don't suppose he ate off 'em much. Probably thought they was too valuable to wear out rubbing against his tongue!

OLD JOE. [*Paying her.*] Two shillings.

MRS. DILBER. Worth twice that much. What yer being so pinchfisted about? Yer a regular miser, as bad as he. [*Angrily, she grabs the money and leaves.*]

CHARWOMAN. [*With confidence.*] Examine me bundle, Joe.

OLD JOE. [*Holds up the coverlet.*] What do you call this? His coverlet?

CHARWOMAN. [*Great pride.*] His coverlet!

OLD JOE. You don't mean to say you took it right off him—with him laying there?

CHARWOMAN. I do. Why not? He ain't likely to take cold without it, I daresay.

OLD JOE. [*Suddenly doubtful.*] I hope he didn't die of anything catching, eh? [*He drops it and picks up the shirt.*]

CHARWOMAN. Don't be afraid of that. I ain't so fond of his company that I'd loiter about him if he did. You can look through that shirt 'til yer eyes fall out, but you won't find a hole in it or a threadbare place. Best he had, and a fine one, too. They'd have wasted it if it hadn't been for me.

OLD JOE. What do you call wasting it?

CHARWOMAN. Putting it on him to be buried in. Somebody was fool enough to do it, but I took it off again.

OLD JOE. Yer a rare one. A rare one! [*He stuffs them in the bag, and pays her. Meanwhile, she produces a crumpled piece of paper from her dress.* JOE *takes it.*] Now, what's this?

CHARWOMAN. [*As he unwraps it.*] That's the prize of it all, that is. Wrapped in a piece of paper, under a pile of old ledgers in the bottom of a trunk.

OLD JOE. [*Carefully holding it up to the light— it's the ring that* BELLE *had returned to* YOUNG SCROOGE *many years before.*] I wonder what he was doing with such a thing. [*Chuckling.*] Think he was going to give it to some lady?

CHARWOMAN. None in their proper mind would have such a one as he was. He was just like the undertaker said: unnatural, from first to last.

OLD JOE. [*Greatly excited over such a valuable find.*] A valuable piece. It'll fetch a nice price and feed old Joseph for a month. [*He pays her for the ring, and puts it on his little finger.*]

CHARWOMAN. This is the end of it, you see. He frightened everyone away from him while he was alive, to profit us when he was dead!

[*They both laugh, and steal away.*]

SCROOGE. Spirit, I see, I see. The case of this unhappy man might be my own. It tends that way now.

[*Recoiling from the scene,* SCROOGE *turns upon the sheeted figure on the bed.*]

Merciful heavens, what is this?

[*The* GHOST *points toward the bed.*]

Is this the man, Spirit, whose belongings these scavengers[10] have plundered?

[*The* GHOST *responds by pointing to the head beneath the sheet.* SCROOGE *understands what is being asked of him.*]

Spirit, this is a fearful place. In leaving it, I shall not leave its lesson, trust me. Let us go.

[*Still, the* GHOST *points with an unmoving finger toward the head.*]

I understand you, and would do it if I could. But I have not the power, Spirit. I have not the power! Surely there is one man or woman or child who will speak kindly of him? Show me that person, Spirit, I beseech you!

[*A pause.*]

Let me see then *some* tenderness connected with a death, or this dark chamber will be forever present to me.

[*The* CRATCHIT *house appears again. The family is quiet.* PETER *sits near the table reading;* MARTHA *is setting the table.* MRS. CRATCHIT *sits by the fire sewing, and* BELINDA *is near her, spooling yarn. By the chimney is the small stool and the crutch.*]

MRS. CRATCHIT. [*Putting her sewing down, and wiping her eyes. To* MARTHA, *who notices.*] The light hurts my eyes. [*A pause.*] It makes them weak, working by candlelight. For the world, I wouldn't show weak eyes to your father when he comes home. It must be near his time.

PETER. Past it, rather. But I think he's walked

---

10. **scavengers** [skav'in jərz]: people who search through trash or other discarded material for usable items; also, animals that feed on corpses.

a little slower these past few nights.

MRS. CRATCHIT. With Tim on his shoulder, he used to walk very fast indeed.

PETER. I've known him to run, nearly.

BELINDA. He galloped. [*A pause.*]

MRS. CRATCHIT. But he was very light to carry. And your father loved him so that it was no bother. [*A sound on the stairs.*] There's your father at the door.

[CRATCHIT *enters;* MRS. CRATCHIT *goes to greet him.*]

CRATCHIT. Merry Christmas, my dear.

MRS. CRATCHIT. Merry Christmas.

CRATCHIT. The goose smells delicious. And the pudding—I think I can taste it already. Did you help your mother, Belinda?

MRS. CRATCHIT. She made the pudding.

BELINDA. By myself, I did.

CRATCHIT. No! You'll have your own bakery shop before you know it.

MRS. CRATCHIT. You were gone a long time, Bob.

CRATCHIT. Yes, I took a longer way. [*A pause.*]

MRS. CRATCHIT. You went today, then?

CRATCHIT. Yes, my dear. I wish you could have gone. It would have done you good to see how green a place it is, even this time of year. I promised him we'd walk there often, of a Sunday.

MRS. CRATCHIT. I'll go soon. When the weather warms.

CRATCHIT. I should be making my punch.

BELINDA. It's already made, father. I wanted to save you the trouble.

CRATCHIT. [*Going to the table. He puts on a cheerful expression, as he pours the punch and passes it around the table.*] It's no trouble. It's always one of my greatest pleasures this time of year. And this is the best time of year, I believe. Am I right? [*No reply from the family.*] Am I right, Peter?

PETER. Yes.

CRATCHIT. Of course. [*Straining a bit more.*] You'll never guess who I met on the street today. Mister Scrooge's nephew. He only sees me once a year, you know. Yet he talked as if we were the oldest of friends, and on the most intimate terms. He'd heard about our—distress—and he said, "I'm mighty sorry for it, Mister Cratchit. And heartily sorry for your good wife." By the bye, how he knew *that*, I don't know.

MRS. CRATCHIT. Knew what, dear?

CRATCHIT. Why, that you're a good wife.

PETER. Everybody knows that.

CRATCHIT. Very well observed, my boy! I hope they do. "Heartily sorry," he said, "for your good wife." [*A pause.*] Now, gather 'round for a toast.

[*The family gathers around him, and they raise their mugs.*]

A merry Christmas to us all. . . . And a healthy New . . .

[*His voice breaks, and he lowers his mug. The family holds him.*]

My little boy . . . my poor little boy . . .

SCROOGE. Spirit, tell me: is there a reason the boy had to die?

[*Nothing from the* GHOST.]

I know not how, but something informs me

that our parting moment is at hand. Tell me . . . what man was that whom we saw lying dead?

[*The sound of tolling bells, thunder, and wind grows progressively louder as the scene goes on. The lights grow dim, and the* CRATCHITS *vanish. The* GHOST *points toward a mound.*]

A church yard?

[*A pause.*]

Before I draw nearer, answer me one question. Are these the shadows of things that *will* be, or are they the shadows of things that *may* be, only?

[*No answer from the* GHOST. *A bell begins to chime.*]

Spirit, hear me. I am not the man I was. I will not be the man I have been. Why show me this if I am past all hope?

[*Loud thunder crash.*]

Good Spirit, you pity me.

[*Another loud crash of thunder, as a light reveals a gravestone, reading "Ebenezer Scrooge, R.I.P."[11]* SCROOGE *falls to his knees in horror.*]

No, Spirit, no!

[*The* GHOST *begins backing away.*]

I will honor Christmas in my heart, and try to keep it all the year. I will live in the past, the present, and the future. The Spirits of all three shall strive within me. I will not shut out the lessons that they teach. Tell me, Spirit, that I may sponge away the writing on this stone!

[*He pulls the stone over; it falls with a crash. He follows the* GHOST *and grabs it to beseech it—and comes away with an empty cloak. He wrestles in its folds and falls into bed as the chimes toll five.* SCROOGE *wrestles with the cloak in bed, as the stage grows brighter.*]

I will live in the past, the present, and the future . . . the past, the present, and the future . . . the past, the present . . .

[*A pause. He wakes, taking a moment to realize where he is.*]

I'm alive . . .

[*Feeling himself to make sure.*]

I'm alive . . . [*Taking in the room.*] and this bed is my own. And this room is my own. . . . And the time before me is my own. The Ghost spared me! I knew it!

[*He jumps on his feet, opening a window.*]

I *will* live in the past, the present, and the future! The Spirits of all three *shall* strive within me! Oh, Jacob Marley! Heaven and Christmas time be praised for this! I say it on my knees, old Jacob.

[*He's on his knees.*]

On my knees!

[*He's up again, careening[12] about the room.*]

I don't know what to do! I'm as light as a feather! I'm as happy as an angel! I'm as merry as a schoolboy!

[*He wheels about, taking in the entire room.*]

There's the saucepan that the gruel was in . . . there's the door by which the Ghost of

---

11. **"R.I.P.":** abbreviation, frequently seen on gravestones, for the Latin term *requiescat in pace*, which means "rest in peace."

---

12. **careening:** running wildly.

Jacob Marley entered . . . there's the corner where the Ghost of Christmas Past sat! It's all right, it's all true, it all happened!

[*He leaps onto the bed.*]

A merry Christmas to everybody! A happy New Year to all the world!

[*He's off the bed again.*]

I don't know what day of the month it is. I don't know how long I've been among the Spirits. I don't know anything. I'm quite a baby! Never mind, I don't care. I'd rather be a baby!

[*Opening another window.*]

Hello! Whoop!

[*A loud chorus of bells.*]

Glorious! Glorious!

[*He sees a* BOY *on the street.*]

Hello there! Hello! What's today?

BOY. [*How could anyone not know?*] Today? Why, it's Christmas Day!

SCROOGE. It's Christmas Day! I haven't missed it! The Spirits have done it all in one night. They can do anything they like. Of course they can! Hello there, my fine fellow!

BOY. [*Trying to figure this strange bird out.*] Hello.

SCROOGE. Do you know the poulterer's,[13] in the next street but one? The one at the corner?

BOY. I should hope I did.

SCROOGE. An intelligent boy! A remarkable boy! Do you know whether they've sold the prize turkey that was hanging there? Not the little prize turkey—the big one?

BOY. What, the one as big as me?

SCROOGE. What a delightful boy! It's a pleasure to talk to him. Yes, my buck!

BOY. It's hanging there now.

SCROOGE. Is it? Go buy it!

BOY. Buy it yourself!

SCROOGE. No, no, I'm serious. Go and buy it, and tell 'em to bring it here that I may give 'em directions where to take it. Come back with the man and I'll give you a shilling! [*The* BOY *turns to run off.*] Come back with him in less than five minutes, and I'll give you half-a-crown!

BOY. Garn![14] [*He runs off.*]

SCROOGE. I'll send it to Bob Cratchit's. He shan't know who sent it. It's twice the size of Tiny Tim! Four times the size of Tiny Tim!

[*He takes off the nightcap and sleeping gown, and struggles into his coat. He is now out in the street. The two* PORTLY GENTLEMEN *enter.*]

FIRST PORTLY GENTLEMAN. [*Recognizing* SCROOGE, *he tries to sidestep him and continue on his way.*] Scrooge and Marley's, I believe?

SCROOGE. [*Stopping them and pumping their hands.*] My dear sirs, how do you do? I hope you succeeded yesterday. It was very kind of you—a wonderful gesture. A merry Christmas to you both!

FIRST PORTLY GENTLEMAN. Mister Scrooge?

SCROOGE. Yes, that is my name, and I fear it may not be very pleasant to you. Allow me to ask your pardon. And will you have the good-

---

13. **poulterer's** [pōl′tər ərz]: shop of a person who sells geese, chickens, ducks, and other poultry.

14. **"Garn!":** British slang expression showing amazement or disbelief.

ness—[*He whispers into the* FIRST PORTLY GEN-TLEMAN*'s ear the size of the contribution he wishes to make.*]

FIRST PORTLY GENTLEMAN. Lord bless me! [*He whispers it to the* SECOND PORTLY GENTLEMAN, *who gasps, and takes out his handkerchief to mop his brow.*] My dear Mister Scrooge, are you serious?

SCROOGE. If you please. Not a farthing[15] less. A great many back-payments are included in it, I assure you. Will you do me that favor?

SECOND PORTLY GENTLEMAN. My dear sir, I don't know what to say to such munificence[16]—

SCROOGE. Don't say anything! Come and see me. Will you come and see me?

FIRST PORTLY GENTLEMAN. I will!

SECOND PORTLY GENTLEMAN. And *I* will! We *both* will!

SCROOGE. Thank'ee. I'm much obliged to you. I thank you fifty times! Bless you!

[*The two* PORTLY GENTLEMEN *are off.*]

NARRATOR. Scrooge went to church, and walked about the streets, and patted the children on the head. He had never dreamed that anything could give him so much happiness. In the afternoon, he turned his steps towards his nephew's house. He passed the door a dozen times before he had the courage to go up and knock.

SCROOGE. Fred . . . [*A pause, as* FRED *must look twice.*]

FRED. Uncle Scrooge? [*Another brief pause.*] It's Uncle Scrooge! It's Uncle Scrooge!

[*He brings* SCROOGE *inside.* MRS. FRED, TOPPER, *and* MRS. FRED'S SISTER *enter.*]

NARRATOR. He was at home in five minutes. His niece looked just the same, so did Topper, so did the sister. Wonderful party, wonderful games, wonderful unanimity, wonderful happiness.

[*The lights dim on this group and come up on* SCROOGE*'s office.*]

He was early at the office next morning. If he could only be there first, and catch Bob Cratchit coming late. That was the thing he had his heart set upon. The clock struck nine. No Bob. A quarter past. No Bob. He was a full eighteen minutes behind his time.

[CRATCHIT *rushes in with the intention of hurrying to his desk—but is stopped cold at the sight of* SCROOGE *waiting for him.*]

CRATCHIT. Good morning, Mister Scrooge.

SCROOGE. [*Feigning[17] his old scowl as best he can.*] "Good morning, Mister Scrooge." What do you mean by coming in here this time of day?

CRATCHIT. I am very sorry, sir. I *am* a bit behind my time.

SCROOGE. I should say you are. Step this way, sir, if you please.

CRATCHIT. [*Approaching* SCROOGE.] It's only once a year, sir. It shan't be repeated. I was making rather merry yesterday, sir . . .

SCROOGE. [*Grasping him.*] Now I'll tell you what, my friend. I am not going to stand for this sort of thing any longer—

CRATCHIT. Mister Scrooge, I—

SCROOGE. And therefore . . . [*A pause.*] and therefore . . . I am about to raise your salary! [*Another pause, as* SCROOGE *lets him go.*

---

15. **farthing:** British coin worth one fourth of a penny.
16. **munificence** [mū nif′ə səns]: great generosity.

17. **feigning** [fān′ing]: putting on or pretending.

CRATCHIT *just stands there, stunned.*] A merry Christmas, Bob! A merrier Christmas, Bob, my good fellow, than I have given you for many a year!

[CRATCHIT *recovers and picks up a stool, to defend himself from this madman.*]

I'll raise your salary, and endeavor to assist your family, and we'll discuss your affairs this very afternoon, over a Christmas bowl of your special punch.

[*Seeing that* SCROOGE *is evidently in earnest,* CRATCHIT *has put the stool down.*]

Make up the fire, and buy another coal-scuttle before you dot another *i*, Bob Cratchit! [*Digging into his pocket, he pulls out some coins and presses them into* CRATCHIT's *hand.*]

CRATCHIT. Yes, sir. Thank you, sir. [*A pause.*] And a merry Christmas . . . Mister Scrooge. [*He exits.*]

SCROOGE. [*Coming downstage.*] Oh, Jacob Marley, I shall remember you as long as I live. A wonderful gift! A merry Christmas, Jacob . . . wherever you are.

NARRATOR. Scrooge was better than his word. He did it all and infinitely more. And to Tiny Tim, who did *not* die, he was a second father. He became as good a friend, as good a master, and as good a man as the good old city knew. Some people laughed to see the alteration in him, but he let them laugh, and paid them little heed. For he was wise enough to know that nothing ever happens for good on this globe at which some people do not have their fill of laughter at the outset. His own heart laughed, and that was quite enough for him. And it was always said of him that he knew how to keep Christmas well, if any man alive possessed the knowledge.

STUDY QUESTIONS

Recalling

1. Who is Tiny Tim? What does Christmas Present tell Scrooge about Tim's future?
2. According to the vision of the future that Scrooge sees, who will "inherit" his hard-earned possessions?
3. What does Christmas Yet to Come show Scrooge in the graveyard? What effect does this sight have on Scrooge?
4. Describe Scrooge's reaction when he wakes on Christmas morning. What does he do for Bob Cratchit on Christmas and on the day after? How does he treat Tiny Tim, according to the Narrator?

Interpreting

5. In what ways are the Cratchits more fortunate than Scrooge as he is at the beginning of Act II? What does Scrooge's interest in Tiny Tim suggest about his character?
6. What does Scrooge's trip to the future reveal to him about other people's opinion of him? What do the scenes at the Exchange and pawnshop tell him about the value of material goods?
7. Scrooge's final speech refers to a "wonderful gift." What is this gift?

Extending

8. What do you think Dickens would make of our world? Would he see it as better or worse than his own world in its treatment of the poor? Explain.

READING AND LITERARY FOCUS

The Total Effect

A director staging a play needs to keep in mind various aspects that contribute to the play's **total effect**—the overall impact of the play as a whole. The **plot,** or sequence of actions, must hold the attention of the audience. The plot presents **con-**flicts, or struggles between opposing forces. These conflicts move the action forward to a **climax,** the point at which we know how these conflicts will finally be resolved. **Characters** must be varied, interesting, and believable. The **setting,** the time and place of the play, must be appropriate to the play's action and should add to the play's power. Finally, the play's **themes,** the ideas it expresses about life, must grow out of the other elements of the play and must be expressed in terms that make a strong impression on the audience.

Thinking About Plot

1. When Scrooge wakes on Christmas morning, he says of his ghostly visits, "It's all true; it all happened." In your opinion did it all "happen"? Or do you think we should view the visits of the ghosts as Scrooge's dreams? Give reasons for your answer.
2. What is the basic conflict that moves the action of the play forward? Is this conflict internal or external?
3. What event is the play's climax? How is the play's conflict resolved?

Thinking About Character

4. How does the character of Scrooge change from the beginning to the end of *A Christmas Carol*? What events and realizations make him change?
5. Most of the other characters in *A Christmas Carol* represent a particular human quality or an aspect of human life. What might Tiny Tim represent? Joe, the pawnbroker? Scrooge's nephew, Fred?

Thinking About Setting

6. What do the Fezziwigs' party, the Cratchits' dinner, and Fred's gathering all have in common? In what ways are these settings different from Scrooge's office and bedroom?
7. What do the pawnshop and graveyard settings add to the impact of the play?

Thinking About Theme

8. What things does Scrooge learn are more important than money?

9. What qualities does this play associate with the true Christmas spirit?

10. What might Scrooge's reform suggest about the ability of people to change?

COMPOSITION

Writing a Drama Review

■ Write a three-paragraph review of *A Christmas Carol*. Begin by relating the most important facts about Dickens and the play, including the setting of the work. Then go on to describe the main characters and to summarize the plot of the play. End by giving your opinion of the play, and support this opinion. *For help with this assignment, see Lesson 9 in the Writing About Literature Handbook at the back of this book.*

Writing a Scene

■ Write a scene for an updated version of *A Christmas Carol*. First decide what aspects of *A Christmas Carol* might apply to life in the 1990s. Then decide what details from modern life you want to use in your version of *A Christmas Carol*. For example, you might set the play in a modern home or business office. The ghostly voices might come from a computer. Be sure to follow the format of the dialogue and stage directions used in the text of *A Christmas Carol*. *For help with this assignment, see Lesson 10 in the Writing About Literature Handbook at the back of this book.*

CHALLENGE

Literary Criticism

■ When *A Christmas Carol* was first published in 1843, the English novelist William Thackeray described the work in the following way:

> It seems to be a national benefit, and to every man or woman who reads it a personal kindness. . . . A Scotch philosopher, who . . . does not keep Christmas Day, on reading the book, sent out for a turkey, and asked two friends to dine. . . .

Why might *A Christmas Carol* inspire such reactions?

COMPARING DRAMAS

1. *Gregory's Girl* is a realistic, comic film about a 1980s high school student. *A Christmas Carol* is a fanciful but serious play based on a nineteenth-century work. Point out some of the specific, concrete differences between the characters and settings of these two works. Which drama do you prefer, and why?

2. For all their differences, *Gregory's Girl* and *A Christmas Carol* have a few basic things in common. Each work is about a character who, led by three guides, goes on a journey that brings about an important change in his life. Compare Gregory's guides, journey, and change with Scrooge's. Who leads each, and where do they go? Why does each need to change? Why and how does each change, and how does the change improve his life?

Active Reading

Drama

Interpreting Details in Drama I

Reading a drama is noticeably different from seeing one performed. When you go to the theater, you remain a part of the audience. Your job is to observe and react to the activity on stage. When you read a drama, however, your responsibilities widen. Not only do you *react* to the proceedings, but you also *act* them out in your imagination. In other words, you provide the performance as well as watch it.

As a good reader of drama, you must pay close attention to the details that help you imagine a performance. Use the stage directions to picture every scene in your mind. Visualize exactly where actors enter and exit the stage. See the lights as they brighten and dim. In your imagination picture how performers move about and gesture. Hear their voices as they speak each line. Also listen to any other sounds that occur on stage or off.

Activity 1 Read the following lines from *A Christmas Carol*. Then, based on the details in the stage directions, answer each question. Be prepared to give reasons for your choices.

> [*Low sound of wind. It quickly fades.*]

SCROOGE: Humbug.

> [*He sits on a stool by the fire and takes a pan of gruel and a spoon from near the fireplace and eats. Suddenly the bells on the wall begin to clang. A loud gong is heard, and the sounds die as quickly as they began.*]

Humbug. It's nothing! It's the wind!

> [SCROOGE *sits rigidly on his stool. Heavy steps are heard. Chains are being dragged up the stairs.*]

It's humbug still! I won't believe it!

> [*A door swings open. There is a crash of thunder, and a bright, eerie light illuminates the doorway.* MARLEY'S GHOST—*in a ragged suit, wrapped in chains—enters.*]

1. Which of these sounds would you *not* hear in the scene?
   a. bells clanging
   b. thunder crashing
   c. sirens wailing
   d. chains rattling

2. What is probably the loudest noise heard in the scene?
    a. the wind
    b. the bells
    c. the chains
    d. the thunder
3. What do you assume causes the loud gong that is heard?
    a. a clock
    b. a ghost
    c. the wind
    d. thunder
4. What overall mood, or atmosphere, do the sounds in the scene help to create?
    a. festivity
    b. suspense
    c. sadness
    d. anger
5. Before the door swings open, how does Scrooge's room probably appear?
    a. dimly lit
    b. completely dark
    c. brightly lit
    d. lit with flashing lights
6. When the footsteps stop, where do you imagine Scrooge is looking on stage?
    a. at the wall
    b. at the fireplace
    c. at the door
    d. at the floor
7. What does Scrooge's posture on the stool suggest?
    a. He is sleepy.
    b. He is in pain.
    c. He is confident.
    d. He is frightened.
8. What emotion is probably expressed in Scrooge's last line?
    a. disbelief
    b. embarrassment
    c. joy
    d. relief
9. Which of these items is Marley's ghost most likely to wear?
    a. a bright red tie
    b. a dusty suit
    c. brand-new sneakers
    d. a green beret
10. Which of the following two pictures more accurately portrays the scene?
    a. Picture A
    b. Picture B

A

B

Interpreting Details in Drama II

To fully appreciate a drama that you are reading, you must always try to *see* and *hear* the details in the script. An important part of seeing and hearing details is imagining the characters. You use the stage directions and dialogue to help you picture characters' facial expressions and gestures and to hear the sound and tone of their voice.

Consider this brief excerpt from a conversation between Menzies and Gregory in *Gregory's Girl:*

MENZIES: I want to make some changes. I want to try out some other people. Switch the team around. Take some people out. [*A pause.*] I was going to take *you* out.

GREGORY: [*Laughing at the silly idea.*] You don't want to do that.

MENZIES: Yes I do.

GREGORY: [*Still a coaxing smile.*] You don't.

MENZIES: I do.

GREGORY: [*Pauses. Serious.*] You don't.

MENZIES: I might.

During the conversation Gregory speaks the words "You don't" three times. Each time the phrase is said in a slightly different manner. The first time Gregory is "laughing at the silly idea." The second time he is no longer laughing but is speaking with a "coaxing smile." His final "You don't" comes after a pause. It is spoken with a seriousness that is absent in Gregory's voice the first two times. By "hearing" Gregory's shift in tone and by "seeing" his face as you read, you can better understand the boy's growing concern with the coach's threat.

Activity 2   Read the following lines from *Gregory's Girl.* Try to see and hear the characters as you read. Then answer each numbered question. Be prepared to give reasons for your answer.

GREGORY: Got your message, Dorothy.

DOROTHY: Good. I just wanted to know what you were up to at lunchtime.

GREGORY: [*A new spark of optimism lights up his face.*] Nothing that can't wait a million years.

DOROTHY: Good. Will you help me out with some goal practice?

GREGORY: Yes—sure.

DOROTHY: Good. It'll speed things up. I want to practice goal shots at different angles.

GREGORY: [*Jokingly.*] I'll bring my compass.

[*Just a look from* DOROTHY.]

GREGORY: [*More subdued.*] Good. See you at half-twelve?

DOROTHY: [*Smiling now.*] Fine.

GREGORY: Good. See you.

[GREGORY *tears off down the school corridor, where he eagerly accosts* STEVE.]

1. In your imagination what tone of voice does Gregory use when answering Dorothy's first question? How do his words help to indicate the tone he uses?
2. What do you imagine Gregory's face looks like when he answers Dorothy's question? How do the stage directions help you envision his face?
3. How do you think Dorothy speaks to Gregory at first? Is she polite? Serious? Demanding?
4. How does Gregory speak the words, "I'll bring my compass"? Is he trying to be funny? Sarcastic? Serious? Why do you think he talks with Dorothy in this manner?
5. Toward the end of the conversation, Gregory changes his tone because of a look he receives from Dorothy. What kind of look do you imagine she gives him? Why do you think she looks at him this way?
6. How does Gregory's manner of speech change for the rest of the conversation? How does his voice probably change when he speaks? Do you imagine it rises or lowers in pitch? Why?
7. How can you tell that Dorothy is satisfied with Gregory's change in tone during their conversation? What kind of look do you picture on her face as they finish the conversation?
8. After Gregory and Dorothy finish speaking, Gregory goes down the corridor toward Steve. What do the stage directions tell you about Gregory's movement? How do you imagine he feels at the moment, based on his gestures?

Literary Skills Review

Drama

Guide for Reading Drama

Of all types of literature, drama seems the most lifelike. Its actions are meant to be performed, and its words are meant to be spoken out loud. Whenever we see a play or film, we are caught up in its "lifelikeness." When we read a play or screenplay, we imagine how it might come to life in front of an audience. However, we also respond to a drama as a work of literature, with features such as plot, characters, setting, and theme. Review the following questions when you read or see a dramatic work. In helping you understand how drama creates its special impact, this guide will add to your enjoyment of any play or film.

1. Is the work a **stage play** or a **screenplay**?
2. What **conflicts** does the **plot** present? What event is the **climax**?
3. Who are the main **characters** in the work? What does the **dialogue** reveal about the personalities of these characters? Do any characters change, and, if so, how?
4. What is the **setting,** or time and place, of the work? How do the **stage directions** help us to see the details of the setting?
5. What **themes,** or ideas about life, does the work present? How do the plot, characters, and setting help reveal these themes?
6. In what ways could **staging**—scenery, props, lighting, costumes, and acting—bring the writer's words to life?

Themes Review

Drama

Many works of literature deal with universal themes, matters that touch most people's lives. For example, many stories, poems, essays, and plays are concerned with the search for identity. However, each writer conveys a personal, specific idea about the theme "identity." For example, by showing us a teenager's comic attempts to be someone he is not, *Gregory's Girl* (page 343) makes the following specific point about identity: "Growing up means trying on different identities and discovering who we really are and what we do well." On the other hand, *A Christmas Carol* (page 372) expresses the following specific view of identity: "Each of us creates his or her own identity through our treatment of others." Note that the general theme can be a word or phrase, while the specific theme can be stated as a complete sentence.

1. In *A Christmas Carol* what specific idea about identity does Dickens suggest by including the characters of Young Ebenezer and Young Scrooge?

2. What specific points do *Gregory's Girl* and *A Christmas Carol* make about the general theme "love"?

3. Tell what *Gregory's Girl* and *A Christmas Carol* show us about the general theme "growth and learning."

4. For *A Christmas Carol* and one story or nonfiction selection below, explain each work's specific view about the general theme "communities."
   Stories: "The Snow in Chelm"   "Rip Van Winkle"
   Nonfiction: "Roberto Clemente"   "Morning . . ."

5. For *Gregory's Girl* and one other work below, explain each selection's specific view of the general theme "heroes."
   Stories: "A Just Judge"   "Rikki-tikki-tavi"
   Poems: "The Highwayman"   "A Song of Greatness"
   Nonfiction: *Growing Up*   "Roberto Clemente"

Preview
Greek Myths and World Folk Tales

Literature is one of the most enjoyable of human inventions. It is also one of the longest lasting. In fact, we still enjoy even the earliest imaginative literature—the ancient myths and tales that tell about the beliefs, histories, and delights of people from long ago.

The word *myth* comes from *mythos*, a Greek word meaning "story." For thousands of years, people all over the world have been telling stories. However, of all the world's myths, those created by the ancient Greeks have had the greatest effect on the literature that we read and write today. By reading Greek myths—like those in this unit—we help ourselves to enjoy and understand the literature of our own time and place.

A myth is a special kind of story, usually involving gods and goddesses. People created myths thousands of years ago to explain how the world worked and to show how human beings ought to act. No one knows exactly when or how the Greek myths began. However, they were already very old when the Greek writer Homer used them in his poems about 850 B.C. Many myths were connected with celebrations and ceremonies. They were a basic part of people's lives and were passed along by word of mouth for many generations.

Like myths, folk tales are stories told by *folk*, people who are not professional writers. Like myths, they change as people tell and retell them over many generations. However, unlike myths, they are not part of a collection of stories about gods and goddesses.

Every country has its treasure of folk tales—practical, enjoyable stories about ordinary people. The folk tales in this unit come from different parts of the world. They remind us that every country has a way of expressing its customs, beliefs, ideals, and attitudes in imaginative literature.

GREEK MYTHS

Greece is a warm, rocky, hilly country pushing out from southern Europe into the Mediterranean Sea. Thousands of years ago, when myths were created, life was difficult there for most people. Kings ruled many different local regions, and wars were common.

A **myth** is an ancient anonymous story, usually involving gods and goddesses, that conveys the beliefs and ideals of a culture. The Greek myths tell the stories of the gods and goddesses whom the people believed lived on Mount Olympus. These myths relate the gods' relationships with human beings on earth.

Myths helped people *understand* how natural events and human actions happened. For example, in order to explain how the sun traveled across the sky, people created a myth about a sun god driving a mighty chariot. Myths also helped people *control* what happened in the world. For example, by telling the story of how a god created rain, people believed they could encourage the god to make rain fall.

Gods and Goddesses of Greece and Rome

When the ancient Romans conquered Greece in the second century B.C., they took many Greek myths home to Rome, but they substituted Roman names for the gods.

Greek Name	Roman Name	Description
Cronus [krō'nəs]	Saturn	ruler of the Titans
Zeus [zoos]	Jupiter	king of the gods
Hera [hēr'ə]	Juno	queen of the gods
Poseidon [pō sī'dən]	Neptune	god of the sea
Hades [hā'dēz]	Pluto	god of the underworld
Ares [ār'ēz]	Mars	god of war
Apollo [ə pol'ō]	Apollo	god of the sun
Artemis [är'tə mis]	Diana	goddess of the moon
Athena [ə thē'nə]	Minerva	goddess of wisdom
Aphrodite [af'rə dī'tē]	Venus	goddess of love
Eros [er'os]	Cupid	god of love
Hephaestus [hi fes'təs]	Vulcan	god of fire
Hermes [hur'mēz]	Mercury	messenger of the gods
Demeter [di mē'tər]	Ceres	goddess of agriculture
Dionysus [dī'ə nī'səs]	Bacchus	god of the vine

As you read this overview of the Greek gods and goddesses, notice that they are much more than ancient names on a list. They have personalities and responsibilities. They direct the forces of nature and govern the actions of human beings. They are the imaginative foundations upon which thousands of stories were built.

■ Which god or goddess do you think had the most interesting responsibilities?

Statue of Zeus, king of the gods.

Olivia Coolidge

An Introduction to Greek Mythology

Greek legends have been favorite stories for many centuries. They are mentioned so often by famous writers that it has become impossible to read widely in English, or in many other literatures, without knowing what the best of these tales are about. Even though we no longer believe in the Greek gods, we enjoy hearing of them because they appeal to our imagination.

The Greeks thought all the forces of nature were spirits, so that the whole earth was filled with gods. Each river, each woodland, even each great tree had its own god or nymph.[1] In the woods lived the satyrs,[2] who had pointed ears and the shaggy legs of goats. In the sea danced more than three thousand green-haired, white-limbed maidens. In the air rode wind gods, cloud nymphs, and the golden chariot of the sun. All these spirits, like the forces of nature, were beautiful and strong, but sometimes unreliable and unfair. Above all, however, the Greeks felt that they were tremendously interested in mankind.

From very early times the Greeks began to invent stories to account for the things that went on—the change of seasons, the sudden storms, the good and bad fortune of the farmer's year. These tales were spread by travelers from one valley to another. They were put together and altered by poets and musicians, until at last a great body of legends arose from the whole of Greece. These did not agree with one another in details, but on the whole gave a clear picture of who the chief gods were, how men should behave to please them, and what their relationships had been with heroes of the past.

---

1. **nymph** [nimf]: minor nature goddess in the form of a beautiful young woman.
2. **satyrs** [sā′tərs]: spirits of the woods who were part man, part goat.

An Introduction to Greek Mythology 415

The ruler of all the gods was Zeus,[3] the sky god, titled by courtesy father of gods and men. He lived in the clouds with most of the great gods in a palace on the top of Mount Olympus,[4] the tallest mountain in Greece. Lightning was the weapon of Zeus, thunder was the rolling of his chariot, and when he nodded his head, the whole earth shook.

Zeus, though the ruler of the world, was not the eldest of the gods. First had come a race of monsters with fifty heads and a hundred arms each. Next followed elder gods called Titans,[5] the leader of whom, Cronus,[6] had reigned before Zeus. Then arose mighty giants, and finally Zeus and the Olympians. Zeus in a series of wars succeeded in banishing the Titans and imprisoning the giants in various ways. One huge monster, Typhon,[7] lay imprisoned under the volcano of Etna,[8] which spouted fire when he struggled. Atlas, one of the giants, was forced to stand holding the heavens on his shoulders so that they should not fall upon the earth.

Almost as powerful as Zeus were his two brothers, who did not live on Olympus: Poseidon,[9] ruler of the sea, and Hades,[10] gloomy king of the underworld, where the spirits of the dead belong. Queen of the gods was blue-eyed, majestic Hera. Aphrodite,[11] the laughing sea-born goddess, was queen of love and most beautiful of all. Apollo[12] and Artemis[13] were twins, god of the sun and goddess of the moon. Apollo was the more important. Every day he rode the heavens in a golden chariot

---

3. **Zeus** [zo͞os]
4. **Olympus** [ō lim′pəs]
5. **Titans** [tīt′əns]
6. **Cronus** [krō′nəs]
7. **Typhon** [tī′fän]

---

8. **Etna** [et′nə]: very active volcano located on Sicily, an island off the southwestern tip of Italy.
9. **Poseidon** [pō sī′dən]
10. **Hades** [hā′dēz]
11. **Aphrodite** [af′rə dī′tē]
12. **Apollo** [ə pol′ō]
13. **Artemis** [är′tə mis]

LD DILLON©84

from dawn to sunset. The sun's rays could be gentle and healing, or they could be terrible. Apollo, therefore, was a great healer and the father of the god of medicine. At the same time he was a famous archer, and the arrows from his golden bow were arrows of infection and death. Apollo was also god of poetry and song; his instrument was a golden lyre,[14] and the nine Muses, goddesses of music and the arts, were his attendants. He was the ideal of young manhood and the patron of athletes.

Apollo was also god of prophecy. There were temples of Apollo, known as oracles, at which a man could ask questions about the future. The priestesses of Apollo, inspired by the god, gave him an answer, often in the form of a riddle which was hard to understand. Nevertheless, the Greeks believed that if a man could interpret the words of the oracle, he would find the answer to his problem.

Artemis, the silver moon goddess, was goddess of unmarried girls and a huntress of wild beasts in the mountains. She also could send deadly arrows from her silver bow.

Gray-eyed Athena,[15] the goddess of wisdom, was patron of Athens.[16] She was queen of the domestic arts, particularly spinning and weaving. Athena was warlike too; she wore helmet and breastplate, and carried a spear. Ares,[17] however, was the real god of war, and the maker of weapons was Hephaestus,[18] the lame smith and metalworker.

One more god who lived on Olympus was Hermes,[19] the messenger. He wore golden, winged sandals which carried him dry-shod over sea and land. He darted down from the peaks of Olympus like a kingfisher[20] dropping to catch a fish, or came running down the sloping sunbeams bearing messages from Zeus to men. Mortal eyes were too weak to behold the dazzling beauty of the immortals; consequently the messages of Zeus usually came in dreams. Hermes was therefore also a god of sleep, and of thieves because they prowl by night. Healing was another of his powers. His rod, a staff entwined by two snakes, is commonly used as a symbol of medicine.

The Greeks have left us so many stories about their gods that it hardly would be possible for everyone to know them all. We can still enjoy them because they are good stories. In spite of their great age we can still understand them because they are about nature and about people. We still need them to enrich our knowledge of our own language and of the great masterpieces of literature.

---

14. **lyre** [līr]: stringed musical instrument.

15. **Athena** [ə thē′nə]
16. **Athens** [ath′ənz]: major city of Greece.
17. **Ares** [ār′ēz]
18. **Hephaestus** [hi fes′təs]
19. **Hermes** [hur′mēz]
20. **kingfisher:** brightly colored bird with a long, pointed bill.

STUDY QUESTIONS

Recalling

1. Name three types of nature gods, and tell where they lived.
2. Describe the place where most of the great gods lived.
3. What did Zeus do to the Titans in order to become king?
4. What did Poseidon rule? What did Hades rule?
5. Name three of Apollo's responsibilities.
6. What were Hermes' responsibilities?

Interpreting

7. Why do you think the Greeks created so many gods and goddesses?
8. Give three examples of the gods' interest in human beings.
9. Why was Apollo an important and powerful god?

Extending

10. If you had been an ancient Greek, which god or goddess would you have preferred to guide your life? Give reasons to support your answer.

READING AND LITERARY FOCUS

Oral Tradition

A **tradition** is a group of beliefs, customs, or skills handed down from one generation to another. Thanksgiving dinner and Fourth of July parades, for example, are part of our country's tradition. Our belief in freedom and equality is another part. Towns, families, and clubs often develop traditions that pass from generation to generation. Years later no one may remember how these traditions began. People simply follow them, often adding to them in one way or another.

Stories, proverbs, superstitions, legends, and folklore are often part of tradition. Many of these are kept alive by **oral tradition**, or word of mouth. The story of George Washington and the cherry tree and many folk songs are part of America's oral tradition. Only after they had been part of our culture for generations did anyone write them down.

In the same way Greek mythology was formed over a long period of time by many people who told and retold the stories to one another. If oral tradition had not kept the myths alive, they would have been lost to us.

Thinking About Oral Tradition

■ According to this selection, which god do you think would have helped the storytellers who kept the myths alive generation after generation?

COMPOSITION

Writing an Evaluation

■ The author's purpose in "An Introduction to Greek Mythology" is to present an overview of the gods and to tell something about each one. Evaluate the author's work. First state in general terms how helpful this introduction was to you. Then identify the paragraphs in which the author talks about the gods as a whole. Next tell what kinds of information the author gives about individual gods. Conclude by suggesting why some gods are given more description than others.

Writing an Introduction

■ Imagine a group of creatures from another world. Write an introduction, or brief overview, presenting these creatures to readers who have never experienced them before. First identify the group and tell what they have in common. Next tell how they are like and unlike humans. Then describe different individuals. Vary the length of the descriptions and kinds of information you give.

Scientists today can explain many aspects of nature that people once explained through myths. The mythological explanations, however, still have a powerful imaginative appeal.

◾ As you read the myth of Demeter [di mē′tər] and Persephone [pər sef′ə nē], notice how in mythology personal emotions such as love and sadness may affect the course of the whole world.

Greek statue of Hermes, messenger of the gods.

Retold by
Anne Terry White

Demeter and Persephone

Deep under Mt. Etna, the gods had buried alive a number of fearful, fire-breathing giants. The monsters heaved and struggled to get free. And so mightily did they shake the earth that Hades, the king of the underworld, was alarmed.

"They may tear the rocks asunder and leave the realm of the dead open to the light of day," he thought. And mounting his golden chariot, he went up to see what damage had been done.

Now the goddess of love and beauty, fair Aphrodite, was sitting on a mountainside playing with her son, Eros.[1] She saw Hades as he drove around with his coal-black horses and she said:

"My son, there is one who defies your power and mine. Quick! Take up your darts! Send an arrow into the breast of that dark monarch. Let him, too, feel the pangs of love. Why should he alone escape them?"

At his mother's words, Eros leaped lightly to his feet. He chose from his quiver[2] his sharpest and truest arrow, fitted it to his bow, drew the string, and shot straight into Hades' heart.

The grim King had seen fair maids enough in the gloomy underworld over which he ruled. But never had his heart been touched. Now an unaccustomed warmth stole through his veins. His stern eyes softened. Before him was a blossoming valley, and along its edge a charming girl was gathering flowers. She was Persephone, daughter of Demeter, goddess of the harvest. She had strayed from her companions, and now that her basket overflowed with blossoms, she was filling her apron with

---

1. **Eros** [ēr′os]: god of love.

2. **quiver:** case for holding and carrying arrows, usually slung over one shoulder.

lilies and violets. The god looked at Persephone and loved her at once. With one sweep of his arm he caught her up and drove swiftly away.

"Mother!" she screamed, while the flowers fell from her apron and strewed the ground. "Mother!"

And she called on her companions by name. But already they were out of sight, so fast did Hades urge the horses on. In a few moments they were at the River Cyane.[3] Persephone struggled, her loosened girdle[4] fell to the ground, but the god held her tight. He struck the bank with his trident.[5] The earth opened, and darkness swallowed them all— horses, chariot, Hades, and weeping Persephone.

From end to end of the earth Demeter sought her daughter. But none could tell her where Persephone was. At last, worn out and despairing, the goddess returned to Sicily. She stood by the River Cyane, where Hades had cleft[6] the earth and gone down into his own dominions.

Now a river nymph had seen him carry off his prize. She wanted to tell Demeter where her daughter was, but fear of Hades kept her dumb. Yet she had picked up the girdle Persephone had dropped, and this the nymph wafted[7] on the waves to the feet of Demeter.

The goddess knew then that her daughter was gone indeed, but she did not suspect Hades of carrying her off. She laid the blame on the innocent land.

"Ungrateful soil!" she said. "I made you fertile. I clothed you in grass and nourishing grain, and this is how you reward me. No more shall you enjoy my favors!"

That year was the most cruel mankind had ever known. Nothing prospered, nothing grew. The cattle died, the seed would not come up, men and oxen toiled in vain. There was too much sun. There was too much rain. Thistles and weeds were the only things that grew. It seemed that all mankind would die of hunger.

"This cannot go on," said mighty Zeus. "I see that I must intervene." And one by one he sent the gods and goddesses to plead with Demeter.

But she had the same answer for all: "Not till I see my daughter shall the earth bear fruit again."

Zeus, of course, knew well where Persephone was. He did not like to take from his brother the one joyful thing in his life, but he saw that he must if the race of man was to be preserved. So he called Hermes to him and said:

"Descend to the underworld, my son. Bid Hades release his bride. Provided she has not tasted food in the realm of the dead, she may return to her mother forever."

Down sped Hermes on his winged feet, and there in the dim palace of the king, he found Persephone by Hades' side. She was pale and joyless. Not all the glittering treasures of the underworld could bring a smile to her lips.

"You have no flowers here," she would say to her husband when he pressed gems upon her. "Jewels have no fragrance. I do not want them."

When she saw Hermes and heard his message, her heart leaped within her. Her cheeks grew rosy and her eyes sparkled, for she knew that Hades would not dare to disobey his brother's command. She sprang up, ready to go at once. Only one thing troubled her—that

---

3. **River Cyane** [sī'an]: river in Sicily, an island off the southwestern tip of Italy.
4. **girdle:** belt.
5. **trident:** spear with three sharp points.
6. **cleft:** opened.
7. **wafted:** carried along.

Detail of stone tablet showing Persephone and Hades.

she could not leave the underworld forever. For she had accepted a pomegranate[8] from Hades and sucked the sweet pulp from four of the seeds.

With a heavy heart Hades made ready his golden car. He helped Persephone in while Hermes took up the reins.

"Dear wife," said the King, and his voice trembled as he spoke, "think kindly of me, I pray you. For indeed I love you truly. It will be lonely here these eight months you are away. And if you think mine is a gloomy palace to return to, at least remember that your husband is great among the immortals. So fare you well—and get your fill of flowers!"

---

8. **pomegranate** [pom'gran'it]: round, golden-red fruit with many small seeds.

Straight to the temple of Demeter at Eleusis,[9] Hermes drove the black horses. The goddess heard the chariot wheels and, as a deer bounds over the hills, she ran out swiftly to meet her daughter. Persephone flew to her mother's arms. And the sad tale of each turned into joy in the telling.

So it is to this day. One third of the year Persephone spends in the gloomy abode of Hades—one month for each seed that she tasted. Then Nature dies, the leaves fall, the earth stops bringing forth. In spring Persephone returns, and with her come the flowers, followed by summer's fruitfulness and the rich harvest of fall.

---

9. **Eleusis** [ē loo'sis]: town in Greece northwest of Athens.

STUDY QUESTIONS

Recalling

1. Who is Hades? What causes him to fall in love with Persephone?
2. Where does Demeter place the blame for her daughter's disappearance? What does Demeter do to gain revenge?
3. Why does Zeus intervene?
4. What does Persephone do in the underworld that keeps her from leaving it forever?
5. How does this myth explain the changing of the seasons?

Interpreting

6. Give at least three examples from the selection of human emotions displayed by gods and goddesses.
7. Do you think the final decision of the gods is a fair compromise for all the characters? Tell why or why not.

Extending

8. Name at least one other aspect of nature that might be explained by the strong emotions of a god or goddess.

READING AND LITERARY FOCUS

Myth

A **myth** is an ancient anonymous story, usually about gods and heroes. Myths originally explained some aspect of nature or accounted for some human action. In other words, most myths grew out of particular historical events. They show us the imagination at work, creating literature out of the events of the real world.

Almost every culture created myths. There are myths about the beginning of the world, the first human beings, great wars, and movements of people from place to place. There are myths about why flowers grow, why birds fly, and why different languages exist. In fact, collections of myths—

called **mythologies**—generally account for everything in the experience of a particular culture.

Thinking About Myth
■ What elements in the story of Demeter and Persephone fit the definition of a myth?

VOCABULARY

Roots
The **root** of a word is its core, or main part. It is the central portion of a word to which either prefixes or suffixes may be attached. For example, in the word *monarch* the root *-arch-* is from the Greek language and means "ruler" or "ruling." *Mono-* is a prefix meaning "one." A monarch is a single ruler, a person ruling alone.

On a separate sheet of paper, identify the roots of each of the following words. The words are from "Demeter and Persephone." Then give one other word formed from each root. Check your answers in the dictionary.

1. intervene
2. dominion
3. preserve
4. descend

COMPOSITION

Writing About Dialogue
■ Examine the dialogue, or spoken words, of a main character in "Demeter and Persephone." First identify important pieces of that character's dialogue. Then tell what the dialogue reveals about the character. Conclude by describing how the character would deliver his or her words. Use vivid adverbs to clearly identify the tone of voice each character uses and the emotion each character expresses.

Writing Dialogue
■ Near the end of the myth, Hades speaks to Persephone, revealing his love for her. Continue that dialogue, having Persephone answer him. In her response have Persephone reveal her true feelings for Hades, her memories of her past life, and her feelings for her mother. Extend the conversation, with each character speaking several times. Be sure to use expressions that are appropriate to each character. Make each line of the dialogue lead naturally into the next line.

CHALLENGE

Collage
■ The myth of Persephone reminds us that we depend on the earth for food. Make a collage with pictures from magazines. Show how bountiful the earth can be during some seasons, and show what happens during periods of excessive heat and rain. You may want to arrange your collage to suggest the never-ending cycle of growth and change in nature.

"Knowledge is power." This old saying is brought to life in the story of Prometheus [prə mē'thē əs]. Imagine the sense of power humans felt when they first learned to build fire.

■ As you read, notice the reasons that Prometheus feels such strong sympathy for mortals.

A modern statue of Prometheus.

Retold by
Jeremy Ingalls

Prometheus the Fire-Bringer

Fire itself, and the civilized life which fire makes possible—these were the gifts of Prometheus to the men of ancient times. Prometheus himself was not of the oldest race of men. He was not alive in the first age of mankind.

Ancient writers tell us there were three ages of men on earth before the fourth age, in which we are now living. Each of the previous ages ended in terrible disasters which destroyed a large part of the human race. A raging fire ended the first age of the world. At the end of the second age, vast floods engulfed plains and mountains. According to the oldest poets, these misfortunes were punishments the gods visited upon men for their wickedness and wrongdoing.

The story of Prometheus, remembered by the Greeks and set down in their books, tells of the days when Zeus was king of the world and Prometheus was his chief councilor. From their ancestors they and their compan-

ions upon Mount Olympus had inherited the secrets of fire, of rain, of farming and metalworking.[1] This knowledge gave them a power so great that they appeared as gods to the men who served them.

After the flood which destroyed many of the men of the second age, Zeus, with the help of Prometheus, had bred a new race of men in Arcadia.[2] But Zeus did not find life on earth so simple for men and gods as it had been in earlier times.

When Cronus, the father of Zeus, had ruled the earth, summer had been the only season. Great land masses toward the north had barred all the icy winds. The age of Cronus was an age of contentment. No man had needed to work for food or clothes or a house to shelter him.

---

1. **metalworking:** process of making objects out of metal.
2. **Arcadia** [är kā'dē ə]: region in ancient Greece noted for the simple and pleasant life of its people.

After the first flood, the land masses were broken. Winter winds blew upon countries which before had known only summer.

The race of gods did not suffer. They warmed their houses, having the secret of fire. And the women of the race were weavers of cloth, so that the gods were clothed and defended from the north wind.

But winter was a harsh season for the men and women who did not live on the gods' mountain. Without defense from the cold, they huddled with the animals. They complained against the gods, whom they must serve for what little comfort they might find of food and warmth. They scarcely believed the stories which their ancestors had handed down to them of a time when men had lived in endless summer weather, when men were friends and favorites of the gods.

Men became rebels and grumblers. For this reason Zeus, seeing winter coming on again, determined to destroy the people of Arcadia. Then Prometheus, his chief councilor, sought to save this third race of man from destruction.

"They quarrel among themselves," said Zeus angrily. "They start trouble in the fields. We must train up a new race of men who will learn more quickly what it means to serve the gods."

Zeus was walking across the bronze floor of his mountain palace. A tremendous, tall figure of a man he was, the king god Zeus. But he who stood beside him, Prometheus of the family of Titans, was even taller.

"Worthless," Zeus was saying as if to himself. "Worthless," he repeated again, "the whole race. They complain of the winters. They are too weak a race for the climate of these times. Why should we continue to struggle with them? Better to be rid of them, every man and woman of the troublesome tribe."

"And then?" inquired Prometheus. "What if you create a new race to provide manpower for the farms and the bigger buildings? That race, too, will rebel while they can see and envy our knowledge and our power."

"Even so, I will destroy these Arcadians," insisted Zeus stubbornly. "Men are our creatures. Let them learn to serve us, to do our will."

"Up here on your mountain," observed Prometheus thoughtfully, "you make men and destroy them. But what about the men themselves? How can they learn wisdom when, time after time, you visit them with destruction?"

"You have too much sympathy for them," answered Zeus in a sharp voice. "I believe you love these huddling, sheepish men."

"They have minds and hearts," replied Prometheus warmly, "and a courage that is worth admiring. They wish to live even as the gods wish to live. Don't we feed ourselves on nectar[3] and ambrosia[4] every day to preserve our lives?"

Prometheus was speaking rapidly. His voice was deep. "This is your way," he went on. "You won't look ahead. You won't be patient. You won't give men a chance to learn how to live. Over and over again, with floods or with cracking red thunderbolts, you destroy them."

"I have let you live, Prometheus," said Zeus in an ominous tone, "to advise me when you can. You are my cousin. But I am not your child to be scolded." Zeus was smiling, but there was thunder behind the smile.

Silently Prometheus turned away. Leaving the marble-columned hall, he went out among the gardens of Olympus, the gods' mountain. The last roses were fading before the time of winter winds and rain.

---

3. **nectar:** drink of the gods.
4. **ambrosia** [am brō′zhə]: food of the gods.

This was not the first time Prometheus had heard thunder in the voice of Zeus. Prometheus knew that someday Zeus would turn against him, betray him, and punish him. Prometheus the Titan had the gift of reading the future. He could foresee the fate hidden and waiting for him and for others and even for Zeus himself.

Climbing among the upper gardens, Prometheus stopped at last beside an ancient, twisted ash tree. Leaning against its trunk, he looked toward the south. Beyond the last canal, the last steep sea wall, he could see the ocean. He looked far out toward that last shining circle of water. Then, with his head bent, he sat down on the tree roots bulging in thick knots above the ground.

It would be hard to tell you all the thoughts in the mind of the Titan—thoughts that coiled and twined like a nest of dragons. In his mighty brain were long memories of the past and far-reaching prophecies of what was to come.

He thought most often of the future, but the talk with Zeus just now had brought the past before him once again. He remembered once more the terrible war in which Zeus had seized the kingship of the gods. He thought of the exile and imprisonment of Cronus, the father of Zeus. He remembered the Titans, his people, now chained in the black pit of Tartarus.[5]

The great god Cronus himself, who had given peace to gods and men, where was he now? And the mighty-headed Titans, the magnificent engineers, builders of bridges and temples, where were they? All of them fallen, helpless, as good as dead.

Zeus had triumphed. Of the Titans, only two now walked the upper earth—he, Prometheus, and Epimetheus,[6] his brother.

And now, even now, Zeus was not content. It was not enough for his glory, it seemed, to have dethroned his own father, not enough to have driven the race of Titans from the houses of the gods. Now Zeus was plotting to kill the race of men.

Prometheus had endured the war against the Titans, his own people. He had even given help to Zeus. Having seen what was to come, he had thought, "Since Zeus must win, I'll guide him. I'll control his fierce anger and his greed for power."

But Prometheus could not submit to this latest plot of Zeus. He would use all his wits to save the men of Arcadia from destruction.

Why were they to be destroyed? Because they were cold and full of fears, huddled together in caves like animals. It was well enough in the warm months. They worked willingly in the fields of the gods and reared the horses and bulls and guarded the sheep. But when the cold days came, they grumbled against Olympus. They grumbled because they must eat and hunt like the animals and had no hoof nor claw nor heavy fur for protection.

What did they need? What protection would be better than hoof or claw? Prometheus knew. It was fire they needed—fire to cook with, to warm them, to harden metal for weapons. With fire they could frighten the wolf and the bear and the mountain lion.

Why did they lack the gift of fire? Prometheus knew that too. He knew how jealously the gods sat guard about their flame.

More than once he had told Zeus the need men had of fire. He knew why Zeus would not consent to teach men this secret of the gods.

---

5. **Tartarus** [tär′tər əs]: place in the underworld for wrongdoers.

6. **Epimetheus** [ep′ə mē′thē əs]

The gift of fire to men would be a gift of power. Hardened in the fire, the spears which men might make to chase a mountain lion might also, in time, be hurled against the gods. With fire would come comfort and time to think while the flames leaped up the walls of hidden caves. Men who had time to think would have time to question the laws of the gods. Among men who asked questions disorder might breed, and rebellion stronger than any mere squabble in the fields.

"But men are worth the gift of fire," thought Prometheus, sitting against the roots of his favorite ash tree. He could see ahead dimly into that time to come when gods would lose their power. And he, Prometheus, through his love for men, must help to bring on that time.

Prometheus did not hesitate. By the fall of night his plans were accomplished. As the sun went down, his tall figure appeared upon a sea beach. Above the sands a hundred caves, long ago deserted by the waters of the ocean, sheltered families of Arcadians. To them the Titan was bringing this very night the secret of the gods.

He came along the pebble line of high water. In his hand he carried a yellow reed.

This curious yellow stalk was made of metal, the most precious of the metals of the gods. From it the metalworkers molded rare and delicate shapes. From it they made the reedlike and hollow stalks which carried, in wisps of fennel[7] straw, coals from the gods' ever-burning fire. The gods who knew the sources of flame never built new fires in the sight of men. Going abroad on journeys, they took from their central hearth a smoldering coal.

Prometheus had left Olympus as one upon a journey. He alone knew he was not going to visit the home of Poseidon, Zeus's brother, lord of the sea—nor going into India, nor into the cold north. He was going only as far as the nearest sea beach.

He knew that, though he was going only to the sea beach, he was in truth starting upon a journey. He knew the hatred of Zeus

---

7. **fennel:** plant with bright green feathery leaves and clusters of yellow flowers.

would follow him. He knew that now he, Prometheus, could never return to the house of the gods. From this night he must live his life among the men he wished to save.

While the stars came out, bright as they are on nights when winter will soon come on, Prometheus gathered together a heap of driftwood. Opening the metal stalk, he set the flame of the gods in the waiting fuel.

Eating into the wood, the fire leaped up, fanned in the night breeze. Prometheus sat down beside the fire he had made. He was not long alone.

Shadowy figures appeared at the mouths of caves. One by one, men, women, and children crept toward the blaze. The night was cold. North winds had blown that day. The winds had blown on the lands of men, even as they had blown on the head of Zeus in his palace above them. Now in the night they came, the people of men, to the warmth of the beckoning fire.

Hundreds there were of them now. Those nearest the tall fire-bringer, the Titan, were talking with him. They knew him well. It was not the first time Prometheus had come to talk with them. But never before had he come late, alone, and lighted a fire against the dark.

It was not the first time men had seen a fire or felt its warmth. More than once a god, walking the earth, had set a fire, lit from the coals he carried secretly. Men reverenced the slender magic wands with which, it seemed, the gods could call up flame. But never before had they stood so near a fire nor seen the fire-wand.

Now men might hold in their own hands the mysterious yellow rod. They said, "Look" and "See" and, fingering the metal, "How wonderfully the gods can mold what is hard in the hands."

For a while Prometheus let them talk. He watched with pleasure the gleam of firelight in their shining eyes. Then quietly he took the metal stalk from the man who held it. With a swift gesture he threw it into the heap of burning wood.

The people groaned. The fire-wrought metal crumpled against the heat. The metal which carried well a single coal melted in the blazing fire.

The people murmured among themselves, "Hasn't he taken away the secret now? Hasn't he destroyed before our eyes the source of fire?"

Patiently, silently they waited. A few asked questions but got no answers. The cold wind cut them as the last of the burning driftwood grayed and blackened in the sand.

While the embers crumbled away, Prometheus rose, calling with him a few of the men who had asked him questions. Watching, they saw him scrape a hollow pit. Wondering, they followed his every movement, his hands holding a bronze knife, shaving chips of wood, taking from the fold of his cloak handfuls of bark and straw.

Next he set in his pit a chunk of ashwood, flat and firm, notched cleanly on one side. Beneath and around this notch he laid in bark and straw. Into the notch he set a pointed branch, slender, hard-tipped, and firm. Then slowly he swung the branch in his palms, twirled it in a steady rhythm, boring, drilling more and more rapidly with his skilled and powerful hands.

The wood grew warm. The dust ground from the ash block heated to smoldering. The straw caught. Light sputtered from the pit. Small sparks glowed, flew up, went out. Tugged by the night wind, smoke curled from the dry straw, from the bark, from the wood shavings fed gently from the heap Prometheus had made ready to his hand. At last, more suddenly than the eye could follow, out of the pit in the sand rose the living flame.

Deftly Prometheus removed the ash block, added heavier kindling. Last of all, the driftwood yielded to the strengthening fire. He knelt beside it awhile, breathing upon it, guarding, urging the blaze. At last he rose, stood back, folded his arms. As if considering a thought, half sorrow, half pleasure, he looked up at the glare of fire invading the night sky.

Whispers and murmuring first, then cries, then shouting. Men ran to scoop new hollows in the sand. They begged Prometheus' knife. The children, running from the beach to the caves and fields, hurried back with fists crammed full of straw and withered leaves.

The people of the caves were breathless with excitement. Here was no secret. The fire-wand did not breed the fire as they had thought. No nameless power of the gods bred the flame.

The hard, pale ashwood passed from hand to hand as men struggled to light their own fires. They despaired at first. New sparks flew up and died. Or the hands were weak, too weak to drill the flame. But at last came triumph. A dozen fires sprang up. Women and children ran with laden arms to feed each growing blaze.

The gods, from their distant houses, saw the glow. There to the south it shone, fighting against the starlight, the glare in the sky. Was it the end of the world? Would the terrible fire consume the earth again?

Hermes, the messenger, came at last with an answer to all their questions.

"Great Zeus," said Hermes gravely in the assembly of the gods, "Prometheus, your cousin, stands in the midst of those rising fires. He took coals from the central hearth as for a journey."

"So?" asked Zeus, nodding his head. Then, as if he were holding an argument with himself, he continued, saying, "But then? What then? The fire will die. It is not a crime for a god or for a Titan to light a fire for himself on a cold evening."

"But that fire will not die," interrupted Hermes. "That fire is not the fire of gods and Titans. Prometheus has taught men the source of fire. Those fires are their own, the fires of men. They've drilled flame out of hardwood with their own hands."

Then the gods knew the end of the world was not yet come upon them. But they knew, and Zeus most of all, that it might be their own great power that was burning away in the fires of men.

STUDY QUESTIONS

Recalling

1. According to the myth, how many ages of the human race have there been? Why did the gods end each age?
2. Why does Zeus consider the people of Arcadia "worthless"? What qualities does Prometheus see in them?
3. What gift does Prometheus want to give humans? What will they be able to do with this gift?
4. What does Zeus fear that humans will be able to do if they have fire? What does Prometheus know is going to happen to the gods?
5. What actions does Prometheus perform to build a fire on the beach? What do the human beings do when they see the fire?

Interpreting

6. How do Zeus and Prometheus differ in their attitudes toward humans?

7. What human qualities does Zeus himself exhibit? What human qualities does Prometheus possess?

8. After teaching humans how to make fire, Prometheus looks up at the sky with "half sorrow, half pleasure." Why does he have mixed feelings?

Extending

9. In what way might this myth be the ancient Greeks' explanation of the beginnings of civilized life?

READING AND LITERARY FOCUS

Allusion

An **allusion** is a reference in a work of literature to a character, place, or situation from another work of literature. For example, if a character in a story is described as *Promethean*, that character is creative, life giving, and courageous—just like Prometheus himself.

Literature contains many allusions to Greek mythology. A character in a modern story may possess the wisdom of Athena or the cleverness of Hermes. A place may be so large and grand that it is called *olympian*. A situation may be so pleasant that it is said to be a *golden age*—a perfect time, according to the myths.

By using allusions a writer can make a work of literature more interesting and full of additional meanings. When you recognize an allusion, you are calling up one of your past reading experiences and enriching your appreciation of literature.

Thinking About Allusion

▦ Write a sentence that contains an allusion to Zeus. In your allusion be sure to refer to Zeus's character traits. For example, "He thought he was Zeus himself, throwing out his commands like thunderbolts."

VOCABULARY

Vivid Words

Vivid words make the places, characters, thoughts, and actions in a story come alive. Sometimes vivid words add sound and color, as in ". . . with *cracking red* thunderbolts you destroy them." Sometimes vivid words create pictures: "I believe you love these *huddling, sheepish* men." We see men in a huddle, frightened like sheep. Some vivid words emphasize an idea: ". . . he looked up at the glare of fire *invading* the night sky."

▦ Find three other sentences with vivid words in this selection. On a separate sheet of paper, write the sentences, underlining the vivid words. Explain what those words add to your understanding or picture of the situation.

CHALLENGE

Survey

▦ Conduct a survey to determine what things people consider essential to civilization. Write out one question, and ask a number of people the question. You may want to provide people with some possible answers, such as *fire, farming,* or *language*. Ask the question exactly the same way each time. Record the responses, and report to the class on your findings.

Many mythologies include a myth of a great flood, a punishment for evil. Prometheus had given human beings the gift of fire, a gift they violently abused. In the face of total destruction, it was Deucalion [dōō kā′lē ən], a son of Prometheus, and his wife, Pyrrha [pir′ə], who were chosen to keep the human race alive.

■ What riddle did they need to solve?

Greek statue from the fifth century B.C. of Poseidon, god of the sea.

Retold by
W. H. D. Rouse

Deucalion and Pyrrha

Now in this Iron Age,[1] Zeus visited the earth, to see whether men were as bad as they were said to be; and he came to the realm of one Lycaon,[2] who was King in Arcadia. Lycaon laughed, on hearing that Zeus had come, and said, "Now then, let us see if he is really a god!" So he killed an innocent man, a hostage in fact, whom he was bound to protect, and cooked his flesh, and set it before Zeus his guest, to see if he would eat it. But Zeus struck the King's house with a thunderbolt, and Lycaon fled terrified to the hills. His rough coat changed into bristling hairs all over his body. He tried to shout, and out came a snarl, for he had turned into a wolf, destined to delight in blood all the rest of his days.

Zeus called a council of the gods, and told them what had been done; and then he declared that he thought it best to destroy mankind. The others said, "But what shall we do? There will be no one to offer sacrifices to the gods." "Never mind for that," said Zeus, "I will provide." The question then came, whether he should launch his thunderbolts on the world and set it afire; but Zeus was afraid that so great a conflagration[3] might rise to the upper air, and set that also on fire, so that the Olympians themselves would be burned up.

It seemed best therefore to use water. The winds were bidden to gather the clouds; the rains descended; and the floods came and overwhelmed the whole country of Greece, so that all who dwelt there were drowned. Men and beasts, wolves and sheep, lions and tigers were carried down to the sea, and seals and dolphins swam about in the forests.

1. **Iron Age:** in mythology the most wicked age of the world, coming after the Golden, the Silver, and the Bronze Ages.
2. **Lycaon** [lī′kā′ən]

3. **conflagration** [kon′flə grā′shən]: very large fire.

Deucalion and Pyrrha 431

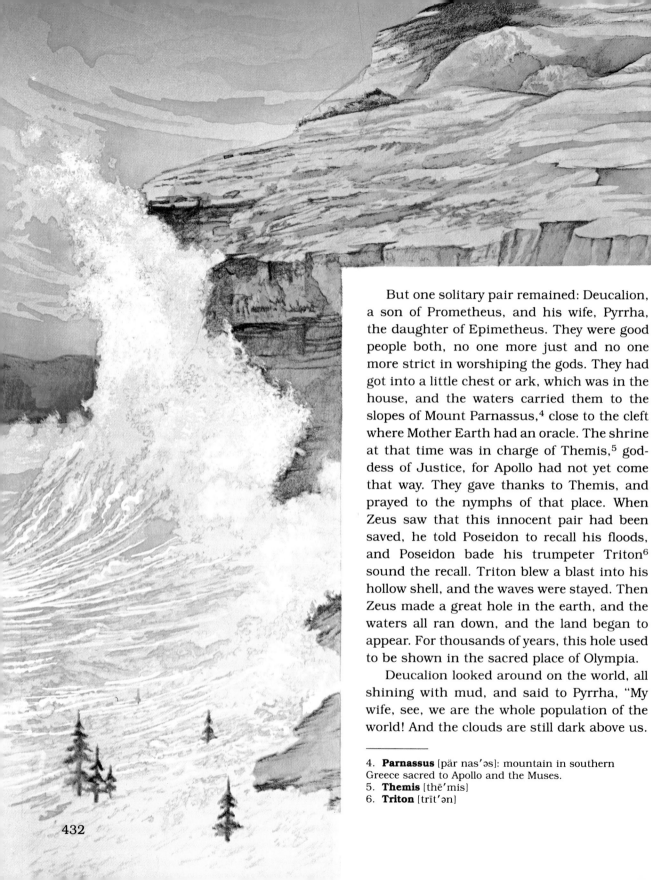

But one solitary pair remained: Deucalion, a son of Prometheus, and his wife, Pyrrha, the daughter of Epimetheus. They were good people both, no one more just and no one more strict in worshiping the gods. They had got into a little chest or ark, which was in the house, and the waters carried them to the slopes of Mount Parnassus,[4] close to the cleft where Mother Earth had an oracle. The shrine at that time was in charge of Themis,[5] goddess of Justice, for Apollo had not yet come that way. They gave thanks to Themis, and prayed to the nymphs of that place. When Zeus saw that this innocent pair had been saved, he told Poseidon to recall his floods, and Poseidon bade his trumpeter Triton[6] sound the recall. Triton blew a blast into his hollow shell, and the waves were stayed. Then Zeus made a great hole in the earth, and the waters all ran down, and the land began to appear. For thousands of years, this hole used to be shown in the sacred place of Olympia.

Deucalion looked around on the world, all shining with mud, and said to Pyrrha, "My wife, see, we are the whole population of the world! And the clouds are still dark above us.

---

4. **Parnassus** [pär nas′əs]: mountain in southern Greece sacred to Apollo and the Muses.
5. **Themis** [thē′mis]
6. **Triton** [trīt′ən]

What should I do, if I were alone? Or you, without me? Let us ask what is the will of God."

So they entered the shrine of Themis, and said, "Themis, if the anger of Zeus is satisfied, tell us how to recover the human race." And Themis said, "Go down to the plain, and cover your heads with a veil, and throw behind you your mother's bones."

They went out, and Pyrrha said to her husband, "I am afraid, my dear husband. How can we find our mother's bones? And if we could find them, would it not be wicked to disturb them?"

But Deucalion was not his father's son for nothing; he had some of his father's wisdom, and he replied, "Wife, the gods often speak in riddles. I think Themis means the bones of Mother Earth, that is, stones. Let us try them, it can do no harm to try."

Then they veiled their heads, and each of them picked up stones, and threw them behind their backs. Perhaps you will hardly believe it, but the stones as they fell took on human shapes. Deucalion's became men, and Pyrrha's became women. Even now we show traces of this origin, for we have veins in our bodies, like the veins in a piece of marble, both called by the same name; and men are called peoples, because they grew out of pebbles.

STUDY QUESTIONS

Recalling

1. What did Zeus do to Lycaon to punish him for his great crime?
2. What reason did Zeus give for using water rather than fire to destroy the earth?
3. Of all the people on earth, why were Deucalion and Pyrrha chosen to survive?
4. What did Deucalion and Pyrrha do to escape the flood?
5. Whom did Deucalion and Pyrrha ask for guidance? What unusual instruction did they receive?
6. How did Deucalion solve the "riddle"?

Interpreting

7. What actions of Deucalion and Pyrrha demonstrate their attitude toward the gods?
8. Why do you think Deucalion was worthy to be called "son of Prometheus"?
9. What do you think this myth suggests about the relationship of people to the earth itself?

Extending

10. In your opinion, why would a culture want to continue to tell this story of destruction and rebirth?

READING AND LITERARY FOCUS

Flat and Round Characters

Characters in a story are called **flat characters** when they show only one trait, or quality, from beginning to end. Deucalion and Pyrrha, for example, are flat characters because they show only goodness. Many myths use flat characters in order to represent the single quality that the myth is trying to emphasize.

Round characters show a variety of traits, often complicated and seemingly opposite ones. For example, a round character may be light-hearted one minute and deadly serious the next. A round character may have doubts, fears, opinions, memories, or any mix of emotions. Most importantly, round characters change just as people do. Round characters are literature's attempt to portray lifelike people.

Thinking About Flat and Round Characters

■ Zeus, though a god, has many human qualities. Tell how Zeus is a round character by listing his different personality traits. Explain how some of these traits contradict one another.

COMPOSITION

Answering an Essay Question

■ Write an answer to the following essay question: "Do you think Zeus was justified in destroying the earth because of the actions of Lycaon?" Begin by restating the question as your topic sentence or thesis sentence. Then give clearly stated reasons to support your opinion. Conclude with a summary of your reasons. *For help with this assignment, see Lesson 1 in the Writing About Literature Handbook at the back of this book.*

Writing a Letter

■ Write a letter to Deucalion and Pyrrha, giving them advice from the twentieth century. Suggest several things they should and should not do to make the human race happy. For example, how should they divide the land on earth?

The tale of Midas [mī′dəs] is one of the most popular myths. It was probably designed to teach a lesson, for it shows us a king learning a very hard lesson indeed.

■ As you read, notice how the power of the gods is balanced by wisdom and mercy.

Statue of Apollo, god of the sun.

Retold by
Bernard Evslin

Midas

There was a king named Midas, and what he loved best in the world was gold. He had plenty of his own, but he could not bear the thought of anyone else having any. Each morning he awoke very early to watch the sunrise and said, "Of all the gods, if gods there be, I like you least, Apollo. How dare you ride so unthriftily in your sun-chariot scattering golden sheaves[1] of light on rich and poor alike—on king and peasant, on merchant, shepherd, warrior? This is an evil thing, oh wastrel[2] god, for only kings should have gold; only the rich know what to do with it."

After a while these words of complaint, uttered each dawn, came to Apollo, and he was angry. He appeared to Midas in a dream and said, "Other gods would punish you, Midas, but I am famous for my even temper. Instead of doing you violence, I will show you how gracious I can be by granting you a wish. What is it to be?"

Midas cried, "Let everything I touch turn to gold!"

He shouted this out of his sleep in a strangling greedy voice, and the guards in the doorway nodded to each other and said, "The king calls out. He must be dreaming of gold again."

Wearied by the dream, Midas slept past sunrise; when he awoke it was full morning. He went out into his garden. The sun was high, the sky was blue. A soft breeze played among the trees. It was a glorious morning. He was still half asleep. Tatters[3] of the dream were in his head.

"Can it be true?" he said to himself. "They

---

1. **sheaves:** large bundles of things tied together.
2. **wastrel** [wās′trəl]: wasteful person.

3. **Tatters:** shreds.

say the gods appear in dreams. That's how men know them. On the other hand I know that dreams are false, teasing things. You can't believe them. Let us put it to the test."

He reached out his hand and touched a rose. It turned to gold—petals and stalk, it turned to gold and stood there rigid, heavy, gleaming. A bee buzzed out of its stiff folds, furious; it lit on Midas' hand to sting him. The king looked at the heavy golden bee on the back of his hand and moved it to his finger.

"I shall wear it as a ring," he said.

Midas went about touching all his roses, seeing them stiffen and gleam. They lost their odor. The disappointed bees rose in swarms and buzzed angrily away. Butterflies departed. The hard flowers tinkled like little bells when the breeze moved among them, and the king was well pleased.

His little daughter, the princess, who had been playing in the garden, ran to him and said, "Father, Father, what has happened to the roses?"

"Are they not pretty, my dear?"

"No! They're ugly! They're horrid and sharp and I can't smell them any more. What happened?"

"A magical thing."

"Who did the magic?"

"I did."

"Unmagic it, then! I hate these roses."

She began to cry.

"Don't cry," he said, stroking her head. "Stop crying, and I will give you a golden doll with a gold-leaf dress and tiny golden shoes."

She stopped crying. He felt the hair grow spiky under his fingers. Her eyes stiffened and froze into place. The little blue vein in her neck stopped pulsing. She was a statue, a figure of pale gold standing in the garden path with lifted face. Her tears were tiny golden beads on her golden cheeks. He looked at her and said, "This is unfortunate. I'm sorry it happened. I have no time to be sad this morning. I shall be busy turning things into gold. But, when I have a moment, I shall think about this problem; I promise." He hurried out of the garden which had become unpleasant to him.

On Midas' way back to the castle he amused himself by kicking up gravel in the path and watching it tinkle down as tiny nuggets. The door he opened became golden; the chair he sat upon became solid gold like his throne. The plates turned into gold, and the cups became gold cups before the amazed eyes of the servants, whom he was careful not to touch. He wanted them to continue being able to serve him; he was very hungry.

With great relish Midas picked up a piece of bread and honey. His teeth bit metal; his mouth was full of metal. He felt himself choking. He reached into his mouth and pulled out a golden slab of bread, all bloody now, and flung it through the window. Very lightly now he touched the other food to see what would happen. Meat . . . apples . . . walnuts . . . they all turned to gold even when he touched them with only the tip of his finger . . . and when he did not touch them with his fingers, when he lifted them on his fork, they became gold as soon as they touched his lips, and he had to put them back onto the plate. He was savagely hungry. Worse than hunger, when he thought about drinking, he realized that wine, or water, or milk would turn to gold in his mouth and choke him if he drank. As he thought that he could not drink, thirst began to burn in his belly. He felt himself full of hot dry sand, felt that the lining of his head was on fire.

"What good is all my gold?" he cried, "if I cannot eat and cannot drink?"

He shrieked with rage, pounded on the table, and flung the plates about. All the servants ran from the room in fright. Then Midas raced out of the castle, across the bridge that spanned the moat,[4] along the golden gravel path into the garden where the stiff flowers chimed hatefully, and the statue of his daughter looked at him with scooped and empty eyes. There in the garden, in the blaze of the sun, he raised his arms heavenward, and

---

4. **moat:** wide ditch, usually filled with water, surrounding a castle.

cried, "You, Apollo, false god, traitor! You pretended to forgive me, but you punished me with a gift!"

Then it seemed to him that the sun grew brighter, that the light thickened, that the sun-god stood before him in the path, tall, stern, clad in burning gold. A voice said, "On your knees, wretch!"

He fell to his knees.

"Do you repent?"

"I repent. I will never desire gold again. I will never accuse the gods. Pray, revoke the fatal wish."

Apollo reached his hand and touched the roses. The tinkling stopped, they softened, swayed, blushed. Fragrance grew on the air. The bees returned, and the butterflies. He touched the statue's cheek. She lost her stiffness, her metallic gleam. She ran to the roses, knelt among them, and cried, "Oh, thank you, Father. You've changed them back again." Then she ran off, shouting and laughing.

Apollo said, "I take back my gift. I remove the golden taint[5] from your touch, but you are not to escape without punishment. Because you have been the most foolish of men, you shall wear always a pair of donkey's ears."

Midas touched his ears. They were long and furry. He said, "I thank you for your forgiveness, Apollo . . . even though it comes with a punishment."

"Go now," said Apollo. "Eat and drink. Enjoy the roses. Watch your child grow. Life is the only wealth, man. In your great thrift, you have been wasteful of life, and that is the sign you wear on your head. Farewell."

Midas put a tall pointed hat on his head so that no one would see his ears. Then he went in to eat and drink his fill.

---

5. **taint:** something evil.

For years he wore the cap so that no one would know of his disgrace. But the servant who cut his hair had to know so Midas swore him to secrecy, warning that it would cost him his head if he spoke of the king's ears. But the servant who was a coward was also a gossip. He could not bear to keep a secret, especially a secret so mischievous. Although he was afraid to tell it, he felt that he would burst if he didn't.

One night he went out to the banks of the river, dug a little hole, put his mouth to it, and whispered, "Midas has donkey's ears, Midas has donkey's ears . . ." and quickly filled up the hole again, and ran back to the castle, feeling better.

But the river-reeds heard him, and they always whisper to each other when the wind seethes among them. They were heard whispering, "Midas has donkey's ears . . . donkey's ears . . ." and soon the whole country was whispering, "Have you heard about Midas? Have you heard about his ears?"

When the king heard, he knew who had told the secret and ordered the man's head cut off; but then he thought, "The god forgave me, perhaps I had better forgive this blabbermouth." Therefore he let the treacherous man keep his head.

Then Apollo appeared again and said, "Midas, you have learned the final lesson, mercy. As you have done, so shall you be done by."

And Midas felt his long hairy ears dwindling back to normal.

He was an old man now. His daughter, the princess, was grown. He had grandchildren. Sometimes he tells his smallest granddaughter the story of how her mother was turned into a golden statue, and he says, "See, I'm changing you too. Look, your hair is all gold."

And she pretends to be frightened.

STUDY QUESTIONS

Recalling

1. What did Midas accuse Apollo of wasting?
2. What did Midas wish? What happened to his daughter?
3. What made Midas ask "What good is all my gold"?
4. What change took place in Midas' body? How did people learn of it?
5. What final lesson did Midas learn? What action showed he had learned it?

Interpreting

6. Why do you think Apollo was the appropriate god to deal with Midas?
7. Explain at least two traits of Midas' character before he learned his lesson. Give examples of each trait.
8. What change took place in Midas' character after he learned his lesson?

Extending

9. Why do you think people often do not think about all the possible results of their actions?

READING AND LITERARY FOCUS

Metamorphosis

A **metamorphosis** is a change in shape or form, and it occurs frequently in Greek myths. It is one of the elements that make the myths such imaginative reading. Some of the gods, like the sea god Proteus, for example, frequently changed themselves into different shapes, such as a fish, a lion, or a snake. Zeus often changed shape and became a bull, a shower of gold, or even a puff of smoke when he visited earth.

However, gods often used their powers of metamorphosis when they wanted to teach someone a lesson. They usually created a magical change of shape that was particularly appropriate to a person's character. In one ancient story, for example, a young woman who cried a great deal was turned into a fountain.

Thinking About Metamorphosis

▓ Tell why the metamorphosis that takes place in Midas' body is especially appropriate for his character.

COMPOSITION

Writing About Description

▓ Write about one of the vivid descriptions of Midas turning an object to gold. First choose one of the descriptions. Then identify the details the author uses. Finally, tell what such detailed description adds to the story.

Inventing a Metamorphosis

▓ Write about a person or an object that is changed into something completely different, such as a person changed into a tree. Be specific in describing the person or object as it changes. You may also want to invent a story explaining why the change takes place.

CHALLENGE

Illustration

▓ The gods and goddesses, the monsters, and the characters who undergo metamorphosis in Greek mythology provide many opportunities for vivid illustration. Illustrate the story of Midas or one of the other myths in this unit.

The tale of Echo and Narcissus [när sis′əs] is one of the most moving stories in Greek mythology. Like the punishment of King Midas, it includes metamorphosis, or shape changing. As you read, notice how the myth imaginatively explains a natural phenomenon—the echo—and turns it into a sad but tender love story.

■ What is Echo's greatest mistake?

Greek statue of a young man, 475 B.C.

Retold by
Katharine Pyle

Echo and Narcissus

At times it pleased great Zeus to take upon himself some earthly form, and so descend from Olympus, and amuse himself among the mortals for a time.

But Hera, his queen, was jealous of these pleasures, and whenever she learned that he had gone, she would follow him and search the whole world through until she found him. Then she would weary him with angry words and with reproaches[1] till, for the sake of peace, he would return with her to his high palace on Olympus.

But once, when Hera followed him there, he hid himself in a deep wood and bade the nymph Echo go to meet his queen and keep her for a while in talk until he could escape unseen back to Olympus.

This Echo did. Of all the nymphs,[2] she was the wittiest and the most cunning.[3] She hastened forth, and meeting the goddess on her way began at once to pour into her ears some curious tale of something she had lately seen. So strange was the tale that, though Hera was in haste, she stayed to listen. Then when the story had reached its end, she would have gone again upon her way, but now it was some even stranger tale Echo had to tell. So she kept Hera listening there till Zeus was safely back upon Olympus. His queen found him there when she returned at last, outwearied[4] from her searching on the earth. He was enthroned again in his high hall in all his majesty and glory.

But Hera guessed the trick that had been played upon her, and in wrath she cried, "Never again shall Echo's cunning tongue be used for deceiving others. All her wit shall now

---

1. **reproaches:** words of blame.
2. **nymphs** [nimfs]: minor nature goddesses in the forms of beautiful young women.

3. **cunning:** clever.
4. **outwearied:** tired out.

avail her nothing, for she shall never again be able to put into words her cunning thoughts," and she took from Echo all power of speech, except that of repeating what she heard others say.

Now piteous indeed was Echo's case, and the more piteous because she loved a youth named Narcissus. He was the fairest youth on all the earth; so beauteous, indeed, that many a nymph had pined for love of him, but Narcissus scorned them all and fled from their sighs and tender looks. Echo might, perhaps, in time have won his love by her wit, if she could have put it into words, but now she could not, and he fled from her as from the others.

But one day she hid herself among the bushes in a wood where he often came, with the hope that, thinking himself alone, he might breathe out some tender word or sigh she could repeat to him.

It was not long before she saw him come. He was weary from the chase,[5] and threw himself down beneath a tree to rest. "Heigho!" he sighed.

"Heigho!" Echo repeated softly.

"Who is there?" cried Narcissus, starting up.

"Is there!" answered Echo.

"Is it a friend?"

"A friend!" replied the nymph.

"Then come to me."

"Come to me," Echo cried joyously, and springing from the thicket where she had lain hidden, she ran to him with outstretched arms.

But Narcissus drew back from her with frowning brows. "I know thee now," he cried. "Thou art one of those who have followed me. I do not want thy love."

"Want thy love," the nymph repeated piteously, holding out to him her arms.

But Narcissus answered more sharply still, "Away and touch me not and never follow me again!"

"Follow me again!" cried Echo. But already Narcissus was gone from her. He had fled away more swiftly than she could follow him, and from that day he hid from her so that she could not find him.

Then the poor nymph grieved bitterly. Day after day she spent in tears and sad complaints until at last her sorrow melted her flesh away; her bones became rocks, and at last nothing was left of her but a wandering voice that haunted caves and cliffs, answering back the calls and cries of others. But before she had vanished quite, the nymph breathed out a silent prayer to Aphrodite that some day Narcissus himself might feel a sorrow like to hers, might pine with love of one who neither could nor would return that love.

Her silent prayer was granted, and thus it came to pass that Narcissus entered once a lonely wood where he had never been before, and there came to a pool as still and bright as polished silver. Never deer or bird or any living thing had found that pool until Narcissus came. Thirsty after his wanderings he knelt to drink, and as he bent above the pool he saw himself reflected in the water, yet he did not know it was his own image that he saw. He thought it was some nymph or naiad[6] who lived there in the pool—one lovelier far than any he had ever seen before.

Filled with delight he gazed, then suddenly plunged his arms down in the pool and sought to seize the lovely thing, but at once the water broke into ripples and his reflection disappeared.

---

5. **chase:** hunt.

6. **naiad** [nī′ad]: water nymph.

Narcissus drew back with beating heart, and breathlessly waited hoping it would again appear, yet fearing that he had frightened it away forever.

Then, as the pool grew still, his image showed again there in the water. More gently now Narcissus moved, stooping down toward it, and always as he stooped near and nearer, so the image seemed to rise up toward him, until it was as though in a moment their lips would meet; but when he thought to kiss those lips, 'twas only the chill water that he touched.

Again and still again he tried to grasp the image, but always at his touch it disappeared. And now the unhappy youth spent all his days there by the pool, filled with hopeless love of his own image. He neither ate nor slept, but pined and pined with love, even as Echo had, until at last he pined his life away.

Then from the fields and woods arose a sound of mourning. Voices cried, "Narcissus, the beautiful, is dead! Is dead!" Youths and nymphs, dryads[7] and fauns,[8] lamented over him, while Echo repeated every sigh and sad complaint she heard.

A funeral pyre was built on which they thought to lay the lovely form of dead Narcissus, but when they went to look for it, it had disappeared; instead they found only, in the spot where it had lain, a snow-white flower; it was a flower different from any they had ever seen before, and guessing that the gods had changed him into this form, they called it by his name, and ever since that flower has been known everywhere as the Narcissus—loveliest of blooms, even as of old that first Narcissus was the loveliest of youths.

---

7. **dryads** [drī′ədz]: wood nymphs.
8. **fauns** [fônz]: Roman word for *satyrs*, spirits of the woods who were part man, part goat.

STUDY QUESTIONS

Recalling

1. What did Echo do to keep Hera's attention while Zeus was visiting earth? What did Hera do to punish Echo?
2. Who was Narcissus? How might Echo "have won his love"?
3. What happens to Echo because of her grief? What does she ask Aphrodite?
4. What did Narcissus see in the pool? What did he think he saw in the pool?
5. What happened to Narcissus' body after he died?

Interpreting

6. Why is Echo's metamorphosis appropriate to the "crime" Echo had committed?
7. Describe the character of Narcissus. Why is his metamorphosis appropriate to his character?
8. Do you think the punishments of Echo and Narcissus were just? Why or why not?

Extending

9. What lesson about human behavior do you think this myth teaches?

COMPOSITION

Writing About Plot

■ Write about the plot of "Echo and Narcissus." First identify the major parts of the plot. Then identify the conflict. Next describe the problems that make it difficult for the main characters to resolve the conflict. Finally, tell how the myth concludes. *For help with this assignment, see Lesson 2 in the Writing About Literature Handbook at the back of this book.*

Writing a Dialogue

■ Write a dialogue in which one character, like Echo, can only repeat the last few words of another character. First write a brief introduction to identify the characters—for example, two people planning a trip.

Mythology is filled with stories of mortals who dare to challenge the gods. Sometimes the gods are amused by these challenges; sometimes they are understanding; sometimes they are angry. Arachne [ə rak′nē] is a young girl who dares to challenge Athena.

■ What is Athena's response?

Statue from 440 B.C. of Athena, goddess of wisdom.

Retold by
Olivia Coolidge

Arachne

Arachne was a maiden who became famous throughout Greece, though she was neither wellborn nor beautiful and came from no great city. She lived in an obscure little village, and her father was a humble dyer of wool. In this he was very skillful, producing many varied shades, while above all he was famous for the clear, bright scarlet which is made from shellfish, and which was the most glorious of all the colors used in ancient Greece. Even more skillful than her father was Arachne. It was her task to spin the fleecy wool into a fine, soft thread and to weave it into cloth on the high-standing loom[1] within the cottage. Arachne was small and pale from much working. Her eyes were light and her hair was a dusty brown, yet she was quick and graceful, and her fingers, roughened as they were, went so fast that it was hard to follow their flickering movements. So soft and even was her thread, so fine her cloth, so gorgeous her embroidery, that soon her products were known all over Greece. No one had ever seen the like of them before.

At last Arachne's fame became so great that people used to come from far and wide to watch her working. Even the graceful nymphs would steal in from stream or forest and peep shyly through the dark doorway, watching in wonder the white arms of Arachne as she stood at the loom and threw the shuttle[2] from hand to hand between the hanging threads, or drew out the long wool, fine as a hair, from the distaff[3] as she sat spinning. "Surely Athena herself must have taught her," people would murmur to one another. "Who else could know the secret of such marvelous skill?"

_____
1. **high-standing loom:** large, free-standing machine for weaving thread into cloth.

_____
2. **shuttle:** device on the loom that moves the thread back and forth through the thread that runs up and down.
3. **distaff:** stick that holds the cotton or wool before it is pulled thin into thread.

Arachne was used to being wondered at, and she was immensely proud of the skill that had brought so many to look on her. Praise was all she lived for, and it displeased her greatly that people should think anyone, even a goddess, could teach her anything. Therefore when she heard them murmur, she would stop her work and turn round indignantly[4] to say, "With my own ten fingers I gained this skill, and by hard practice from early morning till night. I never had time to stand looking as you people do while another maiden worked. Nor if I had, would I give Athena credit because the girl was more skillful than I. As for Athena's weaving, how could there be finer cloth or more beautiful embroidery than mine? If Athena herself were to come down and compete with me, she could do no better than I."

One day when Arachne turned round with such words, an old woman answered her, a gray old woman, bent and very poor, who stood leaning on a staff and peering at Arachne amid the crowd of onlookers. "Reckless girl," she said, "how dare you claim to be equal to the immortal gods themselves? I am an old woman and have seen much. Take my advice and ask pardon of Athena for your words. Rest content with your fame of being the best spinner and weaver that mortal eyes have ever beheld."

"Stupid old woman," said Arachne indignantly, "who gave you a right to speak in this way to me? It is easy to see that you were never good for anything in your day, or you would not come here in poverty and rags to gaze at my skill. If Athena resents my words, let her answer them herself. I have challenged her to a contest, but she, of course, will not come. It is easy for the gods to avoid matching their skill with that of men."

At these words the old woman threw down her staff and stood erect. The wondering onlookers saw her grow tall and fair and stand clad in long robes of dazzling white. They were terribly afraid as they realized that they stood in the presence of Athena. Arachne herself flushed red for a moment, for she had never really believed that the goddess would hear her. Before the group that was gathered there she would not give in; so pressing her pale lips together in obstinacy[5] and pride, she led the goddess to one of the great looms and set herself before the other. Without a word both began to thread the long woolen strands that hang from the rollers, and between which the shuttle moves back and forth. Many skeins[6] lay heaped beside them to use, bleached white, and gold, and scarlet, and other shades, varied as the rainbow. Arachne had never thought of giving credit for her success to her father's skill in dyeing, though in actual truth the colors were as remarkable as the cloth itself.

Soon there was no sound in the room but the breathing of the onlookers, the whirring of the shuttles, and the creaking of the wooden frames as each pressed the thread up into place or tightened the pegs by which the whole was held straight. The excited crowd in the doorway began to see that the skill of both in truth was very nearly equal, but that, however the cloth might turn out, the goddess was the quicker of the two. A pattern of many pictures was growing on her loom. There was a border of twined branches of the olive, Athena's favorite tree, while in the middle, figures began to appear. As they looked at the glowing colors, the spectators realized that Athena was weaving into her pattern a last warning

_____

4. **indignantly** [in dig′nənt lē]: with restrained anger.

5. **obstinacy:** stubbornness.
6. **skeins** [skānz]: strands of yarn coiled into bundles, ready for weaving.

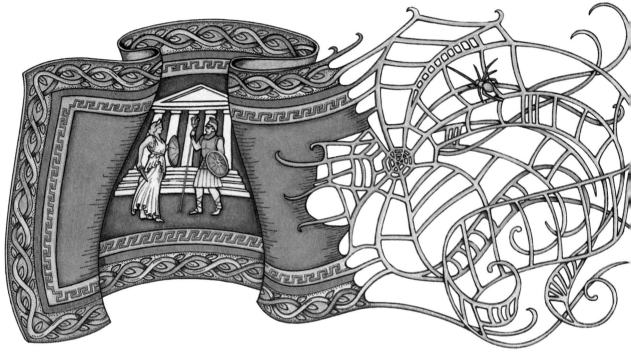

to Arachne. The central figure was the goddess herself competing with Poseidon for possession of the city of Athens; but in the four corners were mortals who had tried to strive with gods and pictures of the awful fate that had overtaken them. The goddess ended a little before Arachne and stood back from her marvelous work to see what the maiden was doing.

Never before had Arachne been matched against anyone whose skill was equal, or even nearly equal to her own. As she stole glances from time to time at Athena and saw the goddess working swiftly, calmly, and always a little faster than herself, she became angry instead of frightened, and an evil thought came into her head. Thus as Athena stepped back a pace to watch Arachne finishing her work, she saw that the maiden had taken for her design a pattern of scenes which showed evil or unworthy actions of the gods, how they had deceived fair maidens, resorted to trickery, and appeared on earth from time to time in the form of poor and humble people. When the goddess saw this insult glowing in bright colors on Arachne's loom, she did not wait while the cloth was judged, but stepped forward, her gray eyes blazing with anger, and tore Arachne's work across. Then she struck Arachne across the face. Arachne stood there a moment, struggling with anger, fear, and pride. "I will not live under this insult," she cried, and seizing a rope from the wall, she made a noose and would have hanged herself.

The goddess touched the rope and touched the maiden. "Live on, wicked girl," she said. "Live on and spin, both you and your descendants. When men look at you they may remember that it is not wise to strive with Athena." At that the body of Arachne shriveled up; and her legs grew tiny, spindly, and distorted. There before the eyes of the spectators hung a little dusty brown spider on a slender thread.

All spiders descend from Arachne, and as the Greeks watched them spinning their thread wonderfully fine, they remembered the contest with Athena and thought that it was not right for even the best of men to claim equality with the gods.

STUDY QUESTIONS

Recalling

1. What was Arachne's great skill? Who did the people think had taught her?
2. What did Arachne "live for"? What did she dare the goddess to do?
3. What was the subject of Athena's weaving? What was the subject of Arachne's weaving?
4. Into what shape did the goddess transform Arachne?

Interpreting

5. Describe Arachne's personality in your own words. What do you think was the greatest fault in her character?
6. Why was the form of Arachne's metamorphosis appropriate to her life and personality?

Extending

7. What human skills do you think are so marvelous that they seem to be "gifts of the gods"?

READING AND LITERARY FOCUS

Character Motivation

One of the questions we ask as we read any story is "Why do the characters do what they do?" In other words, what are their motivations?

Motivation is the idea, emotion, or goal that causes a character to act. Like real people, characters in a story should have clear motivations for their actions. For example, Prometheus gives humans the gift of fire because of his sympathy for the condition of their lives. By giving believable motivations to gods and goddesses, myths make supernatural beings seem like real people.

Thinking About Character Motivation

■ What do you think was Athena's motivation for accepting Arachne's challenge?

VOCABULARY

Antonyms

Antonyms are words that have opposite or nearly opposite meanings. *Early* and *late* are antonyms. The words below in capitals are from "Arachne." Choose the word that is most nearly the opposite of each word in capitals, *as the word is used in the story*. Write the number of each item and the letter of your choice on a separate sheet of paper.

1. HUMBLE: (a) modest (b) proud (c) lowly (d) funny
2. ERECT: (a) straight (b) firm (c) hunched (d) build
3. OBSTINACY: (a) frustration (b) agreeableness (c) rejection (d) defiance
4. VARIED: (a) many-colored (b) plain (c) rare (d) bright
5. SLENDER: (a) heavy (b) narrow (c) slick (d) coarse

COMPOSITION

Writing a Character Sketch

■ Write a character sketch of Arachne or of another character in this unit. First identify the character. Then name the character's outstanding traits, or qualities. Finally, tell how an event in the myth shows one or more of those traits in action. *For help with this assignment, see Lesson 3 in the Writing About Literature Handbook at the back of this book.*

Creating a Character

■ Create a character whose weakness is too much of one particular quality, such as humility, carelessness, or vanity. First describe the character briefly, and explain the character's weakness. Then tell one specific event that is caused by that weakness. Finally, tell the outcome of the event.

Many characters in mythology—like Midas or Arachne—try to challenge, disobey, or even insult the gods. Some characters, however, try to change or avoid **fate**, or destiny. The ancient Greeks believed that fate was so powerful that even Zeus had to bow to it.

■ What clever method does Atalanta [at ə lan'tə] invent to try to avoid her fate?

Greek statue from the third century B.C. of Aphrodite, goddess of love.

Retold by
Rex Warner

Atalanta

The huntress Atalanta, whom Meleager,[1] before he died, had loved, could run faster even than the fastest runners among men. Nor was her beauty inferior to her swiftness of foot; both were beyond praise.

When Atalanta asked the oracle about whom she ought to marry, the god replied: "Do not take a husband, Atalanta. If you do, it will bring disaster on you. Yet you will not escape, and though you will continue to live, you will not be yourself."

Terrified by these words, Atalanta lived in the dark woods unmarried. There were many men who wished to marry her, but to them, in their eagerness, she said: "No one can have me for his wife unless first he beats me in a race. If you will, you may run with me. If any of you wins, he shall have me as a prize. But those who are defeated will have death for their reward. These are the conditions for the race."

Cruel indeed she was, but her beauty had such power that numbers of young men were impatient to race with her on these terms.

There was a young man called Hippomenes,[2] who had come to watch the contest. At first he had said to himself: "What man in his senses would run such a risk to get a wife?" and he had condemned the young men for being too madly in love. But when he saw her—a face and a body like Aphrodite's own—he was lost in astonishment and, stretching out his hands, he said: "I had no right to blame the young men. I did not know what the prize was for which they were running."

As he spoke his own heart caught on fire with love for her and, in jealous fear, he hoped that none of the young men would be able to

---

1. **Meleager** [mel'ē ā'jər]: warrior famous for killing a wild boar sent by the goddess Artemis to destroy the fields of his city in Greece.

2. **Hippomenes** [hi pom'ə nēz]

beat her in the race. Then he said to himself: "But why should not I try my fortune? When one takes a risk, the gods help one."

By now the race had started, and the girl sped past him on feet that seemed to have wings. Though she went fast as an arrow, he admired her beauty still more. Indeed she looked particularly beautiful when running. In the breeze her hair streamed back over her ivory shoulders; the ribbons with their bright borders fluttered at her knees; the white of her young body flushed rose-red, as when a purple awning is drawn over white marble and makes the stone glow with its own color. While Hippomenes fixed his eyes on her, she reached the winning post and was crowned with the victor's garland. The young men, with groans, suffered the penalty of death according to the agreement which they had made.

Their fate, however, had no effect on Hippomenes. He came forward and, fixing his eyes on Atalanta, said: "Why do you win an easy glory by conquering these slow movers? Now run with me. If I win, it will be no disgrace to you. I am a king's son and Poseidon is my great-grandfather. And, if you defeat me, it will be an honor to be able to say that you defeated Hippomenes."

As he spoke, Atalanta looked at him with a softer expression in her eyes. She wondered whether she really wanted to conquer or to be conquered. She thought to herself: "What god, envious of beautiful young men, wants to destroy this one and makes him seek marriage with me at the risk of his dear life? In my opinion, I am not worth it. It is not his beauty that touches me (though I might easily be touched by that); it is because he is still only a boy. And then there is his courage, and the fact that he is willing to risk so much for me. Why should he die, simply because he wants to live with me? I wish he would go, while he still may, and realize that it is fatal

to want to marry me. Indeed he deserves to live. If only I were happier, if only the fates had not forbidden me to marry, he would be the man that I would choose."

Meanwhile Atalanta's father and the whole people demanded that the race should take place. Hippomenes prayed to Aphrodite and said: "O goddess, you put this love into my heart. Now be near me in my trial and aid me!"

A gentle breeze carried his prayer to the goddess and she was moved by it. Little time, however, remained in which she could help him. But it happened that she had just returned from her sacred island of Cyprus,[3] where in one of her temple gardens grows a golden apple tree. The leaves are gold; the branches and the fruit rattle with metal as the wind stirs them. Aphrodite had in her hand three golden apples which she had just picked from this tree. Now she came down to earth, making herself visible only to Hippomenes, and showed him how to use the apples.

Then the trumpets sounded and the two runners darted forward from the starting post, skimming over the sandy course with feet so light that it would seem they might have run over the sea or over the waving heads of standing corn. The crowd shouted their applause. "Now, Hippomenes," they cried, "run as you have never run before! You are winning." It would be difficult to say whether Hippomenes or Atalanta herself was most pleased with this encouragement. For some time Atalanta, though she might have passed the young man, did not do so. She ran by his side, looking into his face. Then, half unwillingly, she left him behind. He, with parched throat and straining lungs, followed after; still the winning post was far in the distance; and now he took one of the golden apples which

---

3. **Cyprus** [sī′prəs]: island off the coast of Turkey.

Aphrodite had given him and threw it in her way. The girl looked with wonder at the shining fruit and, longing to have it, stopped running so that she could pick it up. Hippomenes passed her and again the spectators shouted out their applause. Soon, however, Atalanta made up the ground that she had lost and again left Hippomenes behind. He threw the second apple, once more took the lead and once more was overtaken. Now they were in sight of the winning post, and Hippomenes, with a prayer to Aphrodite, threw the last apple rather sideways, so that it went some distance from the course. Atalanta seemed to

hesitate whether she should go after it or not, but Aphrodite made her go, and, when she had picked up the apple, she made it heavier, handicapping the girl not only by the time she had lost but by the weight of what she was carrying. This time she could not catch up Hippomenes. He passed the winning post first and claimed her as his bride.

Then, indeed, Hippomenes should have offered thanks to Aphrodite, but he forgot entirely the goddess who had helped him, neither giving thanks nor making sacrifice.

Aphrodite was angry and determined to make an example of them both. On their way to the home of Hippomenes they came to a holy temple, sacred to the mother of the gods, great Cybele.[4] No mortal was allowed to pass the night in this temple, so hallowed[5] was the spot; but Aphrodite put it into the hearts of Hippomenes and Atalanta, who were tired from their journey, to rest there all night and treat the temple of the goddess as though it were a common inn. So in the most holy of the temple's shrines, where wooden images of the ancient gods turned away their eyes in horror at the profanation,[6] they rested together. But the terrible goddess, her head crowned with a crown of towers, appeared to them. She covered their necks, which had been so smooth, with tawny manes of hair; their fingers became sharp claws, and their arms turned to legs. Most of their weight went to their chests, and behind them they swept the sandy ground with long tails. Instead of the palace they had hoped for, they lived in the savage woods, a lion and a lioness, terrible to others but, when Cybele needed them, tame enough to draw her chariot, champing the iron bits between their gnashing jaws.

---

4. **Cybele** [sib′ə lē]: goddess of plentifulness.
5. **hallowed:** sacred.
6. **profanation** [prof′ə nā′shən]: act of disrespect.

STUDY QUESTIONS

Recalling

1. What warning and riddle did the oracle tell Atalanta about taking a husband?
2. What method did Atalanta invent to avoid marriage? Why were young men willing to risk their lives for her?
3. Who helps Hippomenes win the race? Explain the trick that he uses.
4. What did Hippomenes forget after winning the race?
5. What profane act did Aphrodite cause Atalanta and Hippomenes to commit?
6. What metamorphosis did Atalanta and Hippomenes undergo because of the anger of Cybele?

Interpreting

7. How did Atalanta's actions show her respect for the oracle and the decrees of fate?
8. Explain how the riddle of the oracle at the beginning of the myth is made clear at the end of the myth.

Extending

9. What do the Greek myths suggest about ancient attitudes toward human behavior when they show the gods directing the actions of people?

READING AND LITERARY FOCUS

Conflict

Conflict, the struggle of two or more forces, makes stories interesting. If characters did not face obstacles, we would not be very interested in them. Conflict creates understanding and sympathy in readers because we all face difficult situations at some time in our lives.

In literature there are four common types of conflict: conflict against nature, conflict against fate, conflict against other people or society, and conflict against oneself. Conflict against nature may take the form of fighting a storm. Conflict against fate occurs in many myths; Zeus himself tries to resist fate when he attempts to prevent Prometheus from giving humans the gift of fire. Conflict against other people may take the form of a battle or a contest. Conflict against oneself may mean being brave or making a mature decision.

Thinking About Conflict

■ Identify the conflicts in the story of Atalanta.

COMPOSITION

Writing About Conflict

■ Write about the conflicts in the story of Atalanta. First tell which conflict you think is the most difficult. Then give your reasons, using examples from the story to prove your point.

Writing a Story

■ Write a brief story in which someone faces a serious conflict. You may want to have the character accept a challenge or make an important decision. Be sure that your story has a logical sequence of events and that you describe the characters clearly. *For help with this assignment, see Lesson 4 in the Writing About Literature Handbook at the back of this book.*

COMPARING MYTHS

■ Choose two or more myths from this unit, and tell what elements or qualities they have in common. For example: In each myth, does the hero or heroine succeed or fail? Is justice done? Is evil punished? Does a metamorphosis occur? You may want to consider comparing the myths in one of the following groups.

"Demeter and Persephone," "Prometheus," and "Deucalion and Pyrrha"

"Midas," "Echo and Narcissus," "Arachne," and "Atalanta"

WORLD FOLK TALES

Folk tales are the world's most popular stories, yet no one knows who created them. **Folk tales** are old stories that were originally told *orally*, or by word of mouth. They were probably first told around campfires and at meeting places by people who were not professional authors. The stories were told and retold, changed and developed, as people moved from family to family, village to village.

Folk tales differ from myths. They are not part of a large system of related stories about the gods, as myths are. Instead, folk tales offer a great variety of down-to-earth, practical tales of how ordinary people live their lives. Folk tales and myths are both part of **folk literature**—the collection of beliefs, customs, and traditions of a people. However, instead of telling about the births of gods and the battles of Titans, folk tales show us how to outwit an unjust neighbor or how to gain fame and fortune by using our common sense.

Most folk tales do not tell of supernatural actions, but they do often include marvelous and magical events. Whether they take place "long ago and far away" or just over in the next town, folk tales keep alive our sense of wonder. The folk tales in this unit come from Greece, Japan, Costa Rica, Afghanistan, and Ethiopia. They show us the vital imaginative life of people all over the world.

Almost nothing is known of the life of Aesop [ē'səp]. In fact, he may not have existed at all. Many different people may have written short tales and signed them "Aesop." It is possible that there was a real Aesop, a Greek slave who lived about 600 B.C. Aesop's immensely popular tales are usually about animals who speak and act like people. Each tale tells an entertaining story and also contains a lesson about human behavior.

■ As you read Aesop's tales, ask yourself what each one teaches. Aesop.

Aesop

The Ant and the Grasshopper

A Folk Tale from Greece, retold by Joseph Jacobs

In a field one summer's day a Grasshopper was hopping about, chirping and singing to its heart's content. An Ant passed by, bearing along with great toil an ear of corn he was taking to the nest.

"Why not come and chat with me," said the Grasshopper, "instead of toiling and moiling in that way?"

"I am helping to lay up food for the winter," said the Ant, "and recommend you to do the same."

"Why bother about winter?" said the Grasshopper; "we have got plenty of food at present."

But the Ant went on its way and continued its toil. When the winter came the Grasshopper had no food, and found itself dying of hunger, while it saw the ants distributing every day corn and grain from the stores they had collected in the summer. Then the Grasshopper knew:

It is best to prepare for the days of necessity.

Aesop

The Shepherd Boy

A Folk Tale from Greece

Retold by Joseph Jacobs

There was once a young shepherd boy who tended his sheep at the foot of a mountain near a dark forest. It was rather lonely for him all day, so he thought upon a plan by which he could get a little company and some excitement. He rushed down toward the village calling out, "Wolf, wolf," and the villagers came out to meet him, and some of them stopped with him for a considerable time. This pleased the boy so much that a few days afterwards he tried the same trick, and again the villagers came to his help. But shortly after this a wolf actually did come out from the forest, and began to worry the sheep, and the boy of course cried out, "Wolf, wolf," still louder than before. But this time the villagers, who had been fooled twice before, thought the boy was again deceiving them, and nobody stirred to come to his help. So the wolf made a good meal off the boy's flock, and when the boy complained, the wise man of the village said:

"A liar will not be believed, even when he speaks the truth."

STUDY QUESTIONS

The Ant and the Grasshopper

Recalling

1. At the beginning of the tale, what is the Grasshopper doing? What is the Ant doing?
2. What happened to the Grasshopper when winter came?

Interpreting

3. Is the Ant or the Grasshopper more practical? Why?
4. Tell in your own words the lesson learned by the Grasshopper.

Extending

5. Why do you think Aesop often used animals as the main characters in his stories?

The Shepherd Boy

Recalling

1. What happened when the boy first cried, "Wolf, wolf"? What happened the second time?
2. What happened when the boy cried, "Wolf, wolf" the third time?

Interpreting

3. Tell in your own words the lesson learned by the shepherd boy.

Extending

4. Do you think this tale applies only to shepherds? Why or why not?

READING AND LITERARY FOCUS

The Fable

A **fable** is a kind of folk tale told to teach a moral, or lesson. For example, the moral of "The Ant and the Grasshopper" is given at the end: "It is best to prepare for the days of necessity." Fables, such as those told by Aesop, are both entertaining and practical. They are fun to read, and they also offer common sense about living our daily lives and making wise decisions.

Thinking About the Fable

■ Which of these two fables do you think is more effective, the one with animal characters or the one with human characters? Why?

COMPOSITION

Writing About a Fable

■ Though fables are brief, they contain all the elements of short stories. Choose one of Aesop's fables, and write briefly about the characters, the plot, the setting, and the theme (or moral). Conclude with your own opinion of the fable.

Writing a Fable

■ Write a fable of your own to illustrate one of the following proverbs: (a) *The early bird catches the worm;* (b) *a stitch in time saves nine;* (c) *haste makes waste.* First decide what point the proverb is trying to make. Then think of a situation in which it would apply. Put human or animal characters in the situation, and have the action point up the lesson of the proverb.

CHALLENGE

Research

■ The morals at the end of Aesop's fables are stated as **proverbs**, or wise old sayings. Use your library to find a collection of proverbs, such as Benjamin Franklin's *Poor Richard's Almanack* or *Bartlett's Familiar Quotations.* Choose five proverbs that you like, read them to the class, and tell why you like them.

One of the most popular subjects of folk tales is how a poor person becomes rich. Some tales tell of a poor person discovering a pot of gold or a magic device. Some tell of a poor person doing a good deed and being richly rewarded. "The Piece of Straw" is a story of a young man who starts with almost nothing.

■ What is the first object he touches that brings him good fortune?

Japanese family emblem.

Retold by
Yoshiko Uchida

The Piece of Straw

A Folk Tale from Japan

Long ago, in the land of Yamato,[1] there was a poor young man who lived all alone. He had no family to care for him, and no friends to whom he could go for help. Each day he watched his purse grow slimmer and slimmer, for there was no one who would give him work. Finally, one day, he saw that his money was almost gone.

"Alas, what am I to do?" he sighed. "The only one who can help me now is the goddess of mercy at the Hase[2] Temple."

So the poor young man hurried to the temple and knelt before the shrine of the goddess of mercy.

"Oh, Kannon-Sama,"[3] he said. "I am without food or money, and I cannot find work to

keep myself alive. I shall kneel here before your shrine until you show me some way in which I can save myself."

The young man sat very still and waited for some sign from the goddess of mercy. "Show me in a dream just what I am to do," he pleaded. And the young man did not move from his place before the shrine. He sat there through the long night and all the next day, and still he had no dream. He sat there for many more days and nights, but still the goddess did not help him.

At last the priests of the temple noticed the young man who neither ate nor slept, but sat quietly in front of the shrine. "He will surely starve to death if he stays there much longer," they said to each other.

Then one of the priests went to question the young man.

"Who are you, my good fellow?" he asked.

---

1. **Yamato** [yä′mä tō]: ancient name for Japan.
2. **Hase** [hä′se]
3. **Kannon-Sama** [kan′non sä′mä]

"And why do you sit here for so many days and nights?"

"Alas, I have no friend or family," said the young man sadly. "And since no one will give me work, I am almost without food or money. I have come here to ask the help of the goddess of mercy, but if she does not help me soon, I know that I shall die here before her shrine."

Now the good priests of the temple felt great pity for the poor young man and decided they would take turns bringing him food and water so he would not starve to death. So with their help, the young man continued to sit before the shrine for many more days and nights. He was growing sad and weary, and began to think perhaps the kind goddess would not help him after all.

At last, on the twenty-first day, as his head nodded with weariness and sleep, he thought he saw a faint dream. An old, old man with a flowing beard seemed to be coming out of the goddess's shrine. The old man stood before him and told him to leave the temple quickly. "The very first thing that your hand touches after you leave the temple will bring you much good fortune," the old man said to him. "So keep safely whatever it is, no matter how small it may be." And then the old man faded away just as quickly as he had appeared. The young man rubbed his eyes and looked around. The goddess of mercy was smiling down at him, just as she had for the last twenty-one days.

"Ah, that dream was her message to me," thought the young man, and he quickly prepared to leave the temple. The priests gave him some food to take along, and the young man hurried out through the temple gates. Just as he was about to turn onto the road, he tripped over a stone and fell flat on the dirt road. As he hastened to pick himself up, he saw that he was grasping a single piece of straw in his right hand. He started to throw it away, but he suddenly remembered what

the old man had said to him: "The very first thing that your hand touches after you leave the temple will bring you much good fortune."

"But surely this little piece of straw can bring me no great fortune," thought the young man, and he was about to toss it on the roadside. Then he thought again, "No, I had better do exactly as the Kannon-Sama instructed me," so he carried the piece of straw carefully in his hand.

As he walked along the road, a horsefly began to buzz about his head. The young man picked up a stick and tried to shoo the fly away, but it would not stop bothering him. It buzzed and it buzzed, and it flew in little circles about his head. Finally the young man could bear it no longer. He cupped his hand, and with one big swoop, he caught the little horsefly. Then he strung it on the end of his stick with his piece of straw and walked on.

Before long, a carriage carrying a noblewoman and her son to the temple came rolling toward him. The little boy was weary and hot and was tired of sitting quietly in his carriage. He was fretting and crying, but he spied the horsefly buzzing on the end of the young man's stick.

"I want the little fly that's buzzing on the stick!" the little boy cried to his servant.

The servant approached the young man and said politely, "I wonder if you would be kind enough to give your stick to the little boy? He has grown weary from the long, hot ride, and this would make him very happy."

"Well, the fly is tied to the stick with a piece of straw which the goddess of the temple told me I must keep, but if it will make the little boy happy, I shall give it to him," said the young man.

"How very, very kind of you," the noblewoman said, as she leaned out of the carriage. "I'm afraid I have nothing with which I can repay you, except these three oranges." And

she held out three large oranges on a beautiful white napkin.

The young man thanked the noblewoman, wrapped up the three oranges carefully, and walked down the road. The sun was hot as it beat down on the dusty road. Before long, he saw a procession of men and women coming toward him. They were walking on either side of a beautiful carriage, and appeared to be the handmaidens and guards of the noblewoman inside. As the group walked by the young man, one of the young women suddenly grew faint and collapsed at the side of the road.

"Oh, I am so thirsty," she said weakly, and held her hand out for some water.

"Quickly, find some water," the guards shouted, but there was no water to be seen anywhere.

They called to the young man and asked if he could tell them where there might be some water.

"I fear there are no wells or streams nearby," said the young man. "But I have three oranges here. Give her the juice from these oranges to quench her thirst," and he handed his oranges to the guards. They quickly gave the young maiden the juice from the three oranges, and before long she felt well enough to go on.

"If you had not come by and given me your oranges, I might have died here on this hot and dusty road," the maiden said to the young man. "I would give you anything to thank you, but I have only these three rolls of white silk. Take them and accept my thanks," she said, as she gave the rolls of silk to the young man.

The young man thanked her for the gift, and with the rolls of silk under his arm, he walked on down the road. "My goodness, one piece of straw brought me three oranges, and now my oranges have brought me three rolls of silk," thought the young man happily.

That night he found an inn where he could spend the night, and he gave the innkeeper one of the rolls of silk to pay for his room. Early the next morning, he started off down the road again. Toward noon, he saw a group of men on horseback cantering toward him. The horses held their heads up proudly, and whisked their long, shiny tails. The young man thought he had never seen such beautiful horses before, and looked at them longingly, for he had always wanted a horse for himself. Then, just as one of the noblemen rode past the young man, his horse suddenly faltered and fell to the ground. The men gathered about the animal and stroked its side and gave it water, but the horse would not move or raise its head.

"I'm afraid it's dead," said the nobleman sadly, and he took the saddle from the horse's back and the bit from its mouth. He then left one of his servants to care for the horse's remains, and rode off on another horse with his men.

The young man went up to the servant who was left to care for the horse. "He must have been a very fine horse," said the young man, as he looked down at the dead animal.

"Oh, yes, indeed he was," answered the servant. "He was such a valuable animal that even though many people offered large sums of money, the master would not think of selling him. It certainly is strange that he died so suddenly," he added, shaking his head.

"What are you going to do now?" the young man asked.

"I can't let the horse just lie here beside the road. I really don't know what to do," answered the servant sadly.

"Well, if you like, I'll give you a roll of silk for the horse. Then you can return home, and I shall take care of the horse," said the young man.

"What a strange person to want a dead horse," thought the servant. "Why, that is a fine bargain, my friend," he said out loud, and he quickly took the roll of silk and hurried away before the young man should change his mind.

The young man knelt down before the horse and prayed to the goddess of mercy that he might come to life again. "Oh, Kannon-Sama," he pleaded, "please give life to this beautiful horse once more." Then, as he watched, the horse slowly opened its eyes. Then it slowly got to its feet, and before long, began to drink water and eat some oats. It shook its head, whisked its long, silky tail, and looked as good as new once again. The young man was so happy he quickly climbed up on the horse's back and rode into the next village. There he spent the night at another inn and used his last roll of silk to pay for his room.

The next day, he rode on his fine horse until he came to the town of Toba. He knew he wasn't far from the big city of Kyoto,[4] when, suddenly, the young man thought of a problem. The nobleman was very well known in Kyoto and many people probably knew his beautiful chestnut-colored horse. "It would never do if I should be accused of stealing the nobleman's horse," he thought, "for no one would believe the strange story of how the horse came to be mine."

So the young man decided he would sell the horse. Just then, he passed by the home of a family who appeared to be getting ready to leave on a journey. A wagon piled high with bags and boxes stood by the front gate. The young man called out to the man of the house, "Good sir, would you like to buy this horse from me?"

"My, what a beautiful horse. I certainly would like to buy it from you, but alas, I have no money," he answered.

Then the man came closer to look at the horse. It was more beautiful than any he had ever seen.

"Ah, what a pity I cannot buy such a fine animal," he said. "But wait, I know what I can do. I can give you three rice fields in exchange for your horse," said the man happily.

The young man thought for a moment. "Well—" he began.

"What's more, since we are going away, I shall leave you the house, and you may live in it until we return," continued the man.

"That's a fair bargain indeed," said the young man. "The horse is yours!"

"In case we decide not to return, the house will be yours too," called the man, and soon he and his family rode off down the road with their wagon rumbling after them.

Now the young man found that one field of rice was plenty to keep himself well fed, so he rented out his other fields. As if by magic, the rice in his field grew and grew, until he had so much rice, he could sell many, many sacks each day. He grew richer and richer, and his purse grew fatter and fatter, and his luck seemed to grow with the years.

Many years went by, and still no one returned to the house, so the young man continued to live there and to raise fine crops of rice. His wealth increased tenfold,[5] and he became an important man in the town. He married a beautiful young maiden of the village, and they had many lovely children. And there they lived happily for many years with their children and with their children's children in the little town of Toba.

So the one little piece of straw which the young man picked up so many years ago outside the temple gate had truly brought him great good fortune and happiness, just as the old man in his dream had said it would.

---

4. **Kyoto** [kyō′tō]: ancient capital of Japan.

5. **tenfold:** ten times.

STUDY QUESTIONS

Recalling

1. At the beginning of the story, what are the young man's problems?
2. Whom does the young man ask for help? What advice does he finally receive?
3. How does he acquire the piece of straw? What does he get in exchange for it?
4. What does he do with the three oranges?
5. How does he obtain the horse, and what becomes of it?
6. What does he do with his rice fields?
7. At the end of the story, what wealth and happiness does the man possess?

Interpreting

8. Describe in your own words the personality of the young man.
9. Do you think luck or personal qualities led to the man's success? Support your answer.

Extending

10. In part this story shows that small actions can make a big difference in life. Do you think this is true? Why or why not?

READING AND LITERARY FOCUS

The Folk Tale

A **folk tale** is an old story that was originally told *orally,* or by word of mouth. In general, folk tales reflect the beliefs, customs, and traditions of a people. They show a way of life through simple plots and with much good humor.

In modern times a folk tale may be retold by a professional writer. For example, "The Piece of Straw" is a Japanese folk tale retold by the Japanese American writer Yoshiko Uchida.

Thinking About the Folk Tale

▪ What specific beliefs, customs, and traditions can you point out in "The Piece of Straw"?

VOCABULARY

Sentence Completions

Each of the following sentences contains a blank with four possible words for completing the sentence. Choose the word that best completes each sentence and that uses the word *as it is used in the selection.*

1. People prayed at the ____.
   - (a) inn
   - (b) shrine
   - (c) alas
   - (d) beard

2. Repeatedly he ____ for help.
   - (a) remembered
   - (b) pleaded
   - (c) found
   - (d) leaned

3. They could barely see the ____ image.
   - (a) faint
   - (b) tenfold
   - (c) thirsty
   - (d) weary

4. He suddenly ____ at the starting gate and fell.
   - (a) whisked
   - (b) gathered
   - (c) faltered
   - (d) increased

5. They tried to ____ the problem away like a fly.
   - (a) cry
   - (b) quench
   - (c) shoo
   - (d) collapse

COMPOSITION

Writing About Plot

▪ Write about the plot of "The Piece of Straw." First identify the main events in the story. Then identify the conflict, and tell what problems make it difficult for the main character to resolve the conflict. *For help with this assignment, see Lesson 2 in the Writing About Literature Handbook at the back of this book.*

Writing a Story

▪ Write a story of your own. First describe your characters and setting clearly. Then invent a logical series of events, one event leading to the next. *For help with this assignment, see Lesson 4 in the Writing About Literature Handbook at the back of this book.*

In many folk tales the characters do not have names. We know them simply as "the poor young man," "the girl," "the grand-mother," "the prince." Folk tales written this way remind us that these stories are indeed universal. "Three Magic Oranges" could have taken place in any country in "those days of magic."

■ What events in this folk tale remind you of stories you have heard or read before?

Detail from pattern on vase from Latin America.

Retold by
Lupe de Osma

Three Magic Oranges

A Folk Tale from Costa Rica

In the old times there was a king who had a son. And as this king was getting on in years, he wished very much for his son to marry, that he might the sooner see his daughter-in-law. And so he held a great feast. And to this feast he invited all the beautiful princesses from far and near, in the hope that his son would fall in love with one of them. But since the prince was in no hurry to take a wife, he found none to his liking.

Now as you may well imagine, this put the old king in a fine temper, and he ordered his son to set out at once and find himself a wife. And he told him that if he fancied ever to wear the crown upon his head, he had better not return without a suitable bride.

Well then, since he knew he must, the prince mounted a fine horse and rode out into the world, in search of a wife. Presently he came to a green forest, at the edge of which

he saw an orange tree with three golden oranges. He plucked the oranges and continued on his way. And he went on, on, and on.

The sun was hot and there was not a single cloud in the sky. And the road was very dusty, for along it rolled many brightly colored ox-carts going to the marketplace with bananas, brown-sugar cakes, and coffee berries. He grew very thirsty; but there was no stream or spring in sight, for it was the summer season and it had not rained for a long time. Just then he remembered the oranges in his pocket. How bright and golden, how full of sweet juice! One, at least, may cool my lips, he thought; so he reined in his horse and cut one in two with his long, sharp knife.

Wonder of wonders! No sooner had he done this than there appeared before him, as if sprung from the earth, a very beautiful maiden with eyes the color of the sky and hair the color of the sun. She begged him for a drink of water, if only a little drop. But he could not give what he had not, and she vanished in the same fashion as she had come.

He stared and wondered, then stroked his chin and said to himself, Well, now I know what sort of oranges these are, and I shall not open them so readily. Then he ate the orange. M-m-m . . . it was sweet! He had never tasted an orange so sweet. And when he had eaten it he felt refreshed and went on his way.

However, it was not long before he was again tormented by thirst, and still there was no water in sight. An hour or more passed by, and still no sign of a stream. And so, since thirst is stronger than good sense, he drew the second orange from his pocket and cut it open. And no sooner had he done this than it was the same thing all over again. But this time the maiden's eyes were green, like a pool of water, and her hair was flaming, like a red hibiscus.[1] She also called for water. But as he had none to offer her, she vanished in the same manner.

"Well," said he, "I still have one orange, and that I will not open unless I have some water handy." And so he ate the second orange and continued along his way.

He had not traveled far when suddenly he was startled by a faint sound, a gentle rippling sound like the murmur of running water. He gave his horse the spur and galloped around a bend in the road, where the sound seemed to be coming from. Then he gasped, for not far off he beheld a lively spring, as clear as the air itself.

He jumped off his horse, filled the hollow of his hand with the cool water, and drank till he was refreshed. When he had done this, he mopped the sweat from his brow and sat down to rest on a convenient grassy bank.

But just then he felt the third orange in his pocket and drew it out. And as he turned it over in his hand he thought, Why, this is the very place to open it! He did so, and on the instant there appeared before him a maiden. Her eyes and her long flowing hair were black as a raven's wing, and her face was soft and white as a jasmine flower. She was beautiful!

Like the others, she asked for water. And losing not a moment, the prince scooped up some water in the hollow of his hand and raised it to her lips. She did not vanish like the others, for the spell was broken.

So beautiful was she and so charmed was the prince that he fell in love with her at sight and immediately asked her to become his wife. She smiled (her little teeth were as white as rice grains), and she consented. Then, being a true princess, she thanked him beyond measure for breaking the cruel enchantment. "You know," she said, "I was once a king's daughter, but an evil witch cast a spell upon me and imprisoned me in that magic orange—until such time as a king's son should break the spell. You are the king's son, and I am set free!"

Full of joy, the prince gently lifted her upon his horse and together they rode home to the royal palace. As they drew near they were followed by many cheering people who came after them, throwing flowers and sombreros[2] in the air. And hearing the cries of the people, the king and all the court came running out of doors.

The prince rode up to them, leaped to the ground as nimbly as you please, and helped the princess down. Then he bowed and said to the king, "Father, here is the maiden of my choice."

Well, the marriage was celebrated at once

---

1. **hibiscus** [hī bis′kəs]: tropical plant with large bell-shaped flowers.

2. **sombreros** [səm brār′ōz]: wide-brimmed hats worn in Hispanic countries.

by a most sumptuous *fiesta*,[3] and everyone rejoiced.

Now the old king's wish to see his daughter-in-law had come true. As time went on he lived out his span of years and died. And the prince and his beautiful princess became king and queen, and wore golden crowns upon their heads.

But misfortune was on their track. Tidings of all these events reached the wicked witch who had enchanted the princess and imprisoned her in the magic orange. Now this witch was exceedingly put out, and to vent[4] her rage she thought of a plan. Disguised as a poor old woman, with a basket full of fruits and fancy pins upon her head, she started for the royal palace without losing any time. And when she arrived there she began to walk up and down the patio, shouting: "Here I bring oranges! . . . Sweet lemons! . . . See what fine mangoes![5] . . . Pins! . . . Pins! . . . Who will buy my fine pins!"

On hearing her cry her wares, the queen looked out of the window. Seeing the old woman standing in the patio with the basket on her head, she asked her to come in, so that she might see the pins. And the witch, who wished for nothing better, went in as fast as she could lay her legs to the ground.

"Here, Señora[6] Queen," she said, as she picked out a pretty hairpin crested with a white pearl. "This will look very fine by your golden crown. Do try it!"

The queen graciously bowed down, and the old woman quickly thrust the pin deep into her head. In a flash the lovely queen was turned into a little white dove and took wing. Through the open window she flew, and on

she went till she vanished into a green forest far away. Well, it was that way in those days of magic!

Now all this happened while the young king was out hunting in that same forest. And as he was aiming his arrow at a bright-plumed macaw,[7] suddenly there was a rustle of wings close by. He looked up and saw a little white dove on a treetop. The king thought the dove so remarkably beautiful that immediately he wished to capture her as a present for his wife, the queen. So with all speed he

---

3. *fiesta* [fē es'tə]: Spanish word for *feast;* celebration.
4. **vent:** release.
5. **mangoes:** sweet yellow-red tropical fruits.
6. **Señora** [sen yôr'ə]: Spanish word for *Mrs.*, a term of respect.

7. **macaw** [mə kô']: brilliantly colored long-tailed parrot of Central and South America.

he mourned over the loss of his beloved queen, and nothing could comfort him.

Time passed as swiftly as the wind in those days, and two years and more went by, till one certain day when the unhappy king—in no mood for pleasures—withdrew into his garden, away from the others. Noticing the little dove, forgotten in her golden cage, he opened the cage door and ran his fingers gently over the bird's head. But as he did this he suddenly felt the pearl, so he brushed the feathers apart and discovered the head of the magic pin. Who could have been so cruel, he wondered, as to stick a pin in such a lovely creature.

Then he pulled out the pin as gently as he could. Behold, the dove vanished, and before him stood the queen, as beautiful and radiant as ever she was in all her life. The king was struck dumb. When he had recovered from his astonishment, she told him all that had happened through the treachery of the wicked witch.

Immediately the king ordered his men to set out and find the witch and bring her to the royal palace so that she might be punished for her evil doings.

But of this there was no need. The witch had made a huge fire in her clay stove that day, planning to make a big lot of tamales.[8] Upon hearing the news of the queen's return, she forgot to tend to her work, and the mighty fire she had built spread through her hut. Both the hut and the witch together went up in smoke, which the wind blew away over the treetops.

And so, from this time forth, the king and his beautiful queen lived in peace and love, and nothing ever again marred their happiness.

dispatched an arrow. It brushed one of the dove's white wings, making her lose her perch and flutter to the ground. Whereupon she was quickly and gently picked up by his men.

When the king reached his castle he placed the little dove in a golden cage and took her to the queen's chamber. But the queen was nowhere to be found, and the whole of the court soon began to buzz with excitement. Questions were asked and answered, up and down they searched, but to no avail—the queen could not be found. She had disappeared as if she had sunk into the earth. All were very sad, but the king was the most wretched man in his kingdom. Day and night

---

8. **tamales** [tə mä′lēz]: Mexican dish of meat, peppers, and cornmeal, wrapped in corn husks and baked or steamed.

STUDY QUESTIONS

Recalling

1. Why does the prince set off on his journey?
2. What happens when the prince opens the first two oranges?
3. What "cruel enchantment" does the prince break?
4. What disguise does the witch use? What does she do to the young queen?
5. How does the king break the second spell?

Interpreting

6. What qualities in the prince's personality allow him to break each of the spells?
7. What elements in this folk tale suggest that things are not always what they seem?
8. What does the tale suggest about the rewards of kindness? About the rewards of treachery?

Extending

9. Like many folk tales this one simplifies real human behavior. What do you think is the advantage of telling a story in this way?

READING AND LITERARY FOCUS

The Hero

The **hero** of a story is the central character. In myths and folk tales heroes often have supernatural abilities. In modern stories heroes are more like ourselves and the people we know.

We are interested in heroes, and we usually sympathize with them. We see ourselves in them, and we see how their defeats and victories are like our own. In "Three Magic Oranges" the hero is a kind prince.

Often the hero goes on a journey, usually in search of something. The hero sets out to attain a goal, to fulfill a desire, to answer a question, to keep a promise, to find the solution to a problem. Hippomenes, for example, in the Greek myth on page 448, sets out to win the race for Atalanta.

Along the way the hero is tested in some way and often suffers. However, by passing these tests, or challenges, the hero triumphs.

The young prince in "Three Magic Oranges" seeks a woman he can truly love. He suffers at first from heat, thirst, and disappointment. He sees two beautiful maidens, but they vanish. In the end, through perseverance, cleverness, and kindness, he saves a maiden and earns her love in return.

Thinking About the Hero

■ The prince and princess later become king and queen. What does the new king do to prove once again that he is a hero?

COMPOSITION

Answering an Essay Question

■ Answer the following essay question: "Do you think folk tales are more like ancient myths or more like modern short stories?" First restate the question as your topic sentence. Then give reasons to support your opinion. End by summarizing your reasons. *For help with this assignment, see Lesson 1 in the Writing About Literature Handbook at the back of this book.*

Inventing a Hero

■ Invent a hero of your own. First list the qualities he or she should possess. Then name a goal that he or she would pursue. Finally, tell what challenge the hero would face and how his or her qualities would help to meet that challenge.

CHALLENGE

Summary

■ Reread "Three Magic Oranges," keeping in mind what you have learned about the hero. Think about the hero's journey and the challenges he faces. Consider the way he answers each challenge. Then summarize this folk tale in one paragraph.

Many folk tales remind us of the hard life of never-ending work faced by the common people who created the folk tales. In stories, however, people could sometimes escape that hard life. Some characters were able to use their wits to defeat injustice and make life easier.

■ In "The Farmer and His Hired Help" what important change takes place at the end of the story?

Depiction of Mithras, Persian god of sun, light, and truth.

Retold by
Eric and Nancy Protter

The Farmer and His Hired Help

A Folk Tale from Afghanistan

Once there lived two brothers who were so poor that they had barely enough to eat. Discouraged with their lot, they sat down together and tried to think of some way to improve their situation. At last the older brother decided it would be best if he went away and tried to find work elsewhere. If he proved successful, he would send his wages to his brother, who would remain at home looking after the family affairs.

The very next morning the older brother set out. He had not traveled far when he came upon a prosperous farm. On the gatepost out front hung a large sign asking for hired help. Immediately he went to the farm building, knocked on the door, and asked to see the farmer.

"I understand you need some help," he said.

"Why yes," answered the farmer cordially.

He looked the boy over carefully and then said, "You look like a strong, healthy lad. I think you'll do."

Though pleased to have found work so easily, the boy became a bit concerned when he heard the conditions of the job.

"I will hire you as a helper," said the farmer, "only if you agree to stay until springtime when the first cuckoo calls. If you should shirk[1] your work, however, or become ill-tempered at any time, you will have to pay me a penalty of fifty pieces of gold. On the other hand," he added, "if *I* should become angry or ill-tempered at any time, then I will pay you a thousand rubles."[2]

"But where will I get the pieces of gold?" asked the boy. "I haven't a penny to my name."

---

1. **shirk:** avoid.
2. **rubles** [roo′bəls]: units of money.

"Oh, that doesn't matter," replied the farmer generously. "If you have no money, you will just have to work for me for seven years without receiving any wages."

The lad considered the bargain very strange. Seven years was a long, long time. Still, he needed the job desperately. "And," he reasoned, "I am a good worker. I shall just have to be extremely careful not to lose my temper. And I should be able to do that for the few months between now and spring."

Agreeing to the conditions, the boy signed the contract the farmer had drawn up.

On the following day, at the first light of dawn, the farmer awakened the new hand and led him to a broad meadow.

"Mow this meadow as long as there is light," he said.

All day long the lad mowed the field and did not return home until late in the evening. By this time he was thoroughly exhausted.

"What?" the farmer exclaimed upon seeing him, "are you back already?"

Somewhat confused by this strange question, the boy replied, "But the sun has been down for several hours now."

"Aha," said the farmer, amused by this reply, "apparently you have misunderstood the terms of our agreement. It is true that the sun is down," he smirked, "but there is still plenty of light. If you'll notice," he continued, pointing to the sky, "there is a brilliantly shining moon tonight."

"This must be a joke," the lad thought to himself, and he could not restrain himself from frowning.

"You are not angry?" asked the farmer, his face contorted by a large grin.

"No, no. Not at all," replied the lad quietly. "But I am very tired and I would like to rest."

The farmer insisted, however, that the hired hand return to the fields, claiming that otherwise he would be shirking his duty. Not wanting to break his agreement, the boy went back to his mowing and he worked all through the night. And hours later the setting moon was followed by the rising sun. By this time, the boy had reached the limit of his strength. In sheer[3] exhaustion he dropped to the ground. As soon as the farmer arrived in the meadow and saw his sleeping farmhand, he urged him up again.

"Can't you see? The sun is up. It's a fine new day."

In his despair, the lad cried out in anger, "Curse your field and curse your bread and money! This is inhuman treatment!"

"You are cursing me," said the farmer. "No doubt you are angry."

Trapped, the boy sobbed with anguish. From where could he get the fifty gold pieces with which to buy his contract? How could he work for seven years for such a man without killing himself? Then he hit upon a solution. Signing a new contract, he promised the farmer that he would pay off his debt in installments. Dejected, hungry, and haggard-looking, he took his leave and returned home to his brother.

"What has happened to you?" his brother asked when he observed the terrible state in which his brother had entered the house.

"I have been duped[4] by a villain," he said, and he went on to explain his bitter experience with the farmer.

"It is a good lesson," replied the younger brother, "and don't be too angry. I believe *I* shall go and look for some work. And don't be too surprised if I turn up at the farm of that very same scoundrel."

The next morning he set off down the road,

---

3. **sheer:** complete.
4. **duped:** fooled.

a mysterious smile curving around his lips. In the late afternoon he arrived at the home of the rich farmer and asked for work. The farmer agreed to take him on and offered him the same proposal he had made his older brother a few days before. However, the young man refused, saying that the offer was not big enough.

"What do you mean?" asked the farmer, somewhat surprised.

"Let us make it a hundred gold pieces or fourteen years of work without pay, if I fail to live up to the agreement."

Delighted with this arrangement, the farmer promptly produced a contract and both he and the hired hand signed it. Each seemed extremely pleased with the stipulations of the agreement.

Cordially the farmer provided the new helper with a good dinner, and then immediately sent him to bed so that he would be fresh for the morning's chores.

As soon as dawn peeped over the horizon, the farmer was up, waiting for the new hired hand to appear so that he could instruct him in his duties. As the sun grew higher and higher in the sky and the boy still did not arrive, the farmer began to get very impatient. Finally, he knocked on the boy's door.

"The morning is well started and you lie in bed dreaming away!" he cried. "Do you think the grass will mow itself?"

"Are you slightly angry?" asked the boy.

Taken aback[5] by the quickness of the reply, the farmer said, "No, no. Of course I'm not angry. I just wanted to remind you that there is work to be done."

"Very well," answered the lad, "I shall start dressing right away." Slowly he put on his

---

5. **Taken aback:** surprised and somewhat confused or embarrassed.

Detail of painting (c. 1525) illustrating *Shah-nameh* by Persian epic poet Firdausi.

pants and shirt, and then laced his boots at a snail's pace. To the farmer standing outside the door, every minute of waiting seemed like an hour.

Anxiously he called out, "Hurry, lad, hurry! I can't wait all day."

"Are you getting angry again?" quizzed the boy.

"No, no, nothing of the kind," replied the farmer, exercising great self-control. "But we have a lot of work to do."

At last, when the sun was very high in the heavens, the lad came out of his room and went with the farmer to the meadow. Upon their arrival there, the new hand noticed that all the other workers were having their lunch.

"Is it worthwhile starting now?" he asked. "Everyone else is eating. Why don't we have our lunch, too?"

Finding it hard to refuse, the farmer agreed reluctantly. It turned out that the young boy was a very slow eater with a very hearty appetite. At last, patting his full stomach, he turned to the farmer and said, "Since there is a lot of hard work ahead of us, I think we need a nap to help gather our strength for the job." With that he lay down on the grass and fell dead asleep until evening.

Shaking his fist in frustration, the farmer cried, "It's getting dark, boy, can't you see? All the other workers have mowed their fields. Wake up! Wake up!" But the lad did not stir.

Finally the farmer shrieked, "May the one who sent you here break his neck."

Suddenly the lad rubbed his drowsy eyes and looked straight at the farmer.

"Are you angry?" he asked.

Forced to protest, the farmer replied, "No, no. I only wished to say that it is dark and time for us to go home."

Instantly the boy jumped to his feet.

"That's different," he said. "Let's go."

When the two arrived at the house, the farmer discovered that he had visitors. Turning to the lad, he ordered him to slaughter a goat for dinner.

"Which one?" asked the boy, feigning total bewilderment.

"Any you find along the path," replied the farmer with annoyance.

Without another word, the lad set out on his assignment.

A short time later all of the farmer's neighbors came running to his house in great excitement.

"What is the matter?" the farmer demanded.

"Your helper has gone crazy!" they exclaimed.

"How do you mean?"

"He has slaughtered every one of your goats! Your entire flock is destroyed!"

"*What!*" screamed the farmer, and he rushed into the yard, where he confronted the farmhand. "What have you done, you idiot?" he roared.

"Why," exclaimed the boy, wide-eyed, "I have done exactly what you have asked me to do. You told me to kill *any* sheep along the path and *all of them* were along the path. I merely followed your orders." Looking directly at the farmer, he continued innocently, "Why, have I done anything wrong? You're not angry, are you?"

"No," replied the farmer through half-clenched teeth, "I'm not angry. It is just a pity that my flock is ruined."

At the end of the month the villainous farmer had lost all his patience. He began to plot a way that would release him from his contract without having to pay the penalty. Reflecting that spring was not too far away, he decided that he would speed up the first call of the cuckoo. Helping his wife into a tall tree, he instructed her to call out like a cuckoo as soon as she saw him and the hired hand enter the woods. Next, he invited the lad to go hunting with him. As they entered the forest, the farmer's wife caught sight of the two and she called out in a clear voice, "Coo-koo, coo-koo."

"Good heavens!" exclaimed the farmer, stopping dead in his tracks, "listen to that!"

"Coo-koo, coo-koo."

"Strange," the farmer said, acting surprised, "spring is here already. Well, this means that our agreement is terminated. The cuckoo calls, and you're free to go."

But the boy, immediately sensing the farmer's plot, was not taken in by such wiles.

"It is unbelievable," he said, "a cuckoo's call in the middle of the winter. That's rather odd, don't you think? I believe I'll look into this."

Quietly stalking through the woods, he stopped directly in front of the tree from where the call had come, and raised his gun as if ready to fire.

"No, no," shrieked the farmer, throwing himself in front of the boy. "Don't shoot, don't shoot!"

Grinning with amusement, the boy lowered his gun.

The farmer, now completely ruined, turned on the boy and screamed, "Go away, get away from here as fast as you can! Get out of my sight! You've driven me out of my mind!"

Very quietly the boy said, "Why, I believe you're angry."

"Yes, yes! I *am* angry. I'll pay you the money. It's worth it to get rid of a scoundrel like you!"

Boiling with rage, the farmer rushed to the house and from a secret place took out a hundred pieces of gold.

"There!" he said, flinging the money at the boy. "Now go, and never come near here again."

"I won't leave until you tear up the contract as well," the boy replied with caution. The farmer did this immediately. Then the boy paid him the fifty gold coins owed by his brother, and the farmer tore up that contract as well. With that accomplished, the young man promptly took his leave, heading home with a joyous heart and richer by fifty gold coins.

The farmer, after surveying his losses, finally decided that he had learned a lesson. Never again did he trick hired hands into unfair contracts, but on the contrary he began to offer better working conditions. He noticed with surprise that a lot more work got done when his men were happy because they were well treated. Eventually, he became known in the area as a kind and just employer, and many people were eager for the chance to work for him.

STUDY QUESTIONS

Recalling

1. For what reason does the older brother go out to find work?
2. What conditions does the farmer set for hiring the older brother?
3. What does the farmer do to make the older brother angry?
4. What contract does the younger brother sign with the farmer?
5. Name three things the younger brother does to make the farmer angry.
6. What does the angry farmer do to end the contract?
7. What kind of conditions does the farmer offer his workers from that day forward?

Interpreting

8. In what ways is the younger brother different from the older brother?
9. Describe the character of the farmer.
10. What do you think this story says about treating people justly and honestly?

Extending

11. Do you think that cleverness is still a useful method of correcting an unjust situation? Why or why not?

READING AND LITERARY FOCUS

Making Inferences About Character from Details

We can deepen our understanding of a character by making inferences. **Inferences** are con-clusions we draw based on detailed information we are given. Making inferences requires us to read with care and attention.

At the end of "The Farmer and His Hired Help," for example, the younger brother says nothing about getting even with the farmer. However, we *infer* from the following detailed description that he is thinking about it: ". . . he set off down the road, a mysterious smile curving around his lips." The detail of the mysterious smile allows us to infer what is going on in his mind.

Thinking About Inferences

■ Find two details of character about the farmer. What can you infer about him from those de-tails?

COMPOSITION

Writing a Character Sketch

■ Summarize the character of the younger brother. First identify his outstanding traits. Then give examples of details and actions that reveal these traits. Conclude with a general statement about the character and his purpose in the folk tale. *For help with this assignment, see Lesson 3 in the Writing About Literature Handbook at the back of this book.*

Inventing a Character

■ Write a description of a character you have invented. First describe the character's physi-cal appearance. Then list the character's qual-ities. Finally, give an example of an event in which the character demonstrates one of those qualities in action.

An ordeal is a difficult test. Folk tales are filled with extraordinary ordeals, tests of strength or cleverness or patience or goodness. Like the heroes of myths, folk heroes sometimes need help to face these tests.

■ In "The Fire on the Mountain" who helps the hero face a difficult challenge?

Painted design on pot from northern Africa.

Retold by
Harold Courlander and Wolf Leslau

The Fire on the Mountain

A Folk Tale from Ethiopia

People say that in the old days in the city of Addis Ababa[1] there was a young man by the name of Arha.[2] He had come as a boy from the country of Gurage,[3] and in the city he became the servant of a rich merchant, Haptom Hasei.[4]

Haptom Hasei was so rich that he owned everything that money could buy, and often he was very bored because he had tired of everything he knew, and there was nothing new for him to do.

One cold night, when the damp wind was blowing across the plateau, Haptom called to Arha to bring wood for the fire. When Arha was finished, Haptom began to talk.

"How much cold can a man stand?" he said, speaking at first to himself. "I wonder if it would be possible for a man to stand on the highest peak, Mount Intotto,[5] where the coldest winds blow, through an entire night without blankets or clothing and yet not die?"

"I don't know," Arha said. "But wouldn't it be a foolish thing?"

"Perhaps, if he had nothing to gain by it, it would be a foolish thing to spend the night in that way," Haptom said. "But I would be willing to bet that a man couldn't do it."

"I am sure a courageous man could stand naked on Mount Intotto throughout an entire night and not die of it," Arha said. "But as for me, it isn't my affair since I've nothing to bet."

"Well, I'll tell you what," Haptom said.

---

1. **Addis Ababa** [ad'is ab'ə bə]: capital of Ethiopia.
2. **Arha** [är'hä]
3. **Gurage** [gōō rä' gä]
4. **Haptom Hasei** [hap'tôm hä sī']

5. **Intotto** [in tō'tō]

"Since you are so sure it can be done, I'll make a bet with you anyway. If you can stand among the rocks on Mount Intotto for an entire night without food or water or clothing or blankets or fire and not die of it, then I will give you ten acres of good farmland for your own, with a house and cattle."

Arha could hardly believe what he had heard.

"Do you really mean this?" he asked.

"I am a man of my word," Haptom replied.

"Then tomorrow night I will do it," Arha said, "and afterward, for all the years to come, I shall till my own soil."

But he was very worried, because the wind swept bitterly across that peak. So in the morning Arha went to a wise old man of his own tribe and told him of the bet he had

made. The old man listened quietly and thoughtfully, and when Arha had finished he said:

"I will help you. Across the valley from Intotto is a high rock which can be seen in the daytime. Tomorrow night, as the sun goes down, I shall build a fire there, so that it can be seen from where you stand on the peak. All night long you must watch the light of my fire. Do not close your eyes or let the darkness creep upon you. As you watch my fire, think of its warmth, and think of me, your friend, sitting there tending it for you. If you do this you will survive, no matter how bitter the night wind."

Arha thanked the old man warmly and went back to Haptom's house with a light heart. He told Haptom he was ready, and in the afternoon Haptom sent him, under the watchful eyes of other servants, to the top of Mount Intotto. There, as night fell, Arha removed his clothes and stood in the damp cold wind that swept across the plateau with the setting sun. Across the valley, several miles away, Arha saw the light of his friend's fire, which shone like a star in the blackness.

The wind turned colder and seemed to pass through his flesh and chill the marrow in his bones. The rock on which he stood felt like ice. Each hour the cold numbed him more, until he thought he would never be warm again, but he kept his eyes upon the twinkling light across the valley and remembered that his old friend sat there tending a fire for him. Sometimes wisps of fog blotted out the light, and then he strained to see until the fog passed. He sneezed and coughed and shivered and began to feel ill. Yet all night through he stood there, and only when the dawn came did he put on his clothes and go down the mountain back to Addis Ababa.

Haptom was very surprised to see Arha, and he questioned his servants thoroughly.

"Did he stay all night without food or drink or blankets or clothing?"

"Yes," his servants said. "He did all of these things."

"Well, you are a strong fellow," Haptom said to Arha. "How did you manage to do it?"

"I simply watched the light of a fire on a distant hill," Arha said.

"What! You watched a fire? Then you lose the bet, and you are still my servant, and you own no land!"

"But this fire was not close enough to warm me, it was far across the valley!"

"I won't give you the land," Haptom said. "You didn't fulfill the conditions. It was only the fire that saved you."

Arha was very sad. He went again to his old friend and told him what had happened.

"Take the matter to the judge," the old man advised him.

Arha went to the judge and complained, and the judge sent for Haptom. When Haptom told his story, and the servants said that Arha had watched a distant fire across the valley, the judge said, "No, you have lost, for Haptom Hasei's condition was that you must be without fire."

Once more Arha went to his old friend with the sad news that he was doomed to the life of a servant, as though he had not gone through the ordeal on the mountaintop.

"Don't give up hope," the old man said. "More wisdom grows wild in the hills than in any city judge."

He got up from where he sat and went to find a man named Hailu,[6] in whose house he had been a servant when he was young. He explained to the good man about the bet between Haptom and Arha and asked if something couldn't be done.

"Don't worry about it," Hailu said after thinking for a while. "I will take care of it for you."

Some days later Hailu sent invitations to many people in the city to come to a feast at his house. Haptom was among them, and so was the judge who had ruled that Arha had lost the bet.

When the day of the feast arrived, the guests came riding on mules with fine trappings, their servants strung out behind them on foot. Haptom came with twenty servants, one of whom held a silk umbrella over his head to shade him from the sun, and four drummers played music that signified the great Haptom was here.

The guests sat on soft rugs laid out for them and talked. From the kitchen came the odors of wonderful things to eat: roast goat, roast corn and durra,[7] pancakes called injera,[8] and many tantalizing sauces. The smell of the food only accentuated the hunger of the guests. Time passed. The food should have been served, but they didn't see it, only smelled vapors that drifted from the kitchen. The evening came, and still no food was served. The guests began to whisper among themselves. It was very curious that the honorable Hailu had not had the food brought out. Still the smells came from the kitchen. At last one of the guests spoke out for all the others.

"Hailu, why do you do this to us? Why do you invite us to a feast and then serve us nothing?"

"Why, can't you smell the food?" Hailu asked with surprise.

"Indeed we can, but smelling is not eating; there is no nourishment in it!"

"And is there warmth in a fire so distant that it can hardly be seen?" Hailu asked. "If Arha was warmed by the fire he watched while standing on Mount Intotto, then you have been fed by the smells coming from my kitchen."

The people agreed with him; the judge now saw his mistake, and Haptom was shamed. He thanked Hailu for his advice, and announced that Arha was then and there the owner of the land, the house, and the cattle.

Then Hailu ordered the food brought in, and the feast began.

---

6. **Hailu** [hī'lōō']

7. **durra** [door'ə]: tall grain grown for food.
8. **injera** [in je'rə]

STUDY QUESTIONS

Recalling

1. What are the conditions of the bet Arha makes with Haptom? What will Arha win if he succeeds?
2. What does the old man tell Arha to do in order to win the bet?
3. What reason do Haptom and the judge give for saying that Arha lost the bet?
4. Who is Hailu? What does he do at the feast to change the judge's decision?

Interpreting

5. What does the way Arha survives the long night suggest about the power of his mind and imagination?
6. Do you think the judge made a fair decision in Arha's case? Why or why not?
7. Why do you think the trick played by Hailu worked better than simply arguing with Haptom?

Extending

8. To what extent do you think the power of the mind and imagination can help people meet challenges?

VOCABULARY

Word Origins

In "The Fire on the Mountain" Hailu tempts his guests with the smells of "many tantalizing sauces." *Tantalize* means "to tempt with something that is withheld." The word comes from the name *Tantalus*. Tantalus is a Greek mythological character who was forced to stand forever near food and water that remained just beyond his reach.

Use your dictionary to find the meaning and origin of the words listed below. Each one comes from the name of a Greek or Roman mythological character. You may have to look up more than one entry for each word. For example, the definition of *tantalize* may refer to Tantalus but may not define him. You would have to look up *Tantalus* to understand completely the origin of *tantalize*.

1. January
2. helium
3. mercurial
4. panic

COMPOSITION

Writing About Conflict

■ Discuss Arha's two main conflicts. First describe each one. Then tell how each conflict is resolved. Finally, tell briefly which conflict is the more difficult one and why.

Describing an Internal Conflict

■ Imagine a situation in which a character you invent must make a difficult decision. First introduce your character. Then explain the situation carefully. Finally, describe how your character resolves this internal conflict.

COMPARING FOLK TALES

1. Compare two or more folk tales. First name some common characteristics of folk tales. Then tell how each tale you are comparing demonstrates those characteristics.
2. For two or more folk tales tell what the characters have in common. Then state the theme of each tale, and tell how the themes are alike and how they are different.

To answer the previous questions, you may want to compare the folk tales in one of the following groups:

"The Ant and the Grasshopper," "The Shepherd Boy," and "The Piece of Straw"

"The Piece of Straw," "Three Magic Oranges," and "The Fire on the Mountain"

"The Farmer and His Hired Help" and "The Fire on the Mountain"

Active Reading

Myths and Folk Tales

Distinguishing Fantasy from Reality

The term *reality* refers to events that actually can happen. The term *fantasy* refers to events that are not true to life. Fantasy involves situations that are highly unusual or seemingly impossible. A goose laying a goose egg is a realistic event; it can happen in real life, and, in fact, does. However, a goose laying a solid gold egg is a fantastic event; it could never occur in real life.

Myths and folk tales combine reality and fantasy. Although the tales are not completely true, some of the characters and events could exist in real life. For example, we can believe that a shepherd boy can alarm a village by crying, "Wolf!" That kind of event is reality. However, we cannot believe that an ant and a grasshopper can have a conversation. That kind of event is fantasy, not reality. To appreciate fully the myths and folk tales you read, you must distinguish reality from fantasy.

Activity 1   The following numbered items describe events that occur in "Three Magic Oranges." Tell whether each numbered item could happen in real life or only in fantasy.

1. A king orders his son to find a wife. The prince mounts a fine horse and rides off in search of a bride.
2. The prince cuts open an orange, and a beautiful maiden magically appears from inside the orange.
3. The maiden vanishes into thin air after the prince is unable to give her a drink of water.
4. The prince eats the orange, which is very sweet. The orange refreshes him, and he goes on his way.
5. The prince opens his last orange, and another maiden suddenly springs from inside it.
6. The prince falls in love with the maiden and asks her to become his wife.
7. A wicked witch had enchanted the princess and imprisoned her in the magic orange.
8. The witch, disguised as an old woman, turns the queen into a dove.
9. The king manages to turn the dove back into a beautiful woman once again.
10. Afterward the king and queen live in peace and love.

Identifying Causes and Effects

The Ancient Greeks invented their myths in order to explain various natural happenings and historic events. Today we can explain these events through science, but we still read the Ancient Greeks' "explanations." For example, we still read "Demeter and Persephone," which presents the Ancient Greeks' explanation of winter. Similarly, we still read "Echo and Narcissus," which suggests how the echo came about, and "Arachne," which gives an explanation for the origin of spiders.

A *cause* is the reason something happens. An *effect* is the result, or what happens. Read the following passage from "Prometheus the Fire-Bringer":

> Men became rebels and grumblers. For this reason Zeus, seeing winter coming on again, determined to destroy the people of Arcadia.

This passage describes an effect and its cause. The effect, or result, is that Zeus determined to destroy the people of Arcadia. The cause, or reason, is that men had become rebels and grumblers. In the passage the words *for this reason* help to indicate that an effect is about to be mentioned. Other words that signal causes and effects include *because*, *therefore*, and *as a result*.

Activity 2 Read each of the following passages from "Prometheus the Fire-Bringer." Answer the question about cause and effect that follows each passage.

1. A raging fire ended the first age of the world. At the end of the second age, vast floods engulfed plains and mountains. According to the oldest poets, these misfortunes were punishments the gods visited upon men for their wickedness and wrongdoing.
    Why were men punished by fire and flood?

2. They [the Arcadians] grumbled against Olympus. They grumbled because they must eat and hunt like the animals and had no hoof nor claw nor heavy fur for protection.
    Why did the Arcadians grumble?

3. He [Prometheus] knew why Zeus would not consent to teach men this secret [of fire] of the gods. The gift of fire to men would be a gift of power.
    Why did Zeus not want Prometheus to give men the secret of fire?

Understanding Character Motivation

Like people, characters in myths and folk tales behave as they do for particular reasons, or motivations. *Motivation* is a feeling or goal that causes a character to act. We can consider character motivations and actions as a specific kind of cause and effect. For example, King Midas wishes, "Let everything I touch turn to gold." What reason does he have for wishing this? What is his motive? The story tells you that what the king "loved best in the world was gold. He had plenty of his own, but he could not bear the thought of anyone else having any." From this information you may infer, or guess, that the king's motive for his wish is greed.

Sometimes in a story a character's motive is stated directly. You do not have to infer the reason for that behavior. However, many times the motive for a particular action is not stated directly. In such cases you must use the details that are given to make an intelligent guess, or inference, as to why a character behaves in a certain way.

Activity 3 Read each of the following passages from "Midas." Then answer the question about motive at the end of the passage. Tell whether the motive is stated directly in the passage or if you must infer it. If you infer it, tell what details in the passage help you identify the motive.

1.   After a while these words of complaint, uttered each dawn, came to Apollo, and he was angry. He appeared to Midas in a dream and said, "Other gods would punish you, Midas, but I am famous for my even temper. Instead of doing you violence, I will show you how gracious I can be by granting you a wish. What is it to be?"
   Why did Apollo decide to grant Midas a wish?

2. He [Midas] felt the hair [of his daughter] grow spiky under his fingers. Her eyes stiffened and froze into place. The little blue vein in her neck stopped pulsing. She was a statue, a figure of pale gold standing in the garden path with lifted face. . . . He looked at her and said, "This is unfortunate. I'm sorry it happened. . . ." He hurried out of the garden which had become unpleasant to him.
   Why had the garden become unpleasant to Midas?

3. The plates turned into gold, and the cups became gold cups before the amazed eyes of the servants, whom he [Midas] was careful not to touch. He wanted them to continue being able to serve him; he was very hungry.
Why did Midas avoid touching his servants?

4. Worse than hunger, when he [Midas] thought about drinking, he realized that wine, or water, or milk would turn to gold in his mouth and choke him if he drank. . . . He shrieked with rage, pounded on the table, and flung the plates about.
Why did Midas shriek with rage?

5.   Midas put a tall pointed hat on his head so that no one would see his [donkey's] ears. . . . For years he wore the cap so that no one would know of his disgrace.
Why did Midas wear a cap on his head?

6.   When the king heard, he knew who had told the secret [of his donkey's ears] and ordered the man's head cut off; but then he thought, "The god forgave me, perhaps I had better forgive this blabbermouth." Therefore he let the treacherous man keep his head.
Why did the king decide not to behead the treacherous man?

Literary Skills Review

Greek Myths and World Folk Tales

Guide for Reading Myths and Folk Tales

As you read myths and folk tales, use this guide to help you understand and appreciate the way ancient tellers related their tales.

Greek Myths

1. What event or belief did the **myth** explain as it was passed down through **oral tradition**?
2. Which **gods** and **goddesses** appear in the myth? What are their roles and responsibilities?
3. What type of **conflict** takes place in the myth?
4. Which **character traits** do the main characters show? What are the characters' **motivations**?
5. What examples of **metamorphosis** can you find in the myth?
6. What is the **theme,** or main idea, of the myth?

World Folk Tales

1. What values and characteristics of society are revealed by the **folk tale**?
2. What human characteristics are given to animals in the **fable**? What is the **moral** of the fable?
3. What are the qualities of the **hero** of the folk tale? What **conflict** or ordeal does the hero face? What qualities enable the hero to triumph?
4. What is the **theme,** or main idea, of the folk tale?

Themes Review

Greek Myths and World Folk Tales

Even in the world's oldest literature, certain general themes occur over and over again. The theme "heroes," for example, occurs in many myths and folk tales. However, each myth or tale that draws on this general theme says something very specific about it. For example, "Prometheus the Fire-Bringer" (page 424) expresses the following specific theme: "A hero is one who uses skill and courage to do a great service to humanity." "Atalanta" (page 448) expresses a different specific theme: "A hero is one who uses skill and courage to win personal happiness."

1. What specific point about the general theme "heroes" is expressed in "Three Magic Oranges"?

2. Choose two of the following myths and folk tales, and explain the specific point that each makes about the general theme "love."

   "Atalanta"   "Three Magic Oranges"
   "Echo and Narcissus" "Demeter and Persephone"

3. Choose two of the following myths and folk tales, and tell what specific point each makes about the general theme "goals and challenges."

   "The Piece of Straw" "The Fire on the Mountain"
   "Arachne"   "The Farmer and His Hired Help"

4. Choose one myth and one story below. Then tell what specific point each work expresses about the general theme "communities."

   Myths: "An Introduction to   "Prometheus the
                Greek Mythology"   Fire-Bringer"
   Stories: "Christmas in Brooklyn" "The Third Level"

5. Choose one of the following myths or folk tales and one other work. Tell what specific point each expresses about the general theme "growth and learning."

   Myths: "Deucalion and Pyrrha" "Midas"
   Folk Tales: "The Shepherd Boy"   "The Ant and the
                                            Grasshopper"
   Stories: "The Fun They Had"   "The Birdman"
   Nonfiction: *Growing Up*   "When Does Educa-
                                            tion Stop?"

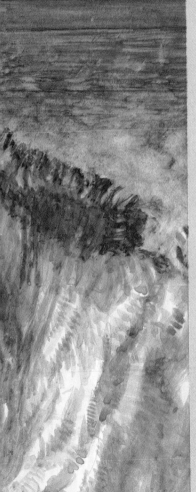

Preview
The Novel

A **novel** is a long work of prose fiction that tells a story. Since it is longer than a short story, a novel may create a fuller picture of life. A novelist can capture a wide range of experiences—good, sad, funny—to make this fictional world seem lifelike.

The same elements that help make a good short story are also present in a novel: plot, character, setting, and theme. Because of a novel's length, an author is able to include more developments in the plot, to introduce more characters, to describe them more fully, and to present more settings than are usually in a short story.

Novels first appeared over two hundred years ago. Since that time the novel has developed and changed as society has. By reading a novel we learn about the world that the author describes. A novel, however, also helps us to understand ourselves and our own world. For example, in *The Red Pony* John Steinbeck describes the life of a young boy living on a California ranch, where his father raises vegetables as well as cattle, pigs, and chickens. Yet this novel goes beyond that one boy and that one place. It shows us the hardships and joys of growing up anywhere.

THE RED PONY

John Steinbeck (1902–1968) was born and raised in the Salinas Valley of California. There he acquired his lifelong love of the outdoors. Like Jody, the main character of *The Red Pony,* Steinbeck loved horses. The day that his horse had a colt, Steinbeck said, was "the most tremendous morning in the world." During holidays from school, Steinbeck worked as a hired hand and learned firsthand about life on a ranch.

Steinbeck gained worldwide praise not only for *The Red Pony* (1937) but also for several other novels. Among them are *Of Mice and Men* (1937), *The Grapes of Wrath* (1939), and *The Pearl* (1947). In 1962 Steinbeck won the Nobel Prize for Literature. In his acceptance speech he said that a writer must "celebrate man's proven capacity for greatness of heart and spirit—for gallantry in defeat, for courage, compassion and love." In many ways the boy Jody has all of these virtues.

The Red Pony covers about two years in the life of a young boy on an isolated ranch. The novel is divided into three chapters. Each chapter deals with a separate incident in the boy's growth. In the first he is given a young pony. In the second he meets a mysterious old man. In the third he learns to care for a mare about to give birth to a colt. Each incident tests Jody and helps him discover new things about the world in which he must live.

Key Ideas in *The Red Pony*

As you read *The Red Pony,* think about the following topics. Keep track of what the novel says about each one. You will then understand the major themes of *The Red Pony.*

- Respect for living things
- Compassion for other people
- The responsibilities of adulthood
- The connection between life and death
- The relationship between people and nature

The Red Pony *takes place near Salinas, a town nestled among the mountains along the central coast of California.*

■ *As the novel begins, notice how the author fondly pictures the beautiful countryside and the simple life of the ranchers.*

John Steinbeck

The Red Pony

I. The Gift

At daybreak Billy Buck emerged from the bunkhouse and stood for a moment on the porch looking up at the sky. He was a broad, bandy-legged[1] little man with a walrus mustache, with square hands, puffed and muscled on the palms. His eyes were a contemplative, watery gray and the hair which protruded from under his Stetson[2] hat was spiky and weathered. Billy was still stuffing his shirt into his blue jeans as he stood on the porch. He unbuckled his belt and tightened it again. The belt showed, by the worn shiny places opposite each hole, the gradual increase of Billy's middle over a period of years. When he had seen to the weather, Billy cleared each nostril by holding its mate closed with his forefinger and blowing fiercely. Then he walked down to the barn, rubbing his hands together. He curried[3] and brushed two saddle horses in the stalls, talking quietly to them all the time; and he had hardly finished when the iron triangle started ringing at the ranch house. Billy stuck the brush and currycomb together and laid them on the rail, and went up to breakfast. His action had been so deliberate and yet so wasteless of time that he came to the house while Mrs. Tiflin was still ringing the triangle. She nodded her gray head to him and withdrew into the kitchen. Billy Buck sat down on the steps, because he was a cow-hand, and it wouldn't be fitting that he should go first into the dining-room. He heard Mr. Tiflin in the house, stamping his feet into his boots.

The high jangling note of the triangle put the boy Jody in motion. He was only a little boy, ten years old, with hair like dusty yellow grass and with shy polite gray eyes, and with a mouth that worked when he thought. The triangle picked him up out of sleep. It didn't occur to him to disobey the harsh note. He never had: no one he knew ever had. He brushed the tangled hair out of his eyes and skinned his nightgown off. In a moment he was dressed—blue chambray[4] shirt and overalls. It was late in the summer, so of course there were no shoes to bother with. In the kitchen he waited until his mother got from in front of the sink and went back to the stove. Then he washed himself and brushed back

---

1. **bandy-legged:** bowlegged.
2. **Stetson hat:** high hat with a wide brim worn by cowboys.
3. **curried** [kur′ēd]: rubbed down and cleaned the horses using a brush, called a currycomb, which has teeth rather than bristles.

---

4. **chambray** [sham′brā]: cotton material.

his wet hair with his fingers. His mother turned sharply on him as he left the sink. Jody looked shyly away.

"I've got to cut your hair before long," his mother said. "Breakfast's on the table. Go on in, so Billy can come."

Jody sat at the long table which was covered with white oilcloth washed through to the fabric in some places. The fried eggs lay in rows on their platter. Jody took three eggs on his plate and followed with three thick slices of crisp bacon. He carefully scraped a spot of blood from one of the egg yolks.

Billy Buck clumped in. "That won't hurt you," Billy explained. "That's only a sign the rooster leaves."

Jody's tall stern father came in then and Jody knew from the noise on the floor that he was wearing boots, but he looked under the table anyway, to make sure. His father turned off the oil lamp over the table, for plenty of morning light now came through the windows.

Jody did not ask where his father and Billy Buck were riding that day, but he wished he might go along. His father was a disciplinarian. Jody obeyed him in everything without questions of any kind. Now, Carl Tiflin sat down and reached for the egg platter.

"Got the cows ready to go, Billy?" he asked.

"In the lower corral," Billy said. "I could just as well take them in alone."

"Sure you could. But a man needs company. Besides your throat gets pretty dry." Carl Tiflin was jovial this morning.

Jody's mother put her head in the door. "What time do you think to be back, Carl?"

"I can't tell. I've got to see some men in Salinas.[5] Might be gone till dark."

The eggs and coffee and big biscuits disappeared rapidly. Jody followed the two men out of the house. He watched them mount their horses and drive six old milk cows out of the corral and start over the hill toward Salinas. They were going to sell the old cows to the butcher.

When they had disappeared over the crown of the ridge Jody walked up the hill in back of the house. The dogs trotted around the house corner hunching their shoulders and grinning horribly with pleasure. Jody patted their heads—Doubletree Mutt with the big thick tail and yellow eyes, and Smasher, the shepherd, who had killed a coyote and lost an ear in doing it. Smasher's one good ear stood up higher than a collie's ear should. Billy Buck said that always happened. After the frenzied greeting the dogs lowered their noses to the ground in a businesslike way and went ahead, looking back now and then to make sure that the boy was coming. They walked up through the chicken yard and saw the quail eating with the chickens. Smasher chased the chickens a little to keep in practice in case there should ever be sheep to herd. Jody continued on through the large vegetable patch where the green corn was higher than his head. The cowpumpkins were green and small yet. He went on to the sagebrush[6] line where the cold spring ran out of its pipe and fell into a round wooden tub. He leaned over and drank close to the green mossy wood where the water tasted best. Then he turned and looked back on the ranch, on the low, whitewashed house girded with red geraniums, and on the long bunkhouse by the cypress tree where Billy Buck lived alone. Jody could see the great black kettle under the cypress tree. That was where the pigs were

---

5. **Salinas** [sə lēn′əs]: city in the Salinas Valley of west central California, lying between the Santa Lucia Mountains to the west and the Gabilan [gə′bi lan] Mountains to the east.

---

6. **sagebrush:** hardy shrub with silvery leaves that grows in dense patches on the dry plains of the West.

scalded. The sun was coming over the ridge now, glaring on the whitewash of the houses and barns, making the wet grass blaze softly. Behind him, in the tall sagebrush, the birds were scampering on the ground, making a great noise among the dry leaves; the squirrels piped shrilly on the side-hills. Jody looked along at the farm buildings. He felt an uncertainty in the air, a feeling of change and of loss and of the gain of new and unfamiliar things. Over the hillside two big black buzzards sailed low to the ground and their shadows slipped smoothly and quickly ahead of them. Some animal had died in the vicinity. Jody knew it. It might be a cow or it might be the remains of a rabbit. The buzzards overlooked nothing. Jody hated them as all decent things hate them, but they could not be hurt because they made away with carrion.[7]

After a while the boy sauntered down hill

---

7. **carrion:** rotting flesh of a dead animal.

again. The dogs had long ago given him up and gone into the brush to do things in their own way. Back through the vegetable garden he went, and he paused for a moment to smash a green muskmelon with his heel, but he was not happy about it. It was a bad thing to do, he knew perfectly well. He kicked dirt over the ruined melon to conceal it.

Back at the house his mother bent over his rough hands, inspecting his fingers and nails. It did little good to start him clean to school for too many things could happen on the way. She sighed over the black cracks on his fingers, and then gave him his books and his lunch and started him on the mile walk to school. She noticed that his mouth was working a good deal this morning.

Jody started his journey. He filled his pockets with little pieces of white quartz that lay in the road, and every so often he took a shot at a bird or at some rabbit that had stayed sunning itself in the road too long. At the crossroads over the bridge he met two friends and the three of them walked to school together, making ridiculous strides and being rather silly. School had just opened two weeks before. There was still a spirit of revolt among the pupils.

It was four o'clock in the afternoon when Jody topped the hill and looked down on the ranch again. He looked for the saddle horses, but the corral was empty. His father was not back yet. He went slowly, then, toward the afternoon chores. At the ranch house, he found his mother sitting on the porch, mending socks.

"There's two doughnuts in the kitchen for you," she said. Jody slid to the kitchen, and returned with half of one of the doughnuts already eaten and his mouth full. His mother asked him what he had learned in school that day, but she didn't listen to his doughnut-muffled answer. She interrupted, "Jody, tonight see you fill the wood-box clear full. Last night you crossed the sticks and it wasn't only about half full. Lay the sticks flat tonight. And Jody, some of the hens are hiding eggs, or else the dogs are eating them. Look about in the grass and see if you can find any nests."

Jody, still eating, went out and did his chores. He saw the quail come down to eat with the chickens when he threw out the grain. For some reason his father was proud to have them come. He never allowed any shooting near the house for fear the quail might go away.

When the wood-box was full, Jody took his twenty-two rifle up to the cold spring at the brush line. He drank again and then aimed the gun at all manner of things, at rocks, at birds on the wing, at the big black pig kettle under the cypress tree, but he didn't shoot for he had no cartridges and wouldn't have until he was twelve. If his father had seen him aim the rifle in the direction of the house he would

have put the cartridges off another year. Jody remembered this and did not point the rifle down the hill again. Two years was enough to wait for cartridges. Nearly all of his father's presents were given with reservations which hampered their value somewhat. It was good discipline.

After supper, Jody sat by the fireplace and his shy polite eyes sought the room corners, and he waited for his father to tell what it was he contained, for Jody knew he had news of some sort. But he was disappointed. His father pointed a stern finger at him.

"You'd better go to bed, Jody. I'm going to need you in the morning."

That wasn't so bad. Jody liked to do the things he had to do as long as they weren't routine things. He looked at the floor and his mouth worked out a question before he spoke it. "What are we going to do in the morning, kill a pig?" he asked softly.

"Never you mind. You better get to bed."

When the door was closed behind him, Jody heard his father and Billy Buck chuckling and he knew it was a joke of some kind. And later, when he lay in bed, trying to make words out of the murmurs in the other room, he heard his father protest, "But, Ruth, I didn't give much for him."

Jody heard the hoot-owls hunting mice down by the barn, and he heard a fruit tree limb tap-tapping against the house. A cow was lowing when he went to sleep.

When the triangle sounded in the morning, Jody dressed more quickly even than usual. In the kitchen, while he washed his face and combed back his hair, his mother addressed him irritably. "Don't you go out until you get a good breakfast in you."

He went into the dining-room and sat at the long white table. He took a steaming hot-cake from the platter, arranged two fried eggs on it, covered them with another hotcake and squashed the whole thing with his fork.

His father and Billy Buck came in. Jody knew from the sound on the floor that both of them were wearing flat-heeled shoes, but he peered under the table to make sure. His father turned off the oil lamp, for the day had arrived, and he looked stern and disciplinary, but Billy Buck didn't look at Jody at all. He avoided the shy questioning eyes of the boy and soaked a whole piece of toast in his coffee.

Carl Tiflin said crossly, "You come with us after breakfast!"

Jody had trouble with his food then, for he felt a kind of doom in the air. After Billy had tilted his saucer and drained the coffee which had slopped into it, and had wiped his hands on his jeans, the two men stood up from the table and went out into the morning light together, and Jody respectfully followed a little behind them. He tried to keep his mind from running ahead, tried to keep it absolutely motionless.

His mother called, "Carl! Don't you let it keep him from school."

They marched past the cypress, where a singletree[8] hung from a limb to butcher the pigs on, and past the black iron kettle, so it was not a pig killing. The sun shone over the hill and threw long, dark shadows of the trees and buildings. They crossed a stubble-field to shortcut to the barn. Jody's father unhooked the door and they went in. They had been walking toward the sun on the way down. The barn was black as night in contrast and warm from the hay and from the beasts. Jody's father moved over toward the one box stall. "Come here!" he ordered. Jody could begin to see things now. He looked into the box stall and then stepped back quickly.

A red pony colt was looking at him out of the stall. Its tense ears were forward and a light of disobedience was in its eyes. Its coat was rough and thick as an airedale's[9] fur and its mane was long and tangled. Jody's throat collapsed in on itself and cut his breath short.

"He needs a good currying," his father said, "and if I ever hear of you not feeding him or leaving his stall dirty, I'll sell him off in a minute."

Jody couldn't bear to look at the pony's eyes any more. He gazed down at his hands for a moment, and he asked very shyly, "Mine?" No one answered him. He put his hand out toward the pony. Its gray nose came close, sniffing loudly, and then the lips drew back and the strong teeth closed on Jody's fingers. The pony shook its head up and down and seemed to laugh with amusement. Jody regarded his bruised fingers. "Well," he said with pride—"Well, I guess he can bite all right." The two men laughed, somewhat in relief. Carl Tiflin went out of the barn and walked up a side-hill to be by himself, for he was embarrassed, but Billy Buck stayed. It was easier to talk to Billy Buck. Jody asked again—"Mine?"

Billy became professional in tone. "Sure! That is, if you look out for him and break[10] him right. I'll show you how. He's just a colt. You can't ride him for some time."

Jody put out his bruised hand again, and this time the red pony let his nose be rubbed. "I ought to have a carrot," Jody said. "Where'd we get him, Billy?"

"Bought him at a sheriff's auction," Billy explained. "A show went broke in Salinas and had debts. The sheriff was selling off their stuff."

The pony stretched out his nose and shook

---

8. **singletree:** wooden bar usually on the front of a plow, to which the ropes of a harness are attached.

9. **airedale's:** referring to a dog having a wiry tan coat.
10. **break:** gradually train a horse to be ridden.

the forelock from his wild eyes. Jody stroked the nose a little. He said softly, "There isn't a—saddle?"

Billy Buck laughed. "I'd forgot. Come along."

In the harness room he lifted down a little saddle of red morocco leather. "It's just a show saddle," Billy Buck said disparagingly. "It isn't practical for the brush, but it was cheap at the sale."

Jody couldn't trust himself to look at the saddle either, and he couldn't speak at all. He brushed the shining red leather with his fingertips, and after a long time he said, "It'll look pretty on him though." He thought of the grandest and prettiest things he knew. "If he hasn't a name already, I think I'll call him Gabilan Mountains," he said.

Billy Buck knew how he felt. "It's a pretty long name. Why don't you just call him Gabilan? That means hawk. That would be a fine name for him." Billy felt glad. "If you will collect tail hair, I might be able to make a hair rope for you sometime. You could use it for a hackamore."[11]

Jody wanted to go back to the box stall. "Could I lead him to school, do you think—to show the kids?"

But Billy shook his head. "He's not even halter-broke yet. We had a time getting him here. Had to almost drag him. You better be starting for school though."

"I'll bring the kids to see him here this afternoon," Jody said.

Six boys came over the hill half an hour early that afternoon, running hard, their heads down, their forearms working, their breath whistling. They swept by the house

and cut across the stubble-field to the barn. And then they stood self-consciously before the pony, and then they looked at Jody with eyes in which there was a new admiration and a new respect. Before today Jody had been a boy, dressed in overalls and a blue shirt—quieter than most, even suspected of being a little cowardly. And now he was different. Out of a thousand centuries they drew the ancient admiration of the footman for the horseman. They knew instinctively that a man on a horse is spiritually as well as physically bigger than a man on foot. They knew that Jody had been miraculously lifted out of equality with them, and had been placed over them. Gabilan put his head out of the stall and sniffed them.

---

11. **hackamore:** halter made of rope that can be tightened around the nose of a horse; used while training horses.

"It isn't much use in the brush," Jody explained. "It'll look pretty on him though. Maybe I'll ride bareback when I go into the brush."

"How you going to rope a cow without a saddle horn?"[12]

"Maybe I'll get another saddle for every day. My father might want me to help him with the stock." He let them feel the red saddle, and showed them the brass chain throat-latch on the bridle and the big brass buttons at each temple where the headstall and brow band crossed. The whole thing was too wonderful. They had to go away after a little while, and each boy, in his mind, searched among his possessions for a bribe worthy of offering in return for a ride on the red pony when the time should come.

Jody was glad when they had gone. He took brush and currycomb from the wall, took down the barrier of the box stall and stepped cautiously in. The pony's eyes glittered, and he edged around into kicking position. But Jody touched him on the shoulder and rubbed his high arched neck as he had always seen Billy Buck do, and he crooned, "So-o-o, boy," in a deep voice. The pony gradually relaxed his tenseness. Jody curried and brushed until a pile of dead hair lay in the stall and until the pony's coat had taken on a deep red shine. Each time he finished he thought it might have been done better. He braided the mane into a dozen little pigtails, and he braided the forelock, and then he undid them and brushed the hair out straight again.

Jody did not hear his mother enter the barn. She was angry when she came, but when she looked in at the pony and at Jody working over him, she felt a curious pride rise

"Why'n't you ride him?" the boys cried. "Why'n't you braid his tail with ribbons like in the fair?" "When you going to ride him?"

Jody's courage was up. He too felt the superiority of the horseman. "He's not old enough. Nobody can ride him for a long time. I'm going to train him on the long halter. Billy Buck is going to show me how."

"Well, can't we even lead him around a little?"

"He isn't even halter-broke," Jody said. He wanted to be completely alone when he took the pony out the first time. "Come and see the saddle."

They were speechless at the red morocco saddle, completely shocked out of comment.

---

12. **saddle horn:** small knob on the front of a saddle to which a rope can be attached.

up in her. "Have you forgot the wood-box?" she asked gently. "It's not far off from dark and there's not a stick of wood in the house, and the chickens aren't fed."

Jody quickly put up his tools. "I forgot, ma'am."

"Well, after this do your chores first. Then you won't forget. I expect you'll forget lots of things now if I don't keep an eye on you."

"Can I have carrots from the garden for him, ma'am?"

She had to think about that. "Oh—I guess so, if you only take the big tough ones."

"Carrots keep the coat good," he said, and again she felt the curious rush of pride.

Jody never waited for the triangle to get him out of bed after the coming of the pony. It became his habit to creep out of bed even before his mother was awake, to slip into his clothes and to go quietly down to the barn to see Gabilan. In the gray quiet mornings when the land and the brush and the houses and the trees were silver-gray and black like a photograph negative, he stole toward the barn, past the sleeping stones and the sleeping cypress tree. The turkeys, roosting in the tree out of coyotes' reach, clicked drowsily. The fields glowed with a gray frostlike light and in the dew the tracks of rabbits and of field mice stood out sharply. The good dogs came stiffly out of their little houses, hackles[13] up and deep growls in their throats. Then they caught Jody's scent, and their stiff tails rose up and waved a greeting—Doubletree Mutt with the big thick tail, and Smasher, the incipient shepherd—then went lazily back to their warm beds.

It was a strange time and a mysterious journey, to Jody—an extension of a dream.

13. **hackles:** hair on the neck and back of a dog.

When he first had the pony he liked to torture himself during the trip by thinking Gabilan would not be in his stall, and worse, would never have been there. And he had other delicious little self-induced pains. He thought how the rats had gnawed ragged holes in the red saddle, and how the mice had nibbled Gabilan's tail until it was stringy and thin. He usually ran the last little way to the barn. He unlatched the rusty hasp of the barn door and stepped in, and no matter how quietly he opened the door, Gabilan was always looking at him over the barrier of the box stall and Gabilan whinnied softly and stamped his front foot, and his eyes had big sparks of red fire in them like oakwood embers.

Sometimes, if the work horses were to be used that day, Jody found Billy Buck in the barn harnessing and currying. Billy stood with him and looked long at Gabilan and he told Jody a great many things about horses. He explained that they were terribly afraid for their feet, so that one must make a practice of lifting the legs and patting the hoofs and ankles to remove their terror. He told Jody how horses love conversation. He must talk to the pony all the time, and tell him the reasons for everything. Billy wasn't sure a horse could understand everything that was said to him, but it was impossible to say how much was understood. A horse never kicked up a fuss if someone he liked explained things to him. Billy could give examples, too. He had known, for instance, a horse nearly dead beat with fatigue to perk up when told it was only a little farther to his destination. And he had known a horse paralyzed with fright to come out of it when his rider told him what it was that was frightening him. While he talked in the mornings, Billy Buck cut twenty or thirty straws into neat three-inch lengths and stuck them into his hatband. Then during the whole day, if he wanted to pick his teeth or merely to chew on something, he had only to reach up for one of them.

Jody listened carefully, for he knew and the whole country knew that Billy Buck was a fine hand with horses. Billy's own horse was a stringy cayuse[14] with a hammer head, but he nearly always won the first prizes at the stock trials. Billy could rope a steer, take a double half-hitch about the horn with his riata,[15] and dismount, and his horse would play the steer as an angler plays a fish, keeping a tight rope until the steer was down or beaten.

Every morning, after Jody had curried and brushed the pony, he let down the barrier of the stall, and Gabilan thrust past him and raced down the barn and into the corral. Around and around he galloped, and sometimes he jumped forward and landed on stiff legs. He stood quivering, stiff ears forward, eyes rolling so that the whites showed, pretending to be frightened. At last he walked snorting to the water-trough and buried his nose in the water up to the nostrils. Jody was proud then, for he knew that was the way to judge a horse. Poor horses only touched their lips to the water, but a fine spirited beast put his whole nose and mouth under, and only left room to breathe.

Then Jody stood and watched the pony, and he saw things he had never noticed about any other horse, the sleek, sliding flank muscles and the cords of the buttocks, which flexed like a closing fist, and the shine the sun put on the red coat. Having seen horses all his life, Jody had never looked at them very closely before. But now he noticed the moving ears which gave expression and even inflection of expression to the face. The pony talked with his ears. You could tell exactly how he

felt about everything by the way his ears pointed. Sometimes they were stiff and upright and sometimes lax and sagging. They went back when he was angry or fearful, and forward when he was anxious and curious and pleased; and their exact position indicated which emotion he had.

Billy Buck kept his word. In the early fall the training began. First there was the halter-breaking, and that was the hardest because it was the first thing. Jody held a carrot and coaxed and promised and pulled on the rope. The pony set his feet like a burro when he felt the strain. But before long he learned. Jody walked all over the ranch leading him. Gradually he took to dropping the rope until the pony followed him unled wherever he went.

And then came the training on the long halter. That was slower work. Jody stood in the middle of a circle, holding the long halter. He clucked with his tongue and the pony started to walk in a big circle, held in by the long rope. He clucked again to make the pony trot, and again to make him gallop. Around and around Gabilan went thundering and enjoying it immensely. Then he called, "Whoa," and the pony stopped. It was not long until Gabilan was perfect at it. But in many ways he was a bad pony. He bit Jody in the pants and stomped on Jody's feet. Now and then his ears went back and he aimed a tremendous kick at the boy. Every time he did one of these bad things, Gabilan settled back and seemed to laugh to himself.

Billy Buck worked at the hair rope in the evenings before the fireplace. Jody collected tail hair in a bag, and he sat and watched Billy slowly constructing the rope, twisting a few hairs to make a string and rolling two strings together for a cord, and then braiding a number of cords to make the rope. Billy rolled the finished rope on the floor under his foot to make it round and hard.

---

14. **cayuse** [kī ūs′]: small Indian horse used by cowboys.
15. **riata** [rē ä′tə]: Spanish for "lasso."

The long halter work rapidly approached perfection. Jody's father, watching the pony stop and start and trot and gallop, was a little bothered by it.

"He's getting to be almost a trick pony," he complained. "I don't like trick horses. It takes all the—dignity out of a horse to make him do tricks. Why, a trick horse is kind of like an actor—no dignity, no character of his own." And his father said, "I guess you better be getting him used to the saddle pretty soon."

Jody rushed for the harness-room. For some time he had been riding the saddle on a sawhorse. He changed the stirrup length over and over, and could never get it just right. Sometimes, mounted on the sawhorse in the harness-room, with collars and hames and tugs hung all about him, Jody rode out beyond the room. He carried his rifle across the pommel.[16] He saw the fields go flying by, and he heard the beat of the galloping hoofs.

It was a ticklish job, saddling the pony the first time. Gabilan hunched and reared and threw the saddle off before the cinch[17] could be tightened. It had to be replaced again and again until at last the pony let it stay. And the cinching was difficult, too. Day by day Jody tightened the girth a little more until at last the pony didn't mind the saddle at all.

Then there was the bridle.[18] Billy explained how to use a stick of licorice for a bit until Gabilan was used to having something in his mouth. Billy explained, "Of course we could force-break him to everything, but he wouldn't be as good a horse if we did. He'd always be a little bit afraid, and he wouldn't mind because he wanted to."

The first time the pony wore the bridle he whipped his head about and worked his tongue against the bit until the blood oozed from the corners of his mouth. He tried to rub the headstall off on the manger. His ears pivoted about and his eyes turned red with fear and with general rambunctiousness. Jody rejoiced, for he knew that only a mean-souled horse does not resent training.

And Jody trembled when he thought of the time when he would first sit in the saddle. The pony would probably throw him off. There was no disgrace in that. The disgrace would come if he did not get right up and mount again. Sometimes he dreamed that he lay in the dirt and cried and couldn't make himself mount again. The shame of the dream lasted until the middle of the day.

Gabilan was growing fast. Already he had lost the long-leggedness of the colt; his mane was getting longer and blacker. Under the constant currying and brushing his coat lay as smooth and gleaming as orange-red lacquer. Jody oiled the hoofs and kept them carefully trimmed so they would not crack.

The hair rope was nearly finished. Jody's father gave him an old pair of spurs and bent in the side bars and cut down the strap and took up the chainlets until they fitted. And then one day Carl Tiflin said:

"The pony's growing faster than I thought. I guess you can ride him by Thanksgiving. Think you can stick on?"

"I don't know," Jody said shyly. Thanksgiving was only three weeks off. He hoped it wouldn't rain, for rain would spot the red saddle.

Gabilan knew and liked Jody by now. He nickered when Jody came across the stubble-field, and in the pasture he came running when his master whistled for him. There was always a carrot for him every time.

Billy Buck gave him riding instructions

---

16. **pommel** [pom′əl]: rounded, front part of a saddle.
17. **cinch** [sinch]: strap fastened around a horse's belly to hold the saddle in place, also called *girth*.
18. **bridle:** gear for a horse's head, used to guide the animal.

over and over. "Now when you get up there, just grab tight with your knees and keep your hands away from the saddle, and if you get throwed, don't let that stop you. No matter how good a man is, there's always some horse can pitch him. You just climb up again before he gets to feeling smart about it. Pretty soon, he won't throw you no more, and pretty soon he *can't* throw you no more. That's the way to do it."

"I hope it don't rain before," Jody said.

"Why not? Don't want to get throwed in the mud?"

That was partly it, and also he was afraid that in the flurry of bucking Gabilan might slip and fall on him and break his leg or his hip. He had seen that happen to men before, had seen how they writhed on the ground like squashed bugs, and he was afraid of it.

He practiced on the sawhorse how he would hold the reins in his left hand and a hat in his right hand. If he kept his hands thus busy, he couldn't grab the horn if he felt himself going off. He didn't like to think of what would happen if he did grab the horn. Perhaps his father and Billy Buck would never speak to him again, they would be so ashamed. The news would get about and his mother would be ashamed too. And in the schoolyard—it was too awful to contemplate.

He began putting his weight in a stirrup when Gabilan was saddled, but he didn't throw his leg over the pony's back. That was forbidden until Thanksgiving.

Every afternoon he put the red saddle on the pony and cinched it tight. The pony was learning already to fill his stomach out unnaturally large while the cinching was going on, and then to let it down when the straps were fixed. Sometimes Jody led him up to the brush line and let him drink from the round green tub, and sometimes he led him up through the stubble-field to the hilltop from

which it was possible to see the white town of Salinas and the geometric fields of the great valley, and the oak trees clipped by the sheep. Now and then they broke through the brush and came to little cleared circles so hedged in that the world was gone and only the sky and the circle of brush were left from the old life. Gabilan liked these trips and showed it by keeping his head very high and by quivering his nostrils with interest. When the two came back from an expedition they smelled of the sweet sage they had forced through.

The Red Pony 497

STUDY QUESTIONS

Recalling

1. List and describe in a few words the four characters who appear on pages 487–497. Describe the ranch where they live.
2. Where do Carl Tiflin and Billy Buck go after breakfast? List at least five things that Jody does while the men are gone.
3. Describe the buzzards that Jody sees. What are Jody's feelings about them?
4. What gift does Carl bring back for Jody? What is the meaning of the name Jody chooses for his new present?
5. Who comes home from school with Jody to see the red pony? How is Jody "different" now in their eyes?
6. Briefly outline the steps that Jody takes to train Gabilan. Who helps Jody train the pony?

Interpreting

7. How are Carl Tiflin and Billy Buck alike? How are they different?
8. What does Jody feel about his routine daily chores? Why do you suppose he smashes the green muskmelon?
9. Why do you think Jody's father gives him the pony? In what ways does Jody show his feelings about his new pony?
10. Describe Jody before he has the pony. Does he change after he receives Gabilan?

Extending

11. From your observations explain how having a pet might teach a person to be less selfish.

READING AND LITERARY FOCUS

Characterization

Characterization can refer to the personality of a character in a piece of literature. Characterization can also refer to the method an author uses to reveal this personality to the reader. Sometimes the author makes clear statements about the character's personality. For example, when Steinbeck tells us that Carl Tiflin is "stern," he is making a direct statement about the character. At other times the author allows the character's own words and actions to reveal personality. For example, we learn that the oil-cloth that covers the kitchen table is "washed through to the fabric in some places." From this fact we may decide that Mrs. Tiflin works hard to take care of the house as well as Jody, her husband, and Billy Buck.

Since a novel is longer than a short story a novelist often shows us the many sides of a character's personality. Well-developed, complex personalities are called **major** characters. Less well-developed, simpler characters, such as Mrs. Tiflin, are called **minor** characters.

Thinking About Characterization

1. Find one direct statement about the character of each of the following: Jody, Carl Tiflin, Ruth Tiflin, and Billy Buck.
2. Describe the "personality" of Gabilan. Include examples from the novel in your description.

Imagery

Imagery is the descriptive language that a writer uses to make characters, places, objects, and experiences vivid and alive for the reader. Imagery appeals to the five senses: sight, sound, smell, taste, and touch. For example, Steinbeck involves the senses of sight and sound in the following sentences:

> The fields glowed with a gray frostlike light [sight]. . . . The good dogs came stiffly out of their little houses, hackles up [sight] and deep growls in their throats [sound].

Thinking About Imagery

1. Find the touch imagery that makes the scene come alive when Jody and the red pony first meet (pages 491–492).
2. Find imagery that refers to three different senses in the description of the farm on page 488.

In this section Jody faces a challenge that threatens his happiness.

■ *What changes will winter bring to Jody and the red pony?*

Time dragged on toward Thanksgiving, but winter came fast. The clouds swept down and hung all day over the land and brushed the hilltops, and the winds blew shrilly at night. All day the dry oak leaves drifted down from the trees until they covered the ground, and yet the trees were unchanged.

Jody had wished it might not rain before Thanksgiving, but it did. The brown earth turned dark and the trees glistened. The cut ends of the stubble turned black with mildew; the haystacks grayed from exposure to the damp, and on the roofs the moss, which had been all summer as gray as lizards, turned a brilliant yellow-green. During the week of rain, Jody kept the pony in the box stall out of the dampness, except for a little time after school when he took him out for exercise and to drink at the water-trough in the upper corral. Not once did Gabilan get wet.

The wet weather continued until little new grass appeared. Jody walked to school dressed in a slicker and short rubber boots. At length one morning the sun came out brightly. Jody, at his work in the box stall, said to Billy Buck, "Maybe I'll leave Gabilan in the corral when I go to school today."

"Be good for him to be out in the sun," Billy assured him. "No animal likes to be cooped up too long. Your father and me are going back on the hill to clean the leaves out of the spring." Billy nodded and picked his teeth with one of his little straws.

"If the rain comes, though—" Jody suggested.

"Not likely to rain today. She's rained her-self out." Billy pulled up his sleeves and snapped his arm bands. "If it comes on to rain—why a little rain don't hurt a horse."

"Well, if it does come to rain, you put him in, will you, Billy? I'm scared he might get cold so I couldn't ride him when the time comes."

"Oh sure! I'll watch out for him if we get back in time. But it won't rain today."

And so Jody, when he went to school, left Gabilan standing out in the corral.

Billy Buck wasn't wrong about many things. He couldn't be. But he was wrong about the weather that day, for a little after noon the clouds pushed over the hills and the rain began to pour down. Jody heard it start on the schoolhouse roof. He considered holding up one finger for permission to go to the outhouse and, once outside, running for home to put the pony in. Punishment would be prompt both at school and at home. He gave it up and took ease from Billy's assurance that rain couldn't hurt a horse. When school was finally out, he hurried home through the dark rain. The banks at the sides of the road spouted little jets of muddy water. The rain slanted and swirled under a cold and gusty wind. Jody dog-trotted home, slopping through the gravelly mud of the road.

From the top of the ridge he could see Gabilan standing miserably in the corral. The red coat was almost black, and streaked with water. He stood head down with his rump to the rain and wind. Jody arrived running and threw open the barn door and led the wet pony in by his forelock. Then he found a gunny

sack and rubbed the soaked hair and rubbed the legs and ankles. Gabilan stood patiently, but he trembled in gusts like the wind.

When he had dried the pony as well as he could, Jody went up to the house and brought hot water down to the barn and soaked the grain in it. Gabilan was not very hungry. He nibbled at the hot mash, but he was not very much interested in it, and he still shivered now and then. A little steam rose from his damp back.

It was almost dark when Billy Buck and Carl Tiflin came back home. "When the rain started we put up at Ben Herche's place, and the rain never let up all afternoon," Carl Tiflin explained. Jody looked reproachfully at Billy Buck and Billy felt guilty.

"You said it wouldn't rain," Jody accused him.

Billy looked away. "It's hard to tell, this time of year," he said, but his excuse was lame. He had no right to be fallible,[1] and he knew it.

"The pony got wet, got soaked through."

"Did you dry him off?"

"I rubbed him with a sack and I gave him hot grain."

Billy nodded in agreement.

"Do you think he'll take cold, Billy?"

"A little rain never hurt anything," Billy assured him.

Jody's father joined the conversation then and lectured the boy a little. "A horse," he said, "isn't any lap-dog kind of thing." Carl Tiflin hated weakness and sickness, and he held a violent contempt for helplessness.

---

1. **fallible** [fal′ə bəl]: capable of being wrong.

Jody's mother put a platter of steaks on the table and boiled potatoes and boiled squash, which clouded the room with their steam. They sat down to eat. Carl Tiflin still grumbled about weakness put into animals and men by too much coddling.

Billy Buck felt bad about his mistake. "Did you blanket him?" he asked.

"No. I couldn't find any blanket. I laid some sacks over his back."

"We'll go down and cover him up after we eat, then." Billy felt better about it then. When Jody's father had gone in to the fire and his mother was washing dishes, Billy found and lighted a lantern. He and Jody walked through the mud to the barn. The barn was dark and warm and sweet. The horses still munched their evening hay. "You hold the lantern!" Billy ordered. And he felt the pony's legs and tested the heat of the flanks. He put his cheek against the pony's gray muzzle and then he rolled up the eyelids to look at the eyeballs and he lifted the lips to see the gums, and he put his fingers inside his ears. "He don't seem so chipper," Billy said. "I'll give him a rubdown."

Then Billy found a sack and rubbed the pony's legs violently and he rubbed the chest and the withers.[2] Gabilan was strangely spiritless. He submitted patiently to the rubbing. At last Billy brought an old cotton comforter from the saddle-room, and threw it over the pony's back and tied it at neck and chest with string.

"Now he'll be all right in the morning," Billy said.

Jody's mother looked up when he got back to the house. "You're late up from bed," she said. She held his chin in her hard hand and

brushed the tangled hair out of his eyes and she said, "Don't worry about the pony. He'll be all right. Billy's as good as any horse doctor in the country."

Jody hadn't known she could see his worry. He pulled gently away from her and knelt down in front of the fireplace until it burned his stomach. He scorched himself through and then went in to bed, but it was a hard thing to go to sleep. He awakened after what seemed a long time. The room was dark but there was a grayness in the window like that which precedes the dawn. He got up and found his overalls and searched for the legs, and then the clock in the other room struck two. He laid his clothes down and got back into bed. It was broad daylight when he awakened again. For the first time he had slept through the ringing of the triangle. He leaped up, flung on his clothes and went out of the door still buttoning his shirt. His mother looked after him for a moment and then went quietly back to her work. Her eyes were brooding and kind. Now and then her mouth smiled a little but without changing her eyes at all.

Jody ran on toward the barn. Halfway there he heard the sound he dreaded, the hollow rasping cough of a horse. He broke into a sprint then. In the barn he found Billy Buck with the pony. Billy was rubbing its legs with his strong thick hands. He looked up and smiled gaily. "He just took a little cold," Billy said. "We'll have him out of it in a couple of days."

Jody looked at the pony's face. The eyes were half closed and the lids thick and dry. In the eye corners a crust of hard mucus stuck. Gabilan's ears hung loosely sideways and his head was low. Jody put out his hand, but the pony did not move close to it. He coughed again and his whole body constricted with the effort. A little stream of thin fluid ran from his nostrils.

---

2. **withers:** highest part of a horse's back, between the shoulder blades.

Jody looked back at Billy Buck. "He's awful sick, Billy."

"Just a little cold, like I said," Billy insisted. "You go get some breakfast and then go back to school. I'll take care of him."

"But you might have to do something else. You might leave him."

"No, I won't. I won't leave him at all. To-morrow's Saturday. Then you can stay with him all day." Billy had failed again, and he felt badly about it. He had to cure the pony now.

Jody walked up to the house and took his place listlessly at the table. The eggs and bacon were cold and greasy, but he didn't notice it. He ate his usual amount. He didn't even ask to stay home from school. His mother pushed his hair back when she took his plate. "Billy'll take care of the pony," she assured him.

He moped through the whole day at school. He couldn't answer any questions nor read any words. He couldn't even tell anyone the pony was sick, for that might make him sicker. And when school was finally out he started home in dread. He walked slowly and let the other boys leave him. He wished he might continue walking and never arrive at the ranch.

Billy was in the barn, as he had promised, and the pony was worse. His eyes were almost closed now, and his breath whistled shrilly past an obstruction in his nose. A film covered that part of the eyes that was visible at all. It was doubtful whether the pony could see any more. Now and then he snorted, to clear his nose, and by the action seemed to plug it tighter. Jody looked dispiritedly at the pony's coat. The hair lay rough and unkempt and seemed to have lost all of its old luster. Billy stood quietly beside the stall. Jody hated to ask, but he had to know.

"Billy, is he—is he going to get well?"

Billy put his fingers between the bars un-der the pony's jaw and felt about. "Feel here," he said and he guided Jody's fingers to a large lump under the jaw. "When that gets bigger, I'll open it up and then he'll get better."

Jody looked quickly away, for he had heard about that lump. "What is the matter with him?"

Billy didn't want to answer, but he had to. He couldn't be wrong three times. "Stran-gles,"[3] he said shortly, "but don't you worry about that. I'll pull him out of it. I've seen them get well when they were worse than Ga-bilan is. I'm going to steam him now. You can help."

"Yes," Jody said miserably. He followed Billy into the grain room and watched him make the steaming bag ready. It was a long canvas nose bag with straps to go over a horse's ears. Billy filled it one-third full of bran and then he added a couple of handfuls of dried hops.[4] On top of the dry substance he poured a little carbolic acid[5] and a little tur-pentine. "I'll be mixing it all up while you run to the house for a kettle of boiling water," Billy said.

When Jody came back with the steaming kettle, Billy buckled the straps over Gabilan's head and fitted the bag tightly around his nose. Then through a little hole in the side of the bag he poured the boiling water on the mixture. The pony started away as a cloud of strong steam rose up, but then the soothing fumes crept through his nose and into his lungs, and the sharp steam began to clear out the nasal passages. He breathed loudly. His legs trembled in an ague,[6] and his eyes closed

---

3. **Strangles:** disease of farm animals in which the breathing organs swell, sometimes becoming so large that the animal can no longer breathe.
4. **hops:** cone-shaped, yellowish-green fruits, which are sometimes used in making medicine.
5. **carbolic acid:** white substance made from coal tar, used to prevent infection.
6. **ague** [ā′gū]: fit of shivering.

against the biting cloud. Billy poured in more water and kept the steam rising for fifteen minutes. At last he set down the kettle and took the bag from Gabilan's nose. The pony looked better. He breathed freely, and his eyes were open wider than they had been.

"See how good it makes him feel," Billy said. "Now we'll wrap him up in the blanket again. Maybe he'll be nearly well by morning."

"I'll stay with him tonight," Jody suggested.

"No. Don't you do it. I'll bring my blankets down here and put them in the hay. You can stay tomorrow and steam him if he needs it."

The evening was falling when they went to the house for their supper. Jody didn't even realize that someone else had fed the chickens and filled the wood-box. He walked up past the house to the dark brush line and took a drink of water from the tub. The spring water was so cold that it stung his mouth and drove a shiver through him. The sky above the hills was still light. He saw a hawk flying so high that it caught the sun on its breast and shone like a spark. Two blackbirds were driving him down the sky, glittering as they attacked their enemy. In the west, the clouds were moving in to rain again.

Jody's father didn't speak at all while the family ate supper, but after Billy Buck had taken his blankets and gone to sleep in the barn, Carl Tiflin built a high fire in the fireplace and told stories. He told about the wild man who ran naked through the country and had a tail and ears like a horse, and he told about the rabbit-cats of Moro Cojo that hopped into the trees for birds. He revived the famous Maxwell brothers who found a vein of gold and hid the traces of it so carefully that they could never find it again.

Jody sat with his chin in his hands; his mouth worked nervously, and his father gradually became aware that he wasn't listening very carefully. "Isn't that funny?" he asked.

Jody laughed politely and said, "Yes, sir." His father was angry and hurt, then. He didn't tell any more stories. After a while, Jody took a lantern and went down to the barn. Billy Buck was asleep in the hay, and, except that his breath rasped a little in his lungs, the pony seemed to be much better. Jody stayed a little while, running his fingers over the red rough coat, and then he took up the lantern and went back to the house. When he was in bed, his mother came into the room.

"Have you enough covers on? It's getting winter."

"Yes, ma'am."

"Well, get some rest tonight." She hesitated to go out, stood uncertainly. "The pony will be all right," she said.

Jody was tired. He went to sleep quickly and didn't awaken until dawn. The triangle sounded, and Billy Buck came up from the barn before Jody could get out of the house.

"How is he?" Jody demanded.

Billy always wolfed his breakfast. "Pretty good. I'm going to open that lump this morning. Then he'll be better maybe."

After breakfast, Billy got out his best knife, one with a needle point. He whetted the shining blade a long time on a little carborundum[7] stone. He tried the point and the blade again and again on his calloused thumb-ball, and at last he tried it on his upper lip.

On the way to the barn, Jody noticed how the young grass was up and how the stubble was melting day by day into the new green crop of volunteer.[8] It was a cold sunny morning.

---

7. **carborundum** [kär′bə run′dəm]: very hard substance used for grinding and polishing.
8. **volunteer**: plants growing from seeds that have fallen naturally to the ground.

As soon as he saw the pony, Jody knew he was worse. His eyes were closed and sealed shut with dried mucus. His head hung so low that his nose almost touched the straw of his bed. There was a little groan in each breath, a deep-seated, patient groan.

Billy lifted the weak head and made a quick slash with the knife. Jody saw the yellow pus run out. He held up the head while Billy swabbed out the wound with weak carbolic acid salve.

"Now he'll feel better," Billy assured him. "That yellow poison is what makes him sick."

Jody looked unbelieving at Billy Buck. "He's awful sick."

Billy thought a long time what to say. He nearly tossed off a careless assurance, but he saved himself in time. "Yes, he's pretty sick," he said at last. "I've seen worse ones get well. If he doesn't get pneumonia, we'll pull him through. You stay with him. If he gets worse, you can come and get me."

For a long time after Billy went away, Jody stood beside the pony, stroking him behind the ears. The pony didn't flip his head the way he had done when he was well. The groaning in his breathing was becoming more hollow.

Doubletree Mutt looked into the barn, his big tail waving provocatively, and Jody was so incensed at his health that he found a hard black clod on the floor and deliberately threw it. Doubletree Mutt went yelping away to nurse a bruised paw.

In the middle of the morning, Billy Buck came back and made another steam bag. Jody watched to see whether the pony improved this time as he had before. His breathing eased a little, but he did not raise his head.

The Saturday dragged on. Late in the afternoon Jody went to the house and brought his bedding down and made up a place to sleep in the hay. He didn't ask permission. He knew from the way his mother looked at him

that she would let him do almost anything. That night he left a lantern burning on a wire over the box stall. Billy had told him to rub the pony's legs every little while.

At nine o'clock the wind sprang up and howled around the barn. And in spite of his worry, Jody grew sleepy. He got into his blankets and went to sleep, but the breathy groans of the pony sounded in his dreams. And in his sleep he heard a crashing noise which went on and on until it awakened him. The wind was rushing through the barn. He sprang up and looked down the lane of stalls. The barn door had blown open, and the pony was gone.

He caught the lantern and ran outside into the gale, and he saw Gabilan weakly shambling away into the darkness, head down, legs working slowly and mechanically. When Jody ran up and caught him by the forelock, he allowed himself to be led back and put into his stall. His groans were louder, and a fierce whistling came from his nose. Jody didn't sleep any more then. The hissing of the pony's breath grew louder and sharper.

He was glad when Billy Buck came in at dawn. Billy looked for a time at the pony as though he had never seen him before. He felt the ears and flanks. "Jody," he said, "I've got

to do something you won't want to see. You run up to the house for a while."

Jody grabbed him fiercely by the forearm. "You're not going to shoot him?"

Billy patted his hand. "No. I'm going to open a little hole in his windpipe so he can breathe. His nose is filled up. When he gets well, we'll put a little brass button in the hole for him to breathe through."

Jody couldn't have gone away if he had wanted to. It was awful to see the red hide cut, but infinitely more terrible to know it was being cut and not to see it. "I'll stay right here," he said bitterly. "You sure you got to?"

"Yes, I'm sure. If you stay, you can hold his head. If it doesn't make you sick, that is."

The fine knife came out again and was whetted again just as carefully as it had been the first time. Jody held the pony's head up and the throat taut, while Billy felt up and down for the right place. Jody sobbed once as the bright knife point disappeared into the throat. The pony plunged weakly away and then stood still, trembling violently. The blood ran thickly out and up the knife and across Billy's hand and into his shirtsleeve. The sure square hand sawed out a round hole in the flesh, and the breath came bursting out of the hole, throwing a fine spray of blood. With the rush of oxygen, the pony took a sudden strength. He lashed out with his hind feet and tried to rear, but Jody held his head down while Billy mopped the new wound with carbolic salve. It was a good job. The blood stopped flowing and the air puffed out the hole and sucked it in regularly with a little bubbling noise.

The rain brought in by the night wind began to fall on the barn roof. Then the triangle rang for breakfast. "You go up and eat while I wait," Billy said. "We've got to keep this hole from plugging up."

Jody walked slowly out of the barn. He was

too dispirited to tell Billy how the barn door had blown open and let the pony out. He emerged into the wet gray morning and sloshed up to the house, taking a perverse pleasure in splashing through all the puddles. His mother fed him and put dry clothes on. She didn't question him. She seemed to know he couldn't answer questions. But when he was ready to go back to the barn she brought him a pan of steaming meal. "Give him this," she said.

But Jody did not take the pan. He said, "He won't eat anything," and ran out of the house. At the barn, Billy showed him how to fix a ball of cotton on a stick, with which to swab out the breathing hole when it became clogged with mucus.

Jody's father walked into the barn and stood with them in front of the stall. At length he turned to the boy. "Hadn't you better come with me? I'm going to drive over the hill." Jody shook his head. "You better come on, out of this," his father insisted.

Billy turned on him angrily. "Let him alone. It's his pony, isn't it?"

Carl Tiflin walked away without saying another word. His feelings were badly hurt.

All morning Jody kept the wound open and the air passing in and out freely. At noon the pony lay wearily down on his side and stretched his nose out.

Billy came back. "If you're going to stay with him tonight, you better take a little nap," he said. Jody went absently out of the barn. The sky had cleared to a hard thin blue. Everywhere the birds were busy with worms that had come to the damp surface of the ground.

Jody walked to the brush line and sat on the edge of the mossy tub. He looked down at the house and at the old bunkhouse and at the dark cypress tree. The place was familiar, but curiously changed. It wasn't itself any more, but a frame for things that were hap-pening. A cold wind blew out of the east now, signifying that the rain was over for a little while. At his feet Jody could see the little arms of new weeds spreading out over the ground. In the mud about the spring were thousands of quail tracks.

Doubletree Mutt came sideways and embarrassed up through the vegetable patch, and Jody, remembering how he had thrown the clod, put his arm about the dog's neck and kissed him on his wide black nose. Doubletree Mutt sat still, as though he knew some solemn thing was happening. His big tail slapped the ground gravely. Jody pulled a swollen tick out of Mutt's neck and popped it dead between his thumb-nails. It was a nasty thing. He washed his hands in the cold spring water.

Except for the steady swish of the wind, the farm was very quiet. Jody knew his mother wouldn't mind if he didn't go in to eat his lunch. After a little while he went slowly back to the barn. Mutt crept into his own little house and whined softly to himself for a long time.

Billy Buck stood up from the box and surrendered the cotton swab. The pony still lay on his side and the wound in his throat bellowsed in and out. When Jody saw how dry and dead the hair looked, he knew at last that there was no hope for the pony. He had seen the dead hair before on dogs and on cows, and it was a sure sign. He sat heavily on the box and let down the barrier of the box stall. For a long time he kept his eyes on the moving wound, and at last he dozed, and the afternoon passed quickly. Just before dark his mother brought a deep dish of stew and left it for him and went away. Jody ate a little of it, and, when it was dark, he set the lantern on the floor by the pony's head so he could watch the wound and keep it open, and he dozed again until the night chill awakened him. The wind was blowing fiercely, bringing the north cold with it. Jody brought a blanket from his bed in the hay and wrapped himself in it. Gabilan's breathing was quiet at last; the hole in his throat moved gently. The owls flew through the hayloft, shrieking and looking for mice. Jody put his hands down on his head and slept. In his sleep he was aware that the wind had increased. He heard it slamming about the barn.

It was daylight when he awakened. The barn door had swung open. The pony was gone. He sprang up and ran out into the morning light.

The pony's tracks were plain enough, dragging through the frostlike dew on the young grass, tired tracks with little lines between them where the hoofs had dragged. They headed for the brush line halfway up the ridge. Jody broke into a run and followed them. The sun shone on the sharp white quartz that stuck through the ground here and there. As he followed the plain trail, a shadow cut across in front of him. He looked up and saw a high circle of black buzzards, and the slowly revolving circle dropped lower and lower. The solemn birds soon disappeared over the ridge. Jody ran faster then, forced on by panic and rage. The trail entered the brush at last and followed a winding route among the tall sagebrushes.

At the top of the ridge Jody was winded. He paused, puffing noisily. The blood pounded in his ears. Then he saw what he was looking for. Below, in one of the little clearings in the brush lay the red pony. In the distance, Jody could see the legs moving slowly and convulsively. And in a circle around him stood the buzzards, waiting for the moment of death they know so well.

Jody leaped forward and plunged down the hill. The wet ground muffled his steps and the brush hid him. When he arrived, it was all over. The first buzzard sat on the pony's head and its beak had just risen dripping with dark eye fluid. Jody plunged into the circle like a cat. The black brotherhood arose in a cloud, but the big one on the pony's head was too late. As it hopped along to take off, Jody caught its wing tip and pulled it down. It was nearly as big as he was. The free wing crashed into his face with the force of a club, but he hung on. The claws fastened on his leg and the wing elbows battered his head on either side. Jody groped blindly with his free hand. His fingers found the neck of the struggling bird. The red eyes looked into his face, calm and fearless and fierce; the naked head turned from side to side. Then the beak opened and vomited a stream of putrefied fluid. Jody brought up his knee and fell on the great bird. He held the neck to the ground with one hand while his other found a piece of sharp white quartz. The first blow broke the beak sideways and black blood spurted from the twisted, leathery mouth corners. He struck again and missed. The red fearless eyes still looked at him, impersonal and unafraid and detached. He struck again and again, until the buzzard lay dead, until its head was a red pulp. He was still beating the dead bird when Billy Buck pulled him off and held him tightly to calm his shaking.

Carl Tiflin wiped the blood from the boy's face with a red bandana. Jody was limp and quiet now. His father moved the buzzard with his toe. "Jody," he explained, "the buzzard didn't kill the pony. Don't you know that?"

"I know it," Jody said wearily.

It was Billy Buck who was angry. He had lifted Jody in his arms, and had turned to carry him home. But he turned back on Carl Tiflin. " 'Course he knows it," Billy said furiously. "Man, can't you see how he'd feel about it?"

STUDY QUESTIONS

Recalling

1. List at least three examples of setting that show what happens to the countryside and ranch as winter comes.
2. Briefly explain why the pony is left outside in the corral. About what was Billy Buck wrong?
3. Why does Jody decide to stay in school even though he wants to go home?
4. Is Billy Buck wrong about anything else? What does he think he must do in order to make up for his "mistakes"?
5. Describe step by step how Billy Buck and Jody care for the pony. Does Gabilan get better?
6. What do Jody's father and mother do to help Jody as he cares for Gabilan?
7. What happens to Gabilan after he escapes from the barn for the second time? What does Jody do when he discovers that Gabilan has escaped?

Interpreting

8. Does Jody's faith in Billy Buck change after Billy Buck is wrong about the rain? Give two examples to support your answer.
9. Choose an appropriate adjective to describe Jody's behavior during Gabilan's illness. Give at least three examples of his behavior that support the adjective you have chosen.
10. Who seems to understand better the way Jody feels about Gabilan's sickness and death, Billy Buck or Carl Tiflin?

Extending

11. What do you think Jody has learned about nature in pages 499–507?

READING AND LITERARY FOCUS

Conflict

Like a short story, a novel has **conflict,** or struggle, between two opposing forces. Conflict can be external or internal. An **external conflict** takes place between a character and some outside force. That force may be another person. For example, two characters may compete against each other in a game. The opposing force may be nature. For instance, a character might try to walk through a furious snowstorm. The opposing force may be society or some other institution. For example, a person may fight against an unjust law. Finally, a character may fight against fate, or circumstances that cannot be changed. For example, a character may try to conquer a fatal illness.

An **internal conflict,** on the other hand, takes place within a character's own mind. For example, a character may feel conflicting emotions: The character may feel happy about being in the game but worried about not scoring enough baskets.

A novel usually has both external and internal conflicts. Because of a novel's length it can contain more conflicts than a short story.

Thinking About Conflict

1. What conflict do Billy Buck and Jody struggle against in this section of the novel? Is the conflict external or internal? Why?
2. What conflict does Jody face when he is in school and it starts to rain? Is the conflict external or internal? Why?

Foreshadowing and Predicting Outcomes

Many authors use hints or clues known as **foreshadowing** to help their readers to predict future developments in the plot. For example, Chapter I ends in a way quite different from what we might have expected. Yet several hints, including the description of the buzzards at the beginning of Chapter I, help us to predict the outcome of "The Gift."

Thinking About Foreshadowing and Predicting Outcomes

■ What remarks about the rain does Billy Buck make? Did his remarks help you to predict the outcome of Chapter I? Why or why not?

Summer has come, and Jody seems to have forgotten about the red pony. He dreams instead of the beautiful mountains around the ranch.

■ *What new lesson about life and death will Jody learn when a strange old man appears one day?*

II. The Great Mountains

In the humming heat of a midsummer afternoon the little boy Jody listlessly looked about the ranch for something to do. He had been to the barn, had thrown rocks at the swallows' nests under the eaves until every one of the little mud houses broke open and dropped its lining of straw and dirty feathers. Then at the ranch house he baited a rat trap with stale cheese and set it where Doubletree Mutt, that good big dog, would get his nose snapped. Jody was not moved by an impulse of cruelty; he was bored with the long hot afternoon. Doubletree Mutt put his stupid nose in the trap and got it smacked, and shrieked with agony and limped away with blood on his nostrils. No matter where he was hurt, Mutt limped. It was just a way he had. Once when he was young, Mutt got caught in a coyote trap, and always after that he limped, even when he was scolded.

When Mutt yelped, Jody's mother called from inside the house, "Jody! Stop torturing that dog and find something to do."

Jody felt mean then, so he threw a rock at Mutt. Then he took his slingshot from the porch and walked up toward the brush line to try to kill a bird. It was a good slingshot, with store-bought rubber, but while Jody had often shot at birds, he had never hit one. He walked up through the vegetable patch, kicking his bare toes into the dust. And on the way he found the perfect slingshot stone, round and slightly flattened and heavy enough to carry through the air. He fitted it into the leather pouch of his weapon and proceeded to the brush line. His eyes narrowed, his mouth worked strenuously; for the first time that afternoon he was intent. In the shade of the sagebrush the little birds were working, scratching in the leaves, flying restlessly a few feet and scratching again. Jody pulled back the rubber of the sling and advanced cautiously. One little thrush paused and looked at him and crouched, ready to fly. Jody sidled nearer, moving one foot slowly after the other. When he was twenty feet away, he carefully raised the sling and aimed. The stone whizzed; the thrush started up and flew right into it. And down the little bird went with a broken head. Jody ran to it and picked it up.

"Well, I got you," he said.

The bird looked much smaller dead than it had alive. Jody felt a little mean pain in his stomach, so he took out his pocket-knife and cut off the bird's head. Then he disemboweled it, and took off its wings; and finally he threw all the pieces into the brush. He didn't care about the bird, or its life, but he knew what older people would say if they had seen him kill it; he was ashamed because of their potential opinion. He decided to forget the whole thing as quickly as he could, and never to mention it.

The hills were dry at this season, and the wild grass was golden, but where the spring-pipe filled the round tub and the tub spilled over, there lay a stretch of fine green grass, deep and sweet and moist. Jody drank from the mossy tub and washed the bird's blood from his hands in cold water. Then he lay on his back in the grass and looked up at the dumpling summer clouds. By closing one eye and destroying perspective he brought them down within reach so that he could put up his fingers and stroke them. He helped the gentle wind push them down the sky; it seemed to him that they went faster for his help. One fat white cloud he helped clear to the mountain rims and pressed it firmly over, out of sight. Jody wondered what it was seeing, then. He sat up, the better to look at the great mountains where they went piling back, growing darker and more savage until they finished with one jagged ridge, high up against the west. Curious secret mountains; he thought of the little he knew about them.

"What's on the other side?" he asked his father once.

"More mountains, I guess. Why?"

"And on the other side of them?"

"More mountains. Why?"

"More mountains on and on?"

"Well, no. At last you come to the ocean."

"But what's in the mountains?"

"Just cliffs and brush and rocks and dryness."

"Were you ever there?"

"No."

"Has anybody ever been there?"

"A few people, I guess. It's dangerous, with cliffs and things. Why, I've read there's more unexplored country in the mountains of Monterey County[1] than any place in the United States." His father seemed proud that this should be so.

"And at last the ocean?"

"At last the ocean."

"But," the boy insisted, "but in between? No one knows?"

"Oh, a few people do, I guess. But there's nothing there to get. And not much water. Just rocks and cliffs and greasewood.[2] Why?"

"It would be good to go."

"What for? There's nothing there."

Jody knew something was there, something very wonderful because it wasn't known, something secret and mysterious. He could feel within himself that this was so. He said to his mother, "Do you know what's in the big mountains?"

She looked at him and then back at the ferocious range, and she said, "Only the bear, I guess."

"What bear?"

"Why the one that went over the mountain to see what he could see."

Jody questioned Billy Buck, the ranch-hand, about the possibility of ancient cities lost in the mountains, but Billy agreed with Jody's father.

"It ain't likely," Billy said. "There'd be nothing to eat unless a kind of people that can eat rocks live there."

That was all the information Jody ever got, and it made the mountains dear to him, and terrible. He thought often of the miles of ridge after ridge until at last there was the sea. When the peaks were pink in the morning they invited him among them: and when the sun had gone over the edge in the evening

---

1. **Monterey** [mon′tə rā′] **County:** county of west-central California.
2. **greasewood:** spiny evergreen bush.

and the mountains were a purple-like despair, then Jody was afraid of them; then they were so impersonal and aloof that their very imperturbability was a threat.

Now he turned his head toward the mountains of the east, the Gabilans, and they were jolly mountains, with hill ranches in their creases, and with pine trees growing on the crests. People lived there, and battles had been fought against the Mexicans on the slopes. He looked back for an instant at the Great Ones[3] and shivered a little at the contrast. The foothill cup of the home ranch below him was sunny and safe. The house gleamed with white light and the barn was brown and warm. The red cows on the farther hill ate their way slowly toward the north. Even the dark cypress tree by the bunkhouse was usual and safe. The chickens scratched about in the dust of the farmyard with quick waltzing steps.

Then a moving figure caught Jody's eye. A man walked slowly over the brow of the hill, on the road from Salinas, and he was headed toward the house. Jody stood up and moved down toward the house too, for if someone was coming, he wanted to be there to see. By the time the boy had got to the house the walking man was only halfway down the road, a lean man, very straight in the shoulders. Jody could tell he was old only because his heels struck the ground with hard jerks. As he approached nearer, Jody saw that he was dressed in blue jeans and in a coat of the same material. He wore clodhopper shoes and an old flat-brimmed Stetson hat. Over his shoulder he carried a gunny sack, lumpy and full. In a few moments he had trudged close enough so that his face could be seen. And his face was as dark as dried beef. A mustache, blue-white against the dark skin, hovered over his mouth, and his hair was white, too, where it showed at his neck. The skin of his face had shrunk back against the skull until it defined bone, not flesh, and made the nose and chin seem sharp and fragile. The eyes were large and deep and dark, with eyelids stretched tightly over them. Irises and pupils were one, and very black, but the eyeballs were brown. There were no wrinkles in the face at all. This old man wore a blue denim coat buttoned to the throat with brass buttons, as all men do who wear no shirts. Out of the sleeves came strong bony wrists and hands gnarled and knotted and hard as peach branches. The nails were flat and blunt and shiny.

The old man drew close to the gate and swung down his sack when he confronted Jody. His lips fluttered a little and a soft impersonal voice came from between them. "Do you live here?"

Jody was embarrassed. He turned and looked at the house, and he turned back and looked toward the barn where his father and Billy Buck were. "Yes," he said, when no help came from either direction.

"I have come back," the old man said. "I am Gitano,[4] and I have come back."

Jody could not take all this responsibility. He turned abruptly, and ran into the house for help, and the screen door banged after him. His mother was in the kitchen poking out the clogged holes of a colander with a hairpin, and biting her lower lip with concentration.

"It's an old man," Jody cried excitedly. "It's an old *paisano*[5] man, and he says he's come back."

---

3. **Great Ones:** peaks of the Sierra Nevada, a mountain chain to the east of the Gabilan Mountains.

4. **Gitano** [hē tä′nō]: Spanish word for "gypsy."
5. ***paisano*** [pī sä′nō]: Spanish word for a person from the same country. Here, a Mexican.

His mother put down the colander and stuck the hairpin behind the sink board. "What's the matter now?" she asked patiently.

"It's an old man outside. Come on out."

"Well, what does he want?" She untied the strings of her apron and smoothed her hair with her fingers.

"I don't know. He came walking."

His mother smoothed down her dress and went out, and Jody followed her. Gitano had not moved.

"Yes?" Mrs. Tiflin asked.

Gitano took off his old black hat and held it with both hands in front of him. He repeated, "I am Gitano, and I have come back."

"Come back? Back where?"

Gitano's whole straight body leaned forward a little. His right hand described the circle of the hills, the sloping fields and the mountains, and ended at his hat again. "Back to the rancho.[6] I was born here, and my father, too."

"Here?" she demanded. "This isn't an old place."

"No, there," he said, pointing to the western ridge. "On the other side there, in a house that is gone."

At last she understood. "The old 'dobe[7] that's washed almost away, you mean?"

"Yes, señora.[8] When the rancho broke up they put no more lime on the 'dobe, and the rains washed it down."

Jody's mother was silent for a little, and curious homesick thoughts ran through her mind, but quickly she cleared them out. "And what do you want here now, Gitano?"

"I will stay here," he said quietly, "until I die."

"But we don't need an extra man here."

"I can not work hard any more, señora. I can milk a cow, feed chickens, cut a little wood; no more. I will stay here." He indicated the sack on the ground beside him. "Here are my things."

She turned to Jody. "Run down to the barn and call your father."

Jody dashed away, and he returned with Carl Tiflin and Billy Buck behind him. The old man was standing as he had been, but he was resting now. His whole body had sagged into a timeless repose.

"What is it?" Carl Tiflin asked. "What's Jody so excited about?"

Mrs. Tiflin motioned to the old man. "He wants to stay here. He wants to do a little work and stay here."

"Well, we can't have him. We don't need any more men. He's too old. Billy does everything we need."

They had been talking over him as though he did not exist, and now, suddenly, they both hesitated and looked at Gitano and were embarrassed.

He cleared his throat. "I am too old to work. I come back where I was born."

"You weren't born here," Carl said sharply.

"No. In the 'dobe house over the hill. It was all one rancho before you came."

"In the mud house that's all melted down?"

"Yes. I and my father. I will stay here now on the rancho."

"I tell you you won't stay," Carl said angrily. "I don't need an old man. This isn't a big ranch. I can't afford food and doctor bills for an old man. You must have relatives and friends. Go to them. It is like begging to come to strangers."

"I was born here," Gitano said patiently and inflexibly.

Carl Tiflin didn't like to be cruel, but he felt he must. "You can eat here tonight," he said. "You can sleep in the little room of the

---

6. **rancho:** Spanish for "ranch."
7. **'dobe:** adobe [ə dōʹbē], house built with sun-dried bricks of clay or soil, coated with paint made of lime.
8. **señora** [sen yôrʹə]: Spanish for "madam" or "Mrs."

old bunkhouse. We'll give you your breakfast in the morning, and then you'll have to go along. Go to your friends. Don't come to die with strangers."

Gitano put on his black hat and stooped for the sack. "Here are my things," he said.

Carl turned away. "Come on, Billy, we'll finish down at the barn. Jody, show him the little room in the bunkhouse."

He and Billy turned back toward the barn. Mrs. Tiflin went into the house, saying over her shoulder, "I'll send some blankets down."

Gitano looked questioningly at Jody. "I'll show you where it is," Jody said.

There was a cot with a shuck mattress,[9] an apple box holding a tin lantern, and a backless rocking-chair in the little room of the bunkhouse. Gitano laid his sack carefully on the floor and sat down on the bed. Jody stood shyly in the room, hesitating to go. At last he said, "Did you come out of the big mountains?"

Gitano shook his head slowly. "No, I worked down the Salinas Valley."

The afternoon thought would not let Jody go. "Did you ever go into the big mountains back there?"

The old dark eyes grew fixed, and their light turned inward on the years that were living in Gitano's head. "Once—when I was a little boy. I went with my father."

"Way back, clear into the mountains?"

"Yes."

"What was there?" Jody cried. "Did you see any people or any houses?"

"No."

"Well, what was there?"

Gitano's eyes remained inward. A little wrinkled strain came between his brows.

"What did you see in there?" Jody repeated.

"I don't know," Gitano said. "I don't remember."

"Was it terrible and dry?"

"I don't remember."

In his excitement, Jody had lost his shyness. "Don't you remember anything about it?"

Gitano's mouth opened for a word, and remained open while his brain sought the word. "I think it was quiet—I think it was nice."

Gitano's eyes seemed to have found something back in the years, for they grew soft and a little smile seemed to come and go in them.

"Didn't you ever go back in the mountains again?" Jody insisted.

"No."

"Didn't you ever want to?"

But now Gitano's face became impatient. "No," he said in a tone that told Jody he didn't want to talk about it any more. The boy was held by a curious fascination. He didn't want to go away from Gitano. His shyness returned.

"Would you like to come down to the barn and see the stock?" he asked.

Gitano stood up and put on his hat and prepared to follow.

It was almost evening now. They stood near the watering trough while the horses sauntered in from the hillsides for an evening drink. Gitano rested his big twisted hands on the top rail of the fence. Five horses came down and drank, and then stood about, nibbling at the dirt or rubbing their sides against the polished wood of the fence. Long after they had finished drinking an old horse appeared over the brow of the hill and came painfully down. It had long yellow teeth; its hoofs were flat and sharp as spades, and its ribs and hipbones jutted out under its skin. It hobbled up to the trough and drank water with a loud sucking noise.

---

9. **shuck mattress:** mattress stuffed with the dried husks of corn.

"That's old Easter," Jody explained. "That's the first horse my father ever had. He's thirty years old." He looked up into Gitano's old eyes for some response.

"No good any more," Gitano said.

Jody's father and Billy Buck came out of the barn and walked over.

"Too old to work," Gitano repeated. "Just eats and pretty soon dies."

Carl Tiflin caught the last words. He hated his brutality toward old Gitano, and so he became brutal again.

"It's a shame not to shoot Easter," he said. "It'd save him a lot of pains and rheumatism."

He looked secretly at Gitano, to see whether he noticed the parallel, but the big bony hands did not move, nor did the dark eyes turn from the horse. "Old things ought to be put out of their misery," Jody's father went on. "One shot, a big noise, one big pain in the head maybe, and that's all. That's better than stiffness and sore teeth."

Billy Buck broke in. "They got a right to rest after they worked all of their life. Maybe they like to just walk around."

Carl had been looking steadily at the skinny horse. "You can't imagine now what Easter used to look like," he said softly. "High neck, deep chest, fine barrel. He could jump a five-bar gate in stride. I won a flat race on him when I was fifteen years old. I could of got two hundred dollars for him any time. You wouldn't think how pretty he was." He checked himself, for he hated softness. "But he ought to be shot now," he said.

"He's got a right to rest," Billy Buck insisted.

Jody's father had a humorous thought. He turned to Gitano. "If ham and eggs grew on a side-hill I'd turn you out to pasture too," he said. "But I can't afford to pasture you in my kitchen."

He laughed to Billy Buck about it as they went on toward the house. "Be a good thing for all of us if ham and eggs grew on the side-hills."

Jody knew how his father was probing for a place to hurt in Gitano. He had been probed often. His father knew every place in the boy where a word would fester.[10]

"He's only talking," Jody said. "He didn't mean it about shooting Easter. He likes Easter. That was the first horse he ever owned."

The sun sank behind the high mountains as they stood there, and the ranch was hushed. Gitano seemed to be more at home in the evening. He made a curious sharp sound with his lips and stretched one of his hands over the fence. Old Easter moved stiffly to him, and Gitano rubbed the lean neck under the mane.

"You like him?" Jody asked softly.

"Yes—but he's no good."

The triangle sounded at the ranch house. "That's supper," Jody cried. "Come on up to supper."

As they walked up toward the house Jody

noticed again that Gitano's body was as straight as that of a young man. Only by a jerkiness in his movements and by the scuffling of his heels could it be seen that he was old.

The turkeys were flying heavily into the lower branches of the cypress tree by the bunkhouse. A fat sleek ranch cat walked across the road carrying a rat so large that its tail dragged on the ground. The quail on the side-hills were still sounding the clear water call.

Jody and Gitano came to the back steps and Mrs. Tiflin looked out through the screen door at them.

"Come running, Jody. Come in to supper, Gitano."

Carl and Billy Buck had started to eat at the long oilcloth-covered table. Jody slipped into his chair without moving it, but Gitano stood holding his hat until Carl looked up and said, "Sit down, sit down. You might as well get your belly full before you go on." Carl was afraid he might relent and let the old man stay, and so he continued to remind himself that this couldn't be.

Gitano laid his hat on the floor and diffidently sat down. He wouldn't reach for food. Carl had to pass it to him. "Here, fill yourself up." Gitano ate very slowly, cutting tiny pieces of meat and arranging little pats of mashed potato on his plate.

The situation would not stop worrying Carl Tiflin. "Haven't you got any relatives in this part of the country?" he asked.

Gitano answered with some pride, "My brother-in-law is in Monterey. I have cousins there, too."

"Well, you can go and live there, then."

"I was born here," Gitano said in gentle rebuke.

Jody's mother came in from the kitchen, carrying a large bowl of tapioca pudding.

---

10. **fester:** cause continuous long-lasting anger or resentment.

Carl chuckled to her, "Did I tell you what I said to him? I said if ham and eggs grew on the side-hills I'd put him out to pasture, like old Easter."

Gitano stared unmoved at his plate.

"It's too bad he can't stay," said Mrs. Tiflin.

"Now don't you start anything," Carl said crossly.

When they had finished eating, Carl and Billy Buck and Jody went into the living-room to sit for a while, but Gitano, without a word of farewell or thanks, walked through the kitchen and out the back door. Jody sat and secretly watched his father. He knew how mean his father felt.

"This country's full of these old *paisanos*," Carl said to Billy Buck.

"They're good men," Billy defended them.

"Oh, they're tough, all right," Carl agreed. "Say, are you standing up for him too? Listen, Billy," he explained, "I'm having a hard enough time keeping this ranch out of the Bank of Italy[11] without taking on anybody else to feed. You know that, Billy."

"Sure, I know," said Billy. "If you was rich, it'd be different."

"That's right, and it isn't like he didn't have relatives to go to. A brother-in-law and cousins right in Monterey. Why should I worry about him?"

Jody sat quietly listening, and he seemed to hear Gitano's gentle voice and its unanswerable, "But I was born here." Gitano was mysterious like the mountains. There were ranges back as far as you could see, but behind the last range piled up against the sky there was a great unknown country. And Gitano was an old man, until you got to the dull dark eyes. And in behind them was some unknown thing. He didn't ever say enough to let you guess what was inside, under the eyes. Jody felt himself irresistibly drawn toward the bunkhouse. He slipped from his chair while his father was talking and he went out the door without making a sound.

The night was very dark and far-off noises carried in clearly. The hamebells[12] of a wood team[13] sounded from way over the hill on the country road. Jody picked his way across the dark yard. He could see a light through the window of the little room of the bunkhouse. Because the night was secret he walked quietly up to the window and peered in. Gitano sat in the rocking-chair and his back was toward the window. His right arm moved slowly back and forth in front of him. Jody pushed the door open and walked in. Gitano jerked upright and, seizing a piece of deerskin, he tried to throw it over the thing in his lap, but the skin slipped away. Jody stood overwhelmed by the thing in Gitano's hand, a lean and lovely rapier[14] with a golden basket hilt. The blade was like a thin ray of dark light. The hilt[15] was pierced and intricately carved.

"What is it?" Jody demanded.

Gitano only looked at him with resentful eyes, and he picked up the fallen deerskin and firmly wrapped the beautiful blade in it.

Jody put out his hand. "Can't I see it?"

Gitano's eyes smoldered angrily and he shook his head.

"Where'd you get it? Where'd it come from?"

Now Gitano regarded him profoundly, as though he pondered. "I got it from my father."

"Well, where'd he get it?"

11. **I'm . . . Bank of Italy:** Carl Tiflin is implying that if he cannot make payments on his loans, his bank will take his land as payment.

12. **hamebells:** bells hung on a wooden piece, called a *hame,* on either side of an animal's collar.
13. **wood team:** pair of horses or oxen pulling a load of wood.
14. **rapier** [rā′pē ər]: long, slender sword.
15. **hilt:** handle.

Gitano looked down at the long deerskin parcel in his hand. "I don't know."

"Didn't he ever tell you?"

"No."

"What do you do with it?"

Gitano looked slightly surprised. "Nothing. I just keep it."

"Can't I see it again?"

The old man slowly unwrapped the shining blade and let the lamplight slip along it for a moment. Then he wrapped it up again. "You go now. I want to go to bed." He blew out the lamp almost before Jody had closed the door.

As he went back toward the house, Jody knew one thing more sharply than he had ever known anything. He must never tell anyone about the rapier. It would be a dreadful thing to tell anyone about it, for it would destroy some fragile structure of truth. It was a truth that might be shattered by division.

On the way across the dark yard Jody passed Billy Buck. "They're wondering where you are," Billy said.

Jody slipped into the living-room, and his father turned to him. "Where have you been?"

"I just went out to see if I caught any rats in my new trap."

"It's time you went to bed," his father said.

Jody was first at the breakfast table in the morning. Then his father came in, and last, Billy Buck. Mrs. Tiflin looked in from the kitchen.

"Where's the old man, Billy?" she asked.

"I guess he's out walking," Billy said. "I looked in his room and he wasn't there."

"Maybe he started early to Monterey," said Carl. "It's a long walk."

"No," Billy explained. "His sack is in the little room."

After breakfast Jody walked down to the bunkhouse. Flies were flashing about in the sunshine. The ranch seemed especially quiet this morning. When he was sure no one was watching him, Jody went into the little room, and looked into Gitano's sack. An extra pair of long cotton underwear was there, an extra pair of jeans and three pairs of worn socks. Nothing else was in the sack. A sharp loneliness fell on Jody. He walked slowly back toward the house. His father stood on the porch talking to Mrs. Tiflin.

"I guess old Easter's dead at last," he said. "I didn't see him come down to water with the other horses."

In the middle of the morning Jess Taylor from the ridge ranch rode down.

"You didn't sell that old gray crowbait[16] of yours, did you, Carl?"

"No, of course not. Why?"

"Well," Jess said. "I was out this morning early, and I saw a funny thing. I saw an old man on an old horse, no saddle, only a piece of rope for a bridle. He wasn't on the road at all. He was cutting right up straight through the brush. I think he had a gun. At least I saw something shine in his hand."

"That's old Gitano," Carl Tiflin said. "I'll see if any of my guns are missing." He stepped into the house for a second. "Nope, all here. Which way was he heading, Jess?"

"Well, that's the funny thing. He was heading straight back into the mountains."

Carl laughed. "I guess he just stole old Easter," he said.

"Want to go after him, Carl?"

"No, just save me burying that horse. I wonder where he got the gun. I wonder what he wants back there."

Jody walked up through the vegetable patch, toward the brush line. He looked searchingly at the towering mountains—ridge after ridge after ridge until at last there was the ocean. For a moment he thought he could see a black speck crawling up the farthest ridge. Jody thought of the rapier and of Gitano. And he thought of the great mountains. A longing caressed him, and it was so sharp that he wanted to cry to get it out of his breast. He lay down in the green grass near the round tub at the brush line. He covered his eyes with his crossed arms and lay there a long time, and he was full of a nameless sorrow.

---

16. **crowbait:** here, a worn-out horse.

STUDY QUESTIONS

Recalling

1. Give three examples of Jody's behavior toward animals at the beginning of this section. Why does Jody feel bad after he cuts apart the bird?

2. What information does Jody get about the great mountains from his father, his mother, and Billy Buck? What does Jody think and feel as he looks at the great mountains?

3. Why has Gitano come to the ranch? What reasons does Jody's father give for wanting Gitano to leave?

4. What similarities does Carl find between Gitano and his old horse Easter? Why does Jody think Gitano is like the great mountains?

5. Explain briefly, using examples from the novel, the way Jody, his mother, his father, and Billy treat Gitano.

6. Where does Gitano go with old Easter? What is Carl's reaction when he learns his old horse has been stolen?

Interpreting

7. Why do you think Jody treats the animals as he does? Give reasons for your opinion.

8. Why do you think Jody is so fascinated by the Great Ones and what lies beyond them?

9. In what ways is Carl's treatment of Gitano like Jody's treatment of the animals? Give examples of both Jody's and Carl's actions and feelings.

10. Why does thinking of Gitano and the Great Ones fill Jody with a "nameless sorrow"? What might that sorrow be?

Extending

11. Has Jody learned new lessons about life by the end of this section? If so, what do you think he has learned?

READING AND LITERARY FOCUS

Comparison/Contrast

When you read, you may often notice similarities and differences in characters, events, or settings in a story or novel. Being aware of these similarities and differences will help you to understand how an author feels about the subject of a work. When you figure out, or analyze, the similarities and differences in a piece of literature, you are **comparing and contrasting.** To **compare** means to examine two or more things in order to discover the similarities between them. To **contrast** means to examine two or more things in order to discover the differences between them.

In stories and novels you can compare and contrast characters, events, or settings. For example, Jody contrasts the Gabilan Mountains and the Great Ones. The Gabilans are "jolly mountains, with hill ranches in their creases, and with pine trees growing on the crests." They make Jody feel "sunny and safe." In contrast, the Great Ones are "a purple-like despair." They are "so impersonal and aloof" that Jody is afraid of the threat he feels from them.

Thinking About Comparison/Contrast

1. Compare and contrast the way Carl Tiflin and Billy Buck feel about Gitano. First list examples that show the way each man feels. Then decide whether their feelings are similar or different.

2. How do you think Steinbeck feels about Gitano? Base your answer on your comparison/contrast of Carl Tiflin and Billy Buck.

CHALLENGE

Classifying

■ **Classifying** is the arranging or grouping of things according to their type. Each group is called a **class,** or category. Within each group are items. For example, one class of books in a library would be fiction. Items in the class of fiction would include short stories and novels. Here is another example of a class and its items:

> Class: riding tack
> Items: cinch, girth, pommel, stirrup

Read each group of words below. One word in the group names the class. The other words are items in the class. On a separate sheet write the word that names the class for each of the numbered groups.

1. buzzard, cardinal, quail, bird, swallow
2. poplar, linden, tree, cypress, oak
3. terrier, hound, poodle, dog, collie
4. apple, fruit, plum, muskmelon, orange
5. pony, mare, stallion, horse, colt

Spring brings new life to the ranch and a chance for Jody to have what he has always wanted.

■ *By the end of the novel, you will discover what Jody must accept before a promise can be kept.*

III. The Promise

In a mid-afternoon of spring, the little boy Jody walked martially along the brush-lined road toward his home ranch. Banging his knee against the golden lard bucket he used for school lunch, he contrived a good bass drum, while his tongue fluttered sharply against his teeth to fill in snare drums and occasional trumpets. Some time back the other members of the squad that walked so smartly from the school had turned into the various little canyons and taken the wagon roads to their own home ranches. Now Jody marched seemingly alone, with high-lifted knees and pounding feet; but behind him there was a phantom army with great flags and swords, silent but deadly.

The afternoon was green and gold with spring. Underneath the spread branches of the oaks the plants grew pale and tall, and on the hills the feed was smooth and thick. The sagebrushes shone with new silver leaves and the oaks wore hoods of golden green. Over the hills there hung such a green odor that the horses on the flats galloped madly, and then stopped, wondering; lambs, and even old sheep jumped in the air unexpectedly and landed on stiff legs, and went on eating; young clumsy calves butted their heads together and drew back and butted again.

As the gray and silent army marched past, led by Jody, the animals stopped their feeding and their play and watched it go by. Suddenly Jody stopped. The gray army halted, bewildered and nervous. Jody went down on his knees. The army stood in long uneasy ranks for a moment, and then, with a soft sigh of sorrow, rose up in a faint gray mist and disappeared. Jody had seen the thorny crown of a horny-toad[1] moving under the dust of the road. His grimy hand went out and grasped the spiked halo and held firmly while the little beast struggled. Then Jody turned the horny-toad over, exposing its pale gold stomach. With a gentle forefinger he stroked the throat and chest until the horny-toad relaxed, until its eyes closed and it lay languorous and asleep.

Jody opened his lunch pail and deposited the first game inside. He moved on now, his knees bent slightly, his shoulders crouched; his bare feet were wise and silent. In his right hand there was a long gray rifle. The brush along the road stirred restively under a new and unexpected population of gray tigers and

---
1. **horny-toad:** horned toad, insect-eating lizard with spiny horns on its head and scales along the sides of its body.

gray bears. The hunting was very good, for by the time Jody reached the fork of the road where the mail box stood on a post, he had captured two more horny-toads, four little grass lizards, a blue snake, sixteen yellow-winged grasshoppers and a brown damp newt[2] from under a rock. This assortment scrabbled unhappily against the tin of the lunch bucket.

At the road fork the rifle evaporated and the tigers and bears melted from the hillsides. Even the moist and uncomfortable creatures in the lunch pail ceased to exist, for the little red metal flag was up on the mail box, signifying that some postal matter was inside. Jody set his pail on the ground and opened the letter box. There was a Montgomery Ward[3] catalog and a copy of the *Salinas Weekly Journal.* He slammed the box, picked up his lunch pail and trotted over the ridge and down into the cup of the ranch. Past the barn he ran, and past the used-up haystack and the bunkhouse and the cypress tree. He banged through the front screen door of the ranch house calling, "Ma'am, ma'am, there's a catalog."

Mrs. Tiflin was in the kitchen spooning clabbered milk[4] into a cotton bag. She put down her work and rinsed her hands under the tap. "Here in the kitchen, Jody. Here I am."

He ran in and clattered his lunch pail on the sink. "Here it is. Can I open the catalog, ma'am?"

Mrs. Tiflin took up the spoon again and went back to her cottage cheese. "Don't lose it, Jody. Your father will want to see it." She scraped the last of the milk into the bag. "Oh, Jody, your father wants to see you before you

go to your chores." She waved a cruising fly from the cheese bag.

Jody closed the new catalog in alarm. "Ma'am?"

"Why don't you ever listen? I say your father wants to see you."

The boy laid the catalog gently on the sink board. "Do you—is it something I did?"

Mrs. Tiflin laughed. "Always a bad conscience. What did you do?"

"Nothing, ma'am," he said lamely. But he couldn't remember, and besides it was impossible to know what action might later be construed as a crime.

His mother hung the full bag on a nail where it could drip into the sink. "He just said he wanted to see you when you got home. He's somewhere down by the barn."

Jody turned and went out the back door. Hearing his mother open the lunch pail and then gasp with rage, a memory stabbed him and he trotted away toward the barn, conscientiously not hearing the angry voice that called him from the house.

Carl Tiflin and Billy Buck, the ranch-hand, stood against the lower pasture fence. Each man rested one foot on the lowest bar and both elbows on the top bar. They were talking slowly and aimlessly. In the pasture half a dozen horses nibbled contentedly at the sweet grass. The mare, Nellie, stood backed up against the gate, rubbing her buttocks on the heavy post.

Jody sidled uneasily near. He dragged one foot to give an impression of great innocence and nonchalance. When he arrived beside the men he put one foot on the lowest fence rail, rested his elbows on the second bar and looked into the pasture too.

The two men glanced sideways at him.

"I wanted to see you," Carl said in the stern tone he reserved for children and animals.

"Yes, sir," said Jody guiltily.

2. **newt** [no͞ot]: small lizard.
3. **Montgomery Ward:** store that sells its goods by mail.
4. **clabbered milk:** milk that has been soured and thickened, used in making cottage cheese.

"Billy, here, says you took good care of the pony before it died."

No punishment was in the air. Jody grew bolder. "Yes, sir, I did."

"Billy says you have a good patient hand with horses."

Jody felt a sudden warm friendliness for the ranch-hand.

Billy put in, "He trained that pony as good as anybody I ever seen."

Then Carl Tiflin came gradually to the point. "If you could have another horse would you work for it?"

Jody shivered. "Yes, sir."

"Well, look here, then. Billy says the best way for you to be a good hand with horses is to raise a colt."

"It's the *only* good way," Billy interrupted.

"Now, look here, Jody," continued Carl. "Jess Taylor, up to the ridge ranch, has a fair stallion, but it'll cost five dollars. I'll put up the money, but you'll have to work it out all summer. Will you do that?"

Jody felt that his insides were shriveling. "Yes, sir," he said softly.

"And no complaining? And no forgetting when you're told to do something?"

"Yes, sir."

"Well, all right, then. Tomorrow morning you take Nellie up to the ridge ranch and get her bred. You'll have to take care of her, too, till she throws the colt."[5]

"Yes, sir."

"You better get to the chickens and the wood now."

Jody slid away. In passing behind Billy Buck he very nearly put out his hand to touch the blue-jeaned legs. His shoulders swayed a little with maturity and importance.

He went to his work with unprecedented seriousness. This night he did not dump the can of grain to the chickens so that they had to leap over each other and struggle to get it. No, he spread the wheat so far and so carefully that the hens couldn't find some of it at all. And in the house, after listening to his mother's despair over boys who filled their lunch pails with slimy, suffocated reptiles, and bugs, he promised never to do it again. Indeed, Jody felt that all such foolishness was lost in the past. He was far too grown up ever to put horny-toads in his lunch pail any more. He carried in so much wood and built such a high structure with it that his mother walked in fear of an avalanche of oak. When he was done, when he had gathered eggs that had remained hidden for weeks, Jody walked down again past the cypress tree, and past the bunkhouse toward the pasture. A fat warty toad that looked out at him from under the watering trough had no emotional effect on him at all.

Carl Tiflin and Billy Buck were not in sight, but from a metallic ringing on the other side of the barn Jody knew that Billy Buck was just starting to milk a cow.

The other horses were eating toward the upper end of the pasture, but Nellie continued to rub herself nervously against the post. Jody walked slowly near, saying, "So, girl, so-o, Nellie." The mare's ears went back naughtily and her lips drew away from her yellow teeth. She turned her head around; her eyes were glazed and mad. Jody climbed to the top of the fence and hung his feet over and looked paternally down on the mare.

The evening hovered while he sat there. Bats and nighthawks flicked about. Billy Buck, walking toward the house carrying a full milk bucket, saw Jody and stopped. "It's a long time to wait," he said gently. "You'll get awful tired waiting."

"No, I won't, Billy. How long will it be?"

"Nearly a year."

"Well, I won't get tired."

The triangle at the house rang stridently.

---

5. **throws the colt:** gives birth to the colt.

Jody climbed down from the fence and walked to supper beside Billy Buck. He even put out his hand and took hold of the milk bucket to help carry it.

The next morning after breakfast Carl Tiflin folded a five-dollar bill in a piece of newspaper and pinned the package in the bib pocket of Jody's overalls. Billy Buck haltered the mare Nellie and led her out of the pasture.

"Be careful now," he warned. "Hold her up short here so she can't bite you. She's crazy as a coot."

Jody took hold of the halter leather itself and started up the hill toward the ridge ranch with Nellie skittering and jerking behind him. In the pasturage along the road the wild oat heads were just clearing their scabbards.[6] The warm morning sun shone on Jody's back so sweetly that he was forced to take a serious

stiff-legged hop now and then in spite of his maturity. On the fences the shiny blackbirds with red epaulets clicked their dry call. The meadowlarks sang like water, and the wild doves, concealed among the bursting leaves of the oaks, made a sound of restrained grieving. In the fields the rabbits sat sunning themselves, with only their forked ears showing above the grass heads.

After an hour of steady uphill walking, Jody turned into a narrow road that led up a steeper hill to the ridge ranch. He could see the red roof of the barn sticking up above the oak trees, and he could hear a dog barking unemotionally near the house.

Suddenly Nellie jerked back and nearly freed herself. From the direction of the barn Jody heard a shrill whistling scream and a splintering of wood, and then a man's voice shouting. Nellie reared and whinnied. When Jody held to the halter rope she ran at him with bared teeth. He dropped his hold and scuttled out of the way, into the brush. The

---

6. **the wild . . . scabbards:** The tops of the wild oat plants were just beginning to appear above the lower part of the leaves that surrounded their stems.

high scream came from the oaks again, and Nellie answered it. With hoofs battering the ground the stallion appeared and charged down the hill trailing a broken halter rope. His eyes glittered feverishly. His stiff, erected nostrils were as red as flame. His black, sleek hide shone in the sunlight. The stallion came on so fast that he couldn't stop when he reached the mare. Nellie's ears went back; she whirled and kicked at him as he went by. The stallion spun around and reared. He struck the mare with his front hoof, and while she staggered under the blow, his teeth raked her neck and drew an ooze of blood.

Instantly Nellie's mood changed. She became coquettishly feminine. She nibbled his arched neck with her lips. She edged around and rubbed her shoulder against his shoulder. Jody stood half-hidden in the brush and watched. He heard the step of a horse behind him, but before he could turn, a hand caught him by the overall straps and lifted him off the ground. Jess Taylor sat the boy behind him on the horse.

"You might have got killed," he said. "Sundog's a mean devil sometimes. He busted his rope and went right through a gate."

Jody sat quietly, but in a moment he cried, "He'll hurt her, he'll kill her. Get him away!"

Jess chuckled. "She'll be all right. Maybe you'd better climb off and go up to the house for a little. You could get maybe a piece of pie up there."

But Jody shook his head. "She's mine, and the colt's going to be mine. I'm going to raise it up."

Jess nodded. "Yes, that's a good thing. Carl has good sense sometimes."

In a little while the danger was over. Jess lifted Jody down and then caught the stallion by its broken halter rope. And he rode ahead, while Jody followed, leading Nellie.

It was only after he had unpinned and handed over the five dollars, and after he had eaten two pieces of pie, that Jody started for home again. And Nellie followed docilely after him. She was so quiet that Jody climbed on a stump and rode her most of the way home.

The five dollars his father had advanced reduced Jody to peonage[7] for the whole late spring and summer. When the hay was cut he drove a rake. He led the horse that pulled on the Jackson-fork tackle, and when the baler came he drove the circling horse that put pressure on the bales. In addition, Carl Tiflin taught him to milk and put a cow under his care, so that a new chore was added night and morning.

The bay mare Nellie quickly grew complacent. As she walked about the yellowing hillsides or worked at easy tasks, her lips were curled in a perpetual fatuous[8] smile. She moved slowly, with the calm importance of an empress. When she was put to a team, she pulled steadily and unemotionally. Jody went to see her every day. He studied her with critical eyes and saw no change whatever.

One afternoon Billy Buck leaned the many-tined manure fork against the barn wall. He loosened his belt and tucked in his shirt-tail and tightened the belt again. He picked one of the little straws from his hatband and put it in the corner of his mouth. Jody, who was helping Doubletree Mutt, the big serious dog, to dig out a gopher, straightened up as the ranch-hand sauntered out of the barn.

"Let's go up and have a look at Nellie," Billy suggested.

Instantly Jody fell into step with him. Doubletree Mutt watched them over his shoulder; then he dug furiously, growled, sounded little sharp yelps to indicate that the gopher was practically caught. When he looked over his shoulder again, and saw that neither Jody

---

7. **peonage** [pē'ə nij]: condition of having to do hard labor as payment of a debt.
8. **fatuous** [fach'ōo əs]: silly, self-satisfied.

nor Billy was interested, he climbed reluctantly out of the hole and followed them up the hill.

The wild oats were ripening. Every head bent sharply under its load of grain, and the grass was dry enough so that it made a swishing sound as Jody and Billy stepped through it. Halfway up the hill they could see Nellie and the iron-gray gelding, Pete, nibbling the heads from the wild oats. When they approached, Nellie looked at them and backed her ears and bobbed her head up and down rebelliously. Billy walked to her and put his hand under her mane and patted her neck, until her ears came forward again and she nibbled delicately at his shirt.

Jody asked, "Do you think she's really going to have a colt?"

Billy rolled the lids back from the mare's eyes with his thumb and forefinger. He felt the lower lip and fingered the black, leathery teats. "I wouldn't be surprised," he said.

"Well, she isn't changed at all. It's three months gone."

Billy rubbed the mare's flat forehead with his knuckle while she grunted with pleasure. "I told you you'd get tired waiting. It'll be five months more before you can even see a sign, and it'll be at least eight months more before she throws the colt, about next January."

Jody sighed deeply. "It's a long time, isn't it?"

"And then it'll be about two years more before you can ride."

Jody cried out in despair, "I'll be grown up."

"Yep, you'll be an old man," said Billy.

"What color do you think the colt'll be?"

"Why, you can't ever tell. The stud[9] is black and the dam[10] is bay. Colt might be black or bay or gray or dappled. You can't tell. Some-

times a black dam might have a white colt."

"Well, I hope it's black, and a stallion."

Billy pursed his lips, and the little straw that had been in the corner of his mouth rolled down to the center. "You can't ever trust a stallion," he said critically. "They're mostly fighting and making trouble. Sometimes when they're feeling funny they won't work. They make the mares uneasy and kick the geldings. Your father wouldn't let you keep a stallion."

Nellie sauntered away, nibbling the drying grass. Jody skinned the grain from a grass stem and threw the handful into the air, so that each pointed, feathered seed sailed out like a dart. "Tell me how it'll be, Billy. Is it like when the cows have calves?"

"Just about. Mares are a little more sensitive. Sometimes you have to be there to help the mare. And sometimes if it's wrong, you have to—" he paused.

"Have to what, Billy?"

"Have to tear the colt to pieces to get it out, or the mare'll die."

"But it won't be that way this time, will it, Billy?"

"Oh, no, Nellie's thrown good colts."

"Can I be there, Billy? Will you be certain to call me? It's my colt."

"Sure, I'll call you. Of course I will."

"Tell me how it'll be."

"Why, you've seen the cows calving. It's almost the same. The mare starts groaning and stretching, and then, if it's a good right birth, the head and forefeet come out, and the front hoofs kick a hole just the way the calves do. And the colt starts to breathe. It's good to be there, 'cause if its feet aren't right maybe he can't break the sac, and then he might smother."

Jody whipped his leg with a bunch of grass. "We'll have to be there, then, won't we?"

"Oh, we'll be there, all right."

They turned and walked slowly down the

---

9. **stud:** father.
10. **dam:** mother.

hill toward the barn. Jody was tortured with a thing he had to say, although he didn't want to. "Billy," be began miserably, "Billy, you won't let anything happen to the colt, will you?"

And Billy knew he was thinking of the red pony, Gabilan, and of how it died of strangles. Billy knew he had been infallible before that, and now he was capable of failure. This knowledge made Billy much less sure of himself than he had been. "I can't tell," he said roughly. "All sort of things might happen, and they wouldn't be my fault. I can't do everything." He felt badly about his lost prestige, and so he said, meanly, "I'll do everything I know, but I won't promise anything. Nellie's a good mare. She's thrown good colts before. She ought to this time." And he walked away from Jody and went into the saddle-room beside the barn, for his feelings were hurt.

Jody traveled often to the brush line behind the house. A rusty iron pipe ran a thin stream of spring water into an old green tub. Where the water spilled over and sank into the ground there was a patch of perpetually green grass. Even when the hills were brown and baked in the summer that little patch was green. The water whined softly into the trough all the year round. This place had grown to be a center-point for Jody. When he had been punished the cool green grass and the singing water soothed him. When he had been mean the biting acid of meanness left him at the brush line. When he sat in the grass and listened to the purling stream, the barriers set up in his mind by the stern day went down to ruin.

On the other hand, the black cypress tree by the bunkhouse was as repulsive as the water-tub was dear; for to this tree all the pigs came, sooner or later, to be slaughtered. Pig killing was fascinating, with the screaming and the blood, but it made Jody's heart beat so fast that it hurt him. After the pigs were scalded in the big iron tripod kettle and their skins were scraped and white, Jody had to go to the water-tub to sit in the grass until his heart grew quiet. The water-tub and the black cypress were opposites and enemies.

When Billy left him and walked angrily away, Jody turned up toward the house. He thought of Nellie as he walked, and of the little colt. Then suddenly he saw that he was under the black cypress, under the very singletree where the pigs were hung. He brushed his dry-grass hair off his forehead and hurried on. It seemed to him an unlucky thing to be thinking of his colt in the very slaughter place, especially after what Billy had said. To counteract any evil result of that bad conjunction[11] he walked quickly past the ranch house, through the chicken yard, through the vegetable patch, until he came at last to the brushline.

He sat down in the green grass. The trilling water sounded in his ears. He looked over the farm buildings and across at the round hills, rich and yellow with grain. He could see Nellie feeding on the slope. As usual the water place eliminated time and distance. Jody saw a black, long-legged colt, butting against Nellie's flanks, demanding milk. And then he saw himself breaking a large colt to halter. All in a few moments the colt grew to be a magnificent animal, deep of chest, with a neck as high and arched as a sea-horse's neck, with a tail that tongued and rippled like black flame. This horse was terrible to everyone but Jody. In the schoolyard the boys begged rides, and Jody smilingly agreed. But no sooner were they mounted than the black demon pitched them off. Why, that was his name, Black Demon! For a moment the trilling water and the grass and the sunshine came back, and then . . .

_____

11. **conjunction:** coincidence.

Sometimes in the night the ranch people, safe in their beds, heard a roar of hoofs go by. They said, "It's Jody, on Demon. He's helping out the sheriff again." And then . . .

The golden dust filled the air in the arena at the Salinas Rodeo. The announcer called the roping contests. When Jody rode the black horse to the starting chute the other contestants shrugged and gave up first place, for it was well known that Jody and Demon could rope and throw and tie a steer a great deal quicker than any roping team of two men could. Jody was not a boy any more, and Demon was not a horse. The two together were one glorious individual. And then . . .

The President wrote a letter and asked them to help catch a bandit in Washington. Jody settled himself comfortably in the grass. The little stream of water whined into the mossy tub.

The year passed slowly on. Time after time Jody gave up his colt for lost. No change had taken place in Nellie. Carl Tiflin still drove her to a light cart, and she pulled on a hay rake and worked the Jackson-fork tackle when the hay was being put into the barn.

The summer passed, and the warm bright autumn. And then the frantic morning winds began to twist along the ground, and a chill came into the air, and the poison oak turned red. One morning in September, when he had finished his breakfast, Jody's mother called him into the kitchen. She was pouring boiling water into a bucket full of dry middlings[12] and stirring the materials to a steaming paste.

"Yes, ma'am?" Jody asked.

"Watch how I do it. You'll have to do it after this every other morning."

"Well, what is it?"

"Why, it's warm mash for Nellie. It'll keep her in good shape."

Jody rubbed his forehead with a knuckle. "Is she all right?" he asked timidly.

Mrs. Tiflin put down the kettle and stirred the mash with a wooden paddle. "Of course she's all right, only you've got to take better care of her from now on. Here, take this breakfast out to her!"

Jody seized the bucket and ran, down past the bunkhouse, past the barn, with the heavy bucket banging against his knees. He found Nellie playing with the water in the trough, pushing waves and tossing her head so that the water slopped out on the ground.

Jody climbed the fence and set the bucket of steaming mash beside her. Then he stepped back to look at her. And she was changed. Her stomach was swollen. When she moved, her feet touched the ground gently. She buried her nose in the bucket and gobbled the hot breakfast. And when she had finished and had pushed the bucket around the ground with her nose a little, she stepped quietly over to Jody and rubbed her cheek against him.

---

12. **middlings:** mixture of bran and coarse bits of wheat used as feed for livestock.

The Red Pony 527

Billy Buck came out of the saddle-room and walked over. "Starts fast when it starts, doesn't it?"

"Did it come all at once?"

"Oh, no, you just stopped looking for a while." He pulled her head around toward Jody. "She's goin' to be nice, too. See how nice her eyes are! Some mares get mean, but when they turn nice, they just love everything." Nellie slipped her head under Billy's arm and rubbed her neck up and down between his arm and his side. "You better treat her awful nice now," Billy said.

"How long will it be?" Jody demanded breathlessly.

The man counted in whispers on his fingers. "About three months," he said aloud. "You can't tell exactly. Sometimes it's eleven months to the day, but it might be two weeks early, or a month late, without hurting anything."

Jody looked hard at the ground. "Billy," he began nervously, "Billy, you'll call me when it's getting born, won't you? You'll let me be there, won't you?"

Billy bit the tip of Nellie's ear with his front teeth. "Carl says he wants you to start right at the start. That's the only way to learn. Nobody can tell you anything. Like my old man did with me about the saddle blanket. He was a government packer[13] when I was your size, and I helped him some. One day I left a wrinkle in my saddle blanket and made a saddle-sore. The next morning he saddled me up with a forty-pound stock saddle. I had to lead my horse and carry that saddle over a whole mountain in the sun. It darn near killed me, but I never left no wrinkles in a blanket again. I couldn't. I never in my life since then put on a blanket but I felt that saddle on my back."

Jody reached up a hand and took hold of

Nellie's mane. "You'll tell me what to do about everything, won't you? I guess you know everything about horses, don't you?"

Billy laughed. "Why I'm half horse myself, you see," he said. "My ma died when I was born, and being my old man was a government packer in the mountains, and no cows around most of the time, why he just gave me mostly mare's milk." He continued seriously, "And horses know that. Don't you know it, Nellie?"

The mare turned her head and looked full into his eyes for a moment, and this is a thing horses practically never do. Billy was proud and sure of himself now. He boasted a little. "I'll see you get a good colt. I'll start you right. And if you do like I say, you'll have the best horse in the county."

That made Jody feel warm and proud, too; so proud that when he went back to the house he bowed his legs and swayed his shoulders as horsemen do. And he whispered, "Whoa, you Black Demon, you! Steady down there and keep your feet on the ground."

---

13. **government packer:** one who transports goods and equipment for the government.

The winter fell sharply. A few preliminary gusty showers, and then a strong steady rain. The hills lost their straw color and blackened under the water, and the winter streams scrambled noisily down the canyons. The mushrooms and puff-balls[14] popped up and the new grass started before Christmas.

But this year Christmas was not the central day to Jody. Some undetermined time in January had become the axis day around which the months swung. When the rains fell, he put Nellie in a box stall and fed her warm food every morning and curried her and brushed her.

The mare was swelling so greatly that Jody became alarmed. "She'll pop wide open," he said to Billy.

Billy laid his strong square hand against Nellie's swollen abdomen. "Feel here," he said quietly. "You can feel it move. I guess it would surprise you if there were twin colts."

---

14. **puff-balls:** round mushroomlike plants that can be eaten.

"You don't think so?" Jody cried. "You don't think it will be twins, do you, Billy?"

"No, I don't, but it does happen, sometimes."

During the first two weeks of January it rained steadily. Jody spent most of his time, when he wasn't in school, in the box stall with Nellie. Twenty times a day he put his hand on her stomach to feel the colt move. Nellie became more and more gentle and friendly to him. She rubbed her nose on him. She whinnied softly when he walked into the barn.

Carl Tiflin came to the barn with Jody one day. He looked admiringly at the groomed bay coat, and he felt the firm flesh over ribs and shoulders. "You've done a good job," he said to Jody. And this was the greatest praise he knew how to give. Jody was tight with pride for hours afterward.

The fifteenth of January came, and the colt was not born. And the twentieth came; a lump of fear began to form in Jody's stomach. "Is it all right?" he demanded of Billy.

"Oh, sure."

And again, "Are you sure it's going to be all right?"

Billy stroked the mare's neck. She swayed her head uneasily. "I told you it wasn't always the same time, Jody. You just have to wait."

When the end of the month arrived with no birth, Jody grew frantic. Nellie was so big that her breath came heavily, and her ears were close together and straight up, as though her head ached. Jody's sleep grew restless, and his dreams confused.

On the night of the second of February he awakened crying. His mother called to him, "Jody, you're dreaming. Wake up and start over again."

But Jody was filled with terror and desolation. He lay quietly a few moments, waiting for his mother to go back to sleep, and then he slipped his clothes on, and crept out in his bare feet.

The night was black and thick. A little misting rain fell. The cypress tree and the bunkhouse loomed and then dropped back into the mist. The barn door screeched as he opened it, a thing it never did in the daytime. Jody went to the rack and found a lantern and a tin box of matches. He lighted the wick and walked down the long straw-covered aisle to Nellie's stall. She was standing up. Her whole body weaved from side to side. Jody called to her, "So, Nellie, so-o, Nellie," but she did not stop her swaying nor look around. When he stepped into the stall and touched her on the shoulder she shivered under his hand. Then Billy Buck's voice came from the hayloft right above the stall.

"Jody, what are you doing?"

Jody started back and turned miserable eyes up toward the nest where Billy was lying in the hay. "Is she all right, do you think?"

"Why sure, I think so."

"You won't let anything happen, Billy, you're sure you won't?"

Billy growled down at him, "I told you I'd call you, and I will. Now you get back to bed and stop worrying that mare. She's got enough to do without you worrying her."

Jody cringed, for he had never heard Billy speak in such a tone. "I only thought I'd come and see," he said. "I woke up."

Billy softened a little then. "Well, you get to bed. I don't want you bothering her. I told you I'd get you a good colt. Get along now."

Jody walked slowly out of the barn. He blew out the lantern and set it in the rack. The blackness of the night, and the chilled mist struck him and enfolded him. He wished he believed everything Billy said as he had before the pony died. It was a moment before his eyes, blinded by the feeble lantern-flame, could make any form of the darkness. The damp ground chilled his bare feet. At the cypress tree the roosting turkeys chattered a little in alarm, and the two good dogs re-

sponded to their duty and came charging out, barking to frighten away the coyotes they thought were prowling under the tree.

As he crept through the kitchen, Jody stumbled over a chair. Carl called from his bedroom, "Who's there? What's the matter there?"

And Mrs. Tiflin said sleepily, "What's the matter, Carl?"

The next second Carl came out of the bedroom carrying a candle, and found Jody before he could get into bed. "What are you doing out?"

Jody turned shyly away. "I was down to see the mare."

For a moment anger at being awakened fought with approval in Jody's father. "Listen," he said, finally, "there's not a man in this country that knows more about colts than Billy. You leave it to him."

Words burst out of Jody's mouth. "But the pony died—"

"Don't you go blaming that on him," Carl said sternly. "If Billy can't save a horse, it can't be saved."

Mrs. Tiflin called, "Make him clean his feet and go to bed, Carl. He'll be sleepy all day tomorrow."

It seemed to Jody that he had just closed his eyes to try to go to sleep when he was shaken violently by the shoulder. Billy Buck stood beside him, holding a lantern in his hand. "Get up," he said. "Hurry up." He turned and walked quickly out of the room.

Mrs. Tiflin called, "What's the matter? Is that you, Billy?"

"Yes, ma'am."

"Is Nellie ready?"

"Yes, ma'am."

"All right, I'll get up and heat some water in case you need it."

Jody jumped into his clothes so quickly that he was out the back door before Billy's swinging lantern was halfway to the barn. There was a rim of dawn on the mountaintops, but no light had penetrated into the cup of the ranch yet. Jody ran frantically after the lantern and caught up to Billy just as he reached the barn. Billy hung the lantern to a nail on the stall side and took off his blue denim coat. Jody saw that he wore only a sleeveless shirt under it.

Nellie was standing rigid and stiff. While they watched, she crouched. Her whole body was wrung with a spasm. The spasm passed. But in a few moments it started over again, and passed.

Billy muttered nervously, "There's something wrong." His bare hand disappeared. "It's wrong," he said.

The spasm came again, and this time Billy strained, and the muscles stood out on his arm and shoulder. He heaved strongly, his forehead beaded with perspiration. Nellie cried with pain. Billy was muttering, "It's wrong. I can't turn it. It's way wrong. It's turned all around wrong."

He glared wildly toward Jody. And then his fingers made a careful, careful diagnosis. His cheeks were growing tight and gray. He looked for a long questioning minute at Jody standing back of the stall. Then Billy stepped to the rack under the manure window and picked up a horseshoe hammer with his wet right hand.

"Go outside, Jody," he said.

The boy stood still and stared dully at him.

"Go outside, I tell you. It'll be too late."

Jody didn't move.

Then Billy walked quickly to Nellie's head. He cried, "Turn your face away, turn your face."

This time Jody obeyed. His head turned sideways. He heard Billy whispering hoarsely in the stall. And then he heard a hollow crunch of bone. Nellie chuckled shrilly. Jody looked back in time to see the hammer rise and fall again on the flat forehead. Then Nellie fell heavily to her side and quivered for a moment.

Billy jumped to the swollen stomach; his big pocket-knife was in his hand. He lifted the skin and drove the knife in. He sawed and ripped at the tough belly. The air filled with the sick odor of warm living entrails. The other horses reared back against their halter chains and squealed and kicked.

Billy dropped the knife. Both of his arms plunged into the terrible ragged hole and dragged out a big, white, dripping bundle. His teeth tore a hole in the covering. A little black head appeared through the tear, and little slick, wet ears. A gurgling breath was drawn, and then another. Billy shucked off the sac and found his knife and cut the string. For a moment he held the little black colt in his arms and looked at it. And then he walked slowly over and laid it in the straw at Jody's feet.

Billy's face and arms and chest were dripping red. His body shivered and his teeth chattered. His voice was gone; he spoke in a throaty whisper. "There's your colt. I promised. And there it is. I had to do it—had to." He stopped and looked over his shoulder into the box stall. "Go get hot water and a sponge," he whispered. "Wash him and dry him the way his mother would. You'll have to feed him by hand. But there's your colt, the way I promised."

Jody stared stupidly at the wet, panting foal. It stretched out its chin and tried to raise its head. Its blank eyes were navy blue.

Billy shouted, "Will you go now for the water? *Will you go?*"

Then Jody turned and trotted out of the barn into the dawn. He ached from his throat to his stomach. His legs were stiff and heavy. He tried to be glad because of the colt, but the bloody face, and the haunted, tired eyes of Billy Buck hung in the air ahead of him.

STUDY QUESTIONS

Recalling

1. What does Jody do with the animals that he captures?
2. What is Jody's reaction when he learns that his father wants to speak with him? What deal does Carl make with his son?
3. Describe the change in Jody after he talks with his father about breeding Nellie. What new chores does Jody undertake?
4. In what ways does the old green water tub comfort Jody? Why does the black cypress tree upset him?
5. What promise does Billy Buck make to Jody? What must Billy Buck do to fulfill his promise?

Interpreting

6. In what ways is Jody's treatment of the captured animals similar to his treatment of animals in Chapter II? In what way has his attitude toward living things changed?
7. Why are the water tub and the black cypress "opposites and enemies" in Jody's mind? What two sides of nature might they represent?
8. Does Jody act courageously when Billie Buck kills Nellie? Support your opinion with evidence from the novel.
9. What must Jody accept before he can be glad about having the colt? What has he learned about nature?

Extending

10. Think of one or two examples of something new being born of hardship.

READING AND LITERARY FOCUS

The Total Effect

A novelist uses plot, setting, characterization, and a narrator to develop **themes,** or general ideas about life. The **plot,** or sequence of events, must capture the interest of the reader. The **setting** is the time and place in which the action of the novel takes place. Descriptions of the setting often add to the overall mood of the work. **Characterization** can refer to the personality of a character. Characterization can also refer to the method an author uses to reveal this personality to the reader. Sometimes one of the characters in a work is also the narrator. The **narrator** is the person who tells the story. Sometimes the narrator is a third-person storyteller who is not involved in the action.

Unlike a short story, a novel is long enough to have several themes that present the novelist's views. All the elements of a novel work together to create a total effect—its impact on the reader.

Thinking About Plot

1. Identify the external conflicts in each of the three parts of *The Red Pony*. What is the outcome of each conflict?
2. What main internal conflict does Jody have? What is its outcome?
3. If you were to make *The Red Pony* into a short movie, which scenes would you be sure to include? Why?

Thinking About Setting

4. Details of the novel's setting can be put into two groups. What does Jody associate with each of the following groups: (a) summer, the Gabilan Mountains, the water tub, the wild quail that eat with the chickens; (b) winter, the Great Ones, the black cypress, the buzzards?

Thinking About Character

5. Name at least four of Jody's personality traits. Give an example of Jody's actions to illustrate each trait.
6. Name Billy Buck's main personality trait. Find three examples of his words to support your opinion.
7. Compare Jody's reaction after the death of his pony with his reaction after the death of Nellie.

In what way has he changed by the end of the novel?

Thinking About the Narrator

8. Who is the narrator of the novel? What are the advantages of having such a narrator?

Thinking About Theme

9. Consider Jody's destruction of plants and animals at various times in the novel. What theme about people and living things is Steinbeck suggesting?
10. Does Jody ever free himself entirely of fear during the novel? Does he face his fears courageously? Give examples to support your answers. What theme is Steinbeck suggesting about the roles of fear and courage in people's lives?
11. Consider the characters of Billy Buck and Jody's parents. What does Jody learn from each one about being an adult? What do you think Steinbeck would say are the responsibilities of adulthood?
12. What two sides of nature does Steinbeck show us? What, according to Steinbeck, must humans learn to accept about the natural world?

VOCABULARY

Prefixes

A **prefix** is a letter or group of letters added to the beginning of a word. The prefix *dis-* often means "not" or "the opposite of." For example, look at the word *disobey*. To what word has the prefix *dis-* been added? What does the combined word mean?

Now practice adding *dis-* to the following words. Do not change the spelling of a word when you add a prefix to it. Tell how the prefix changes the meaning of each base word.

1. appear
2. mount
3. placed
4. orderly
5. satisfy
6. regard
7. agree
8. service
9. interest
10. like

COMPOSITION

Writing a Book Review

■ Write a book review of *The Red Pony*. First present some general information about the book and its author. Then describe the setting of the story and the main characters. Next summarize the plot. Conclude by giving your opinion of *The Red Pony,* backed by examples from the book. *For help with this assignment, see Lesson 9 in the Writing About Literature Handbook at the back of this book.*

Writing a New Ending

■ Write a new ending for *The Red Pony* so that Nellie is saved. In a paragraph describe the scene at the dinner table where Jody, his parents, and Billy Buck talk about the new pony, its mother, and the future.

CHALLENGE

Literary Criticism

■ Author Theodore Hornberger has written:

What he [Steinbeck] had to say, basically, was that life goes on, . . . although . . . individual lives may be snuffed out by the . . . forces of nature. . . . Steinbeck still finds a core of goodness in men and women, a zest for living.

—*The Literature of the United States*

Do you think these statements are true of *The Red Pony*? Explain.

Active Reading

The Novel

Preparing for a Test

When you prepare for a literature test, you must review carefully the material you have read. If the test is on a novel, you should concentrate on reviewing four main elements of the story: *plot, character, setting,* and *theme.* Reviewing, of course, does not mean rereading the entire book. However, it does require skimming (see page 49) each chapter to remind yourself of the most important details in the story.

As you skim, you should take notes on important information you wish to remember. Since your notes will relate to four elements, you may begin your review by dividing a stack of note cards into four piles. At the top of each card in the first pile, write the heading *Plot.* At the top of each card in the second pile, write *Character,* and so on. This way, after you have skimmed the entire book, you will be able to organize your notes easily into an outline.

You can take notes in two ways. You can take phrase notes or sentence notes. *Phrase notes,* as the name implies, are notes that contain only phrases—perhaps just a word or two to represent a particular detail. *Sentence notes,* on the other hand, are written as complete sentences. If, for example, you were jotting down a physical description of Billy Buck, your notes might look as follows:

PHRASE NOTES	SENTENCE NOTES
Character (P. 487) *Billy Buck's physical appearance: small, broad, bowlegged, mustache.*	*Character (P. 487)* *Billy Buck has a small, broad physique. He is bowlegged. He wears a mustache.*

It does not matter which kind of notes you take. You may find phrase notes faster and easier to take, but sentence notes may be clearer to you later when you review the notes. Notice that in both examples of note cards, a page number appears in the upper right-hand corner. As you take notes from a novel, you should jot down the page numbers where the information appears, in case you need to refer to them later.

Paraphrasing Information in a Novel

As you take notes from a novel, you should not copy information word for word. Instead you should write a *paraphrase*, which is a summary or restatement of information in different words. When paraphrasing, you must be careful not to change the meaning of the original text.

Consider the following description of Jody in *The Red Pony* (page 487):

> He was only a little boy, ten years old, with hair like dusty yellow grass and with shy polite gray eyes, and with a mouth that worked when he thought.

If you were taking sentence notes, you might paraphrase the passage in this manner:

> He was a blond-haired, gray-eyed ten-year-old whose lips moved when he thought.

The paraphrase uses several synonyms—"blond" for "dusty yellow" and "lips moved" for "a mouth that worked," for example. The essential information, however, has not been altered. Also notice that the paraphrase shortens the original description and includes only the most vital information.

Activity 1 Read each of the following passages from *The Red Pony*. Write either phrase notes or sentence notes that paraphrase the most important information in the passage. Do not change the original meaning of the passage.

1. A red pony was looking at him out of the stall. Its tense ears were forward and a light of disobedience was in its eyes. Its coat was rough and thick as an airedale's fur and its mane was long and tangled. (page 491)
2. In a few moments he [Gitano] had trudged close enough so that his face could be seen. And his face was as dark as dried beef. A mustache, blue-white against the dark skin, hovered over his mouth, and his hair was white, too, where it showed at his neck. The skin of his face had shrunk back against the skull until it defined bone, not flesh, and made the nose and chin seem sharp and fragile. (page 511)

Making an Outline

After completing all your notes on the novel, you are ready to make an outline from the notes. The outline will cover the elements of *plot, character, setting,* and *theme.* A model follows:

I. Plot
  A. Major events leading to the climax
    1. _____
    2. _____
    3. _____
  B. Climax _____
  C. Resolution _____
  D. External conflicts
    1. _____
    2. _____
  E. Internal conflicts
    1. _____
    2. _____

II. Characters
  A. First main character
    1. Physical appearance _____
    2. Major character traits _____
    3. Motivations _____
    4. Examples of character change, if any _____
  B. Second main character (Cover points 1–4 for each main character.)

III. Setting
  A. First major setting
    1. Time and place _____
    2. Descriptive details _____
    3. Mood created _____
  B. Second major setting (Cover points 1, 2, and 3 for each major setting.)

IV. Theme
  A. First main theme
    1. Statement of theme _____
    2. Major ways theme is revealed (for example, through the title, character changes, etc.) _____
  B. Second main theme (Cover points 1 and 2 for each main theme.)

Activity 2 Prepare note cards for *The Red Pony* on the most important details of plot, character, setting, and theme. Use your note cards to complete the preceding model outline. Follow these steps carefully when doing the outline:

1. Under *I. Plot* list the major events leading to the climax. The model provides room for three examples, but *you may list as many or as few examples as you feel apply.* (The same holds true for the rest of the outline.) Next identify the climax and resolution. Then list the most important external and internal conflicts in the novel.

2. Under *II. Characters* list the physical traits and major character traits for each main character in the story. Also list important examples of character motivation and character change.

3. Under *III. Setting* describe the first major setting in the novel. First identify the time and place, and then list descriptive details about them. Tell what kind of mood is created by the setting. Provide the same type of information in the outline for each major setting.

4. Under *IV. Theme* state the main themes of the novel. For each theme list the ways in which the theme is revealed.

5. Review your outline in preparation for a test on *The Red Pony.*

Literary Skills Review

The Novel

Guide for Reading the Novel

As you read novels, use this guide to help you notice and appreciate the way authors create fictional worlds.

Plot

1. What is the main **plot** and main **conflict** of the novel?
2. Does the novel have **subplots** that are related to the main plot?
3. Does **foreshadowing** help you to predict future plot developments?

Character

1. Who are the **major characters** of the novel?
2. Who are the **minor characters** of the novel?
3. What aspects of the major characters' personalities does the author reveal directly?
4. What aspects of the major characters' personalities does the author reveal indirectly?

Setting

1. **When and where** does the novel take place? Does the setting change?
2. What **atmosphere,** or mood, is created by the setting?

Point of View

1. Does the author use the **first-person point of view,** using a character as storyteller?
2. Does the author tell the story, using the **third-person point of view**?
3. What are the advantages and disadvantages of the author's choice of narrator?

Theme

1. What is the novel's **theme,** or main idea? Does the novel have more than one theme?
2. What themes are stated directly by the author or by characters?
3. What themes are implied in the novel?

Themes Review

The Novel

Authors have written about certain general themes—such as love, nature, heroism, growth—time and again. For example, the general theme "growth and learning" appears in many works of literature. Yet each writer says something special and personal about this theme. For example, consider the different specific views of learning presented in "The Birdman" (page 127) and *The Red Pony* (page 487). Birdman's experience conveys the following specific theme: "By doing difficult things, we learn to master the world around us." On the other hand, Jody's experience conveys this specific theme: "By living through painful ordeals, we learn to accept the good and bad aspects of our world." A general theme can be a phrase, while a specific theme is a sentence.

1. In *The Red Pony* what specific point about the general theme "growth and learning" does Billy Buck convey?

2. For one of the following stories and *The Red Pony*, tell what specific point each work makes about the general theme "families."
   "Last Cover"   "Uncle Tony's Goat"   "Thirteen"

3. Consider one of the following stories and *The Red Pony*. Tell what specific point each work makes about the general theme "the world of animals."
   "Old Yeller"   "Feathered Friend"   "The Sparrow"

4. Explain the specific view of the general theme "the land" expressed in *The Red Pony* and one of the following works.
   Stories: "The Clearing"   "The Wild Duck's Nest"
   Poems: "Flower-Fed   "Bamboo Grove"
   Buffaloes"

5. Explain the specific points about the general theme "goals and challenges" expressed in *The Red Pony* and two of the following selections.
   Stories: "Home"   "The Dinner Party"
   Poems: "Roadways"   "A Song of Greatness"
   Nonfiction: "In Search of Our   "Beneath the Crags of
   Mothers' Gardens"   Malpelo Island"
   Drama: *Gregory's Girl*   *The Speckled Band*
   Myths: "Prometheus"   "Midas"

STUDENT'S RESOURCES
LESSONS IN ACTIVE LEARNING

SPEAKING AND LISTENING HANDBOOK

THINKING SKILLS HANDBOOK

READING AND STUDY SKILLS HANDBOOK

WRITING ABOUT LITERATURE HANDBOOK

READING AND LITERARY TERMS HANDBOOK

SPEAKING AND LISTENING HANDBOOK

LESSON 1: A Speech About Literature

OVERVIEW

You will present a speech to the class. You will compare an incident narrated in one of the selections in this anthology with an incident from your life or the life of someone you know. You will summarize the two incidents and talk about your reactions to each of them.

A short speech allows you to speak without interruption and to develop ideas fully. In conversation—as opposed to a speech—you are not able to be so logical. A speech combines the development and cohesiveness of a written essay with the spontaneity of conversation.

PREPARING THE SPEECH

Most successful speakers spend 80 percent of their time preparing what they are going to say and only 20 percent of their time practicing the delivery of their speech.

The ultimate success of your speech about literature depends on your choosing an effective incident from this anthology. To help yourself choose an appropriate piece of literature for this assignment, ask yourself these questions and ones like them about the piece you are thinking of using:

- Has something like this ever happened to me?
- Have I ever observed anything like the event described here?
- Do I know anyone who experienced something like this?

Jot down your answers to these questions and to other questions you may ask yourself.

ORGANIZING YOUR IDEAS

Now you will have to determine the *order* of your ideas. You will have to decide which incident—the one from literature or the one from your life—you will talk about first. If other students have read the work, you may want to begin with that. On the other hand, the incident from your life may be more immediately familiar to students and a better starting point.

You will also need to decide how you will begin and end your speech.

- It is always a good idea to begin by catching the attention of your audience.
- You can end your speech by summarizing your reactions to the two incidents or by telling why you find the literature so satisfying.

Finally, you will prepare an outline. An **outline** is what you look at, or refer to, while delivering your speech. You write down the key words and phrases of your speech.

A SAMPLE SPEECH

Let us assume that your class has already read Mark Twain's "Glorious Whitewasher" from *The Adventures of Tom Sawyer* (page 146). Let us further assume that as you reread the selection, you remember a personal incident that had something in common with the Tom Sawyer whitewashing episode. Here are examples of the ideas you might think about and jot down.

Example
- My father gave me a weekly chore: washing the family car every Saturday morning.

- My neighborhood friends began playing baseball on Saturday mornings. I was a good pitcher, and they would not start the game without me.
- As my friends stood around, they would complain, "Why don't you hurry up?"
- Sometimes they told me how to wash the car.
- Once they took the hose and got the car all wet and streaked. I became angry.
- I finally got up extra early and finished washing the car before my friends came to play.

Indeed you begin to see similarities between your experience and Tom Sawyer's. Then you realize there are some differences too:

- Tom's whitewashing would have taken most of the day, whereas my chore required less time.
- Tom made the work seem like play and enticed others to do the chore for him. I wish I had been as clever as Tom Sawyer.

The outline of your speech may look like this:

I. Opening
My favorite selection: Tom Sawyer whitewashing the fence

II. Body
   A. Whitewashing the fence
   Recall the episode briefly with a few details to refresh students' memory.
   B. Incident that happened to me
     1. Chore: washing the car on Sat. a.m.
     2. Neighborhood friends waiting for me to finish: their comments, actions
     3. My solution to the problem
   C. Comparison of two incidents
     1. Similarities
     2. Differences

III. Closing
Tom's solution better than mine

DELIVERING THE SPEECH

1. Be seen.
Position yourself where everyone in the audience can see you easily.

2. Be heard.
Speak loud enough for everyone to hear you. Speak to the person farthest away.

3. Be clear.
Pronounce each sound in a word. Be sure not to drop, or omit, final consonants, such as *t*'s and *d*'s.

4. Be interesting.
Vary your tone of voice, pace, and loudness. Let variety in speech reflect your ideas and descriptions. In the sample speech you might let your voice slow down and become quiet as you describe Tom Sawyer looking at the thirty-yard fence he has to whitewash.

5. Be relaxed.
Don't stand too stiffly, but don't slouch either.

6. Practice delivering your speech.
Give your speech for a friend or relative. They will give you reactions to how you sound. Then you can make adjustments.

ASSIGNMENT
Select another piece of literature that contains an incident comparable to an incident in your life or the life of someone you know. Here are suggestions for literature on which to base your speech.

- Shirley Jackson's "Sneaker Crisis"
- Sherwood Anderson's "Stolen Day"
- Betty Smith's "Christmas in Brooklyn"
- Jessamyn West's "Thirteen"
- Russell Baker's *Growing Up*

LESSON 2:   *Asking and Responding to Questions*

▨ OVERVIEW

In this lesson you will learn how to improve the way you listen to oral presentations of literature and to speeches, discussions, and conversations about literature. Although you theoretically already know how to listen, you will see that *active* listening involves more concentration and thinking than you may now be investing. One of the best measures of how well you listen is the kind of questions you ask as well as the quality of answers you give.

To begin with, think about the importance of listening—not just to the listener but to the speaker. A speaker *needs* a listener; otherwise there is no reason for the speaker to speak. By listening carefully and showing interest in what the speaker is saying, you can help the speaker do a better job.

▨ GUIDELINES FOR ASKING QUESTIONS

After someone has made a speech about literature (see Lesson 1 in this handbook) or completed an oral presentation (see Lesson 3), you may have an opportunity to ask questions. Usually, the question-and-answer period for a very short speech runs only about two minutes; for a longer speech the questions and answers may represent as much as 25 percent of the time given to the speech proper.

In general, your questions will probably fall into two categories:

- Questions about the speaker's content: What did he or she really mean by saying such-and-such?
- Questions about the speaker's style

Here are some pointers for effective listening and for good questioning.

1. Listen with an open mind. If you prejudge the speaker, you will not really be able to hear what he or she is saying. You need to be willing to hear the speaker and to change your mind as necessary.

2. Enjoy listening. You cannot fake good listening, and the speaker will quickly realize that you are only pretending to listen.

3. Do not ask a question just to show off your own knowledge. Do not ask a question that you already know the answer to. Do not try to trick a speaker into agreeing with you or make him or her look silly.

4. While listening to the speaker, take a few notes to remind yourself what you may want to ask—but only a few notes because you do not want to be distracted from what the speaker says next. Continue to listen closely so that you will not miss it if the speaker answers your question before the end of the speech.

5. Ask only one question at a time; do not ask a question that includes two, three, or four parts.

6. Make sure that the question is important. Do you really need to know the answer?

7. Make sure the question is really a question and not a long statement. You may make a brief statement preceding your question, but make sure you get to the point as soon as possible. *Examples:* "I think you said . . . , and I was wondering if . . ." "The author of the selection you are referring to says . . . , and I would like to ask you . . . ."

8. Phrase the question so that it will be immediately clear to the speaker and to the rest of the audience.

9. Remember that you are addressing the entire group, not just the speaker. Therefore, speak up loudly and slowly enough so that you will not have to repeat yourself.

10. If the speaker does not answer your question, you may ask it again, perhaps phrasing it a little differently. Or you may state why you think the speaker's answer was inadequate.

11. You may also ask a follow-up question at times, but be careful not to monopolize the question period.

12. After the speaker has answered your question, say "Thank you." This statement signals that you are satisfied with the answer and are turning the floor over to another questioner.

GUIDELINES FOR RESPONDING TO QUESTIONS

As a speaker you should be grateful for questions. Rather than feeling intimidated by questions, think of them as a sign that your audience was stimulated by your presentation.

1. After you have finished your presentation and opened the floor to questions, always wait about five seconds. It may take your audience that long to formulate their questions. If no one asks a question, ask a question yourself to break the ice—and answer it.

2. Plan ahead by thinking about what questions your listeners may ask as a result of your speech. Be ready to answer those questions.

3. Always listen carefully and fully to a question from the audience. Don't assume you know what someone is asking until it has been completely asked. Overcome any temptation to interrupt the questioner.

4. You may repeat the question to make sure you heard it accurately and to make sure the rest of the audience hears it too. Repeating the question also gives you a little more time to prepare your answer.

5. Keep your answer simple, brief, and to the point—giving other listeners a chance to respond too.

6. If you do not know the answer to a question, admit that you do not rather than attempt to bluff your way through. The question actually may be outside your topic; say so. You can always comment on the importance of the question but explain that you had not thought about it. Then move on.

7. Use strong, direct eye contact with the questioner. Begin your answer by looking at the questioner, then move out to include the entire audience, and then finish your answer by coming back to make eye contact with the questioner.

8. Ask the questioner if your answer was satisfactory. Be open to follow-up questions: "Did you have a further question?

9. Thank the questioner, and move on to the next questioner.

10. After the question-and-answer period summarize your speech briefly, perhaps including a few of the ideas brought up through the audience's questions. End with a strong, positive statement, pointing out the importance of your topic.

LESSON 3: *Fundamentals of Oral Interpretation*

OVERVIEW

In this lesson you will improve your ability to read literature aloud to the class. That is, you will learn to engage in **oral interpretation,** which involves communicating your feelings and thoughts about the literature to an audience. Your individual presentation will run from three to five minutes.

PREPARING AN ORAL INTERPRETATION

1. **Select a work of literature.**

    For this introductory assignment in oral interpretation, select literature from any genre: fiction, poetry, nonfiction, drama.

2. **Think about the work of literature.**
    a. Make sure you know the meaning and pronunciation of unfamiliar words.
    b. Think about the various elements of literature. The Guides for Reading in this textbook will help (the short story: page 206; poetry: page 286; nonfiction: page 338; drama: page 410; myths and folk tales: page 482; the novel: page 538).
    c. Make sure you recognize the most important points in the plot, or narrative line, so that you can stress those points. (This reminder does not apply to some kinds of poetry, of course.)
    d. Is the speaker or character calm, slow, and mature or excited, quick, and confused? What is the narrator's or character's attitude toward what he or she is saying?

3. **Adapt or edit the selection if necessary.**

    If you are working with a long piece of literature, cut it so that you can give your oral interpretation in the time specified. Find a beginning and ending for a section of the work. Alternatively, read one part of the work, stop and explain in your own words what happens next,

and then pick up your oral interpretation later on in the selection.

4. **Prepare a manuscript.**

    Type or print the selection double spaced. During rehearsal (see below) you can mark where to pause, which words to emphasize, where and how to change your tone and pacing.

5. **Rehearse your reading.**

    Read the work several times in order to figure out how to reveal what you think and feel through your voice and body. Think about these questions:

    a. How does each character sound at each point?
    b. Is the mood the same throughout the piece, or do I need to show a change in mood?
    c. What parts should I emphasize? What parts should I subordinate?
    d. Where should I vary my rate (e.g., from fast to slow), my volume (e.g., from loud to soft), my pitch (e.g., from high to low)? Where should I pause? (Let punctuation be your guide, but in addition figure out where to pause for suspense or to lend emphasis to a point.)

    Your performance will change as you try out different ways of communicating your interpretation. If possible, perform for your family and friends before you perform for the class.

6. **Prepare an introduction.**

    In your introductory remarks tell the audience the title and the author. If you are performing an excerpt, you may have to give your audience information about the piece as a whole.

Because you want your audience to be attentive to your performance of literature, the introduction should interest them. Ask a question, tell something unusual about the literature or its author, or simply explain why you like this piece of literature.

Prepare a brief outline of your introductory remarks as you do for any speech (see Lesson 1). Then you will have notes from which you can speak extemporaneously.

THE ACTUAL PERFORMANCE

1. Stand where you can be seen and heard.

2. It is human to be nervous. Once you start, you will feel better.

3. Make sure it is clear where your introduction ends and where the literature begins.

SAMPLE ORAL INTERPRETATION

Consider the following pointers for a performance of the short story "After Twenty Years" by O. Henry (page 175).

1. Analysis

This is a sort of detective, or mystery, story—a suspense story. It is about Bob, who returns to New York City to meet a former friend of his, Jimmy Wells, whom he left twenty years before. The friend, now a police officer, arranges for the arrest of Bob, who is wanted as a criminal.

The narrator creates suspense with his eerie descriptions of nighttime, large-city streets.

The story has essentially a two-part structure: (a) the meeting of Bob and a police officer; (b) a scene between Bob and a plainclothes detective. One important point occurs when Bob notices the detective is not his friend, and the detective places Bob under arrest; another essential point occurs at the very end of the story, when Bob reads the note from the real Jimmy Wells.

The theme of the story probably has something to do with friendship, the effects of time, the well-being of a community.

2. Rehearsal

a. Practice capturing an eerie, suspenseful, haunting tone for the narrator.

b. Try different ways of bringing each character to life: Bob might sound a bit like a worldly person, bragging about his life, but also needing a friend; Jimmy should sound like a decent, unpretentious person; the plainclothes detective should sound like a long-lost friend at first but then should sound cold and businesslike.

c. Make the structure of the story clear. Consider how you can use your voice to set off the characters' conversations from the narrator's descriptions. Consider how to read Jimmy's letter. Will it have a greater effect to use a very flat, unemotional tone?

ASSIGNMENT

Selections that lend themselves to oral interpretation by a single person include

- "A Just Judge" (page 92)
- "Christmas in Brooklyn" (page 101)
- part of "Rip Van Winkle" (page 187)
- "The Highwayman" (page 260)
- "The Listeners" (page 278)

LESSON 4: *Group Storytelling*

OVERVIEW

As part of a small group, you will select one of the myths or folk tales in this anthology and retell it orally in terms of today's world. Storytelling out loud is becoming a very popular activity again. Myths and folk tales, always popular, work particularly well as the basis for modern storytelling.

PREPARING TO TELL A STORY

After your group selects the myth or folk tale to modernize, follow these guidelines:

1. Analyze the myth or tale.

Each member of the group should first read the original myth or tale silently. Then as a group you should discuss the story to see what conclusions you can reach about it.

Divide the story into several parts. Give each part of the story a title, and identify an image of some kind that you associate with that part of the story. You should end up with five to eight parts for the story.

2. State the theme or themes of the story.

3. Transform the myth or tale.

You will retain the broad plot outline—the major stages of the original story. Your goal is to update the characters, the circumstances, and the main images.

A SAMPLE RETELLING PLAN

1. Analysis

For the myth "Midas" (page 435), your group might divide the plot line into five parts. The title and image of each part will help you when you go on to modernize the story.

a. King Midas loves gold and is jealous of others who have gold—even of people who receive the golden rays of the sun.
TITLE: greed
IMAGE: Midas surrounded with his gold

b. Apollo grants Midas' wish that everything he touches will turn to gold. Midas touches his daughter, who turns to gold.
TITLE: wish fulfilled
IMAGE: daughter turned to gold

c. Midas realizes his mistake and calls out to Apollo in anguish. Apollo allows Midas to turn things back from gold.
TITLE: anguish
IMAGE: Midas crying out

d. Apollo punishes Midas by making him wear donkey's ears. Midas covers the ears with a large cap to keep them secret.
TITLE: punishment
IMAGE: ears

e. A servant tells others about Midas' ears. Midas threatens to kill the servant but then spares his life. Because Midas shows mercy, Apollo removes the ears.
TITLE: mercy
IMAGE: ears shrinking

2. Theme

The themes of "Midas" include the following:

- Greed can distort other human feelings.
- Life itself is more important than wealth.
- One must accept punishment for being greedy.
- Mercy is important.

3. Transformation

Retell the Midas tale in terms of a modern character who is exceptionally greedy. Everything the character touches will turn to the desired substance. In the retelling the god Apollo might simply be a voice that the character hears.

Working from these suggestions, everyone in the group might write his or her own modernized version, and the group will select the version to rehearse and deliver. Or you can work together to write the modernization. Here is a slightly more developed modernization of the first part of the story—"greed":

"Just before the stock market crash of 1987, a Wall Street businessman who already owned oil wells in seven states and off-shore wells along the Atlantic and Pacific coasts became even hungrier for oil. The government would not let him drill for oil off the Gulf Coast. He schemed in all sorts of ways to get drilling rights. He never spent any time with his family. Instead he spent day and night in his office, where the walls were covered with pictures of his oil fields and with charts showing oil production. There he sat all day, talking on one phone and then on two phones and sometimes on three phones all at once."

The image for this part of the story could be the businessman surrounded by pictures of oil wells (just as for the Midas story it was the king surrounded by his gold).

Going on to the next part of the story, "wish fulfilled," you can tell how the businessman suddenly comes into more oil—how, for example, the earpiece of his telephone starts to spout oil. You can then continue with the transformation of the other parts.

REHEARSING THE RETELLING

1. Divide the story among speakers.

You have two choices. Either everyone in your group can tell a section of the modernized story. On the other hand, one student might take the part of the narrator, and the others may divide the dialogue. In addition, if your story ends with a moral, the group might pronounce it together.

2. Learn the tale.

Your presentation will be more successful if you do not have to read your modernization. Learn the written version well enough that you can tell it without having to read it word for word. To help you accomplish this goal, focus on the key modern-day image that your group creates for each part. The image will help you to remember each part of the story. Make up cue cards with the name of each part of the story and its image.

3. Practice the tale.

Comment on one another's performance.

PRESENTING THE STORY

1. The members of the group might position themselves in a semicircle. As each one speaks, he or she can move to the middle.

2. Speak clearly.

3. Speak faster or more slowly, louder or softer, depending on what you are describing.

4. Speak extemporaneously. Look at the cue cards to remember what image to focus on.

ASSIGNMENT

Continue the retelling of "Midas," and present the modernization to the class. Any of the other myths and the world folk tales in this book can be the basis for a group project.

THINKING SKILLS HANDBOOK

LESSON 1: *Problem Solving*

DEFINITION

Problem solving is a way of thinking. It involves a group of different thinking skills, but two facts are common to all problem solvers. One, a problem solver always has some basic information about the problem. After all, you cannot solve a problem if you know nothing about it. Two, a problem solver thinks in an orderly fashion, following several clearly defined procedures, or steps.

EXAMPLE

A group of five students must make a fifteen-minute oral presentation to the class on the topic "character," using four short stories the class has read.

EXPLANATION

1. **Goal**—what you want
   The goal is to make the presentation on "character" to the class according to the directions of the teacher. Doing this will solve the problem.

2. **Givens**—What you start with
   The five members of the group must speak about "character." They must fit their presentation into a total of fifteen minutes. They must use four stories the class has read as examples.

3. **Obstacles**—Things that get in the way of a solution
   - How can five students talk about four stories and still have each student take part in the presentation?

- Of all the stories the class has read, which four will be discussed?
- How long may each person talk?
- Does each student have the same definition of "character," or will each student have a different focus on the topic?

4. **Methods**—how things will be done
   The group "brainstormed" to come up with a variety of ideas. By considering each obstacle, the students identified the methods they would use to solve the problem.

- Someone suggested that the presentation be done as a group discussion. A group needs a leader; therefore, four students would each talk about one story, and one student would be the leader.

- Another person pointed out that the stories appearing in the subunit called "Character" would probably be good for discussion of character. Each of the four students chose one story from that subunit of the book.

- The fifteen minutes were equally divided; each student would speak for three minutes during the presentation.

- The leader would begin by speaking for three minutes about the definition of "character." The leader's comments would provide a focus for each student's follow-up response.

5. **Carrying out the plan**
   Each student prepared a statement, and the class presentation was rehearsed. After the

practice session, the group made changes as necessary and then made the presentation to the class.

6. Checking the results

The teacher rated the presentation on content, equal participation, clear organization, and length. For the teacher, the presenters, and the class audience, the results were excellent.

▪▪▪ PROCEDURES

1. State a goal.

If you can say clearly what the goal is, you can usually also define the problem clearly.

2. List the givens.

What information is available to you as you start to think about the problem?

3. List the obstacles.

Obstacles are those things that get in the way of a solution. What are the requirements, that is, what must you do? What are the limits, that is, what must you not do? If there are no obstacles, there probably is no problem. Obstacles may be easy to see and clearly stated. They may also be unstated or hidden. You may have to figure them out.

4. Identify the methods.

What are you going to do to reach a solution? What is your plan of attack? What steps will you follow to eliminate each obstacle in your path?

5. Carry out the plan.

6. Check the results.

Have you solved the problem?

▪▪▪ ACTIVITY I. IDENTIFYING A PROBLEM-SOLVING STRATEGY

The purpose of this activity is to identify and describe the way a character in a story solves a problem by looking at it in a different way.

Read "The Glorious Whitewasher" from *The Adventures of Tom Sawyer* by Mark Twain (page 146). Write three sentences describing how Tom solved his problem by looking at it in a different way. In sentence one, describe how Tom felt at first about whitewashing the fence. In sentence two, describe how Tom suddenly saw the problem differently. (Clue: Did Tom define the problem differently? How?) In sentence three, describe how this new way of looking at the problem enabled Tom to solve the problem.

▪▪▪ ACTIVITY II. DEFINING A PROBLEM IN A SHORT STORY

The purpose of this activity is to define a problem faced by a character in a story in this book.

1. Select a story. Identify one character in the story who seems to have a problem.

2. State the character's **goal.**

3. State the **givens** in the character's situation. How does the character begin to think about the problem?

4. State the **obstacles** to solving the problem.

5. Describe the **methods,** or the plan, the character uses to solve the problem.

6. Check the **results** by telling whether or not the character has actually solved the problem. If the problem has not been solved, tell what change in the methods or plan you would make in order to solve it.

LESSON 2: Inductive Inquiry

DEFINITION

Inductive inquiry is a way to *discover* meaning by observation. In fact, it is sometimes called discovery learning. When you inquire inductively, you observe several examples of something and discover how they are alike. You discover what features they share—that is, what they have in common. You also discover how they differ.

EXAMPLE

The Poetry unit in this book includes many poems that are different from one another in a number of ways. However, they are all poetry. Some poems rhyme; some do not. Some tell a story; some do not. The poems differ in shape, subject matter, and style. What, then, makes them poems?

EXPLANATION

In order to **inquire** into the special features of the idea of poetry, you first need to **find some examples** of poems. Your next step is to **identify the general characteristics** of each of the poems you have chosen. Then, after you have identified those characteristics, you **identify which characteristics are common** to all of the poems.

Making a chart to **display** all of the characteristics is often very helpful.

Characteristics	Poem 1	Poem 2	Poem 3
Rhyme	+	−	+
Stanzas	−	+	+
Regular rhythm	+	−	+
Imagery	+	+	+
Complete sentences	−	+	+
Concrete language	+	+	+

The plus and minus signs indicate whether or not a poem has (+) or does not have (−) that characteristic. Looking closely at the chart, you see that two characteristics—imagery and concrete language—are common to all the examples you examined. Once you have identified common characteristics, you can more accurately and easily recognize any new example of poetry.

It is also useful to **test your findings** against examples that you are fairly sure are not likely to share the characteristics. In this case, it would be a good idea to test your findings about poetry against an example of prose. An easy way to follow this step in inductive inquiry is to add one more column to your chart, a column for a prose selection, a non-example. Your chart might then look like this:

Characteristics	Poem 1	Poem 2	Poem 3	Non-example
Rhyme	+	−	+	−
Stanzas	−	+	+	−
Regular rhythm	+	−	+	−
Imagery	+	+	+	+
Complete sentences	−	+	+	+
Concrete language	+	+	+	−

Looking closely at this chart, you see that the non-example does share two characteristics of poetry—imagery and complete sentences. But the chart shows that imagery and complete sentences are not enough to make a poem. The non-example still does not share any of the other characteristics. Adding more examples and non-examples will give even more support to your findings.

PROCEDURES

1. In order to inquire into a particular idea, first **examine several familiar examples** of the idea.

2. **List all the general characteristics** you can think of that are true of each of the examples.

3. **Display the list** in a way that helps you see the pattern of common characteristics.

4. **Identify the pattern** of common characteristics.

5. **Test your findings** by comparing what you found to be true of the idea with the characteristics of a closely related non-example. When you do this, you will find some combination of characteristics which is special to your idea and which does not occur in the non-example.

ACTIVITY I. INQUIRING INTO IMAGERY IN POETRY

The purpose of this activity is to apply the steps of inductive inquiry to discover the common characteristics of images.

An image is a picture, or likeness, that a poet creates with words. Images are most often visual, or related to sight. They help us picture in our minds what a poem is describing. However, images may appeal to any of the senses and may help us imagine how something may look, feel, taste, sound, or smell.

1. Using any of the poems in the Poetry unit of this book, **identify three examples** of images.

2. **List all the general characteristics** you can think of that are true of each image. For example, to which of the five senses does the image appeal? Is the image vivid or dull? Does the image use concrete language or abstract language?

3. **Display the list** in a way that helps you see the pattern of common characteristics. You may want to make a chart or invent another kind of display.

4. **Identify the pattern** of common characteristics.

5. **Test your findings** by comparing what you found to be true of the examples of imagery with the characteristics of a closely related non-example. You may want to use a line of a poem that you think does not contain an image.

ACTIVITY II. INQUIRING INTO THE IDEA OF SHORT STORIES

The purpose of this activity is to apply the steps of inductive inquiry to discover the common characteristics of short stories.

1. A short story is a brief work of prose fiction, usually short enough to be read in one sitting. **Identify three examples** of short stories, using any of the short stories in this book or any short stories you have read.

2. **List all the general characteristics** you can think of that are true of each story.

3. **Display the list** in a way that helps you see the pattern of common characteristics.

4. **Identify the pattern** of common characteristics.

5. **Test your findings** by comparing what you found to be true of the examples with the characteristics of a closely related non-example.

LESSON 3: *Logical Reasoning*

DEFINITION

Logical reasoning is a way of thinking. It is a way of putting together an explanation that can stand up to a challenge. When you reason logically, you state the *conditions that are necessary* for the explanation to hold. You then determine whether there is *sufficient evidence* to conclude that the conditions have actually been met.

In order for logical reasoning to be effective, you and your audience must share the same set of assumptions. **Assumptions** are the ideas you and your audience take for granted without needing any evidence or support. For example, if you were comparing the performance of two different stereos, you would assume that both stereos were plugged in and turned on.

EXAMPLE

Newspaper stories present factual accounts of actual events. Biographies present descriptions of actual occurrences in the lives of real people. Both news stories and biographies are nonfiction. They share a common set of characteristics: They are realistic (they could happen, and they did happen), and they are verifiable (you could find out when and where they did occur).

If you wanted to reason logically to convince someone that a selection you have read is a work of nonfiction, you would begin by identifying the conditions that are necessary for a selection to be nonfiction. (In this case, you would point to realistic and verifiable details.) Then you would show that there is sufficient evidence (details in the selection) to meet these conditions. You would also expect that your audience shares your assumptions about nonfiction.

EXPLANATION

Both you and your audience assume that the conditions that are necessary for a selection to be nonfiction include realistic details and verifiability. In addition, some nonfiction may contain details that are natural, describing the way people really talk or really do things, and commonplace, describing things that happen fairly often. Are these last two conditions as necessary as the others to classify a selection as nonfiction?

It will help you to make a chart to display the features of each example you are trying to classify. On this chart you can examine the features of several selections to see whether they match the necessary conditions. Such a chart might look like this:

Features	Example 1	Example 2	Example 3
Realistic	+	+	+
Verifiable	+	+	+
Natural	+	+	?
Commonplace	+	−	−

Example 1 has all the features of nonfiction. Examples 2 and 3 are realistic and verifiable but deal with situations that are not commonplace. Example 3 also seems to describe a situation that does not reflect the way people actually talk and do things.

The three examples seem to show that it is not absolutely necessary for a literary selection to be natural and commonplace in order for it to be nonfiction. On the other hand, the three examples suggest that realistic and verifiable details are necessary for a selection to be nonfiction. When you demonstrate that any selection meets these *necessary conditions,* you engage in *logical reasoning.*

1. **State what you believe** to be true.

2. **Identify all the conditions that are necessary** for the situation to be true.

3. Show how the necessary conditions have been met. **Give specific examples that constitute sufficient evidence** to support your position.

4. **Identify the important assumptions** you and your audience must share in order for your position to be convincing.

ACTIVITY I. REASONING LOGICALLY ABOUT A WORK OF NONFICTION

Several authors in the Nonfiction unit of this book (pages 289–339) suggest that a parent's or a teacher's ideas of what is good had a significant effect on the main character. The purpose of this activity is to determine whether a particular writer provides sufficient evidence to support this position logically.

1. Choose a nonfiction selection in which you **find an example** of a parent's or a teacher's ideas of what is good. **Describe the behavior** that the parent or the teacher in the selection prefers.

2. **Find a situation** in which the author or the subject of the biography or autobiography must make a choice. Using a chart, **list the necessary conditions** required for that choice to reflect the parent's or the teacher's idea of what is good.

3. On the chart **describe the choice** that is actually made, and **compare that choice** with what the parent would have preferred. Is there sufficient evidence to suggest that the choice does or does not reflect the parent's or the teacher's values?

4. **Identify the assumptions** the author seems to have made about the parent's or the teacher's values. Do you find any evidence to suggest that the author thought the parent was correct?

5. **Write a brief statement** in which you present your position on whether the choice reflected the parent's or the teacher's values. **State the logical reasons** supporting your position—the necessary conditions and the sufficient evidence.

ACTIVITY II. REASONING LOGICALLY ABOUT A LITERARY CHARACTER

The purpose of this activity is to demonstrate logically that a literary character possesses a certain character trait, or quality.

1. **Choose any literary character** you like. Identify one outstanding trait of this character.

2. **Describe the conditions** under which this character would necessarily demonstrate this trait.

3. **Find examples in the story that constitute sufficient evidence** to show that the character's behavior indeed demonstrates that trait.

4. **Describe what you assume to be true** of the character and why that trait would show up under certain conditions.

5. **Write a brief statement** describing your position and the logical reasons for it.

LESSON 4: *Evaluation*

DEFINITION

When you **evaluate** something, you make a judgment about it. We are constantly evaluating—clothing, food, entertainment, cars, and so on. Sometimes our evaluations make sense, but sometimes they don't. Whether or not our evaluations make sense is often determined by the criteria we use as their basis. **Criteria** are the standards, rules, or tests on which a judgment can be based.

EXAMPLE

C. J. is having dinner in a French restaurant. Everyone else orders escargot [es kär gō], so C. J. orders it too. It is delicious, and C. J. finishes his portion. A companion comments on how amazing it is that something as ugly as a snail can taste so good. C. J. feels ill.

EXPLANATION

C. J. based his first evaluation on the opinion of others: Others ordered escargot, so he ordered it too. C. J. based his next evaluation on taste: It tasted good, so he ate it. When C. J. learned that he was actually eating snails, however, he started to feel ill. The probable reason is not that the snails were spoiled but that C. J. used different criteria to judge what he ate. His past experience with food probably did not include snails. In fact, C. J. probably would have said snails were not fit to eat if you had asked him before the meal.

PROCEDURES

1. **Start with a reason or purpose** for your evaluation.

2. **Identify the criteria,** the rules, tests, or standards you will use to judge.

3. **Apply the criteria.**

4. **Draw a conclusion.** Your conclusion will be your evaluation.

ACTIVITY I. EVALUATING CHARACTER CHANGE IN DRAMA

The purpose of this activity is to evaluate the changes that can be observed in characters from the beginning to the end of a drama. Work in groups.

1. **Think of three examples** from movies, television, or literature in which characters *changed* from the way they were at the beginning of the movie, television show, or story.

2. For each example, **decide what caused the character to change.** For example, some characters may have changed because they achieved a victory; others, because they suffered defeat.

3. **Make a list of causes** or "reasons why" characters in the examples changed. Add other causes, or "reasons why," characters change that come to mind.

4. In each example you have mentioned in which a character has changed and for which you have identified a cause or "reason why," **apply the criterion** of being true to real life.

5. Now **apply the test or evaluation** to the selections in the Drama unit in this book (pages 341–411). Ask yourself whether people really change as Scrooge did, or whether people really change as Gregory (or Dorothy) did.

6. **Share your group's evaluation** of Scrooge and Gregory with the class.

◾ ACTIVITY II. USING CRITERIA IN EVALUATION

The purpose of this activity is to practice the general procedures for making evaluations.

1. Your group is a panel of experts. You will **decide in or on what you are experts.** Be sure you pick something with which you are all familiar—music, literature, sports.

2. **List criteria** for making evaluations in your chosen field of expertise. What rules, tests, or standards could you apply?

3. **Identify some thing or things in your field** that you want to evaluate with the criteria you identified in step 2.

4. **Apply the criteria. Make your evaluation.**

5. **Decide on a way to present the results** of your evaluation. For example, if you evaluate only one thing, you will probably describe how you applied your criteria. If you evaluate a group of items, you may want to rate or rank them.

6. **Each group will present its expert evaluations** to the class. Be prepared to defend your method of evaluation.

◾ ACTIVITY III. DETERMINING VALIDITY OF AN EVALUATION

Read Scene 2 of *Gregory's Girl* (pages 345–346) by Bill Forsyth. Phil Menzies makes an evaluation in this scene.

1. **What was the reason or purpose** for Menzie's evaluation?

2. **Identify the criteria** Menzies used to make his judgments. What rules, tests, or standards did he plan to apply?

3. **How did he apply the criteria?** What method did he use to test his players?

4. **What conclusion did he draw? What was his evaluation?**

5. Decide whether or not Phil Menzies made a proper evaluation under the circumstances. Discuss his criteria for judging players. Suggest criteria that would have resulted in a different evaluation from the one he arrived at.

LESSON 5: *Representation*

DEFINITION

Representation involves changing the way that you perceive information. If the information is in words, making pictures or diagrams of the meaning is a way of representing that information. This is called *graphic* representation. If the information is given in some type of picture or diagram, thinking about its meaning in words is another way of representing that information. Representations are usually developed by asking yourself what the important elements are and how they are related. In making graphic representations, different shapes may be used to represent different ideas.

EXAMPLE

"Spider maps" are one kind of representation. They are helpful to pull together what you know about a given concept. The concept word goes in the middle, and information about the concept is placed on lines around the box, resembling a spider with many legs. Spider maps are also useful for representing or mapping a theme, a description of something, or a problem.

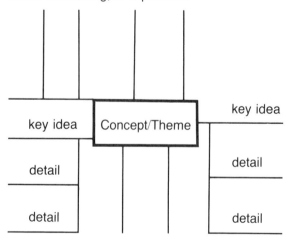

EXPLANATION

Spider maps make it easier to select what is important, integrate and organize the different parts, and summarize.

PROCEDURES

1. **Decide** whether you have to represent a single concept, a problem, a theme, or a description. **State it** in the box.

2. **Brainstorm** alone, with a group of students, or with your teacher to identify categories of information to go on lines attached to the box. Start with what you already know about the concept. Then decide what you would like to know about it. Try to distinguish key ideas from details. **Select** the most important ideas, and place them on the "legs" of the spider map— one category per line.

    Note: In this brainstorming stage consider all categories, but realize that not all of them will turn out to be useful.

3. Keep these categories of information in mind as you **review your textbook** and any notes or activities related to the concept. **Take notes on a spider map.** Add any new categories as you continue your review of the material in the textbook.

4. When you have finished taking notes, ask yourself which categories are most important. **Eliminate unimportant categories.** Ask yourself how the remaining categories are related.

5. You may want to **redraw the map,** placing related items near each other, and think about the overall order of the lines.

ACTIVITY I. REPRESENTING INFORMATION ABOUT MYTHS AND FOLK TALES

Prepare a spider map for any one of the following topics relating to the selections in the Myths and Folk Tales unit of this book:

1. the concept of virtue (behaviors that are rewarded) in "Deucalion and Pyrrha" (page 431) or "The Piece of Straw" (page 456)

2. the concept of evil (behaviors that are punished by the gods) in "Echo and Narcissus" (page 440), "Arachne" (page 444), or "The Ant and the Grasshopper" (page 453)

3. the concept of fate in "Atalanta" (page 448)

4. the concept of justice (and injustice) in any of the above selections or "The Farmer and His Hired Help" (page 467)

5. the concept of cleverness in "The Farmer and His Hired Help" (page 467) or "The Piece of Straw" (page 456)

ACTIVITY II. REPRESENTING INFORMATION ABOUT A LITERARY WORK

Prepare a spider map for any literary work you choose. Follow the procedures for constructing a spider map. Identify a central concept, problem, or theme. Brainstorm, and organize the results into categories. Redraw the map several times if necessary to display the key ideas in the clearest possible way.

LESSON 6: *Synthesis*

DEFINITION

Synthesis involves combining elements from different sources into some kind of organized product. In a synthesis there has to be some evidence of a pattern or structure that was not present before you created it. Synthesis involves the creation of something new.

EXAMPLE

Maria is preparing for an oral report in which she must present both sides of an issue and come to a conclusion.

EXPLANATION

Maria's report is on the topic of a new school building about to be built. One group of local citizens favors one building site; another group favors a different site. The key elements in Maria's report are the two different points of view, the supporting evidence for each point of view and the conclusion she will construct. Her conclusion should be a well-organized statement that did not exist before she constructed it. Her conclusion is the result of synthesis.

Maria's purpose is clear—to examine the situation and clarify it for her audience, presenting a conclusion based on differing points. She identifies the elements she has to work with—the two points of view. She states a relationship between the elements—that they are opposed on the issue of the site but that they agree on many other points. She constructs an original product—an oral report that expresses the relationship between the two sides. Her oral report is a synthesis, a combining of information into something that did not exist before she made it.

PROCEDURES

1. **Establish a purpose** for the product.

2. **Identify the elements** to be combined.

3. **State a relationship** among the elements. **Represent the relationship** in a graphic if possible.

4. **Construct an original product** that expresses the relationship.

ACTIVITY I. COMBINING FICTION AND NONFICTION

The purpose of this activity is to gain a new perspective on a work of fiction by describing it as nonfiction. You will, in effect, be creating something new.

1. **Establish criteria** for identifying literary events that might be newsworthy. For example, they might endanger human life or reveal great discoveries. **List the items** that you finally choose as your criteria.

2. **Select a genre** (the novel, drama, poetry, short stories, myths, or folk tales).

3. **Decide on the event or series of events** to be reported. Try to choose events that would have been reported in the news had they really happened. For example, had the story of the runaway fox in "Last Cover" (page 73) been a true story, it seems likely that its escape might have been reported by the local newspaper. Similarly, the story of Rip Van Winkle (page 187) is indeed a newsworthy topic.

4. After you have chosen an event, **discuss why it is newsworthy** according to your criteria. (Is it life threatening, for example?)

5. **Discuss with other students how the event could be reported** as a news event. **List specific elements** in the story that would have to be changed or eliminated to present the story as nonfiction. Tell why each element needs to be changed.

6. **Construct an outline** of the event as it would be reported in a newspaper article.

7. **Write a brief news story,** describing the event as a news event.

ACTIVITY II. ANALYZING SEVERAL GENRES

The purpose of this activity is to build understanding that many different ways of loving are expressed in literature.

1. **Review various selections** that deal with kinds of love, including friendship. **Select** at least three literary works for your analysis.

2. **Decide** what type of love is discussed or described in each selection. **Construct a definition** of the type of love that is expressed in each selection. (Hint: Identify specific behaviors or actions that you think are loving. Include motivation as a behavior.)

3. **Compare and contrast** the different types of love. In this process you may decide that some types of love you thought were different are really the same. (Hint: Ask yourself how the actions and behaviors are the same or different.)

4. **Construct a written statement** that defines three different types of love.

READING AND STUDY SKILLS HANDBOOK

LESSON 1: *Finding the Main Idea of a Paragraph*

▆▆ EXPLANATION AND EXAMPLES

When you read, it is important that you understand and remember the material. You might want to discuss it later in class or with friends, or you may have to take a test about it. One useful technique that can help you understand and remember information is to find the main idea in a paragraph.

The **main idea** is the overriding or most general thought the writer has about the topic of the paragraph. Although there may be several sentences in the paragraph, each of these usually provides only a *detail* about the topic. When you put all the details together, you will have the one major idea about the subject that the author wants to express.

Finding the main idea is like assembling a jigsaw puzzle. When you first open the box, there are hundreds of little pieces. Once you fit the individual pieces of the puzzle together, however, you have one complete picture—the main idea. For example, little pieces of the puzzle may illustrate part of a sail or some water; only when you combine all the pieces do you have a picture of a ship sailing on the ocean. When you find the main idea in a paragraph, then, you are deciding what the overall "picture" is.

Sometimes, the writer states the main idea for you. When this happens, the main idea usually appears at the beginnng of the paragraph. However, it can also be placed at the end of the paragraph as a concluding remark, and it can even be positioned in the middle of the paragraph. In the following example, the main idea is stated at the very beginning of a paragraph (it is underlined for you).

Poetry is like a circus. It is full of color, motion, and excitement. It entertains, delights, and inspires the audience. Like a circus, poetry appeals to our senses: A poem can please the eyes, sing to the ears, tickle the taste buds, and create a sense of wonder along the way. (page 209)

The writer opens the preceding paragraph with the statement that poetry is similar to a circus. The next four sentences provide examples to support that statement: Poetry entertains—like a circus. Poetry inspires its audience—like a circus. Poetry appeals to our senses—like a circus. These individual details support the main idea stated in the first sentence: Poetry is like a circus.

Many times the author does *not* state main ideas at all. (One study found that only 44 percent of the paragraphs in the textbooks examined contained a stated main idea.) Generally, very few paragraphs in narrative pieces have stated main ideas. Therefore, you have to use information elsewhere in the paragraph to figure out its main idea. In other words, you need to put the pieces of the puzzle together and then decide what the picture is. Some of these details—or pieces—will be more useful than others. Let's experiment with the following paragraph. The main idea is not stated, but there are many details about the subject—the form of a poem:

The form of a poem is its overall pattern. You can get a sense of form simply by looking at a poem on the page. The poem may be broken into even parts, like bread cut into slices, or it may be presented uninterrupted, as a whole, uncut loaf. The lines of the poem may be similar in length or quite different, creating a visual pattern on the paper. Words may even be arranged to form a picture. A poet can construct a poem by using a known pattern or by making one up. In either case the finished creation will have shape and form. (page 244)

In this case the main idea is the *overriding thought that the writer has about the form of a poem*. To figure out what that main idea is, look first at the individual details:

1. The form of a poem is its overall pattern.
2. Look at a poem to get a sense of form.
3. The poem can be broken up into even parts.
4. A poem can be presented without any breaks.
5. Poem lines can be the same length or different presenting a visual pattern.
6. Words can be arranged to form a picture.
7. The poet can use a known pattern or make one up.
8. The finished poem will have shape and form.

The next step is to look for a way to categorize the details. Is there a generalization that explains what all the details add up to? Looking at the eight details above, we can see that some define form (picture, pattern, shape) and that others tell how a poet can give form to a poem. Now we can make up a short statement that expresses the main idea: *Poets can give their poems shape and form by using a variety of techniques*.

Remember, the main idea will always be the overall thought that the writer has about the subject in the paragraph. Sometimes it is actually stated in the paragraph, but most of the time it is only implied, or suggested. You must

1. study the various parts of the paragraph
2. decide what these parts are saying about the subject

3. find or think of the general sentence that best expresses the various details

ASSIGNMENTS

1. Read the following paragraph from Shirley Jackson's story "*The Sneaker Crisis*," and identify the stated main idea:

> Day after day I went around the house picking things up. I picked up books and shoes and toys and socks and shirts and gloves and boots and hats and handkerchiefs and puzzle pieces and pennies and pencils and stuffed rabbits and bones the dogs had left under the living-room chairs. I also picked up tin soldiers and plastic cars and baseball gloves and sweaters and children's pocketbooks with nickels inside and little pieces of lint off the floor.

2. In a story written by Quentin Reynolds (page 169) about a milkman named Pierre and the horse that pulls his milkwagon, the third paragraph on page 170 provides examples about the horse. These examples all support a main idea—which is stated in the paragraph. Read the entire paragraph, and find the one overall idea about Pierre's horse.

3. Turn to page 53, and read the first paragraph in the section Preview: The Short Story. What is the main idea of that paragraph? List the details in the paragraph that support the main idea you identified.

4. Find three paragraphs in this book that have stated main ideas. Identify the sentences that state the main ideas. Find three paragraphs in this book that do not have stated main ideas. For each such paragraph, tell in your own words what the main idea is.

LESSON 2: *Sequencing*

▮▮ EXPLANATION AND EXAMPLES

When you are reading, you will frequently come across stories or articles in which events are related in a certain order—according to a *sequence of events.* The text often signals the sequence for you.

Time sequence

Perhaps the easiest clue is a date or time given by the author. For example, in the following selection from Joan Aiken's story "All You've Ever Wanted," the clues to sequence are the days of the week:

> Matilda was brought up exclusively by her six aunts. These were all energetic women and so on *Monday* Matilda was taught algebra and arithmetic by her Aunt Aggie, on *Tuesday* biology by her Aunt Beattle, on *Wednesday* classics by her Aunt Cissie, on *Thursday* dancing and deportment by her Aunt Dorrie, on *Friday* essentials by her Aunt Effie, and on *Saturday* French by her Aunt Florrie. (page 66, italics added)

Other words and phrases that can signal a sequence of events include *yesterday, today, later, before, after, then, not long after, in the beginning, shortly after,* and *still later.*

Jesse Stuart uses sequence words in his description of four boys' actions. As you read this excerpt from his story "The Clearing," notice how the italicized words indicate the sequence in which the actions occur:

> Finn and I were pruning the plum trees around our garden when a rock came cracking among the branches of the tree I was pruning. *Then* we heard the Hinton boys laughing on the other side of the valley. I went back to pruning.

> *In less than a minute,* a rock hit the limb above my head, and another rock hit at Finn's feet. *Then* I came down from the tree. Finn and I started throwing rocks. *In a few minutes,* rocks were falling like hailstones around them and around us. (page 162)

Another way a writer indicates sequence is by enumerating with words such as *first, second, third, finally,* and *last.* You have probably used enumeration yourself when you explained a procedure—such as how to use a computer—to your parents or a friend.

Cause-and-effect sequence

Frequently one event causes another to happen, giving us a cause-effect sequence. Writers signal this type of sequence by using words such as *because, as a result, since, however,* and *therefore.* James Thurber's classic essay "The Night the Bed Fell" is an excellent example of how one event leads to another.

> Always a deep sleeper, slow to arouse (I had lied to Briggs) I was at first unconscious of what had happened when the iron cot rolled me onto the floor and toppled over on me. It left me still warmly bundled up and unhurt, for the bed rested above me like a canopy. Hence I did not wake up, only reached the edge of consciousness and went back. The racket, *however,* instantly awakened my mother, in the next room, who came to the immediate conclusion that her worst dread was realized; the big wooden bed upstairs had fallen on Father. She *therefore* screamed, "Let's go to your poor father!" It was this shout, rather than the noise of my cot falling that awakened Herman, in the same room with her. (page 306)

In this selection the first event—the iron cot's falling over—causes a definite chain of events: The fall makes loud noise. → Noise wakes mother.→ She concludes that the bed upstairs has fallen on the father. → Conclusion causes her to scream. → Scream wakes Herman.

Logical sequence

Finally, you need to realize that there is a logical order in which events must occur. For example, before you can have your hair cut, you have to have hair. Similarly, before your bike can be stolen, you have to own a bike. Your common sense is a very good tool to use when determining whether the order of events is logical. Ask yourself the question, Does this order make sense?

◼ ASSIGNMENTS

1. On a separate sheet put the following events in correct order from beginning to end. The events are from "Morning—The Bird Perched for Flight," page 18.

   a. It has gone miles into the sky.

   b. We park the car and find a good place to watch the launch.

   c. We wake to the alarm at four-thirty.

   d. With the morning light, Apollo 8 and its launching tower become clearer, harder, and more defined.

   e. We leave the motel at five-fifteen.

   f. "Now only thirty minutes to launch time . . . fifteen minutes . . . six minutes."

2. What words in the excerpt from "Thirteen" signal sequence? List those words on a sheet of paper.

   At first, Cress was so certain of seeing Edwin that she walked along the boardwalk, really observing. What with observing, keeping her hat on straight, and practicing on occasional strangers the look of melting suprise with which she planned to greet Edwin, the first hour went by quickly. Then suddenly the first hour was gone by, it was past three and already the wind seemed a little sharper, the sun less bright, the boardwalk less crowded. It was three-thirty. It was fifteen of four. Edwin did appear, crossing the street a block away.

3. The story "The Shepherd Boy" (page 454) has a definite order of events. Read this short selection, and outline how the first event stated below caused the chain of events to occur.

   The shepherd boy was lonely and came up with a plan to get company and have some excitement.

   a. What did this cause to happen?
   b. What did that cause?
   c. What did that cause?
   d. What did that cause?

LESSON 3: *Taking a Test*

▄▄▄ EXPLANATION AND EXAMPLES

"On Friday I will be giving you a test."

That simple sentence from a teacher will very likely stimulate a chorus of groans from students in the class. Test taking, however, need not cause fear. You can—and should—learn how to deal with tests because you will be taking tests all life long.

- *Do you want to go to college?* You most certainly will have to take many tests.
- *Do you want to drive a car?* You will have to take a written test.
- *Do you want a job?* Don't be surprised if you have to take a test.
- *Do you want a better job?* You will have to take more courses or get more specialized training—and take more tests.

Knowing how to tackle a test—in addition to studying for the test—gives you a decided advantage. Research shows that the more students know about test taking, the better they do on tests.

The rest of this lesson will outline steps for you to follow whenever you take a test. Think back to the last test you took. What did you do? What could you have done differently?

1. **Have a good attitude about taking the test.**
   Instead of thinking about what you don't know, think about what you *do* know.

2. **Survey the test.**
   Look over the whole test before you begin to write. When you skim through the test, think about the following:

   a. What kinds of questions are there?
   - True or false

- Matching items
- Completing a sentence
- Multiple choice
- Short answer
- Essay

   b. How many questions are there?

   c. How many points is each question worth?

   You want to know the types of questions because some questions take longer to answer than others. For example, marking a statement "true or false" takes considerably less time than writing an essay question. In addition, you will want to be sure to answer those questions that are worth the most points.

3. **Read the directions carefully.**
   By not reading the directions you can actually waste valuable time. Suppose the directions advise you to answer only three of the five questions on the test. If you don't read the directions and just start answering the questions, you will end up answering five questions when three answers were all you needed.

4. **If you are given options, choose the questions you are sure you can answer.**

5. **Plan your time.**
   If you must answer two essay questions, decide how much time you will need to write on each one. Perhaps you decide that ten minutes on each essay will be plenty of time. If you have fifty minutes for the entire test and spend twenty on essay questions, you have thirty minutes left to answer the other questions.

6. Answer the easy questions first.

As a result you will have a feeling of confidence and success. To begin with just skip over the questions you don't know. Put a mark by them so that you can go back to work on them later.

7. Then work on the questions that are worth the greatest number of points.

Frequently, these are the essay questions. Keep in mind the amount of time that you have decided you can spend on them.

8. Go back and answer the hard questions.

9. Leave time at the end to go over the entire test one more time.

Make sure you have answered all of the questions you are required to. You may feel a strong urge to change one of your answers at this time. Most people do. Don't make a change unless there is a very good reason.

10. Check to make sure your name is on the test before you turn it in.

■■ **PRACTICE**

The following test is based on the story, "Feathered Friend," by Arthur C. Clarke (page 54). You may have read this story already. For this exercise, take time to read it again, knowing that you are going to answer some questions about it. After you have read the story, take the test. Allow yourself fifteen minutes to take this test.

■■ **SAMPLE TEST: "FEATHERED FRIEND"**

I. *Directions.* You should answer three of the following items. The following statements are either true or false. On your paper label the ones that are true with a *T* and the ones that are false with an *F*.

A. The story takes place on the moon.
B. Claribel is Sven's pet canary.
C. Claribel catches a rare space virus.
D. The storyteller alerts the engineer to a problem with the air purifier.
E. The story ends with the death of Claribel.

II. *Directions.* You should answer four of the following items. Identify each quotation by identifying the character or speaker who says it.

A. "I don't know, I just found her like this."
B. "He's looking for Claribel. Says he can't find her anywhere."
C. "Nonsense. The alarms would have gone off."
D. "Let's have a look at her."
E. "The second alarm circuit isn't connected up yet."

III. *Directions.* You should answer three of the following questions.

A. Who is Claribel? How does she come to be in the space station?
B. Describe Claribel's condition when Sven brings her to breakfast one morning.
C. Name two ways in which Claribel proves to be a friend to the workers in the station.
D. As the storyteller watches Claribel, what does he suddenly realize about the space station? What leads him to this conclusion?

■■ **ASSIGNMENT**

Think about the last test you took.

- What subject was it in?
- What kinds of questions were on that test?
- What did you do when you took the test?
- Would you take that test any differently now?
- Write down the steps you would follow if you took that same test again tomorrow.

LESSON 4:   *Using Graphic Organizers*

■ EXPLANATION AND EXAMPLES

Every time we read, we are bombarded with pieces of information. These details and concepts may be related to information we read earlier in the selection. They may be details to support a major conclusion that comes later. It is important that we know how to keep track of or organize all these pieces of information effectively so we can remember and use them later.

Organization can be very useful. Consider this example: You have an extensive collection of albums by your favorite singers and groups. You invite several friends over to listen to the various albums. Finding the ones you and your friends decide to play is easier if you have organized them in some logical order. One system would be to put albums by female singers on one shelf, those by male singers on another shelf, and those by groups on still another shelf. If you have albums by fifteen different female singers, you may even put these in alphabetical order by singers' names.

We need to do the same type of organizing with the information—the details and concepts— we encounter when reading. One very effective way to categorize information is through the use of graphic organizers. **Graphic organizers** provide a visual representation of key facts or concepts *and their relationships*. Basically, graphic organizers help us distinguish the more important concepts from those that are of lesser importance.

Example: This textbook contains a section that describes myths and folk tales. This section points out how these two types of stories are similar and how they are different. A very simple graphic representation of the relationship of myths and folk tales follows:

Semantic webbing

A very common graphic organizer that you will find useful is semantic webbing or mapping. Read the following paragraph, and study its webs or maps.

Every story has several important elements, including plot, character, setting, and theme. These are the events, people, places, and ideas that make a short story a complete world. In most good stories these elements work together. In fact, we sometimes cannot talk about one element without also mentioning the others. This combination of elements forms a story's total effect, or overall impact on the reader. (from page 53, "Preview: The Short Story")

Example 1: Here is one way the preceding paragraph can be mapped.

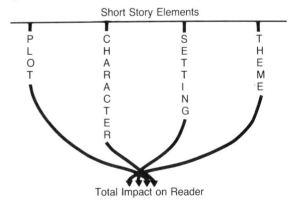

Example 2: This is another way to map the same paragraph.

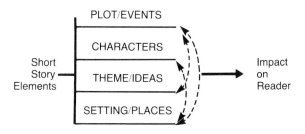

Notice that the first example illustrates the interaction of the four elements by intertwining the lines. The second example shows the relationship between the elements with the use of dotted lines. What these two examples should make clear to you is that there is no one correct way to graphically organize a selection. The organizer that works best for you may be very different from your friend's organizer. Remember that a graphic organizer is a tool to help *you* remember and construct relationships.

Story map

Another very useful graphic organizer for narrative selections is the story map. The story by Mark Twain, "The Glorious Whitewasher," has been mapped using this type of graphic organizer:

TITLE: "The Glorious Whitewasher"

SETTING: By a fence along a sidewalk

CHARACTERS: Tom Sawyer
              Ben Rogers
              Billy Foster
              Johnny Miller
              Other boys

PROBLEM: Tom has to whitewash Aunt Polly's fence instead of doing all the fun things he had planned. All his friends will make fun of him.

EVENTS: 1. Tom decides he doesn't have enough money to pay his friends to whitewash the fence.
              2. Tom gets an inspiration.
              3. Ben comes by and commiserates.
              4. Tom acts as if he's having fun.
              5. Ben gets envious and gives Tom the core of his apple so he will let Ben whitewash.
              6. Other boys give Tom things so he will let them whitewash.
              7. The fence gets whitewashed by Tom's friends.
              8. Tom ends up with a wealth of objects.

SOLUTION: Tom learns an important lesson. To make a man or boy covet a thing it is only necessary to make the thing difficult to attain.

Mapping the story in this way helps you to see the relationship between the various elements and events. This story map will be a very useful resource as you review important information about a short story for a test or homework.

ASSIGNMENTS

1. Examine one or more of the graphic organizers provided on overhead transparencies for this textbook. Explain how the organizer helps you to understand concepts about literature.

2. Read Ivan Turgenev's story "The Sparrow" (page 144). Then graphically organize this story using a story map.

3. Prepare a story map for Ray Bradbury's story "The Sound of Summer Running" (page 151).

4. Prepare a graphic organizer of your choice for any other selection in this textbook.

WRITING ABOUT LITERATURE HANDBOOK

LESSON 1: *Answering an Essay Question*

Writing is a process with several steps. When you follow these steps, any writing assignment becomes more manageable and seems easier. As a result your finished product will be thoughtful, informative, well organized, and polished. This lesson will teach you a step-by-step method to use when you are asked to analyze and write about a piece of literature.

PREWRITING

Before you begin to write, think carefully about the writing assignment, and organize your thoughts. To do so, follow these steps:

1. Read the essay question, copying down important words that tell you what is expected in your answer. Notice the key words that are underlined in the following example. Notice also that there often is a main question followed by a request for details, or further explanation.

Example of Essay Question

Write a short essay in which you tell whether or not you liked a particular work of literature. Then explain your response by answering the following questions: (a) Did the selection hold your attention? (b) Was the outcome of the selection satisfying? (c) Did you care about what happened to the main character? Support your opinions with examples.

main question

request for further explanation

2. Make a chart on which to jot down ideas in note form. The chart below helped a writer develop and organize ideas for the assignment given in Prewriting 1. The chart is based on "Rikki-tikki-tavi" (page 2).

SAMPLE CHART: NOTES FOR ANSWERING AN ESSAY QUESTION		
QUESTION	**ANSWER**	**EXAMPLES**
a. DID THE SELECTION HOLD YOUR ATTENTION?	I wondered who would win—the evil snakes or the loyal Rikki.	Nag plans to kill Teddy and his family. Rikki can save them if he is alert and brave.
	I learned interesting facts about animals.	Mongooses like people. Snakes are natural enemies of mongooses.
b. WAS THE OUTCOME OF THE SELECTION SATISFYING?	The ending was logical.	Mongooses often kill snakes and eat their eggs. Rikki works hard for his victory.
	The friendly, loyal character defeated the evil characters.	Rikki saves the family and all the other animals. He is rewarded by the humans.
c. DID YOU CARE ABOUT WHAT HAPPENED TO THE MAIN CHARACTER?	I cared about Rikki. I wanted him to succeed.	Rikki is treated well by the family, and he vows to protect them.

WRITING PARAGRAPH BY PARAGRAPH

After you have put your thoughts down as notes on a chart or an outline, you may follow these steps to present them in carefully constructed paragraphs:

1. Restate the question as a statement. This sentence will be your thesis statement, a clear statement of your central idea. You may follow the thesis statement with one or more sentences telling how your answer will proceed.

Example of Thesis Statement

"Rikki-tikki-tavi" by Rudyard Kipling is a particularly exciting, absorbing story that holds a reader's attention throughout, provides a satisfying conclusion, and presents a character that a reader can care about very much.

2. Begin each of the middle paragraphs of your answer with a topic sentence, which states the main idea, purpose, or plan for the paragraph. Each sentence that follows the topic sentence should support it. The supporting sentences can be examples, quotations, or incidents taken directly from the selection.

Example of Topic Sentence and Supporting Example for Second Paragraph

The story captures the reader's attention immediately and holds it page after page. With his first sentence Kipling arouses interest by stating that the story is about a "great war that Rikki-tikki-tavi fought single-handed. . . ."

3. Write a concluding paragraph. Begin it with the idea expressed in your thesis statement, but use different words.

Example of Topic Sentence in Concluding Paragraph

From its beginning to its end, Kipling's "Rikki-tikki-tavi" interests the reader with its exciting action and sympathetically drawn main character.

You may round out this paragraph by adding other thoughts about your reaction to the story. For example, who else do you think would enjoy the story?

WRITING A ONE-PARAGRAPH ANSWER

If your answer is limited to one paragraph, begin with a strong topic sentence that restates the question in the essay assignment. Each of your following sentences should develop one aspect of the topic sentence. You must give evidence to support your topic sentence.

REVISING AND EDITING

Now that you have completed the first draft, it is important that you review your work. Use the following checklist to revise, edit, and proofread your written work. Prepare a final version.

I. Content and Organization
   A. Have you turned the assignment question into a thesis statement?
   B. Does each following paragraph have a topic sentence and supporting details?
   C. Does the concluding paragraph restate the thesis statement and perhaps add further insights and comments?
II. Grammar, Usage, Mechanics
   A. Have you used complete sentences?
   B. Have you used correct punctuation, capitalization, and spelling?
III. Word Choice, Style
   A. Have you used appropriate words?
   B. Have you avoided wordiness?
   C. Have you varied sentence length?

ASSIGNMENTS

1. Finish the answer to the question presented in this lesson about "Rikki-tikki-tavi." You may use the information on the chart.
2. Do an assignment called "Answering an Essay Question" on page 14, 58, 135, 434, or 466. Be sure to use examples from the literature to support your opinions.

LESSON 2: *Writing About Plot*

The **plot** of a story is the sequence of events or actions that occurs within the course of that story. The plot usually hinges on a conflict, or struggle, that the story's main character must face.

CONCEPTS TO REMEMBER

A plot is made up of several stages:

1. **Beginning of a story:** Here we learn about the characters, the setting, and the situation in which the main character finds himself or herself.
2. **Conflict:** As the story progresses, we find out about the conflict that the main character faces.
3. **Climax:** At the point of highest interest, or the climax, of the story, we form a good idea of how the story will end.
4. **Resolution:** After the climax the plot moves on to the resolution. Here we see how the conflict is resolved, or settled. We learn what takes place as a result of settling the conflict.

TYPICAL ESSAY QUESTION

When you are asked to write about the plot of a story, you will often have to answer a question like the following one:

Analyze the plot by discussing its major parts. First identify the conflict, and discuss who or what is engaged in a struggle. Explain what problems make it difficult for the main character to resolve the conflict. Tell how the story concludes.

PREWRITING

Break down the assignment into its various parts. Draw a chart with space in which to make notes about each part of the assignment. A sample chart appears at the top of the opposite page. Then think about each part of the assignment. Use the following guidelines and questions as aids to your thinking and note making.

1. Identify the conflict in the story, and clarify for yourself who or what is involved in the conflict. Ask yourself questions such as the following:

   a. Is the conflict between two people? If so, is the conflict about another person? About a place? About a possession? About an event?
   b. Is the conflict between a person and something in nature, such as an animal or an environment?
   c. Is the conflict between a person and society? What is the problem?
   d. Is the conflict within a person's mind?

2. Examine the story closely to figure out why the main character has trouble resolving, or settling, the conflict. Ask yourself questions such as the following:

   a. Is the main character physically unable to resolve the conflict? Is he or she too far away or too weak or handicapped in some way?
   b. Is the main character too confused to resolve the conflict? Is he or she lacking some important information that is necessary to resolve the conflict?

3. Make sure you understand exactly what happens at the end of the story. Ask yourself the following questions:

   a. Does the main character resolve the conflict for himself or herself? If so, does the character use intelligence or physical strength or something else to resolve the conflict?
   b. Does another character come to the rescue and resolve the conflict?
   c. Is the character satisfied with the solution?

SAMPLE CHART: ANALYZING PLOT	
SELECTION: "The Sneaker Crisis"	
PART OF ESSAY QUESTION	**NOTES FOR ANSWER**
1. WHAT IS THE CONFLICT? WHO OR WHAT IS IN-VOLVED IN THE CONFLICT?	The conflict is between Laurie and his mother. Laurie blames his mother for the lost sneaker. The mother blames his carelessness.
2. WHAT PROBLEMS MAKE IT DIFFICULT FOR THE MAIN CHARACTER TO RESOLVE THE CONFLICT?	The conflict can be solved only after the sneaker is found. Laurie insists that he already looked under the bed. The other children interfere. Jannie tries to find a solution in her reading. Sally tries magic.
3. HOW DOES THE STORY CONCLUDE?	The sneaker is found under Laurie's bed. Because Laurie claimed to have looked there already, he is proven care-less.

▮▮ WRITING PARAGRAPH BY PARAGRAPH

You may be able to answer the essay question in a single paragraph, or you may take more space to develop your answer. Refer to the chart with the notes you made in response to the questions suggested under Prewriting. Then convert your notes to sentences and paragraphs, following the steps listed here. (If your answer is just one paragraph long, think of these steps as applying to each sentence rather than to each paragraph.)

1. In your introductory paragraph write a thesis statement, putting the central idea of the essay question into your own words. You may follow the thesis statement with one or more sentences telling how your essay will proceed.

Example of Thesis Statement

In the plot of "The Sneaker Crisis" Shirley Jackson shows us an everyday conflict between a mother and son. Interference by other children makes it difficult for the characters to resolve the conflict.

2. In each of the middle paragraphs present a topic sentence based on your chart notes. Each topic sentence should answer one of the questions on the chart. After each topic sentence, offer supporting details.

Example of Topic Sentence and Supporting Detail

Interference by Laurie's brothers and sisters makes it difficult for Laurie and his mother to find the sneaker. Sally gets in the way with her magic dance through the house. Inspired by one of her detective stories, Jannie suggests "reconstructing the crime." This method takes time and produces a lost hat but not the sneaker.

3. In your concluding paragraph restate your thesis statement, using different words from those in your introductory paragraph. If you wish to include an additional comment about the plot, you may state whether you found the conclusion satisfactory.

▮▮ REVISING AND EDITING

See Lesson 1 for detailed reminders about improving your writing.

▮▮ ASSIGNMENTS

1. Use the chart given in this lesson and ideas of your own to analyze the plot of Shirley Jackson's "Sneaker Crisis" (page 59).
2. Complete an assignment called "Writing About Plot" on page 85, 126, 167, 279, 443, or 461.

Writing About Literature Handbook 573

LESSON 3: *Writing a Character Sketch*

A **character** is a person or animal presented in a work of literature. An author may use several techniques to make a character seem real. For example, an author may (1) describe the character's physical appearance, (2) present the character's speech, actions, thoughts, feelings, and motivations, and (3) illustrate reactions of other people or animals to the character. As a reader you can show your understanding of a character by writing a character sketch.

▓▓ CONCEPTS TO REMEMBER

1. A **character sketch** is a short written portrait of a character from literature or real life. In this lesson we will use the term *character sketch* to refer to writing about characters from literature only. The character sketch zooms in on just a few incidents, scenes, or encounters in order to illustrate those qualities.
2. A character in literature has outstanding traits. *Trait* is simply another word for "quality" or "characteristic." *Outstanding* in this usage simply means "most important."

▓▓ TYPICAL ESSAY QUESTION

When you are asked to analyze a character in a piece of literature, you may be asked to examine that character's personality and patterns of behavior. A typical assignment follows:

Choose a character, and discuss the character's outstanding traits.

▓▓ PREWRITING

1. Think about which character from a particular selection interests you the most. When you have decided on that character, review the selection, asking yourself the following questions:

   a. Who is the character? What is his or her name, age, job, or role?
   b. What does the character look like?
   c. How does the character speak? How does the character act? Which words or actions in particular illustrate what the character is like?
   d. Does the character have any unusual or noteworthy habits?
   e. What details can you mention to illustrate the character's thoughts and feelings?
   f. What motivates, or drives, this character to act the way he or she acts?
   g. Does the character remain the same from the beginning to the end of the literary selection, or does the character change? If the character changes, tell how.
   h. How do other characters in the selection respond to the character about whom you are writing?

2. To help you organize your ideas about the character's outstanding traits, record the answers to the preceding questions on a chart such as the one on the opposite page.

▓▓ WRITING PARAGRAPH BY PARAGRAPH

If your answer is just one paragraph long, think of the following steps as applying to each sentence rather than to each paragraph.

1. Begin your introductory paragraph with a thesis statement in which you identify the character, the work in which the character appears, and the character's outstanding traits.

Example of Introductory Paragraph
   In "Lucas and Jake" the author, Paul Darcy Boles, shows Lucas' three outstanding traits: a desire to be recognized as special, a gift for storytelling, and a tendency to show off a little. Boles allows us to see Lucas' traits by providing details about his appearance, his speech and actions, his thoughts and feelings, his motivations, and the reactions of others to Lucas.

CHARACTER TRAIT CHART

SELECTION: "Lucas and Jake"

CHARACTER: Lucas

OUTSTANDING TRAITS: wants to be recognized as special; a good storyteller; a bit of a showoff

DETAILS USED TO REVEAL OUTSTANDING TRAITS

PHYSICAL APPEARANCE	SPEECH AND ACTIONS	THOUGHTS AND FEELINGS
His teeth are "largely his own." He has hard, "bronzed knuckles." He has white hair which makes him "resemble a tough Santa Claus." His joints creak.	*Speech:* He often speaks in fragments and slang and uses imaginative figurative language, such as "Put him up at the moat . . . he'd eat 'em like cornflakes." *Actions:* He fibs to the boys, saying that Jake is a Cape lion. He reaches into Jake's cage to retrieve the boys' yo-yo.	*Thoughts:* He thinks that as a boy he would feel "footloose and free as a big bird." He thinks that he needs someone to look up to him and that no one does. *Feelings:* He feels young again after gaining the boys' respect. "Lucas could feel the radiance of the day pour itself into his veins as though he . . . were about twelve again."
MOTIVATIONS OR GOALS	CHANGES IN CHARACTER	OTHERS' REACTIONS TO CHARACTER
to feel important and special to entertain the boys	from not feeling special to feeling special: He says, "Jake's my special talent." "Lucas smiled. It was the smile of a man who'd earned something: more than status."	Because the boys are afraid of Jake, they are awed by Lucas' "bravery." Ridefield tries to speak but is unable. Ridefield and Paddy show their respect for Lucas when they shake his hand.

The changes in Lucas also tell us something about the kind of person Lucas is.

2. In each of the paragraphs that follow, present a topic sentence in which you identify one outstanding trait of the character. For the remaining sentences of the paragraph, provide details from the chart that support your topic sentence.

3. In the concluding paragraph restate your thesis, using different words. You may end your character sketch by commenting in general on the character and indicating whether you were impressed or otherwise affected by the character.

REVISING AND EDITING

See Lesson 1 for detailed reminders about improving your writing.

ASSIGNMENTS

1. Use the chart for Paul Darcy Boles's "Lucas and Jake" (page 96) to write about Lucas' outstanding traits. Tell what these traits are and how they are revealed.

2. Complete an assignment called "Writing a Character Sketch" on page 115, 156, 174, 447, or 472.

LESSON 4: *Writing a Story*

A **short story** is a brief work of prose fiction. Important elements in any short story include plot, character, and setting. In order to plan and write an effective story, you must consider each of these elements.

CONCEPTS TO REMEMBER

1. **Plot** is the sequence of events, or what happens in a story. Each event causes or leads to the next. At the center of a plot is a problem, or conflict, that the main character faces. For example, this problem may be a personal goal, a competition with another person, or a struggle against hardship. The story builds toward its point of highest interest, the climax. The character solves the problem and learns something about himself or herself.
2. A **character** is an individual in a story. Most stories have only one or two major characters. They should have believable personality or character traits and clear motivations for their actions.
3. The **setting** is the time and place in which a story happens. Details of setting can give a story mood, or atmosphere. For example, a story may be gloomy or cheerful.

TYPICAL ASSIGNMENT

When asked to write a story, you will often be given an assignment like this one:

Write a short story that has a logical sequence of events. Describe your characters and setting clearly.

PREWRITING

1. To find an idea for your story, try to think of an interesting problem, an unusual person, or a colorful place. Most people write best when they write about things they know. Perhaps your hobbies and interests—for example, baseball or dancing—can inspire you. You may also want to page through a magazine or travel book. Some action, face, or location may give you an idea. Keep in mind that a story can be about very common, everyday occurrences—such as a school election. List some different ideas on a chart like the one that follows.
2. From your chart choose the problem, character, and setting for your story. Ask yourself the following questions: In what ways will your character react to the problem? How will the problem be solved?

POSSIBLE IDEAS FOR A STORY		
PROBLEMS	**CHARACTERS**	**SETTINGS**
lost ticket	sports fan	World Series
limited oxygen supply	deep-sea diver	underwater colony
stolen deed to gold mine	prospector	old West
desire to be human	robot	computer store
strange messages in lunch bag	student	school cafeteria
engine failure	stunt pilot	over a mountain range
lost in a wilderness	camper	mountain forest
escape from a sea creature	swimmer	lake
school play auditions	shy student	school auditorium
drought	farmer	farm in summer
noises in the attic	babysitter	neighbor's house
school election	students	school

CHARACTERS								
CHARACTER	PHYSICAL TRAITS					PERSONALITY OR CHARACTER TRAITS		
	AGE	HEIGHT, WEIGHT	HAIR	DRESS	FEATURES	PERSONALITY	SPEECH	BEHAVIOR
Janet	13	5 feet, 2 inches; 95 pounds	brown, long, worn up	skirts and sweaters	freckles, glasses	enthusiastic, optimistic, hardworking	clear, careful	nice to others, jumps to conclusions
Steven	12	5 feet, 9 inches; 115 pounds	blond, very short	jeans	sloped shoulders	acts tough, determined	not talkative	serious, sometimes abrupt

SETTING			
HISTORICAL PERIOD, YEAR, SEASON, TIME OF DAY	LOCATION (CITY, COUNTRY, INDOORS, OUTDOORS)	WEATHER	OTHER DETAILS
present day, beginning of school year, during school time	a suburban junior high school	rainy	gray hallways decorated with bright campaign posters

3. Try to imagine how your characters look, sound, and act. Then fill in a chart like the one called "Characters" above. You may not use all this information in the actual story, but the chart will help you to picture the characters as believable people. The sample chart contains information about characters that one writer has in mind for a story.

4. Picture your setting. Then fill in a chart like the one called "Setting" above. You may not actually use all this information in your story, but the details will help you to picture the setting. The sample chart contains information about the setting that one writer is planning for a story. Imagine the place and time of the story as well as the weather and other details.

5. Write an outline to help organize your thoughts. In the outline that follows, the sections printed in boldface type are the steps that every story outline should include. The sections in italics are examples from the two charts on this page.

STORY OUTLINE

I. **Beginning**
   A. **Introduce the main character.** *Janet is thirteen.*
   B. **Describe the setting.** *It is a rainy week, the first week of school in a suburban junior high school.*
   C. **Begin the plot.** *Janet is running for class president.*

II. **Middle**
   A. **Introduce the character's problem.** *Janet finds that some of her campaign posters have been destroyed.*
   B. **Introduce minor characters.** *Steven is Janet's opponent. He tells Janet that he will make sure that she loses.*
   C. **Build toward the point of highest interest, or climax.** *On election day Steven wins by a vote of 34–32. Janet tells others that Steven obviously voted twice because the class has only sixty-five students.*

III. Ending

    A. Reach the point of highest interest. *Alice, Janet's friend, admits that she cast the extra vote to help Janet win.*

    B. Wind down the action. *Janet apologizes to Steven.*

    C. Give the final outcome. *Janet vows not to jump to conclusions.*

6. When you have completed your outline, recite your plot aloud. Be sure that your plot builds in interest to a climax and then tells how the problem was finally solved.

7. Plan to use dialogue, or conversation between characters. Dialogue makes your story more realistic and more exciting. Remember the following points when you write dialogue.

    a. All words spoken by characters must be surrounded by quotation marks. A direct quotation can come at the beginning or the end of a sentence.

    b. A direct quotation begins with a capital letter. If a quotation is interrupted, the second part begins with a small letter.

    c. A direct quotation is set off from the rest of a sentence by commas. If a direct quotation is interrupted, commas are placed before and after the interruption. The comma before a direct quotation falls outside the quotation marks. The comma—or any punctuation—after a direct quotation falls inside the quotation marks.

    Examples

    • She smiled and thought, "I think I am going to win this one!"

    • "No, I am the best person for the job," corrected Steven.

    • "Jan," he said with a laugh, "I'm going to make sure that you lose this election."

    d. Dialogue is less formal than other kinds of writing. To make your characters sound natural, you may use short sentences and contractions in dialogue.

    e. In a conversation between characters, start a new paragraph each time the speaker changes.

    f. Be careful not to use the word *said* too often. Use other, livelier verbs, such as *whispered, yelled, mumbled, crowed,* and *confessed.*

8. When you have completed your outline, choose a title for your story. The title may refer to an important event, object, character, or setting in the story.

▄▄▄ WRITING PARAGRAPH BY PARAGRAPH

1. Following your outline, begin your first paragraph by describing your main character and your setting. The first paragraph should also introduce the plot with one important action. You may wish to have your main character speak.

Example

    Janet pinned up her hair and put on her glasses in order to look official. Now that she was running for president of the seventh grade, she planned to work hard and look the part. Later, as she walked down the halls of the Valley Junior High School, she looked at her bright campaign posters on the gray walls. She smiled and thought, "I think I am going to win this one!"

2. In the next paragraph introduce the character's problem. Describe the problem in detail, and include the character's reaction. Describe minor characters who are involved in the problem.

Example

    As she rounded the corner to the math room, Janet spotted two of her posters on the floor. Someone had torn them up. Janet scooped up the colorful scraps of paper. As she walked away with the pieces, she passed Steven, her opponent.

"Jan," he said with a laugh, "I'm going to make sure that you lose this election."

3. In the paragraph or paragraphs that follow, build suspense as the story moves toward the point of highest interest, the climax, and the character tries to solve his or her problem. Be sure that your character acts according to the information in your chart for characters.
4. In the final paragraph or two, present the climax. Be sure that the solution to the character's problem is believable. End by showing what the character learned from the problem.

▉▉▉ REVISING AND EDITING

Once you have finished the first draft, you must take time to polish it into an improved second draft. Read your story aloud. Use the following checklist to revise, proofread, and edit your writing.

I. Content
   A. Does your title point to something important in the story and grab the reader's interest?
   B. Have you included details that describe your characters and setting?
   C. Do you present the main character's problem clearly? Does each event of the plot grow logically from what happened before?
   D. Is your climax a clear solution to the problem? Does your plot end soon after the climax? Do you show the main character's reaction to the climax?
   E. Do you use dialogue to make the story more interesting and realistic?

II. Style
   A. Have you cut out unnecessary details?
   B. Have you used colorful adjectives and verbs wherever possible?
   C. Does your dialogue sound real?
   D. Do you use both long and short sentences for variety?

III. Grammar, Usage, Mechanics
   A. Is each sentence complete (no fragments, no run-ons)?
   B. Are all words spelled correctly? If you are not sure of the spelling of a word, have you consulted a dictionary?
   C. Have you punctuated and capitalized your sentences correctly? In dialogue have you used quotation marks and capital letters correctly?
   D. Do you begin a new paragraph whenever the subject, time, or place changes or whenever the speaker in a dialogue changes?

▉▉▉ ASSIGNMENTS

1. Complete the story begun in this lesson by using the charts. You may follow the outline to the end of the story, or you may create your own ending if you wish. Give the story a title. Be sure that your plot develops as a logical sequence of events. In addition, use vivid details of character and setting.
2. Do an assignment called "Writing a Story" (page 14, 72, 174, 279, or 461). Your plot should be a logical sequence of events. Describe your characters and setting clearly.

LESSON 5: *Writing About Poetry*

Reading or listening to a poem is a rich experience. In addition to engaging your mind, the poet stimulates your senses and stirs your emotions. The full power of a poem does not come merely from its word-by-word meaning. Rather, the power of a poem grows out of the interplay of the many poetic techniques that the poet uses to bring an idea to life. When you analyze a poem, you should consider how these individual techniques add up to produce the poem's overall impact, or total effect.

CONCEPTS TO REMEMBER

1. The **total effect** of a poem is the overall impact that it has on the reader or listener. The total effect of a poem is made up of its meaning, its sound, its images, and its figurative language.
2. **Sound devices:** Many sound devices contribute to the poem's effect. These devices include

   Alliteration: the repeating of consonant sounds, usually at the beginnings of words
   Onomatopoeia: the use of a word or phrase whose sound imitates or suggests its meaning
   Rhythm: the pattern created by arranging stressed and unstressed syllables
   Rhyme: the repeating at regular intervals of similar or identical sounds

3. **Images:** The poet also relies on images, or mental pictures created with words, which appeal to one or more of the senses—sight, sound, taste, smell, touch.
4. **Figurative language:** The poet uses language that stretches words beyond their usual meanings. The most common figures of speech are

   Simile: A simile is a stated comparison between two otherwise unlike things. The comparison uses the word *like* or *as.*
   Metaphor: A metaphor is an implied comparison between two things. The comparison does not use the word *like* or *as.*

Personification: Personification is a figure of speech in which the poet gives human qualities to an animal, object, or idea.

TYPICAL ESSAY QUESTION

When you are asked to write about poetry, you may find yourself answering an assignment such as the following:

Write about the total effect of a poem. First describe the poem's overall impact on you. Explain the poem's meaning. Then give examples of the sounds, imagery, and figurative language that help to create the poem's impact.

PREWRITING

1. Read the poem out loud. Then reread it silently, thinking about its **meaning,** or the central idea or emotion behind the poem. If it will help you, paraphrase the poem, restating it in your own words. If you still have difficulty grasping the poem's meaning, ask yourself these questions:

   a. Does the poem spotlight a person, place, thing, idea, or feeling?
   b. What emotion do you feel when you read the poem?

2. Read the poem again, asking yourself the following questions about the techniques:

   a. **Sound:** What is the rhythm of the poem? Is it regular or irregular? Fast or slow? Gentle or driving? Does the poet use alliteration, onomatopoeia, or rhyme? How does each of these techniques add to the poem's meaning, emotion, and music?

   b. **Imagery:** What images does the poet use? Which seem most vivid? To which senses does each image appeal? What do these images add to the meaning and emotion of the poem?

TOTAL EFFECT OF A POEM			
SELECTION: "This Land Is Your Land"			
MEANING	**SOUND**	**IMAGERY**	**FIGURATIVE LANGUAGE**
Paraphrase: This is a great, vast country. It is rich in beauty and belongs to all of us. *Emotion:* pride, happiness, patriotism	*Rhythm:* regular, rolling *Alliteration:* "land is your land"; "roamed and rambled"; "followed my footsteps"; "sparkling sands"; "diamond deserts"; "wheatfields waving" *Rhyme:* occasional end rhyme: "highway/skyway," "strolling/rolling"	*Images of sight:* "redwood forest"; "Gulf Stream waters"; "endless skyway"; "sparkling sands"; "diamond deserts" *Images of motion:* "wheatfields waving"; "dust clouds rolling"	*Metaphor:* "ribbon of highway" *Personification:* "her diamond deserts"

c. **Figurative language:** What examples of simile, metaphor, and personification can you find? What do these figures of speech contribute to the poem?

3. After you have thought about the meaning of the poem and have looked carefully at the techniques used in the poem, prepare a chart that will help you see how the techniques contribute to the meaning and how the poem as a whole affects you. One reader of "This Land Is Your Land" (page 213) prepared the chart above.

▮▮ WRITING PARAGRAPH BY PARAGRAPH

If your answer is just one paragraph, think of the following steps as applying to each sentence rather than to each paragraph.

1. Begin your introductory paragraph with a thesis statement, which should restate the major points made in the assignment. In other words, the thesis statement should refer briefly to the poem's impact on you, its meaning, and those techniques that the poet uses to create the poem's impact. The introductory paragraph can also include other general thoughts about the poem before you go on to discuss the specifics.

Example of Thesis Statement
In "This Land Is Your Land" Woody Guthrie uses sound, imagery, and figurative language to celebrate this country and to create an inspiring effect.

2. In each of the following paragraphs, focus on one technique. Supply examples of each technique.

3. In the concluding paragraph restate your thesis, using different words.

▮▮ REVISING AND EDITING

See Lesson 1 for detailed reminders about how to improve your writing.

▮▮ ASSIGNMENTS

1. Use the chart in this lesson to finish writing about the total effect of Woody Guthrie's "This Land Is Your Land" (page 213).
2. Do the assignment called "Writing About Poetry" on page 277 or page 281, or choose another poem from this book and write about its total effect. Explain which techniques contribute to that effect. Use specific examples to support your views.

Writing About Literature Handbook 581

LESSON 6: *Writing a Poem*

To write a poem, you should first understand the qualities that make poetry sparkle and sing.

CONCEPTS TO REMEMBER

1. Poetry contains colorful language. **Concrete language** is specific language that appeals to the senses. **Images** are pictures made with words. **Figurative language**—similes and metaphors—makes unusual comparisons. A **simile** compares seemingly unlike things using a comparing word such as *like* or *as*. A **metaphor** compares seemingly unlike things without direct comparing words.
2. Poetry uses several sound techniques. **Repetition** is the repeated use of sounds, words, phrases, or lines. **Alliteration** is the repetition of consonant sounds, often at the beginnings of words. **Rhythm** is the pattern of beats made by stressed and unstressed syllables. **Onomatopoeia** is the use of words whose sounds imitate or suggest their meanings.
3. Every poem has an overall pattern, or **form.** Some poems are broken up into groups of lines, or **stanzas.** Some have a set number of syllables in each line.
4. A poem can be about anything at all, but it should include the poet's attitude or feelings toward the subject.

TYPICAL ASSIGNMENT

When you are asked to write a poem, you may be asked to do an assignment like the following:

Write a poem on any subject. Use at least three of the following techniques: images, figurative language (simile and metaphor), repetition, alliteration, and onomatopoeia. Use concrete language that appeals to the senses. You may choose the form of your poem, but do not use rhyme.

PRACTICING POETIC TECHNIQUES

Practice poetic techniques to prepare yourself to write a poem and to help you find a subject.

1. **Concrete language:** Copy the following chart, and finish filling it in. For each general word or sentence, write a concrete, specific word or sentence. The first two have been done for you as examples.

GENERAL	CONCRETE, SPECIFIC
animal	koala
I feel nervous.	My stomach is churning.
flower	
vacation	
Summer is fun.	
car	
I am tired.	
The lawn is pretty.	

2. **Colorful details:** Choose one of the following items, or name any item you wish: turpentine, a firefly, a tornado, a lemon. Then fill in a chart like the one that follows. On your chart write five sense descriptions of the item. Appeal to all five of the senses. After each description tell which sense is involved.

ITEM	SENSE DESCRIPTIONS	SENSE
peach	1. an orange-pink globe 2. fuzzy and fat 3. cold, crisp skin 4. I slurp its sweet juice. 5. fresh and sweet smelling	sight touch, sight touch hearing, taste smell

3. **Similes:** Write down five of the following items or any items of your choice: a basketball hoop, the sun, a lizard, spring, pizza, homework,

sandpaper, happiness, a dog's ear, a mirror, a comma, carrots, a fire drill. Use each item as the first word of a sentence that you will complete with an unusual comparison, or a simile. Use *like* in three of your answers; use *as* in two.

Examples
- Carrots are like crunchy spears.
- A lizard is as slippery as a wet bar of soap.

4. **Metaphors:** Choose one of the following items, or name any item you wish: a hamburger, a bridge, sleep, hunger, a test, a cloud. Then write five different metaphors for the item. Begin each metaphor by naming the object. Try to make vivid comparisons.

Examples
- A cloud is a cluster of doves.
- A cloud is a wisp of winter breath.

5. **Vivid verbs:** Replace the italicized verbs in the following sentences with vivid verbs.

Example
- The jaguar *walked* through the ravine.
- The jaguar slinked through the ravine.

a. The ice skater *moved* across the lake.
b. The cafeteria tray *fell* to the floor.
c. The dolphin *dove* through the hoop.
d. Snow *covered* the ground.
e. My head *hurt* during the exam.

6. **Alliteration:** Write a three-line nonrhyming poem in which almost every word in a line begins with the same consonant sound. You may change the sound with each line. You may use one of the following subjects, or you may use a subject of your own: winter winds, gossiping geese, silly students, tennis teams.

Example
Frogs *f*requently *ph*one *f*avorite *f*riends.

7. **Onomatopoeia:** Copy the following chart, and fill it in. Beside each item in the chart, write

three words whose sounds imitate the item. The first item has been completed to serve as an example.

ITEMS	WORDS WITH ONOMATOPOEIA		
dripping faucet typewriter diving board chalk on a black-board wolf water boiling	splash	splatter	plop

8. **Repetition:** Write an eight-line nonrhyming poem that uses repetition. Begin the first line with the words "In September I am ____." Complete the line with an imaginative statement. Begin the second line with the words "In June I will be ____," followed by another vivid statement. Repeat and alternate these beginnings through the entire poem.

Example
In September I am a simple sentence.
In June I will be a whole book.
In September I am a shaking mouse.
In June I will be a kangaroo on roller skates.

9. **Form:** Write a two-stanza poem with four lines in each stanza. Do not use rhyme. In the first stanza vividly describe one of the items in column A. In the second stanza describe the matching item in column B.

COLUMN A	COLUMN B
bad weather an elephant's ears the day it snowed sand a tree in winter a vegetable garden	your reaction to it an elephant's trunk the day it rained fish the same tree in spring eating vegetables

PREWRITING

1. An idea for a poem can come to you in many ways. You may see a striking image in your mind. You may want to express a strong emotion. You may hear a word and like its sound. You may begin a brief practice exercise (such as those above) and find yourself writing a whole poem. If you have difficulty finding a subject, the following list of general ideas may help.

    a. a person (you, a stranger, a celebrity)
    b. an animal (real or imaginary)
    c. an object (natural or artificial)
    d. a scene (real or imaginary)
    e. an event (real or imaginary)
    f. an emotion (something you feel or you would like to feel)

2. After you choose your subject, close your eyes, and try to picture it in detail. Ask yourself what you see, hear, taste, smell, and touch when you think of the subject. How does the subject make you feel?

3. To help you to explore your thoughts, prepare notes for your poem. In the following sample of notes, the sections printed in boldface type are advice for every writer of a poem. The sections in italics are examples of one writer's ideas for a poem.

POETRY NOTES

I. **Content**
   A. **State the subject of your poem.** *a visit to a cave in winter*
   B. **Tell how the subject makes you feel.** *moved, frightened, awed*

II. **Language**
   A. **Write specific images that apply to your subject and that appeal to the senses.**
      1. **Write an image of sight.** *icicle fangs*
      2. **Write an image of sound.** *Boots crunch on the snowy cave floor.*
      3. **Write an image of taste.** *The snow tasted salty and metallic.*
      4. **Write an image of smell.** *the smell of oil from the lantern*
      5. **Write an image of touch.** *The ice stings my fingers.*
   B. **Write figurative language.**
      1. **Write at least one simile.** *The cave is as dark as the inside of a bear's belly.*
      2. **Write at least one metaphor.** *The cave entrance is a hungry mouth.*

III. **Sound**
   Decide what sounds fit your subject and your images.
   A. **Write at least one example of alliteration.** B*oots* b*ite the* b*itter snow.*
   B. **Write at least one example of onomatopoeia.** *Icicle fangs drip and drop.*
   C. **Write at least one phrase or line that you will repeat in the poem.** *Still, the ice cave calls me back.*

IV. **Form**
   A. **Describe the form of your poem.** *Free verse (no particular number of beats per line), one stanza, six lines*

WRITING LINE BY LINE

1. In your first line identify your subject. Use concrete language and sense details.

    Example
    I crawled inside the ice cave, clawing snow.

2. In the lines that follow, use the ideas and words that occurred to you when you worked on your poetry notes. Use one of these details per line, or combine two in a single line. Add connecting words *(and, but, or, for, since, because)*, colorful adjectives, and vivid verbs.

    Example
    The cavern smelled of metal and salt.
    It was dark, and ice fangs dripped and dropped.
    Had I been caught inside a hungry mouth?

3. If you have chosen a specific form for your

poem, try to fit your ideas into this form. You may need to change the word order and to leave out some of your ideas. If you have not chosen a specific form, decide whether or not you will break your poem into stanzas. Decide what lines will begin the new stanzas.

4. The last line or lines of your poem should present a striking image. This image should sum up your feelings about the subject, or it should repeat an important phrase that you have used elsewhere in the poem.

Examples
- I am trapped inside an ice cube for the night.
- Still, the ice cave calls me back.

5. When you have finished the first draft of your poem, choose a title. It can be the subject, an important image, or a phrase that is repeated in the poem.

▨ REVISING AND EDITING

Once you have finished the first draft, you must take time to polish it into an improved second draft.

1. Read your poem aloud.
2. Do you use striking images that appeal to several senses?
3. Do you use at least one simile and metaphor?
4. Do you use alliteration, onomatopoeia, and repetition?
5. Do you use colorful adjectives and vivid verbs?

6. Is your poem written in complete sentences and punctuated correctly? Does it flow naturally?

▨ ASSIGNMENTS

1. Complete the poem begun in the lesson. First look at the sample lines, and choose those you want to use. Then add connecting words. In addition, add one striking image, one simile, and one metaphor of your own. Give the poem a title.

2. Do an assignment called "Writing a Poem" (page 233, 240, 250, 254, or 281). Be sure to use at least three of the following techniques: images, figurative language (simile and metaphor), repetition, alliteration, and onomatopoeia. Use concrete language that appeals to the senses. You may choose the form of your poem, but do not use rhyme.

3. Write a tongue twister, a short poem that is difficult to pronounce. Use many examples of alliteration and onomatopoeia. Use concrete language that appeals to the senses. Do not use rhyme.

4. Write a cinquain, a Japanese poetry form. In line one write two syllables. Line one is also the title. In line two write four syllables to describe the item in line one. In line three write six syllables that tell what the item does. In line four write eight syllables that give your feelings about the item. In line five write two syllables that have the same meaning as the title.

LESSON 7: *Writing About Nonfiction*

Nonfiction is factual prose writing. It provides true accounts of real people in real situations. Autobiographies, biographies, diaries, journals, essays, and magazine and newspaper articles are all examples of this kind of writing. Whether a piece of nonfiction is only a few paragraphs or as long as a book, you can analyze it using the same approach. First identify its central idea, and then discuss the various techniques that the author uses to communicate that idea.

▨▨▨ TYPICAL ESSAY QUESTION

When you are asked to write about a piece of nonfiction, you are often asked to do an assignment such as the following:

A piece of nonfiction always has a central idea. To convey the central idea the author may use various techniques. For example, the author may provide facts, describe details, and give examples. What is the central idea in this piece of nonfiction? Mention the general techniques that the author uses to convey this idea, and give specific instances of each technique.

▨▨▨ PREWRITING

1. Think about the central idea of the selection. If you have difficulty determining what the central idea is, ask yourself the following:

   a. What, if anything, does the title suggest about the author's opinion of the subject discussed in the selection?

   b. What opinion about life is suggested by the experiences that the author relates?

   c. What opinion about people in general is suggested by the experiences that the author relates?

   d. What ideas about the world in general are suggested by the details of setting?

2. Once you have determined the central idea of the selection, prepare a chart on which to record specific instances of the techniques that the author uses to convey that idea. After reading "Morning—'The Bird Perched for Flight'" (page 18), you might prepare the chart that appears in this lesson.

▨▨▨ WRITING PARAGRAPH BY PARAGRAPH

If your answer is just one paragraph long, think of the following steps as applying to each sentence rather than to each paragraph.

1. Begin your introductory paragraph with a thesis statement that (1) states the central idea of the selection and (2) indicates in general terms which techniques the author uses to convey that central idea.

   Example of Thesis Statement
   In "Morning—'The Bird Perched for Flight'" Anne Morrow Lindbergh uses facts, descriptive details, and examples to show that humanity can control enormous power.

   The rest of the introductory paragraph may say more about the central idea itself.

2. In each of the following paragraphs, show how the author uses one particular technique to communicate the selection's central idea. Following the topic sentence, give specific occurrences of that technique within the selection.

3. In the concluding paragraph restate your thesis statement from your introductory paragraph, using different words. This is also the place where you can tell whether you think the author supported the central idea as well as possible.

▨▨▨ REVISING AND EDITING

See Lesson 1 for detailed reminders about improving your writing.

ANALYZING NONFICTION		
SELECTION: "Morning—'The Bird Perched for Flight' "		
CENTRAL IDEA: Humanity can control enormous power.		
TECHNIQUES USED TO CONVEY CENTRAL IDEA		
FACTS	**DESCRIPTIVE DETAILS**	**EXAMPLES**
Rocket is thirty-six stories high. Hundreds of birds "rise pell-mell from the marshes at the noise." Launch pad "steams in the bright morning air."	Rocket is a "creation of . . . hard, weighty metal." ". . . the rocket begins to rise—slowly, as in a dream, so slowly it seems to hang suspended on the cloud of fire and smoke." "The earth shakes; cars rattle; vibrations beat in the chest. A roll of thunder, prolonged, prolonged, prolonged." "There . . . reappears the rocket, only a very bright star. . . ."	*Examples of people in control:* "the individuals who man the machine, give it heart, sight, speech, intelligence, and direction; and the men on earth who are backing them up."

ASSIGNMENTS

1. Using the chart provided in this lesson for "Morning—'The Bird Perched for Flight,' " discuss Lindbergh's central idea, and explain how she conveys that idea.

2. Do the assignment called "Writing About Autobiography" (page 295) or "Writing About Nonfiction" (page 312). Discuss the author's central idea and the techniques used to convey that idea.

LESSON 8: *Writing a Nonfiction Narrative*

Nonfiction is factual prose writing. A **nonfiction narrative** tells a true story. Writers of nonfiction present facts. However, they also interpret these facts and reveal their own opinions about them.

▓▓▓ CONCEPTS TO REMEMBER

1. The **purpose** of a work of nonfiction is the author's reason for writing—to entertain, to inform, or to persuade. The **audience** is the type of reader for whom the work is intended. Nonfiction usually contains a **central idea,** or general statement about life.
2. Effective nonfiction uses many techniques of fiction. **Plot** is the sequence of events, what happens in a narrative. At the center of a plot is a problem, or **conflict.** As a person in the narrative tries to solve his or her problem, the plot builds to the point of highest interest, or the **climax.** Nonfiction also uses **dialogue,** or conversation between individuals. In addition, descriptions of people and places help to make a narrative interesting and lifelike.

▓▓▓ TYPICAL ASSIGNMENT

When asked to write a nonfiction narrative, you may be asked to do an assignment like this one:

Write a nonfiction narrative telling about a true experience in which you learned something about yourself or something about another person.

▓▓▓ PREWRITING

1. To find a subject, think about the important people and events of your life. Choose one experience that caused you to learn something about yourself or another person. In choosing an event, consider your audience—for example, your teacher and classmates. The experience you choose should be something that you wish to share with them. You may wish to

choose a happy event. The following chart may help you to remember an appropriate experience.

POSSIBLE SUBJECTS	
first day of school	recital or play
birth of brother or sister	school event
being excluded from a group	moving
something lost or found	serious mistake
accident	school project
trying to improve grades	prize or trophy
learning a new skill	getting lost
helping a friend	helping at home
making a friend	having a job

2. In one or two sentences write the lesson that you learned from the experience. These sentences will state your central idea. The purpose of your narrative is to explain the lesson you learned.

   Examples
   - I learned that fear is a normal feeling and that I should not be ashamed of being afraid.
   - I learned that I can follow through on what I set out to do.

3. Think about the sequence of events that made up your true experience. How did the experience begin? What problem, or conflict, did you face? In what way did you solve it? List events in chronological order. Be sure that each part of the experience leads clearly to the next.
4. Remember how you and the others in your narrative looked, dressed, sounded, and acted. Remember how you felt. Then fill in a chart like the one that follows. The sample chart contains information about one writer's plan for the people in a narrative.

PEOPLE IN NONFICTION NARRATIVE				
PERSON	PHYSICAL TRAITS	CHARACTER TRAITS	BEHAVIOR / REACTION	WHAT I LEARNED ABOUT MYSELF OR ANOTHER PERSON
ME	short, thin, wearing red swim trunks	optimistic, sensitive, easily frightened	frightened, angry, sympathetic	1. I can follow through on what I set out to do. 2. Fear is a common, normal human emotion.
LENNY	tall, muscular, striped swim trunks	tough, a braggart, afraid underneath	boasts, bullies, cries when he fails	A tough image is often a cover-up for fear.

SETTING FOR NONFICTION NARRATIVE							
PLACE	TIME OF DAY / YEAR	WEATHER	DETAILS OF SIGHT	DETAILS OF SOUND	DETAILS OF SMELL	DETAILS OF TASTE	DETAILS OF TOUCH
town swimming pool	early morning, summer	warm, sunny, calm	blue water, diving boards, swimmers	echoes of shouts and laughter	chlorine	chlorine	warm air, cold water

5. Picture the setting, or the time and place, in which your true experience happened. Remember what you saw, heard, smelled, tasted, and touched in this setting. Then fill in a chart like the one above. The sample chart contains information about one writer's plan for the setting in a narrative.

6. Write an outline to help organize your thoughts. In the outline that follows, the sections printed in bold type are the steps that every narrative outline should include. The sections in italics are examples from the two charts on this page.

NARRATIVE OUTLINE

I. **Beginning**
   A. **Describe the setting.** *It was summer at the town swimming pool, the site of tryouts for a pre-junior Olympic swimming team.*
   B. **Give important background information including your age at the time.** *I was twelve years old and had been swimming in competition for four years.*
   C. **Begin to tell what happened.** *I tried out for the team.*

II. **Middle**
   A. **Introduce and briefly describe the other people involved.** *Coach Ruggerio was the large, friendly swimming instructor; Lenny was a bully and a rival for a place on the team.*
   B. **Introduce a conflict, or problem.** *The coach encouraged me to try the high dive. Lenny laughed at me and told me that I could never make the team.*
   C. **Show your reaction to the conflict with a direct statement.** *I became angry but began to doubt my own ability. I became afraid to try the dive.*
   D. **Build toward a climax, the point of highest interest.** *The coach announced that the team had only one opening. Lenny continued to taunt me, and I became more afraid.*

III. Ending

A. Write a climax. *I was afraid of the high dive but pushed myself to follow through with it. Neither Lenny nor I made the team. Lenny broke down and cried.*

B. Give your reaction to the climax. *I was disappointed but proud of having tried. I felt sorry for Lenny and realized that toughness is often a cover-up for fear.*

7. Review the tips for writing dialogue, or conversation, in Lesson 4.
8. When you have completed your outline, choose a title for your narrative. The title may refer to what happens or to the lesson that you learned. It may also refer to a person, object, or setting in the narrative.

▬▬ WRITING PARAGRAPH BY PARAGRAPH

1. Follow your outline. In the first paragraph tell where and when your true experience happens. Use sense details to describe the setting. Then give background information about yourself and the event, including your age at the time.

Example

Two years ago I tried out for a pre-junior Olympic swimming team. The tryouts were held at the town swimming pool. Although bright sunlight reflected off the blue water, I shivered as I waited for my turn. I was twelve years old and had been swimming in competition for four years. Now I wanted to make this team so much that I felt very nervous.

2. In the second paragraph introduce the other people who are involved in the experience. Briefly describe them and your feelings toward them. If you wish, use dialogue.

Example

I watched Coach Ruggerio in his blue jacket; he was patiently giving some younger swimmers tips on breathing. When he looked up and saw me, he cupped his thick hands around his mouth and shouted to me, "Good luck, Champ!" A minute later I felt his hand on my shoulder. "Champ," he said, "I want you to try the high dive later today. I think you can do it."

3. In the third paragraph introduce your problem, or conflict. Be sure to include your feelings about the problem.

Example

Just as my turn approached, I heard Lenny behind me whispering, "Why bother trying out? You can never make this team. Your high dive will make us all laugh." His words broke my good spirits. I turned and glared at him. However, I also began to wonder if he was right about my chances of making the team. I realized that I was afraid to try the high dive.

4. In the paragraph or paragraphs that follow, build suspense as the narrative moves toward a climax and you try to solve your problem. Continue to recount your actions and to reveal your feelings about what happens.
5. In the next-to-last paragraph, present the point of highest interest, or climax. Give your reaction to what happens.
6. In the last paragraph wind down the action, and give the final outcome of the experience. Be sure to tell what you learned about yourself or another person.

▬▬ REVISING AND EDITING

Once you have finished the first draft, you must take time to polish it into an improved second draft. Read your narrative aloud. Use the following checklist to revise your writing.

I. Content

A. Does your title point to something important in the narrative and grab the reader's interest?

B. Does your narrative reveal the kind of person you are? If your narrative concerns another person, do you reveal something about his or her personality?

C. Do you present events in chronological order?

D. Do you use sense details and dialogue to make the narrative more interesting and realistic?

E. Do you use a first-person narrator, referring to yourself as "I"?

F. Do you clearly tell what you learned about yourself or someone else from the experience in your narrative?

II. Style

See Lesson 4 for detailed reminders about improving the style of your writing.

III. Grammar, Usage, Mechanics

See Lesson 4 for detailed reminders about improving the grammar, usage, and mechanics of your writing.

ASSIGNMENTS

1. Imagine that you are the young swimmer in the narrative outline in this lesson. Complete the narrative begun in this lesson by using the charts. You may follow the outline to the end of the narrative, or you may create your own ending if you wish. Give the narrative a title.

2. Do an assignment called "Writing a Nonfiction Narrative" (page 85 or 295). Your narrative should tell about an interesting experience in which you learned something about yourself or something about another person.

3. Choose an important event in history, and write a nonfiction narrative about that event. First identify the event, and clearly tell what happened. Then tell what lesson about people can be learned from the event. You may choose an event from history, but you may wish to use one of the following: the discovery of America, the Declaration of Independence, the first flight by the Wright brothers, the first walk on the moon.

LESSON 9: *Writing a Book or Drama Review*

Reviews of books and of dramatic performances and films appear daily in newspapers and magazines throughout the country. A review provides a quick "guided tour" of a literary work, helping a reader to decide whether to read a book or see a play or film.

A meaningful book or drama review includes the title of the work, brief information about the work's contents, biographical facts about the author that directly relate to the work, and judgments about the content and literary elements in the work.

TYPICAL ESSAY QUESTION

You will often be asked to do an assignment such as the following one:

Write a book [or drama] review in which you begin with facts about the book [or drama]—such as the work's title, critics' opinions of it, date of publication, and awards if any. Describe the setting of the story. Then go on to describe the main characters and to summarize the plot. Conclude by giving your opinion of the book [or drama] backed by supporting details from the work.

You may be asked to write a drama review based on the printed version only or on an actual performance.

PREWRITING

1. Collect as much of the following information about the work and its author as you can find:

   a. whether or not the work is well known
   b. if it is an early, late, typical, or unusual work by the author
   c. what the author's general reputation is
   d. when and where the author lived
   e. what awards the work has received

   This information often appears on the book jacket, in the program of a play, or in a reference book.

2. Ask yourself questions such as the following about each of the literary elements:

   a. **Setting:** Is the setting realistic or at least believable?
   b. **Characters:** Are they believable? Do you come to care about the characters?
   c. **Plot:** Does the plot grow logically out of the characters' actions, decisions, and personalities? Does the suspense build toward a climax? Is the conflict settled in a satisfying way?

3. Prepare an outline for your review. In the suggested outline that follows, the sections printed in bold type are useful for all reviews. The sections in italics are examples based on the film script for *Gregory's Girl* (page 343).

OUTLINE FOR REVIEW

I. **Introduction (General information about the work)**
   A. **Title:** *Gregory's Girl*
   B. **Critics' opinion of the work:** *highly praised when first released*
   C. **Date:** *1981*
   D. **Place of work in author's career:** *his second feature film*
   E. **Awards:** *1981 Best Screenplay award from the British*

II. **Body of Review**
   A. **Setting**
      1. **Where and when:** *at and near a Scottish high school; now*
      2. **Appropriateness of setting:** *soccer field, science lab, shopping mall, cafeteria, and park—all places where students meet*
   B. **Main characters**
      1. **Names and key descriptions:** *Gregory, a tall, awkward sixteen-year-old; Dorothy, a self-confident soccer*

player whom Gregory wants to date; Andy and Charlie, Gregory's friends; Madeline, Gregory's sister; Susan, Gregory's eventual date

2. Believability of characters: *realistic characters, especially Gregory with his self-doubts—checking and re-checking with Dorothy about their upcoming date; joking to cover up discomfort about being stood up*

C. Plot

1. Brief summary: *The film is about a sixteen-year-old's attempts to impress and date Dorothy, a female soccer player. He finally asks her out, but she does not show up for the date. Instead, he ends up on a date with Susan and, unexpectedly, has a good time.*

2. Believability of plot: *The film presents believable conflict, suspense, and resolution. Suspense builds when Gregory talks to his friends and sister about asking Dorothy out and also when Dorothy does not show up for the date.*

III. Conclusion

A. General opinion of the work: *a warm, realistic, funny film with setting, characters, and plot that create an entertaining story*

B. Recommendations to others: *particularly to teen-agers*

▓▓ WRITING PARAGRAPH BY PARAGRAPH

If your answer is just one paragraph long, think of the following steps as applying to each sentence rather than to each paragraph.

1. In your first paragraph begin with a thesis statement. Tell which elements you will review.

Example of Thesis Statement

In *Gregory's Girl*, an award-winning screenplay, Scottish author Bill Forsyth presents a contemporary view of a high school boy by skillfully interweaving setting, characters, and plot.

You can fill out the introductory paragraph with other facts about the work. (See, for example, I.A. on the outline.)

2. In each of the following paragraphs, discuss one literary element and its appropriateness. For each element, give a topic sentence and at least one example to support it. The following paragraph discusses setting. Other paragraphs could take up characters and plot.

Example of Topic Sentence and Detail

Much of the action in *Gregory's Girl* takes place, appropriately, at or near a high school in present-day Scotland. For example, settings include a soccer field, science lab, shopping mall, cafeteria, and park. All are realistic places where students meet.

3. In your concluding paragraph give your overall opinion of the work. Then tell who else would enjoy the work.

▓▓ REVISING AND EDITING

See Lesson 1 for detailed reminders about improving your writing.

▓▓ ASSIGNMENTS

1. Use the outline for *Gregory's Girl* to complete the review of the screenplay.

2. Do one of the assignments called "Writing a Drama Review" (page 45 or 405) or the assignment called "Writing a Book Review" (page 533).

LESSON 10: *Writing a Scene*

Drama is the form of literature that presents stories meant to be performed for an audience.

CONCEPTS TO REMEMBER

1. A **scene** is a very short play or part of a play. A scene usually concerns a single event and happens in a single setting.
2. The script of a play contains (1) **dialogue,** or the conversation of the characters, and (2) **stage directions,** or descriptions of actions, characters, and settings.
3. Drama uses many of the same techniques as the short story. The plot of a play usually concerns a problem, or **conflict.** As the characters try to solve this problem, the play builds to its point of highest interest, or **climax.** The characters in a play should have believable personality traits and clear motivations for their actions. They reveal their personalities by their words and actions.

TYPICAL ASSIGNMENT

When asked to write a scene, you will often be given an assignment like this one:

Write a dramatic scene with believable plot, characters, and setting.

PREWRITING

1. To find an idea for your dramatic scene, think first about characters. Because you will need at least two characters in order to have dialogue, try to think of interesting combinations of people. Then think of a problem, or conflict, that such people might share. List some different ideas on a chart like the one below.
2. From your chart choose the characters and problem for your scene. Ask yourself the following questions: How will a problem occur between the two characters? In what ways will each character react to the problem? How will the problem be solved?
3. Try to imagine how your characters look, sound, and act. Then fill in a chart like the one called "Characters" on the next page. The sample contains information about characters that one writer has in mind for a scene.
4. Picture your setting. When and where does the action take place? What background scenery will your scene need? What furniture and objects, or props, are on the stage? Fill in a chart like the one called "Setting" on the next page. The sample contains information about the setting that one writer is planning for a scene.

POSSIBLE IDEAS FOR A DRAMATIC SCENE		
FIRST CHARACTER	**SECOND CHARACTER**	**PROBLEM**
lion tamer	butcher	enough steak for six lions
young singer	singing coach	stage fright
astronaut	astronaut	who gets to walk in space
fashion model	football fan	what to wear to a game
robot	repair person	getting the robot to obey orders
magician	person in audience	giving away magic secrets
student's parent	teacher	need for passing grade
classical music composer	rock-and-roll fan	different musical tastes
child	child's parent	building a tree house
fossil expert	student	lost dinosaur bone

CHARACTERS

CHARACTER	JOB	AGE	SIZE	FEATURES	GESTURES	DRESS	SPEECH	PERSONALITY
Mike French	student	13	tall, thin	short hair, open, smiling face	waves arms while speaking, paces	neat work clothes	voice becomes high and fast when excited	adventurous, excitable, intelligent
Dr. Regina Phelps	fossil expert	40s	short, heavy	glasses, long hair, little expression on face	calm, picks lint off her clothing	gray clothes, lab coat	slow, careful, speaks as if others will not understand	serious, professional, dedicated

SETTING

HISTORICAL PERIOD, SEASON, TIME	PLACE	BACKGROUND	FURNITURE	LIGHT	PROPS
present day, summer after-noon	dinosaur room, museum of natural history	marble walls, pictures of fossils and dinosaurs	hanging models of prehistoric birds, giant model of dinosaur	bright sunlight from skylight	notebook, large box, small dog, leash, large bone

5. To help you to organize your thoughts, prepare an outline for your scene. In the following sample outline, the sections printed in bold type are steps that every outline for a dramatic scene should include. The sections in italics are examples of one writer's ideas for a scene.

DRAMATIC SCENE OUTLINE

I. **Cast of characters**
   List your characters in order of appearance with some identification for each.
   Mike French, 13, a student
   Dr. Phelps, a fossil expert
   Andrew Kennedy, museum director
   Pete French, 9, Mike's brother

II. **Setting the stage**
   A. **Describe the background scenery, furniture, and lighting.** *The dinosaur room of a museum of natural history has marble*
walls, educational posters, models of pre-historic birds and dinosaurs, and a skylight that lets in bright afternoon sunshine.

   B. **Tell which characters are on stage and what they are doing as the scene begins.** *Kennedy is studying the giant dinosaur model and is taking notes. Phelps and Mike enter through a door on the left. Phelps is carrying a large box.*

III. **Beginning**
   A. **Make it clear who your characters are and how they are related.** *Kennedy welcomes Dr. Phelps and Mike. Phelps introduces Mike as a member of her fossil-hunting club.*

   B. **Give background information that is important to the plot.** *Mike tells Kennedy that he found a rare dinosaur bone on the club's camping trip.*

C. Introduce the problem, or conflict.
Phelps opens the box that should contain the bone, but she finds nothing inside.

IV. Middle

A. Show the reactions of characters to the conflict. *Mike, Phelps, and Kennedy all express surprise.*

B. Build toward the point of highest interest, or climax. *Phelps accuses Mike of carelessness because he kept the package overnight. Kennedy says Phelps was foolish to entrust the bone to a child. Mike insists that the bone was safe all night.*

C. Introduce minor characters, and show their relationship to others. *Mike's brother, Pete, runs into the room in order to meet his brother. He is carrying a dog's leash. As the discussion about the bone continues, Pete begins to look upset. He admits to taking the bone.*

V. Ending

A. Reach the point of highest interest. *The other characters question Pete. He looks around for his dog, who had run after the museum's cat. Gradually each character stops talking and begins to call for the dog. The dog runs in; he has the bone in his mouth.*

B. Show the characters' reactions to the climax. *Pete explains that he thought the bone was worthless. The others express relief and happiness.*

C. Show the final outcome. *The dog is promised a soup bone. Mike is congratulated.*

6. When your outline is complete, practice writing dialogue. Write at least one line for each character. You may want to ask friends for help in writing realistic dialogue. Assign the part of one character to each friend. Then have the group improvise a short conversation as the characters. Write down lines and expressions that sound realistic. Remember that dialogue is less formal than other kinds of writing. To make dialogue sound natural, you may use short sentences and contractions.

7. Choose a title for your dramatic scene. The title may refer to an important event, object, character, setting, or statement in the scene.

WRITING LINE BY LINE

1. Write your title. Beneath it write *Cast of Characters*. Under this heading list the characters in order of appearance. Identify each briefly.

2. On a new line write the word *Scene*. Then state the time and place. Describe the scenery, furniture, and lighting. Tell which characters are on stage. Describe them briefly and tell what they are doing as the scene begins.

Example
Scene: The setting is the dinosaur room of a museum of natural history on a summer afternoon. The marble walls of the room are decorated with posters of fossils and dinosaurs. Sunlight floods in through a skylight. Models of prehistoric birds hang from the ceiling. The giant model of a dinosaur dominates the room. ANDREW KENNEDY, director of the museum, is studying the dinosaur and taking notes. He is dressed in a gray suit. MIKE FRENCH, a tall, thin thirteen-year-old student enters with DR. REGINA PHELPS, a dedicated expert on fossils. She is carrying a large box.

3. Write the name of the first character to speak on the next line, followed by a colon. Then write what this character says. Place stage directions, descriptions of the character's movements and speech, inside parentheses. Begin a new line each time a different character speaks.

Example
KENNEDY: [His voice is pleased.] Dr. Phelps, welcome back! [He puts down his notebook and extends his right hand.] How was your fossil-hunting expedition?

PHELPS: [She shakes KENNEDY'S hand and smiles broadly.] Andrew, I am very happy to be back. I want you to meet a member of the expedition, Mike French. [She gestures MIKE forward. The men shake hands.] Mike has big news for you.

4. Following your outline, continue to use dialogue and stage directions to introduce the problem, or conflict. Clearly develop the sequence of events.
5. In the dialogue that follows, build suspense as the scene moves toward the point of highest interest, the climax.
6. Use dialogue and stage directions to introduce any additional characters.
7. Present the climax. Be sure that the solution to the problem is believable. Show the characters' reactions to the climax. Write final stage directions that tell what the characters are doing as the scene ends.

◼ REVISING AND EDITING

1. Read your scene aloud. If possible, do a dramatic reading with friends or family.
2. Use the following checklist to revise your writing.

I. Content
   A. Does your title point to something important in the scene and grab the audience's interest?
   B. Do you list and identify your characters?
   C. Have you described the scenery, lighting, and furniture? Do you tell what the characters are doing as the scene begins? Does the scene have only one setting?

D. Do your stage directions describe the speech and actions of the characters? Do they include information about props, or objects that the characters use?
E. Does your dialogue provide necessary background information?
F. Does your dialogue clearly show the problem, its solution, and the characters' reactions?

II. Style
   A. Have you remembered not to use quotation marks in dialogue? Have you put colons after the characters' names before they speak? Have you enclosed stage directions in parentheses?
   B. See Lesson 4 for further reminders about improving the style of your writing.

III. Grammar, Usage, Mechanics
   A. Is each sentence complete (no fragments, no run-ons)?
   B. Are all words spelled correctly? If you are not sure of the spelling of a word, have you consulted a dictionary?
   C. Have you punctuated and capitalized your sentences correctly?

◼ ASSIGNMENTS

1. Complete the scene begun in this lesson by using the charts. You may follow the outline to the end of the scene, or you may create your own ending if you wish. Give the scene a title. Be sure that your plot, characters, and setting are believable.
2. Do an assignment called "Writing a Scene" (page 45, 126, or 369). Be sure that your plot, characters, and setting are believable.

READING AND LITERARY TERMS HANDBOOK

ALLITERATION   *The repetition of consonant sounds, most often at the beginning of words.* For example, line 9 of Woody Guthrie's "This Land Is Your Land" (page 213) repeats the sounds of *r* and *f*:

> I've *r*oamed and *r*ambled and I *f*ollowed my *f*ootsteps

See page 219.

ALLUSION   *A reference in a work of literature to a character, place, or situation from another work of literature.* For instance, in "Thirteen" (page 116) the hat that Cress wants to buy reminds her of a poem by John Keats.

See page 430.

ANECDOTE   *A brief account of a true event, meant to entertain or inform.* Anecdotes are often used in nonfiction to help reveal personality. For example, in *Growing Up* (page 290) Russell Baker's anecdote reveals his mother's generosity.

See page 303.

ATMOSPHERE   *The mood, or feeling, that runs through a work of literature.* For example, in "The Sound of Summer Running" (page 151) the vivid descriptions of summertime activities help the reader understand Douglas' determination.

See page 131.

AUDIENCE   *The type of reader for whom a literary work is intended.* For example, in "Roberto Clemente: A Bittersweet Memoir" (page 296), Jerry Izenberg probably wrote for an audience of readers who admire Roberto Clemente.

See pages 47, 289.

AUTOBIOGRAPHY   *The story of a person's life written by that person.* Russell Baker's *Growing Up* (page 290) is an autobiography.

See pages 21, 289, 294.
See also NONFICTION.

BIOGRAPHY   *The story of a person's life written by someone other than that person.* "Roberto Clemente: A Bittersweet Memoir" (page 296) is an example of biography.

See pages 21, 289, 303.
See also NONFICTION.

CAUSE AND EFFECT   *A relationship between events in which one event—the cause—is the reason why another event—the effect—takes place.* Cause and effect plays a humorous role in "The Sneaker Crisis" (page 59).

See pages 72, 479.
See also MOTIVATION.

CHARACTER   *A person or animal involved in a story, novel, or play.* Each character has certain qualities, or character traits, that the reader discovers as the work unfolds. **Major characters** are the more important characters in a work, and **minor characters** are the less important characters. For example, in *Gregory's Girl* Gregory and Dorothy are major characters, and Andy and Charlie are minor characters.

See pages 95, 434, 498.
See also MOTIVATION.

CHARACTERIZATION   *The personality of a character and the method by which an author reveals that personality.* The author may directly state opinions about the characters. For instance, in "Birdman" (page 127) Mari Sandoz explains that Birdman wants to become a buffalo hunter. The author may reveal the character's personality indirectly, through the character's own words and actions. For example, in "Thirteen" (page 116) Mr. Delahanty's sympathetic response to Cress's request to look at the hat indirectly reveals that he is eager to make his daughter happy.

See pages 109, 498, 532.
See also INFERENCE, MOTIVATION.

CHRONOLOGICAL ORDER   *The time order in which events naturally happen.* In a literary work that follows chronological order, the event that takes place first is described first, and so on until the last event. For example, "Old Yeller and the Bear" (page 86) is told in chronological order.

See page 72.
See also FLASHBACK.

CLIMAX   *The point of the reader's highest interest and greatest emotional involvement in a story, novel, or play.* For example, the climax in *The Speckled Band* (page 23) occurs when Holmes and Watson find Dr. Roylott dead in his room with the snake coiled around his head.

See page 65.
See also PLOT.

COMPARISON AND CONTRAST   *A similarity (comparison) or difference (contrast) between two or more items.* For instance, the contrast between the practical, straightforward Matilda and her whimsical Aunt Gertrude adds to the humor of "All You've Ever Wanted" (page 66).

See pages 143, 519.

CONCRETE LANGUAGE   *Specific words that appeal to the five senses and are used to create images.* For example, in Robert Francis' "Seagulls" (page 219) the line "Arc intersecting arc, curve over curve" creates a more specific visual

picture than a statement like "The seagulls are very graceful."

See page 235.
See also FIGURATIVE LANGUAGE, IMAGE.

CONCRETE POEM   *A poem shaped to look like its subject.* The placement of letters, words, lines, and punctuation creates a striking visual effect. John Updike's "Pendulum" (page 255) is a concrete poem.

See page 257.

CONFLICT   *In the plot of a story, novel, or play, the struggle between two or more opposing forces.* An **external conflict** occurs when a character struggles against an outside force, such as nature, fate, or another person. In "The Dinner Party" (page 157) there are two external conflicts: the argument between the guests (person against person) and the threat created by the arrival of the snake (person against nature). An **internal conflict** takes place within a character's mind. In "The Dinner Party" Mrs. Wynnes overcomes her feelings of horror at seeing the snake.

See pages 79, 85, 451.
See also PLOT.

DESCRIPTION   *The type of writing that creates a clear picture of something—a person, animal, object, place, or event.* Description is used in both fiction and nonfiction.

See pages 289, 312.
See also DETAILS, ESSAY, EXPOSITION, NARRATION, PERSUASION.

DETAILS   *Particular features of an item, used to make descriptive writing more precise and lifelike.* For example, in *Growing Up* (page 290) Russell Baker helps the reader to see his first suit by describing it with the following details: "It was a hard fabric, built to endure. The color was green, not the green of new grass in spring, but the

Reading and Literary Terms Handbook   599

green of copper patina on old statues. The green was relieved by thin, light gray stripes. . . .''

See pages 100, 138, 202, 282, 312.
See also DESCRIPTION.

DIALECT *The special form of speech that belongs to a particular group or region.* For example, in ''The Catch-Dog'' (page 309) *bull-bats* is a dialect term for *nighthawks.*

See page 238.

DIALOGUE *Conversation between characters in a literary work.* Dialogue can advance the plot or reveal the personalities of the characters.

See pages 161, 355.
See also DRAMA.

DRAMA *The form of literature that presents a story to be performed for an audience.* The written script of a drama contains **dialogue**—the speeches of the characters—and **stage directions**—the writer's descriptions of settings, characters, and actions.

See pages 1, 44, 341.

END–STOPPED LINE *In poetry a line in which a pause occurs naturally at the end of the line.* The pause may be created by a period or semicolon, for example. Theodore Roethke's ''Sloth'' (page 220) begins with an end-stopped line:

In moving-slow he has no peer.

See page 247.
See also RUN-ON LINE.

EPISODE *A self-contained incident within a novel, story, or play.* ''Christmas in Brooklyn'' (page 101) is an episode, or excerpt, from Betty Smith's novel *A Tree Grows in Brooklyn.*

See page 91.

ESSAY *A short piece of nonfiction that can deal with any subject.* A **narrative essay** (''Beneath the Crags of Malpelo Island''—page 324) tells a story, usually in chronological order. A **descriptive essay** (''The Catch-Dog''—page 309) creates a clear picture of something. An **expository essay** (''In Search of Our Mothers' Gardens''—page 313) explains an idea or presents information. A **persuasive essay** (''When Does Education Stop?''—page 318) seeks to convince the reader to accept the author's opinions and, often, to move the reader to action.

See pages 21, 289.
See also DESCRIPTION, EXPOSITION, NARRATION, PERSUASION.

EXPOSITION *The type of writing that presents facts or explains ideas.* Alice Walker's ''In Search of Our Mothers' Gardens'' (page 313) is an example of an expository essay.

See pages 289, 317.
See also DESCRIPTION, ESSAY, NARRATION, PERSUASION, THESIS STATEMENT.

FABLE *A brief folk tale told to teach a moral, or lesson.* Often, the characters in fables are animals. For example, Aesop's fable of the fox and the grapes teaches the lesson that it is easy to despise what we cannot get.

See pages 145, 455.
See also FOLK TALE, MYTH.

FANTASY *Fictional events and details that could not occur in real life.* For example, in ''All You've Ever Wanted'' (page 66) the magical results of Matilda's birthday wishes represent elements of fantasy. The opposite of fantasy is *reality,* which in a written work consists of details that seem true to life. For example, the surprised or angry reactions of people to the flowers that spring up behind Matilda seem true to life and therefore represent elements of reality.

See page 478.

FICTION *A prose narrative work of the imagination including novels and short stories.*

FIGURATIVE LANGUAGE *Imaginative language used for descriptive effect and not meant to be taken as the literal truth.* In *A Christmas Carol* (page 372) Scrooge's nephew Fred uses figurative language when he says that Christmas is the only time in the year when men and women "open their shut-up hearts." He thus creates a vivid picture of people's rare generosity at Christmas. Instances of figurative language are called **figures of speech. Similes** and **metaphors** are among the most common figures of speech.

> See page 273.
> See also CONCRETE
> LANGUAGE, METAPHOR,
> SIMILE.

FLASHBACK *In a narrative, a scene or incident that breaks the normal time order of the plot to show an event that happened earlier.* For example, in "Beneath the Crags of Malpelo Island" (page 324) Harry Rieseberg explains his decision to dive for the treasure by relating in flashback his earlier conversation with Charlie Boyer.

> See page 85.
> See also CHRONOLOGICAL
> ORDER.

FOLK TALE *An old story that was originally told orally, or by word of mouth.* Both folk tales and myths are part of **folk literature**—the collection of beliefs, customs, and traditions of a people.

> See page 461.
> See also FABLE, MYTH.

FORESHADOWING *The use of clues by a writer to prepare the reader for future developments in a story, novel, or play.* For example, in "Rikki-tikki-tavi" (page 2), when Teddy's father says, "If a snake came into the nursery now—" he foreshadows the arrival of the snake later on.

> See pages 91, 369, 508.

HAIKU *A three-line poem, usually on the subject of nature, with five syllables each in the first and third lines and seven syllables in the second line.* "Bamboo Grove" by Bashō (page 249) is an example of a haiku.

> See page 250.

HERO *The central character of a work of literature.* A hero may be either male or female. In myths and folk tales heroes often have superhuman abilities. In most modern works heroes are more like ordinary people. Francie in "Christmas in Brooklyn" (page 101) is an example of a hero in a modern story.

> See page 466.

IMAGE *A picture or likeness that is created with words.* Images are most often visual, but they may appeal to any of the five senses (sight, hearing, touch, taste, and smell). For example, in "When the Frost Is on the Punkin" (page 236) the line "And the raspin' of the tangled leaves, as golden as the morn" appeals to both the sense of hearing and the sense of sight.

> See page 233.
> See also CONCRETE
> LANGUAGE, IMAGERY.

IMAGERY *Language that appeals to the senses.* Imagery is the combination or collection of images in a work of literature.

> See pages 233, 498.
> See also IMAGE.

INFERENCE *A conclusion that can be drawn from the available information.* For example, in *A Christmas Carol* (page 372) the reader learns that the boy Ebenezer suffered from the unkindness of his father. We can infer that this treatment left its mark on Scrooge, turning him into a bitter man.

> See pages 100, 138, 203, 283,
> 472, 480.
> See also CHARACTERIZATION,
> MOTIVATION.

IRONY *A difference between the way things seem to be and the way they actually are.* For example, irony occurs in "The Glorious Whitewasher" (page 146) when Tom's friends beg him to allow them to whitewash the fence instead of laughing at him for whitewashing it.

See page 178.

LIMERICK *A humorous five-line poem that follows a specific form: three long lines (1, 2, and 5) that rhyme and two short lines (3 and 4) that rhyme.* A limerick also contains a regular rhythm, or pattern of beats. Two examples of limericks appear on page 253.

See page 254.
See also RHYTHM.

LYRIC POEM *A poem that expresses a personal thought or emotion.* Most lyric poems are short and present vivid images. For example, "Miracles" (page 276) is a lyric poem that expresses the joy the poet finds in all of life.

See page 271.
See also NARRATIVE POEM.

METAMORPHOSIS *A change in shape or form.* Metamorphosis occurs frequently to the characters in Greek myths. For example, Hera becomes angry at Echo and turns her into a mimicking voice.

See page 439.
See also MYTH.

METAPHOR *A figure of speech that compares or equates two basically different things.* For example, in "This Land Is Your Land" (page 213) the phrase "that ribbon of highway" is a metaphor equating a highway with a ribbon.

See page 243.
See also SIMILE.

MOTIVATION *A feeling, idea, or goal that causes a character to act in a certain way.* For instance, in *The Red Pony* (page 487) Billy Buck is motivated to save Nellie's colt because he knows that Jody will be heartbroken if he loses a second horse.

See pages 105, 447, 480.
See also CHARACTER, INFERENCE.

MYTH *An ancient, anonymous story that conveys the beliefs and ideals of a culture and usually involves gods and goddesses.* Myths originally explained an aspect of nature or of human life. According to the Greeks, for example, Prometheus gave fire to humans because he was disturbed at Zeus's cruelty. A **mythology** refers to the collection of myths of a particular people.

See pages 413, 422.
See also FOLK TALE.

NARRATION *The type of writing that tells a story.* A narrative work may be either fiction or nonfiction. Types of narrative writing include autobiographies, biographies, narrative essays, short stories, novels, and narrative poems.

See pages 289, 308.
See also DESCRIPTION, ESSAY, EXPOSITION, PERSUASION.

NARRATIVE POEM *A poem that tells a story.* The events are often told in chronological sequence—that is, the order in which they happen. In a narrative poem the theme, or central idea, unfolds as the story is told. Walter de la Mare's "Listeners" (page 278) is a narrative poem.

See pages 258, 264.
See also LYRIC POEM.

NARRATOR *In a short story or novel, the person who tells the story.* A **first-person narrator** is a character in the work who tells the story as he or she experiences it. For example, a crew member is the first-person narrator in "Feathered Friend" (page 54). A **third-person narrator** is an outside observer—not a character in the story—who describes the thoughts and experiences of the characters. "All You've Ever Wanted" (page 66) and *The Red Pony* (page 487) are both told by a third-person narrator.

See pages 115, 126, 532.

NONFICTION *Factual prose writing.* Nonfiction always tells about incidents that really happened and people who really lived. Nonfiction includes **autobiography, biography,** and **essays.**

See pages 21, 289.
See also AUTOBIOGRAPHY, BIOGRAPHY, ESSAY.

NOVEL *A long work of prose fiction that tells a story.* John Steinbeck's *Red Pony* (page 487) is a novel.

See pages 91, 485.
See also FICTION, SHORT STORY.

ONOMATOPOEIA *The use of a word or phrase that imitates or suggests the sound of what it describes.* For example, in "When the Frost Is on the Punkin" (page 236) the words *kyouck* and *gobble* suggest the sound of a turkey.

See page 228.

OPINION *A statement expressing an individual's personal belief.* An opinion is not a *fact,* which is a statement that can be proven true. For example, James Michener states a fact when he says that he consulted thousands of research books in order to write *Hawaii.* He expresses an opinion when he says "The good work of the world is accomplished principally by people who dedicate themselves unstintingly to the big job at hand."

See page 335.
See also PERSUASION.

ORAL TRADITION *The handing down of songs, poems, legends, and folk tales from generation to generation by word of mouth.* The poem "The

Magnificent Bull" (page 239) is part of the oral tradition of the Dinka people.

See pages 216, 341, 418.
See also FOLK TALE, MYTH.

PARAPHRASE *A restatement in the reader's own words of the content of a written work.* By paraphrasing a written work a reader can gain a better understanding of the writer's meaning.

See page 535.

PERSUASION *The type of writing in which an author attempts to make the reader accept an opinion or take action of some kind.* "When Does Education Stop?" (page 318) is an example of a persuasive essay.

See page 322.
See also DESCRIPTION, ESSAY, EXPOSITION, NARRATION.

PLOT *The sequence of events in a short story, novel, or play.* A plot has a **conflict,** or struggle between opposing forces. The **climax** of a plot is the point of the reader's highest interest. The **resolution** reveals the final outcome of the plot.

See pages 57, 532.
See also CLIMAX, CONFLICT, RESOLUTION.

POETRY *Imaginative writing in which language, images, sound, and rhythm combine to create a special emotional effect.* Poetry is usually arranged in lines. Many poems have a regular **rhythm,** or pattern of beats, and some have **rhyme.** Types of poetry include **narrative poetry** and **lyric poetry.**

See pages 16, 209.
See also LYRIC POEM, NARRATIVE POEM.

PROSE *The kind of writing that is used in short stories, novels, works of nonfiction, journalism, and so forth.* Prose is distinguished from poetry.

Unlike poetry, prose is usually written in lines that run from margin to margin across a page. Prose is also divided into sentences and paragraphs and is more like everyday speech than poetry.

See pages 13, 209.

PURPOSE *The author's intention or goal in writing a particular work.* A writer's purpose may be to inform, entertain, or persuade the reader, or to express an idea. For example, Jerry Izenberg's purpose in "Roberto Clemente: A Bittersweet Memoir" (page 296) is to show the reader Clemente's loyalty and integrity.

See pages 47, 289, 295.
See also AUDIENCE,
NONFICTION.

REFRAIN *In some songs and poems a line or group of lines repeated at regular intervals.* For example, in Robert Frost's "Pasture" (page 247) the line "I sha'n't be gone long.—You come too" is a refrain because it is repeated at the end of each stanza.

See page 214.
See also REPETITION.

REPETITION *The repeated use of sounds, words, phrases, or lines.* Repetition emphasizes important items and helps unify a poem or other work of literature. For example, in "Simple Song" (page 268) the word *open* is repeated in the third stanza. This repetition emphasizes the idea that openness is necessary in love.

See page 218.
See also ALLITERATION,
REFRAIN, RHYME.

RESOLUTION *In a story, novel, or play the part of the plot that presents the final outcome.* In "The Dinner Party" (page 157) the resolution occurs when Mrs. Wynnes reveals how she discovered the snake.

See page 65.
See also CLIMAX, PLOT.

RHYME *The repetition of the same or similar sounds in words that appear near each other in a poem.* The most common type of rhymes are **end rhymes,** which occur at the ends of lines. **Perfect rhymes** are words that sound exactly alike except for the first consonant sound—for example, *be, three,* and *key.* Lines 5 and 6 of "This Land Is Your Land" (page 213) contain end rhymes that are also perfect rhymes:

As I was walking that ribbon of *highway*,
I saw above me that endless *skyway*.

See page 221.
See also REPETITION,
RUN-ON LINE.

RHYTHM *The pattern of beats made by stressed and unstressed syllables in the lines of a poem.* A poem's rhythm usually reflects its meaning. For instance, a fast rhythm fits a poem of action, while a slower rhythm is appropriate in a poem that expresses a calm feeling. Rhythm may be regular and follow a repeated pattern, or it may be irregular. These lines of "The Pasture" (page 247) follow a regular rhythm of alternating unstressed and stressed syllables:

I'm going out to clean the pasture spring;
I'll only stop to rake the leaves away

See page 225.
See also LIMERICK.

RUN–ON LINE *In poetry a line in which the meaning continues beyond the line.* The line does not end with a punctuation mark or other break. For example, the very first line of "A Song of Greatness" (page 215) is a run-on line:

When I hear the old men
Telling of heroes

See page 248.
See also END-STOPPED
LINE.

SCANNING *A method of reading in which the reader searches quickly through a work for a* particular word, phrase, or piece of information.

See page 49.
See also SKIMMING.

SETTING   *The time and place in which a story, novel, or play occurs.* For instance, the setting in "Christmas in Brooklyn" (page 101) is a poor city neighborhood. The time is the early part of the twentieth century.

See pages 131, 532.
See also ATMOSPHERE.

SHORT STORY   *A brief account in prose of fictional events.* Most stories have one or more **characters** and happen in a particular time and place, or **setting.** The **plot** is the sequence of events in the story.

See pages 13, 53.
See also CHARACTER, NARRATOR, PLOT, SETTING.

SIMILE   *A figure of speech that uses the words* like *or* as *to directly compare two seemingly unlike things.* For example, line 74 of "The Highwayman" (page 260) describes the face of the landlord's daughter as being "like a light."

See page 240.
See also FIGURATIVE LANGUAGE, METAPHOR.

SKIMMING   *A method of reading in which the reader glances quickly through a written work in order to preview it.* The reader skims through a written work by noting the title, table of contents, headings, any boldfaced or italicized terms, and illustrations.

See page 49.
See also SCANNING.

STAGE DIRECTIONS   *In drama the writer's instructions for performing the work and descriptions of characters, actions, and settings.*

See pages 45, 341.
See also DRAMA.

STAGING   *The acting, costumes, sets, lighting, sound effects, and other special effects that bring a play to life.*

See pages 385, 406.
See also DRAMA.

STANZA   *A group of lines forming a unit in a poem.* The first four lines of John Masefield's poem "Roadways" (page 15) form one stanza.

See pages 16, 252.

STEREOTYPE   *A kind of character who has only a few personality traits and is more a category than a real, individualized person.* Stereotypes are sometimes used in literature to teach a lesson or make a point. For example, in "A Just Judge" (page 92), a story that teaches a lesson about justice, all of the characters, both good and bad, are stereotypes.

See page 200.
See also CHARACTER, CHARACTERIZATION.

SUSPENSE   *The reader's interest in the outcome of a work of literature.* For example, in "Old Yeller and the Bear" (page 86) the reader is eager to learn whether Little Arliss will be rescued from the raging bear.

See page 57.
See also CLIMAX, RESOLUTION.

THEME   *The central idea of a literary work, usually expressed as a generalization about life.* A **stated theme** is one that the author expresses directly in the work. An **implied theme** is one that is not stated directly in the work but is suggested by the work's other elements. For example, in "The Wild Duck's Nest" (page 183) Colm's reverence for the duck's nest suggests the story's theme: "Trust between humans and wild creatures is a rare and wonderful thing."

See pages 145, 156, 267, 269, 368.

THESIS STATEMENT *A sentence or group of sentences expressing the central idea in a work of nonfiction.* The material that follows the thesis statement supports and develops it with facts, incidents, examples, and details. For example, James Michener states the central idea of "When Does Education Stop?" (page 318) in the following sentence: "Adults who are unwilling to reeducate themselves periodically are doomed to mediocrity."

See page 317.
See also TOPIC SENTENCE.

TITLE *The name of a work of literature.* The title sometimes refers to an important character or event or provides a clue to the main idea. For example, the title "Last Cover" (page 73) refers both to Bandit's hiding place in the pool and to the box cover on which Colin draws his picture of the scene.

See page 166.

TOPIC SENTENCE *The sentence that expresses the main idea of a paragraph of nonfiction.* The topic sentence usually appears very early in the paragraph, and the rest of the paragraph develops the idea stated in that sentence. For example, the fourth paragraph of "The Night the Bed Fell" (page 304) relates some of the author's family's strange "crotchets." The paragraph's first sentence announces this topic: "Briggs was not the only member of his family who had his crotchets."

See page 322.
See also THESIS
STATEMENT.

GLOSSARY

The following Glossary lists words that are from the selections but may be unfamiliar to you. Many of the words have several different meanings. However, they are defined here only as they are used in the selections. Some words may be familar to you in other contexts but may have unusual meanings in this text.

Each Glossary entry contains a pronunciation, a part of speech, and a definition. Some words are used in more than one way in the textbook and therefore have more than one definition. Occasionally a word has more than one part of speech. Related words are often combined in one entry: The main form (for example, the adjective *absurd*) is defined, and another form (for example, the noun *absurdity*) is listed after the main definition. Adverbs ending in *-ly* are usually listed after the definition of the adjective form.

Some unusual words or meanings of words are labeled ARCHAIC (old-fashioned). Other special usage labels include INFORMAL, CHIEFLY BRITISH, and so on.

The following abbreviations are used in this Glossary:

n.	noun	*adv.*	adverb
v.	verb	*conj.*	conjunction
adj.	adjective	*n. pl.*	plural noun

A key to pronunciations may be found in the lower right-hand corner of each right-hand page of the Glossary.

A

abandoned [ə ban′dənd] *adj.* left alone; deserted.

abet [ə bet′] *v.* to encourage, help, or support.

abode [ə bōd′] *n.* a home; dwelling place.

abrupt [ə brupt′] *adj.* sudden, unexpected. – **abruptly,** *adv.*

absurd [ab surd′, ab zurd′] *adj.* ridiculous; contrary to reason and common sense. – **absurdity,** *n.*

accentuate [ak sen′choo āt′] *v.* to emphasize; make stronger.

accommodate [ə kom′ə dāt′] *v.* **1.** to have or make space for something or someone. **2.** to help or do a favor for someone.

accordingly [ə kôr′ding lē] *adv.* therefore; as a consequence.

accost [ə kôst′] *v.* to approach and speak to someone.

acquiescence [ak′wē es′əns] *n.* a silent agreement or act of accepting.

adjoin [ə join′] *v.* to be next to; touch on.

admittance [ad mit′əns] *n.* permission to enter.

agape [ə gāp′, ə gap′] *adj.* wide open, usually referring to the mouth, in amazement or disbelief.

alien [āl′yən, ā′lē ən] *adj.* strange; not appropriate.

allay [ə lā′] *v.* to calm; put at rest.

aloof [ə loof′] *adj.* distant; removed; reserved.

alter [ôl′tər] *v.* to change in some way.

anesthetic [an′is thet′ik] *n.* substance that produces loss of pain and physical sensation, with or without loss of total consciousness.

anguish [ang′gwish] *n.* agony; physical or mental distress.

anticipation [an tis′ə pā′shən] *n.* hope; a feeling of excited expectation.

anxious [angk′shəs, ang′shəs] *adj.* uneasy; fearful. – **anxiously,** *adv.*

apologetic [ə pol′ə jet′ik] *adj.* expressing regret. – **apologetically,** *adv.*

apparition [ap′ə rish′ən] *n.* a ghost; phantom.

appointed [ə point′id] *adj.* agreed upon; decided.

appraise [ə prāz′] *v.* to judge the quality of something.

apprehension [ap′ri hen′shən] *n.* state of being anxious and fearful.

approbation [ap′rə bā′shən] *n.* approval; acceptance.

apt [apt] *adj.* likely.

arc [ärk] *n.* a curved line.

archer [är′chər] *n.* a person who shoots with a bow and arrow.

ark [ärk] *n.* a boxlike boat with a flat bottom.

aromatic [ar′ə mat′ik] *adj.* having a pleasant odor; fragrant.

artful [ärt′fəl] *adj.* skillful; clever.

aspiration [as′pə rā′shən] *n.* a desire to achieve; ambition.

assemblage [ə sem′blij] *n.* a meeting of a group.

assess [ə ses′] *v.* to make a judgment about; evaluate.

assume [ə soom′] *v.* to take for granted.

asunder [ə sun′dər] *adv.* in separate parts or pieces.

atmospheric [at′məs fer′ik] *adj.* relating to the air that surrounds the earth or some other planet.

austere [ôs tēr′] *adj.* severe; stern.

avail [ə vāl′] *v.* to help or be of value.

averse [ə vurs′] *adj.* against; opposed to.

awning [ô′ning] *n.* rooflike covering, usually made of cloth.

azure [azh′ər, a′zhər] *adj.* clear blue in color.

B

balmy [bä′mē] *adj.* pleasantly mild; soothing.

bankrupt [bangk′rupt, bangk′rəpt] *v.* to make a person or organization unable to pay debts.

barometer [bə rom′ə tər] *n.* an instrument used to forecast weather by measuring pressure in the atmosphere.

bear [bār] *v.* to carry; take.

beauteous [bū′tē əs] *adj.* having qualities that delight the mind or the senses.

beguile [bi gīl′] *v.* to pass time pleasantly.

belligerent [bə lij′ər ənt] *adj.* ready to fight. – **belligerently,** *adv.*

---

at; āpe; cär; end; mē; it; īce; hot; ōld; fôrk; wood; fool; oil; out; up; ūse; turn; ə in ago, taken, pencil, lemon, circus; bat; chin; dear; five; game; hit; hw in white; joke; kit; lid; man; not; singer; pail; ride; sat; shoe; tag; thin; this; very; wet; yes; zoo; zh in treasure; KH in loch, German ach; N in French bon; œ in French feu, German schön

bequeath [bi kwēth′, bi kwēth′] v. to make a gift of property that is to be delivered to the receiver after the giver dies.

beseech [bi sēch′] v. to beg; plead with.

billow [bil′ō] v. to swell.

bit [bit] n. the metal part of a bridle that is put in a horse's mouth.

bloated [blōt′id] adj. puffy and swollen.

blunt [blunt] adj. without sharp points.

bore [bôr] v. **1.** to make a passageway. **2.** past tense of **bear.**

brand [brand] n. a mark of disgrace.

brandish [bran′dish] v. to shake or wave in a threatening way.

bravado [brə va′dō] n. a show of bravery or confidence to hide a true feeling of uncertainty.

bred [bred] past tense of **breed.**

breeches [brich′iz] n. pl. trousers reaching just below the knees.

breed [brēd] v. to produce or develop.

bribe [brīb] n. money or gifts given in order to persuade someone to do something.

bronze [bronz] v. to become brown or tan.

brood [brood] v. to think in a moody way.

bungalow [bung′gə lō′] n. a small house, usually of one story.

C

capsize [kap′sīz, kap sīz′] v. to turn over, as a boat in water.

captivate [kap′tə vāt′] v. to fascinate; enchant.

cascade [kas kād′] n. flow, as water in a waterfall.

ceremonial [ser′ə mō′nē əl] n. formal activities for a special occasion; ritual.

champ [champ] v. to chew vigorously and noisily; make chewing movements.

cherish [cher′ish] v. to hold dear; to love and wish to take care of.

chronicle [kron′i kəl] n. a history of events in the order that they happened.

clad [klad] adj. dressed; clothed.

clamber [klam′bər, klam′ər] v. to climb awkwardly, using hands and feet.

clamp [klamp] v. to grasp tightly.

clench [klench] v. to press together tightly.

cobble [kob′əl] n. a rounded stone, used in paving streets.

cobblestone [kob′əl stōn′] n. same as **cobble.**

commission [kə mish′ən] n. a share of money from sales that is paid to the salesperson.

commuter [kə mūt′ər] n. a regular traveler, often to and from work.

compel [kəm pel′] v. to force or urge. – **compellingly,** adv.

compensate [kom′pən sāt′] v. to make up for something.

complacent [kəm plā′sənt] adj. satisfied, especially with oneself.

comply [kəm plī′] v. to act in an agreeable way, in accordance with the rules.

comprehensive [kom′pri hen′siv] adj. large; including a great quantity.

compulsion [kəm pul′shən] n. an urge that cannot be resisted.

conceal [kən sēl′] v. to hide.

conception [kən sep′shən] n. an idea; understanding.

concession [kən sesh′ən] n. something granted or conceded.

concoct [kon kokt′, kən kokt′] v. to prepare; put together.

condemn [kən dem′] v. to declare the guilt of; convict.

conducive [kən doo′siv, kən dū′siv] adj. helpful; leading to.

confront [kən frunt′] v. to meet face to face.

conjecture [kən jek′chər] v. to guess or form an opinion.

consequence [kon′sə kwens′, kon′sə kwəns] n. result; outcome. – **consequently,** adv.

considerable [kən sid′ər ə bəl] adj. important; great. – **considerably,** adv.

consolation [kon′sə lā′shən] n. a comfort; cheerful thought.

conspicuous [kən spik′u əs] adj. easily seen; obvious. – **conspicuously,** adv.

consternation [kon′ stər nā′shən] n. a fearful concern; worry.

construe [kən stroo′] v. to consider; understand to be.

consume [kən soom′] v. to destroy; eat up.

contemplate [kon′təm plāt′] v. to consider; look at; give thought to. – **contemplative,** adj.

contempt [kən tempt′] n. scorn; very strong dislike.

continual [kən tin′ū əl] adj. persisting; not ever stopping.

contort [kən tôrt] v. to twist out of shape.

contract [kən trakt′] v. to tighten; make tense.

contrive [kən trīv′] v. to create; invent.

convulsive [kən vul′siv] adj. having violent movements. – **convulsively,** adv.

cordial [kôr′jəl] adj. friendly; in a warm manner. – **cordially,** adv.

correspond [kôr′ə spond′, kor′ə spond′] v. to communicate by writing letters.

corroborate [kə rob′ə rāt′] v. to support; give proof of.

countenance [koun′tə nəns] v. face; features.

counteract [koun′tər akt′] v. to check; oppose.

counterpart [koun′tər pärt′] n. matching persons or things.

covet [kuv′it] v. to want to own or have something.

cower [kou′ər] v. to shrink or huddle, as in fear.

crag [krag] n. rough, rugged cliff or projecting rock.

cringe [krinj] v. to shrink, as in fear.

critter [krit′ər] n. INFORMAL. a creature.

crux [kruks] n. the most important point.

cubic [kū′bik] adj. shaped like a square and having three dimensions.

cultivated [kul′tə vāt′id] adj. prepared for planting and growing crops.

cunning [kun′ing] adj. clever; crafty. – **cunningly,** adv.

currency [kur′ən sē] n. money, either paper or coins.

customary [kus′tə mer′ē] adj. usual.

D

dahlia [dal′yə, däl′yə] n. a large, brightly colored flower.

dainty [dān′tē] adj. graceful; delicate. – **daintily,** adv.

dapper [dap′ər] adj. neat; trim; well-dressed.

dappled [dap′əld] adj. marked with spots.

dazzle [daz′əl] v. to shine brightly.

deduce [di doos′, di dūs′] v. to draw a conclusion from

facts.

deflate [di flāt'] *v.* to lose air or gas and shrink in size.

deft [deft] *adj.* skillful. – **deftly,** *adv.*

defy [di fī'] *v.* to resist boldly.

dejection [di jek'shən] *n.* sadness; lowness of spirits.

deliberation [di lib'ə rā'shən] *n.* careful thought and consideration.

deluge [del'ūj] *n.* anything that overwhelms or rushes like a flood.

deportment [di pôrt'mənt] *n.* behavior; manners.

designate [dez'ig nāt'] *v.* to show; point out.

desolate [des'ə lit] *adj.* lonely; without joy. – **desolateness** *n.* – **desolation** [des'ə lā'shən] *n.*

despondency [di spon'dən sē] *n.* a loss of hope.

despondent [di spon'dənt] *adj.* sad; depressed. – **despondently,** *adv.*

despotism [des'pə tiz'əm] *n.* complete control or authority.

destine [des'tin] *v.* to set apart for a certain purpose.

destiny [des'tə nē] *n.* a future or fate that is sure to come about.

detect [di tekt'] *v.* to notice; discover.

dethrone [dē thrōn'] *v.* to remove from high position.

diffident [dif'ə dənt] *adj.* shy; lacking confidence. – **diffidently,** *adv.*

dilapidated [di lap'ə dā'tid] *adj.* broken; old; neglected.

dilate [dī lāt'] *v.* to open wide; expand.

diminish [di min'ish] *v.* to grow smaller in size.

dip [dip] *v.* to lower, then raise again.

disability [dis'ə bil'ə tē] *n.* a handicap; lack of ability.

discern [di surn', di zurn'] *v.* to see; recognize.

disciplinarian [dis'ə pli när'ē ən] *n.* one who insists on strict rules of behavior.

discreet [dis krēt'] *adj.* careful; having good judgment.

dishearten [dis härt'ən] *v.* to discourage.

dishevelment [di shev'əl mənt] *n.* state of being untidy and rumpled.

disinterested [dis in'tris tid, dis in'tər is tid, -in'tə res'tid] *adj.* not influenced by personal concerns.

dismal [diz'məl] *adj.* gloomy, miserable, without cheer. – **dismally,** *adv.*

dismount [dis mount'] *v.* to get off or down, as from a horse.

disparaging [dis par'ij ing] *adj.* in a critical way or manner. – **disparagingly,** *adv.*

dispel [dis pel'] *v.* to drive away or cause to disappear.

displease [dis plēz'] *v.* to annoy or offend.

dispute [dis pūt'] *v.* to argue; disagree.

dissuade [di swād'] *v.* to prevent by means of persuasion.

distinct [dis tingkt'] *adj.* **1.** different; separate. **2.** definite; noticeable.

distinguish [dis ting'gwish] *v.* to see clearly.

distort [dis tôrt'] *v.* to twist; bend out of shape.

distraction [dis trak'shən] *n.* the act of drawing attention away from a planned action.

distress [dis tres'] *v.* to cause pain or sorrow.

distribute [dis trib'ūt] *v.* to give out in shares.

ditto [dit'ō] *n.* an exact copy.

divert [di vurt', dī vurt'] *v.* to attract; amuse; entertain. – **diversion** [di vur'zhən, dī vur'zhən] *n.*

docile [dos'l] *adj.* quiet; obedient. – **docilely,** *adv.*

doeskin [dō'skin] *n.* leather made from the hide of a female deer.

domestic [də mes'tik] *adj.* relating to home and family.

dominion [də min'yən] *n.* country, territory.

E

eagerness [ē'gər nis] *n.* enthusiasm; state of being impatient and enthusiastic.

eaves [ēvz] *n. pl.* the overhanging edge or edges of a sloping roof.

ecstasy [ek'stə sē] *n.* complete joy or delight.

egotism [ē'gə tiz'əm, ēg'ə tiz'əm] *n.* sense of one's own importance and worth.

embankment [em bangk'mənt] *n.* a bank of material put up to hold back water or support roadbeds.

embed [em bed'] *v.* to stick into and enclose.

ember [em'bər] *n.* hot piece of wood or coal in the ashes of a fire.

emphatic [em fat'ik] *adj.* strong; striking.

encounter [en koun'tər] *n.* meeting, often a chance meeting.

endeavor [en dev'ər] *n.* effort; attempt.

endow [en dou'] *v.* to give or provide.

engross [en grōs'] *v.* to occupy or absorb.

engulf [en gulf'] *v.* to swallow up.

enrich [en rich'] *v.* to improve; strengthen.

enthrone [en thrōn'] *v.* to put on a throne and give authority to rule.

entomb [en tōōm'] *v.* to bury.

entwine [en twīn'] *v.* to twist or twine around.

envious [en'vē əs] *adj.* jealous; feeling resentment.

essence [es'əns] *n.* that which makes a thing what it is.

evolve [i volv'] *v.* to develop; grow.

exasperate [ig zas'pə rāt'] *v.* irritate; annoy.

exclusive [iks klōō'siv] *adj.* complete; entire. – **exclusively,** *adv.*

exile [eg'zīl, ek'sīl] *n.* state of being forced to live away from home and country.

exotic [ig zot'ik] *adj.* strange and very beautiful.

exquisite [eks'kwi zit, iks kwis'it] *adj.* rare and delicately beautiful.

extend [iks tend'] *v.* to stretch out to full length.

extension [iks ten'shən] *n.* allowance of additional time.

extricate [eks'trə kāt'] *v.* to set free or remove.

F

famished [fam'isht] *adj.* very hungry; starving.

fanciful [fan'si fəl] *adj.* imaginary; not real.

farce [färs] *n.* ridiculous situation; absurdity.

feign [fān] *v.* to pretend; make believe.

---

at; āpe; cär; end; mē; it; īce; hot; ōld; fôrk; wood; fōōl; oil; out; up; ūse; turn; ə in ago, taken, pencil, lemon, circus; bat; chin; dear; five; game; hit; hw in white; joke; kit; lid; man; not; singer; pail; ride; sat; shoe; tag; thin; this; very; wet; yes; zoo; zh in treasure; ᴋʜ in loch, German ach; ɴ in French bon; œ in French feu, German schön

ferocious [fə rō′shəs] *adj.* savage; cruel.
fertile [furt′əl] *adj.* able to produce crops.
fiendish [fēnd′ish] *adj.* very wicked or cruel.
fitful [fit′fəl] *adj.* irregular; from time to time.
flamboyant [flam boi′ənt] *adj.* showy; having too much decoration.
fledgling [flej′ling] *n.* a very young bird.
fleecy [flē′sē] *adj.* soft; light.
fleet [flēt] *adj.* swift.
flounder [floun′dər] *v.* to move; plunge.
foreman [fôr′mən] *n.* a supervisor of a group of workers.
foresee [fôr sē′] *v.* to know in advance.
foretell [fôr tel′] *v.* to tell in advance.
forfeit [fôr′fit] *v.* to lose or pay for an error or mistake.
forge [fôrj] *v.* to make or work into shape.
forsake [fôr sāk′] *v.* to leave; desert. – **forsaken** [fôr sā′kən] *n.*
fortitude [fôr′tə tood′, for′tə tūd′] *n.* strength of mind in the face of danger or hardship.
fragrance [frā′grəns] *n.* a pleasant odor or smell.
frantic [fran′tik] *adj.* wild, active, and without control. – **frantically,** *adv.*
frenzied [fren′zēd] *adj.* frantic; greatly upset.
frolic [frol′ik] *n.* a merry activity; party.
frolicsome [frol′ik səm] *adj.* happily playful.
frond [frond] *n.* the leaf of a palm tree or fern.
furnish [fur′nish] *v.* to supply.
fuse [fūz] *v.* to blend or unite by melting together.

G

gait [gāt] *n.* a way of moving on foot.
gallows [gal′ōz] *adj.* criminal; deserving to be hanged.
gambit [gam′bit] *n.* an action, usually designed to gain advantage.
gangly [gang′lē] *adj.* thin; spindly.
garb [gärb] *n.* clothing.
garland [gär′lənd] *n.* a wreath of flowers or vines, usually given to honor the winner of a contest.
gauge [gāj] *n.* an instrument used to measure or to record measurements.
gawky [gô′kē] *adj.* awkward.
gear [gēr] *v.* to regulate something in order to make it conform to something else.
geometric [jē′ə met′rik] *adj.* having straight lines, triangles, squares, and similar forms.
gesticulate [jes tik′yə lāt′] *adj.* using expressive movements of head, body, or limbs to express a thought.
gingerly [jin′jər lē] *adv.* cautiously; carefully.
gird [gurd] *v.* **1.** to fasten or secure. **2.** to encircle.
glisten [glis′ən] *v.* to shine or sparkle.
gnash [nash] *v.* to grind together.
gorgeous [gôr′jəs] *adj.* brilliantly colored; very beautiful.
grave [grāv] *adj.* serious; earnest. – **gravely,** *adv.*
gypsy [jip′sē] *n.* one of an ancient group of wanderers.

H

habitual [hə bich′oo əl] *adj.* customary, happening often out of habit.
haggard [hag′ərd] *adj.* worn and thin from being tired or from suffering in some way.

hamper [ham′pər] *v.* to get in the way of; interfere.
handmaiden [hand′mād′ən] *n.* a female servant.
harness [här′nis] *n.* straps and bands that are placed on an animal's head and attached to the wagon or load the animal is to pull.
harry [har′ē] *v.* to trouble; torment.
haul [hôl] *v.* to transport or carry as in a truck.
haunch [hônch] *n.* part of the body including the leg and hip.
heckle [hek′əl] *v.* to question continually, usually in an annoying way.
henceforth [hens′fôrth′, hens′fôrth′] *adv.* from now on.
hinder [hin′dər] *v.* to hold back.
hollow [hol′ō] *adj.* empty; scooped out.
holocaust [hol′ə kôst′, hō′lə kôst′] *n.* great destruction, especially by fire.
homage [hom′ij, om′ij] *n.* honor; respect.
homewards [hōm′wərdz] *adv.* toward home.
hostage [hos′tij] *n.* a person held as security that certain promises will be kept.
hostile [host′əl, host′īl] *adj.* unfriendly.
hover [huv′ər, hov′ər] *v.* to linger or stay nearby.
hue [hū] *n.* a color or shade.
hulk [hulk] *n.* a large mass, as the body of a wrecked ship.
humbug [hum′bug′] *n.* nonsense.
humiliation [hū mil′ē ā′shən, ū mil′ē ā′shən] *n.* shame; deep embarrassment.
hustle [hus′əl] *v.* to move rapidly and with energy.

I

ignition [ig nish′ən] *n.* the act of starting an engine by setting its fuel on fire.
illuminate [i loo′mə nāt′] *v.* to light up.
illumine [i loo′min] *v.* to make light.
impact [im′pakt] *n.* a force; blow.
imperturbable [im′pər tur′bə bəl] *adj.* calm; not easily disturbed. – **imperturbability,** *n.*
implore [im plôr′] *v.* to beg; plead with.
incantation [in′kan tā′shən] *n.* words used in casting a spell or performing magic.
incense [in sens′] *v.* to anger; enrage.
incessant [in ses′ənt] *adj.* continuing without interruption. – **incessantly,** *adv.*
incoherent [in′kō hēr′ənt, in′kō her′ənt] *adj.* impossible to understand.
incomprehensible [in′kom pri hen′sə bəl] *adj.* that cannot be understood.
incredulous [in krej′ə ləs] *adj.* unbelieving. – **incredulously,** *adv.*
indescribable [in′di skrī′bə bəl] *adj.* beyond description.
indignant [in dig′nənt] *adj.* filled with anger aroused by something unfair. – **indignantly,** *adv.*
ineptness [i nept′nəs] *n.* awkwardness; clumsiness.
inexplicable [in′iks plik′ə bəl] *adj.* that cannot be explained.
infinitesimal [in′fi nə tes′ə məl] *adj.* very small; unimportant.
inflection [in flek′shən] *n.* a change or variation.
inflexible [in flek′sə bəl] *adj.* stiff; rigid. – **inflexibly,** *adv.*
inhabitant [in hab′ət ənt] *n.* a resident; one who lives in a place permanently.

inhalation [in′hə lā′shən] *n.* the act of drawing something into the lungs.

inhuman [in hū′mən, in ū′mən] *adj.* unkind; lacking human feeling.

initiative [i nish′ə tiv] *n.* the first step in doing or beginning something.

inlet [in′let′] *n.* a narrow body of water leading inland from a larger body of water.

inquire [in kwīr′] *v.* to ask. — **inquiry,** *n.*

insecurity [in′si kyoor′ə tē] *n.* a lack of confidence and security.

insignificant [in′sig nif′ə kənt] *adj.* small in size or amount.

insolence [in′sə ləns] *n.* rudeness.

installment [in stôl′mənt] *n.* the portion of a sum of money owed to be repaid on specific dates.

instinctive [in stingk′ tiv] *adj.* natural; unlearned. — **instinctively,** *adv.*

insuperable [in soo′pər ə bəl] *adj.* that cannot be overcome.

interminable [in tur′mi nə bəl] *adj.* endless. — **interminably,** *adv.*

interpretation [in tur′prə tā′shən] *n.* an explanation that reveals the meaning of something.

intervene [in′tər vēn′] *v.* to come between opposing parties.

intimacy [in′tə mə sē] *n.* closeness.

intolerable [in tol′ər ə bəl] *adj.* unbearable. — **intolerably,** *adv.*

intone [in tōn′] *v.* to speak with a single, regular sound; chant.

intricate [in′tri kit] *adj.* complicated. — **intricately,** *adv.*

intrude [in trood′] *v.* to force upon.

invalid [in′və lid] *n.* one who is ill or disabled.

invariable [in vâr′ē ə bəl] *adj.* constant; unchanging. — **invariably,** *adv.*

irresistible [ir′i zis′tə bəl] *adj.* that cannot be opposed. — **irresistibly,** *adv.*

islet [ī′lit] *n.* a little island.

J

jest [jest] *n.* a joke; humorous remark.

jovial [jō′vē əl] *adj.* merry; good-humored.

K

keepsake [kēp′sāk′] *n.* something given or kept to remind one of the giver.

knot [not] *n.* a ribbon worn as an ornament.

L

laborious [lə bôr′ē əs] *adj.* requiring much work.

laden [lād′ən] *adj.* weighed down by carrying things.

lament [lə ment′] *v.* to speak sorrowfully.

languor [lang′ər] *n.* tenderness or softness of mood or feeling. — **languorous,** *adj.*

lapse [laps] *n.* a period or interval of time.

lash [lash] *n.* a whip.

lather [lath′ər] *n.* a state of excitement.

lavish [lav′ish] *adj.* more than necessary; generous. — **lavishly,** *adv.*

lax [laks] *adj.* loose; not firm.

layman [lā′mən] *n.* a person who does not belong to a certain profession.

legacy [leg′ə sē] *n.* something handed down from previous generations.

leisurely [lē′zhər lē, lēzh′ər lē] *adj.* not hurried; relaxed.

liberality [lib′ə ral′ə tē] *n.* generosity.

listless [list′lis] *adj.* without energy. — **listlessly,** *adv.*

literally [lit′ər ə lē] *adv.* actually; really.

lithe [līth] *adj.* bending easily; flexible.

lofty [lôf′tē] *adj.* too proud; haughty. — **loftily,** *adv.*

loiter [loi′tər] *v.* to move slowly or with frequent pauses.

lore [lôr] *n.* knowledge, particularly traditional learning passed on from generation to generation.

lunar [loo′nər] *adj.* of or relating to the moon.

lure [loor] *v.* to attract powerfully.

M

magnitude [mag′nə tood′, mag′nə tūd′] *n.* greatness of size and difficulty.

malice [mal′is] *n.* the wish to cause harm or injury to another. — **malicious** [mə lish′əs] *adj.*

martial [mär′shəl] *adj.* warlike.

masonry [mā′sən rē] *n.* a construction of brick, stone, or concrete.

masterpiece [mas′tər pēs′] *n.* something done with outstanding skill or craftsmanship.

meander [mē an′dər] *v.* to wander; follow a winding course.

mediocrity [mē′dē ok′rə tē] *n.* the state of being ordinary and not outstanding in any way.

meditate [med′ə tāt′] *v.* to think seriously; reflect.

medium [mē′dē əm] *n.* material or technique used for artistic expression.

melancholy [mel′ən kol′ē] **1.** *n.* depression, sadness. **2.** *adj.* gloomy; sad.

mince [mins] *n.* a mixture of chopped nuts, apples, raisins, and meat, used in pies.

ministry [min′is trē] *n.* a department in a government.

moderate [mod′ər it] *adj.* reasonable; not extreme. — **moderately,** *adv.*

moil [moil] *v.* to work hard.

momentous [mō men′təs] *adj.* of great importance. — **momentously,** *adv.*

morose [mə rōs′] *adj.* gloomy; withdrawn. — **morosely,** *adv.*

musket [mus′kit] *n.* a long-barreled gun used before the rifle was developed.

mutilate [mūt′əl āt′] *v.* to deform or injure seriously.

muzzle [muz′əl] *v.* to silence; prevent from speaking.

---

at; āpe; cär; end; mē; it; īce; hot; ōld; fôrk; wood; fool; oil; out; up; ūse; turn; ə in ago, taken, pencil, lemon, circus; bat; chin; dear; five; game; hit; hw in white; joke; kit; lid; man; not; singer; pail; ride; sat; shoe; tag; thin; this; very; wet; yes; zoo; zh in treasure; кн in loch, German ach; N in French bon; œ in French feu, German schön

N

nameless [nām′lis] *adj.* too terrible to be mentioned.

nimble [nim′bəl] *adj.* light and quick in movement. – **nimbly**, *adv.*

nonchalance [non′shə läns′, non′chə läns′] *n.* a lack of interest and enthusiasm. – **nonchalantly**, *adv.*

notwithstanding [not′with stan′ding, not′with stan′ding] *adv.* nevertheless.

nourishment [nur′ish mənt] *n.* food necessary for life and growth.

O

objectionable [əb jek′shə nə bəl] *adj.* not likable.

obscure [əb skyoor′] *adj.* not well known or easily discovered.

obsess [əb ses′] *v.* to occupy or trouble the mind.

obstinate [ob′stə nit] *adj.* stubborn; not easily persuaded.

obstruction [əb struk′shən] *n.* something that blocks a passage.

occult [ə kult′, ok′ult] *adj.* relating to hidden and secret practices.

odious [ō′dē əs] *adj.* hateful; disgusting.

ominous [om′ə nəs] *adj.* threatening, as warning of bad things to come.

overseer [ō′vər sē′ər] *n.* a person who directs working crews.

P

pacific [pə sif′ik] *adj.* peaceful; quiet; calm.

pageant [paj′ənt] *n.* a procession; parade.

pamper [pam′pər] *v.* to treat too well.

pang [pang] *n.* a sharp pain.

parch [pärch] *v.* to make very dry and thirsty.

passive [pas′iv] *adj.* weak; not effective.

paternal [pə tur′nəl] *adj.* like a father. – **paternally**, *adv.*

pathetic [pə thet′ik] *adj.* arousing pity and sadness. – **pathetically**, *adv.*

patriarch [pā′trē ärk′] *n.* an old man who is respected and honored.

patron [pā′trən] *n.* a person who supports, or assists, a place, person, or organization.

patronize [pā′trə nīz′, pat′rə nīz′] *v.* to feel and act superior toward others.

peaked [pē′kid] *adj.* looking sickly; pale.

penetrate [pen′ə trāt′] *v.* **1.** to pass into or through. **2.** to see clearly; understand.

pension [pen′shən] *n.* regular payments of money by a former employer given to someone who has retired.

perfumed [pər fūmd′] *adj.* sweet and pleasant smelling.

periodic [pēr′ē od′ik] *adj.* happening on occasion. – **periodically**, *adv.*

perpendicular [pur′pən dik′yə lər] *adj.* going straight up from a base; upright.

perpetual [pər pech′oo əl] *adj.* constant; lasting forever.

perpetuate [pər pech′oo āt′] *v.* to keep in use; to keep alive.

perplex [pər pleks′] *v.* to fill with uncertainty; confuse.

personage [pur′sə nij] *n.* a person of importance.

perspective [pər spek′tiv] *n.* the effect of distance on the way something looks.

pertain [pər tān′] *v.* to relate; have to do with.

phantom [fan′təm] *adj.* ghostly; unreal.

philanthropist [fi lan′thrə pist′] *n.* a person who gives money or time to good causes.

philosophy [fə los′ə fē] *n.* the study of the basic purpose and nature of humanity, the universe, and life itself. – **philosophic**, *adj.*

physique [fi zēk′] *n.* condition and development of the body.

piercing [pērs′ing] *adj.* shrill; sharp.

pilgrimage [pil′grə mij] *n.* a journey to a special place.

pitch [pich] *v.* to fall forward; plunge.

piteous [pit′ē əs] *adj.* causing feelings of sadness and sympathy.

pliant [plī′ənt] *adj.* easily influenced.

plunder [plun′dər] *v.* to rob, using force.

ponder [pon′dər] *v.* to think carefully; consider.

ponderous [pon′dər əs] *adj.* heavy; clumsy. – **ponderously**, *adv.*

possessive [pə zes′iv] *adj.* in the manner of an owner. – **possessively**, *adv.*

potential [pə ten′shəl] *adj.* possible but not actual.

precipice [pres′ə pis] *n.* a high, steep face of rock.

preliminary [pri lim′ə ner′ē] *adj.* coming before the main event or action.

premium [prē′mē əm] *n.* a high price.

premonition [prē′mə nish′ən, prem′ə nish′ən] *n.* a feeling that something is about to happen.

preside [pri zīd′] *v.* to act as an authority, as at a meeting.

procession [prə sesh′ən] *n.* a group moving forward in an orderly way, often in a line.

profess [prə fes′] *v.* to claim; declare.

profound [prə found′] *adj.* showing great knowledge and understanding. – **profoundly**, *adv.*

profuse [prə fūs′] great in amount; plentiful. – **profusely**, *adv.*

prolong [prə long′] *v.* to make longer, especially in time.

prominent [prom′ə nənt] *adj.* well-known or important; outstanding.

prompt [prompt] *adj.* on time; without delay. – **promptly**, *adv.*

prophecy [prof′ə sē] *n.* a knowledge of the future; prediction.

proposal [prə pō′zəl] *n.* something offered for consideration.

propose [prə pōz′] *v.* to suggest; present an idea.

proposition [prop′ə zish′ən] *n.* something proposed for consideration.

proprietor [prə prī′ə tər] *n.* an owner or operator.

prosperous [pros′pər əs] *adj.* successful; flourishing.

protector [prə tek′tər] *n.* something worn as a shield to prevent damage or injury.

protrude [prō trood′] *v.* to stick out.

prune [proon] *v.* to cut off parts of a plant, usually to improve growth or appearance.

psychiatrist [si kī′ə trist, sī kī′ə trist] *n.* a doctor who treats emotional and mental disorders.

pulp [pulp] *n.* the juicy, soft inner part of certain fruits and vegetables.

pungent [pun′jənt] *adj.* strong smelling.

pyre [pīr] *n.* a pile of wood or other material for burning a dead body.

R

radiant [rā′dē ənt] *adj.* bright; sending out rays of light. – **radiance,** *n.*

radiate [rā′dē āt′] *v.* to move outward from a center.

radical [rad′i kəl] *adj.* extreme; to a great extent. – **radically,** *adv.*

rafter [raf′tər] *n.* a beam that supports a roof.

ratio [rā′shē ō, rā′shō] *n.* a comparison between two things.

rational [rash′ən əl] *adj.* sensible; reasonable.

reaper [rē′pər] *n.* a machine used to cut and gather grain.

reassure [rē′ə shoor′] *v.* to restore confidence and courage. – **reassuringly,** *adv.*

rebellion [ri bel′yən] *n.* an organized resistance to authority.

rebellious [ri bel′yəs] *adj.* refusing to obey; resisting. – **rebelliously,** *adv.*

rebuke [ri būk′] *v.* to scold, usually sharply.

recoil [ri koil′] *v.* to return to; spring back.

recollect [rek′ə lekt′] *v.* to remember; recall.

reconstruct [rē′kən strukt′] *v.* to rebuild in the mind; tell exactly what happened.

recurrence [ri kur′əns] *n.* a repetition.

reeducate [rē ej′ə kāt′] *v.* to teach again.

reflective [ri flek′tiv] *adj.* thoughtful. – **reflectively,** *adv.*

refugee [ref′ū jē′] *n.* one who has fled his or her homeland.

regulation [reg′yə lā′shən] *n.* an order or rule governing behavior.

reject [ri jekt′] *v.* to refuse to accept. – **rejection,** *n.*

relief [ri lēf′] *n.* financial aid, as from government funds, to those in poverty or need.

reluctance [ri luk′təns] *n.* unwillingness; hesitation.

reluctant [ri luk′tənt] *adj.* unwilling. – **reluctantly,** *adv.*

reminiscent [rem′ə nis′ənt] *adj.* remembering or suggesting the past. – **reminiscently,** *adv.*

remnant [rem′nənt] *n.* a remaining piece or part.

render [ren′dər] *v.* to cause to be or become; make.

reorganization [rē′ôr gə ni zā′shən] *n.* an act of putting things in order again or anew.

repent [ri pent′] *v.* to feel deep sorrow or regret for having done something.

repose [ri pōz′] *n.* rest; quietness. – **reposeful,** *adj.*

repress [ri pres′] *v.* to hold back or keep under control.

reproach [ri prōch′] *n.* an expression of blame. – **reproachfully,** *adv.*

repulsive [ri pul′siv] *adj.* causing extreme dislike.

resentful [ri zent′fəl] *adj.* angry; with bitter feelings.

resignation [rez′ig nā′shən] *n.* **1.** a formal notice of leaving a job. **2.** the acceptance of something without protest or complaint.

resolute [rez′ə loot′] *adj.* determined; decided.

resort [ri zôrt′] *v.* to make use of.

restive [res′tiv] *adj.* restless; uneasy. – **restively,** *adv.*

retain [ri tān′] *v.* to have or continue to have; keep.

revelation [rev′ə lā′shən] *n.* the recognition of new information.

reverence [rev′ər ens, rev′rəns] *n.* a feeling of deep respect.

revision [ri vizh′ən] *n.* a change made in order to improve.

revive [ri vīv′] *v.* to come to life or consciousness.

revoke [ri vōk′] *v.* to take back; withdraw.

ridicule [rid′ə kūl′] *n.* words or actions intended to make someone or something feel or seem foolish.

ritual [rich′oo əl] *n.* a routine faithfully followed.

rogue [rōg] *n.* a dishonest person; villain.

rout [rout] *v.* to drive out.

ruthless [rooth′lis] *adj.* without mercy or pity.

S

sanction [sangk′shən] *v.* to give approval.

scallop [skôl′əp, skal′əp] *n.* a curved shape resembling the shape of a scallop shell, forming a decorative border.

scornful [skôrn′fəl] *adj.* showing or feeling low regard for something or someone. – **scornfully,** *adv.*

scoundrel [skoun′drəl] *n.* a dishonest person; villain.

scowl [skoul] *n.* an angry frown.

scrape [skrāp] *n.* a troublesome or difficult situation.

scruple [skroo′pəl] *n.* a feeling of doubt or concern; worry.

scuttle [skut′əl] *v.* to move with short, rapid steps.

sear [sēr] *v.* to burn.

seawards [sē′wərdz] *adv.* to or toward the sea.

seethe [sēth] *v.* to rise; surge.

sever [sev′ər] *v.* to cut off, usually violently.

shaft [shaft] *n.* a beam or ray.

shambles [sham′bəlz] *n. pl.* a place or situation that is not orderly or sensible.

sheen [shēn] *n.* a brightness; shininess.

sheer [shēr] *adj.* **1.** straight up and down; steep. **2.** pure; utter.

shimmer [shim′ər] *v.* to shine or glimmer.

shrine [shrīn] *n.* a holy place.

signify [sig′nə fī′] *v.* to be a sign of something; represent.

simultaneous [sī′məl tā′nē əs] *adj.* happening at the same time. – **simultaneously,** *adv.*

sinew [sin′ū] *n.* a muscular power or strength.

singularity [sing′gyə lar′ə tē] *n.* strangeness; state of being unusual or extraordinary.

sinister [sin′is tər] *adj.* threatening or suggesting evil.

skein [skān] *n.* yarn or thread coiled into a bundle.

smirk [smurk] *v.* to smile in a silly or affected way.

smite [smīt] *v.* to strike hard, often with the hand or a weapon.

smolder [smōl′dər] *v.* to burn with little or no flame.

smote [smōt] past tense of **smite.**

smug [smug] *adj.* too highly pleased with oneself.

snigger [snig′ər] *v.* to laugh slyly and scornfully.

solemn [sol′əm] *adj.* serious; sober; earnest.

solitary [sol′ə ter′ē] *adj.* lonely; without companions.

spacious [spā′shəs] *adj.* large; having much space.

spake [spāk] ARCHAIC. a past tense of **speak.**

sparse [spärs] *adj.* thinly spread; not crowded. – **sparsely,** *adv.*

---

at; āpe; cär; end; mē; it; īce; hot; ōld; fôrk; wood; fool; oil; out; up; ūse; turn; ə in ago, taken, pencil, lemon, circus; bat; chin; dear; five; game; hit; hw in white; joke; kit; lid; man; not; singer; pail; ride; sat; shoe; tag; thin; this; very; wet; yes; zoo; zh in treasure; KH in loch, German ach; N in French bon; œ in French feu, German schön

spasm [spaz′əm] *n.* **1.** a sudden movement caused by tightening of muscles. **2.** a sudden, violent burst of feeling.

speculation [spek′yə lā′shən] *n.* careful thought on a subject in order to form an opinion.

spindly [spind′lē] *adj.* thin and sticklike.

spiral [spī′rəl] *adj.* having a shape that winds upward, as if along a cylinder.

spirited [spir′i tid] *adj.* lively.

spontaneous [spon tā′nē əs] *adj.* happening without planning. – **spontaneously,** *adv.*

squabble [skwob′əl] *n.* a noisy argument about matters of little importance.

squander [skwon′dər] *v.* to spend or use in a wasteful manner.

stark [stärk] *adj.* plain; severe.

status [stā′təs, stat′əs] *n.* the position of one person in relation to others; rank.

stealthy [stel′ thē] *adj.* moving or acting in a secret way. – **stealthily,** *adv.*

stipulation [stip′yə lā′shən] *n.* a condition in a contract that states something signers are required to do.

strenuous [stren′ū əs] *adj.* very active or energetic. – **strenuously,** *adv.*

stricken [strik′ən] *adj.* strongly affected or overwhelmed.

strident [strīd′ənt] *adj.* sounding harsh and grating. – **stridently,** *adv.*

strive [strīv] *v.* to try; make an effort.

strove [strōv] past tense of **strive.**

stubble [stub′əl] *n.* the short stalks of plants, such as corn, that are left standing after plants have been cut for harvest.

submerge [səb murj′] *v.* to overshadow; obscure.

suburban [sə bur′bən] *adj.* relating to an area on the outer edges of a city.

suffocate [suf′ə kāt′] *v.* to die from lack of air to breathe. – **suffocation,** *n.*

sultry [sul′trē] *adj.* hot and humid.

summon [sum′ən] *v.* to send for.

sumptuous [sump′choo əs] *adj.* costly and magnificent.

superstitious [soo′pər stish′əs] *adj.* fearful of the unknown.

supposed [sə pōz′əd] *adj.* considered to be true. – **supposedly,** *adv.*

surge [surj] *n.* a swelling motion like that of waves.

surly [sur′lē] *adj.* rude; bad-tempered.

surmount [sər mount′] *v.* to be above; top.

suspend [sə spend′] *v.* to attach from above.

sway [swā] *v.* to move from side to side or back and forth.

symmetry [sim′ə trē] *n.* equal arrangement of parts around a central point.

T

tantalize [tant′əl īz] *v.* to tempt by seeming to promise something that cannot be had; to tease.

tapestry [tap′is trē] *n.* a design or picture, usually referring to a ruglike hanging for a wall.

tatter [tat′ər] *n.* a torn, ragged piece of something.

tauten [tôt′ən] *v.* to tighten or become tense.

tawny [tô′nē] *adj.* yellowish-brown.

teem [tēm] *v.* to be full; swarm.

tentacle [ten′tə kəl] *n.* a long, thin armlike part of an animal, used for feeling, grasping, and moving.

tentative [ten′tə tiv] *adj.* in an uncertain, hesitant way, as in an experiment. – **tentatively,** *adv.*

terminate [tur′mə nāt′] *v.* to come to an end or to bring to an end.

testy [tes′tē] *adj.* cross; irritated; annoyed. – **testily,** *adv.*

thoroughfare [thur′ə fâr′] *n.* a street; avenue.

thrift [thrift] *n.* careful management of money or other goods and resources.

thrive [thrīv] *v.* to grow rapidly and well.

tier [tēr] *n.* a level or rank, often considered in order of importance.

timeworn [tīm′wôrn′] *adj.* showing the effects of much use.

toil [toil] **1.** *n.* hard work. **2.** *v.* to work hard and for a long time.

torso [tôr′sō] *n.* in humans, the body, from shoulders to hips.

totter [tot′ər] *v.* to shake; move as if off balance.

tousle [tou′zəl] *v.* to put into disorder.

trample [tram′pəl] *v.* to walk heavily in a way that destroys whatever is underfoot.

tranquil [trang′kwəl] *adj.* undisturbed; quiet. – **tranquilly,** *adv.*

transformation [trans′fər mā′shən] *n.* a complete change in appearance or shape.

transient [tran′shənt] *adj.* lasting for a short time; passing quickly.

trappings [trap′ingz] *n. pl.* richly decorated covering for an animal, especially for a horse.

trifle [trī′fəl] *adv.* slightly; somewhat.

U

unabashed [un′ə basht′] *adj.* without embarrassment.

unabiding [un′ə bīd′ing] *adj.* lasting only for a short time.

unaccustomed [un′ə kus′təmd] *adj.* unfamiliar; unusual; not used to.

unalterable [un ôlt′ər ə bəl] *adj.* unable to be changed.

unanimity [ū′nə nim′ə tē] *n.* the state of being in complete agreement.

unauthorized [un ô′thə rīzd′] *adj.* not approved or permitted.

uncanny [un kan′ē] *adj.* strange; weird.

uncoil [un koil′] *v.* to unwind.

undercurrent [un′dər kur′ənt] *n.* an underlying feeling or attitude.

undertake [un′dər tāk′] *v.* to assume or set about doing.

ungrateful [un grāt′fəl] *adj.* not thankful; lacking appreciation.

unhesitating [un hez′ə tā′ting] *adj.* immediate; prompt.

unison [ū′nə sən, ū′nə zən] *n.* complete or perfect agreement, usually in movement or use of the voice.

unprecedented [un′pres′ə den′tid] *adj.* unusual; unexpected; without previous example.

unreliable [un′ri lī′ə bəl] *adj.* not to be trusted or counted on.

unrepentant [un′ri pent′ənt] *adj.* not having regrets for past sins or wrongs.

unstinting [un′stint′ing] *adj.* very generous. – **unstintingly,** *adv.*

unthrifty [un thrif′tē] *adj.* not saving; spending carelessly. – **unthriftily,** *adv.*

urgency [ur′jən sē] *n.* a state or condition calling for immediate attention.

urgent [ur′jənt] *adj.* in an insistent, persisting manner. – **urgently,** *adv.*

V

vague [vāg] *adj.* not exact or clear; hazy.

valiant [val′yənt] *adj.* brave; courageous.

valuable [val′ū ə bəl, val′yə bəl] *adj.* worth a great deal; having importance.

vapor [vā′pər] *n.* floating, steamlike mist.

vehement [ve′ə mənt] *adj.* violent; with great energy. – **vehemently,** *adv.*

veinous [vē′nəs] *adj.* having large veins or blood vessels.

vendor [ven′dər] *n.* someone who sells goods.

veranda [və ran′də] *n.* a porch, usually with a roof.

vibrant [vī′brənt] *adj.* having life and energy.

vicinity [vi sin′ə tē] *n.* a neighborhood; area.

vicious [vish′əs] *adj.* intense; severe.

vigil [vij′əl] *n.* a watch or period of being awake to watch or guard something.

villain [vil′ən] *n.* a wicked, evil, or criminal person. – **villainous,** *adj.*

virtual [vur′chōo əl] *adj.* being so in reality but not in fact. – **virtually,** *adv.*

vixen [vik′sən] *n.* a female fox.

volley [vol′ē] *n.* an outburst of a number of things in quick succession.

voluminous [və lōo′mə nəs] *adj.* large; bulky.

W

wean [wēn] *v.* to accustom a baby or young animal to food other than milk.

whiff [hwif, wif] *n.* slight smell.

wile [wīl] *n.* a trick used to cheat. – **wily** *adj.*

witty [wit′ē] *adj.* clever.

wobble [wob′əl] *v.* to move or sway from side to side.

wrath [rath] *n.* anger.

wrench [rench] *v.* to pull with a sudden motion; yank away.

wrinkle [ring′kəl] *v.* to form or make a crease in.

writhe [rīth] *v.* to move with a twisting or turning motion, as if in pain.

wrought [rôt] *adj.* made or formed.

at; āpe; cär; end; mē; it; īce; hot; ōld; fôrk; wood; fōol; oil; out; up; ūse; turn; ə in ago, taken, pencil, lemon, circus; bat; chin; dear; five; game; hit; hw in white; joke; kit; lid; man; not; singer; pail; ride; sat; shoe; tag; thin; this; very; wet; yes; zoo; zh in treasure; ĸʜ in loch, German ach; ɴ in French bon; œ in French feu, German schön

VOCABULARY REVIEW

In addition to the words listed in the Glossary and the words covered in the word study sections throughout this book, each of the following words is presented to help you prepare for standardized tests of verbal skills. The page numbers at the right tell where you can find these words treated in *Introducing Literature*.

abandoned	22	fanciful	317	reluctance	150
alms	95	fitful	58	ridicule	150
approbation	201	flamboyant	295	rigorously	65
assume	221	formally	65	scornfully	14
billow	22	forsake	186	seawards	17
bronzed	17	gait	14	shimmered	135
brooded	295	haul	115	shoo	461
burden	161	homewards	17	shrine	461
cascade	265	hostile	115	slender	447
clenched	182	humble	447	smug	221
complied	201	illumined	22	sniggering	265
concocted	295	incessantly	201	solitary	186
consternation	135	infinitesimal	58	spiral	115
contracting	158	inquired	65	spirited	158
covet	150	insignificant	150	spontaneously	295
cowered	14	islet	186	squandered	295
cunningly	14	keepsake	65	stark	22
dahlias	317	languidly	186	summons	158
daintily	115	lash	95	swaying	221
dazzling	182	lures	17	tapestry	182
deftly	95	moonlight	279	thrived	58
descended	279	moor	265	torrent	265
desolateness	201	obstinacy	447	trample	135
detect	58	obstinate	161	tranquilly	150
diminishing	22	perplexed	279	turf	279
dipping	17	pleaded	461	uncoiling	182
discern	95	pondered	135	valiant	14
dismount	95	possessively	161	valuable	115
emphatic	161	precipice	201	varied	447
erect	447	radiant	317	veranda	158
exasperating	221	radiating	186	vibrant	317
extension	161	rafters	158	wobble	182
faint	461	reconstructing	65	wrinkling	135
faltered	461	regulation	58		

INDEX OF TITLES BY THEME

INDEX OF SKILLS

Page numbers in boldface italics indicate entries in the Writing About Literature Handbook. Page numbers in italics indicate entries in the Reading and Literary Terms Handbook.

READING AND LITERARY SKILLS

Act, 45
Alliteration, 219, 274, *598*
Allusion, 430, *598*
Anecdote, 303, 323, 325, *598*
Article, ***586***
Atmosphere, 131, 172, *598*
Audience, 47, 289, *598*
Autobiography, 21, 289, 294, 333, *598*

Biography, 21, 289, 303, *598*

Cause and effect, 72, 479, *598*
Characterization, 95, 109, 170, 434, 498, 532, ***574, 598***
  character traits, 95, 170, 434, 498, 532, ***574, 598***
  techniques of, 109, ***574, 598***
Characters, 105, 171, 368, 404, 434, 447, 498, ***574, 598***
  change in, 368, 404
  flat and round, 434
  major and minor, 498
  motives of, 105, 171, 447
Chronological order, 72, 308, *599*
Climax, 65, 172, 308, 332, 404, *599*
Comparison and contrast, 143, 519, *599*
Concrete language, 235, *599*
Concrete poetry, 257, *599*
Conflict, 79, 85, 170, 308, 330, 404, 451, 508, *599*

Description, 289, 312, 327, *599*
Details, 100, 138, 202, 282, 312, 406, *599*
Dialect, 238, *600*
Dialogue, 45, 161, 171, 341, 355, *600*
Drama, 44, 341, 404, ***592, 594,*** *600*

End-stopped lines, 247, *600*
Essay, 21, 289, *600*
Expository essay, 289, 317, *600*

Fable, 145, 455, *600*
Fact, 334
Fantasy, 478, *600*
Fiction, 485, *601,*
Figurative language, 273, *601*
Flashback, 85, *601*
Flexibility, in reading rate, 48
Folk literature, 413, 461, *601*
Foreshadowing, 91, 172, 369, 508, *601*

Generalizations, 317

Haiku, 250, *601*
Hero, 466, *601*
Humor, 308

Imagery, 233, 274, 498, *601*
Inferring, 100, 138, 170, 203, 283, 472, *601*
  about characters, 100, 472
  about setting, 138
Interview, 303
Irony, 178, *602*

Limerick, 254, *602*
Lyric poetry, 271, *602*

Main idea, 317, 324
Metamorphosis, 439, *602*
Metaphor, 243, *602*
Mood, 131
Moral, 455
Motivation, 105, 447, 480, *602*
Myth, 413, 422, *602*

Narration, 308, 324, *602*
Narrative poetry, 258, 264, *602*
Narrator, 115, 126, 532, *602*
  first-person, 115
  third-person, 126
Nonfiction, 21, 289, 308, 312, 317, 322, ***586, 588,*** *603*
  descriptive, 312
  distinguishing from fiction, 21, 289, ***586, 588,*** *603*
  expository, 317
  narrative, 308
  persuasive, 322
Note taking, 534
Novel, 91, 485, *603*

Onomatopoeia, 228, *603*
Opinion, 334
Oral tradition, 216, 341, 418, *603*
Outlining, 536

Paraphrasing, 535, *603*
Persuasion, 322, 336, *603*
Plot, 57, 65, 404, 532, ***572,*** *603*
  and suspense, 57
  climax and resolution, 65
  in drama, 404
  in novel, 532
Poetry, 16, 209, 214, 216, ***580, 582,*** *603*
Predicting outcomes, 91, 204, 369, 508
Prose, 13, 209, *603*
Purpose, 47, 289, 295, *604*

Reading rates, 48
Refrain, 214, *604*
Repetition, 218, 274, *604*
Research, 303
Resolution, 65, 172, *604*

Rhyme, 16, 221, *604*
Rhythm, 16, 225, 274, *604*
Run-on lines, 248, *604*

Scanning, 49, *604*
Scene, 45
Setting, 131, 169, 186, 404, 532, *605*
   effect on plot and character, 186
Short story, 13, 53, **576,** *605*
Similarities and differences, 46
Simile, 240, *605*
Skimming, 49, *605*
Stage directions and staging, 45, 341, 385, *605*
Stanza, 16, 252, *605*
Stereotypes, 200, *605*
Suspense, 57, *605*

Test-taking skills, 534
Theme, 145, 156, 174, 178, 186, 200, 209, 267, 269, 342,
   368, 371, 404, *605*
   implied, 156, 269
   in drama, 368, 404
   in poetry, 209, 267
   in short story, 174, 178, 186, 200
   stated, 145, 267
Thesis statement, 317, 324, *606*
Title, 166, 174, 323, *606*
Topic sentence, 322, 331, *606*
Total effect, 178, 186, 200, 277, 323, 404, 532
   in drama, 404
   in nonfiction, 323
   in novel, 532
   in poetry, 277
   in short story, 178, 186, 200
Word choice, 238

COMPOSITION SKILLS

Page numbers in boldface italics indicate entries in the
Writing About Literature Handbook.

ANALYTICAL
Writing *about* the following:

Autobiography, 295, **586**
Character, 105, 115, 156, 174, 369, 447, 472, **574**
   character sketch, writing, 115, 156, 174, 447, 472, **574**
   comparing, 369
Conflict, 451, 477
Descriptive essay, 312, **586**
Dialogue, 423
Evaluation, writing, 418
Fable, 455
Haiku, 250
Imagery, 233, 240
Limerick, 254
Metamorphosis, 439
Narrative essay, 308
Nonfiction, 295, 312, **586**
Onomatopoeia, 238
Pauses, 226

Persuasive essay, 322
Plot, 57, 72, 85, 126, 167, 279, 443, 461, **572**
Poetry, 218, 269, 277, 281, **580**
Poetry and prose, 265
Setting, 131, 182
Theme, 145
Title, 216

Writing the following analytical essays:

Book review, 533, **592**
Drama review, 45, 405, **592**
Essay question, answering, 14, 58, 135, 434, 466, **570**
Opinion, 150, 257

CREATIVE
Writing the following:

Advertisement, 238
Description, 156, 182, 216, 265, 269, 312
   of character, 447, 472, 477
   of hero or heroine, 466
Dialogue, 150, 423, 443
Diary entry, 105
Ending, 533
Essay, persuasive, 322
Fable, 145, 455
Haiku, 250
Introduction, 418
Letter, 434
Limericks, 254
Metamorphosis, 439
Narrative, 308
Nonfiction narrative, 85, 295, **588**
Poem, 131, 218, 226, 233, 240, 257, 277, 281, **582**
Scene, 45, 126, 369, **594**
Sequel, 135
Story, 14, 72, 115, 174, 279, 451, 461, **576**
Title, 167

VOCABULARY SKILLS

TEST–TAKING SKILLS

Analogies, 182, 317
Antonyms, 135, 150, 447
Sentence completions, 65, 115, 161, 186, 265, 279, 461
Synonyms, 14, 58, 221, 295

WORD STUDY

Context clues, 22, 95, 201
Dialect, 238
Dictionary, 80
Glossary, 138
Jargon and technical words, 369
Modifiers, 235
Prefixes, 533
Pronunciation key, 303
Root words, 423

CREDITS

INDEX OF AUTHORS AND TITLES

E. Dickinson   William Faulkner   Tom Wolfe

Gerard M. Hopkins S.J.   Mark Twain   Rudyard Kipling

Gwendolyn Brooks   Randall Jarrell   Joseph Conrad

Stephen Spender   R M Rilke   Brontë   Virginia Woolf

John Keats   Arthur Conan Doyle   Sidney ___

___   Robert Burns   A Bradstreet   William Shakespeare

A Lincoln   Henry W. Longfellow   Marianne M___

James Joyce   Fredk. Douglass   W Blake   P. B. Shelley

Wallace Stevens   Phillis Wheatley   ___

Brontë   James ___   F Scott Fitzgerald